T0340355

"In *The Fundraising Reader*, the editors have compiled a collection of classical and contemporary pieces that provide an excellent companion to texts such as *Achieving Excellence in Fundraising* for university courses and practitioners seeking to understand fundraising and fundraisers." – *Eugene R. Tempel, Professor and Founding Dean Emeritus, IU Lilly Family School of Philanthropy*

"The editors have brought together thought-provoking and wide-ranging key writings in a format that encourages reflection. A must-have addition to the bookshelf of all involved in fundraising." – *Dr Alexandra Williamson, Australian Centre for Philanthropy and Nonprofit Studies*

"A one-stop resource for those who are driven to succeed in fundraising: whether new to the profession or looking for inspiration, your incredible career starts and develops here." – *Tom Ahern, Fundraising communications expert*

"This Reader contains a treasure trove of inspiration and innovation for fundraisers the world over." – *Ken Burnett, author of Relationship Fundraising*

"Comprehensive and illuminating. This collection of articles and research has so many rich observations and practical application that will guide fundraisers for years to come." – *Dan Fluskey, Chartered Institute of Fundraising*

"This Reader is a monumental work that will be a keystone resource in the fundraising community for years to come." – *Mark Astarita, former Director of Fundraising, British Red Cross*

"People who design and deliver programmes for all types of causes rely on fundraisers – and this book provides a wealth of material, from dozens of authors over the last 100 years, about all aspects of the profession and vocation that make it all possible. So even if you don't consider yourself a fundraiser (and if you work in an NGO you should!) you certainly rely on these professionals, and understanding the opportunities and dilemmas they face will help you and open your eyes to the many challenges ahead." – *Oliver Smith, Deputy Director of Programmes, World Wide Fund for Nature UK*

"*The Fundraising Reader* gives readers a 360-degree view of the core principles of the fundraising field. The volume's carefully selected materials span time, place, and perspective, providing readers with the broad background and comprehensive insights necessary for understanding fundraising in contemporary society." – *Dr Genevieve Shaker, Lilly Family School of Philanthropy, Indiana University, USA*

"Fundraisers today are facing great changes and challenges. The field is under unprecedented scrutiny, yet must meet unprecedented demand. Researchers studying this essential work, instructors teaching it, and professionals looking to learn and improve how they practice it will all find this Reader an invaluable resource. It deserves to be one of the two or three books on every fundraiser's go-to shelf." – *Michael Moody, Frey Foundation Chair for Family Philanthropy, Dorothy A. Johnson Center for Philanthropy*

"This collection of essays and articles illustrates the depth and breadth of scholarly and practitioner writing about the essential role fundraising plays as the enabler of philanthropic giving. If anyone doubts that role, this Reader should change their mind." – *Ian MacQuillin, director, Rogare – The Fundraising Think Tank*

"This Reader provides an internationally comparative view of fundraising which allows researchers, educators and students to analyse contextually appropriate approaches, of value to fundraisers and nonprofit entities alike. Each user, in whatever category they find themselves, will gain valuable insights and be empowered to develop and analyse better fundraising practice." – *Carolyn Cordery, Adjunct Professor Victoria University of Wellington, New Zealand*

"This book is a wonderfully curated and indispensable single-volume reading room that ensures fundraisers have access to the best thinking on their profession." – *Michael Newsome, Regional Chief of Fundraising & Partnerships, UNICEF East Asia and Pacific*

The Fundraising Reader

The Fundraising Reader draws together essential literature establishing a one-stop body of knowledge that explains what fundraising is, and covers key concepts, principles and debates. The book shines a light on the experience of being a fundraiser and answers an urgent need to engage with the complexities of a facet of the nonprofit sector that is often neglected or not properly understood.

This international compilation features extracts from key writing on fundraising, with a comprehensive contextualising introduction by the editors. Uniquely, this Reader shares conflicting positions relating to age-old and current debates on fundraising: Is fundraising marketing? Should donors or the community be front and centre in fundraising? How can fundraisers deal with ethical dilemmas such as 'tainted' donors and money? Best practice and future trends are also covered, including the impact of new technologies and responding to demands for greater diversity, inclusion, and equity in fundraising teams.

This Reader is for those who seek to further develop their own understanding of fundraising and it provides an invaluable resource for academic courses and professional training.

Beth Breeze is the Director of the Centre for Philanthropy at the University of Kent, UK. Beth worked for a decade as a fundraiser and charity manager before moving into academia where she now leads a team conducting research and teaching courses on fundraising and philanthropy.

Donna Day Lafferty is a Senior Lecturer at the University of Chichester, UK. She has worked as a professional fundraiser and project manager since 1997. She is the founder of the first undergraduate degree dedicated to non-profit fundraising, Charity Development BA (Hons.), launched in 2014.

Pamala Wiepking is the inaugural Stead Family Chair in International Philanthropy at the Lilly Family School of Philanthropy, where she teaches Principles and Practices of Fundraising in the online Master program. She is also the inaugural Professor of Societal Significance of Charity Lotteries at the Center for Philanthropic Studies at VU Amsterdam.

The Fundraising Reader

Edited by
Beth Breeze, Donna Day Lafferty
and Pamala Wiepking

Routledge
Taylor & Francis Group

LONDON AND NEW YORK

Designed cover image: AlexRaths

First published 2023
by Routledge
4 Park Square, Milton Park, Abingdon, Oxon OX14 4RN

and by Routledge
605 Third Avenue, New York, NY 10158

Routledge is an imprint of the Taylor & Francis Group, an informa business

© 2023 selection and editorial matter, Beth Breeze, Donna Day Lafferty and
Pamala Wiepking; individual chapters, the contributors

British Library Cataloguing-in-Publication Data
A catalogue record for this book is available from the British Library

ISBN: 978-0-367-70371-4 (hbk)
ISBN: 978-0-367-70370-7 (pbk)
ISBN: 978-1-003-14593-6 (ebk)

DOI: 10.4324/9781003145936

Typeset in Bembo
by Newgen Publishing UK

Access the Support Material: www.routledge.com/9780367703707

Contents

Section 5:
BEING A FUNDRAISER   383

Section 6:
TRENDS AND DEBATES ABOUT MAKING
FUNDRAISING BETTER 471

Editors' introduction: thinking about fundraising

I: The need for a fundraising reader

This Reader contains 88 extracts of key writing on fundraising and fundraisers by scholars, practitioners, and expert commentators living and working in four continents. It is a one-stop resource of insightful and thought-provoking writing that will help to improve the understanding and practice of all those involved in fundraising. There are at least three reasons that this Reader is needed:

First, fundraising is essential yet largely invisible. Nonprofit organisations need to secure resources (including but not limited to money) to fulfil their missions, yet there has long been far greater focus on the causes and their donors rather than on those who work to secure those resources.

Second, there are limited formal ways for fundraisers to acquire knowledge. The lack of accessible and affordable education and training opportunities means that most fundraisers, especially those working in small, resource-deprived organisations, rely on picking up knowledge on an ad hoc and informal basis.

Third, fundraising is often misunderstood and viewed negatively. The act of asking for help, especially asking for financial contributions, has long been viewed negatively despite its essential contribution to causes that do attract broad public support. In the words of Lilya Wagner, whose work features in the first section of this Reader, this creates the commonplace yet illogical combination of "sympathy for causes but antipathy for fundraisers".

We begin this introductory essay by considering each of these three factors in more depth and explaining how this Reader helps to solve the problems they present. In the second section we clarify the aims and intended audience for this Reader, and provide a brief overview of the six sections into which the extracts are organised. The third and final section provides insights into our selection criteria and the process involved in creating this Reader. In addition, each of the six sections begins with an overview written by the editors to introduce the focus of that section, to situate the chosen texts in relation to the overall theme, and to highlight the ways in which the extracts are in conversation with each other to support, contest, and extend knowledge and thinking about fundraising.

It was not an easy task to select and organise this body of work, and we are aware that ultimately a Reader represents the subjective interests and tastes of the editors, which is inevitably rooted in our particular professional and personal experiences. But we believe that the selected extracts best exemplify the nature, scope and diversity of the field and hope that however readers approach it – whether reading from cover-to-cover or dipping in to extracts that catch the eye – that it will help to inform, prompt reflection and draw attention to the issues and debates that concern all of us who care about ethical, effective and enjoyable fundraising.

Fundraising is essential yet largely invisible

Fundraising is the hidden force behind much social good. Resources – especially money – are needed to pay for nonprofit activity including salaries, rent, equipment, programme and project costs, staff training, and ensuring good governance such as paying for financial, legal and managerial expertise. Even an entirely volunteer-run nonprofit likely needs some resources to recruit, support and train those volunteers and to refund expenses.

Despite the importance of donations, the work of finding and sustaining voluntary income streams is often overlooked. Some philanthropists are well-known, as are some nonprofit organisations whose position on certain topics can help sway public opinion. But whilst donors and the causes they support can occupy visible and influential roles in society, the fundraisers, who constitute the third corner of what Cassandra Chapman and colleagues (in Section 5.4) call "the charitable triad" are largely neglected. As Beth Breeze (in Section 1.1) notes: "There are no plaques recording or honouring the contribution of fundraisers, despite giving and asking being two sides of the same coin".

Money and non-financial resources do not magically appear in the bank accounts of nonprofit organisations, and donors do not only make unprompted gifts. The common-sense wisdom that "If you don't ask, you don't get" is supported by decades of research into the drivers of charitable giving. Applied researchers are also engaged in trying to understand how best fundraising can help to produce philanthropy in an increasingly complex world in which the attitudes and behaviours of potential donors, and the broader contexts in which nonprofits operate, are ever-changing. There is skill and hard work involved in identifying potential supporters (which includes individuals as well as institutions such as companies, churches, and grant-making foundations), facilitating their gifts, and stewarding them well so that they decide to give again. The knowledge, techniques, and behaviours needed to undertake successful fundraising, and the type of people who do that work well, is a key focus of this Reader.

Fundraisers are essential because they inspire and enable generosity, which in turn fuels the work of millions of nonprofit organisations worldwide. To ensure this complex and skilled role is delivered to the highest standard, those involved in fundraising need access to resources so that they can develop the knowledge base and ethical compass of a profession. This Reader contributes to advancing the visibility and professionalisation of fundraising by making systematic knowledge and the contours of key ethical debates easily available to those who wish to educate themselves or teach and train the next generation of fundraisers so that they are even better equipped to inspire generous societies.

There are limited formal ways for fundraisers to acquire knowledge

Unlike those pursuing careers in the corporate or public sector, there is minimal-to-non-existent higher education provision for people seeking to work in the nonprofit sector. Almost every university offers degrees in subjects such as business studies, marketing, management, and public policy and administration, but only a handful of universities – primarily in the US – offer degree courses in nonprofit management, philanthropy and fundraising. Business and Politics courses are also commonly offered for 16–18-year-old schoolchildren, but there are no equivalent pre-tertiary educational courses for young people seeking to work in, or gain an understanding of, the nonprofit sector. Fundraising is something that children and young people often do, because extensive fundraising takes place in schools and universities. But they rarely, if ever, have the opportunity to learn about fundraising, or how to do it well.

Beyond educational settings, there is limited professional training that is available and accessible for people who have found themselves in fundraising roles, especially for those outside of the US and UK, which have more developed fundraising training provision. Regardless of location, fundraisers working within organisations that are small and financially unstable – which constitute the majority of nonprofit organisations – typically find their employer is unable to invest in staff development. It is therefore unsurprising to find that most fundraisers report that their main path to acquiring fundraising skills and knowledge has been "on the job" (53%) or by working alongside a more experienced fundraiser (27%) rather than through attending courses (7%) or reading books about fundraising (2%).[1]

Limited opportunities for formal education and training, and the lack of easy access to the body of knowledge about fundraising, does not only result in an under-skilled fundraising workforce. It also contributes to ongoing problems in the supply of practitioners, a situation familiar to anyone trying to recruit a fundraiser. The pressing shortage of skilled and experienced fundraisers cannot be met until there are more people able to teach fundraising. Access to organised knowledge on fundraising is largely confined to the tiny number of people enrolled on rare undergraduate, graduate and accredited courses, but there remains a lack of textbooks to support those teaching such courses. Drawing together the body of empirically grounded literature presented in this Reader, and making it available to a wider readership, represents a key step in establishing the body of systematic knowledge needed to professionalise fundraising. This Reader serves as a core textbook for courses in fundraising at secondary and tertiary level, and is also a primer for practitioners seeking Do-it-Yourself professional development. It provides access to the robust knowledge and debates that help to make the complex decisions on which charities depend to fund their work. It is our sincere hope that the readings encountered in this book will light the spark for some of the fundraising scholars and educators of the future.

Fundraising is often misunderstood and viewed negatively

The third reason that this Reader is needed is to help correct common misunderstandings and negative perceptions of fundraising. Not only is there greater scholarly and public interest in donors and causes than in fundraisers, as noted above, but when askers do attract attention it is often not of a positive nature. Fundraising tends to hit the news headlines because of scandals involving bad practice or fraudulent behaviour. Whilst it is reasonable for these stories to attract public concern, such incidents can be overblown and are rarely balanced by media coverage of fundraising success and best practice.

Extracts in this reader provide useful context for the long-standing problematising of fundraising, from Booker T. Washington's need to explain, in the early 1900s, why "I am not a beggar" (Section 1.3) to Elizabeth Dale's discussion of fundraising's current "low status" in society "due to rare but well publicized, ethical breaches" (Section 5.1).

In addition to the many documented negative perceptions of fundraisers and fundraising, there are also many innocuous but nonetheless unhelpful misunderstandings about what fundraising is and how it works. For example, there is a widespread belief that fundraising is simply a form of sales, marketing or public relations (as discussed in Section 1.3), or involves trying to persuade people to do things they do not want to do. Yet as one senior fundraiser explains "I am not trying to twist donors' arms, rather I have my arm around their shoulder", meaning the job is not about persuasion but about helping donors put their altruistic intentions into action. Others mistakenly think of fundraising as an isolated task or function, separate to the "real work" of the charity. Yet a fundraiser who is stuck in the corner of an office and expected to raise funds without broader organisational support will undoubtedly struggle. Fundraising success relies on there being a "culture of philanthropy" across nonprofit organisations, which means having a general understanding and appreciation of the need for private donors, and providing the investment and support to raise resources (as discussed in the three extracts in Section 2.2, and by Cynthia Gibson in Section 6.1). The real issue, as explained and explored in many extracts in this Reader, is how to create better fundraising organisations, not just better fundraisers.

A further unhelpful yet common perception is that fundraising is an unskilled and easy task. Some people seem to believe that all you need is the names of some rich people and the money will roll in. If you want to know what an exasperated fundraiser looks like, try asking: "Have you thought of asking Bill Gates?", or whichever rich guy first comes to mind. The extracts in this Reader underline that fundraising is almost always a struggle and that there is no magic way to bring in lots of money, but with hard work, creativity, and resilience it is possible to generate a sustainable income stream for most causes.

A final misperception that prompts the need for the better understanding conveyed in this Reader, is the belief that fundraising occurs as an *alternative* to other income streams. In reality, fundraised income is just one funding option available to nonprofit organisations *alongside* earned income and fees as well as government contracts and subsidies. Furthermore, nonprofit activity and organisations are frequently funded by collaborations between donors and public sector bodies, as well as private sector organisations. The reality of negotiating these complex collaborations is far removed from the simplistic image of fundraising as just shaking a tin.

In sum, this Reader is needed because it can help to meet the high demand for good fundraisers, and can help to tackle the general low awareness and lack of understanding of what fundraising is and how it works.

II: What this Reader covers

What we mean by fundraising

The Oxford English Dictionary defines fundraising as "The action or activity of raising, or seeking to raise, money for a charity, cause, or other enterprise". Yet this definition understates the complexity of the task, and the onerous responsibility held by those securing all of the resources – financial and non-financial – that enables nonprofits to pursue their missions. To conceive of the job of fundraising as simply asking for money is misleading and "insultingly narrow" according to Worth and Asp (cited in Breeze, Section 1.1) who describe it as a complex process that includes defining the needs to be met, cultivating the interest and involvement of prospective supporters, matching their interest and desires with the needs and goals of the institution, soliciting the gift, providing feedback on how the gift was used, and stewarding donors to keep them informed and involved. Despite our sympathy with Worth and Asp's position, we embrace the concise definition offered by Henry A. Rosso (Section 1.1) who refers to the practice of fundraising as "resource development". Rosso also coined the memorable phrase that "fundraising is the gentle art of teaching people the joy of giving" by which he means that asking enables giving, and that the practice of gift seeking is justified when it is "a responsible invitation" to encourage and enable contributors to make meaningful gifts.

Aims of this Reader

Our audience

This reader is intended primarily for five audiences:

1. Students of fundraising, philanthropy and the nonprofit sector.
2. People who work in fundraising and related roles.

3. Educators who are teaching fundraising in academic and professional settings.
4. Volunteers who help raise funds, including board members and trustees who are ultimately responsible for fundraising in their nonprofit organisations.
5. Members of the public who wish to learn more about how fundraising works.

Our motivation for creating this Reader

This Reader was created as a result of our own experience as educators who teach fundraising in our "day jobs" in the universities in which we are employed, as well as in the more amorphous sense of being invited (and sometimes expected) to respond helpfully to non-students who seek us out for help. Admitting to expertise on fundraising often prompts hopeful strangers to fish for advice, much like we have seen hairdressers and doctors being quizzed for their professional opinion on flattering hairstyles and worrisome warts. We do our best to help, but the question "how can I quickly, cheaply and easily raise a lot of money for my cause?" does not have a simple or straightforward answer. If all the required wisdom could be easily imparted in one conversation, there would be no need to employ full-time, professional fundraisers on competitive salaries. As Editors of this Reader, we are all passionate about fundraising, get a lot of job satisfaction from teaching existing and aspiring fundraisers, and are happy to share knowledge and insights more widely through the selections we have made in this Reader, and through the overviews at the start of each section.

We are also aware that there is a shortage of people who feel equipped to teach fundraising, both on university campuses and in professional development settings. We know that aspiring tutors often struggle to identify and get access to appropriate texts that can convey the key concepts, ideas, knowledge, and debates in the fundraising field. Meeting this need is one of our core motivations, and each of the six section overviews ends with suggestions for how to incorporate the texts in the classroom, through a set of discussion questions. This Reader is therefore also created for our fellow educators, as a convenient and comprehensive teaching tool.

Finally, we are aware that there is general public interest in the purpose and practice of fundraising. Most people are on the receiving end of requests for support, and many people voluntarily help their favoured causes to secure resources. We therefore hope that this Reader will also be enlightening and interesting to those engaged in fundraising on a more informal and irregular basis.

Sources and further resources

The needs and interests of this diverse readership have guided our selection, which includes a mixture of academic and non-academic sources. We have chosen the most important scholarly writing found in academic monographs, edited collections, and learned journals, as well as influential pieces originally published in journalistic and popular media, both print and online.

The reading selections have been carefully curated, excerpted, and organized into six sections. Section overviews add value to the selections by drawing out the key issues, concerns, and debates within and across the extracts.

Many extracts refer to concepts, ideas, and debates that are also discussed in other extracts. Sometimes other authors provide more information and sometimes they offer alternative perspectives on that same topic. We encourage readers to make use of the index at the back of this book to find out who else has written about the same topic, in order to gain broader insight and understanding.

Note on the international scope of this reader

The selections in this Reader attempt to reflect fundraising as it is practiced internationally, although this effort is grounded in the reality that most research on, and writing about, fundraising takes place in a limited number of geographic places, notably the US and the UK.

We have tried to bring a global perspective into the core content of all six sections, rather than having a separate section dedicated to this topic. However, despite our many attempts to reach out to fundraisers and scholars working across the globe, our attempts did not result in a truly global representation of fundraising texts. The international experts we approached indicated that there are "just no texts on fundraising" written by local fundraisers or scholars, and that they tended to rely on (translations of) key English fundraising texts.

It is therefore important to take into account that texts in this Reader are predominantly written from an Anglo-Saxon perspective, and to keep that in mind because practices of fundraising are always embedded in culture and context. However, we have done our best with what material exists, including contributions from often radically different contexts (such as perspectives on fundraising in the USA in Section 1.1 and in Russia in Section 2.1) to help highlight crucial questions about the universality of fundraising approaches, the variations in cultural assumptions about the proper place of fundraising in relation to the marketplace and government in achieving social ends, the connection of fundraising to faith traditions, and many other issues which are deeply influenced by, and embedded in, specific contexts and cultures. Presenting the international perspectives in this way also invites readers to see how their own cultural context influences how they think and act as students, fundraisers, and practitioners.

Note on embracing debate and dissent

The role and practice of fundraising is complex and contested: the legitimacy of funding some goods and services through donated income is questioned by some people, and the methods by which some funds are raised also invites critique and concerns. Even the basic classification and terminology invites debate: some people view fundraising as a branch of marketing whilst others are adamant that donors should not be treated like consumers. The extent of debate and dissent will likely grow as the field expands within and across countries, as the job of fundraising becomes further professionalised in the years ahead, and as the pace of growth and innovation quickens in relation to developments such as the use of technology, cryptocurrencies, and artificial intelligence. In keeping with our goal to fully represent the reality of the field, we include contentious and controversial issues throughout the Reader. For example, in Section 2.3 we include texts in which Henry Rosso states that clients cannot be expected to make donations whilst Rona Fernandez insists they must be invited to do so. In the section overviews and Discussion questions we highlight where readings engage directly with arguments in other readings, with the intention of providing a balance of perspectives and raising meaty questions for dialogue and reader reflection. We do not intend to endorse any particular perspective but rather to help readers think about fundraising within their own context, and through engagement with a variety of arguments.

Note on responsiveness to the needs and concerns of students and practitioners

As noted above, we – the Editors – are frequently asked for advice and help from those trying to raise funds for a wide range of causes and nonprofit organisations. Despite the great variety in the destination and intended use of the resources that are sought, the same few questions are almost always asked in these encounters such as:

- How does fundraising work?
- How do we get started?
- What's the best way to ask donors to give, and to keep giving?
- What are the rules about fundraising?
- How do I become good at fundraising?
- What are the key trends and debates in fundraising?

These six common question are aligned with the six sections that make up this Reader:

Section summaries

Section 1: What is fundraising?
Section 2: Foundations of fundraising success
Section 3: Understanding fundraising practice
Section 4: Fundraising theory and ethics
Section 5: Being a fundraiser
Section 6: Trends and debates about making fundraising better

Section summaries

Section 1: What is fundraising?

The subject of this Reader – fundraising – is both commonplace and contested, essential and yet often overlooked, historically typical yet continues to be misunderstood. This first section contains extracts that explore all these dimensions of our subject.

Section 2: Foundations of fundraising success

This second section introduces some fundraising basics: the "laws", "cardinal principles" and "first steps" of fundraising. Several foundational ideas and concepts used in fundraising practice are explained and discussed, including the donor pyramid, developing a constituency of supporters, involving the board, and the fundraising cycle. This section ends with some "vital ingredients" for success including the case for support and cultivating diversity.

Section 3: Understanding fundraising practice

In this section we consider the most visible aspects of fundraising: the tasks involved in seeking funds and resources from prospects and donors. Fundraising practice draws together two essential ingredients, donor markets and fundraising methods. Donor markets are the people and organisations interested in supporting nonprofits. Fundraising methods are the ways in which donor markets are engaged. The result is a wide variety of bespoke and choreographed human interactions, which if done well are informed by the theory and findings shared throughout this Reader.

Section 4: Fundraising theory and ethics

In this section we cover some of the key theories that have been developed in fundraising theory, as well as seminal texts on fundraising ethics. The theories presented by the authors in this section help to shed light on what works (and does not work) in fundraising. If anything, fundraising is an ethical profession. This section provides an overview of ethical dilemmas that fundraisers may encounter, and offers tools to help ethically respond to these dilemmas. It ends with three "Bills of Rights", indicating the rights that donors, fundraisers, and beneficiaries have.

Section 5: Being a fundraiser

People become fundraisers both intentionally and accidentally, to earn a living and to pursue a passion. This section explores the job of fundraising and the kinds of people who tend to succeed in it. It also includes extracts that explore the challenges of being a fundraiser, including lack of internal support and external validation that can combine to make a difficult job even more difficult.

Section 6: Trends and debates about making fundraising better

In the final section we make room to explore some of the most important debates about making fundraising better including diversity and decolonising fundraising, the relative power of donors and beneficiaries, and the ethical use of new technology. We end with some crystal ball gazing: while the future is never fully knowable, there is value in looking at current trends and trying to anticipate what might happen next. The featured authors are both playful and serious in seeking to predict challenges and highlight opportunities that might underpin better fundraising practice in the short and longer term.

III: Notes on creating the Reader

Choosing and editing the selections

The selections in this Reader are either partial or full reprints from previously published texts, rather than new pieces of writing or heavily revised extracts. The vast majority are excerpts, with only a few cases where the original was short enough to be reproduced in full.

In choosing the sources and selecting the pieces to use, we had to make many difficult decisions. Often our choices were guided by the intentional scope and aims of the Reader as described above – i.e. to make the content useful, enlightening, and thought-provoking for our intended audience of practitioners, scholars, and educators. We sought to include texts across a broad range of time – over 100 years separate our oldest extract (1901) and the most recent (2022) – and we include authors and texts from four continents though, as noted above, the dominance of both the US and UK in relation to practitioners, scholars, and educators, mean the final selection is skewed towards those two countries.

Where we created extracts from longer texts, all edits were designed to keep the particular excerpt focused on the specific topic of the subsection within which it appears. Other minor editing involved taking out statements that are transient (such as links to then-current affairs), that only make sense in the original published context, or other such reasons. We indicate all places where edits were made using ellipses or brackets like this: [...].

The selections in the Reader do not include bibliographic references, citations, footnotes or endnotes that were in the original published work. This was to allow us to include more pieces of shorter length and to provide a standard format, as well as in recognition that many readers will not have access to follow up citations in books they do not own or in journals that are behind paywalls. However, if a particular author or source is referred to by name in the text, that remains *in situ* but with the citation removed.

We have given each extract a title that reflects the specific topic of the excerpt and how it fits into the flow of topics of that section; in some cases this title is the same as the original piece.

Some key words are subject to different spellings, such as fund raiser, fundraiser, fund-raiser, and nonprofit, non-profit. We used whatever spelling appears in the original publication.

Given the publication date of some extracts, there are some historic quirks that reflect different social norms in existence in earlier periods, such as reference to "manpower" and assumptions that donors are "he". In addition, some terminology is now considered inappropriate, for example "developing world", and some authors have told us they would now use different wording, for example replacing "prospect" with "prospective donor". As with spellings, we left these more controversial variations as they were in the original.

Full information on the original source for each excerpt in this Reader is available in the "Sources and Copyright" section provided at the end of the volume. We **<u>strongly encourage</u>** all readers to retrieve the original piece and read it in full. There are so many other interesting and helpful elements to all the edited readings than we are able to include here, and the full original texts provide greater context, more depth, additional illustrations, complete bibliographic details, and other things that curious readers will find useful.

Acknowledgements

This Reader has been a labour of love for all three editors who hope this collection of readings will help to improve the teaching, understanding, and practice of fundraising.

We could not have produced this Reader without the financial support, academic collegiality, and practical assistance of a large number of people, all of whom we thank most sincerely, especially:

Our funders: Pears Foundation in the UK, especially Sir Trevor Pears and Bridget Kohner, for generously providing the core funding that covered the cost of permissions.

Our International Advisory Committee: Becky Gilbert, Russell James, Ian MacQuillin, Claire Routley, Genevieve Shaker, and Alexandra Williamson for reviewing our draft selections, making additional suggestions, and helping to fill gaps in our knowledge of fundraising around the world.

For inspiration: Michael Moody, whose lead editorship on *The Philanthropy Reader* (with Beth Breeze, also published by Routledge, in 2016) provided a structure and format for us to build upon in this book, which we view as a companion text.

For practical assistance: Yongzheng Yang who worked hard to support the process of applying for copyright permissions whilst completing his own PhD – congratulations Dr Yang, we hope this book is useful in your future academic career. And sincere thanks to Desi Anastasova and Kafui Osuteye in the finance office at the University of Kent who managed the complexities of project financing with grace and good cheer.

For advice and moral support: Our colleagues, especially Ali Body, Lucy Lowthian, and Claire Routley (all at the University of Kent); Kathi Badertscher, Bill Stanczykiewicz, Gene Tempel, Tim Seiler, Sarah Nathan, Patricia Danahey, Dana Doan, the students in P558 (all at the Indiana University Lilly Family School of Philanthropy).

Finally, thanks to our ever-supportive other halves: Michael Breeze, Ben Hall, and Eskild Wikkeling.

Note

1 These statistics are from B. Breeze (2017) *The New Fundraisers: who organises charitable giving in contemporary society?* Bristol: Policy Press, p. 72.

Section 1

WHAT IS FUNDRAISING?

Editors' introduction

Overview

The subject of this Reader – fundraising – is both commonplace and contested, essential and yet often overlooked, historically typical yet continuously misunderstood. Given these somewhat confusing characterisations, we begin by exploring some fundamental questions: What is fundraising? What are its historical roots? And in what ways – and why – is it frequently misunderstood? It is a reflection of the complexity, and mostly understudied nature, of our subject that we need to start with an entire section devoted to these basic, yet revealing, questions.

All the readers of this volume will have some ideas about fundraising. Perhaps you work as a fundraiser, or are studying, researching or teaching about fundraising? If not, you will likely have some experience of being asked – and maybe of asking others – to support good causes. These varieties of experience, by which almost everyone comes into contact with fundraising in some way, are reflected in the readings in this section which explore the longstanding and often mundane presence of fundraising in our daily lives and across the centuries.

The routine nature of fundraising does not result in easy agreement about its purpose or practice. Indeed, disagreement stretches back to its historical roots, with different authors identifying divergent origins (in both time and place) for the "start" of fundraising, and for the invention of what have become standard practices in fundraising such as major campaigns, community appeals, and door-to-door collections. Whilst origin stories are plausibly diverse – recalling the aphorism that "success has many parents but failure is an orphan" – more heated and fundamental debates surround other disputed issues, for example:

- Is fundraising a goal in itself, or is it only undertaken in the service of bigger goals held by donors and the activities they support?
- What is the right role for fundraising from private individuals and institutions in tax-funded democratic welfare states?
- Do people take jobs as fundraisers to pursue their philanthropic passions or due to economic exigency?

DOI: 10.4324/9781003145936-2

- Is fundraising a distinctive field of practice and scholarly study, or is it simply a sub-division of other fields such as marketing, communications or public relations?
- Is fundraising a "necessary evil" that is a type of sales at best and a form of begging at worst, or does it bring happiness, meaning, and "transcendental benefits" (as described by Arthur Brooks in Section 1.3) to donors and askers alike?

Combine the complexity of fundraising as reflected in the fundamental questions outlined above, with the fact that it is also commonplace. Note that it is often connected to deeply personal values, experiences, and preferences that relate to the causes, nonprofit organisations, and projects for which funding is being sought. You will hopefully see why we need to devote this first section to exploring what fundraising is and what it is not.

There is no single answer to the question, "what is fundraising?" for at least four reasons:

Firstly, because most people, including professionals working in fundraising, have a fairly limited knowledge of the field in all its diversity. Knowledge is largely experiential rather than based on robust evidence, and there are minimal opportunities to study fundraising and the nonprofit sector in comparison to the plentiful opportunities to study government, business, or other major spheres of social life.

Secondly, because even though the principles of asking for money may be similar across the world, it is adapted to local contexts that differ due to specific historical, social, and political factors. Fundraising has some commonalities, such as distinct donor markets being able to give different values of gift, but legislation and culture drive many differences. For example, in the US donations from all board members of an organization may be expected (as noted by Thomas Broce in Section 2.1), while in other places that would be uncommon.

Thirdly, people experience fundraising in distinctive ways depending on what type of hat they are wearing at any given time: as professional or volunteer fundraisers, as those being asked, as donors who have better or worse experiences of having given before, as colleagues of fundraisers, and as beneficiaries. Those directing the fundraising strategy may interpret the demands of meeting budgets and reviewing ethical issues from a different perspective to those being asked to participate in fundraising efforts on top of their "day job", for example as a scientist in a philanthropically-funded laboratory. Another interesting "hat" or perspective is that of beneficiaries who are asked to feature in fundraising appeals.

Fourthly, asking and being asked are also experienced differently by people living within the same culture at the same moment. Think, for example, of the different quality of "asks" that are made of those with the capacity to make very large financial donations compared to those from whom only spare change is sought. The former would likely receive detailed and personalised information about the work for which funds are needed, invitations to visit projects, meet key leadership and front-line staff, and make suggestions about the work, and could expect to receive acknowledgement such as a naming opportunity, and ongoing information about how their money has been used and with what impact. The latter would likely get a cheery "hello", a shake of the tin, and a sincere "thank you" with perhaps a cheap recognition device such as a sticker, and would have no expectation of being informed of how their coin was spent. Whilst the difference is clearly rooted in pragmatic proportionality – it is rarely feasible to give a 5-star donor service to a 50 cents donor – and whilst new information technology is enabling lower-value donors to get a somewhat higher-touch experience, the experience of fundraising varies greatly according to each individual's capacity to give.

This also brings in questions of representation and inclusion in fundraising: Who is being asked to contribute? And who therefore holds power over how donated money is spent, how societal issues are addressed and – perhaps of greatest importance – which societal issues are being addressed?

The readings in this section explore many fundamental questions, and help bring to the surface a number of the core issues about fundraising that are addressed throughout this Reader. To address these questions, the readings here are grouped into four subsections, as follows:

1.1 What is fundraising?

The first four readings approach the question of "what is fundraising" from a variety of perspectives whilst sharing some common themes. Most notably they all challenge the dominant view of philanthropy as a donor-centred enterprise, noting instead that giving and asking are "two sides of the same coin" (in Breeze's words), that generosity needs to be prompted, facilitated, tutored, and encouraged, and that these tasks are all part of the fundraiser's purview.

In the first extract, Beth Breeze argues that fundraising is more complex and crucial than most people realise, and that there is a need to better understand who the askers are and what it is that they do. The urgency of this need is rooted in the necessity of fundraising, as she writes "Charities cannot run on goodwill alone", despite the asker's role being "usually either invisible or problematized". Henry Rosso also notes that, "fundraising has never been considered the most popular practice", and he offers a number of memorable words and phrases to convey the positive role of fundraising: "purposive", "values-based", and "the servant of philanthropy". Rosso insists that fundraising has no substance or value unless it serves a larger cause because it,

> draws both its meaning and essence from the ends that are served: caring, helping, healing, nurturing, guiding, uplifting, teaching, creating, preventing, advancing a cause, preserving values, and so forth.

Rosso's thinking has had an enduring influence on generations of fundraisers in the US as he founded the longest established training and educational centre for fundraisers, The Fund Raising School, which is now part of the Lilly

Family School of Philanthropy at Indiana University in the US. The greater success of fundraising and higher levels of philanthropy in that country, may in part be due to the dissemination of Rosso's philosophy and emphasis on establishing a proud, mission-based rationale for the fundraising profession.

Like Rosso, Lilya Wagner takes a US-centric perspective in her exploration of fundraising which sets the scene for many other discussions contained in this Reader including the enduring role of asking over the centuries yet its relatively recently professionalisation, the influential role of women as volunteers, the reality of the nonprofit sector's reliance on fundraising, and the importance of fundraisers being motivated by the missions they serve.

Jeanne Harrah-Conforth and John Borsos shift the focus from fundraising to fundraisers. They suggest that people who raise funds for a living occupy positions on a continuum stretching from those pursuing a calling or vocation to those with more strategic career goals and financial objectives. Across this spectrum of motivations, fundraisers find themselves in an industry that has been unusually accessible due to the lack of barriers relating to specialised education and training requirements. It is also a career that provides "a constant reminder of one's position and privileges in life" because the work involves pursuing public goods, often with a focus on assisting those in need. Whilst the professionalisation of fundraising should raise internal standards and increase external trust it also brings more opportunities to "reap monetary and stature gains" which may attract more entrants with pecuniary rather than passion-based motivations. Critiques of professionalisation also note risks such as displacing and disrespecting existing local infrastructure and volunteer efforts, as well as causing wage inflation (see Section 6.5).

1.2 Historical perspectives on fundraising

Two longer-than-average extracts provide historical perspectives on fundraising.

Redmond Mullin delivers on his promise of "two thousand years of disreputable history" by describing how the sale of indulgences to raise church funds helped motivate Martin Luther to trigger the Reformation in the late sixteenth century. Had the Tetzel award for discreditable fundraising (mentioned by Redmond Mullin in Section 1.2 and named after John Tetzel who was licensed to sell papal pardons in Wittenberg) been in existence earlier, a worthy winner might have been the nineteenth-century fundraiser whose motto is reported as: "Find a Duchess, flatter her and get £500". Mullin also traces the origins of somewhat less controversial contemporary practices including the acknowledgement of big donors with naming opportunities in ancient Rome, the origins of trust law in thirteenth-century Franciscan orders, and the role of Royal patrons in galvanising donations dating back to Henry III.

The second historical perspective, by Scott Cutlip, focuses on the roots of fundraising, primarily in the US. He describes the introduction of what are now considered standard practices such as the major donor campaign to found Mount Holyoke college in 1830s Massachusetts, the success of a "matched gift" offer in 1871 to found Smith College in the same US state, an early example of global mass fundraising by US communities to relieve suffering in the Irish famine of the late 1840s, and the role of securing press coverage to promote the American Red Cross during its founding year of 1881.

Both historical authors also highlight early incarnations of ongoing live debates such as the ethics and efficacy of tugging at heartstrings to open purse strings (see also Jon Dean and Rachel Wood in Section 4.1 on the use of negative emotions in fundraising), the duplication of fundraising efforts, and public distaste for commission-based fundraising where fundraisers get paid a percentage of the amount they raise.

1.3 Misunderstandings of fundraising

This sub-section contains the largest number of extracts (five) in this first section of the Reader, reflecting the degree of interest in identifying and correcting common misunderstandings about fundraising. These include – but are by no means limited to – misconceptions about the purpose of fundraising, how it is undertaken, how success is measured, whose job it is, and why it should be done with joy and pride, rather than with reluctance, fear or apology.

The oldest extract in the Reader is by Booker T. Washington, writing in 1901 from the perspective of being the first leader of Tuskegee Institute, a historically black university in Alabama. Washington firmly refutes the notion that fundraising is a form of "begging", not simply because of the negative connotations of that word but because his experience shows that success relies on taking every opportunity to "make known the facts" about Tuskegee's work and impact so that people who have the capacity to offer all levels of support are given "the opportunity to help". Likewise, both Russell James and Richard Waters seek to clarify that fundraising is neither sales nor marketing but rather is focused on building healthy and positive relationships with those who share the broader goals of the fund-seeking organisation. Re-framing the central purpose of fundraising in this way has implications for the language used in talking to donors, as explained by James. He urges fundraisers to use "social, conversational, family words" and to avoid "technical or contract terms" that evoke market transactions. It also means, as Waters writes, that "contrary to popular perception" of solicitation as its prime task, fundraising success is more likely to result from communicating the value of the nonprofit's work and keeping supporters consistently involved in the creation of specific social value.

In the face of much public disapproval of asking, with particular resistance to seeking money, Arthur Brooks contends that fundraising ought to be appreciated as a "fun" task that enhances well-being and brings meaning to the lives of all those involved: askers, donors, and recipients. Brooks cites psychological research on causal links between problem solving, self-efficacy, and increased happiness, as well as his own experience of the "magic" of securing support for missions in which he is professionally and personally invested. He also argues that fundraising is a positive act because those who take action to tackle problems they care about tend to be happier than those who remain as bystanders or victims of circumstance. Or, in Brooks' more poetic words: fundraisers "empower those with financial resources to convert the dross of their money into the gold of a better society".

The final article in this sub-section is a rousing and unapologetic defence of fundraising, written by Sasha Dichter who became "sick of apologizing for being in charge of raising the money". Dichter's defence is aimed at colleagues, and in particular at the leaders of nonprofits, who mistakenly believe that successful fundraisers can "work in a vacuum" separate to the "real work" of the organisation. Just as successful private sector brands, such as Apple, are led by people who consistently generate energy and engagement by the broader public, so too all nonprofit staff need to "be an evangelist for your idea and [help] to convince others about the change you want to see in the world". Dichter responds to common accusations, arguing that fundraising can help achieve systemic change as well as ameliorating immediate needs, and insisting that causes need not be in competition with each other but rather can "increase the size of the pie" of overall philanthropic contributions. Dichter also acknowledges that fundraisers themselves can hold negative views about their work due to fears of rejection and the difficulty of navigating power relations. Like James, he proposes re-framing how we think and talk about fundraising as an encounter between people who may have different capacities (money, time, expertise) but who are equally keen to achieve change to make the world a better place. The fundraiser is thus "an evangelist, a storyteller, an educator, a translator, a table-pounder, a guy on his soap box, a woman with a megaphone, a candidate for change" – all necessary tasks that are worth defending.

The eleven extracts in this first section of the Reader each shed light on the million-dollar question (meaning: important but also difficult to answer): What is fundraising? In the next section, Thomas Broce insists that all fundraisers must be able to answer a further, literal million-dollar question: "How would you spend one million dollars if it were given to you today?" The frequent inability to provide a swift and clear response to this question suggests that many fund-seekers would benefit from the readings in this section which emphasise the need for fundraising to be "purposive" and pursued with pride in order to achieve nonprofit missions. That point is underlined in Wagner's article when she cites one of the earliest known US professional fundraisers, Charles Sumner Ward, who said: "I would leave this work immediately if I thought I were merely raising money. It is raising men (sic) that appeals to me".

Achieving missions that make the world a better place, and raising up people, are not easy tasks. As we will see in the next section, when Broce goes on to state that "Fundraisers, paid and volunteer, are not magicians. They must be armed with the knowledge and resources to complete their tasks." We believe the extracts in this first section help to answer the question "what is fundraising" and also help to arm those seeking much-needed funds.

Discussion questions

1. Henry Rosso (in Section 1.1) argues strongly that fundraising is, and must be, "values based". What does the phrase "values based" mean to you, in the context of fundraising? Can you give examples of fundraising that, in your opinion, is and is not, values-based?
2. What did you find most interesting to read about in the texts by Mullin and by Cutlip on the history of fundraising, in Section 1.2? Were you surprised to learn that practices such as naming opportunities and other donor benefits are so longstanding? Does that change your view on the merits of using these practices today?
3. Imagine you are at a birthday party, and your aunt starts complaining about fundraising. Based on the readings by Washington, James, Waters, Brooks and/or Dichter (all in Section 1.3 which is focused on misunderstandings of fundraising) can you provide three responses to your aunt, to share the importance of fundraising?
4. Thinking of the professional fundraisers that you know (including yourself if you work as a fundraiser), do you agree with Harrah-Conforth and Borsos that there is a wide range of motivations that stretches from being passionate about a nonprofit's mission to the necessity of paying the bills? How might this spectrum of motives affect the daily practice and decision making of those who work as fundraisers?
5. Are you convinced by the arguments put forward by James and Waters that fundraising is neither sales nor marketing but is rather about aligning the values of supporters with causes that need their help? Can you name some practices and language used by fundraisers that may inadvertently convey a "sales" rather than a "values-based" approach?
6. Pick any three extracts in this first section of the Reader. What are the key points they make that you would use to defend and explain the necessity of fundraising, for example if asked to justify the cost of hiring a new member of the fundraising team, or to increase the budget for fundraising costs?

1.1 What is fundraising?

.

What is fundraising and why does it matter?

Beth Breeze, 2017

The Oxford English Dictionary offers this narrow definition of fundraising: "persuading individuals or organisations to provide financial support for a cause, enterprise, etc." A wider definition is offered by the UK's [Chartered] Institute of Fundraising: "Fundraising is the act of raising resources (especially, but not only money) by asking for it, to fund the work your organisation carries out, including the front-line activity and the overheads". Yet both definitions understate the complexity of the task, and the onerous responsibility held by those securing the financing that keeps good causes in business. To conceive of the job of fundraising as simply asking for money is misleading, even "insultingly narrow", according to Worth and Asp, because it is a complex process that includes defining the needs to be met, cultivating the interest and involvement of prospective donors, matching their interest and desires with the needs and goals of the institution, soliciting the gift, providing feedback on how the gift was used, and stewarding donors to keep them informed and involved.

A further complication when trying to define this activity is that many fundraisers do not use the word 'fundraising'; rather they speak of 'development', 'advancement' or 'partnerships'. While those words can be interpreted as mealy-mouthed euphemisms or, at best, a polite way to avoid mentioning money, they are often a more accurate reflection of how the person doing the fundraising spends their time – developing and advancing their institution by building partnerships with potential supporters. One US study, by Duronio and Tempel, found that 'solicitation' (the equivalent North American term for 'fundraising') occupied just 13% of the typical fundraiser's working week, with the bulk of their remaining time being occupied with administration (33%), followed by interacting with 'constituents' (16%) and volunteers (11%).

Why charities fundraise

Charities cannot run on goodwill alone. They need money to put their charitable missions into practice, whether that is paying the telephone bill to run a helpline, paying for scientific equipment to search for cures for illness, paying qualified staff to tend to the dying, or paying expenses of volunteer lifeboat men and women. However worthy the cause, and however impressive the charity's achievements, it will not attract donations without a concerted and organised effort to raise funds.

DOI: 10.4324/9781003145936-4

There is nothing new about charitable work costing money, but rapid growth in the number of charities seeking voluntary income has intensified competition for donations and new donors, and financial survival in this new charity landscape relies on ever more innovative and attractive fundraising campaigns … But the wider context for fundraising involves more profound change than simply a more crowded marketplace. The new financial pressures also include dramatic cuts in public funding for charities, and the shift towards restrictions being placed on how some income can be used which creates a particularly competitive environment for charities. These new pressures are occurring in tandem with increased scrutiny from the media and from politicians with regard to the management of, and spending on, fundraising. This convergence of factors, described by Walker as a "perfect storm" hitting charities, means that, according to Duronio and Tempel, "the work of fundraising has never been more demanding, more challenging, or more important."

[…]

The essential yet invisible role of fundraisers

The task of asking for donations is one of the most intriguing, and yet largely unexplored, parts of the puzzle of charitable giving. In the UK, around a third (38%) of total charity income is raised from voluntary donations, which is primarily fundraising from individuals but also includes support from charitable trusts and foundations, companies, the National Lottery and funding grants from government. The reliance on donated income is even higher among the vast majority of smaller charities that receive no public funding [government contracts] and have no mechanism for earning income. Yet despite its importance, our awareness and understanding of the role that fundraisers play in securing donations is low.

One reason for overlooking fundraisers is a preference to interpret generosity as entirely innate, viewing it as a personal and private decision to respond to needs that exist in society. Instinctive kindness, and gifts that appear to be freely given, are far more highly culturally valued than reacting to a request, yet the inconvenient truth is that almost all gifts are prompted and facilitated to some degree. This is not necessarily because donors are unwilling to offer spontaneous help, but rather due to lack of awareness of the existence and urgency of some needs, and also lack of clarity about why and how to respond. We do not personally encounter some needs because of geographical proximity, but also because our highly stratified modern lives mean we exist in different social worlds to our neighbours and can easily be unaware of needs a few streets away.

Furthermore, the largely intangible nature of some needs, such as environmental issues, disaster prevention and the search for medical cures, mean that we often only become aware that something important needs funding as a result of someone drawing our attention to it, offering us a viable and trusted means of responding, and making us feel our contribution was worthwhile.

That 'someone' is often a professional fundraiser, and in a nutshell that is what fundraisers do: they foster the philanthropic impulse, frame charitable needs, and facilitate donations.

[…]

Research on the efficacy of fundraising

The direct connection between asking and giving is, unsurprisingly, a truism among professional fundraisers, confirming what Andreoni calls the "iron law": that people are more likely to give and also tend to donate more when they are asked. Experimental studies confirm the positive effect of asking in securing donations, and Meer concludes "that giving is rare without fundraising". Studies also show that, on average, fundraising is very productive.

Capturing figures on the precise extent of fundraising success is not easy because the charity sector is so broad, and methods of fundraising are too various to make global figures particularly meaningful or easy to come by. But a recent study, based on data from 1,200 UK charities, finds that for every £1 they invested in fundraising, £4.20 was raised, indicating a return on investment that would delight any venture capitalist. Furthermore, *not* fundraising is the sure-fire route to *not* raising voluntary income because most people say their reason for not giving is because they were not asked.

However, despite the proven efficacy of fundraising, it is too simplistic to suggest that more asking will lead directly and unproblematically to more giving. As Clark Kerr explains: fundraisers are not like a light bulb "which performs one unambiguous task … at the flick of a switch." There is huge variability in the quality of 'the ask' (as it is called by fundraisers), which is why the complexity and subtlety of the fundraising role is the subject of this book …

Successful fundraisers know that the request for a gift should only come after a lengthy and careful process that begins by developing a strong case for support, conducting research to identify potential supporters, strategic planning of the fundraising campaign, recruiting appropriate volunteers to assist in approaching potential donors, developing mutually beneficial relationships over months and years, then monitoring and evaluating the outcomes. This process requires an investment of time and resources that is far removed from most people's perception of what fundraising involves.

[…]

The need to shift research attention to askers

One way of encapsulating the essential role of fundraisers is to note that the process of making a donation is not friction-free: it is mediated even when the intermediaries are not visible. So-called 'friction-free giving', usually exemplified by online giving or text giving, still requires someone to design and update a website or to set up the text-giving number, to manage the bank account that receives gifts, and (ideally) to let the donor know that their contribution has been safely received and how it has been used.

A shift in focus from givers to askers is not only necessary to redress the existing imbalance in research, but also because fundraisers' responsibility for triggering giving decisions makes them a more fertile locus of analytic attention. Indeed, research solely focused on donors is arguably guilty of what social psychologists call a fundamental misattribution error, which occurs when behaviour is explained with reference to the actor's personal characteristics rather than the situation in which they find themselves. Difficulties in correctly identifying the site of giving decisions is further complicated by the fact, noted by Smith, that:

> There are no 'social laws' that explain who is generous and why. There is no simple list of variables that 'produce' or 'predict' generosity ... Possessing the natural general power for some given practice like generosity does not guarantee that it will be activated and exercised in any given case. Not all human capacities are triggered, cultivated, and expressed. Some, perhaps especially virtues like generosity, need to be actively prompted and tutored in order to become regular practices. That shifts our analytic attention from deep human neurology to more proximate triggering and routin-izing factors promoting generosity.

Most charitable acts are the result of both an 'asker' and a 'giver', but the donor's role is clearly visible, understood to be essential, and largely appreciated (excepting major donors whose gifts can sometimes generate sus-picion rather than admiration), while the asker's role is usually either invis-ible or problematised. The substantially greater interest in philanthropy over fundraising is normative. Donors – especially wealthy donors – are of gen-eral public interest and attention, both historically and contemporaneously, whereas those asking for donations have never yet breached the public con-sciousness. The names of leading philanthropists, such as Andrew Carnegie, John D. Rockefeller, Bill Gates, and Warren Buffett, are well known, but no fundraiser shares a similar high profile. There are no plaques recording or honouring the contribution of fundraisers, despite giving and asking being two sides of the same coin – or, to use a more evocative metaphor, created by John McLoughlin, that also highlights their differences:

> Donors and fundraisers occupy the same landscape yet they carry utterly different maps. Fundraisers maps are full of routes to donors and potential donors. In contrast, donors, would-be donors and their advisers use maps in which fundraisers are non-existent.

The recent flourishing of research on philanthropy is driven by a practical goal: to identify the factors that encourage people to give, in order to encourage more people to become givers, and to encourage those who are already donors to give more. While understandable, given the increasing expectations of phil-anthropically funded goods and services, this creates an expectation that there is a 'donor type' or a set of sociodemographic characteristics and personal motivations that are allegedly typical of those most likely to give. Chasing this elusive donor profile has absorbed much intellectual and practical energy. However, given the global variation in levels of giving, and the fact that people can move from being non-donors to donors while retaining all other personal characteristics, it would seem that efforts to identify enduring and essential qualities of givers and non-givers would be better spent on gaining a better understanding of askers.

A philosophy of fundraising

Henry A. Rosso, 2016 [first published 1991]

Fundraising is the servant of philanthropy and has been so since the seventeenth century, when Puritans brought the concept to the new continent. The early experience of fundraising was simple in form, obviously devoid of the multifaceted practices that characterize its nature in the contemporary United States. These practices now make fundraising more diversified and more complex than ever before.

The American spirit of giving is known and respected in other nations ... Ironically, the practice of resource development that is so much a part of the culture, necessity, and tradition of not-for-profit organizations in the United States is not sufficiently understood, often misrepresented, and too often viewed with suspicion and apprehension by a broad section of our own population, particularly by regulatory bodies. Few will argue with the observation that fundraising has never been considered the most popular practice in this country.

Dean Schooler of Boulder, Colorado, a scholar and student of fund raising takes the teleological view of a vitalist philosophy that phenomena not only are guided by mechanical forces but also move toward certain goals of self-realization. Indeed, fundraising is never an end in itself; it is purposive. It draws both its meaning and essence from the ends that are served: caring, helping, healing, nurturing, guiding, uplifting, teaching, creating, preventing, advancing a cause, preserving values, and so forth. Fund raising is values-based; values must guide the process. Fund raising should never be undertaken simply to raise funds; it must serve the larger cause.

Organizations and their reasons for existing

Organizations of the independent sector come into existence for the purpose of responding to some facet of human or societal needs. The need or opportunity for service provides the organization with a reason for being, as well as a right to design and execute programs or strategies that respond to the need. This becomes the cause that is central to the concern of the organization. The cause provides justification for moral intervention, and this provides justification for fundraising.

The organization may *claim* a right to raise money by asking for the tax-deductible gift. It must earn the privilege to ask for gift support by its

DOI: 10.4324/9781003145936-5

management's responsiveness to needs, by the worthiness of its programs, and by the stewardship of its governing board. An organization may assume the right to ask. The prospective donor is under no obligation to give. The prospect reserves the right to a "yes" or a "no" response to any request. Either response is valid and must be respected.

Each organization that uses the privilege of soliciting for gifts should be prepared to respond to many questions, perhaps unasked and yet implicit in the prospect's mind. These may be characterized as such: "Why do you exist?" "What is distinctive about you?" "Why do you feel that you merit this support?" "What is it that you want to accomplish and how do you intend to go about doing it?" and "How will you hold yourself accountable?"

The response to "Who are you and why do you exist?" is couched in the words of the organization's mission statement. This statement expresses more than justification for existence and more than just a definition of goals and objectives. It defines the value system that will guide program strategies. The mission is the magnet that will attract and hold the interests of trustees, volunteers, staff, and contributors.

The answer to "What is distinctive about us?" is apparent in the array of goals, objectives, and programs that have been devised to address the need of the value system as well as serve as symbols of fidelity to it.

"What is it that you want to accomplish and how do you intend to go about doing it?" is closely linked to "Why do you merit this support?" People give to people with causes. To be worthy of support, the organization must show that it has not only a vision of what it wishes to accomplish but also a clear plan for making the change it wishes to effect feasible and achievable.

"How do we hold ourselves accountable?" is the primary question. It is a continuing call for allegiance to the mission. It acknowledges the sacredness of the trust that is inherent in the relationship with both the constituency and the larger community. The organization is the steward of the resources entrusted to its care.

It is axiomatic that change is a constant. Shifting forces within the environment quicken the pace of change, thus posing a new constant. Not-for-profit organizations must always be prepared to function in the center of whirling pressure.

Organizations cannot afford to be oblivious to the environment that surrounds, and indeed engulfs, them. Forces within the environment such as demographics, technology, economics, political and cultural values, and changing social patterns affect daily business performance, whether this performance pertains to governance, program administration, fiscal responsibility, or fundraising.

To govern or not to govern

Governance is an exercise in authority and control. Trustees, directors, or regents – the interchangeable nomenclature that identifies the actors in governance – are the primary stewards of the spirit of philanthropy. As stewards, they are the legendary "keepers of the hall." They hold the not-for-profit organization in trust to ensure that it will continue to function according to the dictates of its mission.

The trustees must bear the responsibility to define and interpret the mission and ensure that the organization will remain faithful to its mission. Board members should accept the charge that trusteeship concerns itself with the proper deployment of resources and with the accompanying action, the securing of resources. Deploying resources is difficult if the required resources are not secured through effective fundraising practices. It stands to reason that trustees as advocates of and stewards to the mission must attend to the task of pressing the resources development program on to success.

Institutionalizing fundraising

Fundraising projects the values of the total organization into the community whenever it seeks gift support. All aspects of governance – administration, program, and resources development – are part of the whole. As such, these elements must be part of the representation when gifts are sought. Fundraising cannot function apart from the organization; apart from the organization's mission, goals, objective, and programs; or apart from a willingness to be held accountable for all of the organization's actions.

Fundraising is and must always be the lengthened shadow of the not-for-profit entity, reflecting the organization's dignity, its pride of accomplishment, and its commitment to service. Fundraising by itself and apart from the institution has no substance in the eyes and heart of the potential contributor.

Gift making as voluntary exchange

Gift making is based on a voluntary exchange. Gifts secured through coercion, through any means other than persuasion, are not gifts freely given. They do not have the meaning of philanthropy. Rarely will gifts obtained under pressure or through any form of intimidation be repeated. These gifts lose their meaning.

In the process of giving, the contributor offers a value to the not-for-profit organization. This gift is made without any expectation of a material return, apart from the tax deductibility authorized by government. The reasons for making a gift are manifold.

In accepting the gift, it is incumbent upon the organization to return a value to the donor in a form other than material value. Such a value may be social recognition, the satisfaction of supporting a worthy cause, a feeling of importance, a feeling of making a difference in resolving a problem, a sense of belonging, or a sense of "ownership" in a program dedicated to serving the public good.

Trustees, administrators, or fundraising practitioners so often misconstrue the true meaning of this exchange relationship, and they violate the acknowledgement process by offering a return of substantive value. This alters the exchange, reduces the meaning of philanthropy, and diminishes the gift in its commitment to the mission. The transaction is one of a material exchange, a self-centered quid pro quo with none of the spirit of philanthropy in the exchange.

Substituting pride for apology

Giving is a privilege, not a nuisance or a burden. Stewardship nourishes the belief that people draw a creative energy, a sense of self-worth, and a capacity to function productively from sources beyond themselves. This is a deep personal belief or a religious conviction. Thoughtful philanthropists see themselves as responsible stewards of life's gifts to them. What they have they hold in trust, in their belief, and they accept the responsibility to share their treasures effectively through their philanthropy. Giving is an expression of thankfulness for the blessings that they have received during their lifetime.

The person seeking the gift should never demean the asking by clothing it in apology. Solicitation gives the prospective donor the opportunity to respond with a "yes" or a "no." The solicitation should be so executed as to demonstrate to the prospective contributor that there can be a joy to giving, whether the gift measures up to the amount asked for or not. Fund raising professionals must teach this joy by asking properly and in a manner that puts the potential contributor at ease.

The first task of the solicitor is to help the potential contributor understand the organization's case, especially its statement of mission. When a person commits to contribute to a cause and does so because of an acceptance of and a belief in the mission, then that person becomes a stakeholder in the organization and the cause and work for which it stands. This emphasizes that philanthropy is moral action, and the contributor is an integral part of that action.

Fundraising as a servant to philanthropy

Philanthropy is voluntary action for the public good through voluntary action, voluntary association, and voluntary giving. Fundraising has been servant to philanthropy across the millennia. Through the procession of the centuries, the thesis has been established that people want and have a need to give. People want to give to causes that serve the entire gamut of human and societal needs. They will give when they can be assured that these causes can demonstrate their worthiness and accountability in using the gift funds that they receive.

Ethical fundraising is the prod, the enabler, the activator to gift making. It must also be the conscience to the process. Fundraising is at its best when it strives to match the needs of the not-for-profit organization with the contributor's need and desire to give. The practice of gift seeking is justified when it exalts the contributor, not the gift seeker. It is justified when it is used as a responsible invitation, guiding contributors to make the kind of gift that will meet their own special needs and add greater meaning to their lives.

What is fundraising? A USA perspective

Lilya Wagner, 2004

Fundraising can be traced back to biblical times (for example, the building of the tabernacle in Exodus), to classical Greece and Rome, to accounts of the Middle Ages, and to charitable acts and activities of Elizabethan England. In a mostly European and Judeo-Christian context, America grew up with the spirit of philanthropy. Private gifts from the wealthy in countries of origin helped to develop and sustain not just America's colonies but also its early institutions. Government support was also highly influential, but private generosity built the foundations of a philanthropic tradition in the United States.

Some authorities consider the fundraising efforts for the establishment of Harvard College in 1641 as the foundation of professional fundraising. Others also point to the College of William and Mary in Virginia, and still others believe that Jane Addams and the establishment of Hull House in Chicago in 1889 signaled the beginning of organized philanthropy and fundraising.

Although philanthropy played a significant role in the history of the United States, fundraising as an organized and organizational function only dates back to the early 1900s. The early twentieth century is usually identified as the starting point of the professionalization of fundraising. This was partly due to the growth of paid staff, which changed the philanthropic landscape from one directed by volunteers to one of professionals who then directed volunteers. Scott M. Cutlip, who wrote the most definitive history of fundraising in the United States, said,

> Organized philanthropy supported by systematic fundraising is a twentieth-century development in the United States. Philanthropy, in America's first three centuries, was carried along on a small scale, largely financed by the wealthy few in response to personal begging appeals.

According to Cutlip, World War I provided the foundation for organized fundraising; others, however, believe that the YMCA movement, which began in the early 1900s, actually provided the roots for modern fundraising. Some researchers identify distinct eras in twentieth-century fundraising, delineating both change and continuity in a historical context, but others give generational views or ignore the historical context altogether.

Much of what is considered to be standard practice in fundraising actually began as innovative techniques created to meet certain needs. Prior to World

DOI: 10.4324/9781003145936-6

War I, fundraising was still quite unorganized and haphazard. Philanthropy was usually the domain of the wealthiest. During this period, the need to reduce the requests to the few identifiable donors caused federated fundraising agencies [such as the United Way] to emerge. Eventually, fundraising began to involve increasing numbers of citizens, particularly in the area of social welfare where organizations and people had already been active (for example, in black churches and through women volunteers). At this time, fundraising was the function of nonspecialists and volunteers.

Among those who began to lay the groundwork for formalized fundraising were Lyman L. Pierce and Charles Sumner Ward, who have been credited with developing the campaign method for the Young Men's Christian Associations (YMCAs). Others active during this era were individuals who served as leaders of alumni associations, such as William Lawrence, volunteer president for Harvard's association. Included in this era should be evangelists such as Dwight L. Moody and Frederick T. Gates. The latter was able to solicit John D. Rockefeller for a major gift to establish a major institution—the University of Chicago. The first commercial fundraising firm was established by Frederick Courtenay Barber in 1913, but because he charged a commission, his place in the historical annals is usually discounted. The progenitors of today's consulting firms were established in approximately 1919.

In spite of ongoing activity prior to World War I, fundraising was mostly associated with YMCAs. Only as Ward and Pierce began to tutor others did the understanding of fundraising as a function and service expand. Ward is quoted in Cutlip as having said, "I would leave this work immediately if I thought I were merely raising money. It is raising men that appeals to me". The American Red Cross War Council was created at the beginning of the war with the purpose of conducting fundraising for relief efforts. Ward and Pierce, on loan from the YMCA, were hired to help with this effort, and they raised record amounts of money. Another significant figure emerged during this time, John Price Jones, the first to combine experience in newspapers and public relations with fundraising. The YMCA's form of fundraising, which focused on Christian values and stewardship, and Jones's businesslike approach to fundraising now joined to provide a foundation for modern fundraising—a combination of vision and mission with commercial overtones.

After World War I, consultants became more predominant in fundraising. In September 1919, the firm of Ward, Hill, Pierce and Wells was established. This team included recognizable, famous names, and therefore business was brisk. Others who had gained experience in the YMCA and Red Cross campaigns now became the first wave of fundraising counsel — the pioneers. At this time several changes took place in the fundraising field. First, the fixed fee, rather than commission-based fundraising, became accepted. Second, in spite of the name recognition of many who established or worked for fundraising firms, the idea that the consultant must remain in the background so that attention could be focused on the organization came into fashion. Third, the literature in fundraising received a boost in 1966 when Harold "Si" Seymour, who worked for the John Price Jones company, codified a standard practices volume that became the first training manual in fundraising history.

This era of fundraising consultants slowed down with the Great Depression. The campaigns, which had taken an identifiable format, faded, although Americans still gave, particularly for relief programs. Philanthropy now ceased to be the domain of the wealthy, and the average citizen joined with government to provide relief. Because these were desperate days, fundraising practices took on some questionable aspects. As a result, the American Association of Fundraising Counsel (AAFRC) was established in 1935 to preserve the integrity and promote the dignity of fundraising. The founders of the AAFRC, pioneers of fundraising as an organized activity, attempted to position fundraising as a philanthropic effort, an endeavor that saw a merging of ideological and philosophical ideals with sound business practices.

Fundraising matured greatly between the two world wars. At the beginning of World War II, the Red Cross began a blood donor program; this was the result of increasing government intervention in relief funding, which meant the Red Cross's traditional services were no longer required. Because the Red Cross adapted to change and raised great sums of money, Cutlip called it the greatest fundraiser of modern times.

After World War II, the example of the Red Cross caused many other institutions to begin raising money, and for the first time in-house staff began to be hired. This was particularly true for colleges and universities, where administrators saw the need for more funds and increased goals and recognized the need for professionalism to accomplish this. During the post–World War II period, the need for fundraising campaigns soared and organizations began to seriously compete for charitable dollars. Much happened in fundraising, perhaps too much and too fast. There was little understanding of professional fundraising in the general public. America's ongoing discrepancy of opinion and feeling—sympathy for causes but antipathy for fundraisers—may have begun at this point. Lack of standards caused an understandable mistrust of fundraisers, although the public usually exercised its charitable impulses anyway.

The 1950s saw an increase in federal funding programs. The government poured out funds in greater amounts than philanthropy had contributed, yet when the funding programs closed down, private donors who had become accustomed to government programs were not ready to close the gap. The nation did not recover from this effect until the late 1970s.

In 1960, an influential and significant organization was established to serve the growing number of practitioners—the National Society of Fund Raisers, renamed the National Society of Fund Raising Executives in 1978 and renamed again in 2001 as the Association of Fundraising Professionals (AFP). This organization ushered in the era of staff fundraisers, which continues until today. Nonprofit organizations set up development departments and conducted annual and capital campaigns, many of them multimillion-dollar ones. The practice of placing resident consultants from fundraising firms at institutions began to fade with this influx of permanent staff, and consultants became campaign advisers instead. More associations were also founded during this era, with the most recognizable being the Association for Healthcare Philanthropy, established in 1967. One final landmark of the 1960s was the Tax Reform Act of 1969, which subjected charitable organizations to new regulations.

An expansion of fundraising strategies, such as telethons and door-to-door methods, characterized the 1970s. The Council for the Advancement and Support of Education was formed in 1974, and in that same year The Fund Raising School was established by Hank Rosso, Joe Mixer, and Lyle Cook. This was probably the first formalized training available for fundraising practitioners. In the 1970s there was also an increase in government oversight. These highlights of fundraising history show that the knowledge about philanthropy and the organizations that employ fundraisers increased considerably.

The 1980s brought an influx of fundraisers into the nonprofit arena. Much of this was due to government funding cutbacks. Public educational institutions began to seek support from private funds, something many initially resisted, and the race to compete became fierce. The fundraising function was internalized by this time, with consultants serving an advisory role. In 1980, Independent Sector was established. this organization has been successful in representing donors and fundraisers and has served in an advocacy role. Its formation marked a turning point for donors and fundraising professionals, who began to work more collaboratively to achieve their mutual goals.

Many changes occurred in fundraising in the 1990s, including the following:

- Increased professionalism in fundraising, with a proliferation of courses and training programs
- Development of a body of research and literature providing a theoretical and practical base for the profession
- Intensified demand for accountability by nonprofits
- Consistent increases in philanthropic giving (although never higher than 2 percent of the gross domestic product)
- Growth in the number of nonprofit organizations
- Greater public interest in philanthropy and understanding of the nonprofit sector
- More scrutiny of the sector and its organizations, and therefore increased criticism
- A vast jump in the number of publications related to the nonprofit sector and philanthropy
- A shift in how individuals enter the profession; that is, increased participation in formal educational programs in fundraising as a way of entering the profession
- Greater use of technology in fundraising, particularly the Internet
- Changes in the characteristics and behaviors of donors

The professionalization of fundraising began to receive serious attention in the 1990s. Considerable headway has been made in the fundraising field to bolster the argument that it is a profession. There is a growing, credible pool of knowledge on which fundraisers base their practice; professional development opportunities are numerous; the need for special skills is readily acknowledged; collegiality is generally an expected behavior and organizations such as AFP and other professional associations foster this; ethical practice is a qualification for membership in professional associations; and more attention is placed on the service aspect of fundraising than ever before.

Most people enter the fundraising field because it is an environment that serves human needs—needs that are not served by the business and government sectors. People want to heal, to educate, to preserve cultures, to shelter the abused, to inspire, and to preserve. Other objectives may certainly be worthwhile, such as career advancement, involvement in a specific field of interest, and working in a field that has such a significant impact on nonprofit causes, but belief in the causes that a fundraising professional serves is of primary importance. Fundraising should touch souls, not just of those served, but of the professional as well. Fundraising, or development, as some prefer to call it, is a fundamental part of the process that makes institutions successful.

For the fundraiser, satisfaction is derived from results, often intangible or invisible for some time into the future, not from recognition. An orientation to public service is critical and should be a significant motivation for entering the profession. Idealism and enthusiasm must be balanced with accountability, business-like behavior, and practical action. At the bottom of all is this reality: Most work in the nonprofit sector, whether it is advocacy, healing, educating, entertaining, preserving, or some other activity, will not just happen unless someone brings in money. And the more fundraising is integrated into the entire organization, the more successful it will be.

Is professional fundraising a job or a vocation?

Jeanne Harrah-Conforth and John Borsos, 1991

At its heart the debate reflects a tension, inherent in the fund-raising profession, between the profession's position in a larger American philanthropic tradition and the fact that this position is where an ever-increasing number of individuals make their living. In short, professional fund raising contains elements of being both a ministry – a calling in which service to humankind provides the fundamental motivation – and a job – a career whose personnel are found mainly through default and who apply marketing and "people" skills to persuade potential donors. A closer look reveals that this tension, between fund raising as a calling and fund raising as a business, dates its origins to the earliest days of the profession.

[…]

Most historians would date (somewhat arbitrarily) the emergence of organized philanthropy in the United States to 1889 – the year in which Andrew Carnegie advanced his "Gospel of Wealth" and Jane Addams and her benefactors established Hull House in Chicago. Although in the next few decades organised philanthropy would strengthen its organisational structure through the emergence of foundations and federations, in general the field remained highly chaotic right through the period of World War I. In large measure, philanthropic giving was the exclusive reserve of a select group of America's wealthiest citizens and, not surprisingly, fund raising reflected this trend. Driven by a need to rationalize and make more efficient the donation process, however, the newly emerging federated agencies began to pool resources in order to cut down on the number of requests made to wealthy benefactors … But from one perspective things changed very little: The number of individuals contacted remained extremely small.

The emergence of what historians have labelled the Progressive Movement at the turn of the [twentieth] century, however, began to produce fundamental changes among fund raisers. As social welfare and various public agencies proliferated in the epoch, the number of individuals involved in philanthropic activities likewise extended the purview of those citizens asked to contribute to these organizations. To reach more individuals, fund raisers (still amateurs at this point) were forced to create more innovative techniques. Their solution – the campaign method – was, as Scott Cutlip observed, "to change profoundly the nature of social welfare, health, and educational institutions in

DOI: 10.4324/9781003145936-7

the United States by making philanthropy a broad enterprise and not just a hobby of the very rich."

[...]

For practitioners in the field of fund raising today, it is worth remembering that many of the contemporary standard methods of fund raising were at one time highly innovative developments. In short, they had to be invented. Such is the case of the campaign method – a practice that called for the setting of a particular monetary amount to be raised in a defined period of time and was characterized by heavily publicized competition among teams of volunteers. The campaign method and other techniques that define professional fund raising were developed at the Young Men's Christian Association (YMCA) at the turn of the [twentieth] century by two highly motivated individuals, Charles Sumner Ward and Lyman Pierce. Considering the bourgeois purpose of the YMCA, to inspire values of Protestant Christianity as an avenue of individualistic social uplift, one can see traces of the fundamental tension in fund raising.

[...]

The primary method by which members of the over-sixty generation entered the profession and began the path toward leadership as a consultant or CEO was initially through what can only be called default … A profession that was not "chosen", but rather one into which its members "fall" would appear to lack professional substance. Yet, this means of "finding" philanthropy is in keeping with the pioneer generation. A field whose members may have found their career because they "could not make it in another field", or had an unexpected opportunity presented to them in fund raising, is not entirely negative. There is a fortuitous aspect of such a default career. Elitism or professional snobbery has remained in large measure out of reach of even the highest echelons of fund raising leaders. First, the fund raiser's professional objectives – working for causes to assist those in need – serve as a constant reminder of one's position and privileges in life. Second, the requirements, including specialized education and professional training, to "join the club" are fewer in fund raising than for most professions, and there is therefore a greater potential to attract a truly diverse cadre of professionals.

On the other hand, this lack of standards is a serious draw-back. The image of fund raising has suffered immensely for a variety of reasons. Public perception of fund raisers as amateurs is sustained because there are so few formalized professional requirements for entry into the field. There is a dearth of public knowledge about the approaches and standards in the profession. The image of the transient fund raiser, whose career is based on a life-style of travel and constantly changing campaigns, compounds the negative public perception.

The very essence of fund raising – being asked for money by someone making his or her own living through this act – challenges acceptable American middle-class values. For many people, the charitable impulse is very American, yet so is financial privacy and independence, so that a profession whose essential denominator is asking for money, usually for those in need (who can be interpreted as dependent and unreliable), is antithetical to the very nature of what it means to be "American". There is a disturbing imbalance between the altruistic goals imbued in the profession (goals consistent with the intent of many people) and the deeply ingrained value Americans attribute to self-reliance and free enterprise.

Additionally, the public's feeling about professional fund raising may be one of sympathy with the cause yet irreverence toward the fund raiser. Because so few people know about philanthropic fund raising, the profession has lagged behind others in attaining status with the outside world. Professional standards demand that fund raisers hide themselves in order to shift the focus of acknowledgment and interest toward the cause and the donors: therefore, fund raising remains a behind the scenes career.

[…]

Many fundraisers defend their dedication to philanthropic values by pointing to the long working days, time away from family and friends, constant motivational leadership, and (until recently) mediocre remuneration … Fund raisers sought their own rewards from personal satisfaction rather than external benefits … Fund raising can be seen as a continuum extending between philanthropic values and the mere notion of having a job. Professional fund raisers fall everywhere between these two poles. It is here that the newest generation of fund-raising directors, managers and consultants come into play. In fact, the primary impetus for which the research on which this chapter is based was derived from the differences between the over- and under-sixty generations, which mirror the tension between fund raising as philanthropy and fund raising as business.

Repeatedly, interviewees expressed concern that abrupt expansion and changes in fund raising have jeopardized traditional philanthropic values. In the interviews with many of the over-sixty generation, a fear surfaced that the very elements that are enhancing the public image of fund raising and promoting its professionalism are also eroding its underlying values. For example, the motivations and goals for entering and remaining in a field such as fund raising may well be changing. With the slow establishment of a relatively higher profile through special fund-raising events, the reemergence of environmental and social issues, and accelerated salary levels for development positions, fund raising is no longer rewarded solely by personal inner satisfactions but has begun to shape itself into a profession whose participants can reap monetary and stature gains.

1.2 Historical perspectives on fundraising

Two thousand years of disreputable history

Redmond Mullin, 2006

Charities and the fundraising that supports their activities have been established for over 2,000 years. Both originally drew on Jewish and Graeco-Roman traditions. Fundraising throughout its history has depended on leaders, volunteers and a range of methods segmented in relation to target supporters. The principles have remained constant although activity has been affected by circumstances and by the means available – pulpit or television. It seems there have almost always been professional fundraisers and that criticism of them has remained fairly constant, hence 2,000 years of regulation and licensing. Today we are in a period of extraordinary competition, with national and international regulation a crucial topic.

Fundraising in late antiquity

> *There is famine in Palestine; give your support. I am sending Titus to receive the money you promised and have told people how generous you will be. Every week before he arrives, set aside a considered sum, calculated according to your means. It must be ready before I get there, so that there is no fund-raising during my visit. If you are not as generous as you promised to be, I and you will be shamed. There were previous complaints about the handling of funds, so please appoint trustees to account for the money and take it to Jerusalem. If you like, I will go with them.*

That is a paraphrase of part of Paul's letters to the Corinthians, promoting famine relief to Palestine, written less than thirty years after the Crucifixion.

Paul's is a remarkable precedent for fund raising letters. It is also part of one of the greatest world traditions of fundraising and community care. These early Christians were continuing Jewish tradition which survives today. Then it was common practice for the Jews of the diaspora to send funds to Jerusalem, even after its destruction in AD 70. As late as the third century, fundraisers were being appointed to organise this activity.

That was only one aspect of Jewish fundraising and charity. There were people in each community assigned to fundraising; others to the distribution of food, clothes and funds. Rabbi Jose Ben Halafta prayed for the job of fundraiser to avoid the distributor's hard choices. Rabbi Akiba said: 'It is a greater virtue to cause another to give than to give yourself, blessing fundraisers.

DOI: 10.4324/9781003145936-9

Giving was assessed proportionately to means (as Paul suggests) with the object that no member of the community and no visiting Jew should be in need. Care embraced the *ger*, the gentile resident, the non-Jew. As we have seen, it included relief and alms for Jerusalem. The tradition continued and developed over the following centuries.

The European fundraising tradition was already drawing on established structures and practice from its beginning. It drew on the traditions – Roman and Greek – of the Roman Empire as well as on Judaism. Much in that sophisticated world seems familiar. The rich man of Gytheion who, in AD 161–9, gave oils for the baths, did so on condition that three marble pillars publicising his philanthropy be set up at the prominent places in town. So, in the twelfth century, Bubwith of Wells provided 160 craftsmen's salaries on condition that the north tower be named after him. So, today, the name on the building or facility can clinch a gift. Indeed, in the ancient world the funding of public works and social service by the very rich sometimes took the place of taxation. Private gifts often funded civil works, public buildings, poor relief and even the fleet, as well as circuses and public display.

It seems that the early Christian communities provided for themselves and generously for others. They made donations through a kind of community chest from which everyone, especially the poorest, benefited. In 373 Basil (Bishop of Caesarea), a knowing manipulator of the state system, who had set up a large hostel and hospice outside Caesarea about a year before, wrote to the Imperial Prefect's Assistant: "have the kindness to inspect the home for the poor and exempt it entirely from taxation to make the small property of the poor immune from assessment". It was an important (and corrupting) moment for the new religion when Constantine removed distribution of poor relief – in bread and corn doles – from pagan to Christian priests. Even by Basil's time, founding donors' names and portraits were appearing on Christian buildings and by 321 there was a large flow of legacies to the Christian church and its causes. Peter Brown writes: "the ancient search for personal fame through well-publicised giving, had entered the church in a peculiarly blatant form".

The fundraising and giving of the Christian churches reached far away: in 253 Cyprian in Carthage sent 100,000 sesterces to devastated Numidia; and the church in Rome cared for 1,500 indigent people, many of them refugees. Ambrose in Milan sent ransoms for prisoners in the Balkans (selling his Arian enemies' memorial patens and chalices to pay for this). Support of the poor through its charity was to give the strengthening church distinctive influence as the late Roman Empire (East and West) christianised itself. The poor, disregarded by non-Christian communities, became a special factor for the churches', and particularly their bishops', successful bid for power. Among the poor, then as now, lone parents and the homeless were particularly abandoned. The poor without status were a threat in the growing cities. The bishops and churches embraced them, thus offering security to the state and securing their own statutory position. As numbers of the indigent grew, the church listed the approved poor and, after the Council of Chalcedon, issued under a bishop's signature their licences for begging – a practice that was to become familiar again in pre- and post-Reformation Europe.

Much of that early fundraising was managed by people within the Christian (or Jewish) community assigned to this task. Were there professionals as well as volunteers? Perhaps. In the Ecclesiastical History, by Eusebius (260–340), the heretic Montanus is criticised because "It is he who appointed collectors of money, who organised the receiving of gifts under the name of offering". If this is the professionals' first appearance in history, it is in a hostile text – something you will be used to by the end of this chapter.

Fundraising in the Middle Ages

The Middle Ages were a definitive time for charities. It was during this period that trust law was established in Britain. During the thirteenth century, the Franciscan order was founded. Its elected poverty prevented not just its members, but also the order itself from ownership of property. To allow gifts to reach the friars, a 'spiritual friend' outside the order owned and managed property on the friars' behalf. This was the origin of our trust law.

This was also the period during which the 'heads of charity' from the English 1601 Act were gradually formulated. During the Middle Ages they were a statement of priorities for benevolent action and for funding, to which spiritual benefits would be attached as an incentive. They identified the private and communal issues toward which voluntary funding should be directed. Langland (poet laureate for the poor and disabled), writing between 1360 and 1370, cites as objects for charity: hospitals, the unfortunate, the sick, bad roads, broken bridges, help for maidens, the bedridden poor, prisoners, sending young children to school and the endowment of religion.

This was also a high period for fundraising. In 1174, when the monastery of St Evurtius, just outside the walls of Orleans, had been sacked by the Normans, Bishop Stephan sent out two fundraising letters, parts of which I paraphrase:

> Standing in the smoking ashes of our church among the scorched timbers of its walls, soon to rise again, we are forced to approach the general public and shamelessly to ask for support from outside gifts.

For a more detailed description of medieval fundraising, Table 1.1.1 shows the segmentation of giving between sources, methods used and motivations for the building of Milan Cathedral between 1386 and 1391.

That remarkable campaign was described in an article published by Edmund Bishop at Downside in 1899. He describes how the community came together productively at every level to achieve their cathedral. It was a few individuals who started the street and house-to-house collections. It was civic rivalry between guilds and fraternities and between other classes and groups in Milan which brought out the volunteer teams. The fundraising was managed by a committee. There really were jumble sales and school fundraising. There was also an admirable attempt at major support fundraising.

Table 1.1.1 Fundraising for the building of Milan Cathedral

Source	Method and Purpose	Motivations
Very rich individual	Request for marker gift	Memorial
	To ask and be model for the rich	Salvation
Rich individuals	Request for major support	Memorials
(nobles, soldiers,	Pressure from Court	Salvation
lawyers, doctors)	Legacies	Peer esteem
	Sons' volunteer labour	
	Committee membership	
Prosperous individuals	Through confraternities	(Memorial)
	Sponsor craftsmen, navvies	Salvation
	Gifts in kind	Peer group
	Legacies	Citizenship
	Committee membership	
Ordinary people	House-to-house collections	Salvation
	Street collections	Peer group
	Fundraising events and functions	Citizenship
	Jumble sales	
	Volunteer labour	
Young people	Schools fundraising	–

There was uniformity, apparently, in fundraising around Europe in the Middle Ages. These were some of the ways in which the funds were raised:

- Indulgences were effective: in June 1390 the Milan fabric fund raised 2,398 lira; in June 1391, with a Jubilee indulgence, it raised 24,858 lira.
- Collection boxes, common since antiquity, occur everywhere. Poor Friar Elias, succeeding St Francis and cast as a Judas figure, is criticised for installing one on the site of the basilica he was building in Assisi, in 1230, to hold the saint's body.
- It was very usual for there to be matching funding between bishop and chapter for building their cathedral, the chapter perhaps pledging 50 per cent of the bishop's commitment (as, for example, at Exeter and Chartres).
- There was high-society fundraising: at New Sarum, in 1220 noblemen and noblewomen could lay a foundation stone, then covenant a seven-year subscription to the fabric fund.
- There were many major patrons. Bishop Thoresby (between 1352 and 1373) at York funded 650 salaries for the Minster. Bishop Grandisson at Exeter was helping to fund both his cathedral and his bridge (still visible) about 1328. There were foundations by kings and queens. Henry III and Henry VII made major foundations. Nobles such as Henry de Blois were involved: he set up one of England's most ancient charities at St Cross, Winchester. There were merchants such as Gervase of Southampton, who founded God's House and endowed it as a hospital for poor folk there.

- There was endowment through income-earning assets such as shops, markets, mineral assets, fisheries and mills (cf. current charity trading). Thus in the twelfth century the cathedral chapter was co-owner of the Great Quay in Amiens. Dues levied on Jewish families and enterprises might be transferred to a church or monastery. In Barcelona in the fourteenth century income from the mills was intended to secure income for the hospital there, relieving it of dependence on small-scale fundraising.
- There were even records of sponsored bell-ringing at Rouen and in other places.

The guilds were powerful vehicles for medieval, communal philanthropy. They were formed for various purposes: for piety, to mount miracle plays, and most enduringly as mutual-help associations within a craft or trade. That last form of association has survived in the City of London and other livery companies. More pious types of guild were abolished at the Reformation. Guilds were the original community-chest bodies. There were real wooden iron-bound chests, often with strong double locks, which could only be opened by two aldermen with separate keys. Guildsmen looked after each other and their families, visiting the sick (perhaps with a bottle from the guild's ale store) and providing grants and pensions. There was assistance with grants and loans at times of financial difficulty. All guilds had benevolent objects written into their statutes and looked for contributions, sometimes apportioned according to means, from members. The statutes of a York guild declared: "Vain is the gathering of the faithful unless some work of kindliness is done'. Most guilds were also committed to works of mercy for non-members and to altruistic objects: poor, sick and handicapped people; travellers; schools and schoolmasters: roads, bridges and causeways. We have seen how the guilds of a city might rally to the building of their cathedral. In Strasburg, the guilds had crucial welfare roles. There was overlap across Europe between guild activity and the systematisation of relief and statutory limitation to a community's responsibility for relief. In Britain the 1536 Beggars Act threatened penalties for unsystematic philanthropy:

> No manner of person … shall give any ready money in alms, otherwise than to the common boxes and common gatherings … upon pain to lose and forfeit ten times the value of all such ready money as shall be given in alms contrary to the tenor and purport of [the Act].

This was an early attempt at the control of giving and of relief. Medieval fundraisers were conspicuously successful, hence the real corruption and the criticism. The 1215 Lateran Council decreed that *quaestores eleemosynarii*, as they were called, could only operate under licence from their bishop or from the Pope, a formula already guaranteed to stir strife where papal demands for funds were unwelcome. Despite the regulations, the *quaestores'* success attracted fraud. False fundraisers (sometimes brought in by the chapter) would mount appeals, for their own and sometimes the chapter's gain.

Fraud and personal gain were, perhaps, the least damaging criticisms of the *quaestores*. What they offered was the purchase of salvation. It was salvation purchased through gifts that these medieval fundraisers offered, to their own, their licence-givers' and notionally the donors' gains. They bore relics and were probably the first laymen allowed into Christian pulpits. They drew wrath from reformers as well as satire from poets. They could work for a variety of causes. Chaucer's swindling, prospering pardoner raised funds for the hospital of the Blessed Mary of Rouncivalle near Charing Cross.

Fundraising after the Reformation

On 31 October 1517 the Pope's arch fundraiser, the Dominican John Tetzel, came to sell indulgences near Wittenberg. He was raising money for building St Peter's in Rome and to help pay off a huge debt owed by Prince Bishop Albert of Brandenburg to the Fuggers, who were massive money-lenders. The family still has charitable foundations in Europe. At Wittenberg, Prince Frederick the Wise of Saxony had built up his own collection of relics, from which he wanted to see profits. Far more potently, Martin Luther was Professor of Scripture there. When the Saxons flooded across the border to hear Tetzel preach and to pay for pardons and remissions, Luther protested against such purchase of paradise by publishing his ninety-five theses. His was the cause of salvation by faith alone.

Of course the criticism did not begin with Luther; nor did the debate end with him. Yet it was the *quaestor* or fundraiser Tetzel who sparked the Reformation. (In recognition, the American Philanthropy Monthly makes its annual Tetzel Award to the most discreditable fundraising performance each year.)

Roman indulgences were peddled on into our own time; but what was left for the Protestant world? With promises of salvation abandoned, the main elements of technique and leadership could stay in place. In England during the sixteenth and seventeenth centuries the pulpit was a medium through which most people could be reached, week by week. It had been the medium for the pardoners before the Reformation. Now it was used as potently. In 1536, the year in which he issued his Act Against Papal Authority, Henry VIII also decreed in his Beggars Act that "every preacher, parson, vicar, curate of the realm" should use sermons and all other means to

> exhort, move, stir and provoke people to be liberal and bountifully to extend their alms and contributions toward the comfort and relief of poor, impotent, decrepit, indigent and needy people.

Henry VIII did not give the first example. Henry III, among others, had been there before him. Reformed monarchs became regular fundraisers for such causes as the Society for the Propagation of the Gospel. Queen Anne, George I, George II, George III, George IV, William IV and Queen Victoria all wrote appeal letters on its behalf. George III, for example, decreed: "upon this occasion, Ministers in each parish [are to] effectually excite their parishioners to a liberal contribution" which would be collected at their homes during the following week by the church wardens and overseers for the poor.

Royal patronage and the pulpit were only one aspect of fundraising in England after Henry VIII. Printing was a main instrument of Reformation. Print and literacy increased in influence. Here is a direct marketing appeal by the Quaker John Bellers in his *Proposals for Raising a College of Industry* (the origin of the Saffron Walden Boarding School) in 1696. He is itemising the needs in what looks like an excellent appeal:

> For every 300 persons, the raising of:
> £10,000 to buy an Estate in Land of £500 p.a.
> £2,000 to Stock the Land
> £3,000 to prepare Necessaries to Set the Several Trades to Work
> £3,000 for New-building or Repairing Old
> In all 18,000 pound
> A hundred pound a year in such a College, I suppose will maintain ten
> times as many people as £100 a year in alms-houses.

By 1712 the Society for Promoting Christian Knowledge (SPCK) and others were beginning to build their residing and subscribing members' lists, their databases of supporters. Restrictions such as licensing persisted. In 1718 "a little contingent" from St Anne's, Aldersgate, arrived without licence to raise funds in Chislehurst. They were brought before the High Sheriff. He demanded: "By what right are you strolling and begging through the country without a licence?" One of the trustees was sent to gaol.

All the time, social leadership dominated large segments of English fundraising. [The painter William] Hogarth and [the composer George Frederic] Handel devotedly raised funds for the Foundling Hospital [in London] – Handel was anxious for those children even on his death bed. There was a great concern and generosity – and vulgarity: 'Find a Duchess, flatter her and get £500' was the motto of the Press Bazaar News late in the nineteenth century.

Where were the 'professionals'? As usual, they emerge in criticism because of the percentage that professional companies were taking. In the eighteenth and nineteenth centuries, companies like Robert Hodgson & Byrd and Hall & Stevenson were taking 5–7.5 per cent of the sums raised.

Modern fundraising

Professionally designed and managed fundraising probably started about 1883, in the United States, for the Young Men's Christian Association (YMCA). That was the beginning of a new style of professionalism. In 1919, Ward, Hill, Pierce & Wells became the first professional fundraising company of its kind, Wells having previously worked for the YMCA. From their activity emerged two other main fundraising companies, Craigmyle and Hooker. From these came a highly trained generation of professionals.

During the late 1950s and early 1960s, about the time that the Wells company was transforming some aspects of fundraising, a revolution emerged. Before then, Third World causes had a relatively weak impact, except for occasional appeals, often associated with church missionary initiatives, and sometimes combining Christian with imperial expansion. Then independence for North African nations, World Refugee Year and famine in Biafra and the Congo created an impetus which gave their cause priority. Photographs of starving children and adults in the poor world shocked our rich world into its response. For the rest of the century, Oxfam, War on Want, Save the Children, Christian Aid and the Catholic Fund for Overseas Development (CAFOD) would make their powerful arguments for attention, action and funding support. Simultaneously, prosperity in the West increased and a new age of consumption began in the Western democracies.

Such developments also contributed to the competition for funds which became acute from the mid-1980s onwards. Several factors created this competition. In the United Kingdom, there was rapid increase both in new charity registrations and in the number and scale of appeals launched. The full range of marketing techniques had been brought into the more sophisticated charities' fundraising repertory. They competed through highly segmented direct marketing, sometimes controversially through telephone solicitation, and through television advertising, when this was permitted after 1990. Before the mid-1980s, major support fundraising had largely been confined to capital appeals for universities, schools, hospitals and major arts enterprises. After the success of the National Society for the Prevention of Cruelty to Children (NSPCC) [whose Full Stop appeal, launched in 1999, raised the then-highest ever UK single campaign total of £250 million], many more charities added this segment of support and style of fundraising to their strategies. For example, there was the remarkable Wishing Well Appeal for the hospital for sick children at Great Ormond Street. There were at the same time massive exercises that powerfully reached other, sometimes younger segments of the world for support: Band Aid, the Telethon and Charity Projects' Comic Relief. Camelot and the National Lottery added billions of pounds to the resources available. The result was that virtually everyone was receiving better-designed, higher-pitched propositions for support more frequently and from more petitioners for funds than ever before.

Meanwhile, the [UK] government has liberalised our tax regime so that it encourages more widespread and higher levels of giving. Give As You Earn encourages employees to give routinely through their payrolls. Gift Aid allows tax concessions on one-off gifts, introducing an equivalent to the US tax deduction system for UK charities and donors. For charities that have used them these have had very positive impacts on fundraising here. Government policies and provisions also increased demand from not-for-profit bodies of all kinds – from the arts, old and emergent universities and new hospital trusts. Oxford and Cambridge responded with unprecedented appeals, their targets above £250 million.

Charities responded by intensifying their fundraising. Improvement in the quality and standards of charity personnel has been a crucial issue. There has been much to encourage this since 1980. Standards of recruitment have been raised. There have been some increases in remuneration. Training and educational provision for the sector have greatly improved. Numbers of skilled people, particularly in the 30–45 age group, have grown significantly. There are signs that the sector will be able to offer sound internal career progression.

[…]

Over the past twenty years economic shifts, external to fundraising, became opportunities for it. Huge increases in new private wealth have created fortunes, at their highest levels matching, or excelling, those of the established, philanthropic individuals and families. Many of those established fortunes have also grown. At lower levels a new tier of prospects for fundraising, recently prosperous, has emerged.

[…]

Many of these new philanthropists are in their thirties or forties when they engage in giving. Exploitation of these opportunities has been hesitant, patchy. Have too many fundraisers still been so timid, lacking in understanding, too sceptical, unskilled to identify and motivate such new prospects at levels appropriate to them? … The opportunities are there for the great welfare organisations, if only they grasp them.

The deep roots of fundraising

Scott Cutlip, 1965

Generally speaking, organized philanthropy supported by systematic fund raising is a twentieth-century development in the United States. Philanthropy, in America's first three centuries, was carried along on a small scale, largely financed by the wealthy few in response to personal begging appeals. In those years a small amount of excess wealth in the young nation went, for the most part, to the churches, to the pitifully poor, and to found schools and colleges. There were few organized drives, in the modern sense, before 1900. World War I and the decade that followed provided the seedbed for the growth of today's fund raising and today's people's philanthropy.

Nevertheless, America's modern high-pressure, fund-raising drive has its roots deep in the nation's history. As the skills and techniques of fund raising have advanced apace with America's ability to give, so has her philanthropy progressed, from the "begging mission" and lottery of the colonial period to the highly organized, concentrative $10 billion a year enterprise of our times. The public relations practitioner and the professional fund raiser have played vital roles in this advance. The modern fund-raising campaign, carefully organized shrewdly promoted, and aimed at broader segments of the citizenry, has made American philanthropy a people's philanthropy. These methods, regrettably, are abused by charity bandits and sometimes are used for dubious or fraudulent purposes but, in total sum, popular philanthropy in the United States is a great democratic strength.

The first systematic effort to raise money on this continent was for a college. Harvard College, of course! In 1641 the Massachusetts Bay Colony sent three clergymen to England to solicit money for the college ... Historian Samuel Morison recounts:

> The Weld-Peters begging mission, which one may call, in modern terms, the first concerted "drive" to obtain income and endowment for the College, began early. On June 2 1641 the General Court entreated their respective churches to release Hugh Peter of Salem, Thomas Weld of Roxbury, and William Hibbens of Boston "to go to England upon some weighty occasion for the good of the country."

This was seventeenth-century circumlocution for seeking money. The Reverend Mr Hibbens returned before the year was out, bearing some £500

DOI: 10.4324/9781003145936-10

for the college and the colony. Fund raisers Weld and Peter sent back an urgent request for "literature" to set forth the best "selling points of New England." In response to this request came New England's First Fruits, written in Massachusetts but printed in England in 1643. This surely was the first of millions of fund-raising brochures. Morison describes it as a "promotions pamphlet." This trio eventually fell out, and one of them denounced the whole expedition as a "cheat." Hugh Peter wound up on the scaffold and Thomas Weld became a rector in England. Such were the diverse rewards of early fund raising!

[…]

In 1745 Harvard, William and Mary, and Yale were the only colleges in the American colonies. In the next thirty years before the Revolution seven more had been founded: Dartmouth, Rhode Island (Brown), King's (Columbia), Queens (Rutgers), New Jersey (Princeton), Philadelphia (Pennsylvania), and Newark (Delaware). Starting and maintaining these colleges took capital, in colonies where capital was scarce. As McAnear records,

> The colleges were … saved by the development of widespread popular interest in higher education, interest intense enough to impel thousands of individuals, both in America and in the British Isles, to make cash gifts aggregating a very considerable amount.

This did not happen spontaneously in the seventeenth century any more than it does today.

> The collection of funds from private individuals was systematized, and methods of organized effort and personal solicitation directed by persons closely connected with the colleges were developed.

[…]

In fund raising, as in so many lines of endeavor, Benjamin Franklin put his keen wit, capacious mind, and great tact to work for several philanthropic causes. Ben Franklin was a creative and highly successful fund raiser because he shrewdly planned his appeal and carefully catalogued his prospective donors. He would prepare a list of special projects for each cause and then personally call upon each one. When the Reverend Gilbert Tennent came to Franklin to ask his help in raising a fund to build a Presbyterian church in Philadelphia Franklin declined to participate, but he did give Tennent this advice:

> In the first place I advise you to apply to all those whom you know will give something; next, to those whom you are uncertain whether they will give anything or not, and show them the list of those who have given; and lastly, do not neglect those whom you are sure will give nothing, for in some of them you may be mistaken.

Franklin reports that Mr Tennent took his advice "for he asked everybody, and he obtained a much larger sum than he expected."

[…]

To raise sizable amounts of money for a public cause, fund seekers placed their main reliance on personal solicitation, or "begging" as it was apt to be called by those approached for money. In the 1830s a dedicated teacher, Miss Mary Lyon, was determined to launch a college for women where she could put her own educational ideas into effect. She set out to raise, by personal appeals to persons of means, the $30,000 she estimated she needed. She travelled hundreds of miles, visited at least ninety communities, and obtained 1,800 subscriptions totalling $27,000. The gifts ranged in amount from six cents up. The drive for money to found Mt. Holyoke was launched September 6, 1834, when "a few gentlemen met in Miss Lyon's private parlor, in Ipswich, to devise ways and means for founding a permanent female seminary." The first free-will offerings in Ipswich netted $267. Next, Miss Lyon herself

> went from house to house, to solicit subscriptions. She talked now with the lady of the house, now with the husband … She held before them the object dear to her heart – the bringing of a liberal education within the means of the daughters of the common people.

Mary Lyon carried the story of the liberality of the ladies of Ipswich "from town to town" and "she wrote letters to former pupils of the Ipswich School, soliciting their aid." Such was her dedicated perseverance that in less than two months the sum of $30,000 was very nearly raised. Mary Lyon's heroic, singlehanded fund drive, lacking the elaborate organization and intensive public relations that would characterize college drives a century later, was typical of educational fund raising in the nineteenth century.

[…]

The Irish famine of the late 1840s produced another spate of locally organized fund-raising efforts in the United States. Church collections, bazaars and benefits, collections of foodstuffs, and direct newspaper appeals for cash were used by Irish relief committees in all parts of the country. Merle Curti describes this as "in a sense the first truly national campaign to relieve suffering in another land without respect to political and nationalistic considerations."

[…]

But it was the Civil War (1861–1865) that produced an early model of the twentieth-century American high-pressure organized fund drive. Its initiator was the fabled financier Jay Cooke. Parrington calls Cooke the first modern American, "the first to understand the psychology of mass salesmanship." Cooke was largely responsible for the financing of the Union cause through the sale of government bonds to the public in a hitherto unprecedented scale. He pulled out all the emotional stops to "sell patriotism" to the North with thorough organization and effective publicity. His theme was that the soldier at the front must be supported at the rear.

[…]

These "modern methods" brought widespread sale of government bonds – and profit to Jay Cooke & Company. Moreover, Cooke's methods provided a pattern for the sale of Liberty Bonds and other fund raising during World War I.

Also during the Civil War there were fund-raising fairs in northern cities to raise money for bandages for the U.S. Sanitary Commission, forerunner of the American Red Cross.

[...]

The location of Smith College in Northampton was assured when the citizens of that small Massachusetts town met Sophia Smith's condition, set down in her will, that the college be located there "provided the citizens of Northampton within two years ... shall raise and pay over ... to the said Board of Trustees ... the sum of $25,000." This was accomplished by public subscription and the college started in 1871 – one of the earliest examples of the use of the matching gift as a stimulus to public giving.

[...]

Ironically enough, it was the same Jay Cooke who, through his financial manipulations, was indirectly responsible for perhaps the first volunteer door-to-door campaign to raise funds for charity. This is known in social welfare history as the "Germantown Experiment". In the winter of 1873 many of Philadelphia's factories and shops were closed by the depression and panic resulting from the failure of Cooke's baking firm and the consequent fall in security prices. "Continual were the calls at the back doors of the well-to-do for food, money and help." Samuel Emlin, leading citizen in Germantown, a Philadelphia suburb, used the Germantown *Chronicle* to invite a gathering of all citizens of the borough "to provide for the poor of Germanstown during the coming winter." A Unitarian minister, the Reverend Charles Gordon Ames, came to the meeting with a plan in his pocket, which was adopted: to divide Germantown into eight divisions and then appoint a visiting committee of citizens for each division. He also advocated a central office and a paid superintendent. Another public meeting was called, was well attended, and resulted in the formation of the Germantown Relief Society, one of the first societies for organizing charity in the United States.

[...]

The roots of America's developments in charity, welfare work, and fund raising extend back to the soil of the mother country, England. The YMCA movement, which was to have a profound impact on the nature of fund raising and philanthropy in America, was transplanted to North America from Great Britain in 1851, when the first associations were established in Montreal and in Boston.

[...]

In 1868 the first effort to improve philanthropic administration was also born in England, when the Charity Organisation Society was founded in London ... to deal with the age-old problems of pauperism and poverty in London's East End, it was also "to be a center of harmonious cooperation between them and to check the overlapping of relief." Thus the problem of duplication of fund-raising efforts and welfare expenditures emerged early as a central problem of philanthropy – one that still remains to be solved.

[...]

Another central idea of modern philanthropy, that of the financial federation agencies, can also be credited to England ... developed in Liverpool in 1873. A few civic leaders made a study of the contributions to thirty-eight leading Liverpool charities which revealed that these charities were being supported by 6,000 persons although an estimated 20,000 citizens in Liverpool were capable of giving money; that only 50 percent of the contributors were giving to more than one agency, and only 16 per cent to more than two. After analyzing the study, a plan was recommended by which a group of charitable agencies were to make their appeals through one office and on one central pledge sheet. This list of endorsed agencies was circulated to givers, but no steps were taken toward effecting central accounting, central budgeting, or standardization – fundamentals of the present-day Community Chests in the United States.

[...]

What is now generally conceded to be the first earnest effort to centralise and correlate the financing of community charities was made in Denver in 1877. In the closing months of that year four religious leaders – two Protestant clergymen, a Catholic priest, and a Jewish rabbi – joined forces to organize and promote the Associated Charities of Denver ... Both Liverpool and Denver experiments did give impetus to the long-continuing search for a central charity fund, and both certainly were products of the same philosophy and of the same discontent with the chaos which had accompanied charitable activities ... The combined effort in Denver did not realize all the money needed for the support of its affiliated societies. Consequently, a basic feature of a federated appeal, the immunity principle of only one drive a year, was ignored ... By 1898, reflections of disappointment and unrest were showing in the Society's annual reports. Increased pressures, generated by a growing city and its multiplying needs, were being exerted on all agencies. The federated financing drive was not equal to these demands ... Up to this point the alliance had put its faith in volunteer fund raisers. The next year the president of the Denver Society wrote:

> A few of our institutions have received support that is entirely inadequate to their needs ... In their extremity they were persuaded to engage professional solicitors who retained the larger amount of the sums collected.

Thus just before the turn of the century the paid solicitor for charitable funds appears, one on whom great reliance was to be placed by philanthropic and eleemosynary agencies for the next two decades, in many cases with great regret. In the early years of American philanthropy the solicitor was almost always hired by only one organization, often on a percentage basis, which frequently led to abuse and fraud, or at the least to high administrative costs.

The commission-paid solicitor disappeared from the philanthropic scene after World War I, with the emergence of the modern professional fund raiser and the Community Chest. But the stories of cheating by the first paid charity solicitors may well account for the donor's persistent resentment at giving part of his dollars to any paid fund raiser and the public's mistaken notions about today's ethical fund raiser who works for a fixed fee, not on a percentage basis.

[…]

It was in this period that the American Association of the Red Cross was founded, destined from the start to play an influential role in American philanthropy. It came into being in 1881 as the result of the fierce, unyielding dedication and determination of Clara Barton. This strong-willed, resourceful woman had become convinced of the urgent need for an American Red Cross because of her experiences in the American Civil War and in the Franco Prussian War … From the start Clara Barton recognised the value of publicity and knew how to get it. In her little band of organizers were three able newspapermen of the time – Walter P. Phillips, George Kennan, and Colonel Richard J. Hinton.

Even before the infant Red Cross had received its charter from the District of Columbia in October, 1881, Clara Barton had sent it on its first mission of mercy. In September of that year fires ravaged the forests of Michigan, causing great destruction, making hundreds homeless, and creating needs local authorities could not cope with. When the disaster struck, Clara Barton took the simple step of wiring the Associated Press and a few leading newspapers that the Red Cross would accept and distribute contributions. This powerful yet succinct message to the AP brought a national flood of gifts: "Everything is needed; everything is welcome."

[…]

One of the giants in the field of social welfare emerged in this century in the person of Charles Loring Brace who founded the Children's Aid Society of New York in 1853 … Brace was among the first … to rebel against the then common cheap exploitation of human emotions. Tugs at the heartstrings were then, are now, and perhaps always will be an almost surefire method of getting people to open their purse strings. Yet unrestrained exploitation of raw human emotions can create more problems than the money thus raised can ever solve … Writing in 1880 Brace recalled:

> I was determined to put this [raising money] on as sound and rational a basis as possible. It seemed to me, that, if the facts were well known in regard to the great suffering and poverty among the children of New York, and the principles of our operation were well understood, we could more safely depend on the enlightened public opinion and sympathy than on any sudden "sensation" or gush of feeling. Our Board fully concurred in these views, and we resolutely eschewed all "raffles" and pathetic exhibitions of abandoned children.

Brace was among the first of the fund raisers to realize that only an informed public will prove to be a long-term support and that, conversely, emotional support though easily aroused can, and usually does, quickly vanish.

[...]

While it is true that World War I brought intensive, hard-hitting campaigns that raised millions and established philanthropy on the broad, democratic basis that characterises it today, the pattern was set well before World War I ... In the years 1875–1900, America doubled its population, jammed its people, including large waves of immigrants, into larger and larger cities, enthroned the machine and developed mass production of goods, and spanned the nation with rail and wire communications. It was a turbulent, frenzied period of development which made us into an interdependent society of specialists working along one massive national assembly line. These spectacular developments brought with them increasing social and welfare problems that could be met only through the collective efforts of the whole community.

The increasing needs of the poor, the handicapped, and the victims of technological change, resulting from America's head-long jump into the twentieth century as a major industrial nation of urban dwellers, could no longer be financed by nineteenth-century methods. There was increasing disenchantment with the benefit or bazaar as a means of raising funds on the part of both the money givers and the money raisers .... Charity socials and entertainments became so common as to cause grumbling and irritation among the well-to-do who supported such enterprises and were gradually being replaced by subscription and solicitor methods of raising funds. But these, it was soon seen, were not adequate for the job at hand either.

[...]

As the new varieties and types of organizations concerned with man's welfare continued to proliferate in the 1890s and early 1900s, it was inevitable that accompanying the growing demands for philanthropic money there would be pleas for more cooperation and less confusion among these agencies.

[...]

The early federations relied upon letter appeals, upon personal calls on prospective donors by the society's directors, or the paid secretary, and, in many instances, upon paid solicitors. William J. Norton, a pioneer in the federation fund-raising movement, recalls:

> Although this combination of methods, in addition to the publicity programs that were carried on, produced more money than had been raised by the separate agencies previously, the increase did not satisfy the pressure of the agencies for funds. Consequently the campaign method of raising money became ... universal. It produced larger sums than any known means of fundraising.

The "campaign method" of money raising was to change profoundly the nature of social welfare, health, and educational institutions in the United States by making philanthropy a broad public enterprise, not just a hobby of the very rich.

1.3 Misunderstandings of fundraising

I am not a beggar

Booker T. Washington, 1901

During the last fifteen years I have been compelled to spend a large proportion of my time away from the school [the Tuskegee Institute in Alabama, of which he was President], in an effort to secure money to provide for the growing needs of the institution. In my efforts to get funds I have had some experiences that may be of interest to my readers. Time and time again I have been asked, by people who are trying to secure money for philanthropic purposes, what rule or rules I followed to secure the interest and help of people who were able to contribute money to worthy objects.

As far as the science of what is called begging can be reduced to rules, I would say that I have had but two rules. First, always to do my whole duty regarding making our work known to individuals and organizations; and, second, not to worry about the results. This second rule has been the hardest for me to live up to. When bills are on the eve of falling due, with not a dollar in hand with which to meet them, it is pretty difficult to learn not to worry, although I think I am learning more and more each year that all worry simply consumes, and to no purpose, just so much physical and mental strength that might otherwise be given to effective work. After considerable experience in coming into contact with wealthy and noted men, I have observed that those who have accomplished the greatest results are those who "keep under the body"; are those who never grow excited or lose self-control, but are always calm, self-possessed, patient, and polite.

[…]

In order to be successful in any kind of undertaking, I think the main thing is for one to grow to the point where he completely forgets himself; that is, to lose himself in a great cause. In proportion as one loses himself in this way, in the same degree does he get the highest happiness out of his work.

My experience in getting money for Tuskegee has taught me to have no patience with those people who are always condemning the rich because they are rich, and because they do not give more to objects of charity. In the first place, those who are guilty of such sweeping criticisms do not know how many people would be made poor, and how much suffering would result, if wealthy people were to part all at once with any large proportion of their wealth in a way to disorganize and cripple great business enterprises. Then very few persons have any idea of the large number of applications for help that rich people are constantly being flooded with. I know wealthy people who

DOI: 10.4324/9781003145936-12

receive as many as twenty calls a day for help. More than once, when I have gone into the offices of rich men, I have found half a dozen persons waiting to see them, and all come for the same purpose, that of securing money. And all these calls in person, to say nothing of the applications received through the mails. Very few people have any idea of the amount of money given away by persons who never permit their names to be known, I have often heard persons condemned for not giving away money, who, to my own knowledge, were giving away thousands of dollars every year so quietly that the world knew nothing about it.

As an example of this, there are two ladies in New York, whose names rarely appear in print, but who, in a quiet way, have given us the means with which to erect three large and important buildings during the last eight years. Besides the gift of these buildings, they have made other generous donations to the school. And they not only help Tuskegee, but they are constantly seeking opportunities to help other worthy causes.

Although it has been my privilege to be the medium through which a good many hundred thousand dollars have been received for the work at Tuskegee, I have always avoided what the world calls "begging." I often tell people that I have never "begged" any money, and that I am not a "beggar." My experience and observation have convinced me that persistent asking outright for money from the rich does not, as a rule, secure help. I have usually proceeded on the principle that persons who possess sense enough to earn money have sense enough to know how to give it away, and that the mere making known of the facts regarding Tuskegee, and especially the facts regarding the work of the graduates, has been more effective than outright begging. I think that the presentation of facts, on a high, dignified plane, is all the begging that most rich people care for.

While the work of going from door to door and from office to office is hard, disagreeable, and costly in bodily strength, yet it has some compensations. Such work gives one a rare opportunity to study human nature. It also has its compensations in giving one an opportunity to meet some of the best people in the world—to be more correct, I think I should say *the best* people in the world. When one takes a broad survey of the country, he will find that the most useful and influential people in it are those who take the deepest interest in institutions that exist for the purpose of making the world better.

At one time, when I was in Boston, I called at the door of a rather wealthy lady, and was admitted to the vestibule and sent up my card. While I was waiting for an answer, her husband came in, and asked me in the most abrupt manner what I wanted. When I tried to explain the object of my call, he became still more ungentlemanly in his words and manner, and finally grew so excited that I left the house without waiting for a reply from the lady. A few blocks from that house I called to see a gentleman who received me in the most cordial manner. He wrote me his check for a generous sum, and then, before I had had an opportunity to thank him, said: "I am so grateful to you, Mr. Washington, for giving me the opportunity to help a good cause. It is a privilege to have a share in it. We in Boston are constantly indebted to you for doing *our* work."

My experience in securing money convinces me that the first type of man is growing more rare all the time, and that the latter type is increasing; that is, that, more and more, rich people are coming to regard men and women who apply to them for help for worthy objects, not as beggars, but as agents for doing their work.

[...]

I repeat my belief that the world is growing in the direction of giving. I repeat that the main rule by which I have been guided in collecting money is to do my full duty in regard to giving people who have money an opportunity to help.

In the early years of the Tuskegee school I walked the streets or travelled country roads in the North for days and days without receiving a dollar. Often it has happened, when during the week I had been disappointed in not getting a cent from the very individuals from whom I most expected help, and when I was almost broken down and discouraged, that generous help has come from some one who I had had little idea would give at all.

I recall that on one occasion I obtained information that led me to believe that a gentleman who lived about two miles out in the country from Stamford, Conn., might become interested in our efforts at Tuskegee if our conditions and needs were presented to him. On an unusually cold and stormy day I walked the two miles to see him. After some difficulty I succeeded in securing an interview with him. He listened with some degree of interest to what I had to say, but did not give me anything. I could not help having the feeling that, in a measure, the three hours that I had spent in seeing him had been thrown away. Still, I had followed my usual rule of doing my duty. If I had not seen him, I should have felt unhappy over neglect of duty.

Two years after this visit a letter came to Tuskegee from this man, which read like this: "Enclosed I send you a New York draft for ten thousand dollars, to be used in furtherance of your work. I had placed this sum in my will for your school, but deem it wiser to give it to you while I live. I recall with pleasure your visit to me two years ago."

I can hardly imagine any occurrence which could have given me more genuine satisfaction than the receipt of this draft. It was by far the largest single donation which up to that time the school had ever received. It came at a time when an unusually long period had passed since we had received any money. We were in great distress because of lack of funds, and the nervous strain was tremendous. It is difficult for me to think of any situation that is more trying on the nerves than that of conducting a large institution, with heavy financial obligations to meet, without knowing where the money is to come from to meet these obligations from month to month.

[...]

From the beginning of our work to the present I have always had the feeling, and lose no opportunity to impress our teachers with the same idea, that the school will always be supported in proportion as the inside of the institution is kept clean and pure and wholesome.

The first time I ever saw the late Collis P. Huntington, the great railroad man, he gave me two dollars for our school. The last time I saw him, which was a few months before he died, he gave me fifty thousand dollars toward our endowment fund. Between these two gifts there were others of generous proportions which came every year from both Mr. and Mrs. Huntington.

Some people may say that it was Tuskegee's good luck that brought to us this gift of fifty thousand dollars. No, it was not luck. It was hard work. Nothing ever comes to one, that is worth having, except as a result of hard work.

[...]

I have found that strict business methods go a long way in securing the interest of rich people. It has been my constant aim at Tuskegee to carry out, in our financial and other operations, such business methods as would be approved of by any New York banking house.

I have spoken of several large gifts to the school; but by far the greater pro-portion of the money that has built up the institution has come in the form of small donations from persons of moderate means. It is upon these small gifts, which carry with them the interest of hundreds of donors, that any philan-thropic work must depend largely for its support.

Fundraising is not sales

Russell N. James III, 2022

Isn't fundraising just sales? Whether it's a used car or insurance or scholarships, sales is sales, right? Not exactly. Fundraising is different because charitable decisions are different. They're different at a fundamental, neurological, chemical level.

The first brain imaging study of charitable giving revealed some important facts. Giving shares *some* neural processes with other financial decisions. But charitable decisions are different. They trigger a different brain region. It's a region that activates, "when humans looked at their own babies and romantic partners." Further, "This region plays a key role … in social attachment and the release of the neuromodulators oxytocin and vasopressin."

Oxytocin is part of the family-bonding system. (It's the family-bonding hormone.) Philanthropy engages this family-bonding system.

Giving comes from social emotion. Social emotion comes from the "love and family" system. The family-bonding hormone oxytocin affects this system.

Brain imaging was the first piece of evidence to show these connections. Later experiments got more direct. In one, people received a nasal spray. Some got oxytocin. Others got a placebo. Everyone then had a chance to give money. The result? "Oxytocin raised generosity in the [game] by 80% over placebo."

No, this does not mean, "I've found my fundraising answer! Just carry this nasal spray. Now, what excuse can I use to squirt it up the donor's nose?" The point is scientific. Giving links directly with the family-bonding hormone.

There is another solution. We don't have to squirt something up the donor's nose to increase oxytocin. A later study found another way. Human touch, when combined with receiving a small gift, increased oxytocin. This surge in oxytocin also increased giving. It "increased monetary sacrifice by 243% relative to untouched controls."

In fundraising, it's a good idea to shake the donor's hand. Bringing a small gift for a donor can also help. These age-old practices work. What's new is learning *why* they work. They work *through* the family-bonding hormone.

Sales is *not* a dirty word. Effective fundraising uses many of the same tools. But fundraising is different. It's different in the brain. It's different in body chemistry. What do the brain and the chemistry tell us? Fundraising is not just logic and math. It's not just a market/contract transaction. It's about social emotion. Understanding this can change our words.

DOI: 10.4324/9781003145936-13

Jeff Brooks explains,

> Fundraising doesn't live in the cubicles and carpeted offices of the business world. Fundraising belongs to a messier, more passionate world that includes love letters, ransom notes, pleas for mercy, and outbreaks of religious fervor. The standards of business communication are just roadblocks in that world. If you drag your fundraising into the world of professional communications, you'll leave donors cold and untouched.

Fundraising is about social emotion. It's about building family/social relationships. How do we do this? We already know how. Think about it. How do we build a stronger relationship with a relative? We call. We write. We visit. How do we build stronger donor relationships? Same answer. We call. We write. We visit. And when we call, or write, or visit a family member, what words do we use? Do we use formal, technical, contract words? No. Instead, we use social, conversational, family words. We use simple words and stories.

Generosity and sharing come from the social–emotion system. Family/social language triggers the right frame of mind. It works. What is family/social language? Ask this simple question: "Would you have used this phrase in a normal conversation with your grandmother?" No? Be careful. You might be slipping into technical, formal, or contract language. This language can shift the listener's frame of mind. It can shift to a detached, defensive, market-exchange perspective. This inhibits sharing. In fundraising experiments, these word choices can make a big difference.

Complex charitable planning can offer enormous benefits. Effective fundraisers understand these options. They understand how to help their donors. But there's a danger. It's easy to slip into technical or contract terms. Does it matter? One experiment tested this. People read identical descriptions of a charitable remainder trust. The only difference was this. One began with the phrase, "Make a transfer of assets ….". The other began with, "Make a gift ….". The share of people "definitely interested now" in donating this way also differed. It more than *tripled* for the second description.

Another experiment tested even more formal language. One description of a gift annuity began with, "Enter into a contract with a charity where you transfer your cash or property ….". The other began with, "Make a gift ….". The share "definitely interested now" in the gift annuity also differed. It more than *quadrupled* when switching to the simple language. This isn't just a theoretical issue. That last formal phrasing wasn't a lab creation. It was taken from a popular fundraising brochure. It had already been used by hundreds of charities.

Another set of experiments showed the same result in a different way. Some people read about a complex charitable gift *including* its formal name. Others read the same description, but without the formal name. In every case, removing the technical, formal name increased interest.

One test simply removed the name "charitable remainder trust." Otherwise, the gift description stayed the same. This simple act more than doubled those "definitely interested now" in the gift. Removing the name "charitable gift annuity" also dramatically increased interest. Removing "remainder interest deed" did the same. The results were all consistent. Removing formal, financial, contract terms increased interest in the gift.

Another set of experiments asked a different question. What would you like to read about on your favorite charity's website? Formal, insider terms did not fare well. For example, people did not want to read about "Planned giving." But they *did* want to read about "Other ways to give." Even more, they wanted to read about "Other ways to give smarter." Changing to this phrasing quadrupled those, "definitely interested in reading more."

People didn't want to read about "Planned giving." (Only 4.5% were "definitely interested in reading more.") They didn't want to read about "Gift planning. (Only 3.4% were "definitely interested in reading more.") They wanted to read about "Other ways to give." (15.6% were "definitely interested in reading more.") Even more, they wanted to read about "Other ways to give smarter." (19.5% were "definitely interested in reading more.")

[...]

In yet other study, 23% of people were interested now in making "a gift to charity in my will." Only half that percentage were interested now in making "a bequest gift to charity".

In different studies with different tests, the answer is always the same. Introducing giving with formal, technical, contract terms fails. Simple words work.

Effective fundraising story evokes a clear image that:

1. Produces social emotion, and
2. Avoids error detection.

This two-part goal reflects the two brain systems:

1. The social-emotion system is the engine. It drives giving motivation.
2. The math, logic, finance system is the brake. It detects errors that can interrupt giving motivation.

Different words trigger different systems. They can alter the donor's frame of mind. Formal or contract words trigger a market-exchange frame of mind. This world is logical, mathematical, and detached. It is a world of defensive, protective, or aggressive competition.

Social and family settings use simple, conversational words. This is the world of social emotion and social bonding. This is the cooperative world of *sharing*. Even if things may eventually get complex, we don't want to start there. We want to start simple.

Fundraiser David Hall shares this advice. He asks for complex charitable gifts, but he starts simple. In his conversations, there are no CGAs, CRTs, CLTs, or RLEs. There are only "simple agreements" or "special arrangements." The formal terms disappear. Eventually, technical terms may be necessary. But we don't want to start there. We want to start simple instead. Delaying the technical terms helps. It prevents interference with the social–emotional motivation to give.

Ultimately, these gifts may involve legal and financial technicalities. But these should come later. They come *after* establishing the intention to give. They come after the social–emotion "engine" is running. At that point, these details can even help. They can help calm the math, logic, error-detection system. They can keep the donor's foot off the brake.

Sales strategies can be useful in fundraising. But fundraising is not just sales. It's different. It's different at a fundamental, neurological, chemical level. Family/social relationships encourage philanthropy. Market/exchange relationships don't. Use words that trigger the right mindset. Use words that fit the right world.

Fundraising is communication not marketing

Richard D. Waters, 2016

The practice of fundraising – contrary to the popular perception that it is focused on solicitations – is actually centred on the creation and cultivation of relationships. The professional practice literature on fundraising has frequent reference to 'relationship building', 'friend raising', and 'philanthropic partnerships' rather than centred strictly on asking for donations. Indeed, James Greenfield calls fundraising a unique form of communication that is based on social scientific principles that produce healthy relationships between a non-profit and its donors. Kathleen Kelly echoes this by defining fundraising as "the management function of relationships between a charitable organization and its donor publics". This definition sets the tone for my argument that fundraising is not a marketing function; it is a carefully developed communication process that aims to create mutually beneficial relationships. Unlike marketing, there is no *quid pro* quo relationship where an exchange results in both parties receiving a tangible asset. In fundraising, rarely does an interaction result in a donor receiving a product in exchange for a donation. Sally Hibbert, developing this communication theme and overarching purpose, with its implications for philanthropy across its range of forms, emphasizes the prime need to generate a sound and contemporary evidence-base on the features of such communications that both attract donors and help charities respond to dynamic environments. I delve further into those aspects of fundraising communications which are especially salient for fundraising knowledge and practice: the continuing requirement to communicate the specific and overall societal value of people giving up their private resources for the public good.

[…]

Fundraising centres on the creation and maintenance of positive relationships between a non-profit and its donor publics. Although solicitation represents only a small percentage of the fundraisers' tasks, the focus on increasing gift revenue is vital to nonprofits which need to diversify and grow their donor bases. Thus, fundraisers should be advised against taking a pure marketing perspective with fundraising, and recognize the subtle differences between marketing and communications. With a marketing transaction, the customer ultimately receives a product in exchange for the money being given to the firm or non-profit. For a donation, however, there is no tangible product normally being given in exchange, although it is important to acknowledge that there are

DOI: 10.4324/9781003145936-14

times when a free coffee mug or other small scale premium is provided during annual giving campaigns.

[...]

Whether a nonprofit receives a gift out of altruistic or egoistic motivations should not be of concern to a fundraiser as long as the gift does not violate ethical boundaries or create a conflict of interest for organizations and individuals concerned. Nevertheless, the nuances of how ethical boundaries are drawn, and conflict of interests are determined, may be complex and shift over time, requiring fundraiser sensitivity. Thomas Jeavons reminds us: 'mixed motives are the rule, not the exception, of our experiences in philanthropy'.

[...]

Fundraising focuses on the creation and maintenance of mutually beneficial relationships between a nonprofit and a variety of donor publics. Mutual benefit is key to this relationship as the nonprofit ultimately needs contributions to continue delivering its programs and services, but the donor must also feel satisfied with the altruistic and egoistic benefits they receive from the interaction. Continued, cyclical communication is at the core of fundraising. Programs that approach donors only when they need contributions will not succeed over the long run. Donors must be engaged multiple times in between solicitations, and they must be responded to and heard when they have questions and concerns.

While the amount of personalized attention a donor receives is largely connected to their giving history and size of previous donations, fundraisers have a variety of communication channels to provide the donor of even the smallest annual giving contribution some level of individual attention. Ultimately, it is the fundraiser's ability to keep donors involved with an organization that determines the success of the fundraising function. The overall goal of fundraising is not simply to raise funds, but it is to keep the relationships established with donors active and healthy by transitioning them up the levels of the donor pyramid. Some donors will not be able to move past the base of relatively small annual gifts, however, some will. Through donor research and cultivation, fundraisers can determine which donors have potential to transition from annual gift contributors to major gift and planned giving donors. This growth fuels the sophistication of the fundraising function while the nonprofit continues to expand its donor base by recruiting new donors. Communication, not marketing, is at the heart of fundraising success.

Why fundraising is fun

Arthur C. Brooks, 2014

Once, I asked a class full of aspiring social entrepreneurs — all with business plans and ambitions to start nonprofits — how many of them were looking forward to fund-raising. Exactly zero hands went up. The consensus was that raising money might be a necessary evil, but it was a distraction from a social enterprise's "real" work.

To their disappointment, I told them that today, soliciting donations is often the single biggest part of a nonprofit leader's job. For example, I lead a research institution in Washington. Private philanthropy makes up our entire budget, so I travel every week, and the majority of my time is spent fund-raising.

Sound like fun? Actually, it is. Here's why.

In 2003, while working on a book about charitable giving, I stumbled across a strange pattern in my data. Paradoxically, I was finding that donors ended up with more income after making their gifts. This was more than correlation; I found solid evidence that giving stimulated prosperity. I viewed my results as implausible, though, and filed them away. After all, data patterns never "prove" anything, they simply provide evidence for or against a hypothesis.

But when I mentioned my weird findings to a colleague, he told me that they were fairly unsurprising. Psychologists, I learned, have long found that donating and volunteering bring a host of benefits to those who give. In one typical study, researchers from Harvard and the University of British Columbia confirmed that, in terms of quantifying "happiness," spending money on oneself barely moves the needle, but spending on others causes a significant increase.

Why? Charitable giving improves what psychologists call "self-efficacy," one's belief that one is capable of handling a situation and bringing about a desired outcome. When people give their time or money to a cause they believe in, they become problem solvers. Problem solvers are happier than bystanders and victims of circumstance.

If charity raises well-being, there is no obvious reason it would not also indirectly stimulate material prosperity as people improve their lives. By the time I published my results in an academic journal and book about philanthropy, the only real question was why I hadn't intuitively understood this all along.

But studying the link between service to others and happiness changed more than just my research; the evidence led me and my wife to reconsider

DOI: 10.4324/9781003145936-15

our personal behavior. We raised our financial support for the causes we cared about, increased our volunteering, and — proving that the path to the human heart can run through 100 megabytes of social science data — adopted our youngest child. These things have enriched our family beyond imagination, just as the research promised.

I also began working with nonprofit leaders, helping them to understand the transcendental benefit to donors and recipients alike. And after a few years I finally made the leap to fund-raising myself, leaving academia to lead my current institution, an organization with a mission to which I was morally committed: improving policy and defending American free enterprise.

In this role, I have found that the real magic of fund-raising goes even deeper than temporary happiness or extra income. It creates meaning. Donors possess two disconnected commodities: material wealth and sincere convictions. Alone, these commodities are difficult to combine. But fund-raisers facilitate an alchemy of virtue: They empower those with financial resources to convert the dross of their money into the gold of a better society.

Of course, not everyone shares the principles that motivate my institution's scholars and supporters. But with millions of [nonprofits] nationwide, no one needs to wait on the sidelines and hope that politicians will marshal government power in service of their priorities. By investing their own time, talent and treasure, every American can bring his or her core principles to life. That can mean promoting literacy, conserving nature, saving souls or something else entirely.

[...]

Nonprofit leaders serve others, and help build causes. But just as important, by providing opportunities to give, they empower us to breathe more meaning into our lives.

In defense of fundraising

Sasha Dichter, 2008

I'm sick of apologizing for being in charge of raising money.

I work at a great nonprofit organization [Acumen Fund] that is doing great things in the world, one that's attacking daunting problems in a powerful new way. I believe in what we do, and think that we may be catalyzing a shift in how the world fights poverty.

So why did one of my mentors – someone with a lot of experience in the non-profit and public sector – tell me not to take this job? "Be careful," he said, "You'll get pigeon-holed. Once a fundraiser, always a fundraiser."

He misunderstood what job I was taking.

Look around you at great leaders who you know or respect. What do they spend their time doing? They are infused with drive, passion, vision, commitment, and energy. They walk through the world dissatisfied with the status quo. They talk to anyone who will listen about the change they want to see in the world. And they build a team and an organization that is empowered to make that change.

How good is your idea? How important is your cause? Important enough that you've given up another life to lead this life. You've given up another job, another steady paycheck, another bigger paycheck to do this all day long, every day, for years if not for decades, to make a change in the world and to right a wrong.

How much is your time worth? Start at the low end: if, instead, you had worked at a big company or started your own company or worked at an investment bank or a consulting firm, how much money would the world pay you for your skills? A few hundred thousand dollars? A few million dollars?

That's your baseline. Now ask yourself: how important is the problem you're trying to solve? Are you trying to make sure that women have a safe, affordable place to give birth? Creating a way for people to have clean drinking water so they and their children don't fall ill? Protecting refugees from genocide? Providing after school tutoring for at-risk kids? Giving people with chronic disease a place to come together and support one another?

Sounds pretty important.

[…]

What's your theory of change? How much change happens through the services you deliver? And how much change happens by convincing the rest of

DOI: 10.4324/9781003145936-16

the world that the problem you're trying to address, and the way you're trying to address it, is worth paying attention to? It's both, it's not either/or.

Breast cancer has an unbelievable level of awareness in the United States, definitely ahead of all other cancers. Yet breast cancer is actually the 5th leading cause of cancer death in the United States, behind lung, stomach, liver and colon cancer. So why does it get the most attention and the most funding?

It's because of Nancy Brinker. Nancy's older sister Susan Komen died of breast cancer in 1980, at the age of 36, three years after being diagnosed with breast cancer. In her sister's memory, Nancy Brinker created the Susan G. Komen Breast Cancer Foundation, which has since raised $1 billion for breast cancer research, education and health services – and promised to raise another $2 billion in the next decade. Breast cancer research is the best-funded of all cancers, and that is because of Nancy Brinker's leadership. Nancy decided that fighting breast cancer was worth fighting for. Because of her efforts, drastically more resources (public and private) are in play to find a cure.

This is not about competition for resources, this is about increasing the size of the pie. We've seen an unprecedented growth in global wealth in the last two decades: there are currently 95,000 ultra-high net worth individuals in the world – people with $30 million or more of investable assets. On top of that, there are more than $60 trillion worth of investment assets in the market today, with an increasing amount of this money thinking more long-term about the big problems facing the world: energy and water scarcity, greenhouse gases, global commodity shortages, healthcare and education delivery, poverty alleviation … you name it.

The allocation of these resources matters. Convincing the most powerful, resource-rich people you know that allocating some of their capital to the issues you're addressing matters. You're devoting your life, your spirit, your energy, your faith into making the vision you have of a better future into a reality.

So why are you so scared to ask people for money? Why do you feel afraid to say: "This problem is so important and so urgent that it is worth your time and your money to fix it. I'm devoting my whole life to fixing this problem. I'm asking you to devote some of your resources to my life's work too."

Maybe it's because:

1. People think that asking for money is all about asking for money. It is and it isn't. Most of the time it is about inspiring someone to see the world the way you do – with the same understanding of the problems and the same vision of how it can be overcome – and convincing them that you and your organization can actually make that vision into a reality. The resources come second.
2. People think that storytelling is a gift, not a skill. Learning how to do this – to be an effective storyteller, to consistently connect with different people from different walks of life and convince them to see the world as you do and walk with you to a better future – is hard, but it's a skill like any other.

It's true that some people are born with it. But it still can be learned and practiced, and if your nonprofit is going to succeed, you'd better have more than one or two people who can pull this off.

3. Money = Power. Our society has done a spectacular job of creating enormous amounts of wealth. At the same time, wealth is associated with power, and not having wealth can feel like not having power. So going to someone who has money and saying, "You have the resources, please give some of them to me" doesn't feel like a conversation between equals. How about this instead: "You are incredibly good at making money. I'm incredibly good at making change. The change I want to make in the world, unfortunately, does not itself generate much money. But man oh man does it make change. It's a hugely important change. And what I know about making this change is as good and as important as what you know about making money. So let's divide and conquer – you keep on making money, I'll keep on making change. And if you can lend some of your smarts to the change I'm trying to make, well that's even better. But most of the time, we both keep on doing what we're best at, and if we keep on working together the world will be a better place."

4. I'm terrified you'll say 'no.' We all hate rejection. Being rejected when asking for money is a double whammy. You were already scared to ask, and then the person said no. They have all the power. You walk away, head down, empty hat in hand. Get over it. You're still devoting your life to this work. You shared an idea with someone. You didn't convince them today, but you probably got their attention. Maybe you'll convince them tomorrow. Maybe they'll tell a friend. Maybe you learned something that will make your pitch better the next time. At least you got your story out there to the right person. You made a change – you just didn't get any money in return.

I've met too many nonprofit CEOs who say "I hate fundraising. I don't fundraise." If you're being hired as a nonprofit CEO and the Board tells you that you won't be fundraising, they're either misguided or lying.

Tell them they're wrong. Tell them that your job as a CEO is to be an evangelist for your idea and to convince others about the change you want to see in the world. Tell them that if this idea is worth supporting then they should jump in with both feet and support it with their time and money and by telling their friends it is worth supporting.

Spending your time talking to powerful, influential people about the change you hope to see in the world is a pretty far cry from having fundraising as a "necessary evil."

Do you really believe that the "real work" is JUST the "programs" you operate? (the school you run; the meals you serve; the vaccines you develop; the patients you treat?). Do you really believe that it ends there? Do you really believe that in today's world, where change can come from anyone and anywhere, that convincing people and building momentum and excitement and a movement really doesn't matter?

Of course your programs or investments are real work. But so is evangelizing, communicating, sharing, convincing, cajoling, and arm-twisting. So are videos and images and stories and ideas.

If your ideas and programs and people and vision are so great, shouldn't people be willing to reach into their pockets and fund them? If it's worth spending your life doing this work, shouldn't you or someone in your organization be able to convince someone else that the work is worth supporting?

In the for-profit world, nothing happens if you don't have a compelling product with a compelling story that wins out in the marketplace of ideas and gets people to act. People get so excited about Apple's products that they blog about the next release, scour the Internet for registered patents, spread ideas and rumors about what is coming next, and convince the people around them that Apple = cool. Do you think this would happen without Steve Jobs living and breathing the brand each and every day?

So how is it that in the nonprofit sector we create this illusion that growth and change and impact can happen absent this kind of energy and engagement?

There's this unspoken idea floating around that "fundraisers" can go about their work in a vacuum, having quiet, unimportant conversations with nameless, faceless rich people, while all the while the people who do the real work (the program folks) can go about their business, separate from and unconnected to this conversation.

What a waste.

Don't you think that creating a tribe of connected, engaged, passionate evangelists for your cause will create a positive feedback loop that will amplify the change you hope to see in the world? It doesn't matter if that tribe is 300 powerful, smart, wealthy people or 3 million regular folks who believe in you and the change you hope to make. If they are passionate and engaged and you give them a way to help, you will amplify your impact.

If nothing else, then, we need a new word. Fundraising is about a transaction – I raise funds from you, you get nothing in return.

I'd rather be an evangelist, a storyteller, an educator, a translator, a table-pounder, a guy on his soap box, a woman with a megaphone, a candidate for change. I want to talk to as many people as I can about my ideas – whether in person or in newsletters or on Facebook or Twitter or in the Economist or at the TED conference or at Davos – and capture their imagination about the change I hope to see in the world.

Don't you?

Section 2

FOUNDATIONS OF FUNDRAISING SUCCESS

Editors' introduction

Overview

When first getting acquainted with fundraising, the terminology can be a bit overwhelming. The differences between "planned giving" and "annual giving" may not be obvious, and the purpose of "fundraising cycles" and "donor pyramids" will likely not be clear to people new to the field. This second section therefore introduces several of these key concepts which collectively make up the foundations of fundraising success. The first sub-section contains five texts that offer a high-level overview introducing these foundations, which are also referred to as the "laws", "cardinal principles", and "first steps" for successful fundraising. The other three sub-sections focus more closely on specific foundational aspects, such as the aforementioned shapes (cycles and pyramids) as well as explaining and exploring the purpose of many other basic tools and ideas. The fact that they are "basic" does not mean they are uncontested, so we include texts that highlight some ongoing debates and discussions about their relevance and appropriateness for contemporary ethical practice.

While the fundraising profession can feel lonely, and fundraisers are often "running the whole shop", from creating the budget, working with volunteers, to creating relationships with donors, it is by no means a one-person job. It is very important that it is not just the fundraiser or fundraising team that is involved in fundraising. Fundraising can only be done successfully when the whole organization is involved. Organizations need to be "fundraising-ready" with all the right pieces in place, and all the right people prepared to be engaged, involved and ready to play their part in securing the resources needed to achieve the organisation's mission. This readiness includes the (volunteer) board members because, as noted by Henry Rosso (in Section 1.1) trustees can only fulfil their core role of ensuring the proper deployment of resources after they have attended to the foundational task of securing those resources.

We cannot discuss key foundations for fundraising success without discussing the role of donors. Whatever position one takes in the debate on whether fundraising should be donor-centred or community-centred (as explored in Section 6.2), donors are obviously an important component of fundraising and should be treated with respect (see also the Donor Bill of Rights in Section 4.3). Much fundraising advice state that the best fundraising builds relationships with all donors, not just the major donors: as the founders

DOI: 10.4324/9781003145936-18

of "relationship fundraising" advocate, fundraising should be relational and not transactional. However, donors are only one element in the fundraising process, and too much "donor-centric" fundraising can lead to unintended consequences, such as projects that do not serve constituents or – at worst – might even harm them. That is why developing a "constituency" representative of the geographical or issue area in which the organization works is so important. "Constituency" refers to those who are or potentially will be involved with the organization, in any role possible, including volunteers, staff, donors, clients, and service providers. Using "grassroots fundraising" approaches, as discussed by Kim Klein in Section 2.3, and by inviting often overlooked constituents to become involved in an organization (Rona Fernandez, also Section 2.3) organizations can become more representative of those they serve, and therefore work towards their mission in a way that is inclusive and respectful of everyone involved. Cultivating diversity in fundraising is also clearly a key vital ingredient to enhance inclusivity amongst both fund-seekers and the donating public (see Janice Gow Pettey in Section 2.4). More about the issues with donor-centric fundraising and the power of donors can be found in Section 6.

We hope you will enjoy learning more about the different aspects of the foundations for fundraising in the fifteen readings contained in this section.

1.1 Some fundraising basics

The first subsection includes five extracts that convey basic information about the practice of fundraising. These are especially useful for those starting out or keen to be reminded of the essentials. It is important to note that "basic" is not the same as "simple" or "easy". The "laws" set out by Harold Seymour, the "cardinal principles" set out by Thomas Broce and the "first steps" identified by Irina Menshina, all require care, commitment, and ongoing hard work to establish and implement successfully. This is why Broce describes fundraising as "a full-time, never-ending task".

The first extract in this section, by James Gregory Lord, comes from a short book he wrote setting out "Thirty-five Essentials that Every Trustee Should Know about the Raising of Money". In this extract, Lord makes it clear that fundraising is all about people. People give to people, not to an institution, but to the person who asks them. It is interesting to note how Lord's "Essentials" stood the test of time and are still relevant for fundraisers everywhere in the world today.

The second extract, from Michael Worth, offers a framework for understanding many different types of fundraising programmes, methods, and processes including direct mail, phone (telemarketing), e-mail, events, personal solicitations, and proposal writing. All these methods have a role to play in relation to different types of donors at different stages in the fundraising process, though the feasibility of implementing them all depends on the size and resources of the development office. Whilst Worth is clear that: "In general, the more personal the method is the more effective it is likely to be", he acknowledges that the time and cost involved in personal interactions means that less expensive methods tend to be used to secure larger numbers of smaller gifts, and that these may collectively raise a greater value than major gift efforts. Worth also highlights commonalities across different types of fundraising programmes, such as conducting research and involving volunteers, as well as assumptions about how donors progress and evolve in their giving, as illustrated by the classic fundraising pyramid model. As later extracts in this Reader illustrate, such assumptions are a matter of debate.

Harold Seymour's laws were formulated in 1947. Building on points raised in Section 1.3, he begins by noting four common misconceptions that sabotage effective fundraising. Whilst these are anchored in names and phenomena familiar to mid-twentieth century Americans, they continue to be unfortunately familiar today: (1) underestimating the work involved in raising large sums; (2) favouring replication over innovation; (3) lack of careful planning and preparation; and (4) being too easily satisfied by building awareness and new contacts over monies actually banked.

Thomas Broce's first "cardinal principle" is essentially the same as Seymour's first "law": the importance of consulting widely to create a "strong and timely case for support" (see also Timothy Seiler in Section 2.4) that establishes agreed objectives for the fundraising effort. Failing to put this in place at the outset is unfair to the fundraisers who are tasked with attracting funds (because potential supporters will rightly ask: donations for what?) and will not impress potential major donors who want a clear account of how their gift will be used. Broce offers detailed justifications and explanations of how to implement his principles, including the need to align "asks" with potential donors' known interests. This point underlines that made by many other extract authors (such as Russell James and Richard Waters in Section 1.3, as well as Ken Burnett later in this section) that successful fundraising requires building authentic relationships with supporters, in order to learn what might be of interest to them to fund. A final cardinal principle worth highlighting here, which echoes Sasha Dichter's insistence (in Section 1.3) on wider organisational support for fundraising, is the need for board members to contribute to fundraising campaigns. Failure to secure internal support can result in otherwise willing prospective donors to say no until "those who had decided that this was an important program had also decided that it warranted their support", as Broce explains. More on board members involvement in fundraising can be found in Simone Joyaux in Section 2.2.

Irina Menshenina's advice on "first steps in fundraising" draws on her experience of advising novice fundraisers in Russia. It contains vignettes of the kinds of challenges faced by people at the start of their "fundraising journey" and offers tips, illustrated with real examples, on how to start a fundraising effort, where to find potential supporters, and how to approach different types of donors. Menshenina's core message is reassuring: that even the most inexperienced fundraisers for causes with no system in place and only a handful of known contacts, can build support if they take it slowly and follow known best practice.

2.2 Engaging the whole organisation in fundraising

This second sub-section includes readings that situate fundraising in relation to the wider nonprofit organisation, and in terms that can engage and interest non-fundraising colleagues, including – crucially – board members.

The first extract considers fundraising planning. Susan Kay-Williams identifies the five different stages that an organization can go through in delivering fundraising, which she calls "the fundraising lifecycle" of organizations. The fundraising lifecycle begins with passionate appeals made by a few core volunteers and no organizational fundraising infrastructure to speak of, which develop into highly structured and organized campaigns conducted by trained staff and focused on developing long-term sustainable fundraising income. She specifically pays attention to the important role that volunteers play in these different stages of fundraising.

Simone Joyaux provides many helpful suggestions for fundraisers on how to involve an organisation's board in all aspects of fund development. Her advice shows how to put into action Rosso's view, set out in Section 1.1, that trustees have a responsibility to help nonprofits to secure resources, as well as to deploy them. For (beginning) fundraisers it can be challenging to convey this message to an organization's board, not least because of the typical power differences between board members and fundraising staffers. Joyaux's article helps all involved to better understand the role of an organization's board, its individual members, and their responsibilities. She stresses the importance of accountability: when board members do not comply with expectations such as supporting the values, mission, and vision of the organization, or do not attend board meetings regularly, it may be time to separate ways. As Joyaux stresses, board members do more than give money, and this is especially true outside the US, where concepts like "all board giving" [all board members making financial gifts to the organization] are not common.

In the final extract, Redmond Mullin shares a similarly important lesson as that shared by Lord, namely that "fundraising will fail if it only concentrates on money". In "the shortest book on fundraising, ever", Mullin provides a very accessible and to-the-point example of the different steps of the "fundraising cycle": the four elements that he argues any successful fundraising campaign should contain:

1) Identify the need/case for support
2) Identify prospects
3) Determine campaign characteristics
4) Evaluate the success of the campaign

However, as noted above, just because something can be expressed in a concise and straightforward way, that does not mean it is simple to implement. The next two sub-sections therefore provide more detail and worked examples of how to put these foundational elements in place.

2.3 Developing a constituency of support

An organization's constituency includes everyone that is involved with the organization in one way or another. Constituents include individuals, for example donors, staff, volunteers, board members, and those utilizing the organization's services, but can also be organizations, such as (institutional) funders, government entities, (local) businesses, and community organizations. For fundraising nonprofits, it is crucial to understand who their constituents are, and how they can be involved with the organization.

This sub-section starts with an overview article of how organisations can identify and develop their constituencies of individual donors, volunteers, and fundraisers. It was written back in 1991, by Henry Rosso, the founder of the US-based The Fund Raising School. He specifies the L-A-I principle, which is still current practice in constituency development more than twenty years later. L-A-I stands for **L**inkage-**A**bility-**I**nterest, indicating the three conditions that need to be satisfied for someone to be considered a "prospect", also known as a prospective donor or contributor. When a prospective contributor has no connection to the organization (Linkage), or lacks the (perceived) financial capacity to make a suggested gift amount (Ability) or has no meaningful connection to the mission of the organization (Interest), the likelihood of a successful ask will be diminished. Rosso is also the architect of the "constituency circle" concept, which helps organisations to depict their constituents in "ever-widening" circles, with the most involved constituents at the center. Awareness of the full landscape of an organisation's constituents and their placement in the constituency circles allows fundraisers to meaningfully connect with all of their relevant constituents.

Kim Klein offers the very encouraging statement that: "you already know all the people you need to know to raise all the money you want to raise". She argues convincingly that fundraisers may overlook a highly relevant constituency, those with the strongest "Linkage" in terms of Rosso's L-A-I principle: the people with whom fundraisers already have relationships. Rather than focusing on those with the most "Ability" (e.g. financial resources), which is a common pitfall for novice fundraisers, she argues that "starting with who you know" will help an organisation to become more successful in fundraising. However, she also warns that "if our circles of acquaintances are not diverse, we may have a large segment of potential supporters whom no one in our group knows and who don't get asked." It is key therefore that those involved in fundraising, including boards, staff, and volunteers are diverse and especially representative of the community an organization works in. We return to this vital ingredient of cultivating diversity in the final sub-section.

Rona Fernandez writes passionately about a constituent group that is often overlooked in fundraising: people who are served by the nonprofit organization. Fernandez shares five things that organisations can implement to start raising donations from those they serve, of which the most important may – again – relate to assumptions about the "Ability" principle. She advises fundraisers not to make assumptions about people's ability or willingness to donate. As she writes:

> If you assume that some people are just too poor to give or that they should spend their money on something else, not only are you robbing them of the opportunity to show their support and appreciation for your work, but you're not raising as much money as you could be or bringing in all the donors who can and should be supporting your work.

The final reading on developing constituencies is one that discusses a concept that often evokes strong emotions: the donor pyramid. Where Michael Worth (in Section 2.1) describes this as a useful tool, Tony Elischer captures more mixed emotions about the relevance of this tool that fundraisers have been using since the 1960s. The donor pyramid is a graphical depiction of a triangle showing donors' gift potential within an organisation's fundraising programme. In a simplified version the bottom of the pyramid, the widest point, includes the infrequent, low-value donors; the middle of the pyramid includes the regular donors; and the top, the smallest point of the pyramid, includes the major donors. The idea is that fundraisers build relationships with donors at different levels of the pyramid, to "move them up the pyramid" and thereby increase their giving. The beauty of the donor pyramid is its simplicity, and it has proven a useful tool time and again, especially for newly minted fundraisers working at smaller organisations. However, since its invention, many more frameworks for donors and their journeys within organizations have been invented, including the "donor wheel" by Elischer himself, as presented in this extract. The donor wheel moves beyond classifying donors in terms of gift potential, by additionally taking account of their lifestyles and life stages, which fundraisers know is also crucial information in determining gift potential.

2.4 Vital ingredients for success

The final subsection ends with three readings, each covering a vital ingredient for successful fundraising. Clearly, there are many topics that could justifiably be called "vital", more of which will be encountered in the next section of the Reader which focuses on "Understanding fundraising practice".

Echoing Lord's insistence that "people give to people", the first vital fundraising ingredient discussed here is establishing and cultivating meaningful relationships with people. Ken Burnett writes: "Relationship fundraising is an approach to the marketing of a cause that centres on the unique and special relationship between a nonprofit and each supporter." Burnett advocates that fundraisers should move away from a "transactional approach" to a "relationship approach" in order to create meaningful relationships with donors. Burnett presents relationship fundraising as a "philosophy" that takes into account all aspects of the relationship between donors and organizations, and provides nine elements that can help fundraisers use a relationship approach to fundraising, including being honest, being sincere, being prompt, being regular, being interesting, being involved, being faithful, and being cost-effective.

The second vital ingredient for fundraising success covered here is the "case for support". Timothy Seiler writes that the case for support:

> is a sine qua non [an essential element] for nonprofits. It is the rationale underlying fundraising, the reason nonprofit organizations deserve philanthropic support, not why they need money. Without a case for support, a nonprofit does not have a right to seek philanthropic support, to raise money.

Seiler explains in great detail what a case for support is (and is not) and gives practical advice on the key informational components of a case for support, which include among others the ever-important mission statement, as well as fundraising planning and evaluation (as discussed in Section 3), and the organisation's programmes serving its constituencies. Through a set of ten questions that prompt the nonprofit to "tell its story to constituencies" and ten "core components" that must be articulated in the case for support, Seiler's text enables the reader to create their own "case statements" which can be used in fundraising materials targeted at specific audiences such as brochures or direct mail letters.

Janice Gow Pettey shares with us a third and final vital ingredient: cultivating diversity. The philanthropy and fundraising sectors often lack diversity, and there are significant challenges for fundraisers with a diverse background, as also illustrated by Fatou Jammeh (Section 5.4) and Niambi Martin-John (Section 6.1), who write about their personal experiences as Black fundraisers in Canada. Gow Pettey explains the vital need to cultivate a diverse philanthropic sector in order to respond thoughtfully to changing demographics, and also because it will help to create successful organisations that will:

> benefit from enriched understanding and appreciation of others' cultural, ethnic, religious, and other practices. Fundraisers with an enhanced awareness and empathy for other cultures and lifestyles will assist in cultivating that field of philanthropy that thrives on diversity.

Ranging from an introduction to fundraising basics to vital ingredients, the materials in this second section provide a broad introduction to the foundations of fundraising success which can be helpful to novice and experienced fundraisers alike.

Discussion questions

1. Read Lord's "People give to people" closely and make notes of some of the lessons for fundraisers that he includes in this text. How do these lessons change or challenge your thinking about what successful fundraising constitutes?

2. Read the four common misperceptions about fundraising from Seymour. Pick one misperception and explain why this misperception is still relevant/ is no longer relevant, more than 75 years after Seymour wrote about it.
3. Think about a fundraising organisation with a mission that interests you.
   a. For this organization, can you create a two-paragraph profile of a donor who scores high on the L-A-I principles from Rosso? In your profile, include this donor's demographic characteristics, and their connection with the organization's mission.
   b. Read Klein. Would the donor you describe under 3a contribute to the diversity of donors of the fundraising organization? Why do you think this is/is not the case?
4. Burnett specifies nine "keys to building a relationship" with a (prospective) donor.
   a. Which three "keys" do you think are most relevant to relationship fundraising, and why? Write one paragraph explaining why each of these three keys is most relevant in developing a relationship approach in fundraising
   b. Burnett writes that this list of nine "keys to building a relationship" is not exhaustive: Can you think of more elements that are relevant in relationship fundraising? Why are these elements also relevant?
5. Gow Pettey writes about the need to diversify fundraising. Why is this important, other than because it will help raise more money from diverse communities?

2.1 Some fundraising basics

People give to people

James Gregory Lord, 1984

People don't give to an institution. They give to the person who asks them. Often, a contribution is made because of how one person feels about another. The institution may be almost incidental.

People also give *for* people – not for endowments or swimming pools.

Real money cannot be raised without people. At the outset of any campaign, someone will always say, "The money's out there." But the mere existence of money, without people to ask for it, is like a crop with no one to harvest it.

The donor, too, is *always* a person. A foundation, corporation, or committee never makes a decision. Only people make decisions.

It is true, of course, that foundation proposals have to follow the foundation's guidelines. And a corporation needs a case that will justify its investment to stockholders.

But institutions don't submit proposals to boards of trustees: people submit proposals to people.

Once the volunteer and the prospect are together. The volunteer's own personal influence counts more than anything else. What the volunteer says to the prospect, and *how* he or she says it, will have the greatest impact on the outcome. Ultimately, the best tool of persuasion is the volunteer's own sincerity, interest and enthusiasm.

In other words, once the formalities are taken care of, the volunteer can act as the old saying advises: "Words that come from the heart enter the heart."

John D. Rockefeller Jr said it all (it took him a few words to do it, but they're worth reading):

"When a solicitor [fundraiser or volunteer] comes to you and lays on your heart the responsibility that rests so heavily on his; when his earnestness gives convincing evidence of how seriously interested he is; when he makes it clear that he knows you are no less anxious to do your duty in the matter than he is, that you are just as conscientious, that he feels sure all you need is to realize the importance of the enterprise and the urgency of the need in order to lead you to do your full share in meeting it – he has made you his friend and brought you to think of giving not as a duty but as a privilege."

When we ask for money, we are friends, not adversaries. We are counsellors, not salesmen. It's not a game of predator and prey. We are trying to help the

DOI: 10.4324/9781003145936-20

donor do something significant for the community and for society. After all, we're not asking for anything for ourselves.

Unfortunately, many institutions still think of fundraising as a "hard sell." They train a "sales force" and put them in the field with sales objectives, quotas and sales promotion literature. But major prospects – those who have been contributing large sums of money for a long time – will resist. They have become hardened to aggressive, manipulative selling.

The marketing approach is far more appropriate to the *people business* of fundraising. It's also more effective. This approach focuses on providing satisfaction and fulfilment for the donor, rather than getting the donor to take what the institution has to offer.

Businesses have found – and institutions are beginning to discover – that if marketing is done first, then the sales comes easier. The "salesman" becomes an order-taker who helps the "consumer" make very human decisions and take delivery. The job is not to change a nay-sayer into a yea-sayer, but to increase an order or upgrade it. There's no need for begging or arm-twisting.

"The aim of marketing is to make selling superfluous" writes management consultant Peter Drucker. "The aim of marketing is to understand the customer so well that the product or service fits him and sells itself."

In this respect, philanthropy is not much different from business. People buy from companies, invest in them and work for them because they feel that the enterprise can satisfy their human needs and desires, and because they believe in the *people* who represent the enterprise.

Introducing programmes, methods, and process

Michael J. Worth, 2015

Nonprofit organizations raise funds to meet the four types of gifts defined by purpose: unrestricted support for current operations, restricted gifts or grants to support current programs and projects, gifts for physical capital, and gifts for financial capital (endowment). This has been called the four-legged stool of a comprehensive fundraising program. But in practice, an organization's solicitation programs are usually not labeled in exact alignment with these four purposes.

[…]

There are three core solicitation programs: annual giving, major gifts, and corporate and foundation support. Some development offices have a distinct program for soliciting principal gifts, but most encompass that within the major-gifts program. Annual gifts and major gifts are, of course, defined by the size of the gift, whereas corporate and foundation support relate to the donor constituency addressed. Corporate and foundation support are pursued through a distinct program because … such donors are distinctive in their motivations, require particular methods to solicit their support, and are most inclined to make certain types of gifts. Some large development offices establish separate programs for corporate support and foundation support, but most place responsibility for both under one program and staff specialist.

Planned giving is not identified here as a core solicitation program, although in common parlance many development offices have a planned-giving "program." But planned giving is a method used by some donors, and from the fundraising perspective, it is a strategy for the solicitation of major and principal gifts. It is important to clarify that development offices also have programs that encompass other activities that do not directly involve solicitation. For example, prospect research, donor recognition, communications, and stewardship or donor relations are activities often organized as programs. These are important activities, but they support the solicitation programs, which are at the core of fundraising.

In a small development office, some of the solicitation programs may be missing or embryonic, and those that are operational may be managed by one person or a few people. In larger development offices, each program has a dedicated staff of fundraising professionals, and subspecialties have developed and include individuals working in these areas. That is because each program

DOI: 10.4324/9781003145936-21

addresses a somewhat different donor constituency and uses different methods, thus requiring distinct knowledge and skills.

[...]

Annual giving

The annual giving program is defined by the size of gifts and the type of gifts it usually emphasizes -unrestricted gifts to support current operations. Most are relatively small in amount, less than whatever the organization defines as a major gift. The funds raised are called the annual fund, sometimes called the sustaining fund.

[...]

Many nonprofit organizations are constantly developing their constituencies and resolicit current donors multiple times a year. For such organizations, the term annual giving may not seem to be an exactly accurate description of what occurs. But the term is well-established and widely used throughout the non-profit sector to identify programs that solicit unrestricted operating support gifts on a regular basis.

[...]

Major gifts

Major gifts and principal gifts are defined by dollar amount, and the threshold varies among organizations. Corporations and foundations may make gifts or grants that meet the definition by dollar amount, but the major-gifts program is focused on individual donors.

[...]

Planned giving

The planned-giving program addresses only individual donors, since corporations and foundations are not mortal and thus do not have a need for financial and estate planning. Some planned gifts, especially bequests, may be unrestricted: that is, a donor may simply specify that his or her bequest goes to the organization upon death without any further direction as to how it should be used. In that case, realized bequests could be used to meet current oper-ating needs. However, since it is impossible to predict when bequests will be received It is generally unwise to rely on them in planning annual operating budgets.

[...]

Corporate and foundation support

With some exceptions, corporations and foundations are not the most promising prospects for unrestricted gifts or those that address capital needs.

Solicitation programs focused on corporations and foundations often focus on specific programs and projects.

Foundations and corporations (excluding family foundations and smaller privately held businesses) usually have formal guidelines defining what they are willing to support and how to apply for a grant. Some may issue a request for proposal regarding grants they have decided to make in support of established philanthropic priorities. Organizations respond, usually with a formal written proposal, and the foundation or corporation selects grantees that it thinks most capable of advancing their predetermined goals, on a competitive basis. Thus, in these instances, the donor's decision is based more on the capabilities of the nonprofit to advance the donor's priorities than on the organization's own, self-identified needs.

[…]

Matching programs to needs

A nonprofit organization with a comprehensive fundraising program will maintain a full array of solicitation programs. But, as a practical matter, organizations with limited fundraising capacity may emphasize those programs and donor constituencies most appropriate to meeting their most critical needs.

[…]

Solicitation methods

Various methods are employed to varying degrees within all solicitation programs, although each emphasizes some over others.

The most common methods include direct mail, phone (telemarketing), electronic communication (principally e-mail), events, personal solicitations, and proposal writing. Mail, phone, and e-mail are collectively called direct marketing.

[…]

The growth of social media and mobile communications has introduced additional techniques, but the primary method of electronic solicitation is still e-mail. Fundraising using social media and social networks has gained visibility. It includes peer-to-peer fundraising, for example, in which individuals sponsor friends' participation in charity events. From the organization's perspective, the fundraising method is the event, with social media used to promote participation. Additional emerging techniques, for example, crowdfunding, are most relevant as a strategy for raising funds toward a project.

Annual giving programs employ the methods of direct marketing but also may include personal solicitation of annual gifts at higher levels, that is, leadership annual gifts.

Fundraising events are also a method used by some nonprofit organizations to raise current operating support. Corporate and foundation fundraising often involve personal visits but also usually require written proposals. Fundraising for major gifts usually requires personal visits and often written proposals. The planned–giving program uses personal visits, written proposals, direct mail, and other methods to promote planned–giving opportunities.

The various solicitation methods all have advantages and disadvantages, but some are inherently more effective than others. Henry A. Rosso describes a ladder of effectiveness that places various methods on different rungs, from the most effective at the top to the least effective at the bottom. In general, the more personal the method is the more effective it is likely to be. Thus, face-to-face solicitation is the most effective, followed by personal communications using other methods, such as mail, phone, or e-mail. Least effective are impersonal methods, for example, direct mail and phone solicitations using professional callers. But, of course, there are tradeoffs in cost. Personal solicitation is effective but cannot be conducted in large volume, so it is relatively expensive and needs to be confined to leadership annual gifts, major gifts, and principal gifts. Mail, e-mail, and phone are relatively ineffective compared with personal solicitation, but they are also relatively inexpensive methods that can be used on a broad scale, securing a large number of smaller gifts that may be consequential in total.

The fundraising pyramid

[...]

The fundraising pyramid (see Figure 2.1.1) reflects assumptions about how donors evolve in their giving – it suggests a progression – and it also describes how an organization might go about building its fundraising program from the bottom up.

[...]

An important objective for the annual giving program is the acquisition of first-time donors, that is, moving people up one level from the bottom of the

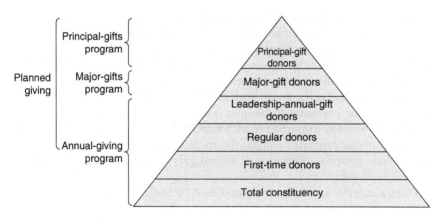

Figure 2.1.1 Fundraising pyramid

pyramid. Once donors have made a first gift, the program's objective for those donors shifts to retention and upgrading, that is, turning them into regular donors and increasing the size of subsequent gifts. If a donor's annual gift reaches a predetermined level, it is defined as leadership annual giving. Again, the latter is defined in dollar terms and varies among organizations.

Donors providing annual gifts at the leadership level may be prospects for major gifts, if they have sufficient interest and financial capability. Some donors, usually after a long, history of annual giving and periodic major gifts, may become prospects for principal gifts; that is, they may reach the apex of the pyramid in their commitment to the organization and its mission. It is important to note that planned giving does not appear in the fundraising pyramid because it is a strategy for major gifts and is not defined by the amount of the gift. Corporate and foundation support also do not appear in the pyramid because they involve a specific donor constituency rather than the amount of the gift and because corporations and foundations generally do not follow the patterns suggested by the pyramid, which relates primarily to individual donors.

[…]

The fundraising process

Fundraising is not synonymous with solicitation. It is a process that begins with the organization or institution itself and includes continuous interactions with donors through a series of planned activities. In her pioneering textbook, Kathleen Kelly emphasizes the latter point, writing, "Success is not attributable to happenstance, miracles, or unexplained phenomena; it is the result of planned action – well researched and systematically implemented".

Various authors, spanning decades of fundraising literature, have described the fundraising process in similar ways. For example, Thomas Broce describes the following steps: institutional goals, fundraising goals, prospect identification and evaluation, leadership and prospect involvement, case preparation, organization of the fundraising program, timetable for execution, and solicitation of gifts. Kathleen Kelly identifies the steps as research, objectives, programming, evaluation, and stewardship, using the acronym ROPES to summarize them. Wesley Lindahl describes a similar model, including research, planning, cultivation, solicitation, stewardship, and evaluation. Timothy Seiler's model includes fourteen steps: examine the case, analyze market requirements, prepare needs statement, define objectives, involve volunteers, validate needs statement, evaluate gift markets, select fundraising vehicles, identify potential giving sources, prepare fundraising plan, prepare communications plan, activate volunteer corps, solicit the gift, demonstrate stewardship, and renew the gift. Figure 2.1.2 provides a simplified illustration of the process, generally consistent with the models described by multiple authors.

[…]

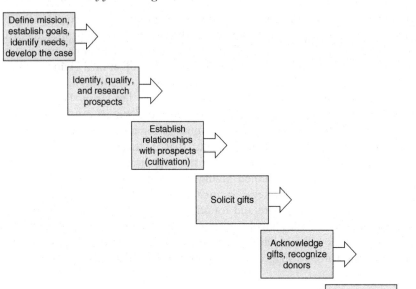

Figure 2.1.2 The fundraising process

The fundraising process is often described as a *cycle,* and indeed it is with respect to a specific donor or group of donors. Stewardship blends into cultivation for the next solicitation of that donor, and the cycle is repeated throughout the relationship. But from the perspective of the organization managing its program, fundraising is an ongoing process, rather than a cycle. The steps may unfold sequentially with regard to a donor or group of donors, but they are all ongoing, concurrent, and overlapping with regard to the nonprofit's overall fundraising efforts.

The laws of raising money

Harold Seymour, 1947

First, then, let us see what we mean when we say "fund-raising campaign." For while Americans use those words more often than any other people in the world, there is still far too little enlightenment or agreement on what the words involve. Here, for instance, are four common misconceptions about effective fundraising:

1. *The William Jennings Bryan Complex.* Before World War I, you oldsters may remember, Mr Bryan thundered his rebuttal to the preparedness warnings of the great Teddy Roosevelt by the confident assertion that "a million men would spring to arms overnight." People who wish to raise money sometimes make the same costly mistake, by assuming happily that if the cause is well publicized, and the people are told where to leave their gifts, the money will roll in.

2. *The Mike and Ike Delusion.* Rube Goldberg's "Mike and Ike – They Look Alike" was a great cartoon idea … But the concept is just so much virulent poison to effective fund-raising, whenever people begin to have the bright idea that everyone should give a dime or a dollar, or that a hundred should give a thousand, or come up with any of those apparently easy schemes that raise money merely by long division and the multiplication table. To be sure, you can raise some money that way, but usually at shockingly high cost.

3. *The Saturday Night Shave.* You'll know what we mean by this if your shave of Saturday morning doesn't look so good when you get ready to go out in the evening; you just give it "the once over lightly." That's all right with a beard, but it is almost always fatal in a fund-raising campaign, for the basic reason that success never comes the easy way, and always requires careful planning and preparation and a lot of hard work.

4. *The Pattern of the Losing Football Coach.* When you can't win, it may be comforting to reflect that you are building character. But those who want nothing less than victory in a fund-raising campaign should always take heed, if not actually do a little viewing with alarm, when the campaign manager starts talking about "the larger, long-term gains in making new friends for the institution." To be sure, a fund-raising campaign is a public relations operation from start to finish; the design, however, should be for giving.

[…]

DOI: 10.4324/9781003145936-22

An organised fund-raising campaign comprises five basic elements ...

First, in chronological order rather than in order of importance, a good campaign needs a strong and timely case.

[...]

Most important of all, but placed second because you usually have to have a good case to get it, is active and influential leadership. Without such leadership many a good cause has withered on the vine; with it, you can accomplish almost anything.

[...]

Third, a successful campaign needs a sufficient number of informed and enthusiastic volunteer workers ...

The fourth essential is a campaign constituency, or field of support, in which the known giving potential is commensurate with the campaign goal.

[...]

The fifth essential, for lack of a better term, we'll call campaign dynamic. If you've made a good watch by qualifying your campaign on the first four essentials, this is what you need to make the watch tick – the catalytic agent to put the mixture to the boil. In its essence, campaign dynamics involves the routines of planning, timing, direction, and operations. But you could just as well say that it involves the skillful manipulation of the laws of human behavior by competent campaign management.

[...]

Here then are the laws of raising money, with which the fund-raising fraternity are believed to be in virtually unanimous agreement:

1. The quantitative result of every fund-raising campaign varies directly with the quality and devotion of the leadership.
2. The effectiveness of any campaign organization can be measured by the extent to which responsibility is decentralized, by the planned distribution of assimilable work units.
3. Personal contacts, whether for the enlistment of workers or the solicitation of gifts, should be established on the same or higher level.
4. Campaigns are best conducted in an atmosphere of universality – a general public impression that everyone will benefit and that nearly everyone will wish to participate ...
5. To paraphrase Shakespeare, if a campaign were to be done, 'twere well it were done quickly; in communities, as in kindergartens, attention periods have their limits.
6. You can't raise money without spending money; within reasonable limits the return is likely to be commensurate with the investment.
7. Every good campaign is essentially a public relations operation – an aggregate of the tremendous trifles by which any enterprise wins and holds public approval; good manners, pleasurable experiences, recognition for achievement, and proof that all the sacrifice anyone made was worth far more than its cost.

The nine cardinal principles of fundraising

Thomas E. Broce, 1986

Throughout this text several basic fund raising principles will appear again and again. They must be highlighted at the outset because they are fundamental to every kind of program, whether a one-time campaign for capital gifts or a drive for annual gifts that must be repeated every year. Because they are so important, I call them the "nine cardinal principles."

Cardinal principle I: institutional or organizational objectives must be established first

Before any successful fund-raising program can take place, the institution or organization seeking funds must determine, define, and articulate its purpose and objectives. As basic as this principle may seem to many, others find it difficult to accept. An organization that hires people and expects them simply to "go out and raise money" cannot expect impressive results. The people may get "donations," but they will not be able to attract substantial funds.

Part of the difficulty lies in a confusion about who is to identify the institution's objectives and why the goals must be reviewed periodically. College presidents, for example, may dismiss the problem, saying that the goals "are in the catalogue," though those goals have not been reviewed in fifteen years. Perhaps the goals are still valid, but for success to be assured, periodic review is wise – and is absolutely essential before a fund-raising campaign is launched. The goals must be current, believable, and salable. In a serious fund-raising effort the solicitors, both staff members and volunteers, must be prepared to describe the institution's goals for the future and how it plans to reach them. Serious prospective donors will want to know.

Since goals reflect and are reflected in policy and direction, the staff in concert with selected organizational directors or trustees should make goal establishment or review a matter of early priority in planning a fund-raising effort – so early, in fact, that it should be considered pre-planning. The fund-raising officer should participate, as should the institution's key leaders, including volunteers. If volunteers do not have a voice in determining the institution's direction, they will have little enthusiasm for selling someone else's program. We will talk about "taking ownership" as a key ingredient to success. This is a significant expression. The persons on whom an organization is depending for fund-raising success must feel that the program is their program. And they

DOI: 10.4324/9781003145936-23

must develop this feeling early. So the preplanning time is the best time to involve the key leaders and prospects.

The planning should not be elaborate or time consuming. Since it has a specific purpose, it should have a specific deadline. It must be accomplished before one can move to the next phase of fund-raising.

It should be remembered that institutional planning is a process that never stops. Fixed long-range planning – beyond five years, for example – doesn't work, because change is always with us, especially in dynamic organizations.

Cardinal principle II: development objectives must be established to meet institutional goals

How I pity people hired to "raise money" without any idea how the money is going to be used in the life of the institution. They might just as well stand on busy corners with tin cups. Once institutional objectives have been established (or re-articulated), it is time to set development objectives.

Donors give gifts to meet objectives, not simply to give money away. Good causes are abounding today, and most all need money. The act of giving away material possessions is not an instinctive one. Most people do so with some reluctance even when the funds are not their own but corporate money. Congruently, few people are born with a natural desire to ask others for money. Many people do like to support worthy causes or efforts, however, and when they are presented with a challenging idea or program that is consistent with their interests, they tend to respond favorably. Likewise, a solicitor has an easier time selling an idea than making a vague request for cash. The institution must know exactly what it plans to do with the gift and must be able to show how such a project or gift will fit in the institution's future. Key questions to consider in this planning stage are: What are we doing or about to do that makes a gift to us important? Why do we deserve support?

Few spokesmen for American institutions can answer in two minutes or less the question: "How would you spend one million dollars if it were given to you today?" Many must stab at an answer (usually naming a building project) or stall for time to hold a meeting. Few can say with authority or confidence how they would use such a windfall. Yet if they can't answer that question, how can they solicit donors for gifts?

Cardinal principle III: the kinds of support needed determine the kinds of fund-raising programs

Whether an institution should expend its staff and resources on an aggressive foundation solicitation program or an aggressive annual gifts program must be determined by the kind of gift support it needs. Again, this decision is based on the institution's goals.

This sounds simple enough, but it is a principle that is repeatedly ignored. For example, how can a church-supported junior college needing supplementary annual support defend a decision to have its chief development officer concentrate primarily on seeking gifts from foundations, despite the fact that most foundations do not make gifts to annual support programs? When a development program is being started, those persons responsible must determine the kinds of gifts needed to meet the institution's objectives and the kind of program that will best attract these kinds of gifts. The donors most likely to support these programs can then be identified, and the development program can be launched.

This principle should not be interpreted to mean that only one phase of a development activity can be conducted at a time. Most development staffs are limited in personnel and funds, however, and the institution deserves maximum return on its investment in development. Institutions should not spend hard-earned dollars on nonproductive programs. Therefore, an institution with a small endowment but a great need for additional operating support should place its prime emphasis on aggressive annual-gifts programs. It also should be active in corporate-support programs with a continuing interest in planned giving programs, but its primary staff and dollar concentration should be on securing operating funds, which come mostly from individuals and corporations. The institution should also be attracting endowment funds, but that should remain a secondary activity. On the other hand, using the same criteria, a research-oriented organization should focus its attention on fund raising from foundations.

I will also make reference to the fund-raising process of "sequencing". The term usually refers to the scheduling of gift solicitation; that is, large gifts should be secured before efforts are directed to smaller gifts. In the context of Principle III, sequencing has another importance: starting various phases of the fund-raising program and building on success. For example, when an organization starts a fund-raising program, I always recommend that it first build a good base of annual support. A hospital, for example, that needs to attract money for medical programs, equipment, and, perhaps, building expansion will do well to start with a high-level, sophisticated, aggressive annual giving program. There are two reasons for this: (1) the volunteer board and close friends will have a chance to make a financial contribution, and the need for financial support can be carried to the broader community; and (2) people who are serious annual contributors are the best prospects for special or capital gifts. By soliciting well, the hospital begins to cultivate well. So, in determining which fund-raising programs to emphasize, the organization begins by building a productive annual giving program with the awareness that it will expand to special program or capital efforts. This is "sequencing" the fund-raising program to meet institutional objectives.

Cardinal principle IV: the institution must start with natural prospects

The "rock in the pond" principle is significant in serious fund raising. An institution cannot expect others to invest in it until those who are closest to the center do so. To illustrate: A distinguished private university did all its pre-campaign work before launching an ambitious program. On the day the campaign plan was presented to the board, the trustees listened attentively, voted unanimously to launch the effort, and then wished the president and his development staff well in their efforts. Most of the trustees agreed that it was just the kind of program many major corporations would like to support.

The staff soon discovered after it hit the road that most prospects did indeed say that they were interested and then asked, "How much has the board contributed?" When told that the trustees had not yet made gifts, the prospects told the solicitors to come back after those who had decided that this was an important program had also decided that it warranted their own support. The campaign bogged down for nearly eighteen months while the staff regrouped.

In establishing priority prospect assignments, it is always necessary to start at the center and work out. The farther from the center, the weaker the interest. This is true in annual as well as capital campaigns. It is also necessary for one's best prospects to be active in the fund-raising organization, where they receive maximum information and cultivation. Such prospects will quickly realize that they must make a gift before they can ask others to do so.

Cardinal principle V: the case for the program must reflect the importance of the institution

The term "case" is used in fund-raising to describe the need for the institution and the program being conducted to support it. For most programs a "case statement" is prepared to convey the value and need to prospective donors. The case statement can be duplicated or printed. But it must be remembered that *the case is more important than the document that describes it*. It must be brief and tastefully prepared, and it must communicate – it must reflect clearly the value of the institution, the worthiness of its objectives, and the undeniable need of funds to meet those objectives.

While the following statements may smack of the melodramatic, reflection on them is essential to success in fund-raising:

1. The members of the fund-raising staff, individually and collectively, must be thoroughly convinced that they are giving the potential donors an opportunity to make a significant investment in a worthwhile cause. Their enthusiasm is contagious. Any doubts or reservations they may have will become apparent to donors.
2. This enthusiasm must be conveyed in every facet of the fund-raising effort, from the preparation of the case statement to the personal solicitation of a gift
3. If this enthusiasm is not shared by professional staff and volunteer workers, the program will never receive the enthusiastic support of others.

The coming preparation of the case for the institution must be constantly in the mind of the chief development officer as he or she participates in institutional planning. The officer must ask himself or herself the questions he or she knows that others will ask later. He or she will want to anticipate as many of those questions as possible in the preparation of the case.

[…]

Cardinal principle VI: involvement is the key to leadership and support

Few people like to be asked to "work for" or "give to" an organization or institution about which they know very little. This is especially true in the fund-raising activities of not-for-profit organizations. If individuals or groups are to be stimulated to make a commitment to a program, they must have the opportunity to be involved in its planning and its operation. The best trustees or directors of an organization are those who are meaningfully involved. The same is true in fund-raising: the best solicitors are those who are most involved. The same is also true of contributors. They will be the ones who are involved in the effort from the conception to victory. They will also be the most aggressive and successful cultivators and solicitors of others.

Most successful people in today's society are busy – they don't need another volunteer job. Therefore, every executive involved in the life of an organization must work with sincerity and consistency in keeping good people meaningfully involved. The meaningful involvement of individuals is a full-time, never-ending task. It must be sincere, it must be constant, and it must be real.

Cardinal principle VII: prospect research must be thorough and realistic

Before significant fund-raising can take place, the staff must identify and evaluate those persons, foundations, corporations, and organizations from which it reasonably can expect to receive support. Blue-sky prospect identification is dangerous. Because people have accumulated wealth does not automatically mean that they will wish to grace your institution with gifts. Because a foundation has made a gift to one college in your state does not mean that it will automatically support yours. The reason for giving may well be no more than geographic, but there must be a reason.

Prospect identification and evaluation should be another continuous staff function. Volunteers can often be used as resources for evaluation, but most of the data must be gathered and maintained by staff. Such research includes collecting information on which to base sound determination about the right prospects for the project (amount and purpose), as well as the right time to solicit from those prospects.

Early in the consideration of a fund-raising program the question must be soberly raised: Who is going to give us the money? It seems to be a rather simplistic question, but I have found many organizational leaders who know that they need financial support but have never pondered realistically where the money is coming from. Answering this question is prospect research.

Cardinal principle VIII: cultivation is the key to successful solicitation

Cultivation of prospects and potential prospects is a process, not a one-time effort. It must be as deliberate and well planned as all other phases of fund-raising. Cultivation again implies involvement both naturally and by design. Prospects are of three kinds: (1) those ready to be solicited, (2) those interested in the institution but not yet meaningfully involved, and (3) those with potential but no known relationship. Prospects in categories 2 and 3 are brought into category 1 by the process of cultivation. In all instances the cultivation must be thorough before sacrificial giving can be anticipated.

Cardinal principle IX: solicitation is successful only if cardinal principles I through VIII have been followed

Many persons engaged in fund-raising think that they can obtain money simply by asking rich persons (or organizations) to give it. Not so. Solicitation is the final (and then often the easiest) step in the fund-raising process. It is at this point that well-motivated donors, thoroughly informed and involved, seize the opportunity to make investments in an organization or institution in whose present operation or future growth they have significant interest and concern.

[...]

In the end, giving depends on the motivation of others to participate. Motivation can often be manufactured, but it is nonetheless real, and the fund-raising process simply provides the mechanism for making things happen.

Fund raisers, paid and volunteer, are not magicians. They must be armed with the knowledge and resources to complete their tasks. From the "cardinal principles" through the mechanics, the most important factors remain honesty, integrity, knowledge, willingness to work hard, and unquenchable optimism. It must be remembered, however, that no one gives unless he or she is asked.

First steps in fundraising – a Russian perspective

Irina Menshenina, 2020

Fundraising in Russia is developing at a rapid pace: non-profit organizations actively hire specialists in raising funds, institutional and private donors allocate money for the development of the infrastructure of non-profit organizations, a consulting practice is emerging, experienced fundraisers transfer their expertise to beginners, technological tools are created.

When starting fundraising every non-profit goes through the first steps of trial and errors. Most of them learn in practice how to expand sources of funding, they move from grant applications to asking for donations from individuals. Some charities already have a donor base, but the inflow of money is weak, while others do not have donors yet, and they need to be found. This chapter provides three practical tips for those who are just starting their fundraising journey.

Fundraising is a complex activity. Where to begin? Write a strategy or shoot a video? Redesign the website or approach all the companies in your city? What are the first steps to take in an organization if there is no system yet? These questions are asked by novice fundraisers who come to me for consultations, as the following three examples illustrate.

Margarita: "I am a successful entrepreneur; I have built several small businesses that work well and bring good income without my participation. For several months now I have been trying to help a charitable foundation build a shelter for homeless animals. I was sure that I would quickly find funding from people like me and sponsors because it's such a good deed! I sent out dozens of letters and presentations, held meetings with those who know me personally from my business. But the result of the "sales" is deplorable. People say: what a fine fellow you are for doing this! But we don't get to the "deal". A couple of times I left the meeting with some small cash in hands, but this depressed me more than pleased me. I'm completely at a loss. My inner businessman doubts whether I can pull this off. I understand intellectually that it is possible to collect money – after all, it works out for others – but something is missing in my system".

Peter: "I am a former drug addict. Fortunately, I am done with it, and now I'm participating in a project to help other guys with this problem. We have opened a camp where a program of labor, sports and rehabilitation is in

DOI: 10.4324/9781003145936-24

place for boys and girls. We have many volunteers, including psychologists, trainers and other specialists. But money is needed for premises, food, transport, equipment, accounting and so on. We wrote letters to the deputies, but this does not lead anywhere. We went to businessmen, asked for sponsorship, but they say there's no money. We contacted local television to promote our number for SMS donation, they said that only appeals for sick children were taken. Sometimes someone agrees to help in kind: a bus is allocated once a month, soccer balls are handed over. But that doesn't save us. How to move on? Who can I ask for money?"

Kirill: "I have been thinking about the transition from the world of big business to the non-profit sector for a long time. In a large company, your personal contribution is hardly noticeable, and the end result of the financial well-being of the company shareholders is not my thing. But it is not clear to me how much I would be able to realize myself as a professional in a charity. I have worked in marketing and sales for many years. But I don't know anything about the life of charitable organizations. Please advise the correct strategy for entering this world."

Sergey: "The task of our charitable foundation is material support for war and labor veterans. From the first day the work has been financed by the founders and members of the Management Board. This is a group of five businessmen who make all key decisions. Six months ago they raised the issue of the need to raise additional funds. I need to present a draft strategy for the development of private fundraising in order to understand what investment will be required for that. There is a certainty that we should aim for small donations from ordinary people. I have worked in advertising and marketing in the past. I don't want to waste time on the way from A to Z by trial and error. I will be grateful if you tell me what to pay attention to right away, what trends in fundraising will become a mass practice in the near future."

First tip: find a foothold in the chaos

Chaos is not an offensive label, but the status quo of an organization at its first stage of development.

Imagine that we entered a teenager's room, which has not been cleaned for a month. Where do we start? Let's find a free island on the floor where you can stand with two feet without risking stepping on or crushing anything. Centimeter by centimeter we will begin to disassemble the mess, putting things in their places and throwing away unnecessary things. And, at the same time, we will find out a lot of new and interesting things.

So, at first with fundraising. It is okay not to have a long-term strategy – short-term tactics are enough at the beginning. Think and choose what you need first: identify your target groups of donors and forms of communication with them, draw a funnel for attracting donors. Plan your first steps. Your island of resilience is something that you do well. For example, writing letters, or organizing events, or building social networks: tasks that simple and clear to you. This will make the first success story. And it is extremely important for the fundraiser himself and for the entire organization to believe in yourself!

Second tip: gather people who have ever helped your organization in some way

Collect all the existing contacts into one list. Do not be worried if there are only a few of them, even just 5 people is enough! Record the information in a table: Excel is ideal for this purpose. This will be the birth of your donor database.

Interview literally everyone in the organization about the people or companies that have been in a relationship with you. I guarantee that even in the most advanced organizations, employees have "their own" such lists that are not included in any database.

I had an experience when I, bit by bit, methodically collected a database of contacts of people who donated for the treatment of seriously ill children. For six months of the new project, there were 700 people in it. I knew the first 100–150 of them by their names.

I also have experience of deleting contacts from a list. When I started working at Downside Up in 2001, I got a base of 500 imaginary donors. Why imaginary? Because it was a list of those the foundation had only hoped to contact at that time. They were not our partners. We sent 500 letters to these companies by mail and asked to give us an answer, whether the organization wants to be in touch (note the wording "to be in touch" – we didn't even ask for anything) with our foundation. To simplify feedback and increase the chances of getting it, we put a ready-made envelope with a postage stamp and a questionnaire in the shipment, where they had to fill in a minimum of information.

We received 19 responses. I didn't know if it was a good result or not at that time because we hadn't heard about "conversion" yet. The foundation is still in touch with someone who then answered positively – they donate and participate in volunteer activities. The rest I then crossed out.

A couple of times I helped small foundations "find" their donors literally over a cup of tea.

Galina, director: "We have no private donors, well, maybe three people. Vorobiev, Sokolov and Galkin. They sometimes send money by bank transfer."
Andrey, administrator: "And that foreigner, Finn, it seems, he brought cash 2–3 times. I have his business card somewhere."
Maria, fundraiser: "We can add to the list those with whom I communicate in companies. They themselves have not yet donated, but we did not ask. And then, their companies are our potential partners. I am just waiting for a response from them to our New Year's appeal."
Me: "Who else gives you funds?"
Galina: "Our founders and members of the board … Well, they also need to be included in the database!"
Me: "First of all".

Bingo! So, we got about 20 names and titles and created a centralized list of donors.

What to do next? Connect with the people on your list and stay in touch with them! Thank them for their support in the past, tell them about your plans, invite them over. Keep in touch with them on a regular basis!

Third tip: if you have no previous experience in fundraising, organize a trial, or pilot, project

It can also be called capsule project. A capsule is a shell that contains various ingredients linked together, be it a medicine or a set of wardrobe items. The capsules are usually small and healthy.

Why am I suggesting this analogy? Because on a small and independent project it is easier to learn, try, test yourself and your approach, check it and correct mistakes. These will be seeds planted in the soil that will sprout. After completing this pilot project, it will be easier for you to make another, following the same rules, but based on experience.

Where does a capsule project start? Always with a description of what the charity plans to do for its beneficiaries. This can be the organization of renovation in an animal shelter, a series of psychological counseling for victims of violence, the distribution of hot food to homeless people.

Describe the project in full and in detail, as if you already have the money to implement it and you just need to inform the whole team about what they have to do. Why is that so? First, careful detailing will help you see all the costs involved. It often happens that a project budget overlooks overhead costs, such as bookkeeping, bank fees, or management. Secondly, a detailed description will help the fundraiser, and therefore the donor, to truly understand what the project consists of. It will be more likely to be correct if the fundraiser receives the description of the project from the person who will directly organize it: the head of the NGO, the manager for work with beneficiaries, etc.

What should be included in the description?

- Name
- Implementation period (the best would be 3–6 months)
- Target group of beneficiaries
- What problem / task does the project solve, why is it necessary
- Expected change: what will change and for whom
- Objectives: what needs to be done by the charity in order for the change to take place
- How the charity will carry out the tasks: schedule of measures and activities
- Estimated costs: expense items and total amount

The next step in a pilot project is a fundraising plan. It involves planning the sources of donations and their amounts. Based on the programmatic description it is much easier to imagine who you can turn to for a donation. When I say "to whom," I do not mean a specific person, but the type of donor.

There are four types of donors:

- Major donors giving large sums
- Mass private donors, which are needed in greater quantity because they make small contributions
- Commercial companies, in working with them it is necessary to take into account a whole range of motivations related to their business interests and philanthropic goals
- Grant-making NGOs, but we do not usually consider them as funders for a pilot fundraising projects. Rather, we use the results of the pilot to make an application to them later.

This fundraising part of the project includes a table listing the types of donors and the estimated donation amounts. I will give an example of such a table (see Table 2.1.1) for a project that requires, say, 192,500 roubles. All figures are imaginary.

Not every nonprofit organisation should or can develop all fundraising sources. In the above examples, it is obvious that it will most likely be possible to attract money from large private donors for psychological support to support victims of violence, who understand the value of such psychological support. Compassionate pet owners will respond to the renovation of the abandoned animal shelter. Sometimes charities would need all three types. To understand who to prioritise in fundraising, the fundraiser needs to think about the motivation of the donors. In other words, why donors of one type or another would want to support your project.

As a next step of your pilot project, you can start listing real people or organizations to contact for support. The right place to start is with those who are already helping you. We talked about this above – see the Second tip.

The final step in preparing to fundraise is to dress your request in a specific format that is convenient and familiar to a specific donor type. So, for a wealthy person, a letter form is suitable, in which the project will be described in detail. Here's where a detailed description comes in! And for ordinary people donating a little, it will take a short but persuasive post on social media. Before launching your communications, be sure to test them on small, safe group of people: friends, colleagues, relatives. Let them give you their feedback. What did they see and hear? Did they want to make a donation? Why or why not?

Table 2.1.1 Types of donors and estimated donation amounts

Type of donor	Number of donors	Average donation	Amount in roubles
Major donors	3	25000	75000
Mass private donors	35	500	17500
Companies	2	50000	100000
Total	40		192500

Remember to show them the format that would suite their type: a letter for a large donor to a rich uncle, and a post on social networks to friends.

When your materials are ready, the stage of active fundraising begins – interaction with potential donors. If you did everything right in the previous steps, then you will quickly feel it – they will begin to donate to you! If the reaction is weak, then I advise you to go back and look for where you might have a failure. It is a small pilot project that gives you such a great opportunity without big risks.

Good luck!

2.2 Engaging the whole organisation in fundraising

The evolution of fundraising practice

Susan Kay-Williams, 2000

Five stages in the fundraising life cycle have been identified. These stages move through three distinct phases, which have been labelled as 'appeals', 'fundraising' and 'marketing'. In using these words, however, no value judgement is implied. It does not mean that the appeals phase is 'bad' and the marketing phase 'good', or that appeals equals 'old-fashioned' and marketing equals 'go-ahead' or 'trendy'. The words are used because they are the most appropriate for each phase and they signify the general progression of fundraising.

Appeals → Fundraising → Marketing

From these three phases, the five stages of fundraising are identified as:

Appeal phase:	Stage One — The passionate appeal
	Stage Two — We need more money
Fundraising phase:	Stage Three — We need some help
	Stage Four — Leave it to us
Marketing phase:	Stage Five — Let's all work on this together

Many variables could be said to play a part in categorising fundraising activity. The key variables selected are those that most specifically define the stage which the fundraising of a charity has reached, in other words the hallmarks of the actual fundraising activity undertaken. For example, the first stage actually comprises committed, passionate individuals trying to interest anyone and everyone in their cause, but the distinctive hallmark of the first stage is that all this activity is undertaken by volunteers.

The four key variables identified are:

- who does most of the fundraising; volunteers or paid staff?
- how, if at all, the opposite group (paid staff or volunteers) are used, which is dominant?
- the involvement and role of the founder or 'torch-bearer' trustees. (The description 'torch-bearer' refers to trustees or other key individuals who take on the mantle or the shared vision of the founder. This may include

DOI: 10.4324/9781003145936-26

Table 2.2.1 The five stages of the development of fundraising within charities

Variables	Appeal phase		Fundraising phase		Marketing phase
	Stage 1: The passionate appeal	Stage 2: We need more money	Stage 3: We need some help	Stage 4: Leave it to us	Stage 5: Let's all work together on this
Who does most of the fundraising: volunteers or paid staff?	A few core volunteers	Lots of volunteer groups	Department of new staff appointed to establish new avenues of income-generation, driven from Head Office	Larger numbers of professionals, but lots more raised by far fewer people overall.	Large team of professional fundraisers to run one-to-one marketing approach.
Are paid staff or volunteers dominant?	Some involvement of the first paid staff member, usually a Chief Executive	May have an administrative staff member with fundraising responsibility or person seconded from another area	Volunteers are more peripheral except for small-scale local fundraising	Volunteers used to spearhead local campaigns, small number of powerful volunteers at the top, with those at the bottom out of sight	Role of volunteers changed – seen as partners. More involved with the charity and sharing goals, therefore extension of HQ team
What is the involvement and role of the founder or 'torch-bearer' trustees?	Will usually include founder and family – may be high level as a result	May include founder volunteers but mostly small volunteer groups	Founder less involved, has moved on from the starting point	The past is past, let it lie.	Revisited past links for connection and re-established on new terms
What is the perceived role and significance of income from voluntary sources?	No targets (unless for major capital appeal). Grateful for anything	May develop other (usually statutory resources)	Growing need for fundraised income as distinct from fees etc	More fundraised income required to do core work	Building long-term reliable fundraised income for the future

some or all of the founder trustees, and also key supporters and trustees later in the development of the charity.)

- the perceived role and significance of income from voluntary sources.

These four variables might sound very simple, if not simplistic, yet it will be shown that they are at the heart of identifying the fundraising stage of the vast majority of charities in the UK.

Table 2.2.1 summarises the four variables and how they develop over the five stages. Each of the stages has been given a popular title to indicate the common themes, although the voice changes from Stage Two to Stage Three, moving from the volunteers to the professional staff.

[…]

Appeal phase: Stage One — The passionate appeal

Stage One is very focused. Its purpose is to get the charity up and running. At this stage the characteristics of fundraising are as follows.

- The fundraising is undertaken solely by volunteers. This will usually be led by the founder and/or the founder's family and the founder trustees.
- Initially there are no paid staff but during this stage, the first staff member is appointed, usually the chief executive or director. Any other 'staffing' needed is undertaken by some of the volunteers, e.g. secretarial work.
- The role of the founder is paramount. He (for ease of reading 'he' will be used throughout although many founders of charities have been female) is the motivating force and will usually be the chairman of the board. Even if a director is appointed he will largely be doing the bidding of the founder. The founder is instrumental in all decisions and is the guiding force for fundraising. At this point the founder considers it very much as his charity and a great deal of personal time and energy will be expended on the fundraising and the cause.
- Reliance on fundraised income is total. Everything has to come from voluntary sources. As a certain amount will be needed to get the organisation off the ground (not least the legal fees to set up and register the charity), the founder will have at least this amount as his personal target although overall targets may not have been set. It is unusual at this stage to have a fundraising strategy. The founder and trustees are grateful for everything that is given.

At this stage there is no organisation as such, so the embryonic culture is that of the founder and his vision … Stage One represents an integrated culture: there is consensus of purpose and vision, consistency of message and no ambiguity.

Appeal phase: Stage Two — We need more money

Once the first tranche of money is raised, there comes a lull as all the volunteers, especially the fundraising trustees, congratulate themselves and turn their attention to the work, the cause. Many volunteers may feel that they have now done their bit as far as fundraising is concerned.

Depending on the other sources of funding now available and the ongoing need for funds (the initial amount raised may enable the work to carry on for some time), charities may stay at this stage for many years.

The characteristics of Stage Two are as follows.

- The number of volunteer fundraising groups has grown, often substantially, but they are at arm's length from the trustees. Inspired by the zeal of the founder or the worthiness of the cause, these small local groups of fundraisers may have begun to flourish. This is particularly noticeable for hospices or other charities that have a strong local presence.
- The chief executive has been directed to begin statutory and trust fundraising as these require a more administrative approach.
- Fundraising help or support from the organisation to the volunteers is minimal. If any support is given it is likely to come from the chief executive's PA or another member of the administrative staff, for whom fundraising is not a principal role.
- New sources of funds are developed, including statutory ones wherever possible, to sustain the endeavour and to reduce the fundraising burden on volunteers, especially the founder trustees.

The founder is, almost always, still driving the organisation at this point … In its early days the operating culture is still being created. Specifically, the culture will be concerned with meeting the need rather than with income generation (this will be referred to in more detail later). The chief executive will still be following the cultural lead of the founder so an integrated culture remains intact.

[…]

Fundraising phase: Stage Three — We need some help

This phase marks the transition from volunteer-led, hand-to-mouth fundraising to establishing a professional department. As with the first phase it splits into two stages. Stage Three is a major transition period; at this stage fundraising is likely to be established as a department. Stage Four takes that transition further by the creation of a larger department with professional specialists for the different areas of fundraising.

The fundraising phase marks the professionalisation of fundraising within the organisation, as well as a move towards giving fundraising the same status as the service departments that are responsible for carrying out the organisation's charitable purpose. At some point during Stages Three and Four (this varies from charity to charity) the head of fundraising will usually become a member of the senior management team. This phase is also characterised by a diminution of the role of volunteers within the day-to-day operation of the charity, especially the fundraising operation.

The characteristics of Stage Three are as follows.

- New funds from voluntary sources are needed more regularly; this creates pressure for formulation of an ongoing plan to acquire the necessary resources and implementation on a proactive, ongoing basis.
- Paid fundraising staff are appointed. This may start with one part-time person, but it is a paradigm shift. Initially the fundraisers are generalists; the post holder(s) need to be able to handle everything from local events to grand balls, corporate and trust fundraising and developing centralised individual fundraising through direct marketing and legacies.
- Fundraising is now driven internally by staff, not by the volunteers, with overall direction from the trustees.
- Volunteers are less important to the fundraising activity. Although most charities do not actively seek to close down their small local fundraising groups the organisation is too busy concentrating on potentially more lucrative initiatives to nurture new local groups.
- Alternatively, charities may rely on many fundraising groups, although still with limited support from the centre and a small number of central income sources, such as legacies. Thus they require a few, more generalised staff at the head office.
- The founder takes more of a back seat in terms of day-to-day fundraising, except for occasional high-level approaches to a company or individual. He usually remains as chairman of the organisation but is briefed by the chief executive rather than maintaining day-to-day contact with the staff and activities of the organisation.

[…]

As Stage Three develops, there may appear some cracks in the overall culture of the organisation with fundraising beginning to be in tension with other departments, especially service delivery, or even with the trustees if they are not willing to take developmental decisions.

[…]

Fundraising phase: Stage Four — Leave it to us

Stage Four represents the professional fundraising charity that does not, on a day-to-day basis need voluntary input, hence the title, 'leave it to us'. Its characteristics are as follows.

- Voluntary income is vital, it is no longer providing the 'icing on the cake' but is funding a growing percentage of core services or charitable purpose.
- Comparatively small numbers of people are raising substantial sums of money at the headquarters.
- The fundraising department comprises a number of people many of whom are professionals in different specialist areas, e.g. direct mail, trusts,

legacies, corporate, shops, membership etc. depending upon the size and nature of the organisation.

- To meet the specialist needs of the fundraising strategy, the staff is often a mixture of experienced fundraisers with charity backgrounds and marketing, sponsorship, sales promotions or advertising people with commercial backgrounds.
- At this stage the types of fundraising are broadened again as the department grows.
- A head of fundraising is appointed and the status of the fundraising department is heightened. Ultimately the head of fundraising is a member of the senior management team.
- Local volunteers are kept at arm's length from head office, relating to the organisation through branch offices; by this stage they may be given annual targets.
- There is a new role for a particular breed of volunteers. These volunteers are people with a profile and positions of influence and power to head major local fundraising initiatives, e.g. major big-gift regional appeals.
- New volunteers replace the founder and torch-bearer trustees, although some of the latter may still be on the board. Generally, the new staff and the new trustees talk more about the future than the past.

Culturally, this is perhaps the most challenging time and may precipitate the departure of the founder and torch-bearer trustees. Often, new staff and trustees directly and indirectly test the fundamental values and beliefs, with suggestions for substitutions or development of the culture that the 'old-guard' find disturbing. It is often, but not necessarily, the time of the largest chasm between fundraisers and the rest of the organisation.

[...]

Stage 5: Let's all work on this together

The essence of stage 5, the marketing phase, is that those charities that have reached it have learnt not only to harness the tools and techniques of marketing to the benefit of fundraising, but have also incorporated the ethos of marketing for the benefit of the charity as a whole. The predominance of a market orientation now positions the donor or member at the centre, harnessing the concept of putting the customer first. To achieve this the fundraising department may have to be completely refigured.

In the marketing phase the fundraising department is instrumental in developing a new culture that permeates not only the fundraising teams but also the whole charity. Fundraising becomes an integral part of the whole organisation, not a nasty but necessary adjunct.

[...]

The characteristics of the Stage Five charity follow.

- The organisation (not just the fundraising department) is building long-term relationships for reliable ongoing income.

- The organisation emphasises planning for the future.
- The fundraising department grows substantially to enable more one-to-one nurturing of key supporters but the long-term return on investment is anticipated to be worth the short-term cost, through more committed supporters.
- In planning for the future, the charity takes the time to look back, revisiting its roots, re-establishing contact with founders and former 'torch-bearers' and major players.
- The charity reviews its relationship with its volunteers at all levels, brings in more staff to encourage and develop local volunteers with the aim of creating partners to meet shared objectives, rather than 'free worker-bees' who can be used or forgotten by the staff on a whim at a moment's notice.
- Donors and beneficiaries/users are also treated as partners and, above all, as individuals.

At this stage, the organisation is not afraid to revisit the past, to learn from the best of it and re-use it for future benefit. In this way the five stages have a cyclical quality, specifically relating to the role of volunteers within the organisation. Of course, by the time some organisations reach this stage all the original trustees may be dead, but there is usually a time in the not too distant past where there was a noted core of torch-bearer trustees whom it would be useful to reinvolve.

[…]

Movement from stage to stage

The starting point of change is always the need for more money from voluntary sources. The main reason why more money from voluntary sources is sought is that this is largely free of constraints on its use or it can be used specifically to develop a new area of work.

One factor, however, remains common throughout. Movement between the stages is not by happenstance or whim. It only comes about as a result of trustee decisions and in the latter stages, staff recommendation to trustees. The inability to take these decisions can cause the charity to be held back in its development. The issue that is often the stumbling block to such decision making is the familiar tension between income and investment. Staff may be ready to move on, or even have started to do so, but as the outward signs of this development are often an increase in fundraising staff numbers (and therefore overheads), this often requires a trustee decision which may not be easily forthcoming.

[…]

Perhaps the most important finding was that neither age nor overall income were reliable indicators of the stage which fundraising had reached in any charity. A charity that had an annual income of many millions per year may still have relied on just two sources of income, one of which was volunteer fundraisers.

Implications for fundraising practitioners

(1) There is a natural progression. It is possible to stay in stages for a very short space of time but that requires committed investment and perhaps also a 'window of opportunity' to be 'the right thing at the right time' so that the donors drive development more than the trustees or staff. In this way, external forces may force the pace of change faster than would have been anticipated by the trustees.

(2) None of this is judgmental but rather it may provide a framework against which a charity can examine its own fundraising, especially for those charities in Stages Three and Four, in relation to internal culture, relationships with volunteers and the need for voluntary income.

(3) The fundraising life cycle is not on a continuous loop … Very few charities that have reached Stage Five would ever go right back to the beginning again. Some charities, however, may find that they move through smaller loops between Stages Five and Four and, especially, between Stages Four and Three, when crises of confidence occur. These can happen with major changes of staffing in the fundraising department, on the senior management team, or with senior volunteers who set in train new assessments of need and the requirements to achieve them.

(4) Is there a sixth stage? The possibility of a sixth stage is currently under review through a longitudinal aspect to the wider research work.

(5) The relationship between staff and volunteers remains important. If there is one underlying given it is this issue. Fundraising may have its tensions between internal departments and volunteers but it is its relationship with the trustees that is a hallmark of the overall health of the charity. Two questions arise: are the professional fundraisers being given enough support to do their job; and are the fundraisers adequately supportive of and encouraging to the volunteers at all levels?

(6) An organisation's culture is not fixed in stone. It will change with time and can be affected by many factors, but it can also be influenced at different points in the organisation's life cycle.

(7) Market orientation goes beyond the fundraising department. The outcome of market orientation is to make the whole more than the sum of the parts and as such the whole process has to start from the top: the trustees and the senior management team.

Involving your board members in fund development

Simone Joyaux, 2010

Role of the board

[...]

The board is a group made up of individuals. The board operates as a collective, with no single board member having any more authority than any other board member. Yes, that means the board chair has no more authority or power than any other board member. (If you have a rogue board chair, get rid of him or her!)

The board is responsible for corporate governance. And corporate governance is the process whereby a group of individuals ensure the health and effectiveness of the corporation. Corporate governance only happens when the board is together, at its meetings. That's why attendance is so critical. And that's why infrequent attendance is grounds for dismissal from the board.

Corporate governance includes things like: articulating values and mission, and standards and controls; defining and monitoring key areas of performance; ensuring that adequate risk management is in place; hiring, appraising, and firing the executive director; and, ensuring that the financial structure is adequate.

To ensure adequate financial structure, the board – at its meetings – does things like: adopt a budget; adopt a fund development plan; define the parameters of board member performance in fund development; set fund development policies. And the board's fund development committee – effectively enabled by the development officer – helps the board do these things.

Role of the individual board member

To create an effective board, you must hold your individual board members accountable. The board adopts performance expectations common to all board members. Yes, those expectations are common to all board members regardless of generation or gender, socioeconomic status or connections, or anything else. And before you nominate anyone to serve on your board, conduct a screening interview and secure commitment to the performance expectations.

Board member performance expectations include things like: support the values, mission, and vision of the organization; regularly attend board meetings and participate in strategic questioning and conversation; support decisions

DOI: 10.4324/9781003145936-27

once made; maintain confidentiality and avoid conflict of interest; and, partici-pate in philanthropy and fund development.

By the way, the best organizations evaluate board member performance annually. These organizations also evaluate governance effectiveness.

Board member role in philanthropy and fund development

What does it mean to participate in philanthropy and fund development? First, every board member must give a personal financial contribution every single year.

Personal ability and level of interest drive gift size. (And if you serve on a board, then your gift to that organization should be one of your most signifi-cant gifts.)

A board member – often the chair – solicits her fellow board members. Personalize the request to each board member, based on his or her financial capacity. For example, you might ask Bob for $25. Bob is the single father of 6 kids. He works in the kitchen of the public school system. On the other hand, you ask Mary for more, lots more. Mary is the head of that big corporation in town.

Board members do more than give money.

Every board member helps identify those who might be interested in the organization. Board members do this over and over, forever.

For example: As a board member of the Women's Fund of Rhode Island, I identified women (and men) that I thought might be interested in leveling the playing field for women and girls. I know what interests my friends. For those who care about women's rights, I introduced them to the Women's Fund. I pay attention to what my professional colleagues talk about, what they do over the weekend, what bothers them in the news. For those who seemed to have an affinity for women's rights, I linked them to the Women's Fund.

A big reminder: Do not ask (or expect) your board members to trespass on their personal and professional relationships. Sure, Mary the head of the big corporation, is on your board. Yes, she does business with corporations and corporate executives. As a board member, Mary identifies those who might be interested in your cause – and Mary facilitates an introduction. Mary does not ask for favors from those she knows. Favor exchanges produce short-term money and bad feelings.

This is a big deal! Don't ask board members to trespass on personal and pro-fessional relationships.

And board members do more.

They help nurture relationships with those who might be interested, with those who are qualified prospects, and with donors. For example: Board members attend your organization's programs and fundraising events. When there, board members schmooze with guests. Board members do not hang out with their friends and dates. Instead, board members mingle and greet people, engage in conversation and listen to guests. Then board members share what they've learned with staff.

Try these practical and successful ideas, too:

*   Invite a board member to visit a foundation with you and share stories.
*   Ask a board member to join you at lunch with a donor.
*   Put some of your strategic thinking board members on the fund development committee.
*   Recruit others to help plan the next fundraising event.
*   Every board member can call donors to thank them for their gifts. This is just a thank-you call, not a prelude to another request.

And finally, board members can help solicit gifts. For example, board members can write personal notes on direct mail solicitation. The board member needn't know the letter recipient. Just write a note: "Thank you for your support. I hope you'll consider giving again." Sign it Mary Smith, board member.

Board members can help sell tickets and recruit sponsors for your fundraising event. Some board members can go on a solicitation call and tell stories; staff can ask. Other board members can go together or alone and personally solicit gifts.

In conclusion

Often – perhaps usually – it's hard to get the board and its individual members involved in fund development. And honestly, I don't blame them. I expect many board members will feel uncomfortable, a bit awkward, and out of their depth.

There are so many bad activities in fund development – like asking people to trespass on their relationships. There are so many silly activities in fund development – like universalizing your own passion and trying to convince others to care.

But competent staff and caring leadership can change the bad dynamics. Good staff don't promote bad activities. Effective enablers overturn unfortunate experiences.

Leaders help board members understand the value that they add to philanthropy and fund development. Leaders know this won't be fun – and they don't sell fun. Leaders help make it easier – or at least less worse – for board members. Leaders help board members care enough to overcome personal discomfort and convenience – and work for the good of the organization.

The fundraising cycle: the shortest book on fundraising, ever

Redmond Mullin, 1987

Fundraising is a function of idealism. It must be sensitive, challenging, technically skilled and efficient; but fundraising will fail if it concentrates only on money.

The reason for this is clear. Fundraising is the activity that makes caring service possible. The urgency of a fundraising message and function is proportionate to the urgency of the cause they support. Unless the values associated with a cause merit response, there is no justification for fundraising. The corollary is that, where the cause demands a response and the response entails voluntary finance, fundraising becomes a critical priority and responsibility for everybody involved.

Here a separate but equally important issue emerges. Those who directly serve need are privileged; but, in the sector that concerns us, they can succeed only with voluntary financial support. The donors who provide such support generally lack the talent, training and opportunity to give service directly. Indeed, it is essential to the service of need that they should continue to create the means through business and commercial activity that will make the funding of service possible.

The voluntary supporter of a cause should be allowed to achieve more than a mere transfer of funds. A gift can express understanding, sympathy, assent to a cause, shared values. It usually depends on the fundraiser to permit this realisation of a donor's latent idealism. For the person at a desk or workbench, a gift may be the only method for sharing in service; but this will not happen if all that is experienced is a cold and lonely transfer of cash from bank to good cause.

This theory can become the foundation for effective practice.

Hold these points in mind, as you read on:

1. It is the cause that gives reason for fundraising.
2. It is the donor whose engaged understanding, heart and will gives substance to fundraising.
3. Dedication to caring service never excuses bad and inexpert fundraising.

DOI: 10.4324/9781003145936-28

The fundraising cycle

There is a basic fundraising discipline that has proved valid for any type of fundraising – spectacular disaster appeals being an exception. It has been applied successfully to local, regional, national and international campaigns, and may be described as a cycle with four cardinal points (see Figure 2.2.1). The cardinal points of the cycle are these:

1.   **Articulate the reasons why the needs you serve are urgent and why your response to the needs you serve merits generous support. Project clearly and fully the capital and revenue requirements.**

     You may be convinced of the merits of your cause and understand why it should receive priority. However, your prospective supporters will subject the arguments you present to stern critical scrutiny, particularly because yours will be one amongst many claims made on them. In terms that are comprehensible and motivating to them, they must be brought to understand why they should respond to you and why the response should be extraordinarily generous. They must assent to your financial targets and be shown how the support they give will make a difference.

2.   **Through research, identify, locate, evaluate and understand the universe of possible supporters relevant to your cause.**

     Such research may embrace companies, foundations and governmental agencies as well as private individuals; but in all cases it is people who decide whether to give or withhold support. Effective communication of your message will depend on your understanding of their knowledge, awareness and prejudices about you. It will depend, particularly with institutions, on the formal constraints which affect their choices. You must

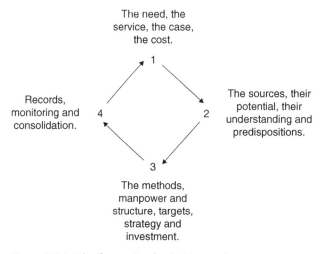

Figure 2.2.1 The four-point fundraising cycle

discover the aptest routes-of access to them: whom do you know who can bring them to you? You must also make a judgement, based on a history of their previous behaviour but more importantly on an assessment of their absolute capacity to give, concerning their financial potential in relation to your cause. One point about them will be almost universally true: however well-disposed they may be, they will be ignorant of how much they should or could give to you.

3. Determine the methods, manpower, organisational structure, strategy and investment required for the fundraising campaign.
Here some simple principles must be intelligently applied:

(a) The various techniques must be ordered strategically so that they complement and do not impede each other. Methods with a higher potential yield will normally be timed for deployment before others that are potentially less productive (particularly where the aim is to offer multiple, ordered, cumulative opportunities for giving). The timetable that governs the sequence of events for a campaign must be designed to realise the fullest potential of its target sources.
(b) There is a scale of effectiveness that can be applied in big-gift fundraising, so that targets may be set for the techniques used as well as for the sources of funds against whom these are deployed (see Table 2.2.2).

Table 2.2.2 Different approaches to big-gift fundraising and their value

Type of approach	Value 1–10
1. Individual to peer with close acquaintance or friendship, the approach being made person-to-person by somebody financially committed at the appropriate financial level.	10
2. Individual to peer group, as above, with personal written or telephoned follow-up.	8
3. Other approaches peer-to-peer, person-to-person as above but without prior personal acquaintance.	6
4. As in 1, but by letter.	5
5. Individual to peer group as in 2, without personal acquaintance but with personal follow-up.	5
6. General, personalised mailing from somebody known to and respected by recipients but not acquainted with them.	4
7. General, non-personalised mailing.	3
8. Leaflet drop with personal, non-peer visit.	2
9. Leaflet drop without personal visit.	1
10. Response to editorial.	1
11. Response to advertising.	0.5
12. Any of the above badly executed.	–1

NB. This table does not deny the value for example, of direct mail or advertising. It considers them only from the viewpoint of big gift fundraising.

(c)   No fundraising programme should be undertaken unless there are the management and skilled, trained staff and volunteers to conduct it efficiently. For a programme of any significant size, the voluntary and paid workforce must operate within an organisational structure that permits optimum attainment.

(d)   Evidently, the cost of a fundraising technique should be justified by the contribution it is likely to yield. However, there must also be realism concerning the interval between the moment investment is made and the time its results emerge. In a sophisticated fundraising programme, there will always be a period, sometimes extended, during which a net outflow of funds has to be endured. Premature demands for results can prevent their achievement. It is legitimate to commit funds this year to secure dependable supporters for the years ahead.

4.   Install efficient systems for records, monitoring and future consolidation.

Committed donors are any not-for-profit agency's most precious assets. Unless there is a system – probably computerised – to maintain a record of your relationship with each of them, you will prevent the realisation of their generosity. The records should give a useful history of the relationship, so that you can segment your lists of donors and communicate sensitively and productively with them. You also need systems to track performance during a campaign, so that you can control progress and make timely, corrective interventions as the situation demands. Finally, you must have vehicles that will permit you to cultivate longer-term relations with donors of various kinds and at various levels of support.

Good fundraising changes realities, for you as well as your supporters.

Targets

It emerges from what has been said in the preceding section that targets for fundraising are influenced by a number of factors:

1.   The urgency of your capital and revenue needs, if these can be established, will obviously be crucial. However, there are some agencies whose needs are virtually limitless.

2.   I emphasise the concept that each fundraising source has a determinable potential.

3.   As do the fundraising techniques you employ, if these are implemented with skill and efficiency.

4.   To allow all sectors of a fundraising universe to perform optimally, the total target must be large enough to generate challenging sub-targets for every segment of the appeal. When translated at local or individual levels, there must still be a strong call to extraordinary generosity.

5.   Perhaps most importantly of all, the agency launching an appeal must have a firm will and determination to succeed. This will be expressed through realistic investment in fundraising and people.

Fundraisers

For reasons that will become clear presently, I personally repudiate the title 'fundraiser'. In a capital campaign my role is to equip others for fundraising. I shall retain the title temporarily, for convenience.

What are the qualities to be sought, then, in so-called fundraisers? They must have basic communications skills. Hence the stress I place on empathy with actual and potential donors. Effective communications work through the eyes and ears, head and heart of the person receiving a message, provided the sender lets this happen.

The fundraiser must be knowledgeable about a broad spectrum of established and emergent techniques, and be skilled and successful in applying at least a few of them. If the skill is not possessed personally, there must be educated experience of the external resources available (e.g. for direct mail, advertising, events, market research etc.) and the ability to harness them. The fundraiser must also have entrepreneurial flair in identifying and exploiting opportunities as they arise.

Many fundraisers will have to be able managers and motivators of staff and volunteers. They will have to administer and control complex programmes calling on a multiplicity of disciplines, including marketing, public relations and advertising, in addition to all the rest. Fundraisers need diplomatic skills in extracting and sustaining support from their own boards, superiors and colleagues.

There will need to be understanding of the context in which fundraising takes place. What is its competitive environment? What are the special tax concessions that may be invoked? What is the broader fiscal frame, as it affects donors and recipients of funds? What are the opportunities for learning and developing skills, for encountering colleagues to make common cause on issues, to co-operate, to exchange experiences?

Above all, though, it is the donor who is important in fundraising. The most fully satisfied donor is the one who has given most generously. This same generous donor is likely, over time, to become increasingly generous. A body of committed donors, involved with the cause through their gifts and through sustained contact, is your most precious, enduring fundraising resource.

Significantly, it is generous donors who personally invite their equals to support the cause at levels similar to their own generosity, who are an appeal's most effective fundraisers. This is why I prefer not to be described as 'fundraiser'. Time and again, successful experience has shown that in a structured campaign, it should be donors who do the big-gift fundraising, qualified for this role by their own generous gifts.

2.3 Developing a constituency of support

Developing a constituency:
where the fundraising begins

Henry A. Rosso, 1991

Whenever a fund raising staff sets out to plan a fund raising program, it begins by searching out from its constituency those individuals who will be willing to contribute, those who will be willing to serve on fund raising committees, and those who will be willing to act as solicitors. That is, the staff endeavors to identify "prospects," or prospective contributors, prospective volunteers, and prospective solicitors.

With this planning exercise, the fund raising staff measures its potential for productivity against whatever goal it is endeavoring to achieve. It does so by analyzing the capacity and the willingness of its constituency to contribute, to volunteer to serve on fund raising committees, and to participate in actual solicitation. These are the important qualities that will lead to fund raising success; these qualities are the substance of a dedicated, involved constituency.

Two terms in the vocabulary of fund raising practitioners confuse this process: *prospects* and *suspects*. Just what is a "suspect"? What is a "prospect"? And what separates one or the other from a contributor? Why are they so important to the fund raising process? Why should the fund raising practitioner be concerned about differentiating between the two? Too often, discussions about potential givers lock on the name of a well-known, influential person who is believed to have considerable assets. This is particularly true when the fund raising committee is seeking to solicit a very large gift. Staff and trustees agree that this person should be seen *immediately*. But neither anyone on the fund raising committee nor anyone on the management team knows or has access to this person. Considering these factors, this person cannot be accepted as a logical candidate for a gift at the level contemplated by staff and volunteers. The person is a suspect, not a prospect. Why? There is no access because there is no *link* to the person. Any time devoted to an effort to solicit suspects for a large gift can be time wasted. It may be wiser to invite this person to make a small gift as a beginning strategy to involve this person as a constituent.

A research concept known as the L-A-I principle of prospect identification will help fund raising planners separate suspects from prospects, thus enabling staff members to direct their solicitation or enlistment energies toward those individuals who are most likely to give or to volunteer their services.

What is the L-A-I principle and what is its function in both fund raising research and constituency development? The principle is timeworn. It is a

DOI: 10.4324/9781003145936-30

heritage of the past, a piece of wisdom passed on from one clan of veteran fund raising practitioners to another, and it is as described below.

L = Linkage: A linkage relates to a contact, a bridge, or an access through a peer to the potential donor. If there is access to the gift source, then this link to the prospect makes it possible to arrange an appointment to discuss the potential of a gift. If accessibility is not a reality, then it would be difficult or downright impossible to arrange for an appointment. Solicitation becomes a matter of a letter or telephone approach, and neither is effective in the production of large gifts.

A = Ability: Through research, it can be determined that the potential gift source has sufficient discretionary holdings to justify a gift solicitation at the appropriate "asking" level. Two perceptions pertain: the asker's perception that the prospect has a gift capability at the level suggested, and the prospect's own perception that such a gift capability is a reality. Some wealthy but financially insecure individuals who are not brought up in the tradition of philanthropy are not sure that they have sufficient resources to give at the level requested. They may not be psychologically prepared to give.

I = Interest: If the potential contributor has no interest in the organization or little knowledge about its work, then the person will be prone to make a small gift or none at all. Interest in the organization and an understanding of its mission and accomplishments are imperative in the identification of valid prospects.

The rules of fund raising, which have been authenticated across the decades, maintain that all three L-A-I principles must apply when separating prospects from suspects during the evaluation of gift potential within the constituency. The elimination of just one of the three principles will invalidate the process and reduce the gift candidate from prospect to suspect.

Constituents are people, people are prospects

Fund raising is an interesting but quite complex art form. Its central force is people. The not for-profit organization must involve itself with people on a constant and continuing basis if it is to justify its existence or, perhaps more important, ensure its future.

The central force in the structure of the not-for-profit organization is its constituency: a heterogeneity of people who give life, purpose, meaning, energy, and a reason for being to the organization. These include the people who need the services provided, those who support the issues espoused, those who sell the organization goods and services, those who are part of its staff or governing board, those who provide regulatory overview, and those who may constitute its philanthropic base as volunteers and as contributors.

The constituency also can be identified as including those who are currently involved with the organization, those who have been involved in the past, and those with the potential for some level of involvement in the future. These people hold a value for the fund raising process in that they can be identified as current and active contributors, past contributors who no longer give, or suspects and prospects who can be induced to give in the future.

Whether the organization is visiting a foundation, a corporation, an association, or a government office for the purpose of seeking a gift or a grant, it is negotiating with a person or a group of people to arrive at a decision that is responsive to the diverse needs of the nonprofit organization. It is asking for money, goods, services, or gifts of precious volunteer time. It is important, therefore, for key people within the organization, particularly fund raising staff members, to know the structure of the constituency and the interests, needs, wants, and requirements of the people who make up that constituency. It is these people who can affect the destiny of the organization in a positive or negative manner.

Since its genesis in the early colonial years of the seventeenth century, fund raising in this nation [US] has preoccupied itself with the selective activation of people as contributors and working volunteers, as well as the advocacy core. Historically, the people who have been most willing to become involved in these activities have been those closest to the organization and most knowledgeable about its work. The rest can be cataloged into three groups: some active, many inactive; some supportive, others disinterested; and others distant and quite detached. All in all, this is the nature of a constituency.

The concept of ever-widening circles

An image of a constituency relationship with the organization can be formed by visualizing concentric or an ever-widening spread of circles (see Figure 2.3.1).

The image can become sharper by envisioning these circles as a set of spreading waves set in motion by the impact of a rock thrown onto the still surface of a pond of water. A wave, a turbulence, a sequence of ever-broadening circles are created on the pond's surface. This is the organization's power center and where the action begins. The waves gradually diminish in force as they move away from the impact point; so, too, does the power of the constituency diminish as it moves away from the center of the organization.

The central circle, where the rock makes violent contact with the still water, depicts the core circle or the energy center of the constituency (see Figure 2.3.2). The bonding to the organization is strongest and more lasting at this point. Its force is dissipated as it moves away from the energy center until it disappears altogether.

At least three primary components of the constituency are in the core circle: the board of trustees, the senior management team, and the major contributors. These constituency components are at the energy center of the organization because they exercise a strong influence on the affairs of the entity. They can significantly affect its progress as it reaches for the future in the following ways:

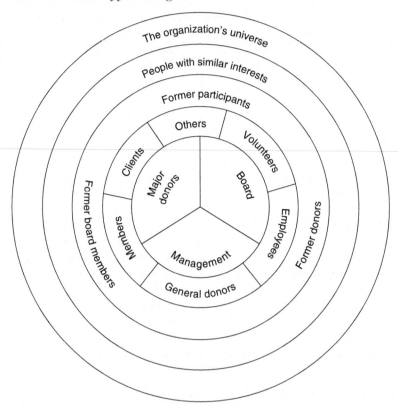

Figure 2.3.1 Constituency circles

- The trustees as custodians of the trust in the public interest approve the mission and the vision, and also set policy.
- The senior management team is the determining force for policy that will be reviewed and approved by the board. This team activates the programs that respond to specific needs.
- Major contributors are among the primary advocates. Their gifts are testimony to their commitment to the cause and its program of services.

Larger organizations with more complex structures may be able to add more than three components to the core circle. Universities, for example, could well place their alumni boards and academic senates in the center circle. Hospitals might consider adding their joint conference committees of physicians and trustees. Organizations with separate foundations would do well to add the boards and executive staffs of each foundation to its core grouping, because foundation boards and executive staffs represent strategic forces in the constituency definition.

The second circle, in an empathic proximity to the energy core, would include administrative and service volunteers, employees and other non-management

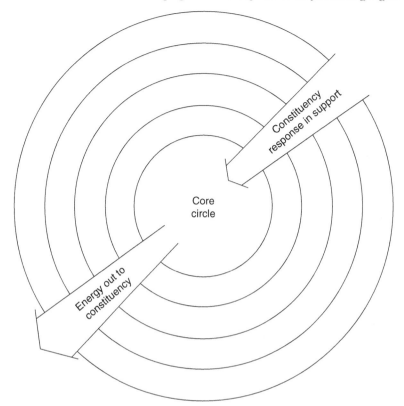

Figure 2.3.2 Energy center in constituency circles

employees, clients who are being served, and vendors. General contributors-those who make smaller gifts – are included in the second circle. They are important because they constitute the contributor base. Gifts in this base can and should be renewed and then upgraded because they represent the best potential for major gift development.

These constituency components are a necessary part of the organization. They are placed in the second circle only because they are not a part of the major policy-making procedure.

The core circle and the second circle of the constituency chart represent strategically important segments of the organization's market: the trustees and senior management staff the clients who are being served, the people who are providing the services, non-board volunteers, employees, and funding sources (individuals, corporations foundations, associations, and governments) who provide the funds to fuel the programs.

The third and fourth circles reflect significant drops in energy as each becomes more distant from the organization's vital core. These are the passive, uninvolved components. They hold a potential only to the degree that they can be activated through a creative outreach effort by the fund raising staff with proper support from the public relations staff, or marketing staff, or both.

Past participants, or individuals with previous involvement with the organization, reside in the third circle. These are former trustees, former staff members, former donors, and former members of a guild, an auxiliary, or an advisory council. Universities have a kindly, friendly title for past donors who are recorded in this quiet third zone. Alumni officers and resources development officers refer to this group as "LYBUNT" (Last Year But Unfortunately Not This Year) or as "PYBUNT" (Previous Year But Unfortunately Not This Year). Activating these constituents is an important assignment for the fund raising program.

The fourth circle presents an amorphous multitude. This is an unknown potential, a large number of people who can be invited to become constituents through the use of mail. When specialists reach out to this diffuse mass through bulk-rate mailings, they endeavor to particularize their lists by identifying people whose interests may parallel those of the organization. List brokers who work with national lists compile these names by demographic and psychograph indicators: that is, by geographic or census distribution or by behavior patterns. Behavior patterns, or psychographic indicators, are useful in identifying "people with similar interests". These interests may signal a possible kinship with the values reflected in the organization's mission. These people may qualify as suspects. The task now is to convert them into prospects and then contributors by exciting their interests through an intelligently conceived and properly directed mail solicitation.

Beyond the fourth circle, there may be a constituency of unknown potential. This fifth and most distant circle is identified as the "universe" of the organization. Its presence should remind anyone who endeavors to evaluate a constituency's giving potential that such potential may be considerably more than any organization dare think. It never achieves final definition.

When judiciously employed, patience, persistence, and creative energy can help to capture this potential. There is quiet, undisturbed potential within the constituency universe of every organization. The size of the gifts may be small during the prospecting stages, but they will increase in value as interest deepens and strengthens through proper cultivation.

Characteristics of a constituency

The Transiency Factor. A constituency is an ever-changing thing. It is as fluid and as transient as the environment in which it functions. Organizations can expect as much as a 20 to 35 percent annual change in the base of its constituency, judging from the comments of development office managers who are charged with the continuing management of data. As the pattern of transiency changes through the 1990s, the character and personality of each organization's constituency will change, thus adding to the complexities of fund raising.

The transitory quality of the constituency may be reflected in a change in residency from an intemperate to a more temperate zone, a conversion in political philosophy, a change in religious affiliations, a financial setback, or a sudden disinterest resulting from lack of attention. Continuing cultivation of a constituency is an imperative for the not-for-profit agency.

[…]

Building a constituency

Some aspect of the constituency comes into being automatically. For instance, the client base becomes an immediate adjunct of the constituency because it acts in response to the services offered. Trustees, management staff, and beginning program staff become an early part of an organization because they must make available the services that are needed by their clients. Contributors, volunteers, and advocates take longer to develop. They must be sought out and invited to become the philanthropic base that will augment and celebrate the organization's work.

The fund raising person must be sensitive to the fact that there is constant interaction within and between the constituency circles and among the elements that make up each circle. Individuals gravitate toward the core circle as their interest is touched and then deepened; they drift away of their interest slackens, if they are ignored, or if their interests change or are neglected. A studied program of constituency involvement and thoughtful cultivation is necessary to maintain the vitality of the constituency base.

A responsible fund raising staff should assert itself continuously to develop an *awareness* within the constituency of the organization's mission, goals and objectives; to foster an *understanding* of the service to that mission; and to invite constituency *commitment* to the organization through the process of making a gift.

An effective, outreaching communication program is the first necessity. In developing any human relationship it is necessary to get the attention of the subject, the person whom the organization wants to involve. The person must be made aware that the organization exists, and that it exists for a purpose that may hold an interest to him or her. Awareness must be converted into understanding, first of the guiding mission that delineates the human or societal needs that must be addressed, and second of the programs that will respond to these needs. From awareness to understanding to acceptance is the direct path to people involvement and the process that is so necessary for constituency development.

People will identify with an organization if they understand and can accept its reason for being, if they accept that the programs are valid and responsive, and if they strongly believe that the people associated with the organization are competent and trustworthy in their service to the mission.

Various techniques are applicable to this process of identifying and involving a constituency, particularly that element that can be induced to contribute funds and to volunteer time.

One of the first and most effective instruments for constituency development is fund raising. The fund raising process is based on intelligent, purposeful communications with the amorphous and unidentified market, including suspects, prospects, and donors. A sensitively managed communication will invite interest in the organization, its mission, its goals, and its programs. The outreach or public relations effort should include quarterly newsletters that contain information of interest to the reader. These publications too often are self-serving informational instruments that extol the accomplishments of staff members while neglecting the concerns, questions, and curiosity of the constituency. Periodic surveys of readers' interests and reactions to the value of the newsletter might well evoke the kind of response that will heal the myopia of an overly abundant self-interest.

Special events offer an opportunity to attract the attention of potential constituents. A special event may be defined as an activity that is designed to accomplish a variety of objectives, one of which is to invite possible constituents to become involved and to learn more about the organization. Events may include open houses, come-and-see tours, 10-K runs, leadership dinners, fashion shows, discussions, seminars, workshops, annual meetings, and book sales.

Properly staged events can serve purposes other than just raising money. They can induce people to become part of the organization's expanding constituency base.

[...]

Conclusion

In summary, the constituency gives meaning to the not-for-profit organization. It is a composite of all individuals who are currently associated with the organization in some manner, those who have been associated in the past, and those who might become involved in the future.

Some organizations protest that they do not have a constituency because they are not universities with alumni, churches with congregations, or symphony orchestras with season subscribers. Let it be established here that every organization that has been qualified as a not-for-profit entity has a constituency. If it does not, then it simply does not exist. These organizations should spend little time in bemoaning their imagined deficiencies and a maximum of time in identifying, cultivating, and bonding constituencies to their missions. Such a constituency holds the potential for service as volunteers, contributors, and advocates. The mission is the message that will provide the bonding influence.

Grassroots fundraising: you already know all the people you need to know to raise all the money you want to raise

Kim Klein, 2000

The second part of the title of this article is taken from a phrase I often use in my fundraising training. It meets with skepticism, denial, laughter, incredulity, and occasionally two reactions that mark people who might actually go somewhere in fundraising: horror and relief. It is obvious why relief would be a great reaction to have to the idea that you already know the people you need to know, but why horror? People who are horrified by this notion realize that their best prop has just been knocked down; the excuse that worked when all others failed has just failed. If they already know who they need to know, what is stopping them? How can they not raise money? Their horror is that they have been found out. But many of them recover from horror and go on to raise money.

What does it mean that you know who you need to know in order to raise the money you want to raise? Simply this: As we point out every year, and sometimes more often, the most money given away in the U.S. comes from middle-income, working-class, and poor families. This happens to be most people. Most people give away most money. This is good news. Imagine if most money were given away by corporations – we would have even more elite universities, a handful of well-funded arts groups, and a lot of funding going to research, scholarships, and cause-related themes. If, similarly, most money were given away by foundations, we would again have a much smaller landscape of nonprofits, with a much greater focus on large organizations. The concept of grassroots fundraising and, consequently, grassroots groups would not exist.

We have a diverse, creative, and extraordinary group of nonprofits because we have a diverse, creative, and wonderful population of people who give away money. In 1995, however, an ominous trend in grassroots giving was tracked and analyzed by the research wing of Independent Sector, a coalition of nonprofit organizations that provides research and advocacy on behalf of the nonprofit sector. Virginia Hodgkinson, vice president of research at Independent Sector, reported that the 68 million households that had made donations in 1995 was 4 million fewer households than had given in 1993, a drop of nearly 5%. Part of this loss was attributed to who was asked for money. The survey reported that only 60% of Americans were asked to contribute to nonprofit

DOI: 10.4324/9781003145936-31

organizations in 1995, down 17% from 1994. Clearly, millions of people who would give are not being asked!

Why aren't people being asked to give?

Nonprofits have themselves caused the problem of people not being asked to give: They focus on the wealthiest potential donors and often pass over lower-income or middle-income households. "If they are targeting more affluent households, they are losing other participants in society," commented Hodgkinson.

Now, one of my own areas of promotion as a fundraiser and trainer is major gifts – how to find them and how to get them. As a consequence, I feel some responsibility when I read a study like this. But perhaps my full message has not been heeded, as I always stress that even your biggest gifts may not come from your wealthiest donors. Giving and having are often unrelated. Havers have. That's why we call them "the haves." Even some very poor people are "'haves." What little they have, they hang onto. Some very wealthy people are also "haves." They hang onto the great deal that they have, and they try to have more.

In fundraising, we must focus on givers. Since most people give when asked and, as corollary studies show, do not give when not asked, we must increase the number of people we are asking.

This brings us to the logical question: Who are we missing? One answer is suggested by Independent Sector's research. They identify the "underasked" as young people and people of color. Furthermore, they find that when these "underasked" are asked, 78% respond. This is a higher percentage than the percentage of givers thought to be in the population at large (about 70%). Since giving and volunteering are habits often developed when young, if we continue to underask young people, we can expect a continuing decline in contributions in the future.

Reversing the trend

How can we make sure to reverse this trend of focusing our asking on affluent households and not asking millions of people who might give?

First, start your fundraising with people you know. Don't focus on posh neighborhoods or major donors to other groups, or act from rumors about how many millionaires are setting up family foundations.

I was recently with a wonderful organization in Oregon that had been grappling with this issue for more than a year. A member of the fundraising committee had carefully researched and compiled a list of business people in town who gave money to various causes. It numbered about 200. Here's an example of her excellent research (with names changed):

- Joe Smith, owner of three hardware franchises, chair of Rotary and active in the Chamber of Commerce. Gifts include $300 to his child's school foundation, $250 plus hardware to a homeless shelter in town, $500 to his alma mater.

- Mary Jones, vice president of a local bank, active in her church and in Rotary, $500 to a battered women's program, $500 to the local symphony orchestra, and a large amount (exact amount unobtainable) to Habitat for Humanity's building program through her church.

And so on, for all 200 names.

All this research had taken about a year to complete. The volunteer who had done it had pored over program books, newsletters, social pages of the newspaper. All of the information was derived from public sources. Once the research was completed, the committee had decided to approach each person on the list individually and divided up the names among themselves. Of the names, 25 were people known to one or more committee members, and those people were asked. Half gave and half declined to give. Those who had given had been asked for introductions to others on the list, yielding introductions to about 20 more on the list.

The remaining people, whom no one on the committee knew personally, did not get asked, despite the committee's intentions and various deadlines set for themselves. In fact, five committee meetings had transpired at which the names were divided up and assigned or reassigned, only to be followed by another meeting at which members reported that for the most part these prospects weren't being approached. This process went on for a full year, so that two years had been devoted to this project – one for the research and one for the follow-up, or lack of it.

In frustration, the group asked me what they should do to motivate themselves to approach the rest of the names on the list. The volunteer who had done the research was understandably peeved that so little had been done with her efforts, although she too admitted that she had not approached any of her designated prospects.

I told the committee something they probably knew in their hearts already: They should give up approaching people they don't know. Nevertheless, the research will be helpful as they are bound eventually to meet some of these people through their known contacts. In the meantime, I suggested, each committee member should make a list of 15 people they know and ask these people for donations. I saw looks of relief on many faces: "It would be a lot faster for me to ask people I know," said one young woman. And another added, "If I ask ten friends and only get $20 each, I'll still have more than I was able to raise from one of these contacts." Then the horror chorus started: "But these are the most prestigious people in town. These are the movers and shakers. We can't ignore them." I pointed out that I wasn't suggesting ignoring them. "I am suggesting that you start with who you know; these are much more likely to be the movers and shakers for your group. Then you can see who these people know."

Finally, the chair suggested a compromise. All those who wanted to ask people they knew should compile a list of those people and bring it to the next meeting so that the group could ensure that no one was being asked more than once. Those who wanted to keep working from the list of 200 could do so. Of 13 committee members, 11 decided to ask people they knew and 2 decided to work the list. Ironically, the volunteer who did the original research was one of the 11 who decided to ask people she knew.

Six months later, 8 of the 11 people who agreed to ask people they knew had done so, resulting in 70 new gifts and $1,900 raised. The two who were plugging away on the original list had asked three more people and raised $750 from two of them. The other three members of the committee had compiled their lists but not quite gotten around to asking.

This is excellent progress.

Starting with who you know

When you start with people you know, start with the person you know best – yourself. Make a gift that feels good to you and then ask your friends for a gift in that range. Much time is lost trying to determine how much to ask people for. The most important thing is to have them feel good about their gift, should they choose to give. A person will feel good about the size of his or her gift if the gift is comparable to the gift given by their friend. Some people may give more and some may give less. You may feel comfortable asking people with considerably more resources for a gift larger than the one you gave, and you probably want to scale back your request when approaching people who have considerably less than you do. Using yourself as a benchmark will save a lot of time. Once a person has given, their gift becomes their own benchmark to start the process of asking for more.

If all of us involved in fundraising ask people we know, we probably won't leave out the millions of households that went unasked in 1995. However, if our circles of acquaintances are not diverse, we may have a large segment of potential supporters whom no one in our group knows and who don't get asked by us. Therefore, it behooves us to make sure that our boards of directors and our staff and volunteers represent the broadest range of demographic possibilities of our communities.

Expanding the fundraising committee

A final point: Make sure everyone in the organization knows how to raise money – staff, volunteers, board, everyone. Any time you notice the faintest enthusiasm about fundraising from a client, a staff person, the janitor of your building, or whomever, bring them on your fundraising committee.

Here is an example: A group was planning its 20th anniversary celebration. The committee was meeting at the home of a board member, whose 16-year-old daughter was eavesdropping on the committee meeting. At one point she piped up, "I have an idea for how you can raise even more money." Committee members smiled and her mother said, "Good-why don't you tell me later." Looking puzzled, the girl left the room. A few minutes later, one of the committee members passed the girl's bedroom on her way back from the bathroom. On a whim, she said, "What's your idea of how we can make more money?" The teenager said, "A lot of people coming to your event will have to hire baby-sitters. I can organize a group of my friends and offer free baby-sitting at the event, and people can contribute what they would have paid for sitters to the organization. It will be much more fun for the little kids and will let me and my friends help." This was a good idea that resulted in an extra $600 being given to the event, and a bunch of 16-year-olds whose ideas will not so easily be overlooked next time.

We have too much money to raise to be able to afford to lose even one household's giving, particularly over something so correctable as that they just needed to be asked.

Fundraising in your own back yard: inviting clients to be donors

Rona Fernandez, 2010

In my work as a fundraising consultant, I'm always surprised at how many nonprofits overlook what seems to be an obvious source of new donor prospects: the people who are served by or are most involved in their program work. For most grassroots organizations, these key constituents are often the backbone of their donor program, but for many other groups, their clients or members are rarely (if ever) asked for money, and they rarely fundraise for the organization either. If your group is one whose donors come mostly from outside your core constituency, then the good news is that you probably have a whole other pool of people you can tap to make your grassroots fundraising program more successful: the people served by your program.

It's not surprising that the people directly affected by your program work would make good donor prospects. In her 2009 article, "Silos Are for Farms," consultant Tina Cincotti quoted researcher Penelope Burk's finding that 93 percent of donors volunteer, and 95 percent of volunteers give money to the organizations they volunteer with. Although statistics for client-based giving are not available, we know anecdotally that the people who benefit the most from your services – whether you provide free health care services or free legal advice, as the two groups that are profiled in this article do, or some other low or no-cost service – would also want to support your work financially.

I spoke to the directors of two San Francisco organizations that have regularly raised several thousand dollars each year from their client base: Belma Gonzalez, former executive director of what was then called the Women's Needs Center (now the Women's Community Clinic), and Marianna Viturro, codirector of St. Peter's Housing Committee. Their stories affirm some of the most basic principles of grassroots fundraising in powerful and inspiring ways.

The Women's Needs Center was a free clinic that provided crucial reproductive health services to low-income women in San Francisco. Although the agency raised the majority of its income from non-clients through a canvassing program and direct mail, they also brought in an average of $3,000 a month from client donations – more than $36,000 a year. However, the original reason behind asking for a donation was not just a financial one – it was that the clinic needed to comply with federal funding requirements. "As a licensed community clinic, we were supposed to get a co-payment from our clients," says Belma Gonzalez, who was the executive director of the clinic for file years in the 1990s. "But as a free clinic, we didn't want to require a co-pay from

DOI: 10.4324/9781003145936-32

folks or be seen as a sliding scale clinic. So, our compromise originally was to ask clients for the co-pay as a donation. The amount was based on the difference between what our funders would pay for the visit which was based on the client's income, and all clients were living below the Federal poverty guidelines – and what the visit actually cost."

St. Peter's Housing Committee, based in the Mission District of San Francisco, a working-class neighborhood with a large Latino immigrant population, provides free tenant counseling, mostly for low-income, Spanish-speaking clients. As at the Women's Needs Center, these services are offered free of charge, but the organization also makes a donation request that has become a standard part of their work.

"It's optional," explains Mariana Viturro, co-director of St. Peter's. "We have taped up on every computer monitor that we are supported by the community and that we suggest a donation of $30. Most people give in that range because that's what we put out." The group receives about $7,000 per year from these donations.

St. Peter's is unique in that it started out as mostly a social service agency and over time evolved into an organization that both provided services and did broader advocacy, grassroots organizing, and movement-building to help preserve affordable housing in San Francisco. As the group's work changed, so did their fundraising strategy – shifting from being funded mostly by government and large institutions to having more individual donors, including their clients, whose donations could be used to support the group's broader agenda.

Drawing from these organizations' experiences, here are five things you can do in your organization to find new donors in your client base. You may not be able to make these changes immediately or all at once, but by doing just one or two of these things you can identify many prospects who have been right in your own back yard all along.

Five things you can do to raise money from your clients

1. Don't assume that people won't or can't donate.

The underlying assumption that many people in social service nonprofits make is that their clients, who are often low-income people, don't have any money to give. But the large majority of people in the United States give money to nonprofits (about seven out of every ten people), and on average, about 60 percent of the total donations given by individuals in this country come from households with incomes of less than $100,000 per year. Even about 20 percent of people who receive Temporary Assistance for Needy Families (formerly known as welfare) give money to charities.

"One of our monthly donors is a client. He gives $25 a month," says Viturro of St. Peter's Housing Committee. "I think he makes $1,500 a month. That $25 is a lot for him." If you assume that some people are just too poor to give or that they should spend their money on something else, not only are you robbing them of the opportunity to show their support and appreciation for your work, but you're not raising as much money as you could be or bringing in all the donors who can and should be supporting your work.

2. Call it what you will ... it's still fundraising!

If program staff in your organization have a mental block around fundraising from your clients – which is common for many groups who are used to seeing their clients as recipients of services only – then by all means call it something else! It's not as important that your staff identify as fundraisers as it is that they carry out the work of bringing in support for the organization.

Viturro's experience at St. Peter's has shown her that calling an activity "fundraising" may make it unnecessarily intimidating. "When I show people spreadsheets with dollar amounts, they just don't relate to it and get bored and think, 'Oh, it's just the fundraising report and it has nothing to do with me.' When we approach it more from how it relates to community building and our services, it's more effective. It makes sense programmatically in terms of bringing people into the organization – it's just one of the ways to do that."

At the Women's Needs Center, Gonzalez says that staff never called their requests for donations from clients fundraising, but that looking back on the experience, she sees that it was definitely a way of raising money for the organization from its clients. Once the practice was firmly in place, however, staff saw the importance of having clients as donors. "Later," she said, "we felt it was important for clients to be on board with us."

3. Educate everyone in the organization about how much it costs to do the work.

All the people who care about your work (donors, board members, staff clients, members) should have a sense of your budget size and what it costs to do the work. Not only is this a good way to build a more democratic organizational culture, but people will be more motivated to fundraise if they know what they are fundraising for and what kind of an impact the donations they bring can make. However, talking about money in your organization can bring up thorny feelings – and sometimes conflict – over how to handle fundraising activities.

At times these conflicts center on whether it's appropriate to even ask low-income people for money (see point #1 above), and can have more to do with staff members' own issues with money and fundraising than about whether clients want to give. Gonzalez emphasized the need for transparency with clients as a way to cut through some of these challenges. "We would be lying to pretend that health care is free," she says about how she responded to staff concerns about asking for donations. "The value I advocated for was transparency," explains Gonzalez. "[I would suggest staff tell clients that] it costs us lots to be here and if you can help us out by donating toward what isn't covered for your visit by our funders, then you're helping to ensure your clinic will remain open."

4. Be respectful of, and value, each person's giving capacity.

"When folks made their appointment, we let them know about the donation and we didn't ask for the donation until their visit was finished," says Gonzalez about the client donations at the Women's Needs Center. "And we made sure the front desk folks were gracious and respectful with folks if they couldn't give."

No matter the size of the donation, it's important to value all donations by your clients and core members, as these are the people who are most committed to your work and most likely to give repeatedly when asked. At St. Peter's, more than 300 of their clients (about half of the people they see each year through their free legal advice service) make donations.

"Some clients give every time they come. It may only be $5 each time but by the end of the year it's $120," says Viturro. "The most incredible donations are when people win a case [thanks to St. Peter's free legal help], which meant they got their deposit back or were compensated for some abuse in their housing. There was one case with three tenants who were able to get their $1,000 deposit back, and they each gave $100 to the organization." Even small donations can add up if you are giving people multiple opportunities to give.

Gonzalez emphasizes the importance of getting clients to see themselves not just as recipients of services, but as part of your work, and to impress this attitude upon program staff who often have the most contact with clients. "I always ask folks to think about how they feel when they contribute to something or help out in some way," she says. "How they then feel a part of something, and are not simply an outsider looking in, or a person being served."

5. Make fundraising a part of everyone's job.

Even if fundraising is not part of everyone's job description, every person – especially program staff who often think of fundraising as something that happens 'over there' in another department, and not as part of their work – should be responsible for at least one key fundraising task.

At St Peter's, the counseling staff not fundraising staff are in charge of collecting donations from clients. "It's part of the counseling ask," she says. The counseling staff also do fundraising asks of the lawyers who volunteer their time to give legal advice to St. Peter's clients. "When new staff come on it's always part of the rap that we teach them, and in our client database there is information to put in about whether they made a donation and the amount."

At the Women's Needs Center, the front desk staff asked for donations. "The phone folks were taught to stress that it was a donation," says Gonzalez, "and to figure out what the donation would be with the client so she could be prepared to bring a donation if she could. If the client had no money it was OK." Gonzalez says that very few clients did not make a donation, and some gave more than the suggested amount.

The main lesson from these two organizations' experiences is that everyone who cares about your work should be asked to make a contribution to your work on a regular basis. Not only will doing so increase the number of prospective donors you have and the amount of money coming in, it will also increase people's feeling of ownership of your organization and make them feel more invested in your work. "Most of the time people feel really invested and honored to be able to contribute," says Viturro. "It helps with their relationship with the organization, and they want to see other people have access to the services that they used."

Rediscovering and climbing the donor pyramid

Tony Elischer, 2008

Mention the donor pyramid (Figure 2.3.3) and most people will either smile, as if to say 'that old thing', feign an understanding or engage to see how something that has been around for nearly forty years may still have a relevance today.

Many years ago I remember being outraged at an article in the professional press that declared 'the donor pyramid is dead' and went on to say very little under the sensational headline. As this was clearly an attempt from someone with very little passion for the thinking that underpins our profession, I decided to respond by pointing out that the pyramid was never alive! And like many such models is designed to stimulate thinking and provide a frame of reference to develop a strategy that moves donors on. The pyramid is simplicity itself, clear stages that can accommodate donors, fewer donors as the value increase and the ultimate destination, if you can steer donors there, of legacies. To add further to this thinking I defined the donor wheels (Figure 2.3.4) that are now widely used by the sector to show how each programme can connect with donors at the different stages of their life and the associated lifestyle. The donor wheels helped illustrate that a successful programme should define the different stages and have them available for donors to connect to as and when

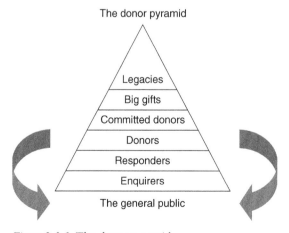

Figure 2.3.3 The donor pyramid

DOI: 10.4324/9781003145936-33

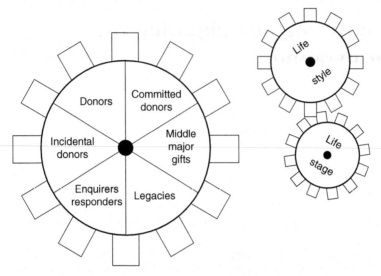

Figure 2.3.4 The donor wheels

they wanted. They could move in and out of a relationship programme and would rarely follow any logical route between levels of relationship. The other significant reminder of this framework was the two wheels that reflected the donor and their constantly changing view of the world and possible needs in terms of a connection with a cause.

The donor pyramid and the donor wheels are two very strong frameworks that have stood the test of time and they present two alternative views with variations of how to develop a programme for individual donors. But they fail to reflect how the digital decade has changed the way many people want to connect with, interact with and possibly build a relationship with a charitable cause. We need to think through how things now happen in real time, how people can access knowledge to any level they require, how speed of service has changed expectations and how the digital world enables people to try more things before deciding what is right for them.

[...]

So where should we be thinking strategically? I don't think it is going too far to think in terms of three separate programmes that are all interlinked but have their distinct approaches and levels of stewardship. ... Charities rightly focus on trying to make as many programmes as possible serve their general funds needs, but this has to be the departure point where the donor is allowed more discretion and control. Remember that smart charities negotiate a system internally that recognises and accounts for three kinds of funding (Figure 2.3.5):

- General funds, which are at the total discretion of the charity in terms of how they are used and are in effect the life blood of the charity serving to

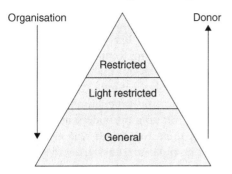

Figure 2.3.5 Three kinds of funding

pay salaries, overheads and often less popular parts of programmes that will not secure earmarked donations.

- Light restricted (or as the Americans would say 'lite' restricted!) funds, which is the new emerging category allowing fundraisers to present theme area of programmes, geographic areas of work or other broad segmentations of the cause. This allows a degree of connection with a project, but is nowhere near as restrictive as the next traditional category of income.
- Restricted income: is exactly 'what it says on the tin', restricted to a specific project or programme of work. Dearly loved by donors for obvious reasons but increasingly not so popular with charities again for obvious reasons in restricting operations and putting pressure on funding general overheads and operations from elsewhere.

Moving from committed givers the first level of HNWI [High Net Worth Individuals] programmes should be **'middle donors'** people giving at the higher level in their existing programme, perhaps with one-off gifts in addition to their regular donations and people generally capable of giving a more significant amount, placing them at the beginnings of the top 5% of a charity's donors, depending on the size of the charity and its donor base. This programme would offer highly personalised direct marketing techniques to cultivate and service the donors.

As some people respond well to the middle donor programme the space to move them to has to be a **'high value programme'** where the charity begins a process of trying to make greater contact, perhaps in small groups, so the donor can literally get closer to the cause, the charity and the brand. This segment is pushing well into the top 5% of the donor base, but again all based on the size and maturity of the database.

Finally our donor segments reach the well known **'major donor'** segment, however with the other two programmes leading up to this, it is likely to be a much smaller group where higher levels of stewardship can be offered to ensure loyalty and ultimately maximum level donations. The distinguishing feature of this programme is the one to one, face to face nature of the programme. We all know that this is the ultimate form of individual fundraising, but extremely labour and resource intensive. In most charities this is likely to be the top 2% of donors, so truly the individuals at the core of giving to the charity.

The other shift over the last few years has been the realisation that programmes for HNWI no longer have to revolve around a capital project or bricks and mortar. Instead of working from the programme out, many charities now work from the donor in, concentrating on understanding their needs and potential, thus being able to link them to a much wider portfolio of projects. We now have enough experience and case studies truly to say that major donor programmes are for every charity; I guess this realisation is what is feeding the staff demand in the area.

The other key strategic factor to having three levels for HNWIs is the fact that the charity has greater control on the cultivation and development process and can cope with far greater numbers of prospects and donors. Once behaviour and research indicates their potential to move between programmes, different approaches and propositions can be tested with the ability to move people back into other programmes. All of which should be seamless to the donor but critical in maximising resources for the charity. In dedicated major donor programmes people talk about the prospect or donor pipeline, an analogy used to remind people of the need to keep identifying people to test within a programme, by defining three levels of programme for HNWIs these pipelines automatically exist and in time can be extremely streamlined and efficient.

So the sixty four million dollar question at this point is, what are the financial giving levels between these different programmes? And the frustrating answer is 'that depends!' But it is true, it is fatal to simply copy others in setting financial bars between different programmes and to complicate this challenge further once financial levels are set they should remain flexible and are likely to change each year for the first few years of growing these programmes. For some people middle donors start at £300, for others £500. To some charities a major donor is £5,000 to other £25,000 so much depends on where you are in your programme and your cause and evolution to date. Charities in the heritage and education field increasingly set their levels much higher than mainstream charities by the nature of their supporters and the projects they are seeking support for. Careful data analysis and research are the tools that will give you the clue to these questions and the conclusions need to be set against the resources you have available.

[…]

So against the background of all the new developments, environmental challenges and most importantly changing donor needs we need a new donor pyramid and donor journey (Figure 2.3.6 and Figure 2.3.7).

[…]

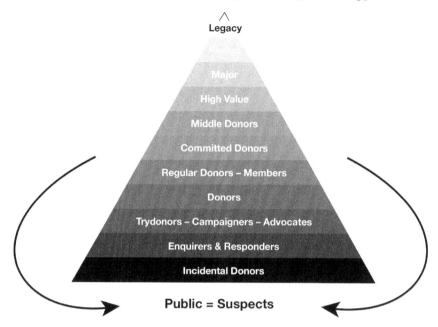

Figure 2.3.6 New donor pyramid

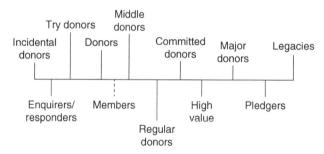

Figure 2.3.7 New donor journey

So our expedition to rediscover and climb the donor pyramid hopefully sets out a new framework for new and more rigorous thinking around the area of maximising the potential of private individuals and their support for our cause, after all globally individuals still represent the largest and most valuable source of voluntary income for our sector.

2.4 Vital ingredients for success

Relationship fundraising

Ken Burnett, 2002

Relationship fundraising is fundraising where people matter most, a sort of Fritz Schumacher [a 20th century German-British statistician and economist] approach to fundraising. Schumacher invented the concept "small is beautiful" and through his book of that name started the appropriate technology movement, which concentrates on using only low-cost, available materials rather than expensive imported technology. Small *is* beautiful. Relationship fundraising advocates a return to the intimacy of the one-to-one relationship between donor and cause but, thanks to the miracle of modern technology, it makes that intimacy possible on a national scale for thousands, even millions of people at the same time.

Above all, relationship fundraising is not just about raising funds. In case you feel a definition would be useful, here is mine. The concept is too complex for one succinct sentence, but a brief paragraph can catch the essence:

> Relationship fundraising is an approach to the marketing of a cause that centers on the unique and special relationship between a nonprofit and each supporter. Its overriding consideration is to care for and develop that bond and to do nothing that might damage or jeopardize it. Every activity is therefore geared toward making sure donors know they are important, valued, and considered, which has the effect of maximizing funds per donor in the long term.

I'm not, incidentally, advocating conversion to relationship fundraising because I'm sentimental about fundraising. I'm advocating it because I speak to a lot of nonprofit supporters and this is the kind of thing they're telling me more and more. Donors generally are distressed to see blatant commercialism from the nonprofits they support. They often resent the repeated process of being asked for money with precious little offered in return. They dislike being written to by a marketing machine and regard the transparent techniques of direct mail and telephone appeals as little short of deliberate deception.

I hasten to say that what I am opposed to are the transparent techniques, not direct mail or even telephone fundraising per se. They are potentially efficient means to a very important end. Donors repeatedly reaffirm their willingness to hear from their chosen nonprofits but they express great concern about *how* that contact will be carried out.

DOI: 10.4324/9781003145936-35

Professional fundraisers of the current generation have been vigorously extending and upgrading their transactions with donors – their "customers." They should have been moving away from a transaction orientation and moving toward a relationship orientation.

People coming into the fundraising profession now are more likely to be trained in an appropriate professional discipline such as marketing or finance, but may perhaps be less well versed in some of the thinking behind the fundraiser's art. This new blood might prove to be of great value to our profession, but if it is unable to appreciate and adopt the theory and practice of relationship fundraising then it is more likely to do lasting damage instead. There are some signs that this has already happened in some communities where, rather like the used-car sales rep, the well-rehearsed and trained professional fundraiser is not always held in great esteem. For fundraisers, increased professionalism doesn't automatically equate to increased status. Unless it is carefully managed, the effect of increased professionalism can be quite the reverse.

[...]

A total philosophy

Relationship fundraising is not a series of isolated incidents, it is a total philosophy. It deals with every aspect of donor contact, channeling that contact toward building a specific lifelong relationship and ensuring that the relationship is as fruitful as possible for both parties. It involves notions that may seem unnecessary or even uneconomic, such as quickly and effectively answering every letter and acknowledging by return of post every donation, however small, sending a personal letter that any donor might wish to receive. The commercial logic in this is simply that small donors leave large bequests. Not all of them, of course. But the relationship fundraiser assumes they all will or at least treats them as if they will.

The relationship fundraiser also notes the warnings in negative, critical letters and responds appropriately and positively. People, even complainers, write because they care. American fundraiser Richard Felton calls it "criticism with love." If they didn't care they wouldn't bother. Worse by far is that they ignore you.

[...]

What relationship fundraising can do for you

In this noisy world, with so many competing promotional voices clamoring for our customers' attention, we all know that our communications have just seconds in which to make an impression. When our carefully prepared and costly appeal package is finally delivered to Mr. and Mrs. Donor, we know the odds are stacked against it even getting opened before it is consigned to the trash. Our attempts to inject compulsion to open and make reading irresistible are, by and large, rather futile and pathetic. If our promotion is read, it is as often an indulgence as an inevitability. Our donors, always drawn from the more intelligent and rational sectors of society, are now among the most sophisticated and aware people on earth – most of them.

They know when they're being sold to and they may tolerate it but they don't like it. They know when they're being written to by a marketing machine and they don't like that either. They may respond to our most recent mailing just as they did the time before because of their commitment to the cause, but that doesn't mean they like the way they've been asked. And while we are congratulating ourselves on achieving a 20 percent response to our latest warm mailing, what about the 80 percent who didn't respond? What do they think of our aggressive fundraising approach and what, ultimately, will they do about it?

But consider what a difference there is when Mr. and Mrs. Donor receive a letter from a friend. We all know the apathy with which most people greet junk mail, but don't forget that millions of people still rush to the mailbox to see what they day's mail has brought. When they see it is from someone they like, they eagerly open that letter first to see what news and information their friend has sent.

Imagine how nice it would be if donors were to telephone you to inquire, rather worriedly, as to why they hadn't received the last issue of your newsletter and to say how much they looked forward to hearing from you. I know of one nonprofit whose donors are so involved and interested that it does get such calls and letters (although less so now that their publication schedules are a little more regular and reliable).

Fundraisers are most often writing to people who have already shown that they believe in the cause. And they are writing about subjects that are almost invariably interesting, dramatic, newsworthy, touching, exciting, and positive. So there is no excuse whatever for fundraisers to produce junk mail or junk anything.

There is every reason for fundraisers to strive to produce interesting, exciting, and relevant information which they can send to friends who share their interest and commitment. But that's just a start. Relationship fundraising can help you to find out all you need to know about your donors, it can help you to locate and recruit others like them, it can encourage your donors to introduce their friends, it can help you to write appropriately and personally to your donors as individuals, it can help you identify the right offer to make them. Relationship fundraising can show you how to avoid making mistakes in dealing with donors, how to avoid wasting money and how to make your promotion pay, how to increase your donors' annual giving and extend their "life" as donors, how to manage your staff and present your organization, how to approach your marketing strategy, how to make your donor your friend, how to increase the value of your donors, and how to ensure a gigantic leap in your income from bequests (also known as legacies).

It can also be very satisfying and rewarding.

Welcome as a letter from a friend

Relationship fundraisers gear their offers to what their donors want to buy, not what they (the fundraisers, that is) want to sell. They recognise that people are different from each other, and also vary in their own response to different appeals over time. As we all know, donors frequently don't give to some appeals, which seems to me to provide an interesting answer to the apparently endless question of how many letters to send. If you listen to your donors, some would receive just one appeal each year, some as many as ten or twelve, and most of the others would receive some number in between.

It depends on the donor. Of course, if you give donors the choice they may choose to receive your appeals less often than you would wish them to. This is where the relationship fundraiser has to get clever ... Fundraisers tend to think automatically of their communications with donors as "appeals". We talk of "mailings" and "packs." I'm as guilty as the next person, but really we should think in terms of *letters* instead – and we shouldn't always expect or ask for a response.

Because each donor is different, the relationship fundraiser is also aware that it makes little sense to send the same mailing package with the same offer, letter, or leaflet to every donor. While the practical difficulties are obvious, technological change is providing fundraisers with the means to do something about this.

[...]

As my experience has grown I have become increasingly convinced that developing a relationship with donors is the key to success in fundraising. Our business is donor development and that is only possible through the formation of a tangible relationship. As donors, by and large, are honest and intelligent people, it is a process that can only be done with honesty and intelligence. You may be able to pull the wool over the eyes of some of your donors for a while, but you can't do it in the long term – and successful relationships are based on trust and confidence, both long-term concepts.

Neglecting the relationship can be expensive too. I once worked with a national nonprofit that, as policy, didn't send any acknowledgement to donors giving less than £5, and sent a preprinted receipt to those giving between £5 and £10. The purpose was to discourage small donors, who probably went to other nonprofits and left their bequests to them.

[...]

The nine keys to building a relationship

The process of building and sustaining lasting and mutually beneficial relationships with hundreds, even thousands, of individual donors, has a number of cornerstones. Inevitably, when written down, these seem trite and obvious – but they are worth listing here. Any fundraiser who can put hand on heart and say "I do all this" is not doing badly.

- *Be honest.* If any business area should be honest, it is fundraising. The public expects fundraisers to be honest. Those that don't view fundraisers as inherently honest and trustworthy certainly don't give, so it pays to be seen as honest.

[...]

- *Be sincere and let your commitment show.* Donors are donors because they care enough to take action and support your cause. Let them see that you care too and that that is why you're there as well. When this happens, immediately you and they are on the same side, with a common concern and aim. Your commitment will then encourage them to go even further for the cause.
- *Be prompt.* Reply quickly and efficiently to any request. Answer letters the next day, or sooner if possible. If the issue is important, telephone the donor and explain what action you are going to take. If it will take time to provide a full answer, write or telephone the donor quickly to say that an answer is being prepared and let them know when to expect it. Prompt response shows you take your donor's concerns seriously.
- *Be regular.* Regular planned communication keeps donors in touch, informed, and involved. If you are irregular in your communications, be aware that other fundraisers are not so lax. They also have access to your donors, so they'll be in touch when you are not.
- *Be interesting and memorable.* By their very nature nonprofits have access to compelling material. Use it to the full; present it well. Fundraising is all about telling stories. Make all your material stand out for its interesting content, style, and presentation. And its unforgettable visuals.
- *Be involving.* Don't allow donors to take a passive role. Ask for their opinions, contributions, and even complaints. Encourage feedback in any way you can. Invite them to events, offer visits to projects. Make the dialogue as two-way as you possibly can.
- *Be cheerful and helpful.* Advertise your helpfulness. Never let donors feel that asking is a trouble. That's what you are there for – to help them. Teach customer care to all your colleagues. I have never forgotten a simple piece of advice from the days when I sold advertising space over the telephone – smile and dial. When you smile on the phone, what you are saying sounds much better at the other end. It really works. Try it. (Tell your colleagues first, otherwise they'll think you've gone mad.)
- *Be faithful.* Always stick to your promises. Let donors see that you are honorable and trustworthy. Stand by your organization's mission and don't compromise what it stands for.
- *Be cost-effective.* Donors expect and appreciate good stewardship of their gifts but are generally well aware of the potential for false economies, which they dislike as much as conspicuous waste. Be open and informative, explain your reasons for financial decisions and show your donors that their money is in good hands.

Of course, this list is not exhaustive. But if you can inject these key elements into your relationships with donors they will not only be encouraged enough to continue their support, they will derive increased satisfaction from their giving and will even go out and tell their friends, encouraging them to do the same. And that, I believe, is what fundraising is all about.

Articulating a case for support

Timothy L. Seiler, 2022

Defining "case for support" and "case statement"

A case for support is a *sine qua non* for nonprofits. It is the rationale underlying fundraising, the reason nonprofit organizations deserve philanthropic support, not why they need money. Without a case for support, a nonprofit does not have a right to seek philanthropic support, to raise money.

It is important to understand that *case for support* as a phrase might be daunting to some, even a cause for panic. Andy Brommel, Director of Communications Consulting at Campbell & Company, fears that the term is fundraising jargon that confuses more than clarifies. Brommel believes that when fundraisers hear case for support, they think, "Oh, no. I have to write some long document." However, the case for support is "not a long document; it's a set of messages that prepare prospective donors and funders for solicitation."

Case for support is an argument or set of arguments explaining why a nonprofit deserves gift support. The case for support is bigger than the organization and relates to a cause being served. The case for support is an encyclopedic accumulation of information, parts of which are used in different iterations to argue that the organization deserves gift support for working in service to the cause.

A *case statement* is a particular articulation of the case for support. A specific case statement is not as large or universal as the case for support; that is, a case statement is a specific illustration of some of the elements making up the case for support. A case statement selects and articulates specific points from the overall case for support.

Preparing the case for support

The case for support is central to an organization's work, and examining the case is the first step in the fundraising cycle, a step-by-step planning and implementation model.

The preparation of the case begins with understanding that nonprofit organizations raise money to meet community needs. Unmet social needs lead to the creation of nonprofit organizations, and the case for support is built on how well the organization meets those needs. The effectiveness of the case depends on how well the organization serves the cause.

DOI: 10.4324/9781003145936-36

The case for support is the bedrock upon which philanthropic fundraising is built. It is the urgent call for a solution to a problem, the meeting of a need. The persuasiveness of the case relates directly to the nonprofit's ability to solve problems and to adjust to changing market or societal needs. The case for support is the expression of the cause, addressing why anyone should contribute to the advancement of the cause. The case is larger than the organization's financial needs; it is larger than the organization.

Preparation, development, and validation of the case begins with staff. Organizations with communications or marketing staff often draw on their writing expertise for case development. For smaller organizations, development staff, or whoever has responsibility for managing development and fundraising, need to take the lead. Development professionals typically serve as interpreters of the concerns, interests, and needs of the external constituencies. The staff must be able and willing to report on constituencies' perceptions of the organization, especially perceptions of prospective and current donors and organizational clients and beneficiaries.

It is not uncommon for fundraisers to discover that not everything is perfect among the constituencies. Occasionally constituencies are misinformed or uninformed. Sometimes there are perceptions that the organization is not effective. Perhaps constituencies lack confidence that gifts are needed or that they make a difference. Finding out how to address these concerns will strengthen the case for support. Fundraising staff must know the organization inside and out and must represent the constituencies as well.

Getting others involved, though, in case development is important. Seeking the ideas of key constituencies – board members, volunteers, donors, and potential donors – is particularly effective in enlisting leadership for articulation of the case in fundraising. Having a role in developing and validating the case increases the enthusiasm of those who will articulate the case. They will question what puzzles them or challenge what disturbs them. If they are representative of others from whom gifts will be sought, their questions and challenges will strengthen the case for support. "Involve those you want to own and use the case. Facilitate structured discussions of key questions and clarify core messages before writing any long document. Test your case via surveys, focus groups, maybe even a feasibility study."

Key information components of a case for support

The development of the overall case for support begins with compiling and collating information components that provide the background for everything a potential donor might want to know about the nonprofit organization. These components probably already exist in the organization. They become an information bank, from which case statements are developed. The information database is a starting point for the development of specific case statements.

The following key components, adapted from Rosso, must be in ready form inside the organization and must be available, accessible, and retrievable when needed for developing a case for support:

1. *Mission statement* articulates awareness of the cause and provides insight into the problem the organization addresses.
2. *Planning and evaluation* illustrate strategic, operational, fundraising, and program plans that demonstrate commitments and provide evidence of strengths and impact.
3. *Goals* articulate what the organization aspires to achieve in solving the problem.
4. *Objectives* state what will be accomplished by reaching the goals.
5. *Governance* illustrates the character and quality of the organization as shown in its volunteer leadership and governance structure.
6. *Staffing* illustrates the competence and qualifications of the staff.
7. *Programs and services* explain how the nonprofit serves its constituencies and the community.
8. *Service delivery* points out advantages, strengths, and effectiveness of how people access the programs and services.
9. *Finances* describe expenses associated with providing programs and services as validation for philanthropic gift support beyond earned income and fees for service.
10. *History* tells of the organization's successes over time and demonstrates legitimacy.

Mission statement

A mission statement is a philosophical statement of the human or societal needs the nonprofit organization meets; it explains why the nonprofit exists. A mission statement is an expression of the values in which the organization believes and around which it does its work.

It is often believed that mission statements express what an organization does, as exemplified by a statement such as "It is the mission of the agency to provide after-school care." This is more a goal or purpose statement rather than a mission statement.

A statement containing an infinitive phrase – to deliver, to provide, to serve – is a goal or purpose statement, telling what the organization does. A mission statement, on the other hand, explains *why* the organization does what it does. An effective mission statement provides a base for identifying beliefs and values. A good mission statement often begins with words such as "We believe" or "We value." For example, a shelter for animals might use the following as its mission statement: *Concern for Animals* believes that all animals deserve humane treatment. Because we care about all animals, *Concern for Animals* provides shelter and food for abandoned and unwanted animals.

Here is another example of a statement that is more of a goal or purpose statement than a mission statement and a suggested revision to reveal more clearly the values/beliefs of the organization.

Original text:

- "The mission of Global Hope is to combine the resources of individuals and organizations around the world to provide emergency relief and economic and social development."

Suggested revision:

- "Global Hope believes that wherever people are suffering, compassion and hope can help them endure and thrive. Global Hope exists to mobilize people and resources to meet the needs of suffering people in a hurting world. This is achieved through a variety of programs including disaster relief and agricultural, education, medical, and economic assistance."

The mission statement gives donors and potential donors an opportunity to find the shared values between them and the nonprofit organization. Because people give to organizations with values they share, it is important for organizations to express their values clearly. Because the first step in the fundraising cycle is to examine the case for support, and the first element in the case is the mission statement, it is critical that the mission statement be one of values. Mission is "why," and even in the corporate world, good business starts with "why." Simon Sinek popularized this idea in his book about how great organizations and great leaders do things differently. Sinek argues that people become deeply involved with a product, service, movement, or idea only when they understand the why behind it. It all starts with why.

Planning and evaluation

This component should describe the process used for planning and the measures taken for evaluation. Program plans precede fundraising plans and validate the need for service. Therefore, the first step in beginning to develop a case for support originates in the organization's strategic plan. The organizational plan articulates where the organization is going and what it takes to get there. Fundraising plans demonstrate the need for philanthropic support for the organization to carry out its strategic plan.

Evaluation provides a means for demonstrating effectiveness and efficiency in programs and accountability and stewardship of philanthropic resources. Evaluation processes must be determined as early as possible and be constantly updated. They need to show responsiveness to those who are served.

Planning and evaluation documents show that the organization takes its work seriously and holds itself accountable. This inspires confidence in donors and potential donors.

Goals

If the mission statement answers "why," goals answer "what." What does the organization do? Goal statements are general expressions explaining what the organization wants to accomplish as it seeks to meet the needs or resolve the problem described in the mission statement. Goals are usually stated in ambitious terms and often come out of strategic planning processes. Goal statements guide the organization towards fulfilling the beliefs expressed in the mission statement. Because organizations frequently have multiple programs, goals will be multiple; that is, the organization will have several program-related goals, some of which require funding, and funding the program goals leads to the formulation of fundraising goals.

Objectives

Objectives differ from goals in degree of specificity. Objectives are more precise and more measurable than goals and explain "how" the organization expects to reach its goals. These too should be defined as part of strategic or annual planning efforts.

A fundraising goal might be "To increase annual fund income." Objectives how to reach that goal might be "To increase annual giving from individuals by five percent in the next fiscal year" and "To increase corporate giving and corporate sponsorship by 15 percent in the next fiscal year."

Governance

The issue of governance of nonprofits is critical in attracting charitable gifts. The governance structure indicates the character and quality of the institution. This component should contain relevant information about how the board is composed and how it functions. Complete dossiers of board members and organizational material such as by-laws and conflict-of-interest statements should be part of the governance component.

Staffing

As governance is a matter of integrity and quality, staffing is an indicator of competence and professionalism. Descriptions of staff should illustrate the credentials and qualifications of staff, paid and volunteer, and include resumes as appropriate. Staffing patterns reveal how the organization delivers programs and services effectively.

Competent, skilled staff, together with dedicated, energetic board members, offer a persuasive case for potential contributors to make charitable gifts. It is essential to keep this component current. Staff should review their resumes at least annually, updating continuing education and professional development activities.

Finances

Financial information about the organization links budgeting with objectives and program descriptions. Information about finances gives a clear picture of how the organization acquires and spends financial resources. This financial overview establishes and validates the need for philanthropic gift support, justifying fundraising. The overview also offers the opportunity to demonstrate fiscal responsibility and accountability for prudent use of funds.

In short, the fundraising plan needs to be based on the organization's full financial plan. Making a case for philanthropic support requires the ability to show a clear picture of all income and expenses for the organization.

Programs and services

The programs and services component should include descriptions of how the organization provides services to its clients and meets community needs.

One of the best ways to show the importance and impact of the programs and services is to collect testimonials from clients and beneficiaries telling their personal stories of how the organization helped them. If confidentiality issues constrain the use of personal testimonials or stories, third-party endorsements provide a helpful substitute, as can anonymous statements and data about the types of people served and the outcomes.

Potential donors and funders are more likely to respond to fundraising appeals when they recognize that people are truly benefiting from the nonprofit's work.

Service delivery

The next component is explaining the delivery of programs and services delivery. This should explain how people access programs and services, in person, online, or through other means.

Occasionally, an organization's facility is a distinguishing factor: visibility, accessibility, and convenience are advantages for both physical and virtual service provision.

This component might include plans for renovation, expansion, or new construction and will help make the case for capital fundraising.

History

In talking about its history, a nonprofit should focus on its accomplishments in terms of how it has served its constituencies and its communities. The history should capture the spirit of the people, both service providers and beneficiaries. The focus should be on the organization's heroes as exemplified by the stories people tell about the organization and its impact. History is the heroic saga of the organization and proves its legitimacy and trustworthiness.

With these components in place, an organization is ready to develop case statements, for fundraising and for informing other types of constituent communications.

Case statements

Case statements order and present information for communications, public relations, and fundraising, and take the form of brochures, foundation and corporation grant proposals, direct mail letters, email messages, website information, campaign prospectuses, news releases, newsletters, speeches, even face-to-face gift solicitations. It is helpful to think of a case statement as the "case at work".

In developing case statements, the focus is on answering these questions:

1. What is the problem or social need central to our concern?
2. What services or programs do we deliver to respond to this need?
3. Why are the problem and the services important?
4. What constitutes the markets (funding sources) for our services?
5. What distinguishes us from others who are seeking support from the same markets?
6. Do we have a written plan with a statement of philosophy (i.e., mission, vision, values), goals and objectives, and programs and evaluation?
7. What are the specific financial needs for which we seek gift support?
8. How do we demonstrate our competence to carry out our defined programs?
9. Who is associated with our organization: staff, key volunteers, trustees or directors?
10. Who is likely to support us?

In writing such case statements, it is helpful to remember that the purpose is to stimulate potential donors and funders to take a series of steps, ultimately ending in the decision to make a gift or grant. Certain qualities of writing must exist to stimulate this sequence:

*   Relevance of the issue – to capture attention
*   Proximity to donors – to engage their interest
*   A sense of the future – to build confidence
*   Immediacy – to instill conviction
*   Excitement – to create a desire to act
*   Importance – to take action

Successful case statements move potential donors/funders to take action; that is, participate in the nonprofit's work by making a gift or grant.

[…]

The process of developing and articulating a case for support takes a series of steps, from creating and/or collating key components to developing "long documents" (see beginning of this text) for information, education, and fundraising.

Tailored to the audience and supporting the mission

Case statements must fit the interests and needs of donors and funders, including individuals, corporations, foundations, and others. Case statements, then, are tailored to the audience – recipients of direct mail like new donors, donors renewing gifts, and donors upgrading their gifts; recipients of email messages and readers of social media posts; corporations and foundations receiving formal grant proposals; and donors being asked for gifts in personal, face-to-face (or virtual) meetings.

While the iteration of the case is specific in each instance, what all case statements have in common is adherence to the mission of the organization. It is the thread that holds everything together.

Effective fundraising case statements must do the following:

1. State a need: a community need, the cause being served
2. Document the need: external evidence that confirms the problem
3. Propose strategies to meet the need: organizational goals, objectives, programs
4. Identify who benefits: recipients, beneficiaries, community at large
5. Demonstrate organizational competence: governance, staffing, mechanics of service delivery
6. Specify resources required: philanthropic support being sought
7. Tell how to make gifts: checks, credit/debit cards, stocks, donor advised funds, online, mobile devices
8. Explain benefits of giving: answer the question, "What's in it for me" as a donor/funder, show what the organization will do with gifts

The answers to the questions should be all be found in the 10 components that help build the case for support.

Conclusion

In articulating the case for support, it is critical to keep the donor/funder uppermost in mind. Case statements must be understandable to the audience; it is unwise to assume the audience knows the organization at all, let alone as well as the creators of the case know the organization. Case statements should avoid "insider language," what Andy Brommel refers to as jargon, and must be written in the clear, precise language of the vernacular.

Developing and articulating a case for support is the first step in the fundraising process.

Reviewing the case occasionally is a way to ensure that it is current and relevant. The following questions can be a starting point for a review:

1. Who are we and why do we exist?
2. What do we want to accomplish?
3. How will we accomplish it?
4. How do we hold ourselves accountable?
5. What distinguishes us from others doing similar work?

Answering these questions regularly validates the organization's case for support and prepares the organization to develop messages that articulate boldly and compellingly why it deserves gift support.

Cultivating diversity in fundraising

Janice Gow Pettey, 2002

A story is told about a southern gentleman who owned a grove of beautiful oak trees. Well established and much admired, these oak trees were a source of great pride. On a trip to another part of the country, the man discovered peach trees. Taken with their lovely blossoms and sweet fruit, he decided that peaches would be a good addition to his grove. Because the grove was filled with oaks, he decided to graft a peach branch onto an existing oak. He studied grafting, soil and climate conditions, and carefully grafted a peach branch onto one of his oak trees. He tended to the grafted tree and patiently waited for the fruits of his work. Spring came and passed, and there was no sign of peach blossoms on the oak tree. After repeated attempts, the man finally admitted that his efforts to graft a fruit tree onto an oak were futile.

Philanthropy in America is well cultivated and bears deep roots. These philanthropic practices as they are known to us have evolved through the growth of the nation reflecting the traditions and interests of the early settlers. The increasing numbers of racially and ethnically diverse people living in the United States now gives us the opportunity to develop new and distinct forms of philanthropy. Our fields of philanthropy will be enriched through the cultivation and appreciation of diversity yielding promise for generations to come.

[...]

Fundraisers work in an ever-changing environment, and we are called upon to address future challenges while responding to current needs. The fast-moving population changes in America require thoughtfulness and creativity from fundraisers in order for the nonprofit sector to remain balanced in delivering services and securing funding constituencies. Creating a vibrant and expanded nonprofit sector is possible through individual and collective effort. Raising more money from diverse communities is the by-product of successful collaborations, understanding, and respect of differences. People will support what they help create.

[...]

The Association of Fundraising Professionals (AFP) defines diversity as "the state of being different among others." By definition, diversity is limitless, and an understanding of the diversity of religious preference, racial/ethnic populations, lifestyle, economic level, education, gender, and age will add to our understanding of prospects, donors, and philanthropists. All of this is required for successful cultivation of diversity in the field of philanthropy and

DOI: 10.4324/9781003145936-37

fundraising. There is an abiding need to recognize the value of cultivating diversity in the field of philanthropy as in every other aspect of our national lives.

[…]

Fundraising as it is practiced today will not be as effective without attention to the needs and interests of our changing population. We don't need to look far to find ways to enhance our fundraising sensitivities. It is a fundamental matter of willingness to learn and adapt. In "Respecting the Individual, Valuing Diversity," Marilyn Fischer writes:

> To overlook traditions of giving in ethnic communities while collecting data on philanthropy is to impose cultural patterns of the dominant society on communities where these do not fit. When giving through voluntary organizations is assumed to be normal and definitional, rather than as "one" way of being philanthropic, other patterns are judged deficient or not even seen.

I agree with Fischer and others who defend the significance of "informal giving" practiced by many ethnic groups, yet not documented or counted in so many surveys measuring time and money given to charitable organizations. In a report issued by the University of San Francisco, Michael O'Neill and William L. Roberts note the "disparity between the findings of survey research on minority giving and volunteering and qualitative studies of this issue." O'Neill and Roberts state, "The latter report extensive and diverse charitable behavior in communities of color, but the former report levels of giving and volunteering substantially below those of whites."

Among the challenges in creating successful models of fundraising in diverse communities is one of definition …

To cite a personal example, my experiences as a Peace Corps volunteer prompted my personal interest in diversity. I was sent to Korea as a public health worker in an isolated fishing village where I was the only American for miles. The program was designed for pairs of volunteers to develop health clinics in the rural Korea of the late 1960s. I was assigned alone, in a particularly isolated area with no paved roads, electricity, or plumbing. There was only one phone in the village, which worked occasionally. I knew I did not earn this assignment because of my Korean language skills, as I had, at best, a marginal grasp of the language. It was not because I possessed technical public health skills, as my degree was in American Literature. It might have had more to do with appearance—an Asian in an Asian country. Korean society, particularly rural Korea at that time, was male dominated and very traditional. This was not a situation where a Chinese-American female could easily and effectively lead others without establishing mutual trust, understanding, and acceptance.

In *Remaking America* author James Joseph says, "the theologian Reinhold Niebuhr suggested that the chief cause of our inhumanity to each other is the tendency to set up 'we' groups and to place them over and against 'they' groups that we assume are outside the pale of our community." Mr. Joseph goes on to suggest, "Whatever cohesion early Americans enjoyed, much of it was based on mutual respect. And that, not surprisingly, is today's missing element. Unless mutual respect is restored, the American society will continue to unravel. ... Few Americans are aware of the extent to which voluntary groups provided a means of economic survival for racial minorities and helped them to make sense of their realities by serving as vehicles for self-help, social cohesion, and a positive group identity." We can and should be proud of the American contributions to the field of philanthropy; but we must not ignore the legacies of the benevolent societies created by Chinese immigrants in the 1800s, or the impact of organized religion on philanthropy evidenced by the acts of charity practiced in African American churches throughout the South during the same time. Philanthropy has a rich heritage, which, if studied and practiced, would only strengthen the fundraising profession. Organizations with interest in the successful cultivation of diverse donor relationships will benefit from enriched understanding and appreciation of others' cultural, ethnic, religious, and other practices. Fundraisers with an enhanced awareness and empathy for other cultures and lifestyles will assist in cultivating that field of philanthropy that thrives on diversity.

Oseola McCarty, the Mississippi laundress turned philanthropist in 1995, was somewhat amazed at the fuss made over her gift to a university she never attended. She inspired many with the generous donation of her life savings, $150,000, to the University of Southern Mississippi (USM). This was not the largest donation the school had ever received, but what distinguished this gift from others was that she had saved the money over the course of a lifetime from her modest earnings ironing other people's laundry. Ms. McCarty had no family to inherit her nest egg, so she chose USM because she herself had dropped out of high school to take care of her family. She wanted to give youth of limited means the opportunity to go to college. Her gift is being used for scholarships. Interviewed by many, her response was modest. She just wanted to help. "I just want the scholarship to go to some child who needs it, to whoever is not able to help their children. I'm too old to get an education, but they can."

In my career as a fundraiser, I worked for a disaster relief organization, assisting at several large disasters. It was energizing to see the philanthropic spirit of the many diverse ethnic groups in Guam following a major typhoon. Their approach was culturally appropriate and successful. There was support for one another without sacrificing individuality. Neighborhood fiestas—we would call them potlucks—created to support one another, and the practice of neighbor helping neighbor, are examples of a comfortable blending of customs used for charitable ends. I have learned to wear the shoes of the residents of the communities I am in, as it is their footprints that will lead the way to successful fundraising.

In choosing to work as fundraisers, we are expected to raise the money, serve as effective administrators, be good with numbers, communicate well, and serve as faithful stewards of the gifts and grants that our organizations receive. Good social work skills can come in handy, too. I believe it is the soul of fundraising that makes the difference. Arthur Frantzreb says this about philanthropy: "The word *philanthropy* has its roots in the Greek language meaning 'love for mankind.' It was never meant to apply only to donors of thousands or millions of dollars." John Gardner's analogy of giving in America being a Mississippi River of small gifts suggests that this flow of generosity comes from many sources composed of large and small gifts, from major donors to those who give less, yet equal in compassion.

The opportunities that exist for us to increase the numbers of donors among diverse constituencies are at the same time challenging and necessary. First, we must understand each other better, and be prepared to learn from others, including those from other cultures that have practiced philanthropy longer than the United States has been a nation.

Evidence of efforts to support diversity and inclusiveness in fundraising are apparent, but one has only to look at the lack of diversity within the fundraising profession to understand the challenge. The number of diverse fundraisers has not changed significantly in the last 10 years, and yet we are looking at an increasingly diverse donor prospect base. Fundraising in the United States has mainly been driven by Western traditions that have shaped philanthropy. It is time for us to broaden our understanding of philanthropic motivation by learning from all those we wish to engage.

Section 3

UNDERSTANDING FUNDRAISING PRACTICE

Editors' introduction

Overview

The material in this section may most closely match expectations of fundraising literature, particularly for readers already actively involved in fundraising. It focuses on the tasks, activities, and programmes that help engage, ask, and retain donors. There is no standard industry typology for organising this branch of fundraising knowledge. Some practitioners will consider the readings in this section in terms of who is asked to give, also described as donor markets in some texts: e.g. individual low or mid-value donors, major-donors, companies, foundations, etc. Others will focus on how the gift request is made, described as fundraising methods in some texts, e.g. through events, sponsorship, grants, regular-giving. Many combine the two, for example the practice title "Major Donors" combines high net-worth donors with the methods of bid writing, and often special events. Some applied practice knowledge is overarching, such as strategic planning and copywriting, which undergird all types of fundraising practice. Much of this book focuses on both the science and the art of fundraising. These are not absent from this section, but here the focus is on application: the practical tasks involved in securing resources (most often monetary) to enable charitable services to be delivered and nonprofits' missions to be realised.

Fundraisers in small organisations often find themselves required to have mastery of every kind of fundraising practice because they must deliver a range of fundraising methods to more than one group of donors. In larger organisations the opportunity to specialise within focused teams exists. Whilst the latter arrangement may sound intuitively superior, there are challenges associated with organising fundraising into teams and programmes. If we organise by *how* we ask, we risk creating teams focused on their particular method, who may neglect to offer donors the full spectrum of giving opportunities. If we organise by *whom* we ask, the challenge arises of managing fundraising methods, such as events, that should have a broad appeal. However, within large organisations, the near universal practice of creating specialist teams, whose remit mixes donor groups and fundraising methods, speaks to the advantage of this approach.

Where focused teams and programmes exist, an additional layer of leadership and skill is needed to avoid silos and to build inter-programme "donor

DOI: 10.4324/9781003145936-39

journeys", thoughtfully engaging with a donor throughout their giving relationship with the organisation. Each fundraising method draws on a broad combination of knowledge and skills, and working with each type of donor requires a range of knowledge and insights gleaned from disciplines such as marketing, sociology, and psychology. There is a great advantage in every fundraiser having a basic knowledge of every method and donor type in order to facilitate collaboration between fundraising teams and offer donors the most relevant and optimal giving opportunities.

In this section we provide an introduction to, and exploration of, many different fundraising practices, although the complexity of fundraising means that not all methods and donor types can be fully covered. For example, this section does not consider earned income such as retail and primary purpose trading. The exception is sponsorship, which has a special status in corporate programmes. This section is divided into four parts as follows.

3.1 Fundraising planning, strategy, and campaigns

This first sub-section is guided by the well-known slogan: "If you fail to plan, you are planning to fail". We therefore begin with four extracts that consider different aspects of laying the groundwork and building the solid foundations on which successful fundraising practice can follow.

In the first extract, Claire Routley and Richard Sved describe the process of strategic planning and implementation. They emphasise the amount of thought, preparation, research, and consultation required, noting that "Your strategy isn't a document. It's a set of mutually agreed decisions, created by all and owned by all. The document is just the receipt."

Mal Warwick's piece reminds us that it is not possible to pursue every desirable goal immediately and simultaneously. Instead, those charged with fundraising planning need to choose between, or at least prioritise, efforts to: grow the donor base; enhance the involvement of existing supporters; increase the visibility of their organisation and cause; improve the efficiency of fundraising operations; and achieve financial stability. Thinking through these five different potential strategies – growth, involvement, visibility, efficiency, and stability (which create the mnemonic GIVES) – can help fundraisers decide how to make best use of their finite time and budget because, as Warwick points out: "a successful strategy is always clear, focused, and directed."

Next, Adrian Sargeant and Jayne George set out how to conduct a "fundraising audit" to determine where the organisation is now, where it wants to be, and how it is going to get there. As they argue, an accurate assessment of "readiness to fundraise" needs to take account of all relevant factors. External factors include macro environmental influences – notably political, economic, and socio/cultural factors – as well as other nonprofits operating in the same field, and the different types of donors that the organisation wishes to engage with. Internal factors relate to the organisation's own activities, including past performance of different fundraising efforts and the present organisation of the fundraising function. This extract ends by explaining and exemplifying a core tool in strategic work: the SWOT analysis. Sargeant and George encourage smaller charities to adjust this framework in proportion to their size and capacity, and to be particularly open to assessing opportunities for collaboration.

The final extract in this sub-section, by Kathleen Kelly, describes the evolution and implementation of big money fundraising campaigns. Kelly provides insights into the structure and organisation of campaigns whilst challenging established wisdom regarding their assumed benefits, noting that they can represent a problematic "fascination with money rather than mission". Instead she advocates replacing campaign strategies with continuous efforts to raise major gifts, which takes us into the topic of our second sub-section.

3.2 Working with major gifts

The second sub-section is focused on fundraising efforts that are designed to result in major gifts, including from individuals during their lifetime and in their wills, as well as from grant-making institutions. These are most often secured through one-to-one relationships between the non-profit organisation and the high-value donor. Therefore, how to initiate, develop and sustain such relationships is of optimum importance.

We turn first to individual major donors who are typically viewed as a greatly desired yet elusive source of income. This degree of interest and apprehension is understandable given the transformational effect that even one major supporter can have on both the balance sheet and organisational morale. The two extracts that are focused on major donors by William Sturtevant and by Angela Cluff provide, respectively, confirmation and consolation in relation to popular assumptions about working with wealthy private donors. They both emphasise that major-donor fundraising is about one-to-one relationship building.

Sturtevant describes major gifts as "stop and think gifts" because the major donor's thought process is far longer and more complex than that required to make a small, one-off, or annual gift. For example, the potential major donor may need to consult family members and financial advisors, and will likely want detailed information on how their gift will be used. Fundraisers wishing to attract the support of major donors therefore need to be prepared to invest the time and attention required, which includes providing good stewardship after the donation so that donors can continue to feel involved and learn how their support made a difference. Sturtevant also outlines the "traps" into which major gifts programmes can fall, including unrealistic and unspecific objectives, and talking at, rather than listening to, prospective major donors. The potential for getting it wrong, and the consequences of "losing" a significant contribution, fuels the fear that many fundraisers feel in relation to working with major donors. Cluff's piece therefore offers some much-needed reassurance by highlighting nine myths about major donor fundraising, including challenging the suggestion that only big and well-known nonprofits are successful in securing this type of income, and that fundraisers only have "one shot" at securing a big gift. However, Cluff also notes five organisational weaknesses that lie behind failure to attract major gifts such as (echoing

Sturtevant) nonprofit boards failing to understand the time and investment required to succeed and (perhaps surprisingly) lack of ambition or "stretch" in the size of gifts requested. For these reasons, Cluff concludes that "major donor fundraising is in theory easy, but in practice very hard".

Nonetheless, Sturtevant's advice to "get real" and set tangible targets, together with Cluff's myth-busting tips, offer the insight and confidence to encourage fundraisers to reconsider received wisdom about building and sustaining major donor relationships and to have a go at pursuing this type of donated income.

Superficially, legacies and major-donor gifts belong in a category together, distinct from foundation and corporate giving because they are high-value gifts from individuals not organisations. There are useful overlaps, but also important differences. Russell N. James III and Claire Routley note that only a minority of current big donors leave a charitable gift in their will, and report on an experiment that shows how sharing stories about living – rather than deceased – legacy pledgers results in generating greater interest in making a bequest gift. James and Routley attribute this finding to people's desire to avoid thinking about their own death when confronted with stories of deceased legacy donors. This finding suggests that fundraisers and their colleagues need to prioritise collecting, storing, and appropriately utilising inspirational stories – clearly this can only be achieved when fundraisers have a strong personal relationship with living pledgers, and when organisations have committed the resources to gathering them.

The final two extracts in this sub-section provide insight into the world of grant-making trusts and foundations, here "foundation" is used as a shorthand for both. Tobias Jung, Jenny Harrow, and Diana Leat offer a bigger picture overview of what a foundation is, while Elin Lindström and Joe Saxton focus on what works in funding proposals that are written to foundations. William Shakespeare's play *Romeo and Juliet* asks "What's in a name?", and Jung et al. suggest "not much" when it comes to foundations. They note that the word can be used in the names of major fundraising nonprofits, such as the British Heart Foundation whilst the word does not appear in the names of major grant-makers such as the Carnegie Corporation of New York. In some countries (such as the UK) there is no legal distinction between "foundations" and other forms of charitable organisations. Many perceive foundations to be a "large body of money" ("surrounded by people who want some of it", as wags have noted) yet there are many important distinctions between different types of foundations, such as those that run their own programmes or offer capacity-building support to grantees, those that operate in defined geographic areas, and those that are run by professional staff versus living donors, including families. Jung and colleagues seek to address this ambiguity by highlighting how foundations differ according to their context (their origins, legal- and socio-political settings); their organisational characteristics (age, lifespan, governance structure, size, and resources); and their strategy (style, approach, and intended beneficiaries).

Diversity in grant-making also informs the extract from Lindström and Saxton whose advice on writing great grant applications is organised around five "hallmarks" that nonetheless contain scope for variety. For example, some grantmakers claim to prefer applications written by nonprofit staff because they better "communicate the soul of the charity", whilst others prefer "skilled applications written by professional fundraisers" which "tend to have much higher success rates". Behind their confusing relationship to the professional fundraiser lies the fact that not all grant-makers are the same, therefore – as emphasised by all the extracts in this sub-section – research to understand prospective donors is vital, and relationships must be tailored and conducted on a one-to-one basis.

Finally, it is interesting to note how the Lindström and Saxton paper predicts contemporary calls for improvements in grantmaking practice, which we return to in Section 6 with an extract written eight years later by Gemma Bull and Tom Steinberg. Lindström and Saxton observed that "Good working relationships and openness to contact can help most other aspects of the grant-making process", but it has taken some time for better grantor systems and policies to come under sector scrutiny.

3.3 Working with many gifts

In the third sub-section another crucial aspect of fundraising practice is considered: asking many people (sometimes described as mass donor markets) for gifts that can range from pennies in a tin, to cumulatively substantial amounts when the lifetime-value of regular supporters is acknowledged. Roger Bennett offers insight into the evolution of this type of fundraising which has, especially in the US and the UK, shifted from transactional to relational strategies. Bennett presents brief overviews of a range of studies into how and why relationship marketing works in the nonprofit sector, including when it doesn't work and ends up recruiting "unprofitable donors": i.e. donors whose recruitment and stewardship is more expensive than the value of their gifts. Bennett also draws attention to the role of organisation branding in donor relationship building and how, despite initial resistance, brand has become an important tool in both the off-line and online worlds of donor engagement, with brand "warmth" positively driving online engagement.

The extracts by both Nina Botting Herbst and Lianne Howard-Dace, and by Pauline Carter, discuss the additional benefits of community fundraising and special events. Whilst there is justifiable concern that these activities typically lead to lower return on investment (ROI), both extracts highlight secondary benefits such as deepening donor engagement, and reaching new groups of donors. In the light of Bennett's observation that donor attrition partly results from "an individual's innate desire for variation" there is a logic in engaging existing donors through a rich offer of fundraising and engagement opportunities, rather than in silos such as "regular giver", "community fundraising volunteer", or "event participant".

Both Botting Herbst and Howard-Dace, and Carter, develop a strong distinction between the volunteer-led world of community fundraising and the professional output of events fundraising, summarised by noting that in community fundraising: "you can maximise your efficiency by seeing yourself and any other staff fundraisers as multipliers of your supporters' energy – not suppliers of it." Here the greatest scope for confusion is the term "volunteer", similar to Jung et al.'s frustration over the ambiguity in naming "foundations". In the previous sub-section, when Cluff writes about the role of volunteers in making major donor asks, she is talking about the well-connected and influential volunteer. By contrast, Botting Herbst and Howard-Dace's community volunteers are drawn from the widest social pool of supporters hosting everything from workplace coffee mornings to, far less frequently, elite dinners. The volunteers associated with special events come in both flavours: members of a "dedicated voluntary steering committee" are more akin to Cluff's volunteers, whilst other types of volunteers are also critical to delivering the event such as stewards, ticket collectors, and those put in charge of social media activity.

Writing skills are clearly key for those who are posting, tweeting, and encouraging engagement online, as well as for those writing copy for more traditional fundraising efforts such as direct mail programmes. Tom Ahern provides advice on how to successfully write text for donors and prospective supporters, including a check list to help ensure text is most likely to prompt a positive response. Ahern's advice includes making intangible nonprofit missions (such as "ending world hunger") as real as possible, using stories and concrete examples to bring nonprofit work and success to life.

The final extract in this sub-section also offers advice on how to help more potential individual donors (from mass donor markets) connect to nonprofit organisations by reaching them via their friends and family. Cassandra Chapman, Barbara Masser, and Winnifred Louis describe and evidence the importance of a phenomenon they call "the Champion Effect". The "champions" are volunteer fundraisers who harness the power of social connections and peer endorsement to raise larger sums. Chapman et al. report on a field experiment which shows that sponsors of fundraising challenges are motivated by supporting their friend or relative who cares about the cause, more than organisational factors such as the efficiency of the recipient nonprofit. In sum: "champions are more important drivers of fundraising outcome in the peer-to-peer domain than charities are." The application of this research to practice is that professional fundraisers should encourage those undertaking sponsored events to clearly signal their investment in the cause by setting a high fundraising target, and by sharing stories of why the cause matters to them personally, with updates and photographs that will motivate their contacts to donate.

3.4 Working with corporate donors and partners

The final sub-section includes three extracts on fundraising from corporations by Dwight Burlingame and Adrian Sargeant, Andrew Peel, and Darian Rodriguez Heyman. Between them they share insight into:

- motives – *why* corporate organizations give;
- mechanisms – *how* corporate organizations give; and

• relationships – *how* the support of corporate organizations can be sought and sustained.

These extracts highlight that companies are complex donors in all three respects because they have a wide range of giving mechanisms, influenced by capacity, motivation, and their relationship with the beneficiary organisation. Burlingame and Sargeant identify different approaches contained within corporate giving that range from "altruistic" models of being a good corporate citizen to "commercial" models where profit and company benefit is the main motive. Fundraisers are advised to keep corporate motives in mind when engaging with companies.

Being realistic about the potential value and extent of corporate support is also key. Peel insists that corporate partners are not "cash cows" because "companies are seldom the vast financial reservoirs that many perceive them to be, and those that are tend to feel more beholden to their shareholders than to their communities." Whilst this will be disappointing for those hoping to quickly and easily secure large cash gifts from corporate organizations, Peel offers a more optimistic take. He highlights the different motivations of corporate organizations and nonprofits, and believes common ground can be found and that there is "no limit" to the opportunities for creative and commercially-minded fundraisers.

Heyman also ends this section on a positive note, reminding us that "corporate sponsorship can yield significant revenues and bolster awareness of your organisation". This is more likely to happen when fundraisers fully understand the needs of corporate partners, and when they follow his seven tips for securing and sustaining relationships with corporate sponsors.

The books and other full sources from which the seventeen extracts in this section are extracted are all well worth exploring for a range of fundraising practice insight, across different donor groups and fundraising methods.

Discussion questions

1. Thinking about the importance of leadership in major donor fundraising (Section 3.2) and mass donor fundraising (Section 3.3), as well as strategic planning (Section 3.1), compare the different emphasis and focus on leadership roles and skills that are needed in different types of fundraising practice.
2. Consider the significance of the different types of volunteers, and the roles they play, across different fundraising methods and donor types. Name tasks that can be given to volunteers in each of: major donors fundraising, community fundraising, and peer-to-peer fundraising.
3. Compare the extracts on corporate fundraising by Burlingame and Sargeant, Peel, and Rodriguez Heyman and make a list of the different ways that companies give, and the different fundraising methods required to realise that support. For example: a method of corporate giving is sponsorship and the accompanying fundraising method would be a pitch-presentation,

based on verifiable data, that evidences the charity's ability to generate goodwill and loyalty among their employees and consumer base.

4. Assume you work for a charity that is researching a cure for bowel cancer, and you have a number of donors who fit the following profile: *female; first donated in response to a direct mail appeal three years ago; makes a regular monthly donation at your lowest value; often "likes" your social media posts; attended a friend's fundraising coffee morning approximately one year ago and posted pictures on her social media tagging your charity's name; lives within three miles of an active local community fundraising group.* Use the extracts in Section 3.3, and insight from Tony Elischer in Section 2.3, to describe a suitable donor journey for this donor over the next three years, explaining why you think the donor would be engaged and inspired by your cultivation and stewardship.

5. Based on the extracts exploring corporate and major donor fundraising giving, discuss the extent to which self-interest is relevant to both types of donor and its impact on the relationship between the donor and the beneficiary nonprofit. You may find it helpful to review the four models of how companies approach their volunteering and giving to nonprofits (as listed in Burlingham and Sargeant, Section 3.4), and the text on "Getting something in return" within Sturtevant (Section 3.2).

6. Many authors discuss the tension between fundraising as a marketing activity that borrows from transactional for-profit sector theories and practices, and fundraising as a relationship building activity that seeks to develop donors as collaborative partners in delivering public good. Looking at a range of authors in this section and across the reader, such as Sturtevant (in 3.2), Bennett (in 3.3), James and Waters (in 1.3), and Burnett (in 2.4) describe the tensions and possible synergies between these two schools of fundraising, i.e. fundraising as marketing and fundraising as relationship building.

7. How is Warwick's "involvement" strategy (described in Section 3.1) similar to, yet also different from, theories of "relationship fundraising" as set out in Ken Burnett's extract in Section 2.4? Which approach do you prefer, and why?

3.1 Fundraising planning, strategy and campaigns

Creating and implementing a fundraising strategy

Claire Routley and Richard Sved, 2021

Henry Mintzberg, a Canadian academic who has written extensively on the subject, argues that there is no single definition of strategy, as the term is used in many different ways. His 'five Ps' of strategy encompass:

- plan: an intended course of action which is made in advance and developed purposefully;
- ploy: a specific manoeuvre designed to get the better of competitors;
- pattern: displaying consistent behaviour, whether or not by conscious intention – can be indicative of a strategy which is emerging;
- position: finding a distinctive place in the wider environment;
- perspective: patterns of thinking or culture, which can be difficult to change.

Mintzberg's five Ps are naturally overlapping and interrelated, and may develop and occur in differing orders. For example, an organisation may fall into a pattern of behaviour, recognise that this is a successful way of working and then build it into a more consciously developed plan.

[…]

Whereas, naturally, some elements of creating your fundraising strategy will come earlier in the process (such as undertaking a fundraising audit) and some will ordinarily take place towards the end of a cycle (such as monitoring and control), there are things which you will need to take into account of throughout the whole process (such as ethical considerations and involving stakeholders). Most importantly, your fundraising shouldn't ever stop just because you are taking time to think strategically about it.

We believe that developing and implementing a fundraising strategy is an involved and involving process that goes far beyond simply producing a document that you can present to others. As charity strategist Wayne Murray puts it, 'Your strategy isn't a document. It's a set of mutually agreed decisions, created by all and owned by all. The document is just the receipt.'

[…]

You can use an audit to understand what external and internal factors might affect your fundraising practice. External factors, clearly, are derived from the world around us, so they might include issues like the impact of a change in legislation or changing economic circumstances. In contrast, internal factors

DOI: 10.4324/9781003145936-41

are derived from within your organisation and might include issues like staffing, budgets or culture. An audit can enable your organisation to gain a picture of its historical performance and where its strengths and weaknesses lie (or indeed previously lay), but also sets up your priorities for the next planning period, making sure those priorities are based on your best estimates about the future. Alternatively, an audit can be both diagnostic and prognostic: you can use it not only to establish any problems in your fundraising performance but also to identify opportunities for future growth and development, and, as you proceed through the planning process, to enable you to set appropriate objectives for your fundraising.

Finally, an audit can play a valuable role as an influencing tool. It can help other stakeholders – such as fundraising team members, senior management team members, trustees or funders – to understand the current situation of your fundraising and encourage them to take an objective perspective, grounded in data.

[...]

If you have completed your audit and there are still significant gaps in your knowledge, you may decide there's a need to carry out some additional primary research. This could be to understand a variety of issues, such as the demographic make-up of your supporter base, the general public's opinion of your organisation or the motives of your supporters.

[...]

Even if you don't feel it's appropriate to carry out a formal research project, it may be appropriate to test your thinking at an early stage with some of your valued supporters who may be affected by your strategy, particularly if they are high-value financial supporters (often referred to as major donors) or people whom you are keen to bring into the fold more centrally. They will be able to give you an indication of whether you are on the right track – and hopefully they will also, if you pitch your enquiry correctly, be flattered that you are keen to hear their thoughts. This may then lead to a deeper relationship with them. In our experience, the old adage 'ask for money, get advice; ask for advice, get money' has often proven true.

[...]

By this point in the strategy development process, you should have a good understanding of the wider situation and your organisation's position within it ... Before you can progress with developing any sort of strategy, it's important to set clear overall objectives ... The value of objectives in management specifically has been discussed throughout the twentieth century, with the principle of 'management by objectives' generally credited to business guru Peter Drucker. He states that every area where performance and results directly affect the survival and prosperity of an organisation should be managed through objectives – and in most charities, surely, fundraising is vitally important to both survival and prosperity! Drucker also points out that to be effective, it's essential that objectives are carefully thought through. However, he argues that in the vast majority of cases, they are not.

[...]

The number of objectives you set is likely to vary according to the complexity and duration of your plan, and the number of income streams you are dealing with. For example, a director of fundraising creating a strategy for multiple income streams may need to include more objectives than someone who is looking after a single type of fundraising. However, it's always worth thinking carefully about your capacity to deliver the objectives. While each might be achievable individually, will they also be achievable collectively? It's better to have fewer, focused objectives than to dilute your efforts across many that you won't have the capacity to deliver.

You might also find it helpful to consider how your objectives interrelate. Some people find it helpful to have an overarching objective (for example, to double event income within three years) and then to break down that overarching objective into a series of sub-objectives (for example, increase the number of event participants by 10% relative to the baseline in year one, a further 40% in year two and the final 50% in year three).

[…]

In practice, regardless of whether you have taken time out to reflect on your strategic approach or have developed a formal written strategy, you will be making ongoing key strategic decisions in two areas:

- which groups of donors to send an appeal to;
- how to make a case as to why someone should support your organisation (for example, as part of a speech to a local group).

Taking the time to think through these strategic decisions in a formalised way ensures your decisions are as considered, effective and co-ordinated as possible.

[…]

Before you begin to develop your message, it can be helpful to have a clear idea in your mind of who you're developing this targeted communication for. That way, you can write with that specific audience in mind, whether it is made up of individual supporters or, for example, key decision makers in companies, foundations or trusts. You might find it helpful to use the information you gathered in the [audit and research stage] to create pen portraits (often termed 'personas') of your supporters, giving each audience you identified a name, age, occupation and so on, so as to be able to develop messaging targeted at a specific (hypothetical) person.

[…]

The first element of messaging is deciding on your position in the market. According to marketing experts Philip Kotler and Kevin Keller, positioning is the act of designing a company's offering and image to inhabit a distinct place in the mind of the target audience. In the charity sector specifically, however, it's been argued that positioning is an underused concept that is often done unconsciously rather than consciously. This could result in organisations being less than ideally positioned: for example, they may not be clearly differentiated from other organisations, or perceptions about them might not align with the reality of their work.

In their seminal text on positioning, advertising executives Al Ries and Jack Trout argue that positioning is not about what you do to your organisation (or, in our sector, your organisation or your fundraising products); it's about each individual supporter – or, more specifically, how you position yourself in their mind. When Ries and Trout were writing around the year 2000, consumers might have seen several hundred ads per day; now the average consumer probably sees more than 6,000 advertising messages daily. Clearly, therefore, positioning your organisation in the mind of your target audience is a key way to make yourself stand out. You need to identify a niche and fill it.

[…]

Closely linked to the idea of positioning is the idea of branding. Brand has been described as a shorthand in the mind of your audience for what your organisation might offer. It can also be thought of as a psychological construct which everyone aware of your organisation holds in their mind.

Often the first things that come to mind when we think about branding are an organisation's logo, the colours or fonts it uses, and its slogan. However, a brand should be embedded much more deeply than that. Writing about nonprofits, authors Adrian Sargeant and John Ford describe brand as an amalgam of everything an organisation is, as well as what it says and does.

[…]

The final key dimension of your messaging is your case for support … According to Timothy Seiler, a case for support is the overarching argument as to why a charitable organisation deserves financial support. Seiler describes it as the foundation of your fundraising: the source from which other fundraising messages flow.

Developing a case for support has several benefits. At a brand level, it can help you to develop an appropriate message (or messages) and use it (or them) consistently throughout your communications. At a practical level, it can help you to save time and have messages ready and waiting to go whenever you have the opportunity to share them. Most importantly, it's the cornerstone of any fundraising activity, which enables you to communicate why you do what you do, and what the results are, to inspire and motivate people to support you.

[…]

So, how do you go about creating a case for support? At an early stage in the process, you will need to decide who will be involved in the process of developing the case. Including stakeholders such as board members, volunteers and donors could help to both gather varied perspectives and, ultimately, achieve buy-in from those people who will use the case for support.

[…]

Mark Phillips, director of the fundraising agency Bluefrog, argues that it's common for organisations to create an internally focused document that doesn't take into account the reasons donors give. He also poses three questions that charities should focus on answering in order to make their case donor-centric:

- What can you offer your donors that other charities can't or won't?
- How can you make your appeal as emotionally rewarding as possible?
- How can you allow your donors to be part of the narrative?

[…]

Having considered the vital strategic issues of who to talk to and what to say, we can now turn our attention to the details of how fundraising is delivered, or fundraising tactics.

[…]

For our purposes, strategy provides the broad principles which underlie your day-to-day fundraising activities and which enable you to achieve your objectives. Tactics, meanwhile, are the details of how you deliver that strategy on the ground. How you approach developing your tactics is likely to depend, in part at least, on your position within the organisation and your ability to delegate to other team members. If you're a director of fundraising responsible for several members of staff (who are, in turn, responsible for delivering specific areas of fundraising) then you might choose to focus on selecting the optimal fundraising mix – a combination of different types of income – for your organisation. You might then delegate the writing of subplans for each element of the mix to the appropriate member of staff, who would address the detail of delivering the strategy … If, however, your strategy is focused on a specific area of fundraising, or you are responsible for the detail of fundraising delivery, then it might be more helpful to you to work through the tactical detail.

[…]

We suggest a framework to help you work through your tactics in a thorough fashion. The framework starts with the donor, which ensures that you build your plans around your audience, and works logically through a set of tactical decisions in the order they're likely to occur, from the immediate gift you would like to receive to the longer-term journey on which you plan to take your donors. The framework should enable you to take a holistic look at how your fundraising is delivered, taking into account not only the obvious issues (such as how you'll promote your offering) but also the less obvious but nonetheless vitally important (such as ensuring that internal teams are briefed about your plans).

[…]

We move on to the level of operations and how to plan out the specific actions you'll need to take to deliver your tactics … Scheduling has been defined as being about the optimal allocation of resources to particular activities over time. It probably won't surprise you to learn that research shows that projects frequently run over, in both cost and time. Pulling together a schedule is therefore a vitally important part of your overall fundraising strategy. Its most obvious benefit is ensuring that you have enough time and resources to deliver your plan, but it also has a number of other benefits. A schedule can:

- be a tool to measure and monitor progress against;
- help to avoid clashes between activities;

- identify interdependencies, so that you can see how a change in one part of your plan may affect other areas;
- act as a communications tool to enable others to see what's planned to happen, where their role fits into the broader picture and, ultimately, whether the plan is on track.

[...]

As well as allocating time for your fundraising, you will need to allocate monetary resources and clarify how much money your activities are likely to bring in. Developing a budget is important for a number of reasons. Budgeting ensures that:

- you have enough money to deliver the fundraising activities you have planned;
- your organisation has enough money to deliver its services;
- you know when money will be coming in and going out;
- your fundraising activities will – eventually – make a profit for your organisation.

Like your schedule, your budget can be a communications tool that you share with the wider organisation to illustrate how much money a particular activity is likely to cost, when those costs may be incurred and how much is likely to be raised.

[...]

Performance management is a series of processes which enable organisations to optimise their strategy. It is part of a sequence encompassing goal-setting, performance measurement, performance diagnosis, and identifying risk (and taking corrective action) ... When planning performance measurement, it is important to be clear what will be measured and why. Consider precisely what needs to be measured. Having too few measures can mean that important information or trends are missed. Similarly, having too many can mean that important information is lost in the noise and that valuable resources are used up in unnecessary measurement.

[...]

You've worked through a thorough process of crafting a strategy, from assessing your organisation's environment to identifying key audiences and messages to planning out exactly what will happen and when and how you'll know whether you have been successful. But two other key aspects of implementing your strategy are to ensure others buy into it and to manage any changes the strategy requires.

[...]

The process of strategy development and implementation is never simple, and success can never be guaranteed. In terms of actually delivering the strategy on the ground, a number of the challenges you encounter may be internal, as you try to implement new ways of approaching fundraising within your organisation. However, if you can ensure that colleagues in fundraising and the wider organisation are on board with your plans, and put in place appropriate processes to ensure that change is managed successfully then your fundraising strategy will be more likely to succeed.

The five strategies for fundraising success

Mal Warwick, 2000

The Five Strategies for Fundraising Success spell GIVES: Growth; Involvement; Visibility; Efficiency; Stability.

[...]

Getting acquainted with the five strategies

The starting point is to make sure you're absolutely clear about your fundraising goals. I don't mean just how much money you want to raise. I also mean when and how and from whom you want to raise that money, and what else you might want to accomplish along the way. There are many different ways to travel the fund-raising road, and the route you choose will have enormous impact on your organization's future.

Not convinced? Look at it this way.

Most people seem to think a fundraising program should achieve several different goals simultaneously:

- Bring in enough money to guarantee the organization's financial stability
- Continue its budgetary growth
- Build the community's awareness of the organization's good works
- Attract large numbers of volunteers, patrons, or other active supporters
- Take back as little money as possible to pay for the fundraising program itself

Unfortunately, your fundraising program cannot achieve all of these goals in equal measure. There are five distinct strategies lurking in the background of these goals. To a considerable degree, these strategies are mutually exclusive ... I make the case for each strategy, one at a time. Along the way, you'll learn some of the reasons why you may trip over your own feet if you try to accomplish all five at once.

I'm well aware that the words 'mutually exclusive' raise hackles in some people. I understand why. Almost all of us would like to be able to achieve all five fundraising goals simultaneously.

In fact, in a mature organization a fundraising program may indeed achieve all five, to some degree. But a strategist in any field (military matters, board

DOI: 10.4324/9781003145936-42

games, sports, business, you name it) will tell you that a successful strategy is always clear, focused, and directed.

Setting a strategy requires making choices. At any time, some things are more important than others.

I hope it's clear that I'm using the term strategy in the classic sense derived from military theory – that is, strategy as distinct from tactics. Big Picture stuff, not the details. Strategy means win the war, don't sweat the battle.

[...]

For a profit-making corporation, strategy is concerned with such overarching concerns as market share, competitive positioning, growth in productivity, stability of the workforce, security of patents and trademarks, and profit margin.

A nonprofit organization's strategy depends on its age, reputation, and accomplishments; the breadth and depth of its financial resources; the quality and spirit of its staff; and most of all, its mission. A nonprofit's strategy is also likely to involve such corporate considerations as market share and competitive positioning.

A for-profit company's strategy has little to do with this quarter's profits. For a nonprofit, too, factors such as the results of last month's fundraising mailing or a favorable story in a major newspaper are unlikely to be strategically significant.

Strategy is writ large.

[...]

Some tactics may indeed have broad implications. When a nonprofit enlists thousands of new members or successfully introduces a top-priority program, that's important. Even though they are legitimate concerns of an institution's top leadership, questions such as these are secondary to the core issues. They're tactical matters – *means to an end*.

Yes, tactical achievements may have strategic implications. In fact, tactics are (or should be) pursued precisely because – ultimately – they do affect strategy. But the question is, which consideration is paramount – the tactic or the strategy? There must be no confusion: strategy takes precedence.

When we boil down the things we fundraisers do and scrutinize what's left, what we find, I believe, is that financial development activities foster five different processes – Growth, Involvement, Visibility, Efficiency, and Stability – each to a varying degree. I call these the five strategies for fundraising success.

[...]

Going for growth

If your organization is new or is supported by too few donors – or if you've bitten off more than your current base of donors can chew – the question you're most likely asking is, how can we get more donors? You're preoccupied by the idea that's at the heart of growth.

For an organization to achieve growth, as I'm using the term, means that its donor base will broaden. If a Growth Strategy works, you'll have a lot more donors next year than this year – and still more the year after that.

[...]

Why large numbers of donors? Because the mission requires broad public outreach in order to come to grips with a problem that's bigger than the organization's founders and their handful of supporters can tackle, and because big numbers afford a broad pool of qualified prospects for such lucrative fundraising operations as major gifts, capital campaigns, and planned giving. In turn, acquiring these large numbers of donors typically requires a substantial investment. Donor acquisition is rarely profitable and usually requires sustained effort over several years to achieve meaningful growth in numbers.

More often than not, a fundraising program guided by a Growth Strategy will employ techniques for acquiring donors by direct mail (because that's normally the most cost-effective way for a nonprofit to recruit large numbers of new donors or members). In small communities or in narrowly based constituencies, volunteer outreach may make more sense. In specialized cases, charities may employ other means to reach a broad universe of prospects – TV, for example, or ads in wide-circulation magazines or extensive door-to-door canvassing. These specialized techniques work well for few organizations. These days, direct mail – and increasingly the Internet – are the donor acquisition methods of choice for most nonprofit organizations determined to grow.

Almost any kind of nonprofit can utilize a Growth Strategy. But it's most often seen in organizations working on broadly popular issues. Obvious examples include nationwide environmental organizations, groups addressing highly emotional issues such as abortion or tax reform, and organizations promoting medical research into the leading causes of disability and death.

Often, however, an organization that addresses a much lower-profile issue may employ a Growth Strategy in its early years – to broaden its base from one or a handful of initial donors to a larger number of sources of financial support. To some degree, this is true of almost any nonprofit that's just starting out. Every organization must invest in fundraising, and that investment may take considerable time to pay off. This is, of course, why fundraising costs typically represent a higher proportion of revenue in younger nonprofits than in older ones.

[...]

Enhancing involvement

Surveys and focus groups repeatedly demonstrate that many of the people who send money to support nonprofit organizations aren't conscious of being donors to these groups. Frequently a large proportion of the donors or members to a nonprofit can't remember the group's name. Sometimes they don't even recognize the name when they see it.

Involvement is the fundraising strategy that wise organizations may adopt to cure that malady and narrow the distance between cause and supporter. Involvement means building stronger relationships with your donors.

Unfortunately, most nonprofits discourage donor involvement, consciously or not. After all, what executive director or board of trustees wants the United Way or the local community foundation to meddle with their independence? What trustee in her right mind prefers gifts with strings attached?

In the real world, however, the strings are usually present, even if in a subtle form. Every donor – whether an individual or an institution – has some expectations about the use to which donated money will be put. These expectations set up a relationship between the giver and the recipient of every philanthropic gift.

[…]

A fundraising strategy built around donor involvement may help an organization increase the number of its donors, gain greater visibility, build a volunteer base, and even, over the long haul, help ensure its financial stability. More importantly, an Involvement Strategy may strengthen the organization's pursuit of its mission – because the mission requires more than just staff work. Others must participate, too. But chances are that the extra cost attached to donor involvement efforts will limit the program's short-term financial efficiency, and the greater demands placed on donors could even limit the organization's growth in numbers. An unencumbered relationship may be more attractive to many donors.

The attribute most commonly associated with an Involvement Strategy is that donors get a lot out of giving. In that way, you could think of this strategy as democratic, with a small d. Whether volunteer work, voting for members of the board of directors, helping set institutional priorities through membership surveys, or signing a postcard to the president of the United States, there's some form of participation in any fundraising program geared to involvement.

[…]

In addition to volunteer programs, techniques frequently employed in pursuing an Involvement Strategy include special events such as meetings, briefings, or tours; membership development programs; telephone fundraising efforts that entail direct, personal contact with donors; and frequent communications with members or donors through such devices as newsletters … or e-mail bulletins.

Involvement devices may be as varied as the imagination will permit.

Some of the most obvious examples of Involvement Strategies occur at museums, performing arts organizations, and grassroots lobbying groups. These are all organizations that virtually require donors to participate.

[…]

Increasing visibility

Museums, symphony orchestras, and other performing arts groups gain more than money by hosting large and splashy fundraising events. They also receive attention from the public and broaden their donor base. They attract patrons as well as contributors. Similarly, advocacy and lobbying groups may enlist thousands of citizens in efforts to sway votes in a state or provincial legislature, the U.S. Congress, or Parliament; or a special event may put the spotlight on a human service agency that depends on funding from local government.

All of these examples illustrate what I mean by visibility.

Just about any nonprofit that receives a significant share of its funds from the United Way is in a stronger position the better known it is, especially in these days when "donor choice" is taking hold in workplace campaigns. Increasingly, donors are choosing individual charities to support through their workplace gifts. If they've never heard of your organization, will they pick you?

[…]

There's no mistaking what a Visibility Strategy is all about. The object is often merely to gain name recognition – to make an organization a household word (even if within just a single community). Visibility is about becoming familiar to the people who matter most.

Organizations devoted to a Visibility Strategy are involved in issues that lots of people care about. The public feels they have a big stake in these organizations' success or failure. These organizations tend to be, or to become, name-brand charities. Public opinion is crucial. Brand identification is a central preoccupation of the organizations' leadership.

Competition with mature, well-established charities is uppermost among the considerations that lead many nonprofits to elect a Visibility Strategy. The public is already familiar with the Red Cross, the Salvation Army, and the American Cancer Society. A more recently established charity that seeks to highlight some less familiar issue or activity may have to go to great lengths to claim what advertisers sometimes refer to as "share of mind." (Don't we all have quite enough things on our minds already?) Because even the most capacious of our brains has limited capacity, and because the instinct to resist change is deep-seated and widespread, it's often difficult for a new idea, a new issue, or a new organization to become established in the public consciousness. This is doubly true if that new organization seeks to enter the same turf as a revered charity that is widely known to address the same issue.

Visibility, then, is more often a strategic consideration when a nonprofit organization is young. In fact, the opportunity to pursue other strategies, such as Growth or Involvement, may depend in the first instance on familiarizing the public with the organization's unique qualities.

Organizations seeking visibility tend to use electronic media and big, splashy public events. They're also most likely to seek (or be sought after for) cause-related marketing programs. A corporation with a large advertising and marketing budget may well find that it can multiply the impact of its expenditures by associating the company or one of its products with a popular nonprofit cause – or even by investing enough to help that cause gain the visibility it needs to grab public attention. Similarly, a nonprofit organization that springs into existence to address an important emerging issue may well discover that the news media are eager to highlight its work because the issue is of obvious concern to the public at large – and there's no better publicity than the free kind.

[...]

Fine-tuning for efficiency

Are you raising money at the lowest possible cost per dollar raised?

That's the question most people have in mind when they talk about a "good" fundraising program. The cost per dollar raised is the most common and most important measure of fundraising efficiency.

Efficiency means raising money by spending as little as possible in the process. It's that simple – and that complicated.

Nonprofits that pursue an Efficiency Strategy typically seek, above all, to come across to the public as trustworthy. Ethics have special meaning to an organization following this strategy, if only because efficiency requires that money be raised with the least possible muss and fuss. Controversy and efficiency don't mix well. Efficiency-driven organizations are cost-conscious, sometimes obsessively so. They literally can't afford trouble.

Of course, the most efficient way to raise money is to secure just a handful of very large gifts. These major gifts are sought through planned giving, institutional fundraising (from foundations, corporations, and government agencies), and monthly sustainer programs involving small donors or members.

Some organizations have little choice but to pursue an Efficiency Strategy. Public pressure – from government regulators, self-appointed charitable watchdog agencies, or the public at large – may force an Efficiency Strategy on such organizations, like it or not.

However, it is sometimes not wise to raise funds at very low cost, and it is frequently not possible to do so. Spending little money on fundraising will probably mean you have to depend on the same old tried-and-true fundraising methods and programs, even when the old ways aren't working so well anymore.

[...]

On the other hand, maximizing your fundraising efficiency could make it impossible for your organization to gain public visibility or to grow, and it could easily threaten your long-term financial stability. Popular convictions notwithstanding, efficiency isn't the be-all and end-all of fundraising!

To a great degree, you cannot control the efficiency of your fundraising program. Efficiency is a function of the size of an organization and its donor base, the popularity of its cause or timeliness of its issue, the length of time it has been in existence, the extent of its public name-recognition, and other factors. But there are many things you can do to raise money either more or less efficiently, and choosing among them calls for judgment.

[...]

Ensuring stability

Board members, bankers, accountants, and others consigned by fate to be professional worrywarts are often most concerned about the long-term stability of a nonprofit's finances. Well, they should be! Proper stewardship of donors' gifts – and of the taxes forgone by nonprofit organizations – cry out for a long-term perspective on an organization's prospects. Few nonprofits fulfil their missions within a finite period. For nearly all nonprofits, financial stability – the ability of an organization to foresee how its bills will be paid next year, in five years, in a decade, or a century from now – is a legitimate and often urgent concern.

How you raise money has a lot to do with your organization's stability. For example:

- Can you reasonably expect to continue receiving as much income in future years if you stick with the same fundraising methods and programs you have in place now? For instance, if you're flush with grants from the United Way or the Rockefeller Foundation this year, can you expect the same level of support next year, and the year after that? If not, where will the money come from?
- Is your fundraising program diversified so that you're not overly dependent on one or very few sources of funds?
- Even if your program is adequately diversified, are you paying enough attention to the differing needs and desires of the donors who support each of your fundraising programs to ensure that their support will continue?

So, here's where we really get down to business.

An organization devoted to stability must seek to convey an image of permanence, of solidity. A stable organization is one that endures.

Normally, organizations that employ a Stability Strategy seem, or try to seem, as though they've always been around – and always will be. Their missions are rooted in unchanging values. Their programs respond to unending needs. They require, and typically attain, a broad financial base.

The most characteristic fundraising technique of a nonprofit guided by the principle of stability is to build an endowment fund that generates investment income. A Stability Strategy may also entail broadly diversified development efforts so that all of the organization's eggs aren't in that one proverbial basket.

More often than not, colleges, universities, and private preparatory schools pursue stability. So do residential care facilities such as nursing homes.

Inevitably, it costs money to achieve stability, at least in the short run. That cost may be well worth paying. For some organizations, stability must be the overriding goal – at any near-term cost to the efficiency or visibility of your fundraising program.

[...]

Interestingly there is a rough correlation between the GIVES hierarchy of fundraising strategies and the traditional "ladder of involvement" or "pyramid of giving". Just as an individual donor climbs up the ladder or scales the pyramid, a not-for-profit may cycle through a sequence of organization-building experiences: building a donor base through growth increases opportunities for involvement and at length improves visibility, too – all of which in turn lends greater efficiency to the organization's fundraising program and ultimately stabilizes its performance.

The fundraising audit

Adrian Sargeant and Jayne George, 2022

We outline a process that may be employed by nonprofits in planning the fundraising activities that they will undertake. Whilst the format may differ slightly from one organisation to another, at its core a fundraising plan has three common dimensions:

1) Where Are We Now? A complete review of the organisation's environment and the past performance of the fundraising function. Only when the fundraising department has a detailed understanding of the organisation's current strategic position in each of the donor markets it serves can the organisation hope to develop meaningful objectives for the future.
2) Where Do We Want to Be? In this section of the plan, the organisation will map out what the fundraising department is expected to achieve over the duration of the plan. Typically, there will be income generation targets for the department as a whole and a series of sub-objectives for each category of fundraising (e.g. individual, trust/foundation and corporate).
3) How Are We Going to Get There? This stage of the plan contains the strategy and tactics that the organisation will adopt to achieve its targets. The strategy specifies in general terms what the broad approach to fundraising will be, whilst the tactics supply the minutia of exactly how each form of fundraising will be undertaken.

[…]

The fundraising audit

The fundraising audit specifically addresses the first element of a fundraising plan ('Where are we now?'). As such, it is arguably the most crucial stage of the whole planning process since without a thorough understanding of the organisation's current position it will be impossible for planners to develop any kind of sense of what they can expect to accomplish in the future. The fundraising audit is essentially a detailed review of any factors that are likely to impinge on the organisation, taking into account both those generated internally and those emanating from the external environment. The fundraising audit is thus a systematic attempt to gather as much information as possible about the organisation and its environment and, importantly, how these might both be expected to change and develop in the medium- and longer-term futures.

DOI: 10.4324/9781003145936-43

Macro factors

It is usual to begin the process by examining the wider or 'macro' environmental influences that might impact the organisation. Often these may be factors over which the organisation itself has little control, but which will nevertheless affect the organisation at some stage during the period of the plan. The framework utilised for this analysis is typically referred to as a PESTLE analysis and comprises the following elements:

- **P**olitical Factors – Political factors impacting fundraising might include local/national government attitudes to the nonprofit sector, the focal cause, and the focal organisation. There might also be government interest in some of the forms of fundraising that an organisation is employing.
- **E**conomic Factors – Economic trends are relevant primarily as predictors of future donor behaviour. Trends in wealth, employment, tax, consumption, and disposable income impact all categories of funders; from corporate givers and foundations to individuals.
- **S**ocio/Cultural Factors – Key data here will include data on demographics and social attitudes, plus evidence of likely behavioural changes or significant shifts in societal values that might occur over the duration of the plan. For example, trends in levels of civic participation, changes in the formation of families, in levels of trust and confidence in the nonprofit sector and in patterns of working would be considered here. Public attitudes to the cause and how these are shifting would also be noted.
- **T**echnological Factors – How are new developments in technology impacting the nonprofit sector and fundraising in particular? These might include advances in database technologies, the creation of new digital channels or developments in payment methods and systems.
- **L**egal Factors – Are there any planned or forthcoming legislative, regulatory or self-regulatory changes that might affect the fundraising environment or fundraising performance e.g. privacy legislation?
- **E**nvironmental Factors – How does an organisation's fundraising practice impact the environment and what public concerns might there be over these practices? Organisations that still rely heavily on print, for example, may be accused of aiding in deforestation. Equally, if an organisation is considering a series of challenge events, what will be the impact of large numbers of visitors on the relevant sites? Increasingly, charities are stepping up to do their bit for the planet and any relevant issues will need to be included here.

The aim in each case is to accumulate a list of all the pertinent factors and how these are expected to change over the planning period. It is best at this point in the process not to spend too much time deliberating over the impact that these factors might have on the organisation, but rather to note them, detail how they might change and move on. For this reason, PESTLE analyses are typically presented in a bulleted list. The danger of precipitating a discussion at this stage is that other clues as to the impact these PESTLE factors might have will tend to emerge as the audit process progresses. It is therefore better to consider potential impacts "en masse" when the audit itself is complete.

[...]

Analysis of competitors

Accurate information on the activities, size and market position of competitor organisations is of vital importance to any nonprofit putting together a fundraising plan ... Throughout this section of the audit, the goal is to see what might be learned from others to inform one's own approach.

Of course, the starting point in conducting an analysis of the competition is to decide which competitors the organisation should profile. There are a number of options:

1) Industry Leaders – Fundraisers will undoubtedly be aware of those competitor organisations that they regard as particularly outstanding in their fundraising activity. From these industry leaders, it may be possible to learn a great deal about successful fundraising practices and to borrow exciting new and innovative ideas in respect of the best ways to solicit funds. These nonprofits may be working in the same field, but could equally be working elsewhere in the sector serving entirely different needs. They are thus selected purely on the basis of the quality/originality of the fundraising they undertake.

2) Other Nonprofits Serving the Same Cause – Some nonprofits will assess the strategy of charities that serve the same broad category of cause (e.g. children, hospice, animal welfare, environmental defence). The goal here is not only to look at what fundraising these organisations do so that this can be compared with the portfolio of the focal organisation but also to identify how this fundraising is approached to see what might be learned. What case for support are they using? How is this being communicated? What opportunities for engagement are there? How does their website compare with ours? Are they raising more money? Why?

3) Nonprofits of a Similar Size – The difficulty with just looking at organisations in the same sector is that these organisations might vary quite substantially in terms of size. A competitor that is much bigger or smaller than the focal organisation will have very different resource levels, so they could be performing better simply because they have a bigger budget and more staff. In such circumstances, it can be more helpful to look at nonprofits of a similar size on the grounds that the resources available to the fundraiser will be similar. Once again, the auditor will look at the forms of fundraising undertaken, the promotional materials produced and how the organisation approaches its fundraising. This can all be used to highlight areas where learning can be identified and improvements made as a consequence.

4) Organisations Using the Focal Forms of Communication Well – So far in this list, we have focused on learning from other nonprofits. Increasingly, and certainly, in the digital space, the best place to look for learning may be outside of the nonprofit sector. For insight on how to use social media well, for example, the best comparators may be for-profit organisations that share a similar target audience of customers. In our experience, a lot of new digital ideas can be "borrowed" or adapted from the commercial sector.

Potential collaborators

Of course, there may be many instances where instead of viewing other nonprofits as competitors it makes more sense to partner with them to mutual advantage. Such partnerships may open up access to new sources of funds, new markets or simply allow the partner organisations to take advantage of economies of scale and thus lower their costs of fundraising. It may not be economic, for example, for smaller nonprofits to undertake corporate fundraising on their own. Forging an alliance with other "complementary" or related nonprofits can create a pool of shared resources that would facilitate fundraising from this potential new audience.

Many forms of community fundraising are also conducted collaboratively; where smaller nonprofits get together to run a joint campaign for the benefit of a focal community and share the costs associated with promoting the campaign and any associated events. As an example, different types of animal charities might work together to hold one major annual event. A gala ball could be established to support a variety of veteran's causes and, equally, a group of arts organisations might come together to run a capital campaign to build a theatre and office accommodation none of them could afford by themselves.

But of course, there aren't always opportunities for collaboration so this section won't always be relevant. But where it is, the auditor might consider examples of where organisations have collaborated successfully in the past and the factors that led to that success. They might look to see what could be learned from these collaborations and whether there might be any way in which the focal organisation could work in partnership with others. If this is possible, it will be instructive to conduct background research into potential partners and to explore how such relationships might develop. An approach to one or more partners could then be suggested in the fundraising strategy/ tactics, later in the plan.

Market factors

The next stage of the audit concerns the gathering of data in respect of the various donor markets the organisation is addressing. It may therefore be sensible to structure this section by considering each market (e.g. Individuals, Corporates, Trusts, Foundations, Community) in turn. Each of these sections should then be further subdivided into identifiable segments or groups of donors, with current performance and likely future developments considered in each case.

Typically, a nonprofit needs to understand:

a)   Who donates to their organisation – Are there certain types of people, corporates or foundations that have elected to offer their support? In the case of individuals, do these individuals have distinctive lifestyle or demographic characteristics that help the organisation understand more about the nature of their target audience?
b)   Donor Motivations – Why do each group of donors elect to support the organisation? How can the organisation best reflect these motives in its fundraising communications? How can donors with specific motives best be stewarded?
c)   Donor Needs/Preferences – What kinds of communications do donors find appropriate? How do they view the communications they currently receive, could these be improved in some way?
d)   Donor Behaviour – Organisations need to understand how donors behave when they give to the organisation. How much does each group/segment of donors give? Do higher value donors have any distinctive characteristics or needs? Are certain types of donors more likely to terminate their support than others? What are the primary reasons why donors terminate their support? Is there anything that may be done to address this?

If the organisation doesn't have this kind of detailed information, a market analysis can still be conducted looking at broader sector trends for each category of the funder. So, if a small charity is raising money from individuals, what do we know about individual giving right now? Are there any sector trends we should be aware of as we look to scope out our own fundraising plan?

In gathering market data, it would again be wise to start with the material that is already available within the organisation. Many nonprofits are able to profile their database to identify patterns in terms of who is giving, giving through specific channels, and giving higher and lower amounts. The organisation may even have conducted some research to learn more about donor behaviour or motivation and this can inform their audit. Likewise, fundraisers dealing with major donors, corporates, trusts and foundations, etc. can have reports on file which provide considerable insight into the nature and distinguishing characteristics of the people or organisations they receive funding from.

This data should then be supplemented through wider desk research, looking at the most recent published sources of information for each market and identifying key issues and trends. Often this broader picture information will identify opportunities to gather further support from some audiences, attract new groups of donors, or in some cases identify audiences which are saturated or shrinking and where the nonprofit might therefore need to consider the possibility of withdrawal.

[…]

The internal environment

Having now summarised the key external influences on the organisation, it is possible to move on to consider an audit of the organisation's own fundraising activity. The aim here is to scrutinise past fundraising performance and to carefully appraise what has worked well in the past and what has not. Current fundraising activities, trends in performance and the current structure and support systems that underpin fundraising activity will all be considered.

It is impossible to be prescriptive about the exact information requirements – they should flow logically from the organisation's circumstances, but it is likely that the auditor will wish to research:

a) The past performance of each form of fundraising undertaken, trends in this performance and whether this might vary by the region in which the fundraising is undertaken. The auditor will wish to examine the revenues that are generated, the costs incurred and the returns generated.

b) This data should also be examined by the group or segment of donors addressed. What success has the organisation had in addressing discrete donor segments? Have some segments proved more responsive than others? If so, why has this been the case? All this data can be valuable in selecting future donors for contact and suggest the optimal ways in which relationships can be stewarded and further funds solicited.

c) A review of the processes that support fundraising is also warranted. In particular, the auditor will want to examine whether these processes are optimal and whether any problems have arisen in caring for donors over the period of the last plan. These processes will include donation processing and handling, thanking and acknowledging, mechanisms for dealing with donor communications and queries, internal co-ordination of strategy with departments such as communications or campaigning and mechanisms for dealing with data protection/privacy issues.

d) The auditor will also want to look at the manner in which the fundraising function is organised and to explore whether this is optimal. In particular, the split between the use of paid staff and volunteers will warrant investigation as will the management reporting structures for each fundraising function. Does it make sense to organise the fundraising department in this particular way, or would it be valuable to explore making changes to these reporting structures?

If the organisation is involved in regional fundraising and managing a network of fundraisers working from home, it may also wish to explore whether the definition of these regions is optimal and whether the number of managers is appropriate given the number and spread of employees/volunteers in the regions.

Data for the internal audit is usually gathered through a mixture of desk research and meetings as well as interviews with staff. Senior staff will be able to provide information on past strategy, tactics, and performance, and will also provide the necessary data on financial performance, human resource strategy and issues concerning governance and the general direction of the organisation. It is often necessary to interview non-fundraising staff at this stage, such as the Finance Director and the CEO, to paint the full background picture of the nonprofit and to establish the positioning and importance of fundraising within the organisation.

It is then necessary to talk to individual fundraising staff to establish an understanding of the current fundraising work undertaken. To understand what has happened in the past and how the organisation has come to have a particular fundraising mix, and to gather information on perceived opportunities and barriers. The auditor undertaking such interviews should also prompt for records and data at these interviews to illustrate, add to and verify the information provided by the interviewee. If external agencies are retained, especially where those agencies give strategic or planning support, it will also be necessary to interview their staff to get a full picture of the fundraising effort.

As with the external audit, the internal data gathering should be an iterative process, with checks being performed throughout to ensure that full and accurate information is being gathered and expressed. The financial, structural and performance information gathered can be used to provide benchmarking data for comparison against other organisations.

[...]

Conducting an audit in a small charity

The framework we offer above is of equal relevance to all organisations irrespective of their size. Even small organisations will be impacted by changes in the macro environment and face the challenges posed by competitors for funds. Small charities will also have an equal, if not greater, need to exploit opportunities for collaboration and they will certainly need to audit their own internal strengths and weaknesses before they will be in a position to fundraise effectively. All that said there will of course be differences in the approach that will be adopted.

Although a PESTLE will still be worth considering there are likely to be fewer macro environmental factors impacting a small day-care centre in Bristol than on a major national charity such as Cancer Research UK. Fundraisers should still take the time to look around at the wider environment to ensure they don't miss any significant changes, but the auditor should not allocate too much time to this section of the audit and/or worry that they have only identified a few points.

It is also true that smaller organisations will find it less useful to look at broad trends in individual or corporate giving taking place at the national level. Published sources will therefore be less helpful than conversations with fellow fundraisers, or the local branches of employer organisations or bodies such as the Chartered Institute of Fundraising. Talking with professional colleagues already working in the area will be likely to give the auditor more of a sense of the picture locally and offer a regional perspective on the reported national statistics.

[…]

The SWOT analysis

Clearly, at this stage, the output from the fundraising audit may be regarded as little more than a collection of data, and in this format, it is as yet only of limited value for planning purposes. What is required is a form of analysis which allows the fundraiser to examine the opportunities and threats presented by the environment in a relatively structured way. Indeed, it should at this point be recognised that opportunities and threats are seldom absolute. An opportunity may only be regarded as an opportunity, for example, if the organisation has the necessary strengths to support its development. For this reason, it is usual to conduct a SWOT analysis (Strengths, Weaknesses, Opportunities and Threats) on the data gathered during the fundraising audit. This is primarily a matter of selecting key information from the audit, analysing its implications, and presenting it under one of the four headings. The important word here is "key." It is important that some filtering of the data gathered at this stage is undertaken so that the analysis is ultimately limited to the factors of most relevance for the subsequent development of strategy.

The SWOT addresses the following issues:

Strengths – What are the strengths of the organisation? What is the organisation good at? Is it at the forefront of particular fundraising developments? Does it have access to a donor segment that is not reached by competitors? Does it have a strong database system/great support agencies/high local awareness?

Weaknesses – What are its weaknesses? In what ways do competitors typically outperform the organisation? Are there weaknesses in terms of internal support or structures? Are the fundraising support systems working well? Is there a strong and compelling case for support? Are there barriers to future development in some areas?

Opportunities – What are the main opportunities facing the organisation over the duration of the plan? Are there new fundraising techniques to test? Are there new audiences to address? Have new ways been found to steward stronger relationships with supporters? Are there opportunities created by changes in the fiscal environment or around Gift Aid?

Threats – What are the major threats facing the organisation? Is a major competitor likely to launch a major new appeal? Will economic changes impact certain core funders and leave them with less to give? Are planned changes to legislation likely to curtail fundraising activity? Are we overly reliant on forms of fundraising which evidence indicates may be facing decline?

Good SWOT analyses have a number of distinctive characteristics:

a)   They are relatively concise summaries of the audit data and are typically no more than 4–5 pages of commentary focussing on key factors only.

b)   They recognise that strengths and weaknesses are differential in nature. This means that a strength is only a strength if the organisation is better at this particular activity or dimension than its competitors. Similarly, weaknesses should be examined from the perspective of where the organisation lags behind others.

c)   They are clear and easy to read. Quality suffers if items are over-abbreviated. For example, we have seen SWOT analyses list "the economy" as a threat. What should the reader take from that? Is it in decline, and if so, by how much and what will be the likely impact on giving over the course of the subsequent plan? The goal is not to reproduce audit data in its entirety, just to be clear over the impact each factor listed will have.

d)   It may help for a separate SWOT to be completed from the perspective of each segment of donor critical to an organisation's future. What may be perceived as a strength in relation to individual donors may well be a weakness when approaching corporate donors. Thus, the global SWOT analyses that are so frequently conducted by fundraising departments can often tend towards meaningless. For all but the smallest and simplest organisations a series of highly focused SWOTs could offer more utility.

e)   Finally, a good SWOT analysis should prioritise rather than merely list factors. So, the list of strengths begins with the strongest strength and ends with the weakest. Similarly, the leading opportunities appear at the top of the list of opportunities. As MacDonald notes: *"if a SWOT analysis is well done, someone else should be able to draft the objectives which logically flow from it. The SWOT should contain clear indicators as to the key determinants of success in the department."*

We have introduced the fundraising audit as the first key component of the fundraising plan [and] introduced the SWOT analysis as a tool to summarise audit data. This is essential since it draws out the key factors driving, or likely to drive, fundraising performance in the future.

Understanding fundraising campaigns

Kathleen Kelly, 1998

At the 1992 National Assembly of CASE (the Council for Advancement and Support of Education), then-President Peter McE. Buchanan exclaimed, "I wish to hell we could get rid of campaigns, I really do". Capital campaigns are an artifact of fund raising's earlier eras when external consultants dominated the field. Increasingly, practitioners and strategic publics are questioning their purpose, the motivations behind them, and their effectiveness. An alternative is a continuous effort to raise major gifts, which is more appropriate for the current era of staff fund raisers.

[…]

Evolving purpose

Capital campaigns were invented by Charles Sumner Ward and Lyman Pierce, founders of the YMCA school of fund raisers and the leading historical figures of the press agentry model. First introduced in 1902, the campaigns concentrated solely on physical assets during the first decades of their use, specifically gifts for new buildings. They properly could have been called physical capital campaigns. They were used by all types of organizations, although the heaviest users were large organizations, such as universities and hospitals.

[…]

By the 1950s, financial capital, or endowment, needs had been added to the purpose of campaigns. Some types of organizations, particularly those with religious missions, however, reserved their use for physical capital (e.g., building a new church). During both periods, consulting firms were hired to manage the campaigns through full-time resident directors. Annual giving, or efforts to raise operating income rather than assets, was the province of staff employees.

[…]

The 1960s introduced the $100-million campaign. The high dollar totals were only possible because the purpose of campaigns, particularly those for universities and hospitals, then encompassed endowment and building needs – an evolutionary factor rarely acknowledged in the literature.

[…]

It was during this decade, according to Harold Seymour, that a new philosophy of fund raising emerged: Money tends to flow to promising programs rather than to needy institutions. The purpose of campaigns moved from

DOI: 10.4324/9781003145936-44

capital needs of the organization to opportunity for raising more money, and a competitive mindset about the strategy was instilled.

Starting in the 1970s, campaigns added annual giving to their purpose and also encompassed planned giving. All gift monies received or generated by the organization during the campaign period, including planned gifts that would not be usable for many years, were counted toward campaign totals. Michael Worth explained, "Today's campaigns represent an intensive cranking-up of all elements of the development program". The definitional issue was addressed by adopting the term *comprehensive campaign* to signify that the effort was for operating as well as capital needs. Again, the change in purpose enabled organizations to set increasingly higher dollar goals.

[...]

During the period when campaigns evolved from capital to comprehensive purpose, the number of organizations employing staff practitioners increased dramatically. Consultants, recognizing the shift in the field, moved away from full-time resident direction to part-time campaign counseling, starting with Maurice Gurin's firm in 1965. Although external fund raisers diversified their repertoire of services, they remained – and currently remain – dependent on campaigns for their livelihoods. Consultant George Brakeley, III described the dependence: "An institution might turn to counsel at almost anytime. Most typically, however, this occurs at one of three junctures: before a comprehensive campaign, during a campaign, or between campaigns".

[...]

What is surprising, given the evolution of the fund-raising function, is that charitable organizations with established internal staffs continue to use a strategy developed for the convenience of consultants, who now play a diminishing role in its use. The campaign structure, with definitive beginning and end dates, was shaped by the needs of external practitioners in the absence of staff fund raisers. Sporadic programming is no longer necessary or desirable.

This was one of three major arguments underlying former CASE President Buchanan's condemnation of campaigns.

[...]

Underlying motivations

The second of Buchanan's three arguments was that campaigns' multimillion-dollar goals represent "fascination" with "money" rather than mission. Goals are determined for competitive reasons, not need. Organizations, particularly colleges and universities, are challenging each other to wage the largest capital campaign .... "Too often, campaign goals are based on what rival institutions report they have raised, rather than on analysis of an organization's greatest needs and careful evaluation of the giving climate among its donors".

The collective result looks much like a game of poker – with million-dollar stakes. While Stanford was in its $1.1 billion campaign, Columbia set its campaign goal at $1.15 billion. When Stanford closed its campaign with $1.27

billion, Yale University launched its campaign for $1.5 billion. Harvard's $2.1 billion goal spurred Columbia to extend its campaign and increase its goal to $2.2 billion.

More serious because it is more common is the "I'll-see-you-and-raise-you" mindset for the hundreds of campaigns with goals of less than $1 billion. A college will announce a $150 million campaign and a fund raiser at another college in the same geographic area will decide the amount for its next campaign must be $175 million, regardless.

[…]

A study by the Walter and Elise Haas Fund, an independent foundation created by heirs of the inventor of Levi's jeans, found that the combined capital-campaign goals of only 49 organizations in San Francisco, California far outstrip the giving capabilities of the city's foundation, corporate, and individual donors.

[…]

As the study concluded, even if receipts for campaigns grew at the same rate of 9.5% per year as they did between 1988 and 1992, there would be more than a $200 million shortfall in performance against targets. For goals to be met, 1997 giving would have to increase to more than 500% of the 1992 level! The author of the study's report, simply stated, "The total appears quite unrealistic".

[…]

The escalating competition is played out in the public spotlight, and Worth, among others, admitted that society's perception of campaigns increasingly is one of organizational greed rather than need. Campaigns have a strong publicity component. Indeed, the CASE campaign standards offered the following definition: "The capital or comprehensive fund-raising campaign is a vehicle for focusing attention upon the needs and aspirations of an institution".

Many experts defend the use of campaigns because of their publicity, or what they call public relations, value. Campaigns, they argue, produce more than gifts; they have spillover effects not specified in programming objectives. Joseph Mixer, for example, stated, "The acceptance of the case and goodwill generated by the promotional efforts of the campaign contribute long-term benefits".

[…]

As campaigns evolved in purpose, their lengths were extended to accommodate ever-larger goals. Whereas Ward spent 5 months to plan a campaign and 10 days to execute it, contemporary campaigns devote about 2 years to planning, 1 to 2 years to the "quiet phase" of raising pace-setting gifts, and 5 or more years to the public phase. The typical time frame for the entire effort is 8 to 10 years, although some organizations have stretched the duration even longer, as attested to by Columbia University's 12-year campaign. … Endeavors sustained over 10 or more years, most experts argue, do not qualify as actual campaigns because a sense of urgency is greatly diminished or absent, among other differences.

[…]

Campaign phases

According to CASE, campaigns consist of four phases: (a) precampaign planning, (b) advance gifts/nucleus fund phase, (c) general public phase, and (d) post campaign accounting. The first phase forces the organization to focus on planning for fund-raising purposes. This may be the greatest advantage of campaigns in that organizations that do not regularly engage in strategic planning and/or isolate fund raising from overall management are obligated to change their behavior before conducting a campaign.

[...]

The advance gifts/nucleus fund phase, also termed the *quiet phase*, marks the official beginning of a campaign. Experts recommend that about 40% of the dollar goal be raised during this period – before the campaign is publicly announced. Henry A. Rosso argued that at least one gift of 10% and two gifts of 5% of the goal must be sought at the campaign's beginning. Therefore, a $1 billion campaign requires one gift of $100 million and two gifts of $50 million. There is strong consensus that 95% of the dollar total will come from 3% to 5% of the donors and that the nucleus fund phase, which concentrates on such prospects, tests the campaign's viability. If advance gifts fall short of expected amounts, the campaign is aborted before the public phase.

Much of the responsibility for successfully completing the second phase rightfully belongs to the organization's trustees. Thomas E. Broce offered a 20/20 rule: "I say that to be successful the board must commit itself to contribute 20 percent of whatever dollar goal is selected and commit to solicit from others the next 20 percent of the goal" ... Broce called these requirements "point-of-no-return checkpoints". Reminding board members of their necessary and extraordinary participation may be the one remaining role best enacted by consultants. Broce explained, "Better than any staff officer, the consultant can face the board squarely and say, 'Unless you will be committed to the success of this program through your own sacrificial giving and enthusiastic leadership, there will be little or no chance for success'". He commented: "This pronouncement makes many board members uncomfortable, especially those who up this point have favored the idea of more money flowing into the coffers from a capital campaign, but have expected the bulk of the gifts to come primarily from new sources. It may be their first collective realization that, on all prospect lists, their names come first".

During the general public phase, both major and lower level gifts are solicited, although efforts still focus on the "critical few" prospects who are able to make major gifts. Programming is guided by the principles of sequential and proportionate giving, with nondonors who have the capability of making only a small gift reserved for the closing months of the campaign. The crucial role of major gifts requires interpersonal communication by a large fund-raising staff ... Harvard University had 271 staff practitioners in the academic year it publicly launched its campaign, 1993–1994. The expense of a campaign is a function of the goal, as well as other factors. Harvard's $2.1 billion goal mandates that its practitioners raise $1 million a day during the public phase (although advance gifts likely reduced that quota to about $600,000). To support campaign programming, the university increased its fund-raising budget by $1.8 million a year, to $24.2 million in 1993–1994. At the conclusion of the 7.4-year campaign, from the beginning of its advance gifts phase in July 1992 to its scheduled date for completion in December 1999, Harvard will have spent around $187 million on fund raising, or 9% of its goal.

Serious problems arise when organizations depend on raising unrestricted outright gifts through the campaign to cover fund-raising expenses. Too often, annual giving dollars are spent for campaign costs, not for announced needs. In such cases, lower level gifts from the majority of donors are used to subsidize the cultivation and solicitation of major donors, who restrict their gifts. Not only are such practices unethical, but they can be financially damaging.

[…]

Effectiveness

Presenting his third and final argument against capital campaigns, CASE President Buchanan stated, "We have the juxtaposition of raising enormous amounts of money at the same time our institutions go into deficit. And then people say, 'What the hell is going on here?'". Too many campaigns, he asserted, cannot answer the question, "Where did the money go?".

A paradox of campaigns is that many organizations successfully reaching dollar goals find themselves facing a deficit or unable to fund announced objectives. Almost all do not meet stakeholders' expectations. Before examining the inconsistency, however, it must be stressed that not every campaign succeeds.

[…]

The Haas Fund study explained: "Organizations that do not reach targets do not typically admit failure. They revise targets downward, slow down or cancel projected construction projects, and delay the finish dates for their campaigns". The study found that of the 41 San Francisco organizations conducting a campaign during the period 1988 to 1992, most extended their deadlines, 8 reduced their goals, and only 18 had completed their campaigns at the time of the study's report. Of those that had finished, four (22%) failed to reach at least 95% of their revised goals.

[…]

The effectiveness of capital campaigns, as measured by dollar production and stakeholder evaluation, is low. Yet most of the literature continues to propagate the opposite opinion, represented by James Greenfield's claim that campaigns are "the most productive, most efficient, and most cost-effective method of fund-raising yet invented". The flawed assessment relies on evidence gathered in the absence of consistent standards and in the proliferation of ambiguous, if not deceptive, reporting.

[…]

CASE Campaign Standards

In April 1994, the CASE Board of Trustees approved new management and reporting standards for campaigns. The standards, which went into effect during academic year 1994–1995, were the result of 4 years of intensive effort. Each organization conducting a campaign is asked to file a report annually with CASE, which will publish and disseminate the information. Although the standards apply only to its members, the association seeks universal voluntary compliance.

According to Peterson, "The impact on campaigns, if these standards are followed, will be to deflate the goals and the announced results of the campaigns." He described the then current work of the advisory group he chaired: "We're trying to do some things that will give us more realistic bases for reporting on our campaigns more honestly." He continued, "I think the era of the mega billion-dollar campaigns could well be over if, in fact, we as a body of development officers nationally adopt these standards and live within them."

The standards depend on three fundamental concepts: (a) campaign reports should separate results by featured objectives and other objectives, (b) they should separate outright gifts and pledges from planned gifts the organization expects to receive after the solicitation and pledge-payment periods end, and (c) they should record planned gifts at both their face value and their discounted present value.

[…]

Replacing the campaign

All serious discussions on capital campaigns – even those extolling their virtues – raise questions about their future use and present the alternative of raising major gifts through a continuous program. The first view, supporting campaigns, is based on the premise that the purpose of fund raising is to raise as much money as possible. As the Haas Fund study pointed out, capital campaigns "have the added appeal of being a proven way to maximize donative revenues". The second view, in support of continuous programming, holds that the purpose of fund raising is to build and maintain relationships with donors and that sporadic campaigns contradict this purpose. Its leading proponent J. P. Smith declared, "Fund raising should be sustained, not episodic".

[…]

J. P. Smith also advocated replacing campaigns with continuous efforts to raise major gifts. The new approach, he argued, is inherently more conducive to … what he called "professional" and "sophisticated fund raising" that "is patient, subtle, and sustained". He anticipated and answered the question …: "Will that kind of sustained program yield as many dollars as campaigns? Maybe, maybe not. But the point I wish to make is that we ought to be asking a different question: Which pattern will provide more support year-in, year-out for the most important objectives of the institution?"

3.2 Working with major gifts

The "stop and think" major gift

William Sturtevant, 1996

Some organizations seem intimidated by major gifts. Somehow they feel incapable or unworthy. This certainly need not be the case. To succeed in major gifts requires (1) a compelling case; (2) sound institutional and lay leadership; and (3) a solid pool of prospects who believe, or could believe, in your mission. If you don't have these three essential ingredients, you have some important work to do. If they are in place, or nearly so – go forward with boldness and confidence.

Until very recently, the dynamics involved with major gifts fund raising have not been well understood. The pioneering work done by G. T. "Buck" Smith and Dave Dunlop has been of signature importance to those seeking a better understanding of cause and effect in the major gifts arena. Impeding our progress has been the reality that such fund raising is more an art than a science. There are many paths to the same outcome, and the process entails the ambiguities, uncertainties, and judgmental requirements that typify a complex process. Yet, there is much that we now know which can assure our successful efforts.

The decision-making process associated with major gifts is far more elusive than that entailed with what we commonly call the "annual" gift. However, because we have little understood the major gifts process, our professional meetings and writings have stressed technique rather than understanding.

It makes sense to talk about techniques in depth when dealing with direct mail or telemarketing. Here the emphasis is on science. But a discussion of major gift fund raising without a thorough understanding of the donor's mental process in reaching a decision is of little value.

From a donor's perspective, the major gift decision is vastly different from the annual gift decision. A colleague who attended one of my seminars told me that the process changes when a donor is asked to make a "stop and think" gift. Inherently we know this to be true. The fact that someone makes an annual gift does not necessarily mean that he or she will convey a major contribution. It doesn't hurt, but it is certainly not sufficient or even controlling. Something else is at work.

Let's agree at the start that it matters not how our organization defines a major gift. From an organizational perspective, the definition of a major gift will change as we gain experience in the fund-raising process. Apart from inflation, based on our track record, we will define a major gift differently five

DOI: 10.4324/9781003145936-46

years from now than what is currently the case. It is also true that we often define a major gift based on a cost-benefit analysis from a budgetary stand-point. That is, it makes little sense for me to fly across the country to secure a $1,000 gift unless, of course, I am cultivating an individual who can donate far more than that. No one ever said that it was precise.

The most important perspective in all of this is the donor's. How a donor defines a major gift is what controls the situation. Obviously, someone's defin-ition of a major gift is influenced by such things as discretionary income, net worth, and the stage in the life cycle.

Prior philanthropic experience is also a crucial factor, regardless of the person's net worth. Making the first major gift is the biggest psychological hurdle, especially for those who have experienced hard economic times.

It is also true that most of us go through an accumulation phase. Only at a later stage in the life cycle will we consider the type of distribution normally associated with a major gift.

The "stop and think" gift

The annual gift is typified by the frequency of the solicitation-contribution process. There is relatively little decision making. On the other hand, the major gift entails extensive decision making and is made on a relatively infre-quent basis. As Dave Dunlop aptly points out, the annual gift fund raiser is always asking. That is not a negative. It merely reflects the task involved. In contrast, the major gifts fund raiser is involved in relationship building, and that is where things become decidedly more complex.

Research tells us that the dynamics of decision making by a donor change significantly when the solicitation moves from an annual gift to a "stop and think" contribution. The process becomes more lengthy and far more com-plex. Here are the reasons:

- It takes longer for a prospect's needs and motives to develop as the gift decision grows in magnitude. This is logical. Someone needs to have a much stronger belief in an organization if, for example, the solicitation is for $1,000 as opposed to $100. The actual dollar amounts are unim-portant, but of significance is the relative magnitude and the need for a much stronger set of motives.
- With a "stop and think" gift, there are likely to be more influences and inputs. This, too, makes sense. My spouse and I might independently render $100 gift decisions, but you can be sure we would consult one another before making a major gift. We might also consult with our accountant, and I would surely consider cash flow and timing. The pro-cess becomes elongated because of more inputs.
- As the gift decision grows in magnitude, the donor is more likely to express decision making parameters in rational terms – even though the decision is increasingly emotional. This is a fascinating finding and one which explains a phenomenon I had observed many times. As the decision

becomes of greater magnitude, we feel it is important to examine all of the rational criteria, whether economic or operational. This is how we primarily justify our decision. However, a decision to make a huge difference in the life of an organization is reached only when there is an incredibly strong emotional tie with the mission. I thought about this when I recently purchased a van. I asked a lot of questions that were very rational and of seeming importance, even though I understand little of auto mechanics. And, frankly, I care little for the subject. What I really liked was the stereo system and the cockpit-like appearance of the dashboard, but I felt it was very important to recite *Consumer Reports* reasons for making my selection. This also explains why so many people give well beyond their capacity to use the charitable deduction generated by their generosity.

- An incorrect major gift decision has far greater negative implications than its smaller counterpart. What this means is that the donor will take longer to decide because he or she does not want to make a mistake. To make a $25 mistake is unfortunate, but a $500 mishap can ruin a day.

What all of this means is that the process of securing major gifts simply takes more time. How much time will depend on the prospect and his or her philanthropic history and relationship with the organization. But we know that relationship building, or cultivation as we commonly call it, is vital to the process. We must secure involvement if we are to be consistently successful with our major gift solicitations.

Getting something in return

The discipline of marketing has much to share with major gift fundraisers. What we know from marketing research is that giving to a charitable organization is an exchange relationship. This is not as well understood as it should be because we are dealing with an intangible. It is easy to understand how the purchase of the microwave is an exchange relationship, but what do I mean by this when I refer to philanthropic activity? It is simply that our donors expect something from the giving relationship and it is up to us to provide it.

"Mega Gifts," the fund-raising classic written by Jerold Panas, teaches us much about donor motives. It is vital to understand these in order to grasp the concept of an exchange relationship. Whether it be finding immortality, seeking prestigious relationships, or just feeling good about one's self … our donors have a right to expect something in return for their gift. If done correctly, both the donor and the institution benefit.

Philanthropy is not a process where one party subtracts and another adds. Rather, it is a matter of the donor feeling wonderful because a shared mission is furthered. If we do not provide the proper satisfaction and meet donor expectations, rest assured that another charitable organization will.

We also learn from marketing that the entire gift giving process is circular. People move through stages in reaching the gift decision. This is often described in marketing literature as AIDA. What this refers to is decision making sequencing from *attention* to *interest* to *desire* to *action*. Building interest and desire is what we commonly refer to as cultivation, and it is the least understood part of the process.

The Moves Management model, created by Buck Smith and sculpted by Dave Dunlop, has done much to assist us in understanding and implementing this key part of the process. The point is that only after securing interest and then desire are we likely to get a positive major gift decision.

In relationship building fund raising, cultivational activities far outnumber actual solicitations. What renders this difficult is the fact that mission-directed relationship building is a rather ethereal process. That is why seminars emphasize solicitation techniques when they really should be addressing methods of cultivation and measurement of the same. The Moves Management concept has helped considerably in this regard.

Implementing a Moves Management program will do much to focus your cultivation and solicitation activities with major prospects. It will also help if you attempt to set objectives for cultivational activities with the prospective donor. This is easier said than done. When surveying institutions with an active major gifts program about the establishment of objectives for cultivational calls, there emerged a general pattern of "traps." These hit home with me because I have fallen into each of these pitfalls on more than one occasion.

Get real

Sometimes we establish a cultivational call objective that is too general. Making someone feel good about our charitable organization is nice and perhaps even necessary, but anyone can feel good about an organization without in any way implying or improving the consideration of a gift. Getting agreement to attend an event or take a tour of a facility is a far better objective for a call.

Our cultivational objectives at times are unrealistic. Securing a major gift during the second meeting with a prospective donor may be asking too much. And even expecting enthusiasm for an endowment campaign among committed volunteers may be ignoring how the process really works.

Don't talk – listen

Perhaps the most common "trap" was that of fund raiser-driven cultivational objectives. Telling someone about your organization is not very helpful. Learning how he or she feels about something is far more significant. This seemingly subtle shift in focus is crucial.

What we recommend in establishing cultivational call objectives is that you consider two parameters along the same continuum. Specifically, (1) describe to yourself the best possible outcome. Then (2) decide on the minimum acceptable outcome.

Let me give you an example. A prospect agreeing to a tour of a hospital might be the best possible outcome, while declining the invitation but considering it later would be the minimum acceptable outcome. Isn't this really what we confront in the major gifts business? Relationships tend to move in small increments rather than in quantum leaps. Because major gift fund raising is an art, measurement is difficult but that does not mean we should not try. This is a framework I have found to be very helpful.

Just keep in mind to avoid the traps, and when setting your cultivational call objectives, remember to be specific, focus on the prospect's action, and seek a measurable and realistic target. You will advance your effectiveness just by going through the process of thinking through your cultivational objectives.

Don't worry about the annual ask

The very best cultivational technique is the good giving experience. I used to operate under the model that my major gift prospects should be free from annual gift solicitations until that magic moment in the future when I asked for a significant contribution.

I was wrong.

First, we now know that the dynamics of an annual gift are vastly different than those entailed with a major gift. Unless the annual gift solicitation is done poorly or is too close to the major gift solicitation, there is no conflict between the two. Second, the process is actually additive. If we make our donors feel wonderful about their gifts, it will serve as effective cultivation en route to the next gift solicitation.

I have even changed my strategy as a result of this realization. Rather than wait for the "magic moment" for a dramatic gift, I sometimes opt for a more moderate gift and the opportunity it provides to further involve a donor with the life of the institution. It helps set the stage for the bigger gift when the time comes.

One final word about circularity. Stewardship is where many of our organizations fail to perform. Thanking a donor seven times, as Jerold Panas suggests, and ensuring good reporting is one of the most effective tools we have in the relationship building process. Further, we now understand that donors go through a post–major gift anxiety period, just as we naturally experience after a major purchase.

Too often our major donors do not hear from us for a while pursuant to a major gift, except perhaps for a perfunctory acknowledgment. This is the very time we should be seeking their further involvement. After all, a major gift is a gesture symbolizing great trust. We give positive reinforcement to the contribution decision when we immediately respond with gratitude and a demonstration of good stewardship. Simple gestures such as calling the day after receiving a gift commitment to thank the donor once again can have a profound impact.

Major gifts fund raising is a rich and rewarding enterprise. It is a process which challenges our mental abilities and allows for much creativity and self-initiative. We can have a lasting impact on important enterprises if we are successful. More importantly, we have an opportunity to associate with people who, by definition, care enough to make a difference. It is a high privilege and an important calling worthy of our every effort to gain greater understanding and efficacy. I wish you well on your important journey.

Dispelling the myths about major donor fundraising

Angela Cluff, 2009

It puzzles me why so many organisations with great major donor potential fail to make the most of that potential. It is especially puzzling since the underlying principles of major donor work are apparently well known and widely published.

[…]

Part of the explanation for this failure is that many initiatives display five common weaknesses – and more worryingly fall victim to nine common myths.

Five common weaknesses

1. Organisations really want money for existing work; major donors want to fund new work

The Holy Grail for most organisations is unrestricted income – income the organisation can choose to spend, however it wants and ideally on existing hard-to-fund work. However, raising unrestricted income rarely works with major donors. Instead major donors want to know exactly how their gift will be spent and the precise difference it will make. Put simply, major donors want to know what their gift *will* do, not what it *may* do.

In our experience, this is where the challenge lies. It is not a fundraising challenge, it is a failure to articulate what the money is *for*. At the heart of every good major donor programme sits a really effective case for support – a compelling and lucid explanation of:

* Why the money is needed?
* What it will be spent on?
* How will it make a difference?
* What will happen if the money cannot be raised?
* Why this organisation is the right organisation to deliver the work?

At its simplest this means *packaging* the organisation's work into 'chunks' that relate to the donor's ability to give.

However, for many significant major donors, even an outstanding case matched to their capacity is not enough. They want an opportunity to be a

DOI: 10.4324/9781003145936-47

part of *shaping the solution* – and for many organisations, this is simply a step too far. And that takes us to the second challenge.

2. Organisations do not really want donors to have the involvement they'd like

Many major donors do not want just to be told an organisation's solution to a particular problem. Rather they want to be part of genuinely *creating the solution.* They want to be asked for their views and ideas. Fundraisers know that this *involvement* is an important and effective step in the solicitation process; it creates a genuine two-way relationship. However, too often the challenge is organisations – especially senior staff on the service side – are not prepared to engage in these debates.

3. Organisations do not ask prospects closest to them to make stretch gifts. So these prospects do not become true leaders, able to leverage further gifts

Most organisations set a financial level for gifts – above which the donor is considered a major donor, below which he or she is not. Major donor status usually means the donor is handled on an individual, personal basis by an 'account' manager. In our experience the common level within mainstream UK charities at which this happens is £5000 or even lower. The actual level set by an organisation is often based on 'top slicing' – taking top performing donors to create a pool of donors that is manageable by the major donor resource available.

This offers a logical and practical beginning to a major donor programme. However, it creates a challenge that can then limit the growth of the programme. Many of the donors categorised as major donors are not actually making major gifts – for them.

For this reason, we prefer to define major gifts as those personally significant to, or perceived as a stretch gift for, the individual. To achieve this, resources need to be focused on those prospects that can be persuaded to make personally important gifts at the highest levels. These are leadership gifts. Such gifts have a key secondary payoff since secured, they can be used to lever more major gifts from other donors.

[...]

4. There are few really experienced major donor fundraisers and even fewer really experienced organisations

Organisations that are really succeeding have a critical mass and sustainability in major donor fundraising. This results from a combination of individual talent and organisational experience.

Major donor fundraising is not just about exceptional fundraisers – though there is a 'cult' of recruiting such staff. Instead it is an organisation-wide process that fully involves the leadership (board and staff) of the organisation and sees donors as partners in achieving the vision. In too many organisations it is the major donor staff that hold the relationships. Without organisational resilience and integration success is uncertain.

The strong market demand for major donor fundraisers compounds the difficulties, with rising salaries and inexperienced staff often over promoted. This pressure can mean that too often major donor fundraisers spend 12–18 months creating an effective case and researching the prospects – and then make their next career move before they have to 'bring home the bacon'.

In a number of consultancy assignments we have found numerous donor files of letters to existing or potential major donors that begin 'I am the new …' This is not good for organisations, donors, or even fundraisers themselves. Organisations and donors in this situation do not enjoy the experience of effective two-way relationships. And fundraisers do not build their own bank of experience in securing major gifts.

5. Too often boards and senior teams think major donor fundraising is a quick fix and then lose faith

Major donor fundraising is a 3–5 year income stream – but you have to start asking early on to create momentum for results later.

To transform those who are warmest and closest into askers themselves means asking them for money first. And that takes time. Those organisations that are succeeding recognise that to keep up momentum it is necessary to create a balanced portfolio that builds in both short-term quick wins and longer-term major asks.

However, it is not just organisational weaknesses that make it hard to get major donor fundraising right. Our research programme also confirmed that some aspects of this approach simply do not work in practice in the way the long-established theory suggests. When this happens many fundraisers feel they are 'failing'. Our research in UK, USA and Australia confirmed nine common myths. We want to dispel them.

Myth 1: Major donor fundraising is for the biggest and best-known charities

Successful major donor fundraising is possible for all organisations if the need is powerfully articulated and the board and senior team are passionate and committed.

Sure, it is easier if you already have a large database of supporters to mine, a network of committed local supporters, you are the brand leader in your sector and have an 'easy-to-understand-and-sell' cause.

However, even the smallest organisation has connections that can lead to potential major donors. The key is to focus on those connections and exploit them relentlessly, working out from who you know *now*, to who you might want to *get to know*. It may take time but you can do it.

[…]

Myth 2: Major donor fundraising is only as good as your prospect research

Our investigation into the value of prospect research revealed very split opinions – from some who regard it as 100% crucial to one very senior fundraiser who told us '90% of research investment is wasted'.

In our view, prospect research is vital if it is focused on gathering information about key prospect characteristics – *capacity, propensity, connection and motivation*. However, too often it becomes an end in itself, an industry to learn everything there is to know about an individual, rather than a means to an end: prioritising prospects. In the worst cases it is actually a *distraction*. So a lack of information means fundraisers hold back on getting out from behind the desk and meeting donors face to face. In fact, getting out to meet real donors in real situations is the fastest, most effective way to find out more and build strong relationships.

[...]

It may seem deeply unfair, but the organisations best able to use prospect research extensively are those organisations who are already the best connected. The more people you know, the easier it is to use network research to connect you to those you might like to know. For many organisations our best advice is to tear up the research and go and talk in an open way to your current best donors.

Myth 3: Your supporter base is the right place to look for prospects

The myth here is that it is only your *financial* supporters who might be major donor prospects. Actually it is also about volunteers, campaigners, beneficiaries, or whoever is closest to you. They may not give you money now simply because you have not asked, but they are passionate about your work, and have networks you may not know about! At worst they are routes to information.

Organisations with a strong community base have a fundamental advantage. It is no surprise that community fundraising is experiencing a renaissance as organisations work out how it can contribute to major donor fundraising.

Myth 4: Asking is the job of the volunteer

It is true that the best asker is usually a volunteer who has made his or her own major gift. It helps too if the volunteer has received training to ask others. In this 'textbook' situation the volunteer can ask beyond the need and lever gifts in relation to their:

•   Own gift.
•   Status in relation to the prospect.
•   Relationship with the prospect.

However, volunteer asking is not the only route – and *you* need to have asked to find your first volunteer asker. Sometimes it is the right – and best – thing for the staff to ask.

As head of major donors at the NSPCC, I experienced this first hand. I went to visit a prospect volunteer fundraising board member. On entering his office he said he had a question for me that had been bothering him. He wanted to know why he and his wife had attended a high profile, glamorous event 6 months earlier and had not been asked for money. I knew the answer. Behind the scenes, we had been working to set up a textbook perfect ask. We had identified the ideal volunteer, who had already made his own major gift. However, we were still working on persuading the volunteer to make the ask. In the eyes of the prospect we were just incompetent. With hindsight it would have been better for a member of staff to ask. Almost certainly, we would have secured a gift (probably a major gift according the NSPCC's definition then) and we would have a relationship that we could have built from.

In our experience, many organisations get into similar situations and do not make progress while they are waiting for the perfect ask opportunity. The perfect ask is not the only ask.

Myth 5: It takes a long time to get a major gift

Sometimes. But only sometimes. In our experience it is possible to achieve major gifts in a relatively short period of time, certainly less than 6 months. These gifts may not be the donor's ultimate major gift, but they may be strategically important to the organisation, particularly if it is in the early days of the programme.

You also need to be aware of the changing situation for a donor – bereavement, or a sudden change in business circumstances might make a change in gift circumstances appropriate.

Myth 6: Successful capital campaigns are about securing the right lead gift early and working top down

Most books and conferences share pyramid-based models of capital appeals that our research suggests do not match successful contemporary practice. In theory, the lead gift will:

*   Be 10–20% of the appeal total.
*   Be secured early.
*   Come from a member of the fundraising committee.
*   Create the cascade of giving through the gift table.

Research – among successful charities it should be noted – leads us to believe that lead gifts are often smaller than 10–20%. Partly this is due to the increased size of campaigns – so for the largest of these 10–20% may simply be unrealistic. (An increasing number of campaigns are in the £100 million + bracket.) Perhaps more challenging, the data also indicate that lead gifts may come late in the campaign, possibly from a surprising source.

Myth 7: Capital campaigns have a sequential private and public phase

The private/public sequencing of a capital campaign is another beloved classic tactic of the theory. This has a purpose, of course. It is designed to prevent *inoculation*. Inoculation happens when a prospect gives a smaller gift than they are capable of, possibly in response to a mass marketing approach. Then, when approached on a personal basis for a large gift he or she is able to say 'I have already given to the campaign'.

Our research shows that there is a consensus that the private/public sequence is more relevant in certain circumstances – especially where the prospect pool is relatively clearly defined and the campaign is limited in size.

However, for campaigns that are potentially wider in scope and more ambitious in scale like the NSPCC's ground-breaking *Full Stop* Campaign – it is rather less clear-cut. These large generic campaigns cannot necessarily know everyone who might be relevant at the outset. They need public awareness of the issue at the start to create opportunities for potential major donors to express an interest in becoming involved. This explains why sometimes very significant gifts come late in campaigns.

[...]

Myth 8: You only have one chance to get the major gift

The concept of inoculation described above is often linked to a second idea. This suggests that, especially within a capital fundraising context, you have just one shot to secure the 'right' gift – a gift that is significant to both the donor and the campaign.

Again, in our experience this is a myth. Major donors, especially those with an emerging sense of philanthropy, often want to make 'test' gifts to try out the relationship they might have with the organisation. And it is possible to build on these first gifts, even within a single campaign.

This concept of the 'test' gift is one that we have found useful when advising charities trying to develop relationships.

Myth 9: 'The rich are different from you and me, yes they have more money' – F Scott Fitzgerald

Are major donors really so different from lower level donors? Not fundamentally in my experience. All donors want to make a significant difference and for their gift to have a real impact ... Granted there is more at stake with major donors. They can and do give more and as a result they can and do demand more. As fundraisers it is our job to build on their interest, show what is in it for them and what is in it for the beneficiaries. (They may also be very interested in who else is involved.) We need to understand and respond to their sophisticated and sometimes changing needs. This is true, however complex and demanding they are. That is why major donor fundraising is in theory easy, but in practice very hard.

Legacy fundraising: let's not talk of death

Russell N. James III and Claire Routley, 2016

Charitable bequest giving is a significant source of income for many nonprofit organizations. In the USA, charitable bequest giving generated over $28bn, exceeding all giving by corporations. Many large charitable organizations in the UK receive more than half of their charitable giving through bequest gifts. Despite this magnitude, the potential for such giving is dramatically larger. Roughly 70 to 80% of the US population engages in current charitable giving, but fewer than 6% leave charitable bequests at death. Similarly, only about one in ten substantial current donors ($500 or more annually) will leave a charitable bequest at death. The magnitude of this difference between current and bequest giving rates suggests the substantial economic potential of any messages that could make charitable bequests as attractive as current charitable giving. Further, the importance of bequest giving will likely grow substantially in the coming years as the population continues to age.

[…]

Previous research demonstrates the enormous difference between the share of those who participate in current charitable giving and charitable bequest giving. What might explain this dramatic behavioral difference? Certainly, the motivations to leave charitable bequests can differ from those for current giving and often emphasize the central role of family in bequest decisions. One distinction between bequest giving and current giving is that bequest transfers occur only at one's own death. Correspondingly, bequest giving decisions may be more likely to generate personal mortality contemplation … it is possible that avoidance of charitable bequest giving (as compared with current charitable giving) is related to the avoidance response to personal mortality contemplation. To the extent that charitable bequest-related marketing messages could downplay the emphasis on personal mortality, it might reduce this natural avoidance response. James found some evidence of this connection. In that experiment, respondents were significantly less likely to express interest in "make a gift to charity in my last will and testament that will take effect at my death," than in simply "make a gift to charity in my last will and testament". The addition of the gratuitous reference to the respondent's death as part of describing the charitable bequest gift had a negative effect on interest.

[…]

Much previous work on charitable bequest giving has focused on tax policy and demographic correlates such as age, gender, education, wealth, and

DOI: 10.4324/9781003145936-48

childlessness. Relatively less work has explored charitable bequest giving motivations. Of course, by researching tax policy, several have thereby explored the motivational effects of estate tax deductibility. Consistent with an avoidance response to mortality salience, we propose the following:

Hypothesis: Otherwise, similar deceased bequest donor stories will be less effective than living bequest donor stories at increasing interest in making a charitable bequest gift.

[…]

All participants [in the research] initially answered a similar set of questions. These included providing demographic information, demonstrating an understanding of the terms "bequest," "will," "last will and testament," and "estate" and answering four questions about preferences regarding treatment of their body after death (in order to induce heightened mortality salience as might be expected in an actual estate planning context).

Deceased bequest donor stories

There were seven vignettes of donors' life stories and their subsequent charitable bequests. The text of the vignettes was used with permission from the "Leave a Legacy" public awareness campaign.

Living bequest donor stories

These were otherwise identical to the deceased bequest donor stories, except they referred to the donor as living (rather than deceased) and the bequest as planned (rather than completed). For example, the deceased donor story beginning, "School janitor Lester Holmes died in 1992. After school today he'll help …," became "School janitor Lester Holmes signed his will today. One day, his charitable bequest gift will help …" with subsequent text placed in the future tense. All donor stories were presented with images consisting of a framed photograph of the purported bequest donor placed on a table or wall in a domestic setting. Identical images were used for both the living and deceased donor stories. In order to include diverse donor examples, the seven donor images included four males and three females. Three pictured donors were white, two were black, and two were Asian. To increase attention to the donor stories, following each story, respondents were asked a question about the content of the story.

Results

[…]

All groups exposed to bequest donor stories reported significantly greater interest in making a bequest gift, relative to their initial interest in making a current gift, than did the control group [the control group did not read donor stories]. Living donor stories were consistently more effective than deceased donor stories at increasing the relative interest in making a bequest gift. The first four living donor stories were significantly more effective than the deceased version of the same stories. The same was true when comparing the two versions of all seven stories. Adding three living donor stories to the initial four stories (either living or deceased) significantly increased relative interest in a bequest gift, but adding the deceased version of these three stories reduced this relative interest.

[…]

As a check on any possible negative effects of the living donor stories on current giving intentions, 325 respondents were asked to re-rate their current giving intentions, rather than rate their bequest giving intentions, after reading the first four living bequest donor stories. The average current giving intention rose by 0.50 points suggesting that there was no negative spillover on current giving intentions from the living donor stories.

[…]

Discussion

Both living and deceased bequest donor stories increased the relative likelihood of making a charitable bequest gift as compared with receiving no stories. These stories may be effective by providing examples that set a social norm encouraging such gifts. Previous research indicates that the use of a social norm statement during the estate planning process ("many of our customers like to leave money to charity in their will. Are there any causes you're passionate about?") increased participation in charitable bequest giving. Similarly, James found that adding a social norm statement ("many people like to leave a gift to charity in their wills") to the description of a charitable bequest gift significantly increased interest in making such a gift. The current results suggest a similarly positive effect from sharing stories of others who have made such gifts. The use of social norms such as these may be particularly impactful for estate giving decisions considering that previous research in terror management theory suggests that mortality salience increases the desire to support social norms.

However, otherwise identical living donor stories were clearly superior to deceased donor stories in increasing bequest giving intentions. The idea that norm adherence is dependent upon perceived similarity with the example actor is relatively well established in psychological research and may partly explain why our results show that more stories are more effective, with more stories offering more opportunity for perceived similarity. In the case of the living examples, the living bequest donor is more similar to the respondent than is the otherwise identical deceased donor, simply by virtue of being alive. This one difference may be particularly powerful given previous research suggesting that personal mortality contemplation (such as making end-of-life distribution choices) may generate a more intense desire to distance oneself from those associated with death or bodily infirmity. More broadly, this provides additional evidence on the benefits of de-emphasizing a focus on death in charitable bequest fundraising messaging.

Implications for professional practice

For the fundraiser, the most practical consequence of this study is that (a) sharing stories appears to increase bequest intentions and (b) concentrating on living donor stories appears more effective. However, in order to tell these stories and to tell multiple stories over time and across channels, fundraisers would need to introduce mechanisms for collecting, storing, and managing donor stories. Some organizations, which take a direct marketing-led approach, now include the facility within their appeals for donors to share their stories, rather than purely ticking a box to indicate their bequest intention. For others, where there is more one-to-one interaction, fundraisers could encourage colleagues to collect donor stories at their meetings or via the telephone. Our results tested the use of a variety of different stories; fundraisers could make a conscious effort to capture stories from people of different demographic backgrounds and perhaps with different motives for supporting that charity.

Although collecting stories may sound like a simple idea, embedding the process of capturing stories with the requisite level of detail, ensuring that those stories can be stored appropriately and utilized when necessary may involve developing new processes, shared across several fundraising teams. There is potentially a wide application for stories in legacy fundraising practice, from case studies in direct marketing material, to stories shared at events, to newsletter features. Digital media offers a particularly exciting space to share stories: for example, by using video to bring donor stories to life.

What is a philanthropic foundation?

Tobias Jung, Jenny Harrow, and Diana Leat, 2018

As one of the most unrestricted contemporary organizational forms, it is difficult to define what constitutes a foundation. Foundations' long and colorful history shows varying perceptions over time: from the legal frameworks of the Roman Corpus Juris Civilis and the German Lex Salica in the sixth century, the establishment and growth of Islamic foundations or waqfs as a juridical form from around 755 ce, to the 1535 and 1601 Statutes of Uses and of Charitable Uses in England. Although foundations' developments across different settings and traditions are usually considered in isolation, there are strong indications of mutual influences, of cross-fertilizations of ideas, practices and frameworks.

Academic, policy and practice discourses often gloss over definitional issues by taking a "common-sense" approach, assuming implicit understanding inherent in the foundation label. Organizational names and labels may be unreliable: few in academic and foundation worlds would consider the British Heart Foundation [a major fundraising charity] to be a "foundation," yet the Henry Smith Charity and the Carnegie Corporation of New York would both be seen as foundations. Legal perspectives have limited use. Many countries, such as the United Kingdom, make no legal distinction between foundations and other forms of charitable organizations. In countries such as in the United States, where foundations exist as a creation of tax law, statutory agencies frequently emphasize exclusion rather than inclusion criteria to determine whether an organization qualifies as a foundation or not. Even foundations' umbrella bodies and associations acknowledge that "the term foundation has no precise meaning".

Notwithstanding these definitional challenges, recurring attempts at characterizing and conceptualizing foundations have been made.

[…]

Within the literature, two of the most prominently referred to definitions are those by Anheier and by Prewitt. The former characterizes foundations as "an asset, financial or otherwise" that is non-membership based, a private entity, relatively permanent, with an identifiable organizational structure, nonprofit distributing, and serving a public purpose; the latter describes them as "a permanent endowment, not committed to a particular institution or activity, that provides a grantmaking capacity reaching across multiple purposes and into the indefinite future". Similar aspects are emphasized by others. Nonetheless,

DOI: 10.4324/9781003145936-49

their application creates difficulties. For example, although Anheier refers to "an asset," Prewitt specifically focuses on an "endowment" as a distinguishing factor. The increasing interest in spend-out, that is time-limited foundations, challenges Prewitt's idea of "indefinite future," while Anheier's nonprofit criterion seems both historically and currently problematic and running into difficulties as a result of the growth in foundation-owned companies. Again, Prewitt's and others' emphasis that endowed foundations do not conduct their own direct charitable activities excludes the entire group of operating foundations – those implementing their own project and programs – including one of Europe's largest foundation, the Bertelsmann Foundation.

To identify different foundation forms, it thus seems appropriate to start off with a broad casting of foundations as grantmaking or operating charities: the former concentrate on the distribution of funds, the latter on running their own programs to achieve their goals.

[...]

Leat demarcates three grantmaking cultures in British foundations, gift-givers, investors, and collaborative entrepreneurs, while Scherer refers to foundations' grantmaking identities as agenda setters, supporters, or community builders. Inherent in both is the differentiation between foundations geared toward making one-off grants, those funding to achieve specific outcomes, and those working collaboratively with grantees and other organizations to pursue their aims.

Distinguishing foundations that focus on "pure" funding from those interested in "funding plus," that is funding supplemented by in-kind resources and support, is a recurring theme. It is implicit in classifications focusing on foundations' "theories of change," that is, how a desired change is to be achieved. Here, "social justice philanthropy" is a prominent concept. Although the precise meaning of social justice philanthropy and its differentiation from related ideas is unclear, it is rooted in the assumption that change comes from the "bottom-up," through giving voice to people. Other theory of change labels include "catalytic philanthropy" to signal foundations' use of "disruptive innovations and new tools", "creative philanthropy" aimed at encouraging debate and experimentation, "venture philanthropy," stressing effectiveness and high performance, and "Total Impact" foundations, those that focus their resources on areas with expected maximum impact. Frequently self-ascribed, the conceptual robustness and practical applicability of such labels seems unclear.

[...]

There are indications that foundations follow an organizational life cycle. As time progresses, the role of founders and their families tend to become more remote; patrician and expert trustees and professional staff gain influence. This seems accompanied by a shift in focus from compassion and relief to improvement and reform, and growing interest in advocacy and research. Alongside age, differences in board composition, governance structures, and industry characteristic are emphasized. Empirical research indicates that these drive strategies and decision making on the types of philanthropic actions under-taken, thus linking back to foundations' approach and role.

[…]

With research and media attention emphasizing mega foundations, such as The Bill and Melinda Gates, Rockefeller, or Ford Foundations, perceptions that foundations are "a large body of money" are widespread. However, as data from the United States and the United Kingdom highlight, a minority of foundations with extremely large assets is followed by increasingly larger numbers of smaller foundations. Based on the understanding that wealthier foundations will have different characteristics and behaviors compared with those that are less well-off, distinguishing between foundations in terms of size and source seems key. For example, Ostrower reports that higher asset levels lead to stronger emphasis on effectiveness and activities beyond grantmaking among foundations, while Boris, Renz, Hager, Elias, and Somashekhar state that foundation type, size, staffing patterns, and operating activities are important drivers in foundations' expenses and compensation patterns.

[…]

What difference geographical span really makes to a foundation's characteristics and behaviors warrants further examination. It appears that geographical span and size are regularly run together such that, erroneously, a "local" founda-tion is assumed to be a small foundation and a "national" foundation large. Furthermore, some foundations give only overseas, or only locally, while others combine national, international, and local giving in different, and sometimes varying, proportions. Even within the community foundations' grouping, necessarily linked to localities, giving frames are cast differently, some mark-edly, as in the case of Silicon Valley Community Foundation's donors regarding the world as their community.

[…]

As the webpages of foundation associations, such as the Belgian Foundation Network, the East Africa Association of Grantmakers, or the Philippines' Association of Foundations highlight, such bodies often do not explicitly define or distinguish between different foundation types. However, there are a number of exceptions: from the Council on Foundations' outline of five broad foundation categories, to a distinction between 16 foundation types by Swiss Foundations. Within such lists, legal forms, where applicable, and other self-ascribed "types" are sometimes mixed together. An examination of foun-dation membership networks listed on the WINGS webpages also highlights that foundations' own thematic clusters mirror those above: foundations' own locations, in the cases of London Funders or the North Carolina Network of Grantmakers; foundations working in specific fields, illustrated by EGA – Environmental Grantmakers Association and IHRFG – International Human Rights Funders Group; foundations with specific styles and approaches, exem-plified by the funders' consortium on social change philanthropy, Grantmakers without Borders; foundations focusing on specific places, such as AGAG – Africa Grantmakers Affinity Group; and membership groups for specific foundations forms, such as the Global Fund for Community Foundations or the League of Corporate Foundations.

[...]

Three broad clusters can be identified. These relate to context, organizational characteristics, and strategy. Within context, the themes of legal and sociopolitical settings and foundations' links and origins can be discerned. In relation to strategy, questions of foundations' style, approach, span, and beneficiaries emerge. Finally, organizational characteristics relate to issues of lifespan, governance structure, age, resources, and size.

Hallmarks of a great grant application

Elin Lindström and Joe Saxton, 2013

In our research, we generally found a great diversity in approaches and opinions of different grant-making trusts. One question stands out as the exception to this diversity: what makes for a great application? There was a near consensus on this. In this section we discuss what charities can do to improve their applications.

[…]

Hallmark 1: Understanding the particular grant-making trust and tailoring applications

Charities need to show they understand and value the potential contribution of a particular grant-making trust.

At the most fundamental level, this means reading the guidelines and criteria carefully to make sure the application is something the grant-making trust would fund. This may be an obvious point, but every grant-making trust we talked to said they sift out a large proportion – anything from a quarter to three quarters of applications – at the first stage simply because they do not fit the criteria. This is often in very obvious ways, like an application for a local project to a grantmaking trust that only works nationally.

Tailoring applications takes more time, but there is also a considerable amount of time to be saved on both sides by reducing the high number of ineligible applications. Fewer, but more targeted applications would benefit both parties.

On a less tangible level, charities can also impress grant-making trusts by showing that the charity understands it. The charity not only needs to read up on the grant-maker, but also to demonstrate in the application that they have done so. A great application shows that the charity's work is in line not just with the criteria, but also with the wider mission and philosophy of a grant-making trust. One grant-maker explained what makes a charity stand out from the crowd:

> *It's very clear when an applicant has tailored their application to us, we can just tell from the language and from the story that's made throughout the application. We know that they've drawn the links between their interests and our interests. They've*

DOI: 10.4324/9781003145936-50

*read our guidance ... very clearly and drawn a link with their own organisation
and mission.*

In addition to understanding a specific grant-making trust, charities can
also make an impression by showing they value and need a particular grant.
Grantmaking trusts, especially smaller ones, are aware that they often make
up quite a small part of a charity's total income. Still, they want to make sure
that they put their funds where they have the biggest possible impact and not
where the grant will be dwarfed by larger funding sources. If the application
demonstrates how a particular, often small, grant will make a difference, it is
in a very strong position.

Hallmark 2: A strong idea

Another vital ingredient of a great application from the grant-makers' viewpoint is a strong idea. Considering the diversity of grant-making trusts, the
form of a strong idea will of course vary greatly, ranging from a tried and tested
delivery of a service to an innovative arts project. There are, however, some
characteristics of a strong idea that apply across this diverse sector.

Most fundamentally, the application needs to show why the work is needed,
what the charity wants to achieve and that they have a robust idea of how to
get there. One grant-maker said:

> *Are they clear about what the project is and what it's trying to do and how they're
> going to measure it and manage it?*

Depending on the particular grant-making trust, they might want a charity to
have the answers to these questions before making the first contact, or they
might be happy to be part of the process of working out a strong proposal.
Either way, by the time the application reaches the board of trustees, it needs
to answer the questions of why, what and how.

A second characteristic of a strong idea is that it takes into account the
wider context, showing that the charity is aware of what is going on around it.
One grant-maker said a charity can have a great idea, but if there are already
nine similar projects running in the area they are very unlikely to fund it.
This is not only because they might think the project is unnecessary, but also
because it does not inspire confidence in a charity if it is unaware of what
is happening around it. In a tough funding context, making sure charities
cooperate to deliver the best results with limited resources has become all the
more important to grant-making trusts.

[...]

Hallmark 3: Competent people

Closely connected to a strong idea are people who come across as knowledgeable about the work and with the competence to put it into practice. In our

research, grant-making trusts said they want to have a single point of contact and they want that person to know the suggested work inside out.

While the idea of what makes for "good people" is highly subjective, there are things that charities can do to make sure they come across in the best light. The most important of these is to do some research into the particular grant-making trust and find out what matters to them. For grant-makers who are open to contact with applicants, asking for their preferences might be a good option.

This is often a matter of understanding the particular type of grant-making trust. For example, do they want contact with someone working on the ground, or do they prefer to talk to a director or trustee? One grant-making trust that tends to fund charities over a long-term period said it was important for them to be in touch with a reasonably senior person. They believe this enables a continuity of contact with a person who is likely to stay for many years and who can speak with authority on behalf of the charity. Other types of grant-makers were more interested in talking to someone working at ground level.

Another factor to keep in mind is the form of grant a particular grant-making trust offers. If it is an unrestricted form of funding, for example for core costs, several grant-makers that we spoke to said that makes it more important for them to trust the people involved. In contrast, if the grant-making trust has very clear objectives and tends to provide restricted funding, the quality of the idea might be more important.

Hallmark 4: Clear and succinct language

No matter how great the idea or the people involved, grant-making trusts are unlikely to know about either unless an application is communicated in a clear and succinct way. One grant-maker said a great application contains:

> *A strong idea. A project that is vital and at a crucial point of that individual or that organisation's development so it's going to make a real difference to them and we're looking for both those things to be clearly communicated, to not waffle or [include] countless pages. I think the best ideas are very succinctly expressed and they come through strongest when someone can do that.*

There was some disagreement between grant-making trusts on who writes the best applications. Many said that it is very obvious when a professional fundraiser has written the application and that they tend to associate these applications with a heavy use of jargon, box-ticking and a lack of knowledge and passion about the work. These grant-makers often said that smaller charities tend to have a better understanding of the work they want to do, which comes through both in the written application and in follow-up questions and visits.

A less tangible quality is that the application needs to not only provide information, but also communicate the soul of the charity. One interviewee said that grant-making is: "*… an act of imagination as well as judgement. You want* *something that stirs the imagination – something that actually gives you some sense of the needs they're meeting and the realities they're working with.*"

The grant-maker continued to explain this, saying that a great application helps bring the beneficiaries' reality to life:

> *The challenge of grant-making is you are a long way from the realities that you're trying to change and the beneficiaries you're trying to help. So, anything that grantees can do to help you imagine and understand those realities before you have a chance to see them, and especially to help you understand changing realities, I think is really helpful.*

In contrast to this, other grant-makers said they prefer the more skilled applications written by professional fundraisers. We know from our previous research with charities that large organisations who can afford professional fundraisers tend to have much higher success rates with their applications to grant-making trusts than smaller charities do. So, while some grant-making trusts say they prefer applications from smaller charities, the overall picture seems to be that professional fundraisers pay off given their higher success rates. In fact, several of the grant-makers we talked to were concerned that smaller charities often struggle to communicate the great work they do. For some, this means they adjust their expectations to accommodate smaller charities' skills. However, others said that sadly they go through hundreds of applications and those that do not grab them straight away are quickly sifted out.

Hallmark 5: Finances in order

The finances and budget included in an application need to add up and they need to sound feasible. This might sound like an obvious point, but most of the grant-making trusts we talked to said they find simple calculation mistakes in the budgets of a large proportion of applications. This obviously does not speak well for the competence and planning skills of the charity.

In addition to adding up, the scope of the project and its budget need to be something that the charity can realistically manage, as shown in the quote below:

> *Is the size of the project appropriate for the scale of the organisation? There's no point in an organisation with a turnover of £50,000 suddenly trying to manage a five-million pound capital project with no more resources, for example.*

Some grant-making trusts said they are happy for charities to contact them before the details of the budget are set. These ones often assist charities in working out the budget, as long as it all adds up by the time the application reaches the board of trustees. However, far from all grant-making trusts have the time or resources for this, so charities need to research the grant-making trust in advance in order to make a tailored application.

[...]

Good working relationships and openness to contact can help most other aspects of the grant-making process. Charities appreciate grant-makers who are open to questions and contact and many of them want to build long-term relationship. From the grant-makers' point of view, it is very important to have an honest relationship where charities let them know if the work that is being funded runs into problems.

[…]

There is plenty to be optimistic about … There are many partnerships between charities and grant-makers that show all the hallmarks of the best collaboration and joint working. There are also a host of ways in which charities and grant-makers can work together better.

3.3 Working with many gifts

Relationship marketing and branding analyzed

Roger Bennett, 2019

Nonprofit relationship marketing is defined by Boenigk as "all strategies and instruments to systematically recruit, retain, and/or reactivate new or lost donors". Activities employed by nonprofits engaged in relationship marketing include telemarketing, database marketing, relationship advertising, mailings of promotional materials, the sale of charity branded products and memorabilia, and 'bonding' events such as open days or gala dinners. These (and other) activities are intended to develop a donor's sense of shared values and affiliation with a nonprofit and to invoke deep levels of organisational attachment among the nonprofit's supporters. "Big Data' (i.e., the speedy collection into computer databases of data from multiple sources in multiple formats) has facilitated nonprofit relationship marketing through the creation of highly specific sub-databases that focus on profiles of the incomes, lifestyles, locations, etc., of various niche segments of potential donors. Hence, differentiated messages can be conveyed to donors according to their known characteristics and preferences.

Academic interest in nonprofit relationship marketing grew sharply following the appearance of Ken Burnett's seminal text *Relationship Fundraising*, which reported the essential differences between nonprofit relationship fundraising and 'transactional' fundraising. The latter aimed at securing 'one-off' donations, provided ad hoc information and limited services to donors, had a short-term perspective, was arm's length and impersonal and focused on attracting as many donors as possible without subsequent attempts to follow-up contacts. Relationship fundraising, on the other hand, sought to establish long-term relationships with carefully segmented individuals and employed customised information useful for satisfying donors' needs. Today, many nonprofits invest heavily in relationship marketing due, inter alia, to the realisation that it is considerably cheaper to retain and satisfy existing donors than it is to acquire fresh supporters. (Normally, the up-front cost of procuring a supporter exceeds the financial value of the person's contributions during the first year of a relationship.) Also, wastage rates among donors are high (typically between 10% and 20% annually of all people who make more than one contribution). Thus, around half of all the individuals who give to a charity more than once are likely to disappear every three to five years.

A number of researchers have sought to develop theoretical frameworks to explain the adoption of nonprofit relationship marketing activities. Sheila

DOI: 10.4324/9781003145936-52

McAllister, for instance, employed Dialogic Theory to analyse the websites of 19 fundraising educational establishments. Dialogic Theory proposes that 'meaning' is best understood via dialogue, as occurs in two-way conversation. Dialogue should be egalitarian, McAllister argued, with neither party dominating. This requires good listening skills on both sides. Information provided should be based on valid claims. Therefore, McAllister suggested, nonprofits must 'foster an air of open dialogue with the public' and treat the donating public as an equal in communications. McAllister examined the 19 websites in terms of their ease of interface, usefulness of information and presence of feedback loops (e.g., chat lines, blogs, discussion forums). Results were mixed, with many fundraising nonprofits in the sample not following the principles of dialogic communication. Websites needed to be open, honest and forthcoming, McAllister insisted.

In a similar vein, Kate Smitko used discourse analysis (which in the present context relates to the analysis of language and language structures occurring within conversations between nonprofits and donors) in order to examine the textual construction of tweets and responses to tweets that the author collected in case studies of two nonprofit organisations. The study searched for patterns of two-way conversations and found that, through Twitter, a participatory culture grew online, and that this culture of participation facilitated strong relationships and produced strong donor engagement with the two nonprofits.

[...]

Another useful paper dealing specifically with online relationship marketing was that of Evie Lucas, who investigated how the UK's three largest charities used Facebook to encourage social interactions among both actual and potential supporters. Facebook was employed by the organisations to "humanise the brand" and to foster feelings of obligation. These objectives were achieved through the application of three strategies, i.e., publicly recognising individual supporters, projecting an organisational image of authority and inculcating a sense of self-efficacy among supporters.

Methods for cultivating relationships with donors in general (not exclusively online) were discussed by Richard D. Waters in an article that reported the outcomes to a survey of 1,830 donors to three nonprofit hospitals. The research aimed to establish managers' and donors' views about relationship cultivation techniques. Specifically, the research applied a 'co-orientation' methodology to assess the degrees of agreement that occurred between the managers of the three hospitals and its donors concerning the importance of various 'cultivation strategies' prominent in theories of interpersonal communication. The main strategies considered were: 'access', i.e., an organisation's willingness to make its people available to donors (e.g., via chat lines and discussion forums); 'positivity', i.e., a nonprofit's attempts to create positive experiences for donors; 'openness', i.e., the provision of honest and direct information and discussion; and 'assurance', i.e., an organisation's commitment to maintaining relationships with donors. Both sides, managers and donors, generally agreed that all these strategies were important and beneficial, although levels of agreement differed. Another interesting contribution to discussions about relationship cultivation was Lesley Alborough's finding that, very often, donors' long-term relationships with nonprofits mainly involved their relationships with individual fundraisers within organisations, rather than with an organisation itself. This conclusion was based on interviews conducted by the author with 44 senior managers and fundraisers in 14 nonprofits examining the details of 'primary relationships' with supporters. The results of the interviews suggested that the efforts of individual fundraisers created a narrative that caused donors to feel both cared for by an organisation and connected with its work. This resulted in supporters wanting to engage in reciprocal relationships.

[…]

Unprofitable donors

Relationships with some donors are more profitable than relationships with others. This is because relationship fundraising activities can attract large numbers of low-value donors who, while giving very little, are expensive to service. The propensity of relationship fundraising to attract large numbers of unprofitable donors who make very small and infrequent gifts, but who thereafter receive expensive materials (welcome packs, catalogues, newsletters, etc.) is a problematic issue that all fundraisers engaging in relations marketing need to address. The cost of servicing small donors is substantial, given that the amount of resources required to process a small donation is about the same as that needed to process a large gift. Noting that fundraising nonprofits commonly implement 'donor priority strategies' (i.e, strategies that deliberately provide favourable treatment to higher value donors), Silke Boenigk and Christian Scherhag investigated the question of how the prioritisation of certain donor groups might affect donor satisfaction and loyalty. The authors surveyed 804 donors to a certain fundraising nonprofit which deliberately differentiated its service provision between 'high' and 'low' donors. Findings from the study revealed that the organisation's priority strategy encouraged higher level donors to give more and encouraged lower level donors to upgrade their contributions. In conclusion, the authors recommended that fundraisers operate service differentiation policies in order to achieve this sort of beneficial result, but with just a few donor differentiation levels.

John Sauvé-Rodd analysed the financial records of 72,000 supporters of a single charity, finding that half of all the donors in the charity's database were unprofitable in any one year. Moreover, 75% of the charity's profit (defined as total revenue from donors minus the total cost of servicing them) came from just 10% of the organisation's supporters. The situation was partly attributable, Sauvé-Rodd claimed, to mass market relationship fundraising campaigns that attracted large numbers of non-monthly donors (i.e., people who had not agreed to monthly bank or payroll standing orders in favour of the charity) who instead made single small value gifts.

[…]

The problem of small and infrequent donors reducing the profitability of relationship fundraising activities can be exacerbated if a relationship fundraising campaign attracts 'slacktivists', characterised by Kirk Kristofferson, Katherine White and John Peloza as people who will make a small donation to a good cause in order to fulfil their altruistic self-perceptions, yet fail to make further gifts or make gifts of very low value. Often a slacktivist will donate online, and perhaps join a Facebook nonprofit support group and/or participate in other relationships with a nonprofit. However, the person's donor lifetime value will be low. Two primary motives lay behind slacktivm, Kristofferson et al. opined, i.e., a desire to present a positive image to others and an internal need to be consistent with personal values. Kristofferson et al. noted that the research evidence on whether slacktivists can be developed into longer term and more substantial supporters has been mixed, although studies have revealed that a high degree of 'observability' of the initial token gift made by a slacktivist appears to lead to higher subsequent donations. Another means for helping to deal with the problem of small ad hoc donations not actually leading to longer term and more substantial support was proposed by Farnoosh Khodakarami, J. Andrew Peterson and Rajkumar Venkatesan, who suggested 'donation variety' as a way of developing long-term relationships with newly acquired donors. People who interacted with a nonprofit by participating in a very broad range of activities would, according to Khodakarami et al., often turn out to be profitable in the longer run, Therefore, a nonprofit should provide new donors with numerous opportunities to interact in disparate ways with the organisation.

[…]

Branding of nonprofit organisations

Nonprofits were initially slow to adopt branding (due mainly to opposition from stakeholders, especially employees and trustees), but branding became widespread in the 1990s and is today practiced by all the large and, in some form or other, by most small fundraising organisations. Branding increased in popularity because it enabled nonprofits to communicate their core values and operations to the donating public, to impel all the stakeholders of an organisation to deliver the same brand promise and to demonstrate the nonprofit's 'professional' approach. The adoption of branding was accelerated by the observation among non-branded nonprofits that nonprofits that engaged in branding were achieving higher financial returns. An early study of nonprofit (charity) branding completed by Tapp defined a charity's brand as 'the complete collection of images of a charity, its products or its cause, that are contained in a donor's mind'. Tapp executed a qualitative investigation of attitudes towards branding that were held by senior marketing executives in large charities, concluding that although many of them used branding, they did not describe it as such.

[…]

Nonprofit brand personality and image

In line with commercial sector branding practices, attempts have been made to relate a nonprofit organisation's characteristics to human characteristics (genuine, strong, energetic, etc.) as a means for identifying the 'personality' of a nonprofit brand, Literature relating to this matter was reviewed comprehensively by Voeth and Herbst, who also developed a nonprofit brand personality scale designed to measure the features of the brand personality of a nonprofit organisation. The authors' 36-item scale contained three components: (i) social competence and trust (which was assessed via 21 items, e.g. professional, trustworthy), (ii) emotion and assertiveness (11 items, e.g., exciting, courageous), and (ii) sophistication (five items, eg. cheerful, glamourous). The scale was tested on donors' perceptions of three well-known nonprofits (UNICEF, Greenpeace and the German Red Cross) and was found to be valid and reliable. In the same year, Sargeant, Ford and Hudson presented another analysis of brand personality, which they tested in relation to nine national UK nonprofits, The authors concluded that the following traits distinguished one nonprofit brand from others: (i) emotional engagement (e.g., exciting, fun, inspiring), (ii) service (e.g., dedicated, compassionate), (iii) the nonprofit's 'tradition', and (iv) voice (e.g., ambitious, authoritative, bold). However, the following traits did not significantly discriminate among the organisations: benevolence, progression (ie., a non-profit's capacity to effect social change), and conservatism. Of all nonprofit brand personality traits, brand 'warmth' was found to be the most important in a study undertaken by Bernriter, Verlegh and Smit. Brand warmth predicted the ease with which nonprofit brands obtained 'likes' on Facebook. This in turn enabled a nonprofit to acquire online endorsements. Images of 'competence', conversely, did not result in 'likes' and endorsements. The warmth effect was enhanced by a brand's ability to communicate 'symbolic value' (i.e., the brand's capacity to state something positive about the person who was contemplating its characteristics) to an observer.

Community fundraising, a jewel in the crown

Nina Botting Herbst and Lianne Howard-Dace, 2019

What is community fundraising?

Community fundraising is perhaps the easiest type of fundraising to identify as it includes many well-known activities, such as coffee mornings, fun runs and quiz nights. However, it is also one of the hardest areas of fundraising to clearly define because organisations categorise and account for their activities differently. For administrative purposes, some organisations might describe community fundraising instead as third-party, public or even volunteer fundraising.

There is no one, widely accepted definition of community fundraising. Harry Brown's definition of it in 2002 as "fundraising carried out by volunteers in their local community" is possibly the most often quoted, but it perhaps doesn't entirely capture how community fundraising has evolved since then. The focus on local communities is not broad enough to encompass what many organisations consider to be community fundraising. The common theme in all attempts to define this type of fundraising, however, is that all community fundraising activities have at least one, and perhaps all, of the following characteristics:

- they are carried out by volunteers;
- they are participatory;
- they raise money from a group, network or community of people (local or otherwise).

As with other fundraising disciplines, there are fashions that come and go in community fundraising in terms of what is offered, with one example being overseas challenge events. Similarly, there are trends in how organisations approach and structure community fundraising – for example, investing in or divesting regionally based staff teams. That said, these external trends are likely to have less impact on how community fundraising is approached than internal factors such as the maturity of the organisation. During an organisation's early years, the type of grassroots support offered by community fundraising can be invaluable. However, as an organisation becomes more professional, it can be difficult to accommodate some of its quirkier aspects.

A trend that has arisen over the past decade or so is a move to focus more on volunteer-led than staff-led activities; this has helped to address the

DOI: 10.4324/9781003145936-53

professionalisation of community fundraising activity. Community fundraising staff now tend to act as professional facilitators who empower and equip volunteers, rather than organising lots of activities themselves. This move has also allowed community fundraising to be more efficient and yield better net incomes.

Why invest in community fundraising?

Community fundraising will almost never have the clear-cut and high return on investment (ROI) of some other income streams. For example, an application to a grant-making charity can elicit a large amount of funding with relatively little expenditure. However, when ROI and effort are maximised, community fundraising can be an important part of a diversified portfolio, and it can also be used to engage new audiences in other types of fundraising.

Community events can be time-consuming and uneconomical for paid staff to run. Your professional community fundraisers' time may be better spent on activities that enhance the efforts of your volunteers. If community fundraising in your organisation has historically involved a lot of staff-led activity, or worse become a dumping ground for less profitable projects which other teams don't consider their primary responsibility, you will need to work on managing both internal and external expectations about the future of your community fundraising programme. ROI can be greatly improved by:

- streamlining your portfolio of activities so as to free up staff members' time to spend on the projects that are most valuable to you;
- empowering your volunteers to organise their own projects.

Community fundraising can be a real jewel in your organisation's fundraising crown. A motivated volunteer can raise more money through fundraising on your behalf than they might afford to donate themselves.

Community fundraising has various supplementary benefits, such as raising awareness and contributing to your organisation's campaign objectives, but these should never be used to justify a programme that is delivering poor financial results. That said, if you start out with a solid rationale for a community event and build these objectives into your key performance indicators (KPIs) from the start, community fundraising can have many secondary benefits, such as:

- increasing brand recognition;
- generating local and regional press stories;
- generating leads for individual giving;
- forging links to potential local corporate sponsors;
- creating a pool of leads for campaigning actions;
- providing a route to high-net-worth individuals;
- providing an alternative offer for lapsed cash givers;
- strengthening engagement and lifetime value.

Types of community fundraising

There are three main types of community fundraising, classified by the way supporters engage with the activity.

1. Mass participation appeals

Many charities have seasonal or annual campaigns that encourage people to hold similar activities during the same month, week or day, such as Breast Cancer Awareness Month or the Poppy Appeal around Armistice Day. The feeling of being part of something bigger can be a significant motivator for people and a great way of both retaining existing supporters and recruiting new ones.

Most community campaigns encourage people to hold an event in their local area – whether that be with their friends and family, at their workplace, or with a society of faith group – and provide resources to help and encourage them. Key to the success of such events is providing enough structure and support to make it easy for people to take part, but with enough scope to scale the event up or down and add their own flair.

2. DIY activities

While having a varied portfolio of events and appeals in which people can take part is a cornerstone of any successful community fundraising programme, there will always be supporters who are sufficiently motivated to develop and carry out their own activities. If you want to encourage this independent activity as part of your strategy, you will need to be able to support and service them – however weird and wonderful their proposed activities may be!

DIY activities are often driven by a supporter's passions, skills and resources. They may want to create events which raise funds through their professional skills, their sports team or their creative hobbies. While the supporter may have expertise in the content of the event, it is the role of the community fundraiser in these situations to offer advice and support – particularly, spotting opportunities to maximise income which a non-fundraiser may not consider and ensuring the charity's brand is acceptably represented.

Having a range of generic resources will help you to efficiently steward and support DIY fundraisers.

[…]

3. Fundraising groups

Many organisations have some sort of volunteer group structure; these are often of long standing, sometimes having existed since the very inception of the organisation. They might have a formal structure with a chair, secretary and treasurer and some sort of signed agreement with the organisation. In some instances, they may also have a role in the governance of the organisation, such as board representation.

The most self-sufficient of these groups will have an established calendar of regular events and activities which could generate tens of thousands of pounds each year, with community fundraisers providing stewardship and encouragement where necessary. These groups could make a significant contribution to your organisation and provide a consistent source of income, as well as championing your mission in their communities. However, the way a group operates will need to evolve over time to continue meeting supporters' needs and have significant longevity. Groups which aren't functioning as well as they might can be very time-consuming for community fundraisers, who may work increasingly hard to keep the group going.

There is a real art to managing the expectations of fundraising groups, and you should clearly articulate how you will support them. For example, setting up a collaboration by saying 'I will help with your next event while we work together to find a new chair for the group' is likely to be more constructive than offering additional support indefinitely. Additionally, for existing groups, there is a tendency for them to be made up of older people who are less active and who may be able to contribute less and less over time. Sometimes, winding up the group and directing former members' support towards other projects is the best way forward.

Some organisations have had success with establishing new supporter fundraising groups, but it is key to have a carefully considered approach and target demographic. It is also important before initiating any such schemes to research whether there is appetite for them within your supporter base. Pilot the idea before rolling out a large scheme and counting on receiving income from it, as this approach won't work for every organisation.

Organisations that provide a local service, such as a hospice, may have more success in starting and retaining these groups, as in such cases there is a more obvious and necessary reason for people to convene locally. Other organisations may have success with more informal groups where people fundraise in memory of a loved one, for medical research on a condition affecting a family member, or to thank an organisation for the care they have received. This type of approach may be more suitable for younger people, who may be less likely to want to be affiliated with a formal group.

Developing a community fundraising strategy

The desired outcome of any strategy is to ascertain where you are, where you want to be and how you're going to get there. The size and complexity of community fundraising in your organisation will play a big part in shaping your ongoing community fundraising strategy

[…]

Objectives and targets

[…]

Income is obviously the key driver of any fundraising programme, but non-financial targets can also help to focus your activity, give direction to staff, manage expectations within your organisation and demonstrate the value of this work. Building on the secondary benefits of community fundraising [as listed above] ... you could measure some or all of the following non-financial KPIs:

- repeat supporter participation;
- conversion rate (from signing up to carrying out the activity);
- referrals (i.e. word-of-mouth recruitment);
- reactivation of lapsed supporters;
- leads generated for other income streams;
- press and media reach ...

[...]

As a rule of thumb, it can take between 18 and 24 months for a new community fundraising programme to show success, so be realistic about when you expect to see a return from your various products and programmes.

[...]

Volunteer-led versus staff-led fundraising

[...]

Using resources well – including direct expenditure but also the time expended by both paid staff and volunteers – can make or break the bottom line of an event. Events can be very labour-intensive, from pre-promotion to set-up on the day, and if you don't include a sensible estimate of staff time in your budget you won't get a clear picture of your likely return on investment.

There are situations where it is most appropriate for staff to run events – particularly in the case of higher-stakes special events – but increasingly fundraisers are moving away from running their own events to playing a more facilitative role. Of course, many staff in community and events roles enjoy running events and have experience of doing this as a volunteer or professionally. It can also be enjoyable to roll up your sleeves and help your volunteer team out on the day to show you are working in partnership with them. However, it pays to be mindful of how responsibilities are shared and where paid staff can really add value to maximise net income for your cause. Therefore, whether you are running a mass participation appeal to encourage supporters to hold their own small events or acting in an advisory role to a volunteer committee running a large event, you can maximise your efficiency by seeing yourself and any other staff fundraisers as multipliers of your supporters' energy – not suppliers of it.

Throughout the process of recruiting and managing volunteers, it is important to remember that there will be certain things which staff must do. For example, your internal governance processes are likely to require a staff member to sign off on a risk assessment. However, paying attention to the skills and talents of your available volunteers will reveal many tasks where they can take the lead or provide support.

Types of volunteer

From the one-off bake sale host to the celebrity who introduces your gala event, volunteers can be the secret ingredient that makes your fundraising really take flight. You may be able to categorise your supporters into different types, such as those below, to help you steward them and develop their relationship with your organisation.

Event organisers

These supporters put on events for your organisation. An event can be relatively simple, such as a quiz night, or a much more complex affair, such as a ball. You will likely have a mixture of people, some who follow their own passions in the events they put on and others who will sign up to work on an existing event or initiative which you promote. Your community fundraising staff can offer their professional expertise to help maximise the income raised and will need to offer different levels of support to event organisers, depending on their experience and the scale of what they are doing for you.

Event volunteers

Whether you are putting on your own flagship event or supporting a volunteer event organiser, it is probable that you will need additional volunteer helpers. Some tasks (such as sending out invitations or fulfilling orders for T-shirts) will need to be done ahead of the event, but much of them will consist of providing on-the-day support. You may need stewards, ushers, refreshment sellers and other similar roles to ensure your event runs smoothly. Make sure you identify and assign distinct roles and brief everyone as to what they need to do.

Office volunteers

There are likely to be tasks which volunteers can take on to enhance the work of your fundraisers and help to keep your programme running. There are a variety of options here, including administrative tasks (such as data entry), research (such as finding potential suppliers) and stewardship of other supporters (such as making welcome calls to people who sign up for your latest community initiative).

Professional volunteers

This type of volunteer supports your programme by donating their professional skills. This could involve marketing your latest event, creating dedicated web pages for a new initiative or running a training session for your staff. It may also be advantageous to join up with your corporate fundraisers and develop pro bono relationships with relevant businesses.

Specialist volunteers

These are people who have an ongoing volunteering commitment to your organisation in a specific role, which may require some initial training. Perhaps the most common type here is volunteer speakers who are trained to talk about your work; they volunteer on an occasional basis, attending specific engagements. The most motivated may seek out their own speaking opportunities.

Celebrities and influencers

Often celebrities and influencers who lend their voice and profile to your cause will do so on a voluntary basis. Making the most of this type of support requires specific consideration.

[...]

Deciding what volunteers can do

Working with volunteers is very rewarding but it can also be time-consuming, and you will need to find the right balance for your programme about what tasks can be supported by volunteers and what needs to be done by an experienced fundraiser. You can coach and train a volunteer to increase their capacity, but this will have to be balanced by the amount of time, both in frequency and longevity, that they are able to offer you. If, for instance, a volunteer can only give time on an occasional basis rather than a regular block of time each week, you will have to decide whether you will always have enough useful work for them to do.

[...]

Stewardship of volunteers

Stewardship broadly refers to the various stages of looking after a group of people – in this case, volunteers. You will need to develop different stewardship plans for each audience or type of volunteer with whom you work. There are essentially three stages in taking somebody from being an interested member of the public to someone who fundraises for or donates to your organisation:

- recruit;
- activate;
- retain.

By taking appropriate action at these three stages, you can get people involved in events and then retain their interest and involvement for the future.

Understanding the pros and cons of special events

Pauline Carter, 2009

What are special events?

There are different views in the sector about what makes a special event, and whether or not to include local community fundraising under that same general umbrella. The definition that I use is:

> A high-profile event, which stands out from normal fundraising events by offering exclusive activities and involving intensive planning and organisation, often using the support of a dedicated voluntary steering committee.

Examples of special events include:

- Sporting events
- Balls and dinners
- Musical and cultural events
- Receptions
- Exhibitions, fairs and festivals
- Conferences and challenge events

[…]

Local 'bread and butter' events such as coffee mornings and jumble sales are not included within the definition of 'special events'. Local community fundraising plays an important part in income generation for a charity because local events can spread the word and reach parts of local communities that central fund raising cannot, but the main difference is that usually they are run by small, dedicated volunteer committees, with minimum central support from the charity. While this can give them some scope to be more adventurous and to be run more frequently, usually they do not require or attract major sponsorship, or have value added tax (VAT) implications. Therefore, on the whole they are similar to organise and run, but this is by no means to denigrate the importance of volunteer and local fundraising.

[…]

When planned well, special events can help support wider organisational strategy, raise the profile of the charity and, of course, raise funds. They can go hand-in-hand with a corporate fundraising programme as a way of encouraging

DOI: 10.4324/9781003145936-54

Table 3.3.1 Special events: pros and cons

Pros of nonprofit special events	Cons of nonprofit special events
Directly rewarding in terms of income generation	Results unpredictable, particularly when insufficient planning has taken place prior to the event
Can support further income generation as part of a fundraising strategy – links to corporate partnerships, major donors	Needs to be planned well in advance
Raises profile of the charity	Requires a great deal of time and effort
Generate publicity and promotion for the charity	Higher-risk element
Manageable as part of a three- to five-year strategy	Potentially high cost to income ratio
Reaches a wide audience not only those already interested in the cause, but those interested in the event itself	Can appear attractive to amateurs, but requires a professional approach to be successful
Attracts new audiences that may be strategically important to the organisation	Results unpredictable, particularly when insufficient planning has taken place prior to the event

companies to get involved and demonstrate their corporate social responsibility, and as a good way to develop a long-term partnership with a company.

[…]

Reviewing your existing strategy

Even if you are working within an established framework, it will be worth your while to take a step back to review your strategy. Look at what your charity has been organising in the way of events in the past. Do you want to continue in the same way? Have previous events achieved their objectives? Is the same format still appropriate, or are there good reasons to change, for example: fewer resource is in your events team; change of key staff; change in the focus of the charity; change in giving patterns; change in profitability?

Key questions to consider

At this stage of thinking, you need to decide on the following.

Should we be doing events at all? Do you have sufficient resource is to invest in an events programme? Are other sources of fund raising more reliable or profitable? Do not carry on doing events just because you have in the past, or start doing them because others are – they are not for everyone, and you need to be clear what your positive reasons are for doing them at all.

How do events fit with the organisation's strategy? What does your organisation exist to do, and is there a natural tie in with particular types of events? Are there things coming up in the organisational plan which could be supported by events, such as a name change, new campaign or project, or a plan to grow the organisation? Remember that events can help to raise your organisation's profile or launch an appeal, as well as raise money for ongoing activity. Creating synergy between your events plan and your organisational plan can maximise the potential of both.

How often will we put on events? Are you just looking at a one-off to support a particular need, or do you want to develop events as a regular source of income for your charity? Do you want one major event on an annual basis or a regular number of smaller events, or both? It takes a lot of effort and expertise to run a successful event, and however many you do, and whatever their profile, you need to make sure you are realistic about the level of resources you will need to do it.

How far ahead will we need to plan and budget for? Many organisations have a three to five year rolling plan, but smaller organisations may plan for one or two years ahead. A three to five-year plan will set a clear direction of travel, but you may need to be flexible and keep it under review as the organisational plan changes and depending on your own progress and external circumstances. However, you do need to allow realistic leading time for organising major events.

[…]

Who needs to sign off or agree the strategy? Because events can be resource-intensive and high-risk, you need to make sure that the overall strategy is known, approved of and supported at the highest level in your organisation. You may need to prepare a paper outlining the overall strategy for events, highlighting the benefits and risks, the assumptions (such as the level of resource provided) and contingency plans, and have it agreed by the trustees, chief executive and/or head of fundraising.

What is your longer term aim for objective for events? … what do you hope to achieve with an events programme: what is your total financial target, and over how long a period? How many new supporters do you hope to enlist, and is there an overall message about your organisation that you want to get across over several events?

What is your past experience with events? How long did they take to organise, how much did they cost, what was the net income? Look at both successes and problem areas, and consider whether they can be replicated or overcome in your current circumstances, especially with regard to staffing and resources.

[…]

Identifying the primary goal or aspiration

Events can have multiple purposes, but you need to know what the primary goal of your event is, so can focus on taking the necessary steps to achieve it. Is your goal:

- fundraising?
- raising the organisation's profile?

- thanking supporters?
- gaining new supporters?

Look at your [special] event in the context of the wider event strategy and decide what the primary goal or aspiration for the event is.

Setting specific objectives and targets

How much do you plan to raise? … Give yourself a specific target, but choose a realistic, even cautious, figure rather than wishful thinking. You have to feel that you can achieve or even exceed it, in order to stay motivated. Make sure that your target figure is the amount you raise after costs, so it represents the real return to your charity. If you plan to increase the level of long-term support arising from this event, put a figure on this as well, and a time frame in which you are going to measure this.

How many people do you want to attend or participate? What messages do you want to get across through the event? How much wider coverage do you hope to achieve, and do you want this in the local, regional or national press? Remember that profile will be about quality as well as quantity, so add a measure that counts how much positive coverage or feedback you get.

How many supporters do you want to attend? The aim here should be for them to enjoy the events, but also to feel even more engaged with the cause, and you may need to find a way to measure this (for example, through feedback forms). If your primary aim is to thank supporters rather than fundraise at the event, you need to be very clear about how much you can afford to spend, but do remember it is an investment in ongoing support.

[…]

Some tools for strategic analysis

There are many tried and tested tools used in the wider strategic planning environment which can be applied equally to help you focus and assess your strategy with regard to special events. These tools provide a framework to help you look at internal factors, such as organisational strengths and weaknesses, as well as prompting you to look at the wider world and how it is likely to impact on what you plan to do.

[…]

PEST analysis

PEST (Political-Economic-Social-Technological) is a well-used method for looking at the overall external environment in which you are operating. It works in the same way as a SWOT analysis [which considers Strengths, Weaknesses, Opportunities and Threats], by listing any key factors under each heading which may have either a negative or positive impact on your plans. The crucial part is to analyse what the overall impact might be, and what your best strategy would be, given the constraints and opportunities that the environment provides for you.

[…]

Boston Matrix

This is a tool you can use to assess the success of previous events in order to decide your future strategy: which ones to invest in more, and which ones to drop and which ones form part of a reliable core activity and income stream. In using this tool it is important to be aware of the product life-cycle and where your events are on this curve – just because an event has been a runaway success in previous years does not mean it will continue to be so forever – you may need to find ways of refreshing or leaving on a high.

To use this tool, first list your current events. Without thinking too deeply about it, write next to each one the reasons why you do it. Be honest: if you do it because it's a fixture, say it's a fixture. If you do it because it's the chair [of the board's] favourite, write that down. If you do it for the income, write it down.

When you have finished looking at the actual reasons why you do these events, find out how much each one costs to put on (remember to include staff costs), and how much income each generates. Then try to fit your current events to their place in the following matrix (Figure 3.3.1).

Cash cows

These are special events that have a higher market share and are easily reproduced. They have a reputation for being excellent events: tickets sell well,

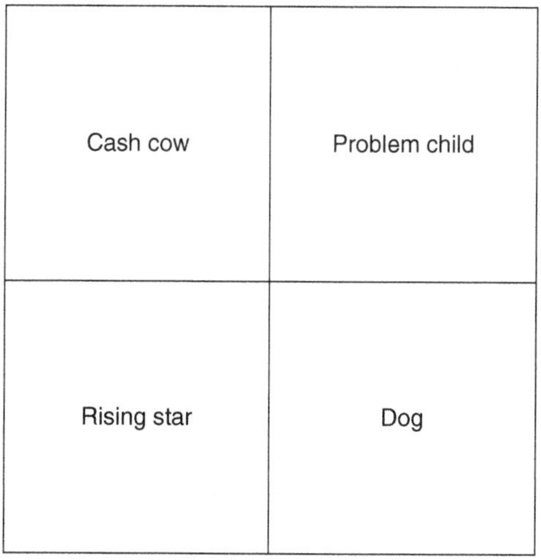

Cash cow	Problem child
Rising star	Dog

Figure 3.3.1 Boston Matrix

the communities are already set up and although they still require a good amount of time and effort, they will not be too much of a problem to organise. There is still a need to look at the product life cycle to avoid being complacent.

Rising stars

These are new events requiring time and effort to reproduce, which have winning prospects of becoming a cash cow, and are worth investing in and developing.

Problem children

These events can consume cash and resources at an alarming rate. They are problems, but can they be turned into cash cows? They cannot be allowed to continue as they are – one option is to get rid of them, but it may be worth spending some time and effort researching how they can be resurrected. You may be able to change around poorly performing events by being clear about your goals, better at marketing and making the most of opportunities.

Dogs

These have a low market share, low growth and do not generally generate significant cashflow: time for the charity to shut its ears to cries of 'But we really enjoy these events!' from supporters and bite the bullet. If they do not sell or achieve their objectives, and are a pain to produce, then kick them into touch. Time is money and the charity would be better off spending that time and money on rising stars and even problem children.

[...]

The product life-cycle

Just like any other product, events tend to follow marketplace rules in terms of a life-cycle: at the planning stage of a new event, you will spend more time and money putting it together, then it will gain its own momentum, popularity and success. However, as with all successful products, interest will tail off and it will become boring unless you spot the right time to change or tweak it in some way.

[...]

Events need to change and develop over time in response to customer needs, competitive activity and perhaps legislation; few (even good) special events will last forever and most will benefit from regular refreshment. There are four phases.

1. Introduction – launch and conception. At this stage you will need to spend more time and more money to get the event off the ground. You

will be taking some risks and trying out new ideas and will need to put a lot of effort into raising awareness and support.

2. Growth – an established event. Event objectives are achieved, awareness has increased, and the event is perceived by supporters to be an excellent event, giving good value for money: 'the place to be'.
3. Maturity – the event is in demand. Everyone who wants to attend has difficulty in acquiring tickets. Tickets go without too much marketing, more via word of mouth. Objectives are overachieved.
4. Decline – too many other charities have jumped on the bandwagon and are copying your charity's event. The event is no longer the novelty or 'the place to be'. Tickets are still selling, but with difficulty. More time and money is being spent on promotion. Objectives are not quite achieved.

The time to change the event is just before maturity: begin to tweak a few elements and then in the following years make further change. Alternatively, you can drop the event altogether and do something completely different. ... Never try to resuscitate an event once it's going [into irreversible decline].

How to make your writing interesting

Tom Ahern, 2007

How to interest people: a checklist

Here's a checklist of some things I consider when I write for donors or prospects:

- Have I said what amazing things the organization did (or would do) with their gifts? Did I mention worthwhile results? Real accomplishments?
- Did I link these accomplishments back to charitable giving?
- Did I celebrate the donor as the hero? (In other words, did I say in some fashion over and over, "This good work would not be possible without your help.")
- Did I talk about the organization's cost efficiency? (In surveys, donors often say that they believe charities are poorly run. And this already high level of skepticism is increasing.)

Am I taking advantage of human psychology?:

- Am I telling (and showing) people things they don't know? That is, does my information have news value? Is it unique or innovative? Are my photos surprising in some way?
- Is it bold, passionate? (Not bland, predictable, or boring.)
- Am I aiming for the heart? Have I included plenty of emotional triggers (fear, anger, greed, exclusivity, scarcity)?
- Is the word "you" used often?

[…]

- Is the tone conversational rather than formal?
- Am I making it easy for skimmers, flippers, and browsers to glean information? If, for instance, someone reads just the headlines, will the person still understand my key messages?
- Is the publication as a whole a quick read? Am I writing short sentences? Am I using action verbs? Have I eliminated jargon?
- Since anecdotes are the fastest way to explain anything, am I using anecdotes to illuminate our most pressing issues?

DOI: 10.4324/9781003145936-55

- Am I using my statistical evidence like a spear, to make a single important point?
- Can I use testimonial anywhere, to inspire the faithful and calm the doubters?
- People want to act. Have I made at least one offer they can respond to?

Secret to response: the offer is king

The purpose of an offer is simple: it gives the reader a reason to respond to you right now.

Every day, you probably weigh dozens of offers yourself.

In every catalogue you receive, each item is an offer. When you buy lunch, "Would you like fries with that?" is an offer. When you visit a website, pretty much anything you can click on, including the word "more", is in fact an offer.

But wait, there's more: The richer you make your offer, the stronger the response. An irresistible offer overcomes hesitance and inertia. That's why challenges and matching gift campaigns often boost fundraising income significantly – people want to take advantage of a limited-time offer. We absolutely, positively adore multiplying our gift to a favorite charity … without in fact spending a penny more. And we don't want to miss the chance.

Direct marketing professionals say, "The offer is king." They mean: Find the right offer, and response pours in.

Conversely, without any offers, expect no response. I mention this because I see, for example, plenty of donor newsletters containing no offers at all. (And you wonder why no one ever calls or writes?).

Don't bury your offer

Making an offer ("Call this number for more information") at the end of a long article guarantees that most people will miss it.

Celebrate every offer you make. Make it big, bold, easy to spot.

What's in an offer?

Remember: the purpose of offers is to stimulate response. And you're probably already making offers. Each appeal letter you send is an offer, for instance. Essentially you're saying: "Send us a gift, and we'll make the world a better place in your name."

Other common offers from fundraisers include:

- "For more information"
- An invitation to join an exclusive society such as a President's Circle
- An invitation to an event …
- A naming opportunity
- A behind-the-scenes tour
- A cow (see below)

Heifer's four-footed offers: making the intangible real

Heifer Project International has a simple plan for ending world hunger: they give poor people livestock that produce food and income, as well as training in how to keep the animals healthy and reproductive. It's the "teach a man to fish" philosophy in action.

In a recent year, Heifer raised roughly $45 million from individuals for its work in 51 countries. How? In part, through offers in what it calls "the most important gift catalog in the world."

The Heifer catalog offers donors the chance to buy an animal suitable for farming ... There is an interesting communications strategy behind these offers. Heifer has taken something fairly intangible (its mission, and the donor's hope that "my gift will make the world a better place") and turned it into something quite tangible: a pig or other bountiful creature put into a person's needy hands. "Nothing's more satisfying than finding exactly the right solution to a problem," says Heifer. "That's the good feeling you get when you give an Asian subsistence farmer a water buffalo."

I can see it. I can almost smell it.

Now in truth you are not buying a specific animal for a specific family in a specific country. Nor are you benefiting a specific child with your gift to a development agency such as Plan International, to give another example. The child's entire community benefits from your gift.

Heifer makes this clear in the fine print: "The prices in this catalog represent the complete livestock gift of a quality animal, technical assistance and training. Each purchase is symbolic and represents a contribution to the entire mission of Heifer International. Donations will be used where needed most to help struggling people." So, yes, it's a symbolic purchase. But the bottom line is, somebody somewhere still gets a cow.

The lesson is this: when you can make your mission more tangible, it's easier for the prospect to imagine the result. In turn, when prospects can easily imagine the result, they're more likely to become donors. They can see the mission in their mind's eye. It's real. It's not a promise. It's a promise fulfilled.

Heifer International has made its mission tangible through livestock offers. What can you offer that will tangibly symbolize your mission? A university selling $2 million endowed chairs offers pictures of 20 assorted chairs, different styles from different periods, throne to recliner, wittily chosen. Each has a space on it labeled, "Your name here."

What's your tangible symbol?

[...]

Anecdotes bring your success vividly to life

Anecdotes in the service of fundraising come in many shapes and sizes, some no more than a few words long. They all share a goal, though: to bring to life in the readers mind a picture of success. Telling people that your program works is nice. But showing them that it works, in the intimate theatre of their very own heads, is far more powerful. Here are some ideas to bring your success to vivid life for the reader:

There's the *"before-and-after"* anecdote. … *Before:* she was a classroom left behind. *After:* she was a classroom champ. Here's another before-and-after example from a case statement:

> Every year more than 3,000 Providence public school students face some kind of learning crisis that could end their chances of a successful school career. And then one of our volunteer tutors walks in the door. (Volunteers in Providence Schools)

A twist on the before-and-after formula is the "now-and-what's-possible" anecdote. This anecdote conveys your vision and invites participation. It has a built-in call to action. Here's an example from Literacy Volunteers of Massachusetts:

> Nearly 880,000 adults in Massachusetts lack functional literacy skills. That means that they can't complete job applications or read newspapers, road signs, or medicine labels. But you can help.

Now there's a vivid mental picture someone in a bathroom somewhere, staring at a prescription bottle, not knowing what it says. *But I can help*, I remind myself.

Testimonial is often anecdotal in nature (it describes a situation in someone's life) and can offer proof that a programme has worked. This testimonial appeared in the Calgary United Way newsletter alongside a photo of a mother and child: "I believe that if I hadn't had SOPHIA house my son and I would not be alive today." A totally persuasive endorsement in a mere 18 words.

Just as persuasive is *"look-at-the-lives-you've-contributed-to"* material. Saint Mary's University of Minnesota inspired prospective donors with a speedy little booklet called "Profiles – Your gifts at work."

The booklet profiled six students who received assistance from various endowed and annual scholarship. The profiles were short and sweet. Each consisted of a beaming close up photo; a statement from the student about how much her or his scholarship meant; add a brief, breezy, bulleted backgrounder that included major, minor, favourite professors, volunteer activities, and last but not least "post-SMU plans." One young woman's intentions: "Politics and the Oval Office." I know I'm impressed. People want to be on the winning team, people including donors.

Then there's the *"Surprise!"* anecdote. The "Surprise!" anecdote overturns expectations. It has a very simple formula, enshrined throughout comedy as well as journalism. It's a formula that hooks not only the Amiable side of the personality but also the Expressive; a two-fer.

Here's how it works: You point the reader in one direction – then you head the opposite way … a first-rate example that ran as a headline in the *New York Times*: Help For The Hardest Part Of Prison: Staying Out. I confess: "Staying

Out" wasn't my first guess (or 100th), so this caught my eye. Surprise me, and I'm yours.

In another example from the Housatonic Youth Service Bureau, the Surprise! anecdote foreshadows doom – yet delivers salvation.

> *For an agency made necessary by drug and alcohol abuse, teen pregnancy, child depression, youth unemployment, truancy and dropping out, family violence, runaways, homelessness, and petty crime … we're remarkably happy. Must be all the changes we see in the people we help.*

The zig: an intense litany of serious trouble. The zag: an organization happy because it has clearly improved its community by helping individuals and families overcome their demons and dangers.

The champion effect in peer-to-peer fundraising

Cassandra M. Chapman, Barbara M. Masser, and Winnifred R. Louis, 2019

Using a unique combination of survey and behavioral data from 1,647 online peer-to-peer fundraisers (whom we call "champions"), we tested empirically the influence of different best practices on fundraising success ... Across two samples, we found the fundraiser's identification with the cause led them to engage in more best practice actions, which in turn led to greater fundraising success. However, not all actions were equally influential.

[…]

We propose that success in the peer-to-peer fundraising context is influenced more by the champion than by the charity – a phenomenon we call the Champion Effect. Thus, while peer-to-peer fundraisers may be motivated by their connection with the cause, their donors are most likely to give because of their connection with the fundraiser. We argue that, if champions are key determinants of fundraising success, then fundraisers will succeed to the degree that they make it clear that success is important to them.

[…]

Peer-to-peer fundraising harnesses the social connections of charity supporters to promote causes within social networks. Individual fundraisers become advocates for their favorite causes by asking friends, family, and colleagues for donations on behalf of a charity, often as sponsorship of fundraisers' participation in endurance or symbolic events. In an increasingly networked society, where consumers are more likely to trust peer endorsement than traditional marketing communications, leveraging peer-to-peer networks is likely to become an increasingly important component of nonprofit fundraising success.

[…]

Outside of the academic domain, the charity sector itself has highlighted particular "best practice" actions that individual fundraisers should take. Best practices are those actions that fundraising professionals identify as being most effective in raising money. For example, industry reports suggest that fundraisers who send more emails to their networks and who tell a story about why they are fundraising are more successful. Blogs targeted at fundraising practitioners suggest diverse tactics, including setting a low initial target, personalizing the fundraising page, asking for specific donation values, sending targeted emails, and sharing fundraising pages via social media.

[…]

DOI: 10.4324/9781003145936-56

While fundraisers themselves may be motivated by their identification with the cause they have nominated, we propose it will be the actions they choose to take in fundraising that will primarily determine their fundraising outcomes. If relational altruism motivates donors in peer-to-peer contexts, any action that signals the importance of fundraising success to the fundraiser will be particularly influential in reaching fundraising targets. Such actions include asking for donations, setting an ambitious target, and making their own identity and motivation a key component of their campaign.

Specifically, we hypothesize the following:

Hypothesis 1 (H1): Fundraisers' identification with the cause, their solicitation efforts, signaled investment, and signaled efficacy will all positively predict amount raised.

Hypothesis 2 (H2): Fundraiser actions (solicitation, signaled investment, and signaled efficacy) will mediate the relationship between fundraiser identification and amount raised.

Hypothesis 3 (H3): Solicitation and signaled fundraiser investment, both of which make the champion salient, will be stronger predictors of amount raised than signaled charity efficacy.

[…]

Across two field samples with online peer-to-peer fundraisers, we find support for all hypotheses related to the notion that fundraising outcomes within peer networks are influenced strongly by the fundraising champions themselves. Specifically, across both samples, we find that fundraisers who identified more with their selected charity, and who took more actions to solicit donations, signal their personal investment, and signal the efficacy of the charity, raised more money (supporting H1). The fundraiser's greater identification with the cause was associated with taking more actions, which in turn was associated with greater fundraising success (supporting H2). All actions are not equal, however. Asking for donations through more channels and, especially, actions that signaled the fundraisers' personal investment in the outcome were stronger predictors of fundraising success than actions that signaled the efficacy of the charity in question (supporting H3), respectively explaining at least 8 and 20 times the variance in amount raised. While these findings will be intuitive to practitioners and to many scholars, they have not been demonstrated empirically before.

[…]

The focal hypothesis that the champion would be an important determinant of fundraising success in the online peer-to-peer context was strongly supported. In both samples, actions that made the fundraiser and their investment salient – such as uploading a photo, personalizing their fundraising page, articulating their reasons for fundraising, and setting a high target – were those most strongly associated with fundraising outcomes. Although we do not test donor motivations, these findings are consistent with Kim Scharf and Sarah Smith's assertion that people give in peer-to-peer contexts because they care about the fundraiser and they know the fundraiser cares about raising money.

[…]

In the fundraising literature, it has been shown that people are more likely to give when they are asked to donate by someone known to them, and that donors tend to respond more favorably to fundraisers who are close to them. In the peer-to-peer domain, fundraisers are almost certainly known to the donors. We argue throughout that signaling investment may make reputation salient to the donor. One important way that fundraisers signal their investment is to ask more often, and through more channels. In this way, solicitation may amplify the perceived relational consequences – whether positive or negative – of the donor's response. Indeed, within the wider literature, concerns about reputation have been observed to affect charitable responses. In the peer-to-peer context, where relationships between fundraiser and donor are personal, solicitation factors may be especially powerful. Beyond mere solicitation, fundraisers can also draw attention to themselves (and indirectly highlight potential reputational consequences) by signaling personal investment in their campaign. It has been argued before that peer-to-peer donors give, at least in part, because they care about the fundraiser, they understand the fundraiser cares about the cause, and they want the fundraiser to succeed. We propose that signalling investment in the campaign evokes reputation because it makes clear that the fundraiser will be paying attention to donor responses. Results here show that actions that signal investment are indeed strong determinants of fundraising success.

Setting a high target was the strongest unique predictor of fundraising success. We interpret this finding as showing that people who are more identified with their cause also set a higher fundraising target, indicating that targets are determined at least in part by fundraiser motivation. Fundraisers could, however, adjust their targets during the campaign, and the current data cannot differentiate between those who set a high initial target and those who set a lower initial target but raised it as their campaign progressed. It must also be acknowledged that targets may also be determined by such pragmatic concerns as perceived wealth and size of the network in question. That is to say, in addition to their personal investment, fundraisers surely consider how many people they know well enough to ask for a donation, and the relative resources those people hold, when determining an appropriate target.

[…]

The perceived efficacy of a charity generally influences fundraising success, and as hypothesized, signaling charity efficacy was associated with greater donations in the two samples here. Yet the role of signaled efficacy was less important in promoting fundraising success than other factors. After accounting for champion-related actions – solicitation and signaled investment – promoting the efficacy of the charity or donations explained no more than 1% of extra variance in the amount raised. These results support the idea that champions are more important drivers of fundraising outcomes in the peer-to-peer domain than charities are.

[…]

Overall, evidence presented in this article supports the assertion that peer-to-peer giving is influenced by a champion effect, where campaign success is determined more by actions highlighting fundraisers than actions highlighting causes. Two factors are of particular importance: asking through more channels (solicitation) and fundraisers' signaling the importance of the outcome to them personally (signaled investment). Fundraisers themselves are likely to be motivated by the cause in question and may, therefore, select tactics aligned to their own motives (e.g., promoting the effectiveness of the charity in achieving its mission) while potentially neglecting tactics that could motivate others (e.g., promoting themselves and their connection with the cause). Our data speak to this phenomenon. Therefore, charities should intervene and educate individual fundraisers to help them to prioritize their efforts. Fundraisers should be encouraged to ask for donations through as many channels as possible and to ensure that their campaigns are personalized with photos, high targets, and articulation of their investment and motives.

3.4 Working with corporate donors and partners

What, why and how do companies give?

Dwight F. Burlingame and Adrian Sargeant, 2010

Data from Giving USA tell us that corporate support of the nonprofit sector represents only a small percentage of donated income, at a mere 5 percent of all voluntary giving. This amount includes the value of cash support, corporate foundation grantmaking, and in-kind donations. It does not include several key forms of corporate support, such as sponsorships and cause-related marketing. These are not included in the Giving USA figures.

[…]

For all practical purposes, corporate support of charitable activities is a twentieth-century invention. In the nineteenth century, most court rulings rendered corporate giving for charitable purposes [in the USA] unlawful unless such giving was business related. Laissez-faire arguments of the time were not unlike the argument put forth by Milton Friedman that company management should not give away stockholders' money because it is the "social responsibility of business … to increase its profits," nothing more.

Many point to business support of the YMCA [Young Men's Christian Association] by the railroads in the early twentieth century in order to provide "safe" housing for workers as the beginning of corporate philanthropy. Indeed, given the consequences of this activity, we might prefer the terms *strategic corporate giving,* or *enlightened self-interest.* The majority of corporate support of nonprofit organizations over the last century could be characterised as self-interested rather than as interest for others or the public good. This is an important realization for anyone conducting fundraising, because it provides the context for building a successful corporate development program – one that is built on seeking gifts that benefit both parties.

[…]

Why do corporations give?

Burlingame and Young developed four models of how companies approach their volunteering and giving to nonprofits. The utilization of these models provides fundraisers with a context in which to approach businesses for support for their missions:

1. Corporate productivity or neoclassical model
2. Ethical or altruistic model

DOI: 10.4324/9781003145936-58

3.   Political (external and internal) model
4.   Stakeholder model

1. Corporate productivity or neoclassical model

This model starts from the basic premise that corporate giving helps companies increase profits and return more value to shareholders. From this perspective, the term corporate philanthropy is oxymoronic, and terms such as corporate citizenship and strategic philanthropy would better convey the purpose of the engagement between the company and the nonprofit. Types of giving that are clearly in line with this model are as follows:

• Projects that help market company products, such as sponsorships, cause-related marketing, and other partnerships
• Projects that improve employee morale and thus increase productivity
• Projects that facilitate the improvement of the public image of the company
• Projects that lower corporate costs, such as grants for research by nonprofits that lower the company's internal expenditures for product development

The opportunity for the fundraiser is to match the organization's mission and activities with the company's desire for improved productivity along the lines just noted. Fundraisers will want to facilitate corporate personnel's understanding of how gifts and support to the nonprofit can contribute to the company's bottom line, whether directly or indirectly. In strategic giving, the benefits sought by a business from its relationship with a nonprofit might include: increased sales; brand differentiation; enhanced brand image; improved employee recruitment, morale, and retention; demonstration of shared values with the target market; enhanced government relations; a broadened customer base; and the ability to reach new customer segments.

2. Ethical or altruistic model

By contrast, the classical notion of corporate philanthropy is based on the premise that businesses and their leaders have a responsibility to be good corporate citizens, and corporate giving and volunteering are ways to demonstrate this responsibility to society. It also assumes that corporations have discretionary resources. When a company is in difficult economic times, one would not expect giving to be based on this model. The giving program must have the capacity to alert corporate leaders to community priorities and to where the company might be a partner in seeking solutions. Types of giving consistent with this model are as follows:

• Projects that address community need where the company operates or has markets
• Projects that appeal to corporate leadership, individually or as citizens
• Projects that engage employees in community efforts to address local issues

Fundraisers need to be keenly aware of how gifts to their organizations will benefit the community through the engagement of employees and corporate leaders.

3. Political model

The political model is played out both externally and internally in many businesses. The external form is based on the idea that corporations use giving to build relationships that protect corporate power and influence, thereby limiting governmental control over companies. Types of giving that are consistent with this model are projects that build closer bonds between the nonprofit and the company. Efforts that substitute for government action are typical, and a joint project between a manufacturer and an environmental charity to benefit the environment would be a good example.

The internal paradigm is built on the premise that the corporate giving officer has a political agenda of his or her own and seeks to justify his or her work to the internal corporate community. From this perspective, corporate giving programs must therefore facilitate the building of alliances with human resources, marketing, research, and public relations so that these aspects of the business can see the value of nonprofit support to them. Giving that is consistent with this model includes employee volunteering, sponsorships, cause-related marketing, partnerships, and educational programs for employees.

From this perspective, fundraisers will want to be strategic in assessing how they engage with all units of the company, not just the corporate giving unit. Projects that are relevant and that meet the needs of the non-profit while also meeting the needs of the company become foremost. Building a multifaceted case for support is crucial in maximizing giving.

4. Stakeholder model

The stakeholder theory of corporate giving is based on the idea that the corporation is a complex entity that must respond to the needs and pressures of a variety of key stakeholders, including shareholders, employees, suppliers, customers, community groups, and governmental officials. Under this framework, managing the company is best accomplished by managing the various stakeholder interests. Thus, to be effective, corporate giving activities need to address various stakeholder interests. Types of giving consistent with this model are as follows:

- Employee benefit or volunteerism projects
- Community education or environmental projects
- Projects that help consumers of company products or services

This model can apply to all businesses, irrespective of size. Whether in a large business or a small one, management interacts with a variety of interested parties. Fundraisers should concentrate their efforts on the identification of key stakeholder groups and on developing project proposals that will articulate the nonprofit mission in a way that appeals to these groups.

These four models provide a theoretical framework for understanding corporate engagement efforts. They are not mutually exclusive. Burlingame and Young recognize that all or some of the models may be operating within a corporation at any one time.

[…]

The Committee Encouraging Corporate Philanthropy [CECP] draws a distinction between three categories of motives:

1. *Charitable*: Little or no business benefit is expected, such as matching gift programs and undirected bulk gifts made to an in-kind distributor.
2. *Community investment*: Gifts serve the dual purpose of supporting the long-term strategic goals of the business and meeting a critical community need,
3. *Commercial*: Benefit to the corporation is the primary motivation, such as cause-related marketing and sponsorship of charity events.

Forms of business support

Whatever the initial motive is for engaging with a nonprofit, there are a variety of forms of corporate support that can be solicited. Following is selection of the most common forms.

Cash donations. These remain the most common form of corporate support of nonprofits, and in many countries (including the United States) they are popular partly because corporation tax benefits can accrue as a consequence of the gift.

Donations of stocks and shares. In some countries, corporations can elect to give stocks and shares to a nonprofit of their choice. Again, this is typically tax efficient, because the gift accrues a tax deduction equal to the value of the shares at the time of donation.

Publicity. Nonprofits can gain from association with a business because the business may promote its link to the cause and thereby heighten public awareness of the issue and the organization. Häagen Dazs, for example, has created a campaign to help endangered bees. It has set up a micro[web]site that promotes the fact that honey bees are in danger and offers the opportunity to help them by buying Häagen Dazs's "bee-dependent" flavors Häagen Dazs then makes donations to Pennsylvania State University and the University of California at Davis, which have two of the world's leading honey bee research facilities.

Gifts of products and services (also known as gift-in-kind). Frequently the goods or services produced by a corporation can be of value to the beneficiaries of a charity. The donation of food at or near its "sell by" or expiration date to soup kitchens is one such example. The donation of computer equipment to schools and colleges is also common, and gifts of office equipment, furniture, computer supplies, or even photocopying facilities have been reported. There are now specialist charities that encourage corporations to provide gifts of this type; they act as clearinghouses for organizations that wish to find appropriate recipients.

Staff time. Some corporations agree to loan staff to a nonprofit where specific expertise, such as management expertise or technical expertise, is being sought, to assist in improving the service provision to beneficiaries. Other corporations are willing to release staff who can work as volunteers with the nonprofit in whatever way is desired. Indeed, some companies have even created their own volunteer departments, complete with budget and staff.

[…]

Sponsorship. Corporations are often willing to sponsor a particular aspect of a nonprofit's service provision in return for an acknowledgment or perhaps placement of the organization's name or logo at an event or on the nonprofit's communications or web site. Organizations may also sponsor events or gala dinners that offer brand enhancement to the corporation while also facilitating fundraising for the nonprofit from those present.

[…]

Employee Fundraising. Corporations sometimes open up access to their workforce for other forms of fundraising. A variety of activities may typically be organized to solicit funds from members of the workforce. Each of these activities may be established either as a standalone program or as part of an integrated pattern of corporate support in which the organization too will participate in giving, perhaps through a variety of the methods already discussed.

[…]

Workplace giving or federated funds… These serve as a contribution vehicle for donors to direct charitable dollars to the groups and issues they care about. A payroll gift to the federation is usually distributed to all of the member organizations, or donors can target gifts to specific groups in the federation. The most familiar federated fund [in the USA] is probably the United Way, but there are many others … Federated funds are popular with businesses because they provide a safe and convenient way for employees to contribute to charities. Companies sometimes match gifts that their employees make through workplace giving programs. The downside of federated funds is that new or small nonprofits or these with unique or offbeat missions are often not included.

Employee matching gifts. Employee matching gifts are contributions from a corporate employer that match contributions to a charitable organization by a corporate employee … Some matching gift programs are open-ended, matching any support that might be offered. More usually, however, an annual ceiling is imposed, either for the program as a whole or for the amounts that individual employees can have matched. There may also be restrictions on the categories of nonprofit that can be supported in this way.

Workplace events. The employer may donate time or space for the hosting of a charity event in which members of the staff may participate. This may be a social gathering or dinner, but it may also be an activity such as a sponsored walk or a golf, tennis, swimming, or challenge event. Although it is the employees themselves who fundraise, often an employer will donate funds too, perhaps matching the funds generated by the employees.

Workplace collections. Where particular members of the staff have a link or commitment to a particular cause, they will often raise funds simply by collecting cash donations from their peers. Typically permission would be sought from the employer for this to happen on the work premises and on the employer's time.

Group presentations. Another common form of employee fundraising involves the nonprofit in making a presentation to groups of staff who have expressed an interest in the cause. The goal here is to explain to members of staff how they can get involved with the work of the organization or in fundraising for it and to suggest activities in which these groups of individuals may engage. Such presentations are usually made on the company's premises and on company time.

Cause-Related Marketing. Rajan Varadarajan and Ajay Menon define cause-related marketing (CRM) as "a process of formulating and implementing marketing activities that are characterized by an offer from the firm to contribute a specified amount to a designated cause when customers engage in revenue providing exchanges that satisfy organizational and individual objectives." McDonalds is credited with being the first organization to develop CRM activity, by linking the purchase of their products to a donation to the Ronald McDonald House Charities. It was not until 1983, however, that the term CRM was used for the first time. American Express partnered with the Statue of Liberty restoration committee and donated one per cent for each transaction on its credit card for a three-month period. The program resulted in a $1.7 million "donation" to the Statue of Liberty fund and a reported 28 percent increase in the use of American Express credit cards over the previous year – truly doing well while doing good … It is important to note that the money spent on a CRM campaign is a business expense, not a charitable donation, and is expected to produce a return on investment.

[…]

Such schemes are not without their critics … Angela Eikenberry refers to this class of giving as consumption philanthropy and has prompted considerable debate by arguing that such arrangements do the following:

- Individualize solutions to collective social problems, distracting our attention and resources away from the neediest causes, the most effective interventions, and the act of critical questioning itself.
- Devalue the moral core of philanthropy by making virtuous action easy and thoughtless.
- Obscure the links between markets – their firms, products, and services – and the negative impacts they can have on human well-being.

[…]

Equally, writers such as Corkery and Levine see CRM as little more than a shallow sales ploy that will leave consumers largely unimpressed. More recent empirical work suggests that how consumers feel about a particular scheme is likely to be a function of the degree of benefit that accrues to the nonprofit. Where only paltry sums are donated relative to the value of the product or service, consumers are significantly more likely to react negatively to the scheme. There is thus a strong case for both partners to a CRM initiative to sit down together to work out a mutually beneficial arrangement. There is nothing to be gained on the part of the business by being seen as exploiting the nonprofit partner.

Corporate partnerships: no cash cow

Andrew Peel, 2017

Corporate fundraising is not a fast track to 'easy' or 'big' money and the path to what funding there is can be a difficult one to navigate. Corporate fundraising can be a slow and labour-intensive process, involving long periods of research and analysis, relationship-building and negotiation within the charity and the company, and many dead ends, pitfalls and frustrations along the way. However, if your charity is prepared to invest time and resources in planning, structuring and managing corporate fundraising, and in understanding what companies want from working with you, the benefits for both parties and the communities you serve can be considerable.

From philanthropic support to strategic partnerships

[...]

There is more to corporate fundraising than simply attempting to secure a financial contribution. In fact, while some charities do manage to regularly land significant corporate donations, large no-strings cash gifts are few and far between. Companies are seldom the vast financial reservoirs that many perceive them to be, and those that are tend to feel more beholden to their shareholders than to their communities.

[...]

Many companies that traditionally provided financial support to charities have shifted their focus from philanthropy towards relationships of a more strategic nature: a move, in other words, from donations towards investment of resources, staff expertise and other assets. This change of emphasis has been driven by the need for companies to be seen to be behaving responsibly and for more tangible business benefits to come out of such projects. Consumers now expect a great deal more from businesses, including meaningful social and environmental impact.

This observation is underlined by a 2015 study which revealed that 91% of shoppers worldwide expect companies to do more than make a profit and that 90% would switch to brands that support a good cause, given similar price and quality. Furthermore, the research found that businesses that are not socially responsible run the risk of alienating their customer base, with 90% of those surveyed saying they would boycott companies found to be engaged in irresponsible business practices.

DOI: 10.4324/9781003145936-59

Unfortunately, this shift in emphasis has increased the scale of the task facing charities that target the corporate sector. It presents such organisations with a considerable set of challenges. And yet, for the creative, astute and commercially minded fundraiser, this new climate means that there really is no limit to the ways in which a charity can engage with a company.

This assertion is borne out by a quick trawl through the annual Business Charity Awards, with the winning partnerships revealing the unprecedented depth and scope of many of today's best charity-corporate tie-ups. The 2016 winners, for example, included a partnership between Unilever's Lynx brand [male toiletries] and the male-suicide-prevention charity Campaign Against Living Miserably, aimed at raising awareness of the issue of young male suicide, and a three-year partnership between retailer Halfords [who sell bikes & spare parts] and the charity Re~Cycle, which has resulted in the public donating more than 20,000 unwanted bicycles to be refurbished and reused in Africa.

Focus on value, not cash

[…]

It is evident, then, that corporate fundraisers who think of themselves simply as 'raisers of corporate funds' are going to be destined for frustration and failure. Some might also argue that the very label 'corporate fundraiser', while remaining a useful generic term, has become something of a misnomer because of the need to think about the role in a broader, more strategic way.

The time has come to regard a corporate partner not as the proverbial cash cow to be milked as rapidly as possible but as a multi-dimensional resource that, if managed skilfully, can present a plethora of opportunities for both organisations. For your charity, as well as being a potential source of income, a company might represent a route to heightened awareness, a source of invaluable pro bono support or gifts in kind, or a new audience for challenge events. For the company, the charitable association might provide benefits such as positive PR, staff development opportunities, access to policymakers or improved sales.

To help clarify your charity's corporate offer, one approach is to take a blank sheet of paper and write down, in a column on the left-hand side, a list of anything that the charity does, owns or has planned which might appeal to a company. This should not only include those activities which are fundable in a traditional sense but also those which could provide more innovative ways to engage companies, perhaps by involving their staff, tapping into marketing budgets or securing gifts in kind. This list of products and assets might encompass, for example, the names of your main programmes, projects or services, along with flagship events, publications, shops and other embryonic ideas which could provide reasons to enter into dialogue with a particular company. Along the top of the page, write in headings describing the various ways in which companies could support your charity in relation to each product/asset heading – for example, with financial donations, staff volunteers and gifts in kind. Then put a mark in the matrix where support is most likely, as in Figure 3.4.1.

⇩ Charity X's products ⇩	Philanthropic corporate support	Marketing-led support (such as sponsorship and cause-related marketing)	Charity of the year or staff fundraising	Volunteering or skills exchange	Networking or profile-raising	Trading or earned income	In-kind support
The cause	✓	✓	✓				
Programmes, projects or services							
Older people's day centre	✓	✓	✓	✓			
XYZ campaign	✓	✓	✓				
Youth outreach	✓		✓				
Playgroup	✓		✓	✓			
Mentoring service				✓			✓
Other activities or properties							
Charity shop				✓			✓
Meeting rooms						✓	
Consultancy (training etc.)						✓	✓
Publications	✓	✓					
Brighton marathon		✓	✓	✓			
Future activities or products							
Quarterly business breakfast		✓			✓		✓
Churches' information pack		✓					
Schools' fundraising pack		✓					
Paris bike ride event		✓	✓		✓		
Three peaks challenge		✓	✓		✓		
Mobile phone and inkjet recycling		✓	✓				

Figure 3.4.1 Product matrix: corporate engagement angles

Research carried out for C&E's annual Corporate–NGO Partnerships Barometer reveals that companies' motivations to get involved in charity partnerships usually differ from NGOs': in 2017, 92% (compared to 91% in 2016) of businesses stated that the reputational benefits of associations with NGOs were their key driver, whereas 93% (compared to 92% in 2016) of NGOs stated that the financial returns were their leading reason for partnering. So the key challenge is: how can this difference be reconciled? The answer is that charities and corporates must work together to identify areas of mutual interest and use these drivers as the basis for initial discussions and joint working. Indeed, one area of mutual interest, as identified in the C&E report, is the opportunity to gain access to people and contacts.

Put the customer first

To keep businesses engaged for longer, charities should aim to adopt a broader, more customer-orientated approach to corporate relationships and seek to open them up on a number of mutually beneficial fronts. This will lead to a more equal and sustainable partnership and may even help to generate some of the funding your charity might have originally anticipated.

The main implication of a more externally focused approach is that a big shift in mindset is usually required. The focal point becomes the company's objectives yet with an added awareness of your organisation's strategy, values, brand and offer. This mindset puts you in a strong position to negotiate and balance your charity's needs with those of the company.

[...]

As a stark indicator of the fruitlessness of cold and untargeted approaches, each year, HSBC bank receives around 10,000 unsolicited sponsorship proposals, of which no more than four (0.04%) are successful. Every other major brand marketer will tell a similar story. The challenge when approaching companies, then, is to do whatever homework is necessary to make it into the top 0.04% rather than the bottom 99.96%. This means forensically examining the target company's needs, engaging its people in dialogue and then creating a tailored proposition. By adopting a more outward-facing and customer-led stance, your chances of success will be significantly increased.

[...]

Adopt an organisational approach

Another key principle is that corporate fundraising is unlikely to succeed in a vacuum. It requires a coordinated, organisational approach and, in particular, the support and buy-in of the senior management team and trustees. They must recognise that they have a pivotal role to play in the development of their charity's corporate relationships, whether that is by fronting approaches or pitches, or by using their networks to open doors.

[...]

You may also find that, to deliver on promises and fulfil obligations to companies, you will be dependent upon the support of a wide range of individuals across your charity. It is therefore important to get key colleagues onside as early as possible by encouraging them to think about how the partnership might work for them and collaborating so that the best offer can be presented to companies. In particular, you may find yourself working closely with colleagues in the communications, public relations or press team; the events team; the finance function; the major giving fundraiser(s); the community or regional fundraisers; and, of course, those who are responsible for delivering your charity's programmes and service delivery.

[...]

Corporate partnerships as a platform

If they are well planned and well managed, corporate partnerships can act not only as an income generator but also as a marketing platform or hub upon which your charity can promote its broader vision, services, products and brand. This is particularly the case when working with blue-chip companies with large workforces and customer bases, though it is just as feasible on a smaller or local level, as long as the resources to manage the relationship are available. What is certain is that one well-chosen and well-managed partnership, whether local, regional, national or even international in nature, can open up a range of opportunities for collaboration and lead to a step-change in your charity's profile.

Seven tips for securing corporate sponsorship

Darian Rodriguez Heyman, 2016

Introduction

Corporations are all around us, every day. We buy their products and services, and increasingly, they're interested in partnering with nonprofits to reach more customers, increase employee loyalty, and improve their image. Billions of dollars a year flow from companies to good causes globally, and when pursued strategically, corporate sponsorships can yield significant revenues and bolster awareness of your organization.

Corporate sponsorships are also a great way to align your organization with a brand that people respect and recognize. This can give you legitimacy with people unfamiliar with your cause and bring attention to your nonprofit, specifically to fundraising events. And while getting corporate sponsorships revolves around the same basic principle of all fundraising – building relationships – it does require a slightly different and unique approach.

Unlike foundations, corporations are not in the business of making social impact. Their focus is on driving profits, which in part comes from generating goodwill and loyalty among their consumer base. Take advantage of this: know your audience and what kind of products and companies they use. Consider also the kinds of companies you want your organization and reputation linked with; the intersections you find will lead to valuable fundraising opportunities. In short, if your nonprofit produces an event that gathers decision-makers of any kind, ideally in large numbers, odds are sponsorships are a promising fundraising vehicle for your cause.

To dive deeper into the secrets to successfully securing corporate sponsorships, I sat down with Maureen Carlson, president of Good Scout, a social good consultancy focused on corporate alliances. Carlson shared seven great tips in a straightforward, step-by-step formula.

1. Dedicate personnel

In order to secure corporate sponsorships, you need to identify a champion in your organization dedicated to the task. This can't be the same person coordinating an event, whether it's a gala, luncheon, conference, or run/walk/ride, as that person will have his or her hands full overseeing logistics. Identify someone who can focus on securing meetings and calls and who's able to speak passionately and articulately about your cause and event.

DOI: 10.4324/9781003145936-60

The person you charge with spearheading corporate sponsorship should have a fundraising or sales background, be able to discuss audience size and demographics with sponsor prospects, identify his or her goals, and frame your event in the context of those. In the corporate world, return on investment rules. That means you'll need a good listener who can clearly identify sponsors' interests and priorities, and then speak in a language that's most compelling to them. He or she should excel at stewardship and will need to ensure you fulfill any promises made to sponsors. Above all, your champion needs to be persistent and willing to follow up with people consistently, even if that means being told "no" often.

2. Price yourself right

Once you have a point person spearheading your efforts, the next step is carefully determining sponsor benefits and pricing levels. Think through the demographics of your audience, and consider what kind of decisionmakers you're mobilizing at your event, and how you can offer sponsors valuable access to them. Your marathon doesn't attract youth; it attracts emerging leaders.

Understand the kind of assets your event has in paid, earned, owned, and shared media and how you leverage those assets in your sponsorship packages. Go beyond simply throwing up a logo or sign and offer key sponsors the ability to address your audience and receive recognition in a relevant and customized way. Identify how many people sponsors will reach through each benefit and how valuable each of them is; ultimately, the combination of reach, audience, and engagement drives corporate decision making.

What companies want more than anything is access to their consumers and potential customers. Offer things like logos and short descriptions or ads in event materials, and through all your marketing channels, including the World Wide Web, press releases, email, and social media. If you've enlisted media sponsors [try to include corporate sponsors in any resulting media exposure]. Let sponsors give out product samples and have a physical presence at your event, like a booth or table, or a branded, customized area.

Offer top sponsors things like experiential access to participants [where appropriate], free tickets, recognition from the main stage, and public, post-event recognition. If you have a VIP event or speaker dinner, invite top sponsors and perhaps let them say a word or two. Offer things beyond exposure; benefits that garner goodwill for the sponsor, such as underwriting scholarships.

Some say it's difficult, if not impossible, to share a rule of thumb for pricing sponsorships. Carlson says it's as simple as doing a valuation of your event to understand the overall combined assets around paid, earned, owned, and shared media, combined with the value of aligning with your cause and providing access to your constituents.

[...]

Most nonprofits offer event sponsor packages (like bronze, silver, and gold), plus a la carte opportunities. To share a couple simple examples of what this might look like, a basic sponsorship package typically includes little more than a couple tickets, a logo and description in the program and on the event page, and perhaps a table. The silver level includes more benefits, like signage, more tickets, an ad in the program, verbal recognition, a VIP ticket, and the ability to distribute samples or products. Finally, top sponsors receive all the other benefits, plus a chance to speak from the main stage, a scholarship fund in their name, and inclusion in media sponsor ads promoting the event, customized owned areas, etc.

A la carte options can include underwriting scholarships, sponsoring specific tracks or portions of the event, such as a VIP reception, the finish line, or simply the ability to include a promotional item in the event goody bag. The key here is scale, meaning making sure you provide your most valuable assets to your highest-level sponsors.

3. Create a killer deck

[…]

Creating a professional, well-designed sponsorship packet is your key to success.

If resources are available, Carlson recommends creating your materials using a digital application that allows you to customize it easily and create related follow-up materials. It's also ideal, she adds, to ensure your deck [the slide presentation, using a package such as PowerPoint] can be accessed online so it can be sent as a link, and for it to have impactful, embedded video and infographics. No matter what format and platform you use, your deck should be a smart, stylish representation of your event and your "brand." Your packet should contain a sign-up form if sponsors want to be involved, and the electronic version should be easy to fill out, save, and return, ideally without requiring them to print it.

[…]

4. Fill the pipeline

[…]

Evaluate which prospects are the best fit, especially those you're already connected to. Then look outside your inner circle and find prospects by looking at who sponsors similar events, who the big companies are in your area, and who's already associated with your cause. And remember, it's important to look at every corporate contact you have in your organization, even if he or she is not a traditional "sponsor" of an event yet. Connections are what matter most, and if your relationships are strong enough, you can often layer on this kind of partnership, to the benefit of both your organization and the corporation.

5. Be flexible

Listen to your sponsors and help them meet their needs by creating customized sponsor packages and benefits whenever possible. For example, if a sponsor is more interested in getting product samples into the hands of consumers rather than logo exposure through media, be prepared to mix and match benefits and price. Being flexible will help you secure more sponsors and unlock additional revenue opportunities, but be sure to document any of these one-off custom arrangements to ensure proper fulfillment. If you work with many sponsors and have a small staff, be prepared to leave some money on the table in order to avoid driving your staff crazy.

6. Have a conversation

When you pitch to a corporate sponsor, don't deliver a cookie-cutter presentation. Your pitch should be a conversation and your deck, a framework. Deals are really closed through dialogue, where you listen to sponsors and present a dynamic opportunity based on the needs and priorities they share. Emphasize the benefits you can offer based on what the sponsor is most interested in. Is it online exposure, association with your cause, or access to live audiences? And don't forget that you are likely not the only organization coming to them with sponsorship requests. Be memorable and make your pitch meaningful. Convey your passion for the cause and your personal connection so that you can begin to build a relationship with the decision-maker.

7. Keep your sponsors happy

Securing corporate sponsorships can be difficult and time-consuming. All the more reason why you want to invest heavily and steward your sponsors, increasing the likelihood they'll sign up again. Make sure you deliver, if not over-deliver, on every detail in the agreement, and that the sponsor is satisfied with the result. Thank your sponsors privately and publicly, and thank participants on the sponsors' behalf.

When the event is complete and you've collected all your data (ideally, within 30 days), create an impact summary for all sponsors. In this report, tell them specifically what impact their sponsorship had, both in terms of the benefits directly to them (how many times and where you gave them marketing exposure, how many people they reached, etc.), as well as the benefits to your cause and the impact the overall event made possible. Don't ever make them guess at what they got out of their sponsorship. Stay in touch with your sponsors throughout the year with brief emails, handwritten notes, or updates on your work so that you aren't only communicating with them when you need money.

Section 4

FUNDRAISING THEORY AND ETHICS

Editors' introduction

Overview

This fourth section covers fundraising theory and ethics. At first sight, that may sound like the least interesting section of the Reader, but we hope we can convince you otherwise. Theory and ethics may be among the most important topics that both existing and future fundraisers can learn about. The Merriam-Wester dictionary tells us that theory means "a plausible or scientifically acceptable general principle or body of principles offered to explain phenomena". Or in other words: ideas about the way the world works, and in this case, ideas about how fundraising works. Theories are just theories, until they are supported by evidence. That is what we present here in this section: tested ideas about fundraising that work – or in some cases, do not work, which is also good to be aware of.

Too often, academic research on fundraising remains inaccessible to fundraising practitioners, either because it is behind a so-called publisher's "paywall" or when it is publicly available, it is written in language that is not very accessible or clear about the practical application. The texts in this section are included in an attempt to bridge the gap between academia and practice for the topics of theory and ethics.

There is a wide and seminal literature related to the role of ethics in fundraising. Understanding what is and isn't ethical in fundraising is of crucial importance to anyone involved with fundraising. Above all else, fundraising needs to be an ethical profession because the organizations the funds are raised for are expected to be "holier than thou", operating for the public good. There are many ethical dilemmas that fundraisers may encounter, ranging from accepting "tainted" gifts described by Moody and Pratt, to O'Neill's exploration of pressuring donors into giving or Fischer's concern with overestimating the outcomes of interventions in communications with donors. Several of the texts selected offer different practical frameworks for decision making to handle ethical fundraising dilemmas, which we hope are helpful to anyone encountering ethical dilemmas.

We end this section with a discussion of the rights of different stakeholders in fundraising: beneficiaries, fundraisers, and donors.

DOI: 10.4324/9781003145936-62

4.1 Theories in fundraising

The first sub-section starts with an overview reading of the different theories that explain how fundraising works. Ruth K. Hansen discusses "the
big picture" theoretical ideas explaining fundraising: systems theory, resource
dependence theory, gift theory and reciprocity, identification theory, social
identity theory, and co-orientation theory. Just reading these names, it may
seem overly complex at first, but Hansen clearly explains these key theories
and their implications for fundraising in an accessible way. For example, when
discussing gift theory she writes:

> Gift theory recognizes that giving gifts is a universal aspect of social human
> behavior, and, further, that receiving a gift generally prompts a social obli-
> gation to reciprocate in some manner ... giving is rarely one-way, but is
> instead a *social exchange* of some type.

This insight is highly relevant in fundraising, as gifts are just one aspect in a
larger social exchange system, where donors, fundraisers, and beneficiaries all
experience social obligations to reciprocate in one way or another. Readers
interested in gift theory should also consider reading Chapman, Louis, Masser,
and Thomas in Section 5.4, which discusses the different roles of donors,
fundraisers, and beneficiaries in this social exchange.

The second reading in this theory sub-section is also authored by Hansen,
this time with Abhishek Bhati. They provide a concise overview of tests of
various fundraising techniques used in practice, and show which fundraising
techniques are actually working well, and which appear to be less helpful.
The techniques they discuss fall across three categories: a) use of images
and messages; b) asking for specific amounts; c) effectiveness of fundraising
events. To highlight one of their more surprising findings: "All else being
equal, using a lottery or raffle prompts people to contribute more than
simply asking for donations – people generally respond well to the chance
to win a prize."

From understanding more general fundraising theories and assessing the
effectiveness of fundraising techniques, we move to more specific theories
about what drives individual donors to give. In "Understanding individual
donors" Pamala Wiepking provides an overview of the different resources that
enable individual donors to give, and the motivations these donors may have
for their giving. The different resources that enable people to make donations
relate to the **A**bility from the L-A-I principle discussed by Henry Rosso in
Section 2.3. In addition to financial resources, these also include education,
social connections, and family characteristics. As Wiepking explains: "Having
a partner and children leads to more social connectedness and thus opportunities and requests for giving, for example through the children's school or
sport clubs." Wiepking also summarises the key giving motivations covered
in the scholarly literature, including solicitation, trust, (social) reputation, tax
incentives, and personal values.

It is well known that donors hate "overhead costs", which are the costs incurred by nonprofit organisations that are not directly related to serving their beneficiaries and running their programmes (the so-called programme expenses). Overhead costs include the costs of fundraising (fundraising expenses), but also costs for the building, electricity, and staff salaries (administrative expenses). When given the option, donors have a strong preference for their donation to be used solely to pay for programme costs, for example helping the children in need, or saving the whales. Charity rating agencies, such as Charity Navigator in the US, often give more favourable rankings to nonprofit organizations with relatively lower overhead costs. However, if fundraising organisations want to achieve their (often) challenging missions, they need a professional organisation, with knowledgeable staff who have the resources to do their job well. In "Are overhead costs a good guide for charitable giving", Jonathan Meer bursts the myth that overhead costs are a good guide for predicting the effectiveness of fundraising organisations. He shows that the use of overhead costs as an indicator of nonprofit effectiveness can actually be harmful, as it leads organisations to limit their expenses on those elements they need to be successful in their mission, such as professional staff.

Emotions are important in fundraising, both as a motivation for giving (for example donors often report feeling emotions such as compassion, empathy or anger when solicited for a gift) and as a technique to prompt more giving (for example by creating emotive fundraising materials that will prompt a generous response). Jon Dean and Rachel Wood describe how fundraisers themselves think about the role of emotions in fundraising. Dean and Wood conducted interviews with UK-based fundraisers to tease out how fundraisers balance the effective use of emotions in fundraising, while also taking into consideration the ethical implications of using these emotions. This research matters because the use of "negative" emotions such as guilt, pity, shock, and anger can raise ethical issues. An example of effective use of emotions in fundraising campaigns which are ethically contested are campaigns raising funds for victims of famine. Using images of starving children, such as those used to raise funds for Ethiopian victims of famine in the early 1980s, has been found to evoke a strong negative emotional response, and lead to increased donations. However, the continuous use of these negative images of starving children has led to stigmatising views of people living in the Horn of Africa, and to donors feeling that their gifts are mere band-aids, and do not contribute to solving the issues their gifts were intended to address.

Abhishek Bhati and Angela Eikenberry conclude this sub-section on theories in fundraising, discussing – among other things – exactly these ethical implications and consequences of portraying beneficiaries as "needy" and "helpless" in order to generate more donations. Using a post-colonial theoretical framework, they examine the experience of beneficiaries in these negative emotional fundraising appeals. This focus on the beneficiary experience is much needed, as Bhati and Eikenberry write: "Fundraisers' focus on donors undermines the importance of beneficiaries who are equal stakeholders and continues to feed into stereotypes of people who are poor as unworthy or lazy."

In the final part of the reading, they provide guidelines and "do's and don'ts" that can help fundraisers to take "an alternative approach to fundraising" in order to ethically and respectfully include the beneficiaries' perspective and voice in any fundraising communication. These "do's" include using story-telling to provide the context for any cause, preferably allowing beneficiaries to share their own story, and showing beneficiaries' "sense of agency": they are not merely helpless victims, but people who actively try to navigate their unfortunate circumstances.

4.2 Ethics in fundraising

In the previous sub-section on fundraising theories, both Dean and Wood and Bhati and Eikenberry addressed some important ethical issues and concerns that fundraisers can encounter in their profession. In this second sub-section, we dig deeper into this topic. In "Rights-Balancing Fundraising Ethics", Ian MacQuillin provides "Ethical theory 101": an overview of the different ethical theories that are relevant for fundraising. These include "trustism", which states that fundraising is ethical when it maintains public trust, "donor centrism", which sees fundraising as more ethical when it respects the donor's intent, and "service of philanthropy", which views fundraising as ethical when it brings "meaning" to a donor's giving. Like Bhati and Eikenberry, MacQuillin addresses the missing perspective and voice of beneficiaries in fundraising ethical theories. He offers a new theory, which he calls the "rights-balancing fundraising ethics theory" which states that: "Fundraising is ethical when it balances the duty of fundraisers to ask for money on behalf of their beneficiaries, with the relevant rights of donors, such that a mutually-optimal outcome is achieved and neither stakeholder is significantly harmed."

In 1994, Michael O'Neill wrote "Fundraising as an Ethical Act", borrowing ethical guidance for fundraising from philosophers Aristotle (Greece; 384 BCE–322 BCE), Kant (Germany; 1724–1804), and John Stuart Mill (UK; 1806–1873). From Aristotle, O'Neill teaches us that fundraisers can help further a donors' personal moral development into virtuous people by inviting them to become givers, especially when they help people "to give wisely and well". Through the "maxim of altruism" O'Neill applies Kant's philosophy into fundraising. Fundraisers can play a key role in "cultivating the general habit of altruism" in such a way that giving may become a universal law. Based on Mills' (and Bentham's) Utilitarian theory O'Neill argues that "fundraisers can bring great good to great numbers of people", and "alleviate pain for great numbers of people". Other ethical themes discussed in the reading by O'Neill include the role of fundraisers in redistributing power in society, in creating responsibility for societal issues, and in breaking down people's "natural wall of selfishness".

In "The Color of Ethics" Marilyn Fischer reflects on the different shades of "grey" that ethical dilemmas can represent. She introduces a framework for ethical decision making, which has been termed "The Fischer Model" in the literature. She argues there are three basic value commitments that guide our ethical decision making: (1) the organizational mission that directs the work; (2) our relationships with the people with whom we interact; and (3) our own sense of personal integrity. Using the Fischer Model, fundraisers encountering an ethical dilemma can explore it in relation to these three basic value commitments, and ideally conduct that exploration in an inclusive way, involving all the relevant people. When trying to resolve ethical dilemmas, storytelling can be helpful, as she argues: "When the full story of the ethical dilemma is told carefully, with sympathetic understanding of each person's perspective ... polarization can be minimized."

Barbara Marion introduces another framework for ethical decision making, The Josephson Institute Model. This model first identifies a set of "values which have transcended culture and time to establish the ethical norms and standards of moral conduct essential to an ethical life", including honesty, integrity, fairness, respect for others, and safeguarding the public trust. Marion herself adds another value that she views as a key ethical value for fundraisers: duty. She writes that it is a fundraiser's duty to act in the best interest of a donor, "to ensure the legitimate interests of the donor are protected, a duty to avoid manipulation or intimidation". Here it is interesting to highlight the shift from donor-centered fundraising in the mid-nineties and early 2000s, when Marion wrote this text, to more community-centered fundraising, as discussed in more recently published texts, such as by Klein and Fernandez in Section 2.3, Zumaya in 6.1, and Vu Le in Section 6.2. The Josephson Institute Model also provides a set of steps to follow when encountering ethical dilemmas. Marion describes these steps in a very accessible way, showing fundraising practitioners how to implement them in their ethical decision making.

Further advice on how to handle ethical fundraising dilemmas comes from Michael Rosen. In "A fundraiser's guide to ethical decision-making" he presents a series of "tests" that fundraisers can use for common-sense decision making when facing ethical dilemmas, including: the Vision Test (can you look yourself in the mirror and tell yourself your decision is ok?); the What Would-Your-Parents-Say-Test (could you explain to your parents what you did and not be sent to your room?); and the Publicity test (are you ok with your decision being front page news?). Rosen highlights that while commonsense is important in solving ethical dilemmas it is also a limited tool, and fundraisers facing ethical dilemmas should also follow local "code of ethics" and ethical decision-making frameworks such as those presented by Fischer and Marion earlier in this sub-section.

The final reading in the sub-section on fundraising ethics is by Michael Moody and Michael Pratt who reflect on one of the most prominent ethical fundraising dilemmas, that of "tainted money" (problems with how money was created) and "tainted donors" (problems with who is giving money). Moody and Pratt raise both conceptual and practical questions that fundraisers should consider when dealing with "tainted" money or donors. These questions include asking about the severity of the ethical issue and who actually gets to decide whether a donor or money is tainted. They make the important point that context matters a lot when deciding whether to accept (or keep) tainted money, as they explain: "What is 'right' might depend on many factors of the situation and the parties involved. For example, might oil companies be considered tainted donors to environmental organizations, but not so much to arts ones?"

4.3 Donor, fundraiser, and beneficiary rights

We end Section 4 with three "Bills of Rights": A Donor Bill of Rights, a Fundraiser Bill of Rights and a Beneficiary Bill of Rights. These three texts address the rights of those involved in fundraising. James Greenfield starts this sub-section with a discussion of the US Donor Bill of Rights. This is a public statement created by a consortium of four US organisations of fundraisers in the late 1980s and early 1990s, reflecting the core of their professional fundraising values and beliefs of what rights donors should be entitled to. By providing "10 moral principles and establish[ing] a covenant donors should expect every nonprofit organization to observe in their behalf", the Donor Bill of Rights intends "to assist donors in making decisions about charities, in the belief that informed decision making would assist donors and charities in forging stronger, more productive relationships that would ultimately benefit the recipients of charitable support."

Some thirty years later, Amelia Garza and Jennifer Holmes address the rights of fundraisers, in their Fundraiser Bill of Rights. Fundraisers can be subject to very challenging working environments, as illustrated among others in the next section of this Reader, 5.4, by Beaton et al.'s writing on fundraiser's experiences with sexual harassment, and by Jammeh who writes about the challenges of being a Black fundraiser. Garza and Holmes argue that fundraisers have the right to be "an equitable partner in creating change for the community", and their "Fundraiser Bill of Rights" creates the conditions for fundraisers of all ethnicities, abilities, and identities to do just that.

The final reading in this section starts with a state-of-the-art summary of the role of ethics in fundraising, supplementing the readings on ethics in fundraising in Section 4.2. We chose to include this reading in this final sub-section, because Anne Bergeron and Eugene Tempel end their text with a proposed "Beneficiary Bill of Rights". They strongly advocate creating "beneficiary-directed" fundraising, "helping donors use their privilege to focus philanthropy on the root causes of inequity and its symptoms". Their Beneficiary Bill of Rights provides ample tools to do this.

Discussion questions

1. Pick one of the fundraising theories described by Hansen (systems theory, resource dependence theory, gift theory and reciprocity, identification theory social identity theory or co-orientation theory) and explain it in your own words in a way that an older relative would understand how this theory is relevant for understanding the way fundraising works.

2. Read Wiepking and then look up materials from a recent fundraising campaign such as a direct mail letter or fundraising video on social media. Find evidence of at least three mechanisms, values or motivations that this campaign is using to entice (prospective) donors to give.

3. In 2013, fundraising consultant Dan Pallotta gave a TED-talk which became seminal in the fundraising world. In "The way we think about charity is dead wrong", he makes a compelling case to evaluate charities based on their achievements and accomplishments rather than on how little they spend on overhead costs. Look up and watch this eighteen-minute TED talk. Based on the TED talk by Pallotta and the reading by Meer, prepare three arguments to share with your friends why overhead costs are a limited criteria for making decisions about which organization to donate to.

4. Based on Dean and Wood and Bhati and Eikenberry, explain why it is important to involve beneficiaries in fundraising. When thinking of your response, the following concepts may be relevant: the use of images in fundraising; stigmatisation of beneficiaries; agency of beneficiaries.

5. Review the following four ethical decision-making frameworks: The Fischer Model (in Fischer), the different tests (vision test; what-would-your-parents say test; etc.) in Rosen, the Josephson Institute model (in Marion and Rosen) and the Markkula Center for Applied Ethics framework (in Bergeron and Tempel). Do you see overlap between the different ethical decision-making frameworks? Which decision-making framework do you think is most helpful for fundraisers facing ethical dilemmas in their work, and why do you think this?

6. Look up a recent media reporting on a fundraising organization that experienced an issue with a "tainted" gift. Based on what Moody and Pratt write, what would you advise the organization to do? Accept or keep the donation? Or reject it? Why would you advise this?

4.1 Theories in fundraising

Theory in fundraising

Ruth K. Hansen, 2022

Philanthropic giving has attracted many theorists, but research on fundraising has been less tied to theory. This text first discusses the role of theory in fundraising practice and then examines several theories that have been used to explain aspects of fundraising.

[…]

Theoretical approaches

The big picture: systems theory, boundary spanning, and resource dependence

Systems theory provides a fundamental theoretical base for understanding fundraising. An organization that isolates itself from its environment can be considered a "closed system." One that is influenced by social and economic trends and needs, and exchanges resources within its community is an "open system." Simply put, charities do not exist in isolation. They exist within an environment and interact with that environment. Typically, strong fundraising programs thrive in relatively open systems.

Individuals who raise funds for an organization function as **boundary spanners**, linking the organization with important resources in the external environment. Boundary spanners are essentially diplomatic liaisons who work to align the interests of those within and those outside the organization. Fundraisers seek to develop financial resources for an organization through cultivation, solicitation, and stewardship activities. They also listen to the interests and concerns of potential donors and look to find good linkages with the organization's mission. By interacting with potential donors on behalf of their organizations, fundraisers perform an important boundary-spanning role.

Resource dependence theory explains why fundraising occurs and suggests some common organizational dynamics. The theory states that for organizations to survive, they must acquire necessary resources, and maintain their supply. This means that organizations are not wholly autonomous in their financial decision making but rely on their environment for various resources. The greater an organization's dependence on voluntary contributions, the more volatile its revenue environment is, and the more likely it is to devote its time and personnel resources to developing financial resources. This illustrates the importance of skilled fundraising.

DOI: 10.4324/9781003145936-64

Dependence on others leads to power considerations. When funding is scarce, the charity is more vulnerable to the demands of prospective funders, which may affect the organization's decision-making autonomy. For instance, nonprofits that receive relatively high levels of government funding are less likely to have nonprofit boards that strongly represent their client constituents. This dependence dynamic is also seen in an increasing focus on donor-centered philanthropy, particularly for major donors. If a donor (or grantor) is providing significant financial support, they may be keenly interested in affecting the design and administration of that program or the organization as a whole, and less attentive to the needs of the community or the organization's beneficiaries. Discerning the point at which a donor's engagement crosses the line into unwelcome or inappropriate territory can be difficult. Organizations may choose to diversify their revenue sources, including fees, dues, or commercial activities in order to lessen their dependence on any one funding source, and in so doing potentially diminish threats to control over financial and programmatic decision making.

Social exchanges: gift theory and reciprocity

Gift theory recognizes that giving gifts is a universal aspect of social human behavior, and, further, that receiving a gift generally prompts a social obligation to reciprocate in some manner. The gifts may vary greatly – they may include money or physical items; favors such as use of resources like a boat or equipment, helping with yard work or childcare, or preferential treatment; or appreciation expressed through a thoughtful note, loyalty, or even prayers. Thus, giving is rarely one-way, but is instead a *social exchange* of some type. Many factors affect what is considered an appropriate gift: cultural traditions, the relationship and relative social status of each party, and time and place. These social considerations apply whether one is considering an initial gift, or a reciprocal expression. Breaking the social norm of *reciprocity* is viewed as a lack of appreciation and makes future giving less likely. Gift theory tells us that giving results in reciprocal obligations, and that these create and maintain webs of both mutual interest and mutual responsibility.

One implication of this theory is stewardship. Demonstrating to donors that their generosity is appreciated and impactful fulfills the expectations of reciprocity. When fundraisers acknowledge gifts and demonstrate stewardship, they are speaking to the social exchange aspect of giving, fulfilling the social norm of reciprocity, and maintaining a relationship of mutual interest. Gift theory explicitly recognizes the importance of relationship building in fundraising.

A second implication of gift theory concerns donor status. As noted by Lindahl, "… making generous donations confers high status on the donor and benefits the recipient organization and the community at the same time". The norms of reciprocity between peers suggest that the gift or favor eventually reciprocated should be of similar value. However, those of high status are often perceived as having higher social obligations to their communities (*noblesse oblige*), while those of lower status are required to reciprocate with their appreciation, which might take the form of loyalty. Thus, gift theory explains instances of conspicuous generosity, in which a person might give significantly to a cause to be recognized publicly as a member of a socially elite group.

Positive identification: the identification theory of care and social identity theory

The **identification theory of care** focuses on relationships and meaning to explain why people give. Its attention to encouraging the process of engagement makes it highly applicable to the work of fundraising. The essential idea is that "voluntary assistance derives from identification, identification derives from encounter, encounter derives from relationship, and relationship derives from participation". This process is illustrated in Figure 4.1.1.

The core of this model is the idea of *communities of participation* – that people care most about family members, friends, and those they know well from the communities in which they participate. This may include those joined in attendance at religious services, or shared membership in formal and informal groups. The social relationships formed in these communities prompt shared frameworks, or ways of thinking about the world. These frameworks influence preferences and commitment to causes. When a person identifies with others – that is, they view others as being similar to them, part of "us," or similar to those they care for – they are likely to help the others by volunteering money, time, or resources. The first important implication of this idea is that generosity is born not of selflessness, but instead of acting in accordance with values and priorities that are essential to self-identity. The second implication, and one of direct significance to fundraisers, is that encouraging an expansion of generosity means recognizing and encouraging people's current expressions of care, broadly construed. Another major implication for fundraisers is the importance of engaging potential donors with a cause and with others who support the cause.

Related to this idea, **social identity theory** helps explain how people identify as members of groups. The tendency to categorize people into groups is a *heuristic* – a mental shortcut that helps in navigating a complex world. If

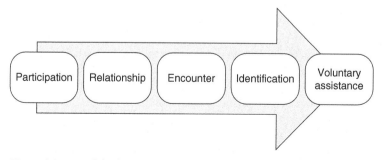

Figure 4.1.1 Model of identification theory

someone sees themselves as belonging to a group, that group is an "in-group"; other groups are "outgroups." People tend to favor others who they see as sharing a *social identity* – belonging to the same "in-group". Applying this idea to fundraising, fundraisers may activate prospective donors' social identities that overlap with others affiliated with the organization. These might include mentioning other donors with similar identities, such as gender; mentioning a tie to an organization, such as alumni status; reminding the donor of their past giving history and, therefore, their status as a donor to the organization; or encouraging the individual to identify with the group or cause that will directly benefit from the donation. Fundraisers can also encourage identification with *moral identities*, such as someone who is "helpful" or "generous." If these adjectives already describe how an individual would like to think of themselves, a fundraiser can encourage behavior that reflects that identity by recognizing that attribute in the donor.

Encouraging prospective donors to identify with a group can make them more willing to help that in-group, and to support what others within that group also support. On the downside, this identity activation can also make people more aware of who is not a member of that group and depress their willingness to help outsiders. However, as donors and volunteers become more involved with an organization, their affiliation with the group will become a greater part of how they view their own personal identity.

People who spend time together and value their relationship tend to find points of agreement and to share many priorities. **Co-orientation theory** explains how people who are within a community of participation will tend to either come to share views and priorities, or step back and spend less time and energy on their mutual relationship. As applied to fundraising, this suggests that peer solicitation – that is, asking an existing donor to help solicit their friends and acquaintances for a cause – is likely to encourage serious consideration on the part of the prospective donor. However, this should not be done lightly. If the gift opportunity is not a good match for the prospective donor, then involving the peer solicitor can potentially damage the friendship.

[…]

Conclusion

Many theories address why people engage in philanthropy as donors, and these also inform fundraising. For example, empirical evidence shows that being asked is key to the act of making gifts. Less attention has focused on theories of how fundraising functions, and its social implications. As Russell James III notes, theoretical guidance is perhaps less important for quick, transactional models of fundraising, but can contribute greatly to aspects of fundraising that rely on developing longer term, nuanced relationships.

The process of developing and testing theoretical frameworks to help understand fundraising is ongoing. Many of these theories are extensions or refinements of theories originally used in other situations. Systems theory is a reminder that organizations are part of a greater environment requiring boundary spanning to ensure adequate financial resources. Resource dependence theory highlights potential power implications of revenue portfolios. Gift theory examines the social exchange aspects of philanthropy, indicating that fundraisers and donors live in a relational society. Identification theory looks to the importance of affirming a donor's sense of self and the role of communities of participation in expanding how a donor identifies with others.

Taken together, these theories undergird the importance of relationships in fundraising. They imply a duty of care to donors, to treat them as whole people with personal values and preferences. They also imply a duty of care to the organizations and those who benefit from fundraising efforts.

Testing fundraising practices and techniques

Abhishek Bhati and Ruth K. Hansen, 2020

Studies of fundraising techniques may vary one aspect of an appeal in order to observe donor behaviors such as participation or size of donation …. We include three categories that are prominent in both the collected experimental literature and in fundraising practice: (a) usage of images and messages; (b) suggested ask amount; and (c) fundraising events: auctions, raffles, and walks/runs.

Usage of Images and Messages. We found two prominent themes emerging that focused on the relationship between images in solicitations and giving: (a) sad versus happy children, and (b) a single child versus a group. Studies suggest that images of children with sad faces increase sympathy and guilt for not giving among donors, thereby increasing donation intentions. In a laboratory experiment with university students and staff, participants were more willing to donate when they saw a sad child versus a happy child's face. Studies by social psychologists argue that the image of a child with a sad face makes viewers feel guilty or sad, and giving gives them an opportunity to convert such negative feelings into a positive emotion; so, images of a sad child increase giving. Fisher & Ma found using images of attractive children in fundraising appeals also led to a negative effect on empathy and actual helping behavior.

Cockrill & Parsonage argue that shocking images, in isolation, decrease the viewer's intent to agree with the cause. They found emotions most associated with an increased likelihood of helping the charity financially were compassion, relief, interest, surprise, and shame. However, Albouy argues that negative emotions such as fear, sadness, and shock increase intent to donate. In a dictator game [an economic game where participants have to make decisions about keeping or sharing resources, often the monetary rewards received for participating in the game], Van Rijn, Barham, & Sundaram-Stukel found that using videos that highlight the situational difference between donors and beneficiaries ("negative/ traditional" approach) fosters guilt in viewers, and is more effective in raising donations than using "positive" videos that highlight similarities. Cao & Jia found that sad images versus happy images garner stronger donation intentions among participants who were less involved with the charity, but the reverse was true for highly involved participants. This suggests that committed donors are more able to think through a problem and

DOI: 10.4324/9781003145936-65

need of beneficiaries, and hence happy images make committed donors feel their donation is making a difference.

Studies have suggested that the framing of fundraising written appeals also affects how donors perceive the cause, and their subsequent decision to give. A negatively framed fundraising message (the consequences of not giving) was found to be more effective when coupled with the use of statistical information about the beneficiaries, while a positively framed message (the outcomes of making a gift) was more effective when coupled with the use of emotional information. In addition, participants' giving intentions were higher for messages that addressed goal attainment. Chou & Murnighan found that using a "loss message" (e.g., your action can "prevent a death" – which is still an outcome of positive action) is more likely to increase intentions to volunteer and donate than a positive message (e.g., your action can "save a life"). Erlandsson, Nilsson, & Västfjäll argue that donation behavior and attitudes towards charity appeals do not always go hand in hand. They argue that it's "possible to hate a negative charity appeal and be angry at the organization behind it but still donate money after seeing it or alternatively, to love a charity appeal and the organization behind it but still refrain from donating". In summary, these studies highlight the cognition discontinuity among donors making a decision to give based on seeing images of beneficiaries. At one level, donors like to see children in a positive light; but they may donate to a sad faced child if that image induces sadness and guilt.

Attribution also plays a role in how messages are perceived. Across experiments, Zagefka, Noor, Brown, de Moura, & Hopthrow found that more donations are given to victims of natural disasters than to those affected by human-caused disasters, such as genocide, because donors feel that natural disasters could happen to anyone, and that the victim has no blame in the situation.

Adding to this tension, Hudson, Vanheerde-Hudson, Dasandi, & Gaines, examined the common practice of "traditional" fundraising appeals that intentionally appeal to guilt and pity with depictions of "poor, malnourished, suffering, and typically African, children" to prompt donations to international development organizations. Using a survey experiment (N=701) Hudson et al. confirmed that this practice does tend to generate giving, while also priming negative emotions such as repulsion that drive potential donors away and may diminish future engagement. "Alternative" fundraising appeals, which highlight commonalities between the recipients and donors, activate hope rather than guilt and anger. "Alternative" appeals also increased the likelihood of a donation and improved readers' sense of personal efficacy. Hence, nonprofits using "traditional" approaches may be trading long-term effects for short-term donations, and should consider the long-term effects their fundraising appeals may have on donors.

Other scholars have focused on the phenomenon known as "identified victim effect," where participants are more likely to respond emotionally and help single beneficiaries than they are to help wider groups of individuals.

Using a student population (N=121), Small et al. found that discussing the details about the full scale of a large problem reduced sympathy towards "identified victims" or single victims, and did not generate sympathy for the larger number of victims. Adding to the findings of Small et al., Kogut & Ritov found that identifying a single victim increases the participant's generosity only when the victim is from a participant's in-group (i.e. sharing participants' identity name representing certain region). Smith et al. added that donors may donate to multiple victims when they perceive them as entitative – comprising a single coherent unit, such as a mother with four children. Cryder et al. using three field and lab experiments found donors' perception of impact of their donation increases giving as they feel their money is making a difference in the lives of the beneficiaries.

Västfjäll et al. re-tests the findings by designing different experiments testing one or more components together, and finds that affective feeling toward a charitable cause is highest when the victim is single. They argue that as the number of victims increases, donors feel their contribution will be less impactful. However, in a different study by Soyer & Hogarth, donations increased with the number of potential beneficiaries, but at a decreasing rate. It seems that there is more to learn about this phenomenon, as we try to understand the circumstances that affect readers' perceptions.

Suggested Ask Amount. Several experimental studies have focused on the relationship between suggesting an amount to give, and the resulting behavior. In one study, Edwards & List (2014) asked US college graduates to donate to their alma mater. Those who received a specific ask amount were more likely to respond, and to send a gift near the suggested number. Similarly, Fielding & Knowles found that a verbal invitation to donate is more impactful than visual clues in isolation, as it acts as peer pressure on the donor. Also, the effect of a verbal invitation is larger if participants have more loose change, as it is more convenient to give change and reduce the peer pressure and guilt of not making a donation.

Often, response cards enclosed with a mailing will have a range of suggested donation amounts, with the first amount referred to as the "anchor," because of its ability to anchor perceptions relative to it. Evidence suggests that providing a relatively low anchor will increase the amount of response to the appeal, although it may also result in lower giving per donor than a response card with no anchoring amount. De Bruyn & Prokopec find that is it possible to counteract the effect on gift size by increasing the amount between each suggested gift, so that there is a steeper increase. However, fundraisers may want to keep the suggested amounts in multiples of $5 or $10, as donors seem to prefer round numbers, and it is easier to give a suggested amount than to pick another one. In fact, response may be suppressed if "strange" numbers are suggested, because it is easier to not give than to write in one's own amount.

Donors seem to have internal reference points, to which suggestions are compared: ask too little or too much, and the request will not be persuasive. Fundraisers can use the last gift received for guidance in establishing the anchor amount. However, introducing any default may also distract from other positive information about the charity that is included within the appeal. It should also be noted that donors' giving standards – expectations about appropriate donation amounts – vary across different methods of solicitation, such as door-to-door or direct mail.

Fundraising and Events: Auctions, Raffles, and Walks/Runs. Special events are commonly used in fundraising, which may relate to social motivations such as solicitation (being prompted to attend, and subsequent asks throughout an event); costs and benefits (as in a dinner, entertainment, or a chance to win something); altruism (when they care about the organization's activities); reputation (as in being seen as a charitable person); psychological benefits (such as contributing to one's self-image, or enjoying the company of others); and values (when the cause being supported aligns well with the individual's priorities). While no experiments addressed the gala-type event, we did find experiments that addressed three aspects commonly associated with special events: auctions, raffles, and walks/runs for charity:

Auctions. Multiple forms of auctions exist, for example: oral auctions, in which an auctioneer calls out ascending bids; silent auctions, in which bids are written down or communicated electronically; sealed, or blind, auctions, in which bidders have no knowledge of others' bids. Lab experiments have tended to support the theory that an all-pay format – in which everyone bidding must pay their bid for an item whether or not they win – will result in higher contributions than the common winner-pay auction. However, all-pay auctions are not commonly used in fundraising. This may be because outside the lab, people are more likely to perceive a choice as to whether or not to participate. In natural field experiments within an existing fundraising event, more people participated, and more was raised, in an auction in which only the winner paid the highest bid. Both the prizes offered and charitable inclination are factors affecting bidding. Evidence shows that, within an auction, some prizes generate more interest than others. Separately, when identical items were placed for auction in both a non-charitable context and a charitable context, those in which a charity or charities benefitted from the higher price paid sold for a higher price.

Raffles. All else being equal, using a lottery or raffle prompts people to contribute more than simply asking for donations – people generally respond well to the chance to win a prize. In a lab experiment using a "self-financing" (or 50/50) raffle, in which money is collected in a short period of time while participants are present, and half the money contributed (the "pot") was donated to charity, sharing information about the size of the pot after a first round of ticket sales increased the tickets sold in a second round. Another common form of raffle is one in which tickets, each of which represents one chance to win, are available over a longer period of time, often several weeks, with proceeds benefiting a local charity. In a field experiment in which proceeds benefited local poverty relief, Carpenter & Matthews found that two variations performed better than the standard linear raffle (in which each ticket sells for the same price). The highest income resulted from pricing with discounts for purchasing more tickets. Another variant, in which people received the same number of chances for any amount donated over a floor amount, also resulted in higher income than simply selling tickets at a fixed price.

Charitable Walks/Runs. When people are suffering, such as from cancer, Alzheimer's disease or another chronic illness, or depression leading to suicide, they will donate more when there is effort or discomfort, such as physical exertion, involved in their donation compared to a similar event that is purely social. This decision is mediated by individuals' perception of the act as meaningful, suggesting a psychological benefit.

[...]

This paper updates and consolidates knowledge of experimental studies across multiple behavioral and professional disciplines that inform the practice of fundraising and we offer suggestions to both researchers and practitioners in the area of charitable fundraising.

Understanding individual donors

Pamala Wiepking, 2022

Resources for giving

People need a variety of resources in order to make charitable donations. First among these is access to income or wealth. Research consistently finds that people with higher levels of income and wealth give more to charity. However, all people deserve the opportunity to participate in philanthropy. Fundraisers should seek contributions from people across the financial resource spectrum, not just those with high levels of income and wealth. People across all income levels give to charity, and there is even evidence that those with lower incomes donate relatively more: they give a higher percentage of their income.

Absolute income and wealth are also not the only financial resources that matter. Wiepking and Breeze show that people's *perception* of their financial resources may be an even more important factor in giving behavior. People need to feel that their and their family's financial future are secure, before considering making substantial donations. Surprisingly, even people with access to multiple millions can feel financially insecure, and hence will not give much to charitable causes.

There are several other key resources people hold that potentially enable higher charitable giving. Table 3.1.1 lists three of these resources, and briefly explains why they influence individual donor giving.

How socio-demographic characteristics relate to giving

Resources enable people to give, but personal experiences lead them to give in certain ways and to specific causes. While every donor has their own unique motivations for giving, trends can be identified among similar groups of people. Lived experience is of course an important motivation for people to connect with a specific cause or organization. Think for example about someone who experienced a serious illness themselves or within their family, or someone who experienced a traumatic event like a school shooting, or someone whose child has a disability and encounters barriers for participation in society. These experiences may motivate them to make donations to associated charities.

DOI: 10.4324/9781003145936-66

Table 3.1.1 Individual donor resources that can enable charitable giving

Resource	Why it can enable charitable giving
Education	Education typically increases people's income and wealth. Through education people also learn about social and societal needs, not just in their own community but also across the world. They also typically develop stronger personal values that motivate caring about others. Those with higher levels of education also are typically more socially connected, which leads to more opportunities for giving and gift requests.
Social connections	Those who are connected with a greater number and a more diverse range of people are more likely to come across opportunities for giving and receive gift requests.
Family characteristics	Having a partner and children leads to more social connectedness and thus opportunities and requests for giving, for example through the children's school or sport clubs.

The complex dynamics of individual giving behavior

Both resources and socio-demographic characteristics influence individual donor behavior. But knowing which people are more likely to give, and give more, to an organization does not always reveal *why* they give to an organization. For fundraisers, understanding *why* people give is highly relevant for building long-term relationships with donors.

Donors may have a multitude of motivations that exist simultaneously. Motivations for giving can be either *intrinsic* or *extrinsic*. Charitable behavior based on intrinsic motivations derives from care for others and desire to contribute to human and societal wellbeing, including concern for the natural environment. People who give to charity out of intrinsic motivations give because they care about the needs of others (altruism) or because their personal values align with the values of the charitable organization. Giving based on extrinsic motivations results from the personal benefits to be received, including feeling good about one's self, increasing one's social reputation, and receiving tax benefits.

Scholars have worked to develop a more comprehensive understanding of the complex dynamics of giving motivations and two articles provide structures for organizing and using that knowledge. The first is a seminal article by Konrath and Handy, in which they reviewed the academic literature, surveyed 800 Americans, and developed the "Motives to Donate"-Scale. This scale includes six key motivations for donors:

Trust. Trusting that organizations will make a difference with their gift.
Altruism. Giving to help others in need, caring about the beneficiaries.
Social. Giving because others also give, or because they know that giving is important for others.
Tax. Lowering the absolute costs for giving through the use of fiscal incentives.

Egoism. Giving to receive benefits, including increasing your social reputation or experiencing the joy of giving.

Constraints. Perceiving financial constraints that limit peoples' charitable giving.

These are easy to remember, as Konrath and Handy devised a clever acronym: "a **TASTE** for **C**harity."

In a second academic article that sheds light on donor motivations, Bekkers and Wiepking conducted an extensive review of the academic literature examining charitable giving behavior. They distilled eight *mechanisms* that drive people's charitable donations. Simply put, mechanisms relate to all the different processes that lead to a certain outcome, in this case charitable giving. Mechanisms also include personal motivations for giving, like the six key motivations included the "Motives to Donate"-Scale, but mechanisms also include other external influences on donor behavior, such as the influence of a gift solicitation.

Figure 4.1.2 shows the eight mechanisms for giving, clustered in four categories: the opportunity to give, values for giving, costs and benefits in relation to giving, and efficacy motivations for giving.

The opportunity to give

The first cluster relates to the opportunity to give. People need to be *aware of a need* and of a way to donate money – typically through *solicitation* – to relieve this need, before they can consider making a donation. Awareness of need increases with the urgency of a need. People can become aware of needs through (social) media. For example, news coverage of a natural disaster often inspires people to make a donation to a nonprofit organization like the Red Cross. When friends post a message on social media about the needs of a local

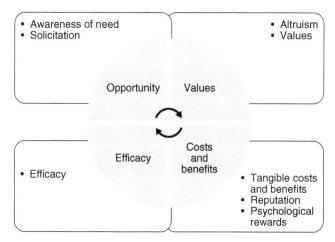

Figure 4.1.2 Eight mechanisms that drive charitable giving

animal shelter, people become aware of this need, and can decide to donate to support that cause.

The opportunity to give is often created by fundraisers through solicitation. Both volunteer and professional fundraisers play a major role in individual donor behavior by asking people to donate. Research estimates that up to 85 percent of donations are made in response to a request. Breeze puts this markedly in her seminal work on the fundraising profession: Charitable gifts are not just given, they are asked for. An increasingly common form of solicitation is through peer-to-peer crowdfunding on behalf of nonprofit organizations.

Values

The second cluster includes mechanisms that drive giving through a donor's personal *values*. People want to change the world in line with their values, and they can use charitable giving for this purpose. When a donor's values align with the organization asking for their support, and they give to this cause out of *altruistic* motivations, that can help facilitate a long-term relationship between the donor and the organization. When people give because of altruism, they give out of intrinsic motivations, to benefit the cause and its beneficiaries, and not for extrinsic motivations such as feeling good themselves or enhancing their reputation. Research shows that in actuality people are *impure altruists*: they do not give out of pure altruistic motivations, but in combination with other, often extrinsic and more self-serving, motivations.

Another key personal value for giving is *empathy*. A first form of empathy is cognitive empathy, which can be defined as understanding how someone else is feeling, and what they may think. The second type is emotional empathy, where people physically feel what someone else is feeling. Both of these types of empathy can motivate charitable giving. However, one specific form of emotional empathy, empathic distress, hampers rather than helps giving behavior. When a person physically takes over the emotional distress of someone in need, this can lead to feeling 'paralyzed' by the other person's emotion. And when people are focused on relieving their own distress they will (and can) not help or give money. Fundraising organizations need to be careful to avoid generating empathic distress with intense negative emotional appeals, as these may be counterproductive.

Other personal values that motivate giving include religious values, biospheric values, 'noblesse oblige', and social injustice. All major world religions advocate to support others in need. When people have stronger religious values, they typically also have stronger altruistic values, motivating them to give money to both religious and secular organizations. Biospheric values relate to caring about nature and environmental protection, which people find increasingly important in times of climate change. 'Noblesse oblige' includes motivations to give back, out of gratitude of what you have received from others and society. Addressing social injustice is also a strong motivation for giving, as shown by the influx of donations to the Black Lives Matter movement in 2020.

Costs and benefits

The mechanisms identified in the third cluster relate to costs and benefits. First, people are more inclined to give, and give more, when the *tangible, absolute costs* of a gift are lower, and the *benefits* are higher. Tax incentives lower the absolute costs of a gift, as do matching and multiplication schemes where a third party increases a donor's gift amount. Tangible benefits of donations include small items like a pen or t-shirt, but also substantial benefits like season tickets to the opera. Social costs and benefits are also relevant: Bekkers and Wiepking call this the *reputation* mechanism, others sometimes refer to this as 'image motivation'. Through charitable donations people can strengthen their social reputation. Giving is typically seen as positive behavior, and hence socially rewarded. People like to see themselves as 'prosocial persons', who care about others and contribute to their lives in positive ways. People also typically want to be perceived as being prosocial by others; this can also motivate them to make charitable donations, especially when other people will see their giving. Failing to give, in front of others and especially in settings where giving is expected (i.e., charity events, peer-to-peer crowdfunding), can also harm one's social reputation.

There are also *psychological costs and benefits* of giving. Giving makes people happy. Moreover, not giving when asked, can damage a person's own self-image and belief that they are prosocial. This sometimes causes people to become 'sophisticated altruists'. When given the opportunity to avoid a gift request, people will do this in order to escape the dreaded anticipated guilt for not giving. Examples include taking a different exit at the supermarket to avoid the Girl Scouts selling cookies or declining a meeting where a gift request is anticipated. As Andreoni et al. put it: "Just as a sophisticated eater will avoid exposure to the chocolate cake, a sophisticated altruist can avoid being asked."

Efficacy

The fourth cluster only includes a single, but important, factor: the perceived *efficacy* of giving. People who believe that their gift makes more of a difference, are more likely to give and give higher amounts. The perceived efficacy of giving can be increased by endorsements or leadership gifts from other trusted donors, including celebrities. Interestingly, donors are less concerned about the actual effectiveness of their chosen charitable organizations, in part because this information is so hard to come by and interpret.

Donors do typically care about the 'overhead' costs, which can relate to the percentage of an organization's income that is spent on staffing, facilities, and fundraising. Donors prefer their donations to go directly towards the programs the organization runs, and not towards sustaining the organization itself. They dislike having their gifts spent on overhead costs, under the assumption that charities with higher overhead costs are less effective than those with lower overhead costs. Ironically, research shows that organizations with higher overhead spending can be just as effective in achieving their goals, suggesting that this concern by donors may be misattributed. In his famous TED talk, fundraiser Dan Palotta explains why fundraising costs in particular can actually contribute to increased organizational effectiveness.

Implications for practice: assessing donor motivations

Ideally, a donor's motivation for giving becomes clear through his or her involvement with an organization or through personal conversations with fundraisers or board members. When lacking information about a donor's specific motivations for giving to an organization, it can be helpful to assess (and document) their motivations based on the broad mechanisms developed by Bekkers and Wiepking, and distinguish between intrinsic and extrinsic motivations. For example, is a donor intrinsically motivated because their values align with those of the organization? Or did the donor start giving to the organization because they participated in a gala event with lots of exposure, allowing them to increase their social reputation and fueling their extrinsic motivations?

When building a relationship with a major donor, it is also important to take their motivations into account. If a donor who gives to an organization out of extrinsic reputational motivations is approached for a gift using a value-based proposition, without opportunities for social exposure, this limits the likelihood that this donor will give. The same holds true for donors who give

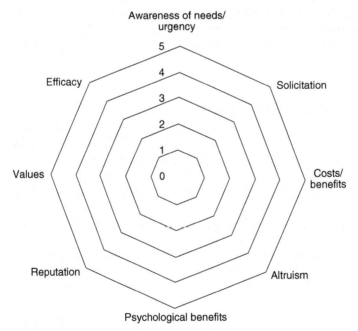

Figure 4.1.3 Spiderplot of mechanisms for giving

out of altruistic motivations. They want their donation to benefit the end-beneficiaries and goals as much as possible. Providing them with tangible benefits for their donation, such as a small token of thanks, will not be appreciated as they feel that the costs of this present should have gone to the cause.

One way to assess which mechanisms from Bekkers and Wiepking are most relevant for a specific donor, is to complete the spiderplot included in Figure 4.1.3. Typically donors will be motivated by a few of the mechanisms, not all. Based on the completed spiderplot, fundraisers can easily assess the most prominent mechanisms that drive a specific donor's charitable giving behavior. This information can be used to continue to develop the relationship by developing specialized opportunities to resonate with their motivations.

Are overhead costs a good guide for charitable giving?

Jonathan Meer, 2017

A commonly used metric for evaluating charities is their overhead cost ratio – that is, the amount the charity spends on administrative and fundraising expenses as a proportion of their total spending. Many charity ratings guides, like Charity Navigator, focus on these measures in their recommendations. Coupled with donor complaints about salaries for the senior staff of some large non-profit organizations, which are considered by some observers to be excessive, it is not surprising that a recent survey by Grey Matter Research found that nearly two-thirds of Americans believe that non-governmental organizations (NGOs) spend excessively on administrative costs. However, limiting overhead costs, through donor or regulator pressure, can have a particularly pernicious effect on a charity's ability to attract highly qualified workers. An inability to pay competitive wages in the marketplace due to a need to limit administrative costs leaves charities at a disadvantage in the labor market, even if the compensating differential of working for a cause one believes in partially makes up for some of this disparity.

[...]

Do donors care about overhead costs?

A survey by Hope Consulting indicated that, among donors who do research on charities prior to donating, the most frequently sought-after data revolve around administrative efficiency. It seems evident that the decades-long emphasis on overhead costs as a metric of quality has had an impact on donor behavior: academic research suggests that donors tend to be quite sensitive to administrative costs, even when these costs have no relationship to the quality of the charity. This latter finding is based on data from an online giving platform. Donors could choose from numerous very similar charities – namely, projects posted by school teachers requesting funds. The platform itself added certain costs, but these costs were explicitly unrelated to the quality of the project. Yet, donors were still less likely to give when these costs were higher relative to the size of the request amount, showing strong preferences for projects with lower costs. In other words, projects received less donor funding when the administrative costs related to collecting funding were relatively higher in comparison to the projects' costs, despite the administrative costs having no

DOI: 10.4324/9781003145936-67

direct connection to the actual projects. Similar results have been found using workplace giving campaigns. Using variation over time in the overhead cost ratio of the same set of charities, prospective donors were less likely to give and gave smaller amounts to charities when their overhead cost ratios went up.

Most strikingly, a recent field experiment showed the degree to which donors focus on overhead costs, finding that the most effective use of a large donation is to cover administrative costs and to promote the charity on this basis (i.e. charities advertise the fact that large individual donations are used to pay administrative costs). In this study, potential donors were solicited with one of several possible approaches based on random assignment. Random assignment (or natural circumstances that lead to as-good-as-random assignment) is crucial, as merely observing that individuals behave in a particular way when faced with a certain situation is insufficient to draw inference about their general behavior and preferences. For instance, it could be that potential donors who are interested in charities that happen to emphasize low administrative costs are particularly generous, leading to a spurious correlation between low overhead ratios and generous donations. In this particular field experiment, individuals were assigned to one of four groups: (i) a control group who were simply asked for funds; (ii) a group who was told (truthfully) that a private donor had made a large donation; (iii) a third group who were also told that the private donor's funds were being used to match additional donations; and (iv) a fourth group who were further told that the private donor's funds were covering the overhead costs associated with the project. … this last treatment (iv), in which donors were told the administrative costs were covered by the large donation, raised three times as much as the control group and twice as much as the other two treatments, even though, in reality, the large donor's funds were fungible across the charity's activities – after all, it is merely an accounting exercise to designate certain funds, but not others, for a particular activity. It is clear, and perhaps not surprising, that donors look for shortcuts to gauge a charity's quality (in this case the concept of a large donor funding the charity's administrative costs appears to serve as a sufficient qualifier), given that even small costs associated with finding reliable information about charities can deter donors from giving.

Should donors care about overhead costs?

Having established that donors are, in fact, responsive to administrative costs, the natural question is whether this metric is useful. Of course, in extreme cases, in which a charity spends nearly all of its donations on staff compensation and other non-programmatic activities, overhead ratios can provide an important indicator of fraudulent activity. However, this does not appear to be the norm.

Some research suggests that overhead ratio metrics are nearly useless, since they represent average rather than marginal expenses. That is, the presence of fixed costs for a charity's operations, like rent for office space or basic office support services, means that an additional dollar donated will not be allocated primarily to administrative costs, or at least not at the same rate as the average ratio.

[…]

More importantly, successful delivery of the programs on which a charity is focused requires administrative support, and expanding these activities requires fundraising expenditures – indeed, using donations to fundraise and spread awareness may, in fact, be a particularly effective use of funds. A charity with a low overhead cost ratio that fails in its stated mission should not be judged more highly than one with a higher ratio that succeeds.

[…]

What effects does the focus on overhead costs have?

Since donors' decisions are affected by overhead costs, despite strong indications that measures of these costs may be counterproductive, it is instructive to examine the effects that this focus has on charities' operations. Administrative expense ratios (but not fundraising ratios) have fallen substantially in recent years, primarily driven by reductions in the proportion of funds spent on staff wages. Since staff wages generally make up a large part of administrative costs, an emphasis on reducing administrative costs almost necessarily means paying below-market salaries and providing less generous fringe benefits. This is particularly worrisome, as charities may find it difficult to compete in the labor market for talent. Paying wages that are low relative to similar jobs in the private sector means that the most talented workers are unlikely to choose to work for charities. While those working for charitable organizations may receive a so-called compensating differential from the "warm glow" that they may feel as a result of working for a cause in which they believe, this can only go so far in limiting the talent drain. For example, employees who are directly involved in the delivery of services with a social mission, such as case workers at a homeless shelter, may feel a great deal of personal satisfaction from helping the less fortunate. It stands to reason, though, that the IT support staff in that organization will experience less direct satisfaction compared to the case workers, since the IT workers will not typically be involved in the hands-on tasks that elicit the aforementioned warm glow. This implies that employees like those in the IT field may not be willing to accept a reduction in pay to work for a charity, and may instead choose the typically higher-paying private sector jobs. As such, charities may find themselves having to employ lower-quality workers in important support positions.

[…]

As a result of being less able to use higher compensation as a means of competing for desirable employees, charities may underinvest in necessary infrastructure. This is exemplified in a series of case studies that illustrate the pitfalls of keeping overheads low, with staff required to cover administrative roles outside of their purview and a general lack of support for key functions. Even large charities did little to no tracking of how funds were being spent, let alone how donors were being solicited, and the non-program staff had little experience in administration, accounting, or finance. For example, one charity outlined in the study did not have any staff with finance or accounting experience and found itself missing invoices and making bookkeeping errors; moreover, it was unable to track its donors or analyze fundraising, obviously inhibiting its overall effectiveness.

Unsurprisingly, misreporting of expense data among charities is therefore rampant. Public disclosure documents frequently improperly allocate expenses across different categories, perhaps unintentionally at times, but often in an attempt to reduce the all-important overhead cost ratio. This can, for example, take the form of classifying administrative expenses as program-related; a recent study found that one-quarter of US-based charities listed accounting fees as a program expenditure, despite instructions from the Internal Revenue Service to include them in overhead costs. Somewhat astonishingly, one-fifth of charities with total donations in excess of five million dollars reported no fundraising costs whatsoever. Yet, stricter standards are a double-edged sword. Regulatory burdens on charities, like requiring extensive governmental filings on finances, can, perversely, increase administrative expenditures owing to a greater emphasis on compliance. This can, in turn, reduce giving as donors are put off from donating in the face of higher overhead costs.

Potential alternatives to overhead cost ratios

The use of a single statistic like the overhead cost ratio is limiting and can often be misleading. Yet donors clearly want a simple metric by which to judge charities. In an effort to provide more meaningful measures, charity rating groups have moved towards more holistic approaches to evaluation. For example, the Better Business Bureau Wise Giving Alliance examines 20 standards, including whether a charity has board oversight and whether the charity assesses its own effectiveness in a formal way. Administrative and fundraising costs are included among these standards, but the threshold is relatively high and appears to be primarily used to screen out illegitimate charities. Similarly, Charity Navigator now evaluates the financial health and transparency of charities using multiple criteria; adjustments are made for the size of a charity and its area of focus to reflect differences in expectations for, say, a small, local animal shelter and a global aid agency. It has also begun an initiative to survey charities on their effectiveness and is planning to add these data to their ratings.

Limitations and gaps

While the burgeoning effective altruism movement [which is concerned with impact and cost-effective donations] focuses on better metrics of effectiveness for the evaluation of charities, it is not clear how to weigh immediate charitable needs, such as alleviating poverty, against investment in future potential, like biomedical research. Much of the existing academic research focuses on donors' taste (or distaste) for overhead costs and, to a lesser extent, the effects of this focus on the charities themselves; moreover, most of these papers study non-profit organizations in the US. It is unclear how the results might generalize to other countries, though donors' interest in the impact of their money is likely universal.

Finally, few studies have focused on how charities are actually organized and managed, which leaves a significant knowledge gap on this topic. Existing research is also insufficient when it comes to evaluating the impact that the single-minded focus on reducing overhead costs has on charities' operations.

Summary and policy advice

Due in large part to third-party ratings agencies' focus on relatively easy-to-measure metrics like overhead cost ratios, donors tend to believe that these measures are a useful way to decide how to direct their charitable funds. Donors clearly respond to overhead cost ratios to an excessive degree, with research showing that the aversion to high overhead costs can shift donor behavior to a great extent. However, this focus hurts non-profit organizations' effectiveness by limiting their ability to compete in the labor market and by altering their administrative structure in a counterproductive way.

Rather than making decisions driven by the value of a particular investment in staff or support, charities must also consider the impact on their cost ratio and, by extension, donors' willingness to give. Policymakers should resist the temptation to use these metrics to regulate charities' activities, even as they police against fraud. Alternative measures based on the true impact of a charity's activities would be far more useful, but they require substantial investigation and are often difficult to compare across different fields. For instance, it is far easier to gauge whether a food pantry is effective in feeding the hungry than whether a charity funding long-term research in disease prevention and control is spending its money wisely.

While better data is needed for more rigorous evaluation, policymakers should be mindful of the burdens imposed by strict reporting practices, particularly on smaller charities.

Conflicts and strategies of eliciting emotions for fundraisers

Jon Dean and Rachel Wood, 2017

Charity is inherently emotional work. Vast numbers of non-profit and voluntary sector organisations exist to tackle the most appalling social and individual suffering. Fundraisers are presented by some as overly virtuous figures – "moral trainers" acting as midwives to virtue and generosity, helping move money from those who have a surplus of it, to those who need it. Appealing to emotion sits at the heart of this process, as Martin Campbell put it in a blog for the [UK, Chartered] Institute of Fundraising. "It doesn't matter which, be it concern, worry, fear, affection or love, emotions are at the heart of our charitable giving, and are the essential starting point for engaging with our donors."

This article presents findings from interviews with 23 fundraisers, fundraising managers, and voluntary sector workers to argue that decisions around how, why, and when to invest in the elicitation of emotion in fundraising are often difficult and conflicted in a battle between questions of ethics and effectiveness. Interviewee concerns around the role of emotion in fundraising can be understood at the macro level of the voluntary sector, at the meso level of the organisation a fundraiser works for, and at the experiential micro-level of individual fundraisers themselves. The ethics of emotion and the strategic practice of how fundraisers and fundraising organisations negotiate utilising emotion are revealed, … with fundraisers making careful decisions about how and with whom to mobilise certain emotions at specific times, but ultimately with little certainty about how to balance competing ethical and practical interests, beyond analysing and being led by the context of individual situations.

[…]

Emotions and the practice of fundraisers

In this article we focus on what fundraisers think about the role of emotions in their work. Fundraisers frequently choose to use a comprehensive gamut of emotional approaches, from evoking nostalgic memories among potential donors to asking celebrities to suffer on screen for good causes. Emotions play an important role in donation decisions, and as social beings, donors will have different interpretations as to what constitutes "rational" behaviour in a giving situation than will fundraisers. Therefore, fundraisers need to be strategic in how they elicit emotional responses. Bennett found that fundraising adverts that are emotional and affective have the potential to generate mixed emotions

DOI: 10.4324/9781003145936-68

in the general public, with a complex and often unpredictable set of negative and positive emotional responses. Therefore, he surmises, perhaps unsurprisingly, fundraisers need to craft advertisements that arouse "desirable" emotions and avoid evoking "undesirable" ones.

Fundraisers also have to make choices about balancing emotional appeals, with more logical-rational appeals based on presenting an overview of need. In his content analysis of direct mail fundraising, Ritzenhein finds that fundraisers are more likely to rely on emotional arguments than logical arguments. Furthermore, over 60% of the emotion-centred materials did not provide any supporting statistics, examples, or testimonies, whereas only 25% of the logic-centred appeals failed to include these. Instead, emotional appeals centred on stressing beliefs and attitudes, persuasive or demonstrative language, or on showing gratitude to potential donors.

In terms of "what works," Chang found that "guilt appeals" can be more persuasive than non-guilt appeals, although the influence is complex and contingent on the products that are marketed and the size of the donation. Similarly, Chang and Lee, in an experiment examining the effectiveness of the framing of child poverty framing, showed that negative framing is effective and that "framing a charitable message negatively leads to higher persuasion than framing it positively." Slightly conversely however, Kerkhof and Kuiper found that when fundraising materials featured positive information regarding the attainment of a campaign's goal, donations were increased. Merchant, Ford, and Sargeant, in their analysis of the emotional processes involved when potential donors experience a fundraising appeal, found evidence to support a particular journey: That after exposure to a "problem statement" in an appeal, potential donors feel negative emotions, followed by positive emotions when they are given the opportunity to help solve the problem through making a contribution. These positive emotions can be built on by voluntary organisations by giving donors feedback on the charity's work, in turn improving the likelihood to give again. Therefore, the relationships that fundraisers make with donors, a cornerstone of their professional practice, is bound up with decisions about stressing emotional messages. Tindall and Waters' research showed that fundraisers found that fundraiser–donor relationships that relied on "emotional manipulation" may exclude detailed dialogues and conversations, lack insight into the true motivations for donors, and resultantly may stifle successful fundraising when compared to those that utilised detailed two-way dialogues. Pressing emotional buttons therefore can be seen as a risky short cut for fundraisers, but with obvious potential rewards: There is evidence that fundraising campaigns for disability issues are often successful in raising donations when using the dependence of people with disabilities to elicit feelings of sympathy, guilt, and pity in potential donors.

As this summary of the literature suggests, arousing or eliciting such emotions can be problematic ethically. In research on the accuracy of images used in homelessness fundraising appeals, Breeze and Dean found homeless participants felt misrepresented by stereotypical images, but were willing to accept these portrayals if donations were maximised as a result. This balance between accuracy and meeting fundraising targets is a concern and constant struggle for fundraisers: Naturally, the achievement of both would be preferable, but as one fundraising expert said in response, "It is incredibly lucky if you can find a creative, or team of creatives, who can combine the two principles, especially as normally in the charity sector there are limited funds, timescales and staff". This suggests that in making decisions about how to utilise emotions in fundraising materials, fundraisers face professional choices, which they address through their own trained judgement, but also mundane and practical elements, which are the often forgotten limitations of any job.

[…]

Findings

[…]

Ethics and effectiveness

Perhaps the first emotion that comes to mind when thinking of fundraising is that of guilt. Although interviewees agreed that guilt was a feature of fundraising's emotional "toolkit", they also identified a number of other emotions including pity, anger, empathy, shock and inspiration. As one fundraising consultant explained: "you can try to press different emotional buttons". The idea of "pressing buttons" is a useful one, as it suggests that emotion is seen as something of a "quick fix", or, as another fundraiser put it, a way to "prompt an instant response". Although some emphasised the convenience and efficiency of shocking emotional campaigns – "they work, it's that simple" – others focussed on the previously discussed unpredictability of trying to provoke emotional responses in the hope they will lead to actual gestures of support: "you don't know what emotion somebody is experiencing … you can't govern how people will respond to how they feel."

Although the effectiveness or predictability of using emotion was one area of debate, the rights and wrongs of doing so, particularly in terms of longer term consequences for public perceptions, was perhaps more central to respondents' accounts. Given that Merchant et al. found that both negative and positive emotions have a role to play in donors' responses, fundraisers wanted to make a clear distinction between the two, with "positive" emotions seen as a more ethical approach by many:

> *We just don't use [negative] visuals really, we talk about the positive side of things … 'Look what we've done for this person', essentially. (Fundraiser, homelessness voluntary organisation)*

> *It's got to be a balance of the positive and the negative. The best fundraising, it's about stories, it's about inspiring. (Policy officer, voluntary sector infrastructure organisation)*

> *I think an 'empowerment' or, 'Look at what we could do together" ... or, 'Look at the difference you can make by supporting', is a better positive narrative around it. (Policy officer, youth volunteering organisation)*

In contrast to these perceptions, one professional fundraiser we spoke to was of the view that sending supporters positive messages about organisations' achievements "doesn't work" because it fails to demonstrate an "ongoing need" for support, suggesting a preference for [a] logical-rational approach to appeals detailed by Ritzenhein. As these different views indicate, ethical questions for fundraisers and senior voluntary sector workers are never far away from the concern of effectiveness or "what works", with the two debates often in conflict with one another (with the extra complication that effectiveness can also be an issue of ethics, where ineffective fundraising materials are a waste of donations). As another interviewee, a policy director with a national voluntary sector infrastructure body, noted, fundraising is "the bit of the sector that is the most fraught with moral, managerial, quandaries." These "quandaries" we argue can be understood to operate at three levels of analysis, moving from the macros level of the wider voluntary sector to the meso level of the voluntary organisation, and, finally, to the micro level of the individual fundraiser.

Conflict at the level of the voluntary sector

Much of the conflict surrounding the use of emotion at this level emerged from political and economic changes that have led to a greater reliance on public rather than state funding. One fundraiser noted his perception that the fundraising market has increasingly become "more competitive and more saturated" as a result, leading to what he understood to be a more "transactional" or "procurement" based approach to fundraising. [...] There was a perception in several interviews that such "mass business" tactics were not trustworthy and may lead to unethical and manipulative elicitations of emotion.

[...]

Conflict at the level of the voluntary organisation

Respondents described fundraisers and fundraising departments as under increasing pressure from the rest of the organisation to raise substantial funds quickly and reliably. At the same time, participants stated that other departments within organisations could be critical of the fundraising strategies used. As a fundraising consultant told us:

> *Internally, fundraisers get it in the neck from their policy wing or programme wing for oversimplification, dumbing down, not telling it how it really is.*

This "dumbing down" could involve debates around the ethics of how emotion was being used in fundraising. A male interviewee who ran a private fundraising firm for voluntary sector clients spoke in some detail about this issue: he imagined the response of a direct marketing fundraiser explaining the situation to the board of a voluntary organisation:

> *Yes, we can give you a return of 4:1 on your money over 2 years. But we can't talk to people about all that boring policy stuff, we have to just show them the big-eyed kiddies and tell them that they're homeless or hungry or ill or starving.*

He felt that workers in other roles in voluntary organisations have come to view fundraisers and fundraising generally not only as "dumbed down" but also as the morally and ethically "grubby end of the organisation". His account points to the disparity of priorities between fundraising and other sectors of the organisation:

> *The fundraising department are the ones saying, "We need to raise the money." And everywhere else in the organisation they will say, "You're stereotyping, You're perpetuating people's negative perceptions."*

These divisions may originate in, and be perpetuated by, the organisational structure of charities in which fundraising and policy may not be adequately integrated. The fundraiser described a situation in which workers in different roles may have backgrounds, qualifications, and employment trajectories that are so different as to make them "poles apart … from completely opposite ends of the spectrum." Being distant from the conflicted choices within fundraising, however, also meant sector workers and commentators could be critical of the ethics of emotion while not having to have the difficult yet necessary discussion between "what's right' and "what works", or make choices in this regard.

One example of respite from conflict was provided by a female participant who had worked as a fundraiser for an international development organisation and now worked within the field of youth volunteering. Citing VSOs [Voluntary Service Overseas] guidelines on representing the developing world, she saw her approach to the potentially ethically "dangerous" nature of stereotypical campaigns as supported by an established precedent in her sector […]. She described how using "shame and guilt" in fundraising would mean her organisation would be "doing ourselves a discredit". Here, established parameters set following long standing debates on the ethics of representation can provide some release from potential conflicts around emotions in fundraising, at both the level of the sector and the organisation, at least in the field of international aid.

Conflict at the level of the individual fundraiser

Questions around the use of emotion in fundraising often appeared to be ongoing, unresolved, and even potentially troubling for individual fundraisers. In interviews, it was clear that a great degree of personal and reflexive internal wrestling occurred, with participants often finding it difficult to express exactly how the conflicts presented previously in this article could be adequately solved.

> *I don't know. Maybe ... I'm torn ... It's really complicated. (Policy director, voluntary sector infrastructure organisation)*
>
> *I think it's a real tension that charities [face] – it's a conundrum. There's no right or wrong, I think. (Fundraising consultant)*
>
> *I do [think it's a problem], yes I do, I suppose. But then they've got to do it, haven't they? I don't know how else they would get the money. I don't know. (Director, Advocacy organisation)*
>
> *It's exceptionally difficult. It's difficult to know what to do for the best. (Project worker, homelessness organisation)*

Although these extracts might seem insignificant, they do point to a notable degree of irresolution and personal conflict below the surface. In contrast to these ongoing internal conflicts, some interviewees did make clear statements of ethics surrounding the ways they would use emotion in fundraising:

> *[Another campaign] was all about guilt ... I am not interested in fundraising like that ... We could make everybody feel bad, and say that, and I won't do that. (Chief executive, children's health charity)*
>
> *I would seriously question if I wanted to go and work for a charity that only played on that one form of fundraising approach ... It's just that that doesn't feel like why I joined the charity sector – to shame and guilt people into giving. (Research director, youth volunteering organisation)*

These personal values also intersect with professional choices in how interviewees had chosen to deploy emotion strategically, especially when working closely with high net worth donors rather than wider facing public campaigns. As a fundraiser for a homelessness organisation stated, she was able to control the targeting of emotion due to the "close relationship" that such donors seek with the charities they support. The interviewee described this kind of relationship in more detail in the context of a homelessness charity:

> *We had two long-term corporate supporters ... they are local companies who were started separately by one guy here, one guy there ... Basically, they say to us that if it hadn't worked out, they could have ended up homeless themselves ... They can really see themselves there. So, that's kind of quite an important point about who we are going to then target with this, because I think with these visuals and video stuff, if you send it to someone like them they go, "Yes, I get that" straight away. So yes, it's all about targeting the right people.*

[...]

This account suggests that the knowledge that comes from a closer relationship with a supporter allows emotion to be deployed in ways that have more knowable outcomes, allowing "desirable" emotions to be elicited and creating a less conflicted context for the use of emotion. Emotion could also be deployed strategically depending on the intention of the message, or, as a fundraising consultant put it, "different communications have different functions", suggesting that emotional buttons could be pressed to secure an initial engagement.

Conclusions

Designing and operationalising fundraising appeals is difficult. There is no one guaranteed tool to raise donations, and although the literature presented here generally shows that emotionally negative appeals may be more successful in raising donations (an assertion supported by interviewees even if they were personally against such approaches), all emotions are personally interpreted and experienced. The new UK Fundraising Regulator's (2017) Code of Fundraising Practice does have some professional guidance on what is not acceptable: placing undue pressure on a person to donate; generating donations out of financial guilt or embarrassment, or sending communications that are indecent or grossly offensive, or are intended to cause distress or anxiety. (In contrast, the [US] Association of Fundraising Professionals, 2014, Code of Ethical Standards does not mention emotion explicitly instead focusing on causing "harm" or "exploiting" relationships with donors, volunteers or clients.) But the [UK] Fundraising Regulator argues that fundraisers must be able to demonstrate that the purpose of a direct mail was "to enhance the message and/or the emotional engagement in the cause." Terms such as "undue pressure" are liable to be interpreted differently by potential donors: One person's "indecent or grossly offensive" is another's "emotional engagement." What this article has shown is that fundraisers and those working to create, or having oversight of, fundraising campaigns in a range of voluntary organisations in the UK are aware of and live out the debate between ethics and effectiveness. This affects their work in different ways within the wider voluntary sector, within their organisation, and how it affects them as an individual with their own professional opinions and values. As MacQuillin discusses in detail, ethical fundraising involves a search for balance, "balanc[ing] the duty of fundraisers to solicit support on behalf of their beneficiaries, with the right of the donor not to be subjected to undue pressure to donate." Our research shows that individuals working in voluntary organisations are well aware of this need and outline the conflicts that may impede this balance.

A critical fundraising perspective: understanding the beneficiary experience

Abhishek Bhati and Angela Eikenberry, 2018

Most of the research in fundraising can be divided into the investigation of two main areas: *who gives,* looking at demographics such as age, gender, and income status; and reasons for *why people give,* looking at factors such as personal attitudes, beliefs, faith, or values.

[...]

Both of these areas studied – who gives and why – primarily seek to understand ways to get people to give more, and are focused on relationship formation between donors and nonprofits or on mechanisms to increase giving. The vast majority of research leaves out examining or questioning *who benefits, who decides,* and the *experience of beneficiaries,* who are equally important if not more important within the philanthropic relationship. Beneficiaries are critical stakeholders to NGOs and the main reason most NGOs exist. A critical, post-colonial theory lens would help us to examine questions about who benefits from philanthropy and fundraising and who decides what is being given, to whom, and in what ways, as well as understand how to incorporate the voice of beneficiaries into NGO and donor decision making, particularly beneficiaries in developing countries.

Who benefits

One reason people support NGOs is their belief that their support benefits people who are poor and who are the most disadvantaged in society. However, giving in the United States goes primarily to religious organizations (32% of total) and education (15%); human services receive only 12 percent of contributions and health only 8 percent. Other studies have found that less than one-third of all charitable contributions in the United States go to aid the poor. Organizations serving people of color receive a very small percentage of contributions – only 3.6 percent of U.S. foundation dollars are granted to minority-led NGOs and estimates are that between only 5 and 7 percent of foundation giving is earmarked specifically for programs and activities benefiting women and girls. Among individual donors in the United States, 14.6 percent report giving to a particular area that impacts women and girls. Only around 6 percent of total giving in the United States goes to international

DOI: 10.4324/9781003145936-69

causes and most of this money goes to investment in social infrastructure such as roads, sewage disposable systems, and education-related activities.

In the UK, religious causes also receive the largest percent of individual contributions (14%), followed by medical-related areas (13%), children (12%) and overseas (12%). People who are homeless (4%), people with disabilities (3%) and elderly people (3%) receive a much smaller percentage of total contributions (even fewer than animals at 7% of the total). Organizations working in the area of racial or ethnic justice represented only 4 percent of total spending in the UK. In a study of European foundation giving, which included the UK, just over one-third of foundations (37%) said at least some of their programmatic activities are specifically intended to benefit women and girls; however, most of the surveyed foundations devoted less than 10 percent of their expenditures in support of women and girls. Mohan and Breeze show only a small percentage of charitable giving is directed to people who are poor. Similarly, a small percentage of total global aid goes to people in need of assistance in developing countries as most of the money goes into administrative overhead, domestic campaigns, and debt forgiveness programs.

What explains these giving trends? According to Mohan and Breeze, donors in the United States and the UK tend to "support beneficiaries with whom they identify as a result of personal connections, common experiences and shared membership of social networks". Thus, wealthy philanthropists – who provide the bulk of philanthropic dollars – tend to give the majority of their donations to organizations from which they or their family directly benefit, such as the symphony, church, or their alma mater as well as to amenity services such as education, culture, and health. This self-interested giving helps explain why more is not given internationally and to the poor. A post-colonial perspective can help us to also understand that the systematic exploitation of the colonies of European empires and also the Othering of people living in these colonies as "inferior," "barbaric" and "savage," and thus, "undeserving," explains why Western donors may explicitly or implicitly be influenced by such colonial stereotyping and think of people in developing countries as not worthy and give less to people who are poor and living in developing countries.

Further, a post-colonial perspective adds that colonialism played a vital role in the current state of poverty in developing countries by looting colonized countries of their material and human resources. For example, the slave trade depopulated Africa for four centuries and Africans were transported to different countries to build the nations once ruled by European colonizers. Nonetheless, charitable giving by relatively wealthy donors from Western/developed (colonizer) countries is often presented as an antidote to the inequities created by colonization. This is part of why it is problematic that donors are enabled to hold so much power over who benefits from NGOs and philanthropy.

Who decides?

In most democratic countries, citizens pay taxes and legislators decide where and how to spend the money for various social problems, such as to address poverty. These decisions occur among legislators through engaging in political discussions with each other and through this process, citizens contribute toward public policy decisions. If citizens do not like the decisions made by policy makers, they can cast their vote for someone else in the next election. However, in the case of philanthropy, the decisions regarding helping any segment of society, either domestic or international, does not come under any legal scrutiny as donors are spending their private money and are not elected by citizens to make such decisions. Thus, wealthy individuals like Warren Buffet or Bill and Melinda Gates have a strong influence on the resolution of public or social problems. For instance, in the case of the Bill and Melinda Gates Foundation, which has made public health a funding priority, it has, according to Nickel and Eikenberry, "the governing capacity to decide which diseases are eradicated – who lives and who dies – not because they represent the public and collective will, but because they have accumulated massive profits". As Reich notes: "citizens can unelect their representatives if they are dissatisfied with the spending programs of the state; the Gates Foundation also has a domestic and global spending program, partly supported through tax subsidies, but its directors and trustees cannot be unelected".

Philanthropists have long been criticized for being unaccountable and having unequal and unfair influence on public and social policy, eroding support for governmental programs, and exacerbating the same social and economic inequalities that they purport to remedy. These concerns are worsened by the influence of neoliberal discourse on donors, who increasingly seek out new approaches to philanthropy that are dedicated to "solving the world's problems" through market-like, individualized means and data-driven solutions with measurable outcomes – what has become known as "effective" philanthropy. Over twenty-five years ago, Ostrander and Schervish warned about an increasing *donor-centric* philanthropy that "runs the risk of obscuring issues that are of concern to recipients and therefore to philanthropy as a whole". Ostrander also argued that trends have further shifted to the supply side, that is becoming more donor focused, "raising donor influence and directly running counter to a mutual and reciprocal framework between donors and recipient groups". In other words, in an ideal scenario, beneficiaries and donors are equal stakeholders in the eyes of NGO leaders, but organizations often place far more importance on (Western) donors because they keep organizations financially afloat.

A post-colonial perspective also shows that one of the reasons NGO leaders may give more importance to donors is that often Western donors are portrayed as superior and "helpful," even as for centuries Western colonists systematically exploited people living in developing countries through the slave trade and stealing natural resources. As noted earlier, post-colonial theorists also argue that colonizers maintain unaccountable power over the colonized, typically propagated by several stereotypes such as framing the colonized as wild, barbaric, lazy, or helpless. These stereotypes rationalize colonizers' use of power or control to trade humans as slaves and steal the natural resources of colonies. In the current context, philanthropy is one response to the stereotypes, putting

Western donors in a "helpful" position to bridge inequalities between the developing countries (as most of them were colonies of European empires) and developed countries even while they exploit. Fundraisers' focus on donors undermines the importance of beneficiaries who are equal stakeholders and continues to feed into stereotypes of people who are poor as unworthy or lazy. In the next section, we shift the focus of fundraising from a donors' perspective and focus on the experiences of beneficiaries.

The experience of beneficiaries

Theories and practices of fundraising tend to primarily look at the relationship of donors and NGOs and completely leave out beneficiaries. For example, Kelly defines fundraising as the management function of relationships between an NGO and its donors, and Greenfield calls fundraising a unique form of communication based on "social scientific principles" that produces healthy relationships between a NGO and donors. The literature on fundraising also has frequent references to "relationship building", "friend raising" and "philanthropic partnerships", but these focus only on the organization doing the fundraising and the donor. Why are beneficiaries left out? Looking at this question from a post-colonial perspective suggests this may be due in part to power asymmetries between beneficiaries and NGOs or donors.

There are only a handful of studies in the fundraising literature that try to capture beneficiaries' perspectives about their experiences in fundraising. Breeze and Dean interviewed people who are homeless in the UK and asked them what they felt about their representation by nonprofit organizations. Participants expressed that they wanted NGOs to tell their whole story, and not focus on mere sympathy shots. Similarly, in a study of the representation of destitute children by NGOs in India, Bhati and Eikenberry found that children wanted to be seen as happy and in a "good light" telling the whole story about their lives but also generating awareness about the hardships they face, such as child labor or marriage.

However, NGOs frequently face competition from other organizations working toward similar missions, thereby competing for the same donors. This competition feeds into an NGO portraying beneficiaries as "exhibitions" that is, showing them in a poor light to gather sympathy from donors to generate more dollars. Studies have suggested that the portrayal of beneficiaries has an impact on recall and attitudes toward supporting and giving. Several studies have found that NGO organizations' fundraising advertisements foster guilt or pity to elicit donations.

Research also suggests that fundraising images portraying beneficiaries as "needy," such as images of victims of disasters, women, or children, tend to generate more donations.

[…]

These images of neediness attract donors, as they are simplified, and stereotypical, and focus on evoking emotions of donors to give by NGO. This approach reduces beneficiaries to mute spectators, where their utility is just to pose in photographs as models that are often stereotypical and lacking in context, thus undermining the aim of philanthropy. For instance, when we see the image of a boy who is crying and covered in soot and tar, which creates a difference between the viewer (often Western donors: clean, hygienic, happy, and comparatively well-off) and the person projected (people from developing countries: dirty, unhappy/crying, and poor). Overwhelmingly, NGOs use such images because they still prove to be highly effective fundraising strategies. The effectiveness of images of people who are poor, especially of children, can be witnessed in the fact that three of the largest fundraising NGOs in Canada that sponsor children, for example, generate almost ten times more funds than the top three nonchild-sponsorship organizations.

Scholars and practitioners have criticized such negative imagery as "pornographic" and that reinforces negative stereotypes about people living in developing countries. Cohen argues that the sight of a half-naked emaciated child, not ashamed to plead, places the audience – typically living in developed countries such as the United States and the UK – in a position of superiority and as a savior. Viewers in the West do not tend to witness such a level of poverty and unhygienic living conditions. This kind of imagery automatically puts donors in a superior role. Thus, this representation of people who are poor contributes to increasing the perceived differences between people living in a developing country such as India and a developed country such as the United States or the UK. Fundraising can construct beneficiaries in ways that perpetuate colonialist stereotypes; that is, as helpless victims.

Ideally, most NGOs' missions should seek to empower beneficiaries and promote social equity through fundraising imagery. NGOs might implicitly undermine their own mission and values by stereotyping beneficiaries. Hence, fundraisers should constantly be aware of how they engage and portray beneficiaries.

An alternative approach to fundraising

Fundraising is essential to the survival of NGOs and to the delivery of NGO programs. Scholars and practitioners have argued that the practice of fundraising is about creating and cultivating relationships; from a sustainability perspective, NGOs should foster relationships with donors on a long-term basis rather than solely focusing on soliciting more donations as standalone transactions. However, fundraising is not only about donors and relationship-building with them for organizations' survival. Fundraising is equally, if not more so, about the beneficiaries that NGOs are helping and serving. As noted earlier, the fundraising imagery used by NGOs to generate awareness and donations has been criticized for fostering stereotypical attitudes against people of color. It is important to understand the "unintended" consequences generated from using such imagery. As such, fundraisers in any country might benefit from truly engaging with and listening to beneficiaries.

The European NGO Confederation for Relief and Development (CONCORD) issued guidelines that state choices of images and messages should be based on principles of: 1) respect for the dignity of the people concerned; 2) belief in the equality of all people; and 3) acceptance of the need to promote fairness, solidarity, and justice. Related to this, Lentfer has

Table 4.1.2 List of dos and don'ts in representing beneficiaries in fundraising advertisements

Do	*Don't*
Layer Information. Build opportunities for people to "dig deeper" through multiple layers of information on development issues.	**Use Jargon**. If you can help it.
Analyze voice. No one is "voiceless." People no longer want to hear *about* people in need in poor countries, but *from* them.	**Supercoat Poverty**. Don't build on ignorance or romanticism of poor countries or what it is to be poor. Poverty sucks, but it doesn't mean people are victims.
Seek Out Story. Use storytelling to provide context and connection. Enable people to tell their own stories whenever possible.	**Skip the Boring Stuff**. Acknowledge and show complexity. Portray multiple factors and long-term perspectives.
Show People's Sense of Agency. There's no need to underestimate or fail to represent people's abilities, skills, or commitment. Root out stereotypes, generalizations, victimization, and exploitation.	**Highlight the problems without offering a "way forward."**
Take Two on Technology. Avoid the hype of "solutions" and demonstrate the demand side for technology.	**Be afraid to take more risks.**
Bridge the "Us" vs. "Them" Divide. Create opportunities for people to connect with the universality of the human experience without relying on pity, guilt, or shame.	**Ignore criticisms and different perspectives about your work**. Be aware of the potential for self-congratulatory and self-righteous tendencies that are often part of international development work.
Results & Failure: Make the Connection. Don't underestimate how much donors want to see how you learned from failure and that you are making adjustments to your strategy approach, or programs.	
Show Who's Driving. Accountability is no longer just about reporting to donors, but more importantly demonstrating how people's own initiatives, feedback, and decision making are incorporated in your work.	

developed a list of specific dos and don'ts for fundraising communications. The dos focus on engaging donors for deeper discussions about poverty and adding context to images by telling a fuller story of the beneficiaries. Similarly, they focus on reducing the divide between poor beneficiaries and rich donors. See Table 4.1.2.

[...]

A positive example demonstrating CONCORD's and Lentfer's guidelines is a fundraising advertisement campaign for Syrian children called the "Most Shocking Second a Day." Since 2014, this video has had over 57 million views. The ad creates awareness about the suffering of Syrian refugees without negatively portraying them and by using a powerful narrative focusing on the hardships and life-threating situations refugees, especially children, go through on a daily basis while living in a war-torn country like Syria. This campaign bridges the gap between people in developing and developed countries as it uses the case of a British girl trapped in a home and imagines London being bombarded with missiles and bombs, not Syria. Similarly, another campaign focuses on generating awareness about the forced marriage of girls before they turn eighteen, in Burkina Faso. This campaign highlights the consequences of early marriage, which robs thousands of girls of their childhoods, and it does so in a dignified way. The campaign allows a young girl, Zalissa, to tell her own story about convincing her father not to marry her off at a young age and how she is now inspiring other parents to do the same.

Alternative approaches such as these might go a long way in telling a more holistic story about the beneficiaries of NGOs. Although such positive images of beneficiaries might negatively affect the revenue of NGOs in the short term – since the research discussed previously shows, donors tend to give more to sad images – in the long term, this more holistic strategy might help in building more equitable relationships with donors to engage them more in the lives of beneficiaries, rather than just giving standalone donations. Furthermore, showcasing beneficiaries in a stereotypical manner may ultimately lead to negative consequences for NGOs. As discussed previously, it may lead to mission misalignment as showing people living in developing countries as weak and needy may not align with some NGOs' missions of promoting equity and welfare among the people they serve. Fundraising professionals should be aware of the unintended consequences of how they fundraise, and be mindful when tactics that are effective at raising funds may actually be inconsistent with the organization's stated goals.

4.2 Ethics in fundraising

Rights-balancing fundraising ethics

Ian MacQuillin, 2019

How do you know what is and isn't ethical in fundraising? Not only is it not an easy question but in fundraising we don't possess nearly enough of the tools we need to be able to answer it.

[…]

Think of an example of an ethical dilemma in fundraising … Got one?

I bet a pound to a penny most readers came up with a corporate donor that conflicts with the charity's mission, such as a tobacco company that wants to support a cancer charity. Many books, articles and conference presentations use just such an example.

Or if you didn't think of the mission-conflicting corporate donation, were you thinking of a particular form of fundraising that you find distasteful – 'chuggers' perhaps, or maybe telephone fundraisers?

What these two examples have in common is that the answers are fairly black and white, but for different reasons.

A mission-conflicting corporate donation is prohibited by many codes of practice. It is therefore easy to say this is wrong.

And if you think 'chuggers' are unethical, that is equally black and white, to you, because that is something that you would never do. But just because you would never do something, does that therefore mean that it would be unethical for anyone else to do it? It might seem black and white to you, but someone else might see it as white and black – or more likely, grey.

Between the certainties of what the rules say you can and can't do and your personal belief system is where we encounter the myriad shades of grey of the ethical palette.

And fundraisers are just not well equipped to deal with these grey areas, in large part because we don't have enough ethical theory that we can draw on to help us understand and resolve professional ethical dilemmas. This is why fundraising ethics is often presented in such black and white terms – by fundraisers either wanting to be told what is right and what is wrong, based on the codes; or someone who is not a fundraiser (it's usually a non-fundraiser) telling them what is right and what is wrong, based on their personal moral conviction.

But there are many ethical dilemmas in the grey regions that neither the codes nor your personal conviction are well equipped to resolve. Here are just a few.

DOI: 10.4324/9781003145936-71

- Is it OK for a person to feel guilty if they decline to give in response to being asked? They might feel guilty simply because they *are* guilty, because they know they should be doing more. ...
- Should you refrain from using images of beneficiaries that show the stark reality of their situation, if using that image impinges on the beneficiaries' 'dignity'? ...
- Should you contact donors only if you have their consent to do so? ...
- Would you engage in fundraising that aims to position your cause as preferential or more deserving than a different cause? ...
- Would you tell donors that you had absolutely no fundraising costs at all – because a different group of donors had already paid for them – and so 'every penny' they gave you would go 'directly to the cause'? Would you be concerned that this might be fostering among the general public a totally unrealistic expectation about the true costs of fundraising that could ultimately undermine trusts in charities?

These are all big questions that the rules give little insight into. But it is equally hard deciding what the right thing is, simply based on what you 'feel' to be right: the more complex the issue, the harder it is to 'feel' your way through it.

And this is not to mention the plethora of day-to-day ethical dilemmas any fundraiser faces in professional practice, such as when to contact donors, how much to ask for, where to contact them, in which ways to contact them – all of which have ethical as well as best practice dimensions. Just because something is tried and trusted best practice doesn't mean you ought to do it every time you could do it. And you have to know when you ought and ought not do it.

As a professional it is incumbent upon any fundraiser to resolve these ethical challenges and arrive at a decision about the 'right thing' that is based on your professional knowledge, not just your personal opinion.

[...]

Ethical theory 101

It's important to understand the difference between so-called 'normative' ethics and applied ethics.

Applied ethics helps you to work out what you ought or ought not do in particular situations; most codes of practice contain much of a profession's applied ethics. By contrast, normative ethics which is where we encounter theories about what is right and wrong and general ideas about how we ought to live – helps you to understand why you ought or ought not do those things.

At its core ethics is about doing the right thing for the right recipients, while normative ethical theories provide ways to answer the questions 'what is the right thing?' and 'for whom are we doing the right thing?'.

[...]

Two of the main branches of normative ethics are what are known as consequentialism and deontology.

Consequentialism, as the name suggests, tells you that the right thing to do is what has the best consequences or best outcomes, specifically actions that promote good and avoid harm.

Deontology is about doing the right thing because it is the right thing, because it conforms to a pre-existing moral principle, such as always telling the truth and never lying. Because it is not contingent on outcomes, deontology is sometimes called non-consequentialism.

[…]

Most – in fact almost all – fundraising ethics is applied ethics and it's to be found in various codes of practice.

Codes of practice tell you what you can and can't do and so they create ethical prescriptions for professional practice. Doing something forbidden by your code is, by definition, unethical. But not all ethical dilemmas will be covered by the code. There will be lots of grey areas the code can't help you with – such as whether it is acceptable that someone feel guilty if they decline a solicitation request – and when you encounter those, you need some kind of normative theory to help you to decide what to do.

[…]

From what has been written about fundraising ethics, we can pull out three candidates for a normative theory of fundraising ethics: trustism, donor centrism, and service of philanthropy.

Trustism

This says the right thing to do in fundraising is the one that maintains public trust. So fundraising is ethical when it does this and unethical when it does not. The question you must ask in trying to resolve an ethical dilemma is whether your proposed resolution would maintain or undermine public trust. But this is a consequentialist idea, so it needs evidence about what the effects on public trust actually are (or likely to be). You can't just assume or believe that trust would be damaged.

Donor centrism

Most fundraisers will be familiar with this idea as a form of best practice. From an ethical perspective, this says that the right thing to do in fundraising is basically do what your donors want – to put their needs, wants and desires at the heart of everything you do as a fundraiser. But this comes in two variants.

The consequentialist version of donor centrism requires you put the donor at the heart of your activities because this is the best way to raise more sustainable income: the better an experience you give them, the more they will give. This is how Ken Burnett describes relationship fundraising in his eponymous book.

But the deontological variant requires you to put the donors' wants and desires at the heart of what you do because this is morally the right thing to do for the donor. And strictly speaking, this is the case even if doing so doesn't result in raising more money.

[...]

Service of philanthropy

US fundraising guru Hank Rosso said fundraising is the servant of philanthropy and so the ethical role of fundraising is to bring 'meaning' to a donor's giving. Fundraising is thus ethical when it brings this meaning, and unethical when it does not. This idea – which casts fundraisers in the roles of philanthropy advisors – has a bit more transaction in the USA than the UK.

[...]

I would suggest that most codes of practice are predicated on trustist and donor centrist fundraising ethics. Both these, and service of philanthropy, confer most of a fundraiser's ethical duties on donors (or even non-donors). It's actually quite staggering – and a little bit shocking – that in almost everything written about fundraising ethics, beneficiaries are rarely mentioned, to the point you could easily conclude that fundraisers owe no ethical duty to their beneficiaries at all.

So to correct this and bring the beneficiary back into ethical decision making, I developed a normative theory of fundraising ethics I call rights-balancing fundraising ethics.

This states that:

> Fundraising is ethical when it balances the duty of fundraisers to ask for money on behalf of their beneficiaries, with the relevant rights of donors, such that a mutually-optimal outcome is achieved and neither stakeholder is significantly harmed.

One of a donor's key rights will be the right not to be subjected to 'undue pressure' to donate. This is the phrase used in the Fundraising Regulator's code of practice in the UK and mirrors the term used in the Charities Act 2006. But what counts as 'undue' pressure isn't defined anywhere, while the use of the word 'undue' implies that some kind of pressure is 'due', or permissible.

So in everyday, professional practice, perhaps the main way this ethical balancing act will be used will be when fundraisers aim to balance their duty to ask for money with the right of donors not to be subjected to undue pressure to give.

But fundraisers won't want to go back to first principles every time they encounter an ethical dilemma in fundraising. It's time-consuming and intellectually intensive trying to weigh all the factors to achieve a balance and the answer probably suggests itself without going through this whole rigmarole. People use rules of thumb all the time to help them make decisions and navigate professional and social life. We can do that in fundraising ethics too.

In any practical ethical dilemma in fundraising, the rule of thumb will probably be to do what you think the donor will want. That'll probably prevent harm to the donor (such as feelings of guilt and other negative emotions), protect sustainable income, and maintain public trust, while any potential harm to beneficiaries from foregoing a possible donation is likely to be minimal to non-existent. The challenge of course, is whether you can say with confidence what your donor really wants – based on your professional judgement and experience, which hopefully includes hard evidence – or are you just guessing or being swayed by your own personal views.

But rules of thumb can only take us so far. There will be times when we'll need a much more tailored and sophisticated solution to the challenge before us and this will be especially true when we move the ethical dilemma out the domain of day-to-day professional practice and into sector-wide policy-making, where bad decisions have the potential to seriously harm beneficiaries.

Fundraising as an ethical act

Michael O'Neill, 1994

Most discussion of ethics is narrow and negative, as if morality were worth talking about only when people are immoral. In the media and at the market-place, people talk about ethics when a corporation hides information on the harmful effects of its products, when a government official gets caught with his or her hand in the till, when Reverend Y or Rabbi Z fools around with a member of the congregation.

If discussion of ethics in general is narrow and negative, discussion of ethics in fundraising is doubly so. The usual topics are lying about the cause, accepting tainted money, using high-pressure tactics, misusing prospect infor-mation, concealing fundraising costs, raising money on commission, and so forth. These are real problems – where there is money, there will always be temptation and often sin – but the ethics of fundraising deserves broader, deeper, and less sin-oriented reflection. One way to do this is to examine the relevance of general ethical theory to fundraising. There is no reason why the young profession of fundraising should ignore the ancient and rich tradition of philosophical and religious ethics. The potential relevance of that tradition may be illustrated by a brief foray into three great ethical theories – Aristotle's, Immanuel Kant's, and the utilitarian theory of Jeremy Bentham and John Stuart Mill – as well as some major themes found in all ethical systems.

Fundraisers can serve as moral trainers

Aristotle said that we are born with the *capacity* for virtue but not with virtue itself; that can be developed only through repeated virtuous acts. By telling the truth we become truthful; by repeatedly showing courage, we become courageous. He also taught that virtue stands in the middle, atop the diffi-cult peak of human behavior; in the chasms of either side lie vices. He uses the virtue of generosity as an example: a person who gives wisely and well is generous; a person who gives nothing or too little is miserly; a person who gives too much is irresponsible. Generosity, we might add, is important in any society and extremely important in a society such as the United States, where human needs far outstrip the capabilities of families and the will of govern-ment. Aristotle noted that generosity is not something that comes easily or automatically to most people: "most men are fonder of getting money than of giving". Most of us have to be pushed, prodded, motivated, led. Moral virtue,

DOI: 10.4324/9781003145936-72

he held, is developed by training. We can add that in the case of generosity, there are various trainers – parents, one would hope; religious leaders; friends; spouses; and so forth. But the need for generosity in society is so great, the potential so great, and the trainers so few – and are being weakened all the time – that more help is needed. The relatively new profession of fundraising has, in this sense, added to the societal pool of moral trainers. Fundraisers give people needed opportunities and incentives to practice generous acts and therefore become generous. They also help people make good decisions about giving. As Aristotle noted, the virtue of generosity means not just giving, but giving to the right persons in the right amounts at the right time, and even with pleasure.

[...]

At their best, fundraisers help people give wisely and well, avoiding the pitfalls or vices of miserliness on the one hand and irresponsibility on the other.

[...]

Fundamental relationship between fundraising and moral development

Aristotle taught that the fundamental goal of ethics was happiness, and that happiness came primarily from the full exercise of one's faculties along lines of excellence .... Happiness, Aristotle said, assumes a reasonable amount of material and social goods – a home, certain amounts of money, family, friends; but most of all happiness depends on the development and exercise of the moral and intellectual virtues, for they pertain most closely to the nature of human beings. It is somewhat pleasurable to wiggle your big toe, but it is more pleasurable to run, and more pleasurable still to talk with friends, listen to music, read, think, help someone in need. The closer you get to the essence of being human, the more potential for happiness there is.

Fundraisers often help people with means raise their sights a little, become better human beings, focus less on material and social goods and more on intellectual and moral virtue – in other words, exercise their faculties along lines of excellence. Throughout history many have amassed great wealth, but few have seriously attempted to use their wealth to benefit society, as did Andrew Carnegie, Margaret Olivia Sage, the Rockefeller family, and the Haas family or the Levi Strauss fortune. These individuals, unlike most rich people, rose above the simple accumulation of wealth and sought to use wealth in what Aristotle would call a virtuous manner, to make full use of their faculties along lines of excellence. These people shared their wealth largely on their own initiative, but most rich people could use a little push. Enter the fundraiser.

This is not to say that fundraisers are therefore virtuous people, they may or may not be. The point is that the *act*, or practice, of fundraising has moral significance: some dimensions of the fundraising act are fundamentally and directly related to moral or ethical development, whatever actually happens in individual cases.

Charitable giving and the maxim of altruism

Immanuel Kant expressed his famous "categorical imperative" in this way: "Act in such a way that you would want the maxim, the underlying principle, of your action to become a universal law". Thus, you repay money you have borrowed because you would want everyone to act the same (especially everyone who owed you money). ... Kant notes that the best way to test a maxim is to imagine the effect of its opposite. The ethical power of the maxim, "One should always tell the truth," is revealed by reflection on the consequences of everyone lying at will: trust in personal relations would end; society would be in chaos. A maxim is unethical if, led to its logical conclusion, it self-destructs.

Similarly, the ethical power of the altruism maxim, "One should help others, share one's good with others" may be tested by imagining the effect of its opposite, "One should keep all of one's own goods at all costs." A world without charity, without altruism, would, humanly speaking, self-destruct. The maxim of altruism is not an easy one and is far from being a universal practice, but the spread of that maxim, the effort to make it more universally accepted, is certainly a work of ethics.

The cultivation of the general habit of altruism – not only the solicitation of this particular gift at this time – is, of course, an important part of the work of fundraisers. The very word "cultivation" implies this: one must get used to the idea of giving and then become more and more accustomed to giving through progressively more generous gifts, before the maxim underlying a charitable act is fully realized, before it truly becomes willed as a universal law.

Kant's second great ethical principle is "Act so that you treat humanity, whether in your own person or in that of another, always as an end and never as a means only". He elaborates: "Everything has either a price or a dignity", that is, either relative worth or absolute worth. The idea that only human beings have absolute worth, that material goods have only relative worth, has clear implications for the fundraiser's role.

Fundraisers can bring great good to great numbers of people

The utilitarians Bentham and Mill were uncomfortable with Aristotle's assumption of a definable human nature and thought that Kant was too idealistic. Bentham and Mill wanted a more concrete and measurable basis of ethics, so they taught that ethics equals the greatest good for the greatest number of people. If your action will bring more pleasure than pain to more people, it is good; otherwise, it is bad. Far from being selfish hedonism, this theory, according to its proponents, called human beings to put the good of the community before their own personal good: What will bring the greatest good to the greatest number, and therefore how should I act?

The ethical theory of utilitarianism relates directly to the fundraiser's task. The ethical imperative here is acting to produce the greatest good for the greatest number of human beings. It would be harder to imagine an ethical rule more supportive of the fundraiser's work. Bentham defines "utility" as "that property in any object, whereby it tends to produce benefit, advantage, pleasure, good, or happiness or to prevent the happening of mischief, pain, evil, or unhappiness". What is ethical is that which produces the greater utility for the community, what will bring about more good and alleviate more harm for more people, including oneself, of course. Most fundraisers try to obtain money to support projects that bring pleasure and alleviate pain for great numbers of people. The pleasures sought may be physical healing, educational growth, artistic enjoyment, environmental safety; the pains fought may be discrimination, homelessness, mental illness, poverty.

Fundraisers can redistribute power

General themes found in every ethical theory also throw light on the ethics of fundraising. The ethical significance of power is one example.

[...]

Fundraising is significantly related to power in society. Wealthy and powerful individuals and institutions – Exxon, the federal government, Bill Gates, David Packard – don't fundraise; they have plenty of money and ways of getting more. While there are important exceptions, most fundraising is for society's weaker, less affluent members – Salvation Army, United Way, international relief organizations, beneficiaries of religious philanthropy, and the like. So part of what fundraisers do, cumulatively, is help redistribute power in the society. Certainly that's not always the effect of fundraising, and fundraising has far less redistributive potential than the government's taxation system, but at $125 billion a year in charitable gifts, as the man said, "it's not nothin'."

The Ford Foundation is a striking if complex example of the redistributive potential of philanthropy and fundraising. In the 1930s the Ford family was one of the richest, most powerful families in the United States. Anyone who has studied the political opinions of Henry Ford understands that this very rich, powerful family was not always a positive force in American society. Facing the threat of new inheritance taxes, which Congress passed with families like Ford's very much in mind, Henry Ford created the Ford Foundation in 1936 – not as a liberal, generous, high-minded act, but as a mechanism to keep control of the Ford Motor Company within the family. But a funny thing happened on the way to the forum. After Henry and Edsel Ford died, and after all the governmental and legal dust had settled, Henry Ford II decided to make the Foundation a mechanism of social betterment. So in 1951, when the Ford Foundation *really* began, with an endowment that, overnight, made it bigger than the Rockefeller Foundation and the Carnegie Corporation combined, Ford embarked on a process of grantmaking that had the effect of significant redistribution of power: the creation of hundreds of minority rights organizations, of public radio and television, of public interest law firms, of community development experiments that led to many of the Great Society programs, the support for the "Green Revolution," the support that helped turn around the economy of India, and so forth. The Ford Foundation could have remained a highly selfish, small-minded, family-centered operation (several examples come to mind) or, perhaps as futile, could have disappeared into the revenue machine of the federal government. Its turn to altruism, and the redistribution of power that this set in motion, constitute an example of the ethical significance of such acts.

There's another sense in which fundraising has to do with power. Many of the causes for which people raise money – education, physical and mental health care, equal opportunity for minorities and women, and so forth – have to do with empowering people: "micro-power," as distinguished from the macro-power of the Ford Foundation example. Micro-power is very important, in two senses. First, for the individuals directly affected: as someone has said: chicken feed is greatly appreciated by the chickens. The empowerment of just one human being is a deeply important thing. Second, cumulative micro-power becomes macro-power: all those individuals educated, trained, healed, freed, encouraged. Fundraising, indirectly as always, has much to do with the delicate balance of power in human relationships, that constant source of ethical challenge.

Certainly not all but many instances of philanthropy lead to a healthy redistribution of power in society; and to the extent that fundraisers make that happen, they are engaged, it seems to me, in profoundly ethical work.

Fundraisers can enable humans to feel responsible for one another

Another factor that introduces ethics into the human situation is responsibility.

[...]

Responsibility begins with those closest to us, those who have become in some way "the other half of our soul," but it extends outward, in a series of concentric circles. As we grow ethically, we come to feel responsibility to our neighbors, our city, our organization, our profession, our ethnic or religious group, our country, even our world; we come to feel responsible even to abstract ideals like truth, beauty, and honor. We not only feel such things; we behave in remarkable ways out of such feelings and commitments. People give their time, their talents, their worldly goods, sometimes even their lives, out of such feelings of responsibility.

Fundraisers deal constantly with responsibility, in at least two important ways: First, they create or help create feelings of responsibility – for political prisoners, for starving children, for the mentally ill. Second, fundraisers connect already existing feelings of responsibility with opportunities for responding. In poll after poll Americans have said they would give more if asked, that the primary reason they don't give, or don't give more, is that they're not asked. In other words, fundraisers help connect the supply of charitable feelings with the demand for charitable dollars, balancing the equation of human responsibility.

Fundraisers can break down our natural selfishness

A third factor that creates ethical dimensions is more elusive than power or responsibility, but probably more important. It is the paradox of "becoming what you are" as a human person. Aristotle described this paradox when he said, "Moral excellence is the result of habit. The virtues are not implanted in us by nature, but nature gives us the capacity for acquiring them, and this is accomplished by training". St. Augustine in his *Confessions* described the same impulse in a religious context, saying to God, "Thou hast made us for Thyself, and our hearts are restless till they rest in Thee." Kant described the paradox when he said that to be moral, a human being must become a quasi-divine lawgiver: "Man is subject only to his own, yet universal, legislation, and he is bound to act in accordance with his own will, which is, however, designed by nature to be a will giving universal laws". And Jean-Paul Sartre, explaining existential angst, wrote: "The man who involves himself and who realizes that he is not only the person he chooses to be, but also a lawmaker who is, at the same time, choosing all mankind as well as himself, cannot help escape the feeling of his total and deep responsibility". The work of fundraising is clearly related to this phenomenon, in that at its best it assists people in responding to the deep ethical call within them, the call to go out of themselves for others.

Aristotle noted over 2,000 years ago that people prefer to get than give money, and not much has changed since. A good fundraiser helps break down that natural wall of selfishness. Fundraisers and the organizations and people they represent are an essential part of the economic and moral exchange system of American society. This should be the starting point for thinking about the ethics of fundraising, not the moral lapses and pitfalls of this work.

The color of ethics

Marilyn Fischer, 2000

"It's such a grey area" we often hear, when difficult ethical situations come up. Grey is the colour of fog, of cloudy dull skies without clarity or edges. In ethical reflection, we sometimes feel as if we are navigating in a fog with no landmarks and no sense of direction. Grey is also a colour made by mixing black and white. Sometimes, in our ethical reflections, we see no clear, right answers; every alternative is tinged with negativity, evil taints the good.

'Ethics as grey' is a potent metaphor, and as with all things potent it needs to be used with great care. Some ethical choices are clearly right or wrong and to call ethics 'grey' in these cases is a way of hiding from ethical truths and ethical responsibilities. But in other cases choices are not so clear, and it is important to identify and acknowledge the ways in which ethics can be grey. In some cases, it may be true that no alternative course of action is ethically pure, and all alternatives require uncomfortable compromises. A second type of greyness arises when ethically decent people prioritize their values differently. Some members of a social service agency may want to emphasize relieving immediate needs for food and shelter; others may want to stress education and job training as long-term self-sufficiency skills. A third type of greyness arises from the way that the same acts can accomplish both ethical and unethical purposes. For example, in the early twentieth century, the Phillis Wheatley Home in Cleveland offered shelter, safety, friendship and job training to young black women. Many white women contributed financial support to the Wheatley home, but historian Darlene Clark Hine sees a racist underside to their generosity. It gave them a way to keep the Young Women's Christian Association exclusively white and to get more highly trained maids for themselves.

[...]

When ethical situations look grey, it is important to sort out just which sense of greyness applies. If the real difficulty is that morally decent people prioritize their values differently, but those involved think the greyness results from good mixed with evil, organizations may become needlessly polarized.

When an ethical quandary feels grey, thinking of ethics as story-telling can be helpful. When the full story of the ethical dilemma is told carefully, with sympathetic understanding of each person's perspective, this sort of polarization can be minimized. A method of ethical decision-making is presented here that will help fundraisers construct stories in a way that clarifies the greyness and brings basic ethical commitments to the foreground. The method

DOI: 10.4324/9781003145936-73

encourages sympathetic understanding and imagination as tools for resolving ethically troubling situations.

[...]

For fundraisers in their professional capacity, three basic value commitments can be identified:

1. The organizational mission that directs the work
2. Our relationships with the people with whom we interact
3. Our own sense of personal integrity

The fundraiser, acting with integrity, has the task of creating and maintaining a supporting network of relationships in order to further the mission of the organization. We bring ethical sensitivity to decision-making when we place particular decisions in the context of these three basic value commitments. The ethical decision-making model takes these three value commitments and uses them to conduct stories about alternative ways of resolving ethically troubling situations.

[...]

1 Organizational mission

Every philanthropic organization has a mission – a social need it is trying to meet, a human good it is trying to achieve. Such purposes range from providing disaster relief to preserving rainforests; from meeting basic survival needs to enriching our spirits through artistic excellence or religious devotion. The mission justifies and directs daily tasks and decisions.

Ethical difficulties often involve misalignments between the organizational mission and daily decisions. Decisions about a university athletic programme may bring glory to the school, while the athletes remain poorly educated. Professors may favour outside consulting to the point of neglecting their students. In some organizations, when glamorous fundraising events net little income, one has to ask if their primary function is to serve the organizational mission or to provide high-class entertainment for the organization's supporters.

Many organizations have more than one fundamental purpose. A hospital, for example, may define its mission in terms of patient care, medical research, and educating future medical practitioners. While a given daily decision may not further all three goals, we can at least take care that a decision furthering one purpose does not unduly slight or injure another. Soliciting funds for long-term basic research is fine, as long as that emphasis does not diminish the quality of patient care.

Each non-profit's specific organizational mission is embedded inside the larger framework of philanthropy. Although it is good to review and revise the mission statement periodically to make sure it advances philanthropic values, it is also helpful to assess even small-scale decisions in light of their impact on philanthropy as a gift economy. Does a particular decision revitalize the spirit of giving and move the gift along its way?

2 Relationships

The slogan goes that fundraisers raise friends as much as funds. Networks of relationships with donors, colleagues, volunteers, and community members are the medium through which organizational missions are furthered. The second basic value commitment, then, is concerned with the character and quality of our relationships to each of these groups. Many ethically troubling situations are caused by, or may cause, fractures in workplace relationships.

Think of the qualities that characterize healthy, long-term professional relationships. Respect, honesty and open communication are high on the list. Sensitivity, caring, and a good sense of humour also figure prominently. And trust, no doubt, is a central value – trust in the goodwill and integrity of the other, and trust that one is respected and that one's basic concerns are taken seriously. When thinking through alternative ways of resolving ethical difficulties, try to enter imaginatively into other people's way of experiencing the world. How do others, with their own idiosyncratic concerns, priorities, and values view this alternative? How would it strengthen or weaken the relationship? Not all relationships can or should be preserved; even in ethically sound decisions, some relationships may still get bruised. The point is to incorporate sympathetic understanding as much as possible, and maintain the possibility of a future healthy relationship.

3 Integrity

The third value commitment is to preserve and strengthen one's own sense of integrity, to express basic values in everyday actions with courage and compassion. 'Ethics' comes from ethos, the ancient Greek word for character. Aristotle defined an ethical person as someone with a virtuous character, in whom virtues reside as deeply internalized personality characteristics. Virtues, like skills and habits, are acquired through practise. Just as a pianist acquires habits of skilful playing through daily practice, so we can practise being generous, fair, brave, thoughtful and honest. Through using daily decisions as opportunities for practice, we gradually nurture and develop the ethical qualities of our character.

Often, a sign of ethical trouble is that gnawing feeling that a given path of action would compromise one's integrity. You know that few of the clients in your drug rehabilitation clinic achieve the glowing success portrayed in your TV spot. Your stomach turns a bit when a donor tells you he was so moved by the spots that he wants to double his pledge. Is your fundraising success based on dishonest portrayals? To maintain a long-term perspective it is helpful to think of integrity as a lifetime project, always in the making. In a sense, we are continually engaged in writing our own autobiographies. Each decision, each encounter adds a few lines. The question 'How should I act now?' is layered inside the larger question 'How would I like this page of my autobiography to read when I look back at it many years from now? What sort of a person will this decision incline me to become?'

Using the ethical decision-making chart

Ethical reflection is an activity, carried out through conversations. Because ethically troubling situations generally involve several people, practising ethics as a social activity enables the participants to hear the others' perceptions and ways of dealing with the difficulty. It also creates the space for collaborative decision-making. Even when done alone, ethical reflection often takes the form of conversations with oneself, in which other voices are imagined and projected. Using the ethical decision-making chart shown in Table 4.2.1 can guide us in constructing stories and using our imaginations to think about the characters and the setting of the workplace dramas.

Making a good ethical decision rests, in part, on whether the participants have asked enough good questions. Placing daily decisions in the context of these three basic value commitments [the organizational mission; relationships; personal integrity] is one way of ensuring that enough good questions are asked. After gathering all relevant information, you are ready to use the ethical decision-making chart. Begin by writing in a few alternative ways of resolving the case. It is all right to start with alternatives as obvious as 'do it' and 'don't do it'. Include alternatives with which you are pretty sure you disagree. Analysing obviously unethical alternatives often brings out insights that can be applied to less clear-cut solutions. Participants often find that additional and often more creative resolutions arise as they discuss the case.

Now work your way down the chart. For each alternative resolution, ask yourself:

- How does this alternative promote or detract from the organization's mission? How does it promote or detract from basic philanthropic values?

Table 4.2.1 Ethical decision-making chart

Alternatives	1	2	3	4
Organizational mission				
How does this alternative promote or detract from the organization's mission?				
Basic philanthropic values				
Relationships				
How does this alternative affect long-term relationships with colleagues, donors, volunteers and community members?				
Personal integrity				
In what ways does this alternative help or not help you develop into the person you want to become?				
How does it strengthen or weaken your own integrity?				

- How does this alternative affect long-term relationships with colleagues, donors, volunteers, and community members?
- In what ways does this alternative help or not help me develop into the person I want to become? How does it strengthen or weaken my own integrity?

There is no equation or formula that, if applied correctly, will yield an 'ethically correct' decision. This is not a flowchart; you do not insert facts, add values, push a button, and wait for a correct solution to emerge at the other end. Ethics always involves judgement, and people of goodwill often disagree on how to interpret the facts or assess the values of a given situation. For many situations, there may be no one right answer; the ethics may be 'grey' in one of the senses discussed above. But there are plenty of wrong answers, and the hope is that after reflection the wrongness of the wrong answers will be clear. One will then be able to choose among the others with sensitivity and good judgement. If an alternative supports all three basic value commitments, you can be assured that it is ethically sound.

Decision making in ethics

Barbara H. Marion, 1994

Decision making in ethics is not a challenge when there is a clear distinction between right and wrong, good and harm. Those choices are obvious and easy. In actuality, most ethical dilemmas present competing values, differing opinions, and varying solutions with positive and negative consequences.

The purpose of this text is to inspire the reader to identify the values that might play a role in decisions that have an ethical component and to plan, in advance, what process to follow when choosing between conflicting values.

[…]

The Josephson Institute for the Advancement of Ethics has proposed that a study of history, philosophy, and religion reveals a consensus as to certain core ethical values which have transcended culture and time to establish the ethical norms and standards of moral conduct essential to an ethical life. The values identified by the Institute, which provided the basis of decision making about ethical issues, are:

1. Honesty
2. Integrity
3. Promise-keeping
4. Fidelity/loyalty
5. Fairness
6. Caring for others
7. Respect for others
8. Responsible citizenship
9. Pursuit of excellence
10. Accountability

Josephson added an eleventh value for nonprofit organizations and their fundraising development professionals: safeguarding the public trust.

Everyday application of values

If we take Josephson's list of ten, plus safeguarding the public trust, and suggest how they affect the decision process within the development profession, some very real, everyday issues spring to mind.

DOI: 10.4324/9781003145936-74

Honesty. The value of honesty affects such things as communications with donors, funders, and institutions. Fundraisers should be open, honest, and clear, avoiding exaggerated claims of performance and misleading descriptions of activities. Proposals should be forthright about the organization's capability, about who else is involved in the work or in the funding, and about how much was raised. The recruitment process should avoid misleading potential volunteers as to their role and the expectation that the board members will be responsible for fundraising. Development staff should avoid ingratiating themselves with a donor through false friendship, making exaggerated claims of professional experience, taking credit for the work or ideas of others, or shifting blame onto others.

Integrity. The value of integrity affects such things as bending the institution's mission to get funding; allowing program activities to drag the organization away from its mission; "looking the other way" at bad policies or questionable tactics.

Promise-keeping. The value of promise-keeping affects such things as failing to live by the spirit of the terms of a gift; misusing restricted funds or continuing to use restricted funds after the purpose has been met or the project finished; or using the precise terms of an agreement to be rigid instead of fair.

Fidelity/loyalty. The value of fidelity in development affects such things as violating the confidentiality of the donor or of the organization; dealing with conflicts of interest; putting personal interest above organizational interest, and organizational interest above mission interest.

Fairness. Josephson suggests that another word for the value of fairness is justice. The value of fairness in development affects such things as manipulating prospects or donors who are vulnerable; being overly demanding of the time of staff; exploiting donors; seeing them as lonely people who can be reached by professional "friends"; making exceptions for major donors that would not be made for others.

Caring for others. According to Josephson, avoiding harm is the linchpin of the application of ethical values. Often, the ethical dilemma is not avoiding harm but choosing between who will be harmed or who will be harmed the most.

Respect for others. The value of respect requires honoring the motivation of donors. Many, if not most, donors are interested in solutions to society's problems. Respect requires candor about the need and the manner in which the organization's program will or will not solve the problem. Respect means being cautious about how prospect and donor research is done; being diligent about how information on clients and donors is protected; cherishing the time and energy expended by volunteers; giving volunteers a clear indication of their role and responsibility before recruiting them. Respect means giving equal access to all: to donors, to service beneficiaries, to volunteers, and to staff.

Responsible citizenship. The value of citizenship requires adherence to all laws, social consciousness, and public service. Good citizenship includes living up to the rules of conduct for the profession and adhering to the code of ethics of your professional organization.

Pursuit of excellence. The value of excellence includes concern with the quality of one's own work, diligence, reliability, industry, and commitment to do one's best. It also requires instilling within each board member the importance of the mission, goals, and the role of leadership in achieving them, as well as integrating each member of the board into a productive and functioning team. Along with that is a requirement for advocacy, a show of commitment to excellence, and a display of belief in the organization. Excellence means recognizing the areas in which you are less strong and working to strengthen those areas so that you can meet your commitment to the organization and its mission.

Accountability. The value of accountability includes acceptance of responsibility for decisions and the consequences of actions or inaction. It requires alerting the appropriate people to a problem; fully divulging how funding was used, including fundraising and administrative costs; being a scrupulous steward over contributed dollars; confronting issues, even difficult ones, directly and quickly; planning for the future of the organization; laying the groundwork to meet future goals by projecting future demands and cultivating future support.

Safeguarding the public trust. According to Josephson, this includes the special obligation to lead by example, to safeguard and advance the integrity and reputation of those organizations that depend on voluntary support, and to avoid even the appearance of impropriety or self-dealing.

Duty. This is my suggestion for a twelfth ethical value for development professionals. Much thought has gone into suggesting a development professional's hierarchy of loyalty, which sequentially prioritizes philanthropy, donors, organization, profession, and self. My definition of the role of a development professional is to facilitate the transfer of available dollars from a willing donor to a worthy cause. I believe development professionals have a special duty to donors, a duty to act in the best interests of the donor, a duty to act as advocate for the donor. It means we have a duty to give information that allows an informed decision, a duty to ensure that the legitimate interests of the donor are protected, a duty to avoid manipulation or intimidation, and a duty to seek funds only for worthy organizations.

When a gift is unencumbered, when the furthering of mission is the value sought by the donor, fairness requires that duty to donors take precedence over duty to organization. Development professionals are skilled in the art of making compelling cases for support of the causes they serve. They have made careers out of being persuasive. The organizations they serve have superior knowledge of the issues and facts surrounding the case and the reasonable outcomes resulting from successful solicitations. With few exceptions the donor is the outsider, the innocent (as in without knowledge or guile) player in the exchange, a financial resource that relies on the integrity of the organization (as relayed by the development professional) to fairly and truthfully state the societal need and the promised solution. Such innocence, connected, as it most often is, without expectation of material return, deserves the extra ounce of duty.

[…]

Decision-making process

Josephson, Pastin, Freeman, and Donahue have developed steps for ethical decision making, some of which are adapted for purposes of this text.

Clarify the problem. What are the driving forces in the situation? Where is the pressure originating? Are the sources of the pressure reliable or may the pressure be without merit? Upon whom is the pressure being put? Given the options, what course of action will send the pressure in what direction? Are there directions in which the damage would be intolerable? Identify the specifics of the predicament. Bring it down to its essence. Remove all extraneous issues from consideration. Remove as much emotion as possible. Identify the number of players affected. Remove personalities, yours and others', from consideration; use position titles: Donor A, Staff Member D, Board Member B, and so on. Identify the critical facts of the situation and the issues at hand. Write them down-not the rumors, but the facts. Review them. Have someone else review the facts for or with you. What else do you need to know? How serious is the issue?

Identify the key, competing values at stake. Is this an issue of honesty, of respect, of justice, of accountability, of fairness, or all of these? Rank the values in priority order by importance and impact. Rarely do all merit the same weight. Identify the organization's values and policies pertinent to the decision. Is there an existing policy? Does it cover the problem? Is the policy current and compatible with the organization's stated values? How many different policies and values are pertinent to the issue? Do any take precedence over others?

Identify the players and stakeholders. Who should have a role in making the decision? Does the dilemma involve donors, clients, staff, the community, volunteers, oneself, or philanthropy? Who is most vulnerable? Are there stakeholders who merit more protection than others? Try to rank these in priority by the weight of their value in the dilemma and the relative negative impact on each stakeholder.

Identify the most plausible alternatives. Plot the differing solutions that could resolve the problem. Note the values, policies, and players affected by each solution.

Imagine the potential outcomes. For each alternative solution, imagine the probable outcomes, both positive and negative. What are the short-term effects? What are the long-term implications? What is the worst-case scenario? Note the effect each outcome has on the players or stakeholders as well as on the organization's mission. Are there stakeholders who would be more damaged? How would justice, or lack of justice, affect each stakeholder?

Evaluate the potential outcomes. Rank the potential outcomes according to the positive and negative results, the harm or good each would cause, the number of players affected, the short-term effects, and the long-term implications.

Decide on a course of action. Take all of the information on balance. Take your time and allow all facets of the dilemma to come into view. Try to back your own emotions and prejudices out of the process. Think, read, roll it over in your mind. If it is not an emergency, sleep on it a few days; problems tend to show other dimensions over time, and the mind often finds solutions when at rest. Select from the alternatives the course of action that is ethically better, the alternative that is least damaging, more in concert with higher tier values. Write down your decision. Have a clear understanding of why you believe this is the best course of action.

Test the decision. James Donahue suggests that the decision be tested for the following:

Consistency: Is this decision consistent with previous actions for which the organization, or the person, have become known? Does the decision fit with the organization's history? Would you apply the same principles to future actions?

Coherence: Is this decision in line with the decisions of other segments of the organization? Do different parts of the organization reflect a unified decision-making process?

Communication: Has the discussion that led to the decision been open and candid? Have all the right people been involved in the decision?

Conviction: Is the decision consistent with the mission and purposes of the organization? Does the decision reflect the values of the organization's culture?

Creativity: Does the decision take sufficient account of new ideas and discoveries that might lead to new advances and rewards for the organization, for society?

Share the decision with someone else. Ethical decisions that affect organizations are best when they are shared, preferably within the organization. However, if you feel that you are more right than the others grappling with the dilemma, remember Barnard's view that we need to continually strengthen our "capacity of being firmly governed by moral codes in the presence of strong contrary impulses, desires, or interests."

Implement the decision. While implementing, try to minimize the negative impacts on the various stakeholders; when possible make them privy to the procedure that resulted in the decision, the evidence of concern for their rights and comfort, and the equity of the decision.

Evaluate the results or consequences. After closure, when all the results are known, evaluate the consequences and results of the decision. Also evaluate the process that led to the decision. Identify weaknesses and strengths within the procedure.

Modify policies and procedures. Develop or modify any policies or procedures found to be lacking in the course of evaluating the decision-making process.

A fundraiser's guide to ethical decision-making

Michael J. Rosen, 2005

True development professionals want to behave ethically. Most believe they are already behaving ethically and striving to make correct choices. However, great challenges stand in the way between the desire to make ethical decisions and the ability to actually do so. Extreme goal pressures, lack of experience, dilemmas without clear solutions, superiors who do not understand fundraising and the ethical standards associated with it, and other complications conspire to complicate the life of even the most ethical of fundraisers. The unfortunate result can be less than ideal decisions that are difficult to justify and which keep a nonprofit organization from realizing its full fundraising potential. Fortunately, by relying on a strong code of ethics and a sound decision-making model, those who want to behave ethically will be well equipped to make highly ethical, defensible, and productive decisions. By making the best possible decisions, development professionals will generate more donors and raise more money for their organizations while enhancing their own marketability as ethical and highly successful professionals.

[...]

Believing that "good" people do not need to worry about ethics training, many often ignore the subject, relying instead on their reflexes when challenged. The reality is that learning about ethics and sound decision-making helps good people to take the kind of action they aspire to take when faced with complex situations. In addition, by following a code of ethics and taking a deliberative approach to decision-making, fundraising professionals will be able to make the best possible choice even when faced with no clear correct answer and will be in a better position to justify that decision to the organization's stakeholders.

For many, making sound ethical decisions is simply a matter of common sense. These people believe Walt Disney's Jiminy Cricket when he says, "Let your conscience be your guide."

The Association of Fundraising Professionals offers a number of relatively simple suggestions for testing decisions:

> The Vision Test – Can you look yourself in the mirror and tell yourself that the position you have taken is ok? If not, don't do it.
> The What-Would-Your-Parents-Say Test – Could you explain to your parents the rationale for your actions? If you could look them in the eye and not get a quizzical response, or be sent to your room, then proceed.

DOI: 10.4324/9781003145936-75

The Kid-On-Your-Shoulders Test – Would you be comfortable if your children were observing you? Are you living the example you preach?

The Publicity Test – Would you be comfortable if your decision appeared on the front page of the newspaper tomorrow? Or was mentioned on the nightly news?

However, while common sense is important to resolving ethical dilemmas, it is a limited tool. "Testing" decisions is also of limited value unless a sound decision-making process has preceded it. Frequently, an ethical dilemma will involve conflicting values for the individual or a conflict between the individual's personal values and those of the organization. Also, an ethical dilemma could involve an issue that is beyond the individual's experience and, therefore, beyond "common" sense.

Others believe that if something is legal, it is ethical. The reality is that society first decides what is ethical or unethical, and then may choose to codify that into law. Therefore, many things remain unethical despite the fact that they might be perfectly legal. For example, development staff members who receive commission-based compensation linked to the money they raise are operating legally in virtually all countries despite the fact that most fundraising codes of ethics from around the world frown on this practice.

[...]

Perhaps the most dangerous misconception about ethics is the belief that it is a soft issue that does not directly impact organizations. The reality is that organizations that are perceived of as ethical will attract more volunteers, recruit better staff, and even raise more money than would otherwise be the case.

[...]

Codes of ethics

Codes of ethics provide valuable guidelines for ideal behavior. Maintaining an organizational ethics code and communicating it to all stakeholders can enhance trust in the organization. In particular, it is important for those responsible for resource development to subscribe to a fundraising ethics code as staff try to enhance relationships with donors and prospective donors. Subscribing to an ethics code and making ethically sound decisions can build public trust.

Professional fundraising associations around the world maintain ethical codes. In 2003, the [US] Association of Fundraising Professionals, the [UK] Institute of Fundraising, and the Fundraising Institute of Australia hosted the first international summit meeting of professional fundraising associations from 21 nations. A review of the 10 ethics codes submitted revealed great similarities despite the cultural differences among participants.

[...]

Using a code of ethics can help fundraising professionals make sound decisions. Codes provide clear answers to some questions on what is right or wrong. For example, the [US] AFP Code of Ethical Principles and Standards of

Professional Practice are quite clear on the question of whether development staff should be compensated with commissions based on monies raised; AFP clearly rejects commission-based compensation. Sometimes, codes are less specific but nevertheless provide useful guidelines when dealing with an ethical dilemma.

> I tell people all the time that a code is a guide and while it sets parameters for behavior, there will almost always be gray areas. Ethics is about everyday choices, some are clear and others are not. For this reason, no code can address all ethical dilemmas. The code can provide guidance, but it is not definitive. [quote by Paulette V. Maehara, President and CEO of AFP]

While ethics codes can inform the decision-making process, codes cannot be relied on to always provide the answers themselves. To make the best possible decisions when the answer does not rest explicitly in a code and when a clear answer is not readily at hand, a decision-making methodology can help the perplexed and ensure all stakeholders that the ethical dilemma will be resolved with great thought rather than whim.

Decision-making models

To help maintain and enhance the public trust, organizations must make high quality decisions. Arriving at the best possible outcome, rather than a merely satisfactory solution, requires a detailed decision-making framework. It requires taking the necessary time, gathering critical information, and involving the appropriate stakeholders. "Organizations that routinely utilize ethical decision-making practices will be much better prepared to handle a crisis when it hits".

Marilyn Fischer believes, "Making a good ethical decision rests, in part, on whether one has asked enough good questions." When making decisions, she argues that one should consider three ultimate areas of concern: organizational mission, relationships, and personal integrity.

[...]

The Josephson Institute has developed another model for ethical decision-making. While not specifically designed for fundraising professionals as the Fischer Model was [for the Fischer Model please see the "Ethical decision-making chart" in the text authored by Fischer in this section], it nevertheless can be of value to the profession and, in some ways, complements the Fischer Model. The first step is to "Stop and Think." Many inappropriate decisions are the ones made in haste. By taking a pause, one is less likely to make a rash decision based upon anger, convenience, pressure, or other urgent stimuli. Taking the time to actually think through a situation is what engages an effective decision-making process.

The second step is to "Clarify Goals." This is an important step because it allows one to consider both the short- and long-term impacts of one's actions.

In the case of fundraising, it allows one to consider fundraising goals as well as broader institutional goals, both short- and long-term.

The third step is to "Determine the Facts." One should identify what one knows and then what one needs to know. Once information is compiled, the credibility of sources must be considered. Also, information from different sources may present different and, at times, conflicting details about the same topic. Determining what information is valid is part of the decision-making process.

The fourth step is to "Develop Options." One should identify as many potential options as possible given the facts at hand. To develop a more complete list, one can consult with other stakeholders. The objective is to try to identify several options and not just one or two.

The fifth step is to "Consider the Options." By visualising the consequences of each option, one can better identify the best solution. When considering the various options, one should consider how it would impact all stakeholders. Also, one should filter the options using the following values: trustworthiness, respect, responsibility, fairness, caring, and citizenship.

The sixth step is to "Choose." In other words, this is the step where one actually makes the decision by selecting one of the options to implement. To help with the decision, one can enlist the input of well-respected individuals. One can also test the quality of the decision by asking: What would the most ethical person you know do? What would you do if you were sure everyone would know? Does it fit the Golden Rule: do unto others as you would have them do unto you?

Although the sixth step involves choosing an option, the process does not end there. The seventh step is to "Monitor and Modify." "Since most hard decisions use imperfect information and 'best effort' predictions, some of them will inevitably be wrong. Ethical decision-makers monitor the effects of their choices. If they are not producing the intended result, or are causing additional unintended and undesirable results, they reassess the situation and make new decisions."

Conclusion

Maintaining and enhancing public trust is essential for organizations that want to raise money. One way to build trust is to consistently make high-quality decisions.

[…]

By committing to a code of ethics or standards of professional conduct, by communicating this commitment, and by using these tools among others to inform a sound decision-making process, nonprofit organizations can achieve stronger fundraising results.

The benefits for development professionals are many. By utilizing a decision-making methodology, one will make better decisions. This in turn will help the individual be more successful in their professional efforts while remaining sensitive to one's own values. It will also help the individual to defend contro-versial decisions and to withstand pressure from other stakeholders with more narrowly defined agendas. This will enhance the fundraising professional's job security and professional reputation thereby enabling smoother career advancement.

The public trust is essential for nonprofit organizations to provide their services in an effective way. Trust is also essential if charities are to raise the financial resources necessary to achieve their missions. By building a reputation for making consistently good ethical decisions, nonprofit organizations and the individuals who work for them, will be better positioned to work with the public. The success this breeds will further engender greater levels of trust and, therefore, a cycle of increasing trust and success will be engaged.

Tainted money and tainted donors

Michael Moody and Michael Pratt, 2020

Just about every major arts institution – from the Guggenheim to the Louvre – has received sizable funding from the Sackler family. Until recently, this arts patronage was how most people knew the Sackler name – if they knew it at all.

But the Sacklers, and their company Purdue Pharma, makers of the addictive painkiller OxyContin, are now becoming much better known for a different reason – their aggressive marketing of the drug despite its known dangers, and their complicity in fueling the nation's deadly opioid epidemic. Museums with a Sackler-named wing, and other nonprofits supported by the Sackler family, now find themselves facing tough questions and ethically complex choices.

Unfortunately, the Sackler family's fall from grace is not an isolated case. New examples of this sort of "tainted donor" or "tainted money" problem seem to keep popping up: the boiling controversy over financier and convicted sex offender Jeffrey Epstein's contributions to MIT's Media Lab, and the Lab's handling of this uncomfortable fact; the University of Southern California's rejection of a $5 million gift from former film producer and accused sexual predator Harvey Weinstein, meant to support female filmmakers; and questions about the prominent board seats occupied by tear gas-maker Warren Kanders. In some circles, the "cleanliness" of *any* money gained through current, predatory capitalist practices should be considered suspect.

All of this puts the nonprofits who depend to varying degrees on private donations in an ethically complicated spot.

These concerns harken back to ethical questions raised about major philanthropists in the past, such as the famous controversy over John D. Rockefeller's gift to the missionary arm of the Congregationalist Church in 1905. In fact, the term "tainted money" was popularized in that debate, mainly by Congregationalist minister Washington Gladden. Gladden was the leading voice for rejecting Rockefeller money because of concerns over how it was made.

Even at that time, ethical opinions were mixed about whether charities should accept tainted money. William Booth, founder of The Salvation Army, is often quoted as saying at the time, "the problem with tainted money is there t'aint enough!" Whether Booth actually said that or not, we know he was strongly in favor of accepting such money, saying tainted money was "washed clean" when used for the greater good.

DOI: 10.4324/9781003145936-76

In today's hyper-connected world, concerns about supposedly tainted donors or money are more easily raised and more rapidly spread. Yet nonprofits and donors have never really developed a sophisticated way of addressing the thorny ethical questions raised in these cases. And this might be the silver lining in the current wave of controversies. They can force us to think and debate more deeply about the ethics of giving and receiving, and to develop better conceptual tools for handling these sorts of challenges in our field.

To do so, we first need to better understand these challenges and their context.

First, what exactly "taints" the money or the donor, and what variations are there in these claims? The distinction between tainted *money* (problems with how money was created) and tainted *donors* (problems with who is giving money) seems a primary one to clarify. Also, are there variations in severity that might matter – e.g., the stigma attached to donors accused of child abuse might be more problematic than that attached to donors accused of not paying their workers a living wage? And perhaps most important, who gets to decide whether a certain donation or donor is tainted or not?

Beyond these conceptual questions, and even more urgent, are the practical questions, especially for nonprofits – questions about the range of possible responses, the process of deciding how to respond, and protocols to preempt or mitigate the risk of future tainted donations. What choices do nonprofits have beyond just refusing or returning the donation? And who should be consulted? How should the decision be communicated, especially when the ethical questions are blurry or disputed? What policies or procedures should nonprofits adopt to guard against the risk posed by tainted money and donors?

There are some resources in the field to help nonprofits and donors find their way through this ethical thicket. Nonprofit membership and philanthropy support organizations, like the U.S. Independent Sector and the Association of Fundraising Professionals, have Codes of Ethics that address the tainted money/donor issue. But while useful, these often do not provide explicit advice for nonprofits who find themselves facing this sort of challenge. U.S. nonprofits can find some guidance by looking to the U.K., where regulators have developed some detailed, actionable guidelines for how and when to accept (or reject) a donation [see the Charity Commission for England and Wales and the Fundraising Regulator].

Examples of practices that would enable nonprofits to anticipate, mitigate, and/or respond to this challenge include investing more resources in vetting donors, creating standing ethics committees, and developing and implementing formal policies and procedures for accepting (or rejecting) donations. These policies and procedures address variables like how the extent of due diligence might change with a gift's size, the conditions under which a donation should be rejected, and contingency plans for when a previously accepted donation becomes tainted.

"Context matters in every case. What is 'right' might depend on many factors of the situation and the parties involved."

Finally, we need to always remember that establishing general policies and procedures is not enough to find our way through these ethical quagmires. Context matters in every case. What is "right" might depend on many factors of the situation and the parties involved. For example, might oil companies be considered tainted donors to environmental organizations, but not so much to arts ones? Will an organization on the brink of insolvency be more willing to accept suspect donations just to keep its doors open? And if a nonprofit has accepted donations from a donor repeatedly in the past, does this change their decision about whether to continue to accept donations when new allegations are made against that donor?

Whatever the specifics, we know these sorts of tainted money and tainted donor questions will continue to arise, and will continue to trouble both nonprofits and the donors who support them. We should use this trend as an opportunity to have a more complex and sophisticated conversation about the ethics of philanthropy. This better conversation will help all parties around the philanthropic table be more accountable and have greater impact.

4.3 Donor, fundraiser, and beneficiary rights

A Donor Bill of Rights

James M. Greenfield, 2013

In the late 1980s, four trade organizations representing professional fundraising practitioners began to develop a set of principles known today as A Donor Bill of Rights. Their goals included "to assist donors in making decisions about charities, believing informed decision making would assist donors and charities in forging stronger, more productive relationships that would ultimately benefit the recipients of charitable support."

[…]

The value of this covenant, which has been endorsed by nonprofits everywhere, is a "united public voice for fund raising and philanthropy fundamental for the strength and health of the field. Professional organizations must continue to help practitioners understand and implement ethical standards of practice and treatment of donors." Further, "the bill emphasizes disclosure, social responsibility, two-way communication, truth, and interdependency … Its 10 tenets, in many ways, are stronger than the codes of ethics of the individual associations … It identifies philanthropy as an American tradition of giving and sharing. It acknowledges the dual levels of accountability to the 'general public,' as well as to the specific publics of donors and prospective donors. Finally, it advances self-regulation by assuming that charitable organizations must continually demonstrate their worthiness of confidence and trust." The preamble for A Donor Bill of Rights captures all the reasons for this good effort:

> Philanthropy is based on voluntary action for the common good. It is a tradition of giving and sharing that is primary to the quality of life. To assure that philanthropy merits the respect and trust of the general public, and that donors and prospective donors can have full confidence in the not-for-profit organizations and causes they are asked to support, we declare that all donors have these rights.

The tenets in A Donor Bill of Rights specify 10 moral principles and establish a covenant donors should expect every nonprofit organization to observe in their behalf, as follows:

DOI: 10.4324/9781003145936-78

I. To be informed of the organization's mission, of the way the organization intends to use donated resources, and of its capacity to use donations effectively for their intended purposes.

The purpose is full disclosure to donors of how their funds will be used to meet mission objectives based on prior year results and sound plans for the future. Mission is the guiding statement for donor decision making and expresses the purposes donors' gifts will serve, such as direct services to others or advocacy of the cause. The cause is the attraction that donors exercise with their support – that's the covenant between donor and nonprofit. The traditional "case statement" used in solicitations for annual, capital, or planned giving purposes usually contains details that answer to these needs.

II. To be informed of the identity of those serving on the organization's governing board, and to expect the board to exercise prudent judgement in its stewardship responsibilities.

Providing the roster of board members on all its publications and solicitation materials (letterhead, brochures, website, etc.) will satisfy this "right," but names alone may be insufficient. Adding board position, employer, and city and state of residence offers more complete details for donors and prospects to assess. In addition, while the duties and responsibilities of board members are broad and legally enforceable, evidence of routine practices (e.g. board size and terms, frequency of board meetings, committee structure, etc.) along with principles of governance (e.g. conflicts of interest policy) also should be disclosed. Stewardship of any nonprofit organization is a large and demanding task and includes all of the following:

1. Determine the organization's mission and purpose.
2. Select the Chief Executive.
3. Provide proper financial oversight.
4. Ensure adequate resources.
5. Ensure legal and ethical integrity and maintain accountability.
6. Ensure effective organizational planning.
7. Recruit and orient new board members and assess board performance.
8. Enhance the organization's public standing.
9. Determine, monitor, and strengthen the organization's programs and services.
10. Support the Chief Executive and assess his or her performance.

III. To have access to the organization's most recent financial statements.

This tenet applies to annual budgets, audited financial statements, and IRS Form 990 Annual Information return. Federal law requires copies of these documents for the most immediate three years to be provided upon request at any time along with the organization's original application for tax-exempt status. Any donor requesting these documents is acting as an "investor" who is seeking to understand the capability of the organization to manage its fiscal affairs competently before making a decision to share personal funds and/or assets (i.e. real estate, stocks and bonds, personal property, etc.). The organization also should offer to discuss its financial reports and should be available to answer questions about their content.

IV. To be assured their gifts will be used for the purposes for which they are given.

This "right" speaks directly to the donor's issue of public confidence and trust in what we say and what we do with a donor's money. "It is always harmful to divert charitable assets from their intended purposes; it is wrong for the poor or sick consigned to an organization's care to be abused or neglected; it is immoral for the administrators of philanthropic institutions to enrich themselves; it is tragic for wasteful and inefficient uses of scarce charitable resources to be tolerated."

This covenant is the bond of trust invested in the organization's faithful adherence to using all donor funds exactly as stated in its appeal. More importantly, if a donor specifies a purpose for use of funds that an organization accepts, it cannot change its use without the express written consent of the donor. "These restricted funds must be spent for their designated purpose. Nothing is more certain to damage a nonprofit organization's ability to attract funds that for it to be found using restricted funds for purposes other than those specified by the donor. An organization that received restricted gifts must account for the funds carefully so that it can prove their use for the purpose intended."

The rise in the number of donor-advised funds is a direct consequence of donors' concerns that their wishes will be observed faithfully; to that end, they attached strings to reinforce this bond.

V. To receive appropriate acknowledgment and recognition.

Receipt of each and every gift requires a timely acknowledgment. At the same time, each gift opens the opportunity to develop a binding relationships with donors. Recognition elements such as benefits and privileges can be added that are guided carefully by board-approved written policies and procedures appropriate to the size and purpose of the gift, donor history of giving, how all other donors are treated, and other factors. "It is of the utmost importance to thank every donor, accurately and promptly, for every contribution, as well as to ensure that donations are recorded in such a way that donors are able to take any tax advantages that accrue to them for their gifts." Much more is possible so long as it is appropriate. The guiding principle is the relationship. How can the recipient organization cultivate its donors to expand their involvement? What are the elements of donor satisfaction?

This can be achieved in several ways including:

- Strive to satisfy current donors. Satisfying current donors is critical, because dissatisfied donors are highly likely to spread negative word of mouth on the charity network and to discourage other prospective donors.
- Undertake a program of asking donors for regular feedback on how they view relationships with the nonprofit and how satisfied they are.
- Create a response management program to act on all negative feedback received. Experience with affluent individuals on other settings indicated that it is possible to turn dissatisfied people into loyalists again if the response to a complaint is appropriate and thorough. Given the high costs of new donor development, even extreme efforts to protect the donor base are usually worthwhile.

VI. To be assured that information about their donation is handled with respect and with confidentiality to the extent provided by law.

The bond of trust between donors and their chosen charities includes the presumption that all these transactions are personal, private acts involving money and are not for public disclosure. It is common practice by nonprofit organizations to publish rosters of donors and prepare forms of visible displays (i.e. donor walls) that list donors by a range of size of gifts, usually with congratulatory labels such as "Patron" or "Benefactor". With this knowledge, donor decisions to make gifts can be presumed to reflect their acceptance of this practice, except when they request their gift be anonymous. On another front, in the United States, there is an IRS requirement that organizations must report all gifts by name of donor and amount if $5,000 or more as part of their annual IRS Form 990 return. However, the IRS does not release this list, nor is it to be included in any distribution of this tax form by the organization.

VII. To expect that all relationships with individuals representing organizations of interest to the donor will be professional in nature.

Respect each donor and treat him or her accordingly. Donors represent not only a reliable fiscal resource but also the potential to support the organization and its mission, vision, and values. Examples include advocacy of the cause, attendance at benefit events and public affairs, voluntary service, and more — all based on their personal interest and commitment that may rise to the role of board membership and other leadership services over time. To achieve any of these enhanced levels of relationships, there must be consistent and respectful communications.

The type and level of communications will be a function of the nature of the relationships between the fundraiser and the donor. A number of elements must characterize this relationship:

- There must be mutual trust between individuals.
- The relationship also depends on respect.
- The relationship must be sincere.
- The fundraiser must give something as well as receive something.

VIII. To be informed whether those seeking donations are volunteers, employees of the organization or hired solicitors [fundraising consultants].

Donors must be informed at the time of each solicitation of who is making this request and what their position with the nonprofit organization is. Volunteers [and non-fundraising] employees are unpaid for their help in solicitation. This tenet is in response to the several states that have fundraising and solicitation regulations requiring registration and public reports by hired solicitors, be they commercial fundraisers, paid solicitors, or in other categories. The donor's concern is linked to the solicitor's compensation, which often is tied to the gift amount and has been the source of many abuses and fraudulent practices. Several state laws and regulations require these for-profit firms to have a signed contract with a nonprofit prior to soliciting the public, approval by the state authority (usually the office of the Attorney General), and the requirement to provide a full report of funds raised, expenses, and net proceeds delivered to the charity. Organizations that hire paid solicitors must be vigilant and observe strict ethical and professional practices in these matters and use only a fee-for-service basis for their compensation to avoid any impropriety and resulting media attention.

IX. To have the opportunity for their names to be deleted from mailing lists that an organization may intend to share.

One of the great benefits that donors and organizations share is open communications. Donors expect to receive newsletters, magazines, annual reports, and other information from the organizations they support, which also is important to the charity in maintaining and enhancing the involvement and relationship with its donors. However, the practice of exchanging, renting, or selling lists of donors is used by some organizations to expand their donor base. Any organization that observes these practices must offer their donors the option to have their names, addresses, and other information deleted from these lists and withheld from any such exchange.

X. To feel free to ask questions when making a donation and to receive prompt, truthful and forthright answers.

The act of solicitation implies disclosure of several details: why the funds are needed, how they will be used, when they will be used, what are the intended outcomes, actual results achieved, and more. Solicitation materials and solicitors should be prepared to offer this information first and should also be prepared to respond with any added details the donor requests. This tenet, among all the others, speaks directly to the need for transparency as well as to open and full disclosure by nonprofit organizations as a matter of principle and daily practice by all its representatives. Open communications is the recommended practice at all times so that "you build loyalty to your organization by focusing on the ways in which you effectively manage gifts to deliver the highest possible program return on the investment, but you provide the true return on values when the donor sees how her investment is affecting larger community or global issues."

[…]

Conclusion

The great beauty of A Donor Bill of Rights is its clear language. In this era of increasing attention to accountability by nonprofits for all their actions, it is equally important to retain close attention to the rights of all donors. Donors are the best friends any nonprofit organization can hope to have. Perhaps if donors are treated as friends in the way each of us would like to be treated, we will honor their support and merit their confidence and trust. Because, in the end, that is the covenant – to use their gifts to do good works that benefit others.

The Fundraiser Bill of Rights

Amelia Garza and Jennifer T. Holmes, 2021

In years past, the fundraiser/donor relationship has often taken a submissive/dominant role. With a growing shift of this binary toward a community centric fundraising model, it has become even more vital for charitable organizations to examine the fundraiser/donor relationship and further define the fundraiser's rights as an equitable partner in creating change for the community. The rights of fundraisers consist of the following:

I. Fundraisers have the right to a decision-making role in determining if a donation should be declined if the gift has conditions that contradict the organization's mission and/or the clients the organization serves.

A fundraiser's role is to secure funding to fulfill the mission of the organization they serve. Should a donor make restrictions around their gift that contradicts an organization's commitment to equity or require the organization to compromise the needs of the individuals it serves, the organization and fundraiser have the right to decline the acceptance of the donor's gift.

II. Fundraisers have a right to a respectful, equitable and transparent professional relationship with the organization they serve and with the donors of the organization.

Whether it be by the organization they serve, the organization's staff or the donor community, each fundraiser should be treated with the assumption of intellectual and professional competence. According to a recent study, fundraisers of color were found to have the additional responsibility of proving their competence to both donors and their teams. This additional obstacle was particularly troubling for fundraisers of color when creating trusting relationships with donors. The study concluded that fundraisers of color would need another 1–2 conversations with donors before they could start philanthropic discussions. The totality of the obstacle of proving their intelligence and professionalism was then reflected in metrics. It would often take more work and more conversations for fundraisers of color to get the same results as white fundraisers.

DOI: 10.4324/9781003145936-79

Nonprofit organizations are encouraged to make a clear statement that their fundraising teams are not beholden to donors but are, instead, committed to fulfilling the organization's mission. Subsequently, the organization will support Fundraisers' decisions to refrain from any dialogue or interactions with donors that are clearly outside of their responsibilities to the organization. These interactions include, but are not limited to, conducting personal errands for donors or leveraging the organization's influence to benefit donors.

III. Fundraisers have a right to be included in the continuous audit of an organization's policies and practices to ensure equity and protection.

Charitable organizations should undergo an inclusive review of policies and practices to ensure that fundraisers of color and professionals from other systemically nondominant cultures are recruited, retained, promoted and have the ability to thrive equitably to their white counterparts. Organizations should also review and reformulate the narratives told about communities of color and create affirming language to describe problems, solutions, and visions for change. Leaders of charitable organizations have a responsibility to their organization's fundraisers not only in evaluating their practices but also in including fundraisers in their evaluations.

Fundraisers of color are often called upon to educate their colleagues, institutions and donors about race, power and privilege while their roles typically hold less positional power and autonomy. By taking on the additional work to create diversity, equity and inclusion values for their institutions, fundraisers of color find themselves in a position of balancing their fundraising goals and workloads with the non-paid work of building the organization's awareness in understanding and addressing racism. It is imperative that charitable organizations that have a commitment to diversity, equity and inclusion secure external consultancy on practices to ensure equity and not assume that the work would be better handled by an internal fundraiser of color.

IV. Fundraisers have a right to develop a "response" plan that the institution will support.

Similar to how an organization develops a response plan for emergencies (i.e., fire evacuation, tornado response, active shooter, etc.), each fundraiser has a right to establish how they will respond to a donor should the donor engage in discriminatory or harassing behavior. As such behavior can be presumed to have a higher chance of occurring than an organization needing to respond to an emergency, the organization has a duty—and is accountable—to make sure their fundraisers are supported when they respond to discriminatory and harassing behaviors. Should the fundraiser's response plan need to be enacted, the fundraiser then has a right not to be reprimanded by their organization.

V. Fundraisers have the right to stop working with a donor based on the donor's behavior toward their gender, sexual orientation, race, ability or any identity based cause for discrimination.

In developing a response plan, organizations should also validate a fundraiser's option to cease interactions with a donor based on the donor's explicit or implicit discriminatory behavior. Fundraisers should not be forced to decide whether to confront or comply with disrespectful treatment (conscious or unconscious) for the sake of achieving fundraising goals. Should a donor behave in a discriminatory or harassing way, the organization should then step forward in protecting the rights of the fundraiser to cease partnering with the donor based solely on the fundraiser's accounts with or without substantial evidence.

The organization is responsible for providing guidance and support for helping the fundraiser navigate discriminating and harassing encounters. It is highly recommended that organizations provide clear statements for fundraisers to use with donors during such situations, as well as clear guidelines for how the organization will support fundraisers in their decision to end a relationship with a donor due to their behavior.

Moving forward in shifting the fundraising rights narrative

The rights of fundraisers have, until now, been considered a subsequent and an assumed concept. It is time to disrupt the notion that acquiescing to the donor is an unquestionable priority. As the philanthropy industry moves away from its traditional and donor-serving framework toward a community-centric approach, it is imperative for charitable organizations to take steps in evaluating their organization's policies, procedures, and values. The Fundraiser Bill of Rights aims to keep organizations accountable and in favor of serving the community above serving their donors while keeping in mind the many obstacles fundraisers of color face within a donor-centered philanthropic approach.

Although the Fundraiser Bill of Rights pertains to fundraisers in general, its approach to a more equitable and community-serving model is conducted through an interdisciplinary lens inclusive of fundraisers of color, fundraisers of differing abilities, and nonbinary fundraisers. In remaining accountable, organizations should work toward disrupting the status quo that creates ostracism of fundraisers of color, tokenism and unrealistic expectations to balance assimilation. Organizations have a responsibility to their staff and the communities they serve to continue working towards an equitable and just structure. As this work continues, additions can and should be made to the Fundraiser Bill of Rights to help ensure the continuation of progress towards an equitable, inclusive, and diverse philanthropic industry.

Ethical fundraising and beneficiary rights

Anne Bergeron and Eugene R. Tempel, 2022

Fundraising is a noble profession, supporting organizations in the voluntary sector – arts, humanities, education, health and human services, religion, social justice, international aid, animal welfare, and the environment. Individuals, including fundraisers, are often drawn to these fields over other public-facing occupations out of service and commitment to enhancing civil society. Fundraisers wield influence in their facilitative role developing relationships among organizations, donors, and beneficiaries. They are responsible to their organizations for helping to realize institutional missions, to donors for fulfilling their gift intentions as agreed, and to beneficiaries for representing their best interests. With these responsibilities come the obligation to act ethically with care and good judgment, and create trust, the foundation of philanthropy. Ethics is not commonly discussed for fear of sounding preachy or old-fashioned. But understanding and applying ethics is as important for fundraisers as technical skill.

[…]

A foundation of trust

The nonprofit and philanthropic sectors are built on a covenant of trust that serves the public good. Trust anchors nonprofit organizations, the constituencies they serve, and the patrons who support them. Although there is a correlation between trust and donor generosity, recent studies express some contradictions. One report finds that trust in nonprofits is high among educated, upper income, urban residents, but low among those from underserved, impoverished, rural communities. Another finds there is little trust in institutions worldwide due to systemic injustice and bias, while a third indicates that nonprofits are viewed as more trustworthy than for-profits and government, but overall trust has declined among donors.

Trust is the foundation on which philanthropy is developed and sustained. Donors must be assured that their contributions will be used as promised and applied in ways to generate the impact intended. Benefactors and beneficiaries expect transparency and accountability from public benefit organizations. The nonprofit sector has not been immune from scandals or stories of abuse and mismanagement, and the inevitable result is an erosion of the public's confidence. Faith in the sector is restored through "stewardship of the public good"

DOI: 10.4324/9781003145936-80

when nonprofit leaders and fundraisers practice ethical behavior and maintain organizational cultures that honor "… a set of core values that are in keeping with the historical, philosophical, moral, and religious roots of the voluntary sector".

If public trust is so critical to the nonprofit sector, then how does one engender trust? Trust is gained by consistently practicing the highest ethics and values. Ethics is defined as "how a moral person should behave" and values as "the inner judgments that determine how a person actually behaves".

[…]

Professional ethics

The Association of Fundraising Professionals (AFP) fosters ethical and best practices for fundraisers through education, training, advocacy, and research. Its "Code of Ethical Standards" guides the profession today in ways that engender trust. The "Donor Bill of Rights" respects those whose philanthropy makes the voluntary sector viable.

Fundraisers must embrace these professional principles and think critically and carefully about ethical issues. As the "consciences of the philanthropic community," fundraisers must bring ethical courage to their work and "create communities of moral deliberation" in the organizations they serve. While codes are guides to professional behavior, ethical fundraising is more about a right way to act than do's and don'ts.

[…]

Ethical behavior

In Obedience to the Unenforceable, a report on ethical practice for non-profit and philanthropic organizations, Independent Sector (IS) clarifies three types of ethical behavior that guide nonprofits: complying with applicable laws; doing the right thing, even in the face of hardship or discomfort; and choosing the ethical path between competing goods or conflicting values. The last, called ethical dilemmas, are the most difficult situations to address, often pitting core values against one another, so there is no easy right answer. There are commonly four types of "right versus right" ethical paradigms: truth versus loyalty, individual versus community, short-term versus long-term, and justice versus mercy.

IS offers guidance to nonprofits in maintaining an ethical culture by adopting these shared values:

*   Commitment beyond self, service to the public at the core of civil society.
*   Obedience of the laws, a fundamental responsibility of stewardship, including those governing tax-exempt philanthropic and voluntary organizations.
*   Commitment beyond the law, or "obedience to the unenforceable," the higher calling of personal responsibility to society accepted by nonprofit

professionals. This phrase is taken from a speech given by British barrister and judge Lord John Fletcher Moulton (1844–1921).

- Commitment to the public good, requiring "those who presume to serve the public good ... [to] assume a public trust".
- Respect for the worth and dignity of individuals, a promise that all voluntary sector staff and volunteers must fulfill.
- Tolerance, diversity, and social justice, reflecting civil society's rich heritage and the fundamental protections afforded to individuals in a democracy.
- Accountability to the public, a central responsibility of public benefit organizations.
- Openness and honesty, essential qualities of organizations that seek and utilize public or private funds to serve public purposes.
- Responsible stewardship of resources, a duty of care governance requirement that nonprofit organizations vow to uphold.

[...]

Attitude and language matter. Fundraisers are not salespeople and donors are not targets. The dignified process of inviting someone to give is not hitting them up. Philanthropy is a voluntary act, so guilt and undue pressure have no place in communications between fundraisers and donors. And organizations and beneficiaries are not beggars, but active agents in addressing community needs.

Conducting oneself with integrity, demonstrating moral character, and exercising good judgment can help to avoid ethical issues common in nonprofits. These include:

1. Conflicts of interest, when trustees, executives, or fundraisers benefit materially from insider relationships to their organizations, such as contracting services from a board member's business, or when fundraisers compromise professional relationships by accepting personal gifts from donors. Because engendering trust is crucial, nonprofits and fundraisers should avoid even the appearance of conflicts of interest.
2. Accountability and reporting, when solicitation materials or reports are inaccurate in describing the purpose of fundraising efforts and the use of funds. Transparency and candor are expected traits of nonprofits, without which trust declines.
3. Tainted money, when conflicts arise between an organization's mission and values, or social mores in general, and the source of donated monies. For example, a number of universities and museums were forced to reckon with gifts from the Sackler family, owner of pharmaceutical company Purdue Pharma, which helped to fuel the opioid addiction crisis.
4. Donor privacy, when the confidentiality of donor information is violated, shared with those who have no need to know, or when fundraisers or consultants take donor information with them from one job to the next. Donor privacy is sacrosanct, protected by the AFP code of ethics, and donor relationships belong to the nonprofit, not the fundraiser.

5. Compensation, when excessive salaries and benefits awarded to senior staff or perks to trustees and high-level volunteers fall outside of what is acceptable to the IRS or breach a nonprofit's duty of care responsibility for prudent management of assets; or when fundraisers are paid a commission on monies raised, which contravenes AFP standards.

6. Financial integrity, when restricted funds are not applied as directed by patrons or are accepted with compromising strings attached; or when holdings in investment portfolios are at odds with institutional missions or values.

Applying ethics

While it is vital to understand moral philosophy and to have good moral character and judgment, that is often not enough to ensure ethical behavior. Ethical issues can be complex and cause even the most principled person to falter. A disciplined approach to ethical decision-making can help prevent missteps while determining the best outcome for the circumstances.

The Markkula Center for Applied Ethics at Santa Clara University offers a useful framework for ethical decision-making in fundraising. First, objectively state the ethical issue at hand. Is there a conflict of interest or the appearance of one? Is there an ethics code violation or a legal compliance concern? Has there been a misappropriation of funds or lack of transparency in reporting? Does the situation present a controversial donor offering tainted funds?

Second, summarize all the relevant information and consider everyone with a stake in the issue – trustees, staff, donors, volunteers, beneficiaries, and the public. Confer with stakeholders, determine if the concerns of some carry more weight than others, and discuss why this might matter. "Good decisions take into account the possible consequences of words and actions on all those potentially affected by a decision".

Third, articulate various alternatives for action and their probable outcomes, assessing each relative to organizational mission and values, plus institutional relationships and one's own personal integrity.

Fourth, decide how to act and apply intuition to the decision. If it becomes front page news, can the decision be defended to one's peers or children?

Finally, take action, monitor the result, and then reflect on the outcome. Doing this in a consistent manner helps to build ethical muscle, which can be relied upon when the next ethical dilemma arises.

[…]

Ethics and social justice

Contemporary society perceives deep disparities and bias in the world's economic, political, and social systems, with calls for those in power to combat structural inequities, including within the voluntary sector. Ford Foundation President Darren Walker urges philanthropists to use their capital to address systemic imbalances that create the need for charity over giving to institutions that support their privilege. Grantmaker Edgar Villanueva favors dismantling colonialist structures inherent in the foundation world by utilizing Indigenous customs that share power and foster participatory decision-making around wealth redistribution. Poet, scholar, and institutional philanthropist Elizabeth Alexander has refocused the Andrew W. Mellon Foundation from conventional arts and humanities funding to social justice initiatives that support community libraries, reading and literacy programs, and educational opportunities for the incarcerated.

Applying social justice perspectives to nonprofit leadership and fundraising means generating new resources that offer the potential to succeed to those lacking opportunity. It means building inclusive workplaces with diverse boards and staff that reflect regional demographics and communities served. It means pursuing equity-based prospect research and cultivation programs that prioritize women and people of color alongside traditional white male corporate donors. It means retooling the annual fund as a catalyst for community building. When fundraising and philanthropy is shared by many, "collective action enables people to achieve results through building equal and mutually-supportive relationships" that advance organizations and causes.

The field of fundraising has long taught that philanthropy is a donor-directed choice, motivated by the interests and intentions of the giver. The astute fundraiser finds the fit between organizational need and donor passion. How might fundraising change to enable justice-focused philanthropy? What if fundraisers are also taught to be beneficiary-directed, helping donors use their privilege to focus philanthropy on the root causes of inequity and its symptoms? Here, the lessons are about humility, empathy, listening, learning, deep community engagement, and trusted partnership.

Community-Centric Fundraising [a US movement focused on evolving "how fundraising is done in the nonprofit sector"], guided by leaders of color and their allies, offers these core principles of socially-just fundraising practice:

1. Fundraising must be grounded in race, equity, and social justice.
2. The collective community is more important than individual organizational missions.
3. Nonprofits are generous with and mutually supportive of one another.
4. All who engage in strengthening the community are equally valued, whether staff, donor, board member, or volunteer.
5. Time is valued equally as money.
6. Donors are treated as partners, and this means being transparent, assuming the best intentions, and occasionally having difficult conversations.
7. Collaborative voluntary actions foster a sense of belonging, not othering.
8. Everyone personally benefits from engaging in the work of social justice – it is not just charity and compassion.
9. Social justice work is holistic and transformative, not transactional.
10. Healing and liberation require a commitment to economic justice.

Reorienting fundraising from donor-centered to community-centered encourages power sharing in philanthropic relationships in ways that foster racial and economic justice. The authors propose the following "Beneficiary Bill of Rights" (see Box 4.3.1) to ensure that the recipients of benevolence have agency and are active participants in collective community enrichment.

Box 4.3.1 Proposed Beneficiary Bill of Rights

Philanthropy is based on longstanding global traditions of offering assistance and support to people and causes beyond oneself. It is a human activity that brings individuals together around common concerns that seek to enhance the quality of life for all. To ensure that philanthropy best serves those intended to benefit from charitable giving, we declare that all beneficiaries of philanthropy have these rights:

1. To be assured that donors and philanthropic and nonprofit organizations are acting in good faith to serve the best interests of the community.
2. To inform leaders of philanthropic organizations, plus donors and fundraisers, of community needs, concerns, and customs by engaging with, listening to, and being responsive to beneficiaries.
3. To be informed of and have access to the leadership of philanthropic and nonprofit organizations engaged in work designed to benefit the community.
4. To expect organizations to embrace an inclusionary practice of community development through collaborative governance that gives agency to all stakeholders.
5. To be at the center of community conversations and involved in framing issues, making plans, taking action, and evaluating outcomes through collaborative decision-making.
6. To have access to philanthropic and nonprofit organizations' most recent financial statements.
7. To be treated with dignity and respect, with opportunities for direct engagement and a voice in the decision-making process, which may include board or committee service.
8. To be free to ask questions and offer commentary without reprisal and to receive timely, honest responses.
9. To have the opportunity to participate anonymously, with personal information protected to the extent provided by law.
10. To be appropriately acknowledged for one's community advocacy, if desired.

Beneficiaries are defined as individuals or a group of people who receive direct benefit from philanthropic or nonprofit organizations working on their behalf to serve the public trust.

Conclusion

Fundraisers play a pivotal role in the nonprofit organizations they represent. Beyond securing the philanthropic resources needed to further institutional missions, fundraisers also serve as moral compasses for their organizations. By embodying moral character, observing the AFP Code of Ethical Standards, being transparent, and embracing accountability, fundraisers build the very trust that is needed to ensure the public good. Doing so takes discipline, courage, and principled action, but the rewards of living and working ethically justify the commitment.

Section 5

BEING A FUNDRAISER

Editors' introduction

Overview

The first four sections of this Reader have focused on what fundraising is, and what the tasks of fundraising involve in terms of key concepts, practice, theory, and ethics. It may therefore seem that our current focus has already been covered: surely "being a fundraiser" is simply implementing those tasks? You will not be surprised to learn it is a little more complicated than that.

The act of "raising funds" may provide the elements that gives the profession its title (i.e. fund-raising), but the parameters of the job are far wider – and often far more imprecise – than that compound word suggests. The extracts in this section show that the work requires implementing a broad range of skills, expertise and knowledge, deployed with high levels of emotional intelligence, in order to secure the resources needed by nonprofit organisations to fulfil their mission. However, that is not all. As fundraisers serve both their nonprofit employer and their donors, the work also involves ensuring that the experience of donating these resources brings greater meaning, purpose, and satisfaction to their supporters. Achieving the alchemy of turning financial transactions into fuel for both good work and good lives, is closer to an accurate description of what is involved in being a fundraiser than the misleadingly simplistic suggestion that it simply involves "raising funds".

This intrinsically tricky task is complicated even further by the high standards that fundraisers often set for themselves, as well as the sometimes idealised and unrealistic expectations that others hold about them. Meeting the ever-escalating demands of colleagues who may see no contradiction in raising fundraising targets whilst decreasing investment in the fundraising function, and also whilst trying to be "all things to all supporters" is exhausting, and may help explain observed patterns in high turnover and burn out in this profession.

In this section we look closely at what exactly it is that people do when their career involves raising funds for good causes, beginning with three extracts that explore what kind of people enter this profession.

5.1 Who raises funds for a living?

We begin with an extract from Kim Klein's rousing argument that more people should choose fundraising as a career. Klein insists that fundraising is "exciting",

DOI: 10.4324/9781003145936-82

"sexy", and "cool" because no significant social change can happen without it, and because those generating much-needed income are still on the front lines of pursuing social justice. She also highlights the attractions for those doing this job: constantly learning about new things, meeting new people, empowering volunteers, and helping donors to feel useful and connected to causes they care about. Klein claims that fundraisers make a further contribution by helping to break down the taboo of talking about money: who has it, how much, and what they do with it. This taboo facilitates ongoing sexism, racism, and the class structure, as Klein insists: "people who cannot talk about money, who will not learn to ask for it and deal with it, actually collaborate with a system that the rest of social change work seeks to dismantle. That alone makes fundraising not only a way cool profession, but also a dangerous one."

The next article, by Elizabeth Dale, continues the theme of exploring the relationship between fundraising and sexism, though arrives at a less celebratory conclusion. Dale studies the job through a gender lens to highlight the "feminization of fundraising" and its implications for those doing this work. She notes the significant entry of women into the profession, especially within certain specialities such as events organising and community fundraising which draw on "so-called" female characteristics, skills and traits such as caring, communication, hospitality, entertaining-type skills, and willingness to accept lower wages. Dale shows how this gendered skill differentiation leaves men to dominate better-paid specialities such as working with major donors, and makes for an easier male pathway to senior positions in management. Dale argues that "the similarity of many day-to-day fundraising tasks with stereotypically female work place women at a systematic disadvantage in the profession and enable men to maintain a disproportionate share of the most financially lucrative and executive-level positions".

The final extract in this sub-section is by Genevieve Shaker, who was part of a major research project that studied the career paths and experiences of 1,600 US fundraisers. Shaker focuses here on one aspect of that data: whether or not those who work as fundraisers "walk the talk" of being generous with their time and money outside of their job. She finds that the professional commitment to generosity and philanthropy does indeed extend beyond the working day, with fundraisers being more likely to give, to give larger amounts, and to volunteer more hours than the norm.

These three extracts show that the kind of people who raise funds for a living are doing exciting, taboo-busting work, which nonetheless is subject to the same gendered constraints found across society, and which attracts people who live generous lives.

5.2 What do fundraisers do?

In the second sub-section we move our attention from focusing on the employees to considering the nature of the work that they do.

The first extract, by Beth Breeze, argues that the job of fundraising is far more complicated than is generally appreciated and includes three broad types of work: (1) fostering a philanthropic culture within the charity and in wider society; (2) framing the needs being met by the charity; and (3) facilitating donations. She notes that the level of intimacy and personal investment required to interact with potential and current donors in order to foster, frame and facilitate donations means that fundraising is a form of "emotional labour" in which practitioners must regulate, and sometimes repress, their own emotions in order to succeed in their work. Fundraisers describe investing their whole self in their work, and trying to maintain an "upbeat" and "happy façade" in order to give donors a positive experience that will sustain their engagement with the nonprofit organisation. Breeze identifies gratitude as a key emotion to be marshalled and managed by fundraisers. This includes creating opportunities for people to give back to organisations they have benefited from (such as educational, health and arts institutions), and extends to cultivating new reciprocal obligations by providing engaging activities such as enjoyable social events and behind the scenes tours that impel donors to repay through further donations. Breeze highlights a further task taken on by fundraisers: absorbing obligations that arise from each new donation in order to minimise power imbalances inherent in philanthropic transactions so that it is the fundraiser, rather than the end beneficiary, who absorbs any "stigma, stress and humiliation of asking for help".

The next extract, by Joseph Mixer zones in on a crucial aspect of fundraising work: maximising the likelihood of achieving positive responses from potential donors while coping with the inevitable – and more frequent – rejections. Mixer offers sound advice for "getting to yes whilst dealing with no" in a resilient and constructive way. He focuses on fundraising work that involves in-person interactions with major donors, describing the four stages of effective solicitation meetings: establishing rapport; engaging the prospective donor in dialogue about the needs to be met; conveying the organizational needs and why meeting them will be satisfying for the donor; and making the ask. Mixer notes that solicitations rarely progress smoothly through these four stages and provides useful ideas for "defusing objections ... with judgment and discretion". Objections and concerns vary from the need for more information, inability to afford the requested gift, and dislike of some aspect of the nonprofit's programme, staffing or approach. Suggested strategies include empathising and sympathising with the prospective donor's perspective, switching the topic, diffusing strong emotions, reframing the concern and refocusing on the value of the nonprofit's impact. Mixer's advice therefore illustrates in practice Breeze's argument that the work of fundraising involves a lot of emotional labour.

In the third extract exploring what fundraisers do, James Hodge explores questions first raised by Robert Payton who was one of the founders of philanthropic studies:

> Do we live for philanthropy, or do we live off of philanthropy? Do we have an occupation in philanthropy or do you pursue a passion for philanthropy?

Hodge takes the higher ground, viewing fundraising as "a noble calling" that is best fulfilled by focusing less on the amounts of monies that need to be raised and instead focusing on the good that fundraisers can achieve together with benefactors. He argues that "chasing meaning rather than money" will not only propel philanthropy to new levels but will also reduce job churn and burnout amongst fundraisers.

5.3　The ideal fundraiser

The third sub-section takes a step back from the day-to-day reality of being a fundraiser to explore instead how others – including non-fundraising colleagues, donors, and the general public – think about this work and the people who do it.

The concept of a singular, "ideal" fundraiser does not make much sense when we consider the great diversity of nonprofit organisations that they work in, and the wide variety of tasks they undertake. A fundraiser writing applications to grant-making bodies for a well-known service-providing non-profit will likely need, and have, a different skill set and personal characteristics to a fundraiser masterminding a social media campaign for a small start-up that is seeking radical reform. However it remains instructive to read about studies that have sought to catalogue the skills, knowledge and characteristics that are found in fundraisers who successfully manage to balance the needs of their organisation, donors, beneficiaries, and all others involved.

Margaret Duronio and Eugene Tempel conducted a major survey of the US fundraising profession to identify the characteristics, skills, and knowledge believed to underlie a fundraiser's performance. Their motivation was partly instrumental: to help those tasked with recruiting fundraisers, and partly motivational: to identify the special expertise that would promote a positive image of the profession. A question asking respondents their view on the primary characteristics of competent and successful fundraisers generated eleven thousand responses. Analysis of this data identified seven groupings of personal characteristics, such as having a sincere and cheerful personality, being hard-working and team-oriented, and having integrity; five types of skills, such as communication skills and cognitive skills; and three clusters of professional knowledge focused on fundraising, management, and general background knowledge. In something of an under-statement, Duronio and Tempel conclude their study indicates that fundraisers have "high expectations" of each other, describing the "best" fundraisers as:

> ethical, smart, committed people who were also friendly and sincere. They were knowledgeable about fund raising and also about their organizations. They were skilled in all forms of communication, interpersonal relationships, and fund-raising activities.

The theme of high standards continues in the next extract, in which Jerold Panas notes the lack of realism when looking for "the ideal fundraiser": "Outgoing, people-oriented, backslapping, extremely well organized, goal oriented, brilliant." It's no wonder that, as Panas jokingly concludes: "This magnificent creature probably doesn't exist." Despite this, he offers 63 observations or "verities" about the qualities, temperament, habits, and practices that he believes will help guide those looking for, or wanting to be, a great fundraiser. There is much overlap in Panas' verities and Duronio and Tempel's research findings, including an emphasis on integrity, working hard, and being a good communicator. There is also commonality with Breeze's finding that fundraisers commit their "whole self" to achieving positive results, with Panas claiming that, "The winner is always the one who gives body and soul, totally and unreservedly, to the joys and passion of the task." Whilst Panas' verity that "You have a way of getting 'yes' for an answer – even before you ask the question" echoes the outcome at the heart of Joseph Mixer's advice.

The final extract that explores what "ideal" fundraising looks like is written by Lisa Greer who sets out how fundraisers can provide donors with "the connection they crave" to organisations that they want to love. As a major donor herself, Greer shares insights into what it is like to be on the receiving end of poor communications, including two fascinating tables that compare the kinds of things that fundraisers frequently say, how badly they can land, and how they could be better phrased.

If the extracts in this sub-section depict an impossibly high bar for the "ideal" fundraiser, the final section comes back to ground with a bump, focusing on the challenging realities that face those doing this work.

5.4 The challenges of being a fundraiser

The first extract that is focused on the challenges of being a fundraiser is by Jason Lewis who offers an "honest but hopeful critique" of professional fundraising. His central point is that most people mistakenly believe nonprofit success is primarily hampered by a "lack of donors with dollars" when in fact the core issue is the "lack of fundraising talent" working in contexts that enable them to succeed. Lewis contends that understanding the true nature of the problem is liberating because nurturing and supporting talented fundraising professionals is within the control of nonprofit leaders, whereas focusing on the absence of generous supporters leads to "learned helplessness" and failed missions. Despite his frustration with nonprofits that over-focus on accumulating new donors whilst neglecting to invest in developing more meaningful relationships and support from those they already have, Lewis' message is ultimately hopeful. He believes that fundraisers who are motivated by their organisation's cause and are also motivated by working with donors who have a passion for that cause, will "jump out of bed in the morning" and achieve the results needed for their organisation to fund and fulfil its mission.

The next two extracts focus on the profound challenges caused by sexism and racism. Fundraising occurs within social contexts and is not immune from the problems that affect broader society. Erynn Beaton, Megan LePere-Schloop and Rebecca Smith share the findings of their study which uncovers multiple types of sexual harassment that occur as a result of fundraisers and their organisations being dependent on those with the ability to provide funding. Their findings highlight the sexualised nature of some fundraising activities (especially events such as gala dinners and golf tournaments) as well as examples of donors taking advantage of the power imbalance to behave inappropriately. The complicity of some employers in encouraging their fundraising staff to do "whatever it takes" to bring the money in, is accompanied by more heartening examples of nonprofits taking a stand against inappropriate and unacceptable behaviour which, as Beaton et al. note, point "to the possibilities of a better approach".

Next, Fatou Jammeh offers a compelling personal account of her experience as a black fundraiser. Noting that the word "philanthropy" means "love of humanity" she describes how the prevalence of institutionalised racism means that "love in the philanthropic sector for a Black fundraiser like myself is a feeling that is hard to find". Jammeh describes many manifestations of poor treatment of non-white fundraisers: when managers and colleagues are oblivious to racially fraught power dynamics, when those who speak up are censored, and when interactions with donors are made harder because "the wealthy are comfortable making pledges to fundraisers who look like them". Despite the barriers that evidently exist, Jammeh's motivation in choosing this career – to pursue equity and a level playing field for those served by philanthropy – also drives her efforts to pursue systemic shifts within the philanthropy sector so that "the love of philanthropy applies to all".

The next extract shifts gear to explore the pressing challenge of finding new fundraising ideas, given the speed at which novelty emerges, peaks, and disappears. Roger Bennett and Sharmila Savani published their paper four years before that trajectory was exemplified by the Ice Bucket challenge, a viral fundraising effort that raised over $100 million for the ALS (amyotrophic lateral sclerosis) association in July–August 2014. The pressure to replicate that stunning fundraising success exemplifies the challenge facing those looking for the next big idea that will inspire millions of people to raise and donate millions of dollars, with minimal cost to the recipient cause. Bennett and Savani's analysis of "the idea generation field" identifies twenty-eight sources of ideas, including internal sources such as informally and formally consulting supporters, volunteers and colleagues, and – less intuitively – analysing complaints received, as well as external sources such as attending conferences, hiring consultants, and reading books and websites on fundraising. Bennett and Savani make a point familiar to many fundraisers that "the ideas that senior managers put forward may be aspirational rather than practical", and they conclude that "monitoring and evaluating the activities of comparable organisations in a charity's own and other fields" (much like the "competitor analysis" advocated by Adrian Sargeant and Jayne George in Section 3.1) is the most common route to obtaining fresh ideas for fundraising.

The challenge identified in the final text in this section resonates with points made in many of the extracts in earlier sections that highlight the invisibility of fundraisers and fundraising. Cassandra Chapman, Winnifred Louis, Barbara

Masser, and Emma Thomas describe fundraisers as an essential yet neglected element in the "charitable triad" – by which they mean donors, beneficiaries, and fundraisers – whose presence, characteristics, and interactive relationships all have an important influence on charitable giving decisions. They note that much research on why people give assumes a dyadic model consisting solely of a donor and a beneficiary, whereas:

> Triadic theory draws attention to the neglected fundraiser and offers a new theoretical approach to understanding charitable giving that actively considers the three key actors involved in any giving exchange: donor, beneficiary, and fundraiser.

It is fitting that this section ends with a theoretically dense extract, as it serves to remind us of the core point running through all the extracts in this section: that "being a fundraiser" is a complex and multi-faceted, idealised yet neglected, and ever-challenging role.

Discussion questions

1. If you are working as a fundraiser, consider your own pathway into this career. To what extent does Klein's positive description of the job reflect your feelings about it?
2. If you are not working as a fundraiser, do the readings in Section 5.1 make you more or less likely to consider this career? What would be the main reasons for or against pursuing this line of work?
3. Thinking of the issues raised by Dale, and by Beaton et al., in relation to the gendered nature of the fundraising profession, think of at least three ways that fundraising practices and activities can be redesigned to minimise opportunities for gender stereotyping and sexual harassment.
4. Make a list of the tasks that fundraisers typically do – this can refer to either generalist or specialist fundraising posts. Which of these tasks do you think require the greatest amounts of expertise, technical knowledge, or emotional resilience?
5. Considering the readings in Section 5.3 by Duronio and Temple, by Panas, and by Greer, do you think that the expectations held of fundraisers are reasonable? How would you account for the idealised nature of these expectations when considered in relation to texts in Sections 1.3 that detail misunderstandings of fundraising?
6. Does Jammeh's account resonate with your experience as a black fundraiser, or as a colleague of black fundraisers? Identify at least three barriers that exist in your organisation and/or the wider philanthropy sector, that must be dismantled to ensure equity for all in the profession.
7. Do the texts on the challenges of being a fundraiser in Section 5.4 contain any points that surprise you? In your experience, are these challenges openly discussed and/or well understood amongst the fundraising profession?

5.1 Who raises funds for a living?

Why more people should choose a career in fundraising

Kim Klein, 2000

What would you say if you could have a career that paid you a salary from $10,000–$150,000? Where your work had fairly measurable outcomes? Where talking about your values and writing about what you believe are part of the job? Where all the people you work with agree that what you do is really important?

Sounds like a great career, doesn't it? It is: it's a career in fundraising.

I have had many goals in my life, but my new goal is to have more people make fundraising their career. I have several reasons for wanting this:

- I have too much work, much more than I can handle. In another 10 or 15 years I want to retire knowing that there are many other people able to do the work I was doing.
- I want fewer phone calls from headhunters, desperate executive directors, friends who sit on boards of directors, all saying: "Do you know anyone who can take our development job? We've looked everywhere. We've extended the deadline for applications indefinitely."
- I want to see good organizations succeed in their fundraising, and one thing many groups need in order to succeed is someone who is paid to coordinate the organization's fundraising efforts.

Of course, my goal is more specific than simply bringing new people into fundraising. What I really want is to bring a new generation into fundraising for progressive social change, which is at the lower end of the salary scale I mentioned above.

> "But fundraising isn't a cool career," I hear you say. "Not like actually doing advocacy or service, or maybe even being a public interest attorney – being on the front lines of changing society."

A woman I worked with in the past recently wrote to tell me that she had just left her fundraising position to take a job as an advocate in an agency serving homeless mentally ill adults. "I'm glad to have had this fundraising experience," she wrote, "but it will be good to be out on the front lines again." Her letter came on the same day as a phone call from another colleague who said, "I just have to get back into doing the real work. I can't do this fundraising anymore."

DOI: 10.4324/9781003145936-84

I know that we need organizers and attorneys and social workers. But none of these positions needs to be exempt from fundraising, and someone needs to be the main person in charge of their fundraising.

Before you dismiss a fundraising career as for nerds only, consider the following facts: Fundraising allows you – in fact, requires you – to talk to people whom you would probably otherwise never meet about what you believe in and the difference their money will make in translating those beliefs into action. Fundraising gives you the chance to experiment with strategies. Will this letter work? Can you raise money on the internet? Would people pay to come to this kind of event? While some strategies are formulaic – you follow a recipe and you can predict the result (comforting, but often boring) – others are a combination of good luck, timing, and creativity.

Of course, fundraising does have its drawbacks. As with any difficult job, you have to be able to handle lots of tasks at the same time. In most organizations the fundraising staff has a lot of responsibility with very little authority. People tend to blame the fundraising department for everything that goes wrong in the organization. People who have no knowledge of fundraising have unrealistic ideas of how much money can be raised in short periods of time. And worse, they tend to believe that all the organization's problems can be solved by finding previously unknown, but very large foundations to get grants from, or by meeting lonely, generous, and previously unsolicited rich people.

Why fundraising is cool

Now I'm going to tell you why people think fundraising isn't cool, and why they're wrong. Let's admit it, fundraisers are regarded with the same mixture of admiration, loathing, suspicion, and awe with which we in America regard money itself. And this explains some of the problems in attracting people to fundraising positions. Money is one of the great taboos of our culture. We are taught not to talk about it or ask about it, except to a very limited number of people in a very limited number of circumstances. As with the subjects of sex, death, mental illness, religion, politics, and other taboos, people say little about their experiences with money. If people are so carefully taught that it is rude to talk about money, it's certainly not going to be easy to ask for it.

Yet, as George Pillsbury points out: "Although money cannot buy social change, no significant change can happen without it." Organizations cannot do their work without money. An organization that does not have enough money to accomplish its goals winds up wasting the time of its volunteers and staff, and possibly hurting the constituency it claimed to be working for.

When I decided to make fundraising my career 20 years ago, it wasn't because I liked fundraising. In fact, like most people drawn to working for social change, I had wanted to do advocacy work. But I found that the advocacy work was not going to happen unless someone brought in money, and if I wanted to do work that was important and useful for the groups and movements that I cared about, fundraising was one of the most useful things I could do.

I also chose fundraising because it meant that I would have to talk about money, which, in a small way, could begin to break down the taboo that surrounds it. This taboo, I believe, helps promote both racism and sexism. If you can't ask others at your workplace what they are earning, you will never know if minorities there are being paid less than whites or women less than men. That way, management has no fear that workers will seek more equitable salaries. The taboo supports the class structure in other ways as well. If only a tiny handful of ruling-class people understand how the stock market or other forms of investing work, they need not fear any threats to the economic system they control.

In fact, people who cannot talk about money, who will not learn to ask for it and deal with it, actually collaborate with a system that the rest of social change work seeks to dismantle. That alone makes fundraising not only a way cool profession, but also a dangerous one.

Here are some other reasons fundraising is exciting, sexy, and cool:

1. Although there are technical aspects to fundraising, it does not require years of education. In fact, the three main requirements for success can be found in people of all educational backgrounds: common sense, a basic affection for other people, and a passionate belief in a cause.
2. Fundraising requires you to learn new things all the time, while perfecting the set of basic skills you bring.
3. Fundraising connects donors to an organization. Many donors have little relationship to the organizations they support aside from giving money. They don't have time to volunteer, or they are not part of the constituency. A fundraiser helps them continue to feel connected and useful so that they will want to continue to give.
4. Fundraising is organizing. Good fundraisers organize teams of volunteers to help with fundraising, and they should be teaching organizers how to ask for money too. Organizers usually ask people only for time – go to a meeting, plan a strategy, come to a demonstration. Good fundraisers teach people fundraising skills and give them confidence that they actually can raise money. With a combined strategy of fundraising and organising, people are asked for time and money – as much of either or both as they can give. A much wider range of gifts and talents and abilities can be brought out in our constituents by adding fundraising strategies to the mix.
5. Fundraising will allow you, perhaps even force you, to confront basic issues of class in yourself, in your organization, and in the people you raise money for and from.

Becoming a fundraiser

You can get into fundraising in a variety of ways. One of the best ways to learn fundraising is to volunteer to help with fundraising tasks at one of your favorite organizations. Fundraising is in fact one of the few jobs for which volunteer experience qualifies you. Being on the fundraising committee of a board of directors or helping put on a special event has launched many a fundraising career. Interning with the fundraising department or staff person at an organization is another form of volunteering that can be very instructive.

You can also learn about fundraising in college classes and courses, but they only have merit if you have a way to apply what you have learned in a real-life setting. Working in a large organization as an assistant to the development director will give you a range of experience without requiring you to take on a lot of responsibility.

If you are serious about fundraising as a career, find a mentor. Many development directors enjoy mentoring people new to the field and can help you find your way through the difficult times.

And don't hesitate to jump in at the deep end. Take a job that you are not totally qualified for, then read, take classes, use your mentor, and wing it. I have often encouraged organizations to stop looking for the person with perfect skills who may not exist, and instead to find a bright, hardworking, quick learner. Give that person a solid team of volunteers to work with and watch what happens. With enough support and a little latitude, this person is likely to be successful.

Join the front lines

As you can see, when I say I want people to make fundraising their career, what I really mean is that I want people to say, "My role in working for social justice will be to help generate money." Fundraising cannot be separated from its context. It is a necessary and central part of developing an organization and fulfilling its mission. It is real work, and though it takes place on a slightly different set of front lines, they are front lines all the same. The more fundraising is integrated into the rest of the organization, the more successful it will be, and the more fundraisers we can hope to have in the future.

Why is fundraising seen as women's work?

Elizabeth Dale, 2017

Even though men occupied the majority of fundraising positions until recently, I argue that two central elements have served to feminize the profession: first, the day-to-day job of fundraising is closely aligned with the stereotypes of women's work; and second, nonprofit executive-level culture has been based on traditionally masculine models of management. Further, the contemporary push for nonprofits to adopt more business-like practices and for-profit values, which are traditionally male domains, present a tension that limits women's potential to transform the profession into one that recognizes and values women's contributions and roles.

Looking through a gender lens at fundraisers' daily work

The foundation of fundraising is based on interpersonal relations, skillful communication, and managing emotions and motivations, in essence, a set of job functions that personify "traditional" female characteristics and traits … The description of fundraising work assumes such characteristics as genderless, when in fact, they are not. Instead of viewing occupational changes as a result of labor theory or human capital theory, Anker argues that

> gender theory makes a valuable contribution to explaining occupational segregation by sex by showing how closely the characteristics of "female" occupations mirror the common stereotypes of women and their supposed abilities.

Anker groups stereotypical female occupational characteristics into positive, negative, and other. The positive stereotypes are a caring nature; skill and experience in household-related work; greater manual dexterity; greater honesty; and an attractive physical appearance. The five negative stereotypes are disinclination to supervise others (which leads to vertical occupational segregation); lesser physical strength; lesser ability in science and mathematics; lesser willingness to travel; and lesser willingness to face physical danger and to use physical force. Finally, three other stereotypes for women are presented: greater docility and lesser inclination to complain about work and working conditions; greater willingness to accept lower wages and less need for income (presumably because of a male earner); and greater interest in working at home.

DOI: 10.4324/9781003145936-85

Fundraising work mirrors a number of these so-called female occupational characteristics including a caring, relational approach; an emphasis on communication; a need to put others before yourself; and the production of events that draw on hospitality and entertaining-type skills. Similarly, fundraising does not pose significant physical danger, require physical strength, or rely on extensive scientific or mathematical knowledge. In fact, in a popular fundraising textbook, Jim Greenfield suggests that fundraising is female-dominated because it "matches well with women's natural ability to engage people in social settings, to cope with diverse personalities, and to nurture relationships". Such essentialist positions only reinforce the idea that women are better suited for a position that was, at one time, occupied by nearly all men.

In interviews, women who work as development officers often mention "female" characteristics as being helpful in their work, but those same traits also pose constraints. Beneficial skills include listening, nurturing, being open, being empathetic, building relationships, and attention to detail. However, these skills are not valued equally to the "male" characteristics of being direct, making quick decisions, focusing on outputs, and increasing profits. Reskin argues that such skill differentiation is fundamental in hierarchical systems and serves as basis for differential evaluation and, thus, differential rewards. With occupational sex segregation, men's activities are valued above women's, and both men and women come to devalue women's efforts. In particular, Reskin writes,

> Task differentiation generally assigns to lower-status groups the least desirable, most poorly rewarded work .... This practice symbolizes and legitimates the subordinate group's low status, while making it appear to have an affinity for these undesirable tasks. As an added benefit, members of the dominant group don't have to do them!

In contrast, women may have less visible roles in making presentations, may be seen as less able to comment on financial matters, and were taken less seriously or had difficulty being heard because of their gender.

Within fundraising, the most economically rewarded tasks are those directly related to securing gifts at the highest dollar amounts. Taylor writes, "Access to money brings power and prestige". Executive-level and major gift work are valued above all else, whereby fundraisers work with leadership volunteers and donors (often wealthy individuals and/or those with public prominence) to secure contributions ranging from the thousands to millions of dollars. As compared with men, women report having less access to top-tier donors and prospects and occupy fewer planned giving, major gifts, or management positions. Instead, women dominate less-highly valued roles, including prospect research, grant writing, event management (a sociability function), or the annual fund, which is composed of soliciting modest-sized gifts from large groups of people, often via phone or mail. Women also can be pigeonholed into working with just women donors or women's programs, which are typically areas of limited advancement and recognition.

Although fundraising may be an essential function for nonprofit organizations, it still competes for status and recognition, both among non-fundraisers in the organization as well as the general public. Unlike service delivery, it is an administrative function, even termed a "necessary evil" to maintain the organization's ability to provide services. It is also assigned low status in society as a result of a lack of understanding among the public about fundraising, combined with a negative public perception, in part, due to rare but well publicized, ethical breaches.

Further, fundraisers often remain behind-the-scenes whereas other individuals play more prominent roles. Many fundraisers are responsible for preparing volunteers or executives before visiting with current or potential donors, debriefing with staff and volunteers afterward, and handling any follow-up work. In this way, fundraising may be a role more women than men may be willing to take, as they end up supporting, and occupying a subservient role to, executives and board members who are disproportionately male.

Additionally, many female fundraisers must balance their paid work with the demands of family and child care roles and negotiate this tension on a daily basis. Gibelman found that although nonprofits' personnel practices generally adhere to equal opportunity hiring and federal affirmative action guidelines, organizations take a broad-brush approach that fails to acknowledge women's child-care obligations and, increasingly, elder care as well. Fundraising and working with volunteers may involve significant work time during evenings and weekends, and many gift officers engage in frequent travel to visit donors in person. Career advancement can also require fundraisers to relocate to achieve greater responsibility, which may limit women's opportunities if they are unable to move due to family responsibilities

Looking through a gender lens at fundraising management

The second way we can conceive of fundraising as women's work is the disparity between men and women in positions of management and preference for masculine characteristics at the executive level. Stivers writes that a "cultural masculinity" predominates in our images of managers and leaders, which inhibits women's pursuit of executive-level positions as well as their management styles, should they achieve such positions. Even though women represent a majority of the nonprofit workforce, the dominant executive-level culture requires female nonprofit executives to adapt to "traditionally masculine models of management," which emphasize directness and focus on the bottom line. Should a woman rise to a management position, she is often the exception and may even be required to function as what Acker termed, "a biological female who acts as a social male" adopting masculine characteristics and traits in order to succeed. Nonprofit organizations are not immune from this culture.

Further, the characteristics of female work, described above, are not seen as directly transferable to advancing into management, thereby further reinforcing the hierarchical segregation of women fundraisers as the "technicians" whereas men are the "managers". Characteristics such as being cooperative, collaborative, and inclusive may limit women's ascension into executive positions. Nonprofits also tend to be structurally flat organizations, which limits the number of pathways to managerial positions and opportunities for internal advancement. Conry quotes Phyllis S. Fanger, one of the founders of Women in Development, a Boston-area organization for women fundraisers, as saying,

> Women are not yet on an equal footing with men in top management in development. Our strength is in the numbers, but the perception is not yet widespread that women can handle the top positions. ... On the way up, women are too often given roles that are out of the spotlight, have lower gift dollar potential, or are gender-defined.

Therefore, the day-to-day work of fundraisers and its similarity to stereotypically female work place women at a systematic disadvantage in the profession and enable men to maintain a disproportionate share of the most financially lucrative and executive-level positions.

Looking through a gender lens at for-profit "professionalization"

Finally, a gender analysis cannot ignore the recent trends of both nonprofits and funders to place greater emphasis on adopting more business-like practices and the values of the private sector, which reflect the masculine bias of society at large. As Gibelman writes, "The underlying values of the nonprofit sector, which include humanitarianism, charity, human rights, and human well-being, suggest that representative organizations would voluntarily and systematically seek to adhere to principles of affirmative action and nondiscrimination in their labor force practices". However, these organizations are not immune from larger societal pressures and, thus, may still discriminate against women and favor the dominant, sociocultural model. Although a number of values within the nonprofit sector align with the characteristics of women's work and may have even served to draw women into paid fundraising roles, the values of the private sector are closely aligned with a masculine culture that is taken for granted as neutral. For example, the essence of major gift work is relationship building; however, this can be contested by organizations that follow a sales or marketing model. Dominant approaches to management also emphasize hierarchy, achievement, and results. Although behaviors that are inclusive, participatory, and transformative are acknowledged in management literature as important to organizational success, the external expectations from funders for a more business-like environment are in opposition to these values. Even contemporary nonprofit management education reflects both the preference for entrepreneurship and professionalization instead of community-based, care-related work.

In addition to values, the language of fundraising is also male-oriented. The term "campaign," one of the original fundraising inventions, is borrowed from a military model. Taylor writes that "to 'solicit' someone has been used in a context that is derogatory toward women". Even "moves management" emphasizes a sales approach and may devalue women's more relational communication styles. In short, what this analysis shows is that, although the nonprofit sector offers the potential to revalue care-centered work and women's contributions, the existing structures, positions, language, and pressures are forcing it to comply with patriarchal models. Acknowledging these structures is the first step required to enable women's equality in the fundraising profession.

Are fundraisers philanthropic?

Genevieve G. Shaker, 2021

"Never ask someone to do something that you wouldn't do yourself," is common leadership advice." In fundraising this idea translates easily to, "Don't ask others to give without giving first."

The message is clear. Fundraisers should be givers themselves. This shows a fundraiser's authenticity, brings added legitimacy to their "right" to ask, and puts fundraisers in donors' shoes. But, do fundraisers live up this advice?

To find out, I was part of a team that analyzed data from more than 1,600 U.S. fundraisers about whether they give and volunteer and how much. We discovered that fundraisers in the study were more generous with their money and time than people in general, with some nuances.

Researching fundraisers

Our survey, conducted in 2015, asked fundraisers a broad range of questions about their career paths and experiences. It was one effort to continue to build knowledge about the fundraising profession and the central role fundraisers play in raising mission-central funds for nonprofits. This research, on the philanthropy of fundraisers, is one outcome of the larger project. We anticipated that that fundraisers would give differently than the general public. This is because professional norms and ethics for fundraisers include a commitment to the public good and a belief in their own responsibility to be philanthropically generous.

Our survey had limitations – including most who responded were members of fundraising professional associations (i.e. the Association of Fundraising Professionals, the Association for Healthcare Philanthropy, the Council for the Advancement and Support of Education), so they were part of national fundraising communities rather than fundraisers without that connection to one another. Like all other studies of fundraisers, our sample was not nationally representative. Therefore, the research suggests information about all fundraisers but is not definitive beyond our participants.

Fundraisers' charitable behavior

We discovered that 98.5% of the fundraisers had donated the previous year and had given an average of US$2,359. In that same year, according to the

DOI: 10.4324/9781003145936-86

Philanthropy Panel Study, 55.4% of the U.S. population donated an average of US$1,364 (includes nondonors). This means that the fundraisers were nearly 80% more likely to give and gave 73% more dollars. When we took out people who didn't give at all and considered only the donors in both groups, fundraisers gave 5% less than all U.S. donors (US$2,397 compared with US$2,514). Considering giving as a percentage of income (fundraisers' salary), we found that fundraisers were more generous.

Shifting from donations of money to time, 82.9% of the fundraisers volunteered as compared to earlier Panel Study of Income Dynamics data showing that 33.7% of Americans were volunteers. A large number of "super volunteers" in the general public (those who volunteered at least 100 hours per year) meant the general public volunteered more hours on average annually than fundraisers (41.1 hours versus 11.0 hours). However, when the super volunteers were removed from the calculations, fundraisers volunteered more (10.1 hours versus 5.9 hours). Interestingly, fundraisers at the lower end of the pay scale were most likely to volunteer, and volunteered the most hours, compared with those making more money.

Giving before asking

In this study, we examined what fundraisers do with their own money and time. We learned that our fundraisers were indeed philanthropists. They did what they asked of others—they gave and volunteered, often more than other people.

We concluded that that the expectation of generosity is deeply embedded in fundraisers' understandings of their work. In a chicken or egg moment, we also wondered if people who were already charitably-inclined gravitated to fundraising or if as fundraisers they became acculturated to the norms of giving. Either way, there is much more research to do about the individuals who choose fundraising as their profession.

Empowered fundraising means asking others to give with pride rather than apology, according to Hank Rosso, founder of The Fund Raising School. Knowing that nearly all fundraisers are givers will make "prideful asking" that much easier.

5.2 What do fundraisers do?

Fundraising as emotional labour and gratitude work

Beth Breeze, 2017

When I first began researching what fundraisers do, and asked someone that very question, they responded with this joke:

> Did you hear the one about the doctor, the lawyer and the fundraiser who all die at the same time? When they reach the pearly gates of heaven, St Peter offers the doctor, who arrives first, a single wish as a reward for doing so much good on earth. The doctor asks for a million pounds and walks through the gates into eternal paradise. The lawyer, who is second in line, overhears the conversation and when his turn comes he asks for – and gets – a billion pounds. Next up comes the fundraiser. When St Peter asks what reward she'd like, she says: "I know it's a big ask, but could I have the business cards of the two people who were just in front of me?"

This joke is appreciated within the fundraising world because it acknowledges and celebrates the all-consuming nature of the job, and highlights many of the qualities that fundraisers need, such as tenacity, opportunism and confidence in their interpersonal skills.

There is one simple truth that underlies any discussion of what fundraisers do: they are proactively working to do whatever it takes to legally and ethically secure the resources their charity needs to fulfil its mission. As the UK's Institute of Fundraising, somewhat wearily, notes, "This money does not appear by magic – donors need to be asked for donations." It ought to be unnecessary to state this basic fact, but given the lack of awareness of the fundraising function, it is worth emphasising that fundraisers are not sitting on the side-lines watching surprise donations come in.

The job of fundraising is often assumed to be exclusively focused on asking for money, but such a restricted definition is unhelpful and misleading. Indeed many, especially those who work closely with major donors and other personalised forms of fundraising, do not use the word 'fundraiser' or 'fundraising' in their job title or on their business card, preferring instead to use terms such as 'development director', 'partnerships' or 'head of philanthropy'. While this could be interpreted as simply reticence to mentioning money, it accurately reflects the reality of the daily tasks of the most successful fundraisers, whose work goes far beyond the isolated task of solicitation.

DOI: 10.4324/9781003145936-88

I draw on existing literature and the new data collected for my study on both the 'art' and the 'science' of fundraising, to describe a new, comprehensive model that depicts what it is that fundraisers do. This model captures the diversity and complexity of the fundraising role, subsuming the multifarious tasks and goals under three broad types of work:

[...]

The three 'Fs': a new framework to explain what fundraisers do

My proposed new model to explain what fundraisers do has three elements:

1. Fostering a philanthropic culture – both within the charity and in wider society.
2. Framing needs – to establish the legitimacy of the cause and educate potential donors about the existence of credible voluntary solutions.
3. Facilitating donations – provide a trusted and, where possible, enjoyable way for donors to respond to needs.

The Foster-Frame-Facilitate triad encompasses the multiplicity of tasks undertaken by fundraisers, which are not sequential: fundraisers must simultaneously foster, frame and facilitate, because fundraising is not a linear process.

[...]

Fundraising as a form of emotional labour

The level of intimacy and personal investment required to interact with potential and current donors in order to foster, frame and facilitate donations is why fundraising can rightly be described as a form of emotional labour. The term 'emotional labour' was coined by the sociologist Arlie Hochschild, who wrote about 'the managed heart' of many employees in the service economy, who are required to manage their personal feelings in order to fulfil their contractual duties: for example, air stewardesses being compelled to smile while working, regardless of any personal sadness they may be experiencing or any obstreperous passengers they may be dealing with ...

Expectations of how paid fundraisers must behave, and the emotions and related behaviours that are required for success in their job, are often quite explicit. These include the need to be passionate, cheerful and open; to be courageous, to be energetic, self-confident and curious; to have patience and tact; to have 'unbridled, unflinching, undying enthusiasm'; to be positive, funny, and humble; to have 'a sincere interest in the donor as a person'; and even to 'love' their donors, because they 'have to feel you care about them'. How-to books for fundraisers note that giving is an emotional act rather than a financial transaction, and advise readers to 'harness the power of emotion ... to open people's hearts and minds'.

In the present study, many fundraisers recounted situations where they felt required to use or manage their emotions in the course of their work, with a typical comment being: "when I'm having a bad day in my personal life, then I do still need to maintain a happy façade in front of the donors". Other interviewees confirmed that being upbeat was necessary for all types of face-to-face fundraising, not just with major donors. An interviewee who began her career as a street fundraiser explained: 'Donors read the emotions of the askers, so if I showed that I was feeling down then people would steer around me, whereas happy street fundraisers attract donors'.

Working with major donors requires more emotional labour than other types of fundraising because it is conducted face-to-face and often involves extensive socialising outside of the office and office hours. The demands of these social occasions exert a particular emotional pressure, as an interviewee explains:

> One does put an awful lot of one's own self into a fundraising role in a way that I think you perhaps don't have to in a more technical role. I put a huge amount of my own self into each donor. The personal investment that fundraisers need to make is very high and underrated.

Stories of soldiering on in the face of personal and professional misery were common, as were the opposite scenarios where fundraisers deployed positive emotions, such as happiness, in order to demonstrate shared personal commitment to the cause:

> I almost cried when a donor announced she was ready to make a big gift. I got very tactile and hugged her. I was worried it might be inappropriate but it seemed to reassure her that I was equally passionate about the cause and not just 'doing my job'.

Fundraisers also recounted how they enjoyed using their personal skills to positively influence the emotional experiences of others, as this example illustrates:

> It's amazing to be able to offer that to somebody, to facilitate that and to say, 'Actually, because I'm here you've had a really great experience'. I know I can make a difference to the tone of a party, and that's just a lovely thing. I quite enjoy the event organising side of the job for that reason: you can be in charge of somebody's happiness.

Other interviewees discussed the difficulty in maintaining the upbeat personality that they feel is expected of them, and which can be dented as a result of interacting with the very people who hold those expectations:

> Donors drain you, they sap your energy. Sometimes I just disappear. Sometimes I'm having a down day and I don't feel like effervescing, but

you have to put your 'game face' on. You feel so responsible – for the cause and for the donors and guests at events. So however tired I am, I put on another layer of make-up and I don't let myself yawn.

This is a classic illustration of emotional labour: masking and regulating one's own emotions because the job demands it and because the worker's personality is now a commodity like any other, available to 'effervesce' for the security of a salary. However, the 'commodification' argument advanced by Hochschild is not unproblematically transferable from a for-profit to a non-profit setting. Air stewardesses may 'sell their smiles' for a wage and other perks, such as free travel, but people who are paid to work in charities often also claim to be driven by higher motivations such as affinity with a particular cause or desire to make a positive difference, and see their job as a 'vocation' or a 'calling'. It may, therefore, be difficult to distinguish when a fundraiser is doing emotional labour because they have to, or because they want to. In many ways the distinction is irrelevant, as fundraisers are clearly engaged in frequent regulation of their emotions in order to succeed in their jobs, as a further quote illustrates:

You do have to be 'on', you know, you have to be engaged and engaging and that takes effort. And actually if you think of fundraisers, you know, it takes a lot … it can take a lot of you.

[…]

Fundraising as gratitude work

While fundraising involves marshalling and managing a wide range of emotions, as described above, the emotion that recurs most frequently in my data is gratitude. This involves more than saying 'thank you' (though it is essential to do so clearly, swiftly and sincerely); it is about expressing gratitude in attitudes and actions as well as in words. Expressing gratitude also involves demonstrating that the gift was meaningful by giving the donor information on how their money was put to work as intended. Successful fundraisers describe being alert to, and able to create, opportunities to express thanks and give meaningful feedback, as well as devoting effort to identifying and cultivating reciprocal obligations so that their charity can benefit from the urge of others to 'repay'.

[…]

As with any emotion, gratitude is manifested in both acts and attitudes. Organising thank-you letters (ideally with a thoughtful signature from someone the donor respects and admires, such as the CEO, Chair or a celebrity patron), and hosting events to thank supporters, are two of the most tangible types of 'gratitude work', but it is also manifested in the fundraiser's demeanour and willingness to use any communication or interaction as an opportunity to reinforce gratitude, as this example illustrates:

One of our major donors is very keen on baking, so whenever I'm in a hotel (for work or pleasure) I always take the free plastic shower caps to give her when we next meet, as she says they're useful for putting over dough whilst it rises! I know she appreciates that I remembered her hobby, and handing them over is a little token of thanks as well as a good excuse to set up a meeting so I can share our latest developments and successes.

This exemplifies good gift-giving practice, as recommended in the how-to literature, as explained by Matheney:

Choosing a gift [for a donor] requires careful thought. Your decision on this point can enhance or destroy a relationship. Begin with your knowledge of the donor, his or her likes and dislikes, hobbies and activities. Instead of an expensive but impersonal gift, try to select a gift that reflects the personality of the donor.

Gratitude is also carefully embedded in the physical life of many charities by naming buildings and staff posts (such as 'the Smith Chair in Physics') in honour of donors, which sends a clear, public signal of recognition and gratitude that is often deeply appreciated.

Gratitude figures in the daily work of fundraisers in two distinct ways. First, and most obviously, fundraisers need to convey sincere gratitude on behalf of the organisation and its beneficiaries to all those who voluntarily provide resources so that the charity can fulfil its mission. This includes expressing gratitude simply for being given the time to discuss the charity. Second, fundraisers need to identify and generate opportunities where others feel a sense of gratitude to the charity, in order to build a constituency of potential donors who may decide to 'pay back' to an organisation from which they have benefited. This latter type of gratitude work is exemplified by the focus on alumni by university fundraising departments: after graduation, alumni typically receive regular updates via emails and magazines, invitations to reunions, help to stay connected with fellow alumni, and opportunities to be involved in the ongoing life of the university, for example, by providing mentoring or career advice to current students …

Hospital fundraising is often explicitly focused on previous beneficiaries: in the US, this is called 'grateful patient fundraising'. In countries without privatised medicine, this may seem an unnecessary, and even objectionable, phenomenon, but despite the existence of the National Health Service, UK donors continue to prioritise donations to hospitals. Furthermore, studies indicate that one function of fundraising from patients and former patients is to empower those who may be feeling disempowered by experiencing ill health. This is because grateful patient fundraising "offers [patients] a way to give back, from which many gain a valid sense of meaning, contribution, and fulfilment". The cycle of gratitude is clearly evident in this example: it feels uncomfortable to take (in this case, excellent medical care) without giving back, and fundraisers provide a mechanism for return gifts.

Charities without such an obvious 'constituency' of potential supporters as alumni and former patients can use other strategies to inculcate gratitude. In my first job as a fundraiser for a Catholic charity that helps young homeless

people we held a 'thank you' mass for our supporters. It was a beautiful celebration with excellent music and a buffet reception afterwards, prepared by
some of the people helped by the charity. I assumed we would pass around
a collection plate during mass to receive donations, but my much-more
experienced fundraising boss said it was better to let the supporters leave
the building feeling indebted to us, having enjoyed the event and the food
and drink. He knew they'd be keen to pay us back and that we'd get bigger
donations if we let that feeling grow for a few days. Of course, he was quite
right!

Another important aspect of gratitude work is that fundraisers are willing
to do 'the labour of gratitude' so that the real recipient doesn't have to …
Fundraisers receive donations on behalf of the charity and the end beneficiaries, and thereby absorb any stigma, stress and humiliation of asking for help.
As Offer explains: "Giving gives rise to obligation, in other words a debt: the
giver notches up an emotional and material credit, in the form of a bond on
the recipient." By inserting themselves between the donor and the recipient,
fundraisers accept both the gift and its concomitant obligations, which helps
to avert problems inherent in the power imbalance between those with
resources and the – often powerless – end beneficiaries. Playing this role makes
fundraisers 'heroes of social interaction', to use Gouldner's term, because they
are willing to bear the burden of unrepayable debt in a society where people
prefer to avoid becoming indebted.

Fundraisers can sometimes share the burden of gratitude work with
colleagues, and with non-vulnerable beneficiaries. For example, an orchestra
may strike up 'happy birthday' for a major donor attending a concert, or a
postgraduate student may meet with the donor funding his or her studies.
But many fundraisers are working on behalf of beneficiaries who cannot
express gratitude: not just in the case of children and vulnerable people whose
privacy must be protected, but also recipients who live in distant countries;
non-human end beneficiaries, such as the environment or historic buildings;
charities working to prevent future harm, such as vaccination programmes and
early childhood interventions; and charities working on behalf of those facing
future needs but who have not yet, for example, contracted a disease or faced
drowning at sea. Part of the historical development of fundraising involves the
widespread raising of funds for imagined and as-yet nonexistent beneficiaries,
which is far removed from centuries of giving alms to visible paupers in the
street. In all cases, the fundraiser has to represent and embody the end beneficiary, accept the gift and convey the gratitude that spurs further gifts.

Getting to 'yes' and dealing with 'no'

Joseph T. Mixer, 1993

All effective solicitations contain four stages …

1. An introduction in which social amenities and relationships between the parties are covered.
2. A dialogue that allows the prospect to express his or her personal views regarding the need, the agency, and his or her individual values.
3. A description of the needs to be met and the benefits for the prospect and the asking of questions that can be answered positively.
4. A conclusion in which a gift is requested.

The exact format for a solicitation will vary with the characteristics of the persons involved. However, to produce the desired results, the content of the four stages must satisfy the donor's personal motivations, present suitable donor stimuli, and cite potential donor rewards. The following sections describe how the four stages apply to face-to-face solicitations.

The setting for face-to-face solicitations usually involves two persons, the prospect and the asker, although when a major gift is expected a second asker may be present and the prospect's spouse or trusted advisor may sit in. The prospect knows either directly or indirectly that a request for funds will be made. This message is conveyed during the telephone call for the appointment or in mailings sent in advance. The amount of the request is not announced but is left to be introduced strategically during the presentation.

1. Introduction of solicitation meeting

In a very brief time, the solicitor should establish a rapport with the prospective donor by discussing existing relationships, mutual involvement with the agency, and shared values. The purpose of the visit is clearly stated: to talk about the prospect's interest in the need to be met and the opportunity for the prospect to be a part of the solution. A brief assertion of the agency's capacity to deal with the need reassures the prospect. In a minute or so, by following this format, the asker can reduce the prospect's concern over any unknown factors by stating the nature of the visit and encouraging the prospect to concentrate on the message instead of on questions about what is going to happen.

DOI: 10.4324/9781003145936-89

The recitation of common affiliations reinforces the social bonds between the asker and the prospect.

2. Dialogue during solicitation meeting

Since a social exchange is the desired result of the meeting, a discussion must ensue to determine the prospect's knowledge, feelings, and interest about the need and the organization working on it. Low-key questions posed to the prospect serve this end. By encouraging the prospect to express his or her views, the solicitor helps mutual understanding and common concerns to evolve. Furthermore, the solicitor can draft a mental road map of the points he or she should cover in the subsequent descriptions.

The dialogue portion of the meeting ends with the solicitor's summing up the areas of agreement and asking the prospect if the points are correct. The dialogue process is based on psychological studies that demonstrate the importance of a person's ventilating concerns and feelings before another person suggests a change in behavior. In this case, the desired behavioral change is from taking no action to making a donation. Additionally, the prospect's assent to the correctness of the summation begins the vital process of encouraging the prospect to agree with the solicitor's statements. This getting-agreement strategy is further enhanced when the solicitor asks the prospect if the solicitor can proceed to talk about some of the agency's accomplishments in meeting the need at hand.

3. Description of the needs to be met and donor benefits

Before making a decision to give, prospects want reassurances that their money will achieve a worthwhile end and not be wasted. They want confirmation that the organization can carry out the proposed project. Thus, the solicitor must have in mind several agency project examples that match the interests and feelings the prospect cited during the dialogue. Recitation of the ways agency work has benefited individuals or improves situations causes the prospect to sense the potential personal power, status, and achievement that can result from a donation. At this point, the solicitor can reinforce the prospect's feelings by mentioning some satisfactions the donor will receive. Again, the solicitor employs the principle of getting agreement by asking the prospect if the service or plan of action seems to be a good idea. Once two or three activities have been described, along with their client and donor benefits, and once confirming questions have been asked and answered, the prospect will be stimulated to wonder what the bottom line is, what is expected in the way of a donation. Any delay in satisfying this curiosity will disrupt the conditioning that has taken place.

4. Conclusion of meeting: requesting the Gift

The effective donation question is worded to address internal motivations and to incorporate external influences as well as to state a specific sum. For example, a solicitor could say, "Because of these benefits, would you join me in making a gift of $1,000 to help these people do X?" or, "Would you become a part of this effort (or plan, or activity) to achieve these benefits by making a gift of $1,000 along with me?". The effectiveness of these questions lies in their intimation of achievement ("do X"; "achieve these benefits"), affiliation ("become a part"), status and group endeavour ("join with me"), and self-esteem. If the presentation has touched on other personal, social, or negative motivations felt by the donor, added leverage is obtained. With a commitment in hand, the solicitor thanks the prospect, reassures the person that positive results will occur, and leaves promptly.

Defusing objections

Rarely will a solicitation proceed as smoothly as this outline shows. Objections and concerns arise quite naturally in prospects' minds as the individuals process a request for action that may or may not have been anticipated. Reactions can include such defensive tactics as temporizing or stating a need for more information and rationales. Prospects who do this are striving to preserve their sense of self-worth by fending off perceived invasions of their images of themselves. Initially, they may consider the idea of making a gift as a threat, a move into the unknown, or an additional frustration. To a prospect these feelings are real; the solicitor who denies the feelings increases the prospect's negative reactions.

The solution to this defensiveness requires that the asker acknowledge and empathize with the objection. The prospect must clearly feel the asker's consideration and feel that the asker is truly listening to the prospect's concern. Such empathy allows the existing rapport to continue and grow. As the emotional aspect of the concerns is being addressed through empathy, the cognitive aspect can be handled in several ways. A frequent prospect objection is lack of money. The asker can express sympathy, not rejection, and build on the objection by suggesting that he or she has faced a similar situation and found the answer in pledging a donation on a monthly or quarterly basis. Other objections may center around dislike for a particular program, personality, or seemingly unjustified need. In these cases, the solicitor can switch the topic after sympathizing with the prospect. This technique allows the solicitor to introduce, for example, a new agency activity to occupy the prospect's mind, thus removing the disliked activity from the prospect's attention and easing the tension, or the expression of sympathy for the prospect's concerns can be followed by a supposition of what could happen to clients, programs, or agencies if there were no support to correct the situation. These two responses to objections are less stressful and more constructive than direct confrontations.

A more forceful tactic is to ask the prospect a direct question. This is particularly effective when the person has no interest in the need presented or states interest only in another field. A pertinent question at this time is, "What would it take for you to become interested in this project?" This question causes the prospect to provide more information about his or her values and feelings, which the solicitor can then address. If the prospect voices a particularly vehement objection, another helpful tactic is to ask the person to repeat the statement. Usually, individuals find it difficult to sustain an emotional outburst a second time. Also, the repetition can help the prospect recognise that the statement was unrealistic or inappropriate.

An additional method of dealing with strong concerns is for the solicitor to rephrase the objections with a slight overstatement or emphasis. For example, in response to a prospect's worry that an agency is not well equipped to deal with the need, the solicitor might say, "As I understand it, our agency does not have any solution to this problem?" The slight exaggeration prompts the prospect to clarify the objection and, in doing so, to gain a better perspective on what is at issue. This procedure helps diffuse emotion and focuses the prospect on the value of the services to be supported. Also, when the solicitor restates the objection, it is important that he or she avoids attributing it to the prospect. Otherwise, the prospect will feel compelled to defend the objection rather than enabled to step back and look at it objectively.

The handling of any objection requires judgment and discretion to adapt the remedy to the rapport existing in the relationship. Harsh response stiffens opposition. As already mentioned, objections to requests for funds frequently take the form of delaying tactics. Prospects may say, "I need more time to think about this," or "I need to consult with my wife (or husband)." An empathetic response by the solicitor and further dialogue softens the objection and allows rapport to develop further. If the delaying tactic cannot be overcome, the solicitor should establish a definite time to return, bringing back the pledge card and one or two new pieces of literature. The return visit appears more necessary and comfortable to both parties when the solicitor has some new items to show and discuss.

Living for, or off, philanthropy?

James M. Hodge

If it is a truism that "what we focus upon we become," then perhaps we need both a vastly wider aperture as well as a more relevantly focused system of metrics for philanthropy. If we only focus on money, we will not only raise less money, but also we will devalue the noble role that philanthropy can play in well-examined lives.

When our work is primarily directed toward raising money, we chase money rather than meaning in philanthropy. We become less aspirational for our institutions and less inspirational to our benefactors.

There is another way. I contend there is a higher path for our work and that the creation of a relationship-based system of mentoring, coaching, and leading the philanthropic process will result in philanthropy well beyond our present levels, and indeed beyond our highest hopes. A focus on shared value systems, on the good that can come from combining visionary nonprofits and committed philanthropists, will propel philanthropy to new levels, resulting in a greatly expanded third sector in our economy. Philanthropy is more about openings rather than about closings. It is about mutual aspirations of what is important and valuable to society. Gifts of significance are not so much about money as they are about meaning.

[…]

Money applied to philanthropic ends is a medium to serve others, to do purposeful work, to empower people to help themselves, to make an impact, and to improve the lots of others and the very health of our planet. Our philanthropic focus, therefore, must be on ideas and ideals and the power that they can have not only on the improved lives of those served but also on the quality of lives of philanthropists and those who work in the nonprofit world. For as Bob Payton once powerfully inquired, "Do we live for philanthropy, or do we live off of philanthropy? Do we have an occupation in philanthropy or do you pursue a passion for philanthropy?"

We indeed become that which we direct our attention to in life. Let us change the picture and start focusing far more attention on relationships with philanthropists and those with a philanthropic nature, rather than merely on money: on qualitative rather than quantitative metrics. Let us bring the relationship aspect of our profession to the foreground rather than assuming it is always the backdrop of our work.

DOI: 10.4324/9781003145936-90

But how do we take idealism into action through philanthropy? How do we explore the "moral dimensions of philanthropy," as Paul Schervish contends is the true purpose aspect of our work? Seen as a spiritual exercise, philanthropists create their own moral biographies, according to Schervish. But are professionals in philanthropy trained to be "moral biographers," asking crucial questions and entering into dialogues that significantly shift philanthropic conversations from money to meaning? Schervish has observed that "most wealth holders will benefit from engaging in what I call extended archaeological conversations with trusted advisors, including development officers." Attending to benefactors' needs to create moral biographies requires building genuine relationships based on trust. This is the genesis of relationship-based metrics.

Such metrics do not replace setting financial targets for our work, but they bring out the "better angels of our natures," as [US President Abraham] Lincoln once said, and alter the focus of our work. The currency of our profession is in the enduring good we do together with benefactors, not in the amount of money we raise from benefactors.

By altering our stance toward benefactors, we avoid potential philanthropists thinking, "Do you love me, or do you love my money?" A more powerful reflection might be, "Think of the walk we can take together to make lives and communities better." When we focus on ever-deepening relationships as outcomes, we open our apertures, we change lives and find better ways to "dilute the misery of the world," as Karl Menninger suggested was the purpose of life.

[…]

James H. Gilmore and B. Joseph Pine, in the book Authenticity, teach us that,

> Today participating in meaningful experiences represents the largest unmet needs of Americans, more precious than economic capital: religion, country, art, and family and education, these are the resources that are literally priceless, from which we draw distinctions regarding our purposes in life.

A system of relationship-based metrics would also be important to the continued energy and passion of development officers. Rather than a practice or orientation of "scheming for money," development officers would both dream of and aspire to a world of possibilities with benefactors … Burnout would be reduced, job hopping would lessen, and the nobility of our work would be palpable and efficacious. In such a system we would become more like moral trainers, as Michael O'Neil once described our work in philanthropy, or "agents of change," as Sheldon Garber viewed our profession at its best.

[…]

A relationship-based model of metrics is not only possible, it is essential to the work we do in the long haul, and it will transform managers of solely dollar-based metrics into mentors and coaches for transformational philanthropy.

Lynn Twist implores us to,

> Renew our sense of a noble calling, not to settle into mediocrity, but to strive for our own personal form of greatness. If we could come to appreciate the meaning of life as a creative striving with love, we would be preparing ourselves to take on a new outlook toward the phenomenon of change.

A change in the spirit of our work in philanthropy and a change in what we teach, coach, and measure in our profession, the strategies, the techniques, the details, the methods, and the metrics, for a qualitative relationship-based model of philanthropy will ensue from such dialogues and will attract and retain the best in our philanthropic profession. We owe it to ourselves and our benefactors to further explore the 'why' for giving instead of merely the 'how' or 'what', to examine the core values of potential benefactors and how they intersect and overlap with our institutional missions. For in the end, philanthropy has little or nothing to do with money and everything to do with meaning and purpose in a well-examined life.

5.3 The ideal fundraiser

What are the best fundraisers like?

Margaret A. Duronio and Eugene R. Tempel, 1996

There is a keen interest among many fund raisers in identifying what good fund raisers are like, what they know, and what they can do ... A profile that specified the qualities of effective fund raisers would assist in selection and promotion of fund-raising staff, help define the special expertise and contribution of the field, and promote a more positive image of fund raisers.

[...]

One of the most problematic aspects in specifying the criteria of effective performance in fund raising is the dramatic diversity of the environments in which fund raisers work. Large, affluent nonprofit organizations acquire more money in private support and have more resources – including funds for higher salaries for fund raisers – to expend in the process of raising money. Therefore, what first appear to be rather straightforward measures of a fund raiser's success – total money raised and salary earned – must be interpreted in the context of the nonprofit organizations in which they were achieved.

[...]

Most experienced fundraisers agree that an organization in a start-up phase, an organization just completing its first major campaign, or an organization with a fully mature comprehensive fund-raising program require different fund-raising approaches. Clearly, some individuals could be outstanding in one of those situations and failures in another. Perhaps some individuals could be successful in any of those situations, and some individuals could not be successful in any of them.

Relative to the task of specifying what measures actually define effective performance in fund raising, in addition to the way in which nonprofit environments can vary and the impact this variation can have on their work of fund raising, there is the additional complexity of the variety of roles fund raisers perform in their organizations. After a thorough review of the fund-raising literature, Worth and Asp determined that authors in the field generally conceptualised fund raisers as:

- Salesperson (the fund raiser's primary function is direct solicitation);
- Catalyst (the fund raiser brings about the direct solicitation but stays in the background);

DOI: 10.4324/9781003145936-92

- Manager (the fund raiser focuses primarily on management, organization, and direction of internal resources);
- Leader (the fund raiser may function in any or all of the first three roles but also serves as a key participant in organizational decision-making)

Although all those who identify themselves as fund raisers are engaged in some way in raising money from private sources, how they function in those roles and what they actually do varies a great deal. As fund raisers' roles vary, so will the qualifications and skills necessary to perform those roles.

Although it was not possible to demonstrate an empirical relationship between characteristics of fund raisers and successful performance, it was possible to collect information about the characteristics, skills, and knowledge believed to underlie successful performance.

What fund raisers see as their best

In our survey we asked participants: "Think of the fund-raising professional that you believe is the most competent and successful of all those you know. Please list up to three (A) personal characteristics or traits, (B) learned skills, and (C) areas of professional knowledge that you believe have contributed most to this person's effectiveness." A footnote defined professional knowledge as "facts and concepts that practitioners in a certain field know, often learned in formal training, that are generally not considered to be common knowledge among those not in the field."

We wanted to know what fund raisers themselves thought were the primary characteristics of the most competent and successful people in their field. Instead of asking them to describe an ideal fund raiser, that is, to think of what fund raisers should be like, we framed the question to call on respondents' actual experience and first-hand knowledge … We hoped to capture what fund raisers most admired in each other … We used content analysis techniques to organize, summarize, and analyze the individual responses – more than eleven thousand in all – this survey item generated. We developed seven categories for responses for personal characteristics, five categories for skills, and three categories for professional knowledge [as follows]:

Personal characteristics

Personality characteristics. Traits describing demeanor and manner, including items such as personable, sincere, and cheerful.

Workstyle characteristics. Traits describing approaches to work, including items such as hard working, prompt, and team-oriented.

Ethical characteristics. Traits describing character as differentiated from personalities, including items such as integrity, is ethical, and honorable.

Commitment characteristics. Traits describing commitment, including items such as committed to organization (fund-raising field, mission), desire to help people, and zealous.

Cognitive characteristics. Traits describing mental characteristics, including items such as intelligent, intuitive, and scholarly.

Self-concept characteristics. Traits reflecting respondents' ideas of the self-perceptions of the fund raisers they described, including items such as self-confident, has self-esteem, and self-demanding.

Background characteristics. Traits regarding personal background, including items such as wealthy, graduate of the school, and lifelong member of the community.

Skills

Communication skills. Items such as overall communication, public speaking, and listening.

Management skills. Items such as organizational skills, planning, and time management – which may refer to the handling of one's own job, the oversight of programs, other staff, and volunteers, or both.

Fund-raising skills. Items such as solicitation, working with board members, and getting appointments.

Cognitive skills. Items such as memorizing, analyzing, and clear thinker.

Other skills. Items falling into a catch-all category; for example, can sleep on airplanes, good golfer, and works within system.

Professional knowledge

Fund-raising knowledge. Items such as all aspects of fund raising, tax and legal knowledge, and gift administration.

Management knowledge. Items such as finance, computer technology, and organizational behavior.

Background knowledge. Items falling into a catch-all category; for example, human behavior, a specific educational background (such as law degree, business degree, degree in the arts), and private sector experience.

[…]

As described by their peers, the best fund raisers were ethical, smart, committed people who were also friendly and sincere. They were knowledgeable about fund raising and also about their organizations. They were skilled in all forms of communication, inter-personal relationships, and fund-raising activities.

[…]

Overall, what have we learnt about how respondents conceptualized "the right stuff" of fund raising, and what is the value of this information? In general, the data indicate that respondents had high expectations of their fund-raising colleagues, prized traits that indicate strong characters and warm personalities, and acknowledged the importance of skills and knowledge in successful fund raising. Respondents also conveyed a strongly value-driven orientation to the field and insight about the sensitive interplay of the art and science of fund raising.

What makes an ideal fundraiser?

Jerold Panas, 1988

> *There are three irrefutable rules which will assure your success as a fundraiser. Unfortunately, no one has ever discovered what they are. John Russell*

Is there a "fundraising type"? Outgoing, people-oriented, backslapping, extremely well organized, goal oriented, brilliant … This magnificent creature probably doesn't exist. It's really hard, perhaps impossible, to know what makes an ideal fundraiser. If you were designing the perfect fly-catcher, you probably wouldn't design it to look like a frog!

[…]

What I offer here are some observations and findings about fundraising and fundraisers – the verities of our profession. Canons to work by. Tenets you can count on. These are truths and principles that will assure your being the best you can be …

It's a potpourri. I have listed these at random, with no order of priority. Most of the items are of equal importance. On a scale of 1–10 they're all tens. A few are elevens! They're off the graph.

Here they are, the [abridged] verities. Sixty-three in all. Each important. Many, a virtual strike of lightening:

1. **Common linkage appears to connect all of the great fundraisers**. You have high ambition, are driven to achieve, and have immense inner motivation. There is a very high level of optimism, a medium to medium-high intelligence level, a willingness to work long and hard, and what can only be termed "a robust ego". You are self-confident.
2. **You read everything in sight**. You read incessantly and compulsively.
3. **You are undaunted**. Your life's philosophy, professionally and personally, is: "I Can Do It". There is brazen belief and fiery faith in the possible – anything can be done! You can do it, and even more divine – you understand that you must.
4. **Above all, is triumph**. The ultimate challenge is not to endure, but to prevail. You accept that challenge and win great victories for yourself and your institution.
5. **Creative planning wins.** You cannot increase the size or the quantity of the gift without enhancing the incisiveness of the planning and the

DOI: 10.4324/9781003145936-93

decisiveness of the strategy. Planning is the seed from which winning takes root and grows.

6. **You are a communicator**. You must be able to communicate clearly and compellingly the goals of your organization and its priorities. Your first task is to be the trumpet that sounds a clear and dramatic sound. It must be a resonant call to action.

7. **Success is always coupled with perseverance**. We in fundraising understand that success is a long race, conducted in inches. We face rejection and refusal head-on and respond with even greater dedication and determination.

8. **You ask for the order.** Markita Andrews is 13 years old and is the champion seller of Girl Scout cookies – 12,000 boxes last year. She says: "You can't just stand around and chat. You've got to lean forward, look them in the eye, and ask for the order."

9. **You are high-touch, low tech**. You have a great appreciation for all of the latest electronic equipment available, but you understand that the computer does not take the place of calling on someone personally for a gift.

10. **Great fundraisers are winners.** We persevere and achieve from our desire to win and from the pride we have in vanquishing all.

11. **You have decisive resolve.** Nothing significant has ever been accomplished unless some man or woman dreamed it should be done. Someone believed it could be done. And then, most importantly, someone decided that it must be done.

12. **You delight in the premise that fundraising provides fulfilment to deeds not words.** It forces us to believe in the promise of the future, but it pays great tribute for what we achieve today. And every day is a new adventure. That is the promise.

13. **You have presence.** If there is one single factor that explains 'presence' best of all, it would be charisma. Yes, I know! I'm sorry to use that overworked word. The energy, the force, the vigor. It's not physical appearance, dress, or funny stories. The single quality that sets those "who have it' apart from those who don't is energy. It shows and it glows.

14. **Boldness has genius, power, and magic to it.** The courage to dare, to step out – that's what wins the contest and gets the gift. The great fundraisers are infused with boldness and courage. An awesome audacity. There must be the willingness to brave the unexplored – and to attempt the unthinkable. The challenge! The great ones in the business thrive on it. It is the one button to push to get them started, and running.

15. **You have an unwavering commitment to the institution, and a near-militant belief in its mission**. Your commitment to the institution must be unshakable. That doesn't mean without question or constructive challenge. That would be faith without thought. But your commitment to the cause must glow and glitter for all to see.

16. **You have a quality of leadership.** Having a great vision and being able to communicate it. That's what it's all about. You've got to lead the way

and take the action. If you want to attract volunteers and dollars, you have to exhibit a quality of leadership.

17. **If you can conceive it, you can achieve it.**
18. **You understand that every grand opportunity is simply masquerading as a problem.** If you don't understand the problem, then explain it to someone and listen to yourself discussing it. Make certain that you never state a problem in the same terms as it was originally brought to you. Studying the reverse always helps. Don't worry about an approach that transforms one problem into another – you're probably taking the first step towards an exciting solution.
19. **You inspire others to action.** If inspiration is the rudder, action is the engine that propels the program. Inspiration must be combined with action in indefatigable proportions.
20. **You must stand on tiptoes.** High expectations impel and drive action. Don't reach for what you can. You must reach for what you cannot!
21. **You can be satisfied – but only with the very best.** You are driven by your goals and objectives. The motivation comes from within. You combine momentum, passion, and a need for market position. You are intensely competitive.
22. **You know it has to benefit the donor.** Even the highest level of altruism is selfish to a great extent. You've got to give your donors WIIFM – What's In It For Me! You can secure most any gift you seek, if you help a prospect get what they want.
23. **Perfection is not a perfect solution.** The difference between excellence and perfection goes virtually unnoticed and almost certainly will not cause either you or the institution to lose or win a gift. But the cost of pursuing perfection is enormous. Striving for perfection is an impossible and debilitating state of mind in an imperfect world.
24. **You must sacrifice.** Our work is demanding. Reaching your objective is knowing what it is others want. But to be successful also requires knowing what you want. And what you are willing to give up to get it. The best work is often done under duress and at great personal cost.
25. **You work hard, think big, listen carefully.**
26. **The quality of the experience is what counts.** Experience is important but it is most certainly not the number of years that count, it is the quality of experience.
27. **You practice the principle of ready, fire, aim.** Some in our field are guilty of spending all of their time preparing for a campaign, or analyzing the most effective way to call on a prospect, or evaluating their plans. They never seem to have time to actually go out and make the call for the gift. I call this: "Analysis Paralysis". The prognosis is not good. The patient will almost certainly pass away, or eke out their profession in the most lackluster sort of way.
28. **Your life is encircled with objective.** You are goal-driven and goal-oriented. Objectives are dreams – visions with deadlines.
29. **Details guide and gird your work.** "God is in the details".

30. **You have focus**. A single-mindedness on an objective. Nothing gets in the way.

31. **No pain, no gain**. It requires intense motivation. Long hours, Long days. But somehow there seems to be only joy and exhilaration. You seem to be willing to pay the price, and you love it!

32. **You recruit the strongest**. Build around you the greatest, the most effective people. Not only staff, but volunteers, recruit those who are leaders in their field, who are themselves driven by the passions and qualities that make one successful. You'll be amazed at how much you can accomplish by learning, listening, and following. And if you don't care who gets the credit, you will be able to accomplish unbelievable achievements.

33. **Follow my rules of the eight 'I's"**. If you have five of this group, you'll be good in this field. If you have seven or eight, you're almost certain to be great!: Integrity, Instinct, Intelligence, Imagination, Intestines, Irreverence, Intensity, and "Inthusiasm"!

34. **Wait to worry**. Worrying is the single most unrewarding of all human emotions. It tears you down, it tears you apart, and worst of all it doesn't accomplish anything. If you've come across a problem with a prospect, you have to deal with it. If it doesn't look like you're going to be able to meet budget, worrying won't help. If you're not going to make the campaign total, worrying won't help you reach it. What is required is some creative problem solving.

35. **Your dictum is grow or go**. You live in a constant state of self-renewal. You have the capacity to acknowledge errors, and treat them as learning experiences. You are curious and you learn from everything, even failures.

36. **You never have enough time**. You abhor procrastination and consider it the art of keeping up with yesterday. You are jealous with your time and guard it with your life. You understand how to use your time most efficiently.

37. **You seek role models**. Look for men and women to pattern your life and work after. Learn from what others do right and you will be establishing your course on the map of success.

38. **Common sense is a prime requisite**. It enables you to analyze a very complex situation and somehow develop a solution and design which cuts through the fat and gets to the very nub of the situation. It turns out that common sense is not so common after all. It's the ability to discern the facts from the fancy. High intelligence is not critical, common sense is.

39. **You know the twelve characteristics most important to success**. These are identified by George Gallup, Jr. in a study he conducted among 1,000 men and women he considered to be "the most successful in their field." They are listed in the order of their priority: Common sense; Special knowledge of your field; Self-reliance; General intelligence; Ability to get things done; Quality of leadership; Knowing right from wrong; Creativity and inventiveness; Self-confidence; Oral expression; Concern for others; Luck.

40. **Creativity and innovation depend heartily on trust**. It means that you trust your instincts, and you have the courage to pursue vigorously your intuition ... Creativity is the ability to join one idea to another, and come up with a new answer. It's old ideas into new combinations that win. Put your imagination into over-drive. It is doubtful that anyone has had a totally original idea. The re-potted flower grows the highest and healthiest.

41. **You have a concern for people – a compassion, a love**. The pull is so strong, it is nothing short of ministerial in its approach and commitment.

42. **You have a great joy in what you are doing**. In one of his speeches, Will Rogers said: "If you want to be successful, it's pretty simple. There are only three things to keep in mind: Know what you are doing. Love what you are doing. And believe in what you are doing." I am certain that success is due less to experience than ardor. Less to intelligence than zeal. Less to the mechanics of the job than enthusiasm. The winner is always the one who gives body and soul, totally and unreservedly, to the joys and passion of the task.

43. **You are unremittingly opposed to the status quo**.

44. **You love calling on people**. You enjoy most aspects of your work – but calling on people, confronting them with the immense opportunity to share in great works and deeds – for you, that's the pinnacle.

45. **You understand that survival is inherent to our profession**. You achieve your high objectives one year, but you are measured by next year. The board remembers the past, but they relish the present and cherish the future. You may not be pleased with this day-to-day surveillance but you accept the process as part of your work.

46. **You pull up the roots to see if the flower is still growing**. In fundraising impatience is a virtue. You are never satisfied. You have a very low tolerance with the pace of your program and the progress. You are itchy by nature! You do not suffer easily standing still or treading water. It's the race you favor, and most of all, the winning.

47. **You are men and women of ideas and ideals**. You understand that your ideals represent true force and energy. It is the foundation which prods you to greater achievement.

48. **You are results-oriented**.

49. **It takes rigorous discipline**. Discipline in all you do – your time, your priorities, your attention to myriad details that make a successful program. Discipline propels dreams and visions and action into success.

50. **You have soaring spiritual values**. Somewhere in your background, in your early childhood, there was a value system – both stringent and joyful – that was imposed upon you.

51. **Memory is monumental**. You never forget anything. Especially regarding prospects, donors, and everything to do with the raising of gifts.

52. **You have a high degree of self-confidence**.
53. **You believe in the promise of tomorrow**.
54. **You are delighted with the specialists in your field**. You understand how important these men and women are to an effective development office. Those who have immense expertise in phonathons, research, computer technology, and response mail – they make things happen. You know how to use each speciality to your advantage. You know a little bit about many things, but claim no specialism as your own. You revel in your overall understanding and expertise. You are a four-star Generalist!
55. **You have a way of getting "yes" for an answer – even before you ask the question**. You understand your donors. You are sensitive to what compulsions drive them, what instincts dominate their life and giving … The fundraiser with the keenest insight for motivation understand what compels a donor to action. The ability to motivate.
56. **Long tenure in a position is essential**. You don't jump from job to job. You stay at your institution. How long? As long as it takes. Sufficient time to conceive the bold dreams, develop the plans, know your constituencies, and achieve your objectives.
57. **You make your own luck**. There is a saying that the harder you work, the luckier you get. But evidence suggests that some are luckier than others. It isn't inadvertent. You plan for it and you seek it. What assures luck is eternal vigilance to new opportunities, a restless spirit, and an irreverent attitude to the obvious.
58. **Your work and life excite you – and it shows**. Because you are happy in your life's work, you are more likely to be happy in your personal life.
59. **You are charged with energy**. Energy begets enthusiasm and is a first cousin to charisma. People seek those with energy. They respond to them. Energy is infectious, creates invincible potency, and invigorates and inspires all around you.
60. **The work burns like fire in your bones**. To you it isn't work, it is sheer joy.
61. **Research is important, but action will prevail**. You must move forward, even if you do not have all of the research about a donor you feel would be desirable. You depend on research, but you are not dependent on it. You know that research alone will not get the gift. I know of one institution that has a glorious research component. It has been gathering detail and data about prospects for years. But it hasn't yet made its major calls. It's been getting ready for war, but hasn't yet waged it.
62. **Listen – and you'll get the gift**. The most important of the communication faculties is that of listening. Meaningful, creative silence! Listening is not passive, it is active. You know that if you give others what they want, you will get what you want. You have heard about people who talk too much – but you have not heard of anyone who listens too much. In fundraising, it is impossible to listen too much. It is what wins the gift.

63. **Nothing is more important than integrity**. I can assure you that integrity is the mightiest weapon in your arsenal. Its power is explosive. It brings together uncompromising individualism and blinding honesty. And it must be combined, too, with compassion – for without grace and love, integrity is without heart and life … Integrity alone is no assurance of the ticket to the top, but without it you can't even begin the journey.

A major donor's view on good communication for all donors

Lisa Greer, 2020

Communications experts worth their salt will tell you that the most important thing you can do, after determining the goals and objectives of your communications, is to know your target audience. For fundraisers, that audience is donors.

'Always make the audience suffer as much as possible' was [film maker] Alfred Hitchcock's motto, and as anyone who's seen [his horror-thriller film] *The Birds* will attest, it worked like a charm. I'm sure it's nobody's intention to reprise that motto in the full-hearted world of fundraising. Still, a great many donors are uncomfortable with how the organizations they support are communicating with them, and 'uncomfortable' is putting it mildly.

As you're no doubt aware, more than 60% of one-time donors (some put it closer to 70%) fail to contribute to an organization a second time. If you're trying to generate funding in order to keep a nonprofit alive, that's terrifying. So … we're going to explore how to build relationships with existing donors.

Because here's what I know: These donors *want* to continue to love you. They even want to hear from you – just not always in the ways that you might think.

[…]

Naturally, most fundraisers follow the money. They spend the bulk of their time on donors with the capacity to give in the range of $10,000 or more. Fundraising jobs depend on these donors and lately, so does philanthropy … Unfortunately, however, everyone is now competing for these mammoth gifts and not everyone is going to be successful. What happens to the sector then?

Worst case, it tanks. That's why it's imperative that we stop heeding the advice, so prolific in fundraising, that 'cultivation' is for the big givers only. Time is finite, of course, and quarterly targets are real. But directing all of our resources (which, let's face it, are famously limited in fundraising) at one, rarified group of supporters – well, it pretty much sacrifices everyone else. At least on the level of relationships.

There are loads of ways of providing regular donors with the connection they crave – communications tactics, for example, that can help to align them with your organization's mission or keep them abreast with your success without making them feel like they're always a 'mark'. Knowing your donors

DOI: 10.4324/9781003145936-94

will help you deploy these tactics, which aren't nearly as crass as they sound and also don't always require a major reallocation of resources.

[…]

Let's say you're an organization that only *really* cultivates your biggest donors. Does this mean you ignore your supporters whose gifts are more moderate?

In my experience, organizations actually do the opposite. Regular donors are often overwhelmed from the nonprofits they support – especially on Giving Tuesday or at the end of the year; sometimes even *all* year – and much of this communication is impersonal. It doesn't reflect the way that the donors are known in any way by the organizations they support, or that their giving history and habits are known. On the contrary, now that these donors' names are on the mailing lists of organizations they've contributed to, they often get sent stuff (mass solicitations, for example) indiscriminately.

Asking for money again and again won't increase your chances of getting it, and nor will it encourage loyalty from the donors you want to retain, as illustrated in Table 5.1.1. So why am I compelled to repeat … the most overused cliché of all time? You probably know it – it's the one about doing the same thing over and over and still expecting a different result.

Nonprofits, I'm looking at you.

[…]

Here's a typical me-and-my-charity relationship arc:

- I engage with an organization that's new to me by donating a modest amount. I'm happy about it! I make a real effort to learn more about the organizations and to deepen my relationship with it, almost always to the extent that I start to feel invested and aligned with its mission.
- Somewhere between months three and twelve post-donation, I'm asked to increase my gift. Frequently, I'm even asked to increase my *annual* gift. But not once have we had a discussion about my gift being annual! The old me might have given more at this point but these days I'm far more likely to just tell the fundraiser that I never intended for my gift to be annual. I'll tell her straight out that I'm only willing to give what I gave last year. Then (and here's what should be concerning to you [the fundraiser]) I'll trust her a little bit less going forward.
- There's still a scenario in which I might give more after being asked to increase my gift, but only if I really love the organization and feel good about how it's run, what it's doing, and how it has handled the ask for more money. (Remember, our relationship at this point spans three to twelve months.) In fact, I will often give *more* in this scenario, and that's a lesson too.
- If I *do* give more, and then am asked again to increase my already-increased gift – well, that's when I start to think that I've been had. I may suspect that the 'respectful' relationship I believed we were building was just a ruse. I may even find myself apologizing for the 'inadequate' size of my gift. Do I feel good about apologizing. No. Do I continue to do it when

approached in this way? Yes. A part of that is on me. But what my apologies also speak to is the fact, frankly, that I'm being manipulated.

And so it goes. I actually had a terrible epiphany the other day about how easy it would be to avoid these scenarios, or at least the worst of them, by limiting my giving to the wholly sporadic. If I were to give off and on, for example, I'd be immune to the assumptions fundraisers often make about recurring donors. Organizations would court me and thank me – first gifts are much more likely to be appropriately acknowledged – and then, after I ignored their subsequent advances, they'd let go of the idea that, as a 'regular' donor, I owe them. They'd finally leave me alone. After skipping a year or two, I could even start the process all over again with the same organization and be thanked as if I were a brand-new donor.

Table 5.1.1 Common communications traps and what they net

Action	Reaction
Thrice-weekly emails from the same organization.	I stop reading emails from the organization and get annoyed.
Any piece of communication I receive from an organization with which I have a relationship that comes via a channel other than the one I typically use.	Either you know (and are ignoring) how I prefer to receive communications from your organization, or you haven't bothered to ask. In each case, I feel disrespected.
Any piece of communication with the words, 'Donate now!' Or 'Before it's too late!'	I worry that the situation at the organization sending me the email is as dire as the email suggests. Then, I wonder why I should give again. Clearly, my initial gift made little difference.
Any piece of communication asking me to give a smaller amount 'today!' than the amount I gave recently.	Since you appear not to be capable of parsing your lists, I start to wonder how professionally your organization is run.
Seemingly arbitrary phone calls and/or voicemail from organizations I don't personally know.	I'm suspicious of unscheduled phone calls and am far more likely to respond to an email with detailed information.
Ads or canned copy at the bottom of every email, with stock directive such as 'Join now!'	Hasn't everyone on your recipient list *already* joined? Have I been sent this email in error?
An ask in every email.	You're making it very clear that I'm nothing more than a dollar sign, and every aspect of the message now reads like a 'hook'. It's not necessary to make an ask in every communication.
'It's Giving Tuesday!' Or 'It's December 31st!'	I know what day it is, and I'm already overwhelmed. Please give me a reason to keep reading.

But do I really want to play that game? No. Nobody wants that, me included.

[...]

Fundraisers: put yourself in a donor's shoes ... I'm an avid reader and I want to do good. I also want to fall in love with the organizations I support. So I do feel compelled, especially as a donor, to carefully and responsibly read everything.

The email I got from you is one of dozens just like it, most of which have totally generic subject lines and a ton of verbal clutter, as illustrated in Table 5.2.2. Do I read or do I *not* read?

These days it's mostly the latter ... Sometimes, even a small change can affect how your communication resonates. It's the same with a change in perspective. If *you* were to get the email you're writing, would its subject line compel you to open it? Would you read it right to the end?

[...]

Table 5.2.2 Connecting with existing donors

The usual way	How it's received	How to do better
You made your annual commitment at around this time last year. Would you please send us your annual gift?	What annual gift? We haven't had that conversation.	Let's talk and review how your goals have evolved and how we can be a part of your giving going forward.
You gave $5,000 last year. This year, can you swing $10,000?	Exactly when will you be satisfied with my support?	Let's talk and review how your goals have evolved and how we can be a part of your giving going forward.
We want to be among the top three organizations that you support.	Why is it necessary for me to choose three?	How does our organization fit into the larger context of your giving?
We're asking you to give until it hurts, and then give a bit more.	Why would you want me to hurt myself?	We appreciate that you give in a meaningful way.
We're aware that you've already given this year, but this is a different campaign. Will you give again?	Exactly when will you be satisfied with my support?	We have a new initiative that feels like a good match for you. Absolutely no pressure. If you're interested, I'm happy to get you more information.
Lunch ... fawn... socialize... fawn. And then the requisite, 'Before you go ...' followed by a pitch.	I will never get back those two hours.	Let me know in advance that our meeting will involve an ask. At the meeting, engage in friendly conversation, but please don't fawn. Introduce your new initiatives and ask for my support.

Table 5.2.2 Cont.

The usual way	How it's received	How to do better
We'd love to catch up and get your thoughts on our new initiative.	My thoughts or my money?	We'd love to see if you have interest in supporting an initiative we're launching or can connect us to people who might.
I'd love to get together to see how you're doing.	Is this a pitch or do you actually care about me?	I'd love to get together to see how you're doing. I promise no pitches.
There's a thought leader in town, whom we think you'd like to meet. We're having a small gathering.	I'd love to hear that thought leader speak, but the gathering will end with a pitch.	We appreciate your past support and think you might enjoy meeting this thought leader. We're having a small gathering that won't include a pitch.
I realize that you told me 'no' last month. What about this month?	What does the word 'no' mean to you?	I respect your giving priorities and I won't ask you again until next year.
Let's have lunch. Our development director will be joining us.	Can't we get together to talk about the organization without a babysitter present?	We want to give you an update on our work. Would you like to schedule a call or a meeting with our director of development?

Be professional where professionalism is warranted. But don't ever forget the heart in this work. Donors and fundraisers can enhance – or squander – the human touch in each and every communication.

5.4 The challenges of being a fundraiser

Fundraising's identity crisis

Jason Lewis, 2017

If we were to ask nonprofit executives what their greatest challenge is in accomplishing the organization's mission, many would point to fundraising as number one. Even those with budgets large enough to employ dedicated fundraising professionals aren't spared. But the problem isn't the money itself.

The grisly reality for nonprofits is that talented fundraising professionals are in high demand – and in short supply. High demand and short supply leads to a trifecta of problems. Today's nonprofit organizations, especially those relying on charitable giving as a primary source of revenue, are finding it increasingly difficult to identify, hire, and retain qualified fundraising professionals. Locating people who share a passion and commitment to the mission while able to consistently achieve their goals makes the search even more difficult.

[…]

The war for fundraising talent can be won with two strategies: First, nonprofits must retain more of our existing supply of talented fundraising professionals. Second, nonprofits must empower new recruits with an understanding of how both they and their employers can achieve success.

This will require that the perks of becoming a fundraiser include more than the opportunity to receive an extraordinary compensation package and the promise of changing the world. The sector has an obligation to tip the scales so there are more places where fundraisers can find success. Organizations of all shapes and sizes must share a common understanding of how effective fundraising really works.

[…]

Two camps differ in understanding what effective fundraising really looks like. One camp recognises that any *lack of fundraising talent* becomes the primary disadvantage; the other camp believes the *lack of donors with dollars* is always the scarcest resource. This amounts to an ideological debate over how nonprofits grow and thrive; the former camp tends towards attracting talent because of its understanding of effective fundraising, seeking the advantages of a mature fundraising operation with talented individuals who can consistently achieve their goals. In contrast, the latter camp has inherited a learned helplessness and loyalty to a system designed to fail them and their missions.

[…]

If we go by the size of their mailing lists, most organizations have more than enough donors. The accumulation of donors over years (if not decades) has

DOI: 10.4324/9781003145936-96

created opportunities to establish the kinds of relationships that lead to meaningful gifts. Our challenge is not to ensure we have enough new donors. Our challenge is neglecting to establish a culture where more meaningful relationships can thrive and where more meaningful support can be the expectation.

[...]

The fundraising profession continues to contend with an identity crisis it can't shake. There are many in the field today who have spent years, if not decades, struggling with their identity as fundraising professionals. They prefer other titles and miss the opportunities to convey the importance of their task, fearing that the essence of their job description might be exposed and misunderstood. Many fundraisers have become quite good at what they do, have achieved remarkable goals, and yet have relied on a forced, obsessive passion, rather than a passion that aligns with who they are.

[...]

Recently I spoke to young fundraising professionals about their career aspirations. As they introduced themselves, I was hoping someone would say her decision to be a fundraiser wasn't solely based on passion for a cause. No luck. One after another, each participant espoused an affinity of some sort to make a difference in a cause.

Now, there's nothing wrong with this. But as a motivator, it won't lead to a long fundraising career. Researchers who study other professional paths have come to the same conclusions about the role passion plays – or does not play – in our careers.

Enticing 'career' advice is tossed about regularly these days. "Follow your passion." "Do what you love." With empty promises like these we've convinced ourselves and the generation behind us that pursuing the work you love is the path to career utopia.

Cal Newport, a professor at Georgetown University, developed what he calls a 'passion hypothesis' explaining why turnover in the workplace is so high among young people today. He says the passion hypothesis has risen to the status of an absolute since Steve Jobs' commencement address at Stanford University in 2005.

While Jobs' address encompassed everything from his adoption as a child to dropping out of college, and from founding multiple companies to his diagnosis with cancer, all people seemed to hear was "follow your passion". They surmised that the key to occupational happiness was to figure out what you were passionate about – and then simply find a job that matches that passion.

What's evident if you read Jobs' commencement address is something else altogether. Just as Jobs did, we're more likely to *stumble* onto life passions rather than being able to *follow* them.

Miya Tokumitsu, author of *Do What You Love: And Other Lies About Success and Happiness*, warns that "Do what you love," synonymous with "follow your passion", makes exploiting employees much easier, because they can be convinced what they're really doing is fulfilling a passion – rather than earning a wage. This way of thinking easily leads to the belief that work is *not what we do for compensation*, but something that is an act of love. While "do what you love" sounds harmless, it is ultimately inward-focused, to the point of narcissism, absolving us of any obligation to acknowledge or improve the world.

But is passion only about doing what you love? Passion can fuel motivation, enhance well-being, and provide meaning in everyday life. However, passion can also arouse negative emotions, lead to inflexible persistence, and interfere with achieving a balanced, successful life. So, is passion only good or only bad? Let's consider the two kinds of passion: *harmonious* and *obsessive*, and see how they differ.

When we freely engage in an activity because it is important to us – not because we anticipate rewards (such as potential income) – we're often embodying harmonious passion. We are generally not compelled by external pressure or obligation; we participate in the activity voluntarily. Harmonious passion can occupy a significant part of our identity, but *it doesn't create an imbalance in other areas of our lives.*

Obsessive passion, on the other hand, means we're responding to pressure to meet expectations beyond our control. It very quickly demands a disproportionate part of our identities and causes conflict with other meaningful areas of our lives. This kind of passion doesn't contribute to satisfaction with our work; instead, it raises the likelihood of burnout – or worse. Many of us are familiar with the stories of leaders whose determination to change the world has wreaked havoc in their personal and professional lives.

It's questionable whether the young fundraisers that I mentioned speaking to earlier were passionate about raising money, achieving their goals, or even building relationships with donors. They may be devoted to their nonprofit's mission. Even so, I suspect they may be relying on a forced passion to continue in their fundraising work. Harmonious passion is the kind that aligns itself with our identities and well-being without conflict. It's much more promising for staying the course. Let's face it: our sector has a passion predicament. To resolve this – and to ensure long-term employment and commitment – we must cultivate a harmonious passion for fundraising.

First, our sector needs to raise up a new generation of fundraising professionals who don't question the legitimacy of their roles. Neither should they dismiss the contribution they make within the nonprofit and for the greater good of society.

Second, nonprofits can't rely on the demand for talent and earning potential to compel young professionals into the field of fundraising. We need to make sure both existing and up-and-coming fundraising professionals learn to be inspired by more than simply their passion for the cause. Otherwise, it's unlikely we'll be able to shake our identity crisis, reduce turnover and reach the goals required to accomplish our mission.

I have found the most talented fundraising professionals develop a complementary passion oriented toward donors who have a passion for the cause. These individuals jump out of bed in the morning to interact with individuals who want to demonstrate, through their generous support, a commitment to effective change and a confidence in those who can carry it out. I sometimes refer to this as a dual orientation to the mission: fundraising professionals are oriented toward those whose relationship with the organization is to give rather than receive.

[...]

If there's anything my two decades of fundraising in the nonprofit sector has taught me, it is that generous donors and talented fundraisers generally expect the same thing. They want to be recognised and admired for the unique and meaningful contributions that they make towards mission accomplishment. The War for Fundraising Talent is already being won by those organizations that understand this similarity in expectations.

The War for Fundraising Talent *will not be won* by organizations that continue to mistake their scarcest resource as *donors with dollars*. After years of obsessively accumulating new donors, most organizations have more than enough donors to keep them busy for quite some time.

The War for Fundraising Talent will be won by organizations that can identify, train, and retain a new generation of fundraising talent characterized by higher expectations of themselves and their donors. Once the initial gift has been received, it will be the fundraiser's responsibility to discern who will be asked to give again. In asking for donors' renewed support, we are committing ourselves to a meaningful relationship with them, and we are expecting a meaningful commitment in return. It will be our distinct and deliberate practices, those that begin with a meaningful relationship and lead to meaningful support, that the fundraising profession can be recognised and admired for.

[...]

Fundraising affords citizens of our modern society an opportunity to experience two of the few things that make us uniquely human. To give and to receive are distinct human experiences. It is our responsibility as fundraising professionals, and those who employ them, to ensure that generosity and gratitude are meaningful opportunities expressed and experienced to the fullest.

Fundraisers' experiences of sexual harassment

Erynn E. Beaton, Megan LePere-Schloop,
and Rebecca Smith, 2021

Fundraisers, who are predominantly female, operate at the boundaries of their organizations as they interact with powerful, mostly male donors and board members attempting to mitigate their organization's resource dependencies. [Resource dependency theory suggests that those providing resources enjoy power and influence over those dependent upon those resources.] Contexts such as these, where the boundary spanners are predominantly women and the third party tends to be a man of resources, are ripe for sexual harassment.

Bringing together research on resource dependency and sexual harassment leads us to ask the research question: How do boundary spanners experience sexual harassment in the context of efforts to mitigate organizational resource dependencies? Approaching this empirical study from a feminist perspective, we engage in interviews with professional fundraisers about their experiences. Our findings suggest that fundraisers do experience sexual harassment at the hands of donors. In addition, some fundraisers feel their employers, in concert with fundraising professional norms, sexually exploit them by putting them in vulnerable positions, treating them as "bait," and asking them to do "whatever it takes" to obtain donations.

[…]

Sexual harassment, gender, and power

Sexual harassment, defined broadly as unwanted sexual attention and/or relationships, can be understood from a legal, behavioral, or psychological perspective.

[…]

Sexual harassment results from asymmetrical power relationships. Power differentials create opportunities for harassers to engage in inappropriate exchanges with their targets. Therefore, to understand and remedy sexual harassment, one must understand the bases of power upon which harassers draw.

[…]

Sexual harassment has been discussed most extensively in terms of supervisory harassment. In this form, sexual harassment stems from the target's position in the organizational hierarchy relative to the harasser. Hierarchical power

DOI: 10.4324/9781003145936-97

in sexual harassment is related to gender because women are often in subordinate positions to men.

[…]

New research on "third-party" harassment suggests that sexual harassment is an issue for boundary spanners. Sexual harassment has been called "an occupational hazard for women who work at the boundaries of organizations". Boundary spanners often spend significant time outside their organizations or work in close proximity to external stakeholders, such as customers or clients. These employees and their organizations depend on third parties for sales, commissions, tips, and performance evaluations. Thus, third-party relationships are significant because boundary spanners depend on them for professional success and personal income, while organizations depend on them to meet their bottom line. As a result, boundary spanners may have little to no formal authority or recourse in the relationship. Boundary spanners are obligated to look, act, and talk in a certain way and are "expected to enact deference and respect to customers". The working conditions and social norms of these environments create opportunities for third parties to engage in sexually harassing behaviors and discourages boundary spanners from reporting or filing complaints with their organizations.

[…]

We focus on the fundraising profession because … fundraising is a boundary spanning position and a context in which organizational resource dependency is explicit. There is also some evidence to suggest that the sexual harassment of fundraisers by donors is a problem.

[…]

Resource dependency endows donors with "hyperagency" whereby donors enjoy a heightened ability to make decisions for themselves and others. Susan Ostrander argues that donor control is growing. The professionals tasked with managing the relationships with these philanthropic hyperagents are fundraisers. Research has characterized the fundraising profession as "women's work," due to the gendered devaluation of relationship-building and because it is female dominated. These characteristics make the fundraising profession an ideal research context for understanding sexual harassment amidst gender power and resource dependency.

[…]

In 2018, the Association for Fundraising Professionals (AFP) commissioned a survey about sexual harassment in the profession. The results suggest that 20% of respondents agree that sexual harassment is "rampant" in the fundraising profession. A full 48% of respondents reported they have been sexually harassed, witnessed harassment, or heard about someone being sexually harassed in the profession. Of the 21% that had personally experienced sexual harassment, 65% reported harassment by a donor compared to 39% by a colleague. These statistics suggest that sexual harassment is a problem in the fundraising profession and that donors sometimes harass fundraisers.

[…]

Recruiting research participants to partner in data production proved challenging. We identified several reasons this was the case. First, accusing donors of sexual harassment could be precarious for fundraisers' employers and for their own careers. Second, sexual harassment is a sensitive topic that many survivors would prefer not to revisit, particularly with a researcher whom they do not know. Lastly, many fundraisers that informally disclosed stories to us believed their experience was not egregious enough to warrant an interview—this tended to mean that they had not been assaulted.

[…]

Ultimately, we conducted interviews with 36 fundraisers. Though this research is influenced by feminist principles, all genders and identities were encouraged to participate. Of the participants, 31 identified as women and five as men. The majority describe themselves as Caucasian or White (27), but some participants identify as African American, Hispanic, Southeast Asian-American, Latinx, or Puerto Rican. The average age of our participants is 42 years old, ranging from 24 to 62. The individuals are all professional fundraisers (now or at some point in their career), and have personally experienced sexual harassment, observed sexual harassment, and/or advised a colleague who experienced sexual harassment in the course of their work.

[…]

We asked participants to tell their stories of sexual harassment in their own words, with as much detail as possible. As they told their stories, we interjected only when necessary to achieve clarity or to empathize. If the participant had multiple stories to tell, we discussed each of them in the order the participant chose until they had recounted all their stories. The narratives detail instances of sexual harassment (experienced, observed, or heard about), and describe decisions to report (or not), and whether they felt their organization supported them and made them feel safe (or not).

[…]

Our participants comprise a purposive sample and do not represent the full spectrum of the fundraising profession. We suspect that fundraisers who experienced more egregious sexual harassment behaviors or felt more strongly about sexual harassment in the profession were more likely to participate in the study. While our results cannot be generalized to the population of fundraising professionals, there is evidence that a portion of the fundraising population feels exploited by their work.

[…]

Findings

Our findings reflect four themes which, together, encapsulate fundraisers' experiences of sexual harassment and exploitation as unintended consequences of resource dependency mitigation strategies.

[…]

Table 5.4.1 Fundraisers' experiences of sexual harassment and exploitation as unintended consequences of resource dependency mitigation strategies

Themes	Description	Example
The sexual nature of fundraising	Many aspects of the fundraising profession are sexualised, creating a context conducive to sexual harassment.	Fundraising events sometimes include young "scantily clad" women serving beverages or tending the golf flag.
Donors wielding power	Due to resource dependence, donors have a great deal of power over the nonprofit and fundraiser, which they can use to achieve their personal aims or pleasure.	Donors use their power to get fundraisers to do errands or to stay silent when they sexually harass the fundraiser.
Employer pressure or complicity	Some employers encourage fundraisers to put themselves at risk, and/or turn a blind eye when fundraisers are mistreated, putting the fundraiser at further risk.	A manager may encourage a female fundraiser to wear certain clothes or high heels to meetings with male donors.
An impossible situation with no way out	When fundraisers experience sexual harassment, they are put in a situation with no recourse; as a result, each fundraiser responds in their own way.	A fundraiser resigns herself to doing "whatever it takes" to get the donation.

1. The sexual nature of fundraising

At the beginning of our interviews we asked each participant to describe their career background. Susan introduced herself this way: "I'm a development director, which means developing relationships for monetary income. [laughs]". As Susan's introduction indicates, the act of fundraising requires relationships and intimacy. For instance, many fundraisers spoke about how people in the field like to hug. Sometimes that intimacy can be a slippery slope and fundraising can also become about sexuality. "For you to do your job, you're developing relationships and getting to know people, and I think there can be this weird perception from somebody else that like, 'Oh, she's into me or interested in me.' And it's like, well, no, I'm just working".

Sex came up in unexpected ways during our interviews. For instance, it was used as a metaphor in a required training described by Kate. The instructor of that training was conveying the importance of building relationships with donors over time. He stated: "If we're out on a date, I'm not going to just immediately ask you to have sex with me. We're going to go on dates and then we'll …". Kate stopped short of finishing the sentence. A fundraising consultant explained to another research participant, Victoria, that "you have to become the entertainment" for donors. It is common for fundraising events to have women as entertainment—tending flags at golf tournaments or serving drinks at galas. Virginia was asked by a donor to plan a poker tournament. The donor directed her to:

> Make sure all the ticket sellers are really cute, maybe put them in little short skirts and they can go around and sit on the guys' laps to sell tickets. That way we'll sell a lot of tickets.

Carrie explained the implication, "there's this expectation that your entire body is up for grabs when you're doing this work". Several women spoke about how they were hired because of how they look instead of their experience, and how they have to dress for the job. Angelina said when she works, "I'm dressed to the nines ... I know that what I am selling is partly me."

2. Donors wielding power

Our participants described the fundraising profession as having high expectations of them that often involved tolerating distasteful, sexual jokes and inappropriate greetings from donors. Describing the comments she would endure, Angela explained donors would say things such as "I've never had a black woman". Many fundraisers also had to endure persistent advances and even assault. Stephen had a donor put his hands down his pants at a bar. As May reflected, "there were unfortunately way too many for me to remember, but often from older males, either donors that were considering large gifts, or donors that had been with an organization for a long time". Fundraisers are "between a rock and a hard place" when they are harassed or assaulted. "When that donation is a tenth of the [organization's] budget ... I don't know, it just felt really weird confronting it from that standpoint". Our participants spoke about how they feel a lot of pressure because it is their responsibility to keep the organization's lights on, to fund colleagues' salaries, and to ultimately serve the disadvantaged. This pressure was felt by women and men alike.

[...]

Susan is responsible for organizing fundraising events and managing the volunteers to staff them. One of her male volunteers and in-kind contributors was very committed, but he also kept asking her out on dates. She explained:

> it's a fine line of pushing them away and laughing it off, when really you just want to destroy them, because every time you talk to them, they're either saying something demeaning or telling you that, "You could have gotten this, if you would have done this with me".

Susan describes resisting the urge to tell donors what she was thinking and feeling because she wants to maintain the relationship and the funding for the organization. This example illustrates the tension between self-respect and personal safety versus job performance and mission commitment that some participants described experiencing when harassed by a donor.

3. Employer pressure or complicity

Many of the fundraisers we spoke with felt they were taken advantage of by their employers. Fundraisers have the sense that they are regularly put in vulnerable or compromising positions because donor interactions often occur in informal settings outside of the boundaries of the organization. They described how meetings take place at bars, restaurants, and even in donors' homes.

[...]

In perhaps the most explicit example of exploitation, Ruth described a conversation at a fundraising event with her boss—a female director of development:

> One of the directors of development came in and she said, "So-and-so saw Renee and said he would pay a million dollars if he could get a chance to get with her." She said to me, she's like, "Yeah, I don't care. If he'll give me a million dollars, I'll give him whoever he wants." ... That was such an example of women, another female fundraiser, willing to put their female colleague out there as bait ... It was just this reinforcement for me, that it's not just the men in the industry that are a problem. Some of these women are perpetuating this idea that we're glorified prostitutes. That's how it can feel. It can feel that way. It feels a little bit like [the film] Pretty Woman. You're going out with somebody who's rich, wealthy, has money, and wants to have a pretty girl sitting next to them at a dinner, but it comes with the expectation that there's something attached. That is not going to go away if we have women like that in leadership positions in organizations who will not deal with these problems head-on, or make jokes about it.

As Ruth describes, a female fundraiser was willing to sexually exploit a female colleague for a donation. If sexual harassment were solely about gender power, we would expect that men might act exploitatively, but that women would ally with female fundraisers in such situations. In this case, however, resource dependency, and/or perhaps goal attachment, seem to have created strong disincentives for female allyship.

While some of the organizations these fundraisers worked for had sexual harassment policies, many did not, in part because they were too small to have a human resources person. When organizational policies were in place, they rarely included donors. Victoria was sexually harassed by a board member who contributed to the organization. She explained:

> My first thought was, "Well, he's a volunteer, he's a board member. If it was a colleague of mine harassing me, I would have an avenue with which to report that and be responsible for reporting that. Does that really apply to volunteers?" My understanding then was that it doesn't.

Not only was there an absence of structures to allow for reporting, but fundraisers were also limited in how they could protect themselves. Lucy told us about how she and other fundraisers at her organization created a secret code to flag inappropriate donors in their donor management software. Fundraisers use secret codes because donors are able to request their file.

4. An impossible situation with no way out

[…]

Fundraisers generally feel powerless when they experience sexual harassment from donors and have a difficult choice to make regarding how they will respond. They weigh many factors in their decision. Often these questions run through their mind in a split second during the heat of the moment:

> I started going through this ladder of decision-making. Literally, within 20 seconds, I'm like, "All right. Who does he know? What does the executive director think of him? What does the chair of the board think of him? What does it mean for me to confront him right now? What are the possible consequences?"

Several fundraisers we spoke with regretted their decision, wishing they had reacted differently in the moment or reported the incident later. Victoria contemplated whether the board member who harassed her has "treated other women at the [organization] that way? I have no idea. By not reporting it, did I perpetuate a cycle of harassment? I have no idea. I've never heard any stories about this particular man. I don't know".

There was a sense from many fundraisers that "we gotta do what we gotta do to close the deal" or … "whatever it takes to get the job done", which is also reflective of their organizations' mentality.

[…]

Some reported that their managers engaged in victim-blaming. After reporting sexual harassment by a board member, Matilda's boss "didn't care" and told her that she needed to be sure she wasn't "sending mixed signals". Others reported that organizational representatives merely dismissed the seriousness of the situation:

> It was a perfunctory, "Sorry, that happened to you. Now press on." It's like when your child gets hurt on their knee, and you say, "Here's a Band-Aid, you'll be fine." As opposed to sitting with them and saying, "I'm really sorry that happened to you. Tell me about it".

[…]

In addition to disheartening stories, there were also some glimmers of hope. Elizabeth's boss who witnessed a donor touch her inappropriately, came to her afterward, and said, "I didn't like the way he greeted you". She went on to ask Elizabeth what she wanted to do about it. "It wasn't a sweep-it-under-the-rug kind of place". Zelda told us that her manager held a meeting with the entire fundraising staff. During that meeting the manager said,

We just want to be very clear on what our policy is here. Nobody ever expects you to be in a vulnerable position with the donor. We don't want a gift so badly that we're willing to put our frontline fundraisers at risk, or where you feel like you have to behave a certain way to get something.

Some of the better approaches we came across were shared by fundraisers who, after experiencing sexual harassment themselves, now protect their direct reports. Lucy said when she found out a donor had shown one of her fundraisers inappropriate photos on his phone, she immediately informed HR and "cut the connection ... because nobody should have to go through that". Some talked about how they had to come to accept that they may lose donations as a result of their zero-tolerance policies. So, while there were relatively few examples of organizations responding constructively, there are some examples pointing to the possibilities of a better approach.

[...]

Conclusion

This study brings together resource dependency theory and research on sexual harassment. By examining fundraisers' experiences of sexual harassment by donors, we contribute to resource dependency research by exposing important unintended consequences of resource dependency mitigation strategies and the mechanisms— professional norms, organizational support or exploitation, and social position differentials—that enable those consequences. Identifying such unintended consequences and perverse incentives is paramount to comprehensive theorization, effective organizational strategy, and the achievement of diversity and social equity efforts.

My love for philanthropy as a black fundraiser

Fatou Jammeh, 2021

I can still remember the first time I held a cheque for one million dollars in my hand.

As a young fundraiser making less than five percent of this cheque a year, I couldn't begin to imagine what. this amount of wealth meant. Yet here I was, holding a piece of paper as light as a feather with enormous power to change lives, even the lives of those of us in the headquarters. Thinking back now about how this gift was secured through a simple coffee conversation is alluring for me. I too wanted to talk to wealth, see what this sector of philanthropy was about and how it could effect change.

Pursuing philanthropy has been an interesting journey. For a long time, my heart longed to advocate for resources for those in need. In the beginning I wasn't sure what area I would do this work in, but my first two jobs as a fundraiser were with women's rights organizations. At the time, I thought this was it; my desires have been met.

Little did I know that my journey had just begun. Since then I've had various roles and have come to realize that it's not simply about the cause or the particular organization. It is also about my motivation, my love for humanity, my wish for equity and my quest for a level playing field.

The Greek etymological meaning of the word "philanthropy" involves love (*phil*) of humanity (*anthropos*). Love in the philanthropic sector for a Black fundraiser like myself is a feeling that is hard to find. Outwardly, we do excellent work, and in some instances we "save lives". Today, five years into the profession, when I ask myself if I feel the love I can say yes. But it hasn't always been that way. It took me four years of tackling barriers and challenges to get to this point.

Early in my career, I saw firsthand how nonprofits treated their employees, especially Black and brown people. This treatment did not align with their stated values. Institutionalised racism was an overt fact against which little action was taken. When I spoke to an executive leader about the revolving door of people in their organization and the lack of diversity among their leaders, the answer was that the qualified prospective leaders could not be found in persons from diverse backgrounds. What a remarkable and revelatory response!

How could I really love this sector when I had to fight to have love reciprocated? It was difficult for me to view philanthropy as love for humanity

DOI: 10.4324/9781003145936-98

when predominately white people, who hold the power to give this love through monetary resources, are the same people using it to exclude and disadvantage people like me.

When I spoke up about the marginalization of Black and brown bodies in the charitable sector, the organization's response was to censor my voice, even as they perpetuated an external image of bestowing love. I was really shocked and stunned at the hypocrisy. It was a traumatic lesson. The organization was supposed to be committed to fighting for the rights of people who lack a platform from which to speak out. Ironically, there I was speaking up and being shut down.

Talking about love in a space where love is absent is hard, but I came to understand the structure of philanthropy, its resources, and the allocation of wealth. And what I have discovered is how the wealthy are comfortable making pledges to fundraisers who look like them. And they are uncomfortable making pledges to fundraisers like me, a Black African woman who does not look like them.

At one point, I really didn't know if I would continue on a path in the philanthropic sector. As a Black African fundraiser, I have not encountered the wealth of individuals like Gates, Rockefellers or Carnegies. In fact, I didn't even know who they were until my work in philanthropy began. Growing up, my trajectory was to obtain a position in a traditional role such as a teacher, doctor or lawyer, with the goal of enhancing my life and my family's. I am the first fundraiser in my family and saw this as an opportunity to extend love further into my community. I also know this is true for many other Black people in the sector.

I, like other Black fundraisers, experience ostracization as I navigate racially-fraught power dynamics and endure affronts to my dignity. But I still have a firm belief that Black fundraisers are well aligned and suited to command space in this sector. It is critical that we use our collective voices to advocate for the interests of people who sit on the margins within our communities. In doing so, we can find healing and love in our collective strength. Together, we occupy a position of influence. Not only do we raise money, but also we can guide where it goes and what gets funded.

One thing I know about the power of love is that it has the ability to heal us. And I find healing through my ability to meet the needs of others. I am grateful when I am able to share love by holding healing space for other fundraisers of colour. It's important to me that I can be an advocate and a support. Another contribution I am currently supporting is the auditing of policies in my organization for gaps in relation to equity, fairness and racial diversity ... issues that will affect the inclusion of Black fundraisers.

As I journey forward, I am aware of the barriers that still exist for Black fundraisers. The key to a systemic shift critical in achieving the change we desire is to understand our power and our value in the nonprofit sector. I'm now convinced that for any real change to happen, we must contribute to the dismantling of systems and institutions, and I'm doing my part by starting within my own realm of influence. As Edgar Villaneuva concludes in [his book] *Decolonizing Wealth*, "philanthropy as the sector most ostensibly responsible for healing, could and should lead the way."

I will continue on this journey of healing and love through philanthropy. I will continue to create spaces where we all feel that we belong, where our opinions matter, where philanthropy is used as a tool for liberation and where we have equal access. Here's to the love of the work of philanthropy for the sake of humanity and to welcoming love with open arms.

"When we engage in acts of love, we humans are at our best and most resilient" – adrienne maree brown

Finding new fundraising ideas

Roger Bennett and Sharmila Savani, 2011

A management in search of new fundraising ideas needs to decide where it will look for ideas and whether to concentrate on certain types of sources, e.g., internal or external; resource intensive (such as commissioned external consultants) or financially inexpensive (such as informal discussions with stakeholders). A review of academic literature in the idea generation field suggested a number of considerations that might affect this matter, as follows.

We list here the main possible internally and externally focused sources of ideas identified by academic and practitioner literature in the area:

Internal sources of new fundraising ideas

(a) Informal discussions with supporters.
(b) Informal discussions with employees and/or volunteers.
(c) Analysis of complaints received.
(d) Focus groups with supporters.
(e) Focus groups with stakeholders such as government agencies, major corporate donors, trustees, etc.
(f) Organized team-based brainstorming sessions.
(g) Individual brainstorming, without using a brainstorming computer software package.
(h) Individual brainstorming using a software package.
(i) Organized creativity sessions using techniques other than brainstorming (e.g., lateral thinking, SWOT analysis, an idea generation template obtained from outside the organization, environmental scanning or similar techniques).
(j) Senior managers' insights.
(k) Accidental discovery and/or by-products of existing activities.

External sources of new fundraising ideas

(a) Informal discussions with people in other charities.
(b) Analysis of the activities of other charities.
(c) Attendance at exhibitions, conferences or conventions.
(d) Perusal of professional magazines (e.g., Professional Fundraising Magazine) and other publications.

DOI: 10.4324/9781003145936-99

(e) Information from a professional body or trade association (e.g., the Institute of Fundraising).
(f) Foreign partners.
(g) Other foreign sources, e.g., foreign visits, foreign literature.
(h) Internet pages dedicated to ideas for charity fundraising.
(i) Internet pages dedicated to idea creation for general business purposes.
(j) Internet information exchange forums (e.g., fundraising chat forums; Facebook's 'Ideas on Fundraising' forums).
(k) Books devoted to fundraising.
(l) Advertising agencies.
(m) Ideas consultants.
(n) Charity fundraising consultants.
(o) Marketing or general business consultants.
(p) Market research firms.
(q) Suppliers of charity promotional merchandise.

A review completed by Pavia of the (then) prior research literature on the generation of successful ideas revealed a substantial amount of evidence suggesting that between two-thirds and three-quarters of winning ideas (i) arose from internal rather than external sources, (ii) were based on a close understanding of clients' requirements, and (iii) were in some way unique. Pavia reported, however, that studies had not discovered any consistent relationship between success and specific sources of ideas. Internal sources have the general advantage that (at least in principle) they should be close to an organization's mission, vision, objectives, capabilities and circumstances. Consequently decision makers should be better equipped to determine what they need to have ideas about.

Some internal sources are known to have disadvantages nevertheless, especially those involving internal employees. Employees might possess a very limited focus and hence suggest only small variations to existing activities rather than radically new proposals. Mechanisms for rewarding and recognizing employees' inputs need to be established and resources provided to convert ideas into action. Pressures placed on employees to come up with ideas might simply lead to the espousal of a plethora of implausible suggestions. Top managers are, of course, highly influential in relation to idea generation, but the ideas that senior managers put forward may be aspirational rather than practical. A senior manager might not understand marketing or what is feasible in marketing terms. Also top management might relinquish control (and accountability) immediately after their ideas have been implemented.

[...]

Kelly and Storey reported a number of studies which claimed that successful organizations were more likely to operate formal and systematic procedures (involving, for example, brainstorming, focus groups, systematic gap and SWOT analysis or environmental scanning) for stimulating the production of ideas. Skilton and Dooley argued that procedures of this kind can help an organization to create new ideas on a regular basis, as opposed to ideas being evoked 'on demand' in ad hoc manners. Also, Skilton and Dooley continued, lessons learned from the creation of successful ideas relating to one project can be carried through to subsequent idea generation activities. Moreover, the employment of systematic procedures transmits a message to everyone in the organization that the creation of new ideas is to be regarded as a top priority. This could contribute to the nurture of an innovative and idea-rich culture within the organization.

Systematic procedures can facilitate the 'selective probing' of ideas rather than 'the production of a flood of ideas, most of which will be impractical'. Additionally they might develop participants' self-confidence and analytical skills. According to Dick et al., the application of formal methods helps avoid the problem of 'unconscious self-reinforcement' that often arises from ideas not being subjected to rigorous interrogation. On the other hand, formal methods allegedly lack flexibility in that they tend to concentrate on one problem at a time. Also their successful application requires expert leadership and the presence of a 'certain corporate atmosphere' within an organization.

External sources

Managers of organizations sometimes look to the outside world for inspiration. For example, fresh ideas for innovative fundraising campaigns might be obtained through a charity manager attending conferences and conventions (e.g. the annual convention of the Institute of Charity Fundraising Managers, which routinely attracts over 1,200 delegates and devotes much of its content to successful fundraising ideas), trade fairs for charity promotional goods, or meetings of relevant professional bodies. Likewise, new ideas might be acquired from articles in professional magazines, including publications in foreign countries (especially those with a non-profit sector similar to that of the UK).

Marketing managers in general are known to be voracious consumers of information on marketing methods obtained from 'grey literature', notably literature available on the Internet. The major Internet search engines are replete with websites carrying titles such as 'Free Fundraising Ideas' and 'Great Charity Fundraising'. Numerous hard copy and online books on ideas for fundraising campaigns are also available: a brief Internet search completed by the authors identified more than 50 British titles currently in print.

Another possible source of ideas is the practice of monitoring and evaluating the activities of comparable organizations in a charity's own and in other fields. This process might enable an organization to copy successful fundraising ideas applied by other charities, although some critics have alleged that imitation can result, in the words of Kelly and Storey, 'in a dangerous focus on me-too products with most development being reactive and defensive in nature'. Conversely, Allen claimed that copying allows an organization to build on the expertise of other organizations and then to generate fresh knowledge and further new ideas. Many large UK charities place on their websites (often very extensive) lists of fundraising ideas for use by their supporter groups. This material can be accessed by anyone, including of course other charities.

The search for new ideas may extend to the examination of the activities of any type of organization in any country. The current practices of exceptionally high status organizations often receive particular attention as they may be assumed to have superior value. As Ansari, Fiss and Zajac pointed out, however, this could lead to the adoption of inappropriate practices.

A charity's management might approach an advertising agency or business consultant and ask for fresh fundraising ideas. Agencies and consultancies employ creative people directly or know where and how to sub-contract in this regard. The main Internet search engines carry details of around 1,200 British firms operating under the title 'Fundraising Consultants'. There is a professional Institute of Fundraising Consultancy organization, some members of which specialize in the development of campaigns. Additionally there exist 'Fundraising Companies' (which help charities to find grant opportunities and assist with bidding) and dedicated 'Ideas Consultants'. Hundreds of firms supply promotional merchandise to charities and, for a fee, will also proffer advice on the development of fundraising campaigns. An advantage of employing a consultant is that an outsider might possess broader perspectives and experience than in-house charity personnel and ought not to be affected by change resistant internal organizational cultures. On the other hand, outsiders might not truly understand a charity's mission and aims or the financial implications of the outsider's ideas for campaign implementation. Also an agency or consultancy will want to retain its client's business and hence might avoid being too adventurous, seeking instead to elaborate on existing campaigns.

[...]

This exploratory study examined the idea sourcing behaviour of a sample of organizations, many of which (by virtue of their competitive environments and circumstances) must continuously implement innovative fundraising campaigns and hence need constantly to acquire fresh ideas for inducing members of the public to make donations.

[...]

It emerged that nearly half of the sample organizations analysed the activities of other charities to obtain fresh ideas for fundraising. This is not entirely surprising given that information on the campaigns of other charities is readily available via direct observation and from articles in newspapers and magazines and in the charity trade literature. Thus, analyses of this type constitute a convenient and relatively low cost means for maintaining a competitive position. The practice of monitoring other charities enables a management to benchmark its activities against comparable organizations, to identify its own vulnerabilities and to plan the resourcing of measures necessary to overcome deficiencies .... Internet websites devoted to charity fundraising also represented a major source of fresh ideas for campaigns (a finding in line with evidence which suggested that marketing managers in general are heavy users of 'grey' literature [often Internet based] to inform their activities) ...

Further major sources of new ideas for fundraising were information gathered from professional or trade associations in the charity area and from attendance at exhibitions and conventions. This outcome underscores the value of the roles played by professional bodies (e.g., the Institute of Fundraising) and professional magazines in helping charity managers devise new and innovative campaigns. Around one in five of the charities involved an advertising agency or outside consultant in the development of fresh ideas for fundraising. Overall, therefore, in-house (and presumably less expensive) idea sourcing was preferred over the purchase of external consultancy services.

A factor possibly contributing to this result is that many of the sample organizations needed to search for new ideas on an almost continuous basis (for the reasons previously outlined) so that very often (and particularly in the case of smaller charities) the ongoing commissioning of external assistance would not be financially viable.

Most of the antecedents of extensive idea sourcing suggested by prior literature in the (general) idea generation field exerted significant influences in some way or other on the organizations in the present study. Risk aversion encouraged a charity to examine a broader range of sources and to focus on internal sources that were more resource intensive. Larger charities employed a more extensive range of sources than smaller charities and were more likely to use resource intensive sources. Innovative and open-minded organizations and charities high in strategic intent tended to use more sources than the remainder of the sample. Organizational formality was associated with the employment of resource intensive sources, though it did not have a significant impact on the range of sources consulted. There was no evidence that formal behavioural control, in the words of Poskela and Martinsuo, "kills creativity" at the front end. Environmental volatility exerted effects on all the dependent variables.

Satisfaction with the quality of the new ideas obtained and with the financial returns from these ideas rose as the overall extent of idea sourcing increased and as the sample organizations intensified their employment of resource intensive sources. Heavy use of convenient and inexpensive sources was negatively associated with satisfaction. The results imply, therefore, that the formal application of resource intensive approaches to the process of sourcing new ideas in conjunction with the consideration of a wide range of sources yields superior outcomes. It follows that charities high in the antecedents of extensive idea sourcing and of the use of resource intensive sources should possess advantages vis-à-vis the implementation of novel fundraising campaigns.

Neglected fundraisers in the charitable triad

Cassandra M. Chapman, Winnifred R. Louis, Barbara M. Masser, and Emma F. Thomas, 2022

Whether trying to cure cancer, protecting human and animal rights, caring for the sick or elderly, or advocating for the environment, charities are critical to the functioning of human society. Most nonprofits rely on voluntary financial contributions to achieve their social goals, and it is the task of nonprofit marketers to secure these donations. Understanding how to target potential donors and communicate with them most effectively is therefore an essential task for nonprofit marketers and fundraisers.

Evolutionary theories for human altruism—including reciprocity, reputation-seeking, and cultural group selection—understand altruism to be dyadic (i.e. involving two actors). There is a help giver (e.g. donor) and a help receiver (e.g. beneficiary), and these approaches have identified different motives for helping different kinds of beneficiaries (i.e. kin vs. non-kin others). In the modern world, however, donors can help many different beneficiaries, including those far outside their immediate communities. To facilitate helping, potential donors receive information about a vast array of potential beneficiaries. Such information is distributed by intermediaries (i.e. fundraisers), which are often large organizations whose entire existence is predicated on successfully mediating help between donors and beneficiaries. The existence of professional fundraising is a relatively modern phenomenon, which has not yet been factored into theories of prosocial behavior.

[…]

The key tenets of Charitable Triad Theory are as follows. First, giving is *triadic* because the characteristics of three actors—donors, beneficiaries, and fundraisers—influence charitable decisions. Second, the characteristics of each of the three actors may be necessary *but not sufficient* to promote charitable giving. Third, giving is *relational* because interactive relationships between the triad determine charitable choices. In other words, donors may give (or fail to give) because of: (1) their own characteristics; (2) characteristics of the beneficiary in question and/or of the person or organization asking for donations; or (3) the interactive (dyadic and triadic) relationships among these three actors. *Dyadic* here means involving two of the Charitable Triad actors (i.e. donor, beneficiary, fundraiser), while *triadic* means involving all three actors.

[…]

DOI: 10.4324/9781003145936-100

We conducted a systematic review of the interdisciplinary literature to test the evidence base for the novelty and value of the Charitable Triad approach, and specific propositions of the triadic theory. The systematic review allows us to: (1) provide a comprehensive overview of the scholarship on charitable giving, (2) illustrate the ways that both characteristics of actors and the relationships between them can influence charitable giving, and (3) identify important gaps and future directions.

A very large number of articles were identified by our review ($N = 1,337$) ... The data show vast asymmetries in attention paid to the three actors. The literature on charitable giving and fundraising has been growing rapidly, but with an accentuating relative emphasis on donors. Considering only the articles that can be understood using the triadic approach, we found that three-quarters of the articles (75%) considered giving from the perspective of the donor, compared to 15% that considered the fundraiser and just 8% that considered the beneficiary. Of those that studied characteristics of fundraisers, most (87%) studied characteristics of fundraising organizations; only 22 published articles considered the role of individual fundraisers.

Even more stark was the relative deemphasis on relationships between the actors. Only 11% of articles considered interactions between the characteristics of different actors. Of those, most considered relationships between the donor and either the beneficiary ($n = 70$) or the fundraiser ($n = 61$), again highlighting the predominance of donor-centric research.

[...]

Charitable Triad Theory consists of seven overarching propositions for the ways that donors, beneficiaries, and fundraisers influence giving; individually and in combination.

[...]

Proposition 1: *Supportive donor characteristics are necessary but not sufficient to promote charitable giving.*

There is ample evidence that certain types of people are more generous than others. Donor behavior is influenced by characteristics like sociodemographics, individual differences, costs and benefits, emotions, and the donor's social world. For example, women, older people, and those with higher incomes and more education are all more likely to give to charity and are more generous when they do so. People who are higher in empathy, trust, and religiosity are also more likely to be donors. Donors can be motivated by the possibility of receiving emotional benefits or material rewards (e.g., thank you gifts or tax rebates). Donor emotions also influence giving, including guilt, compassion, gratitude, anger, happiness, disgust, regret, and sadness. Finally, people's identities influence their giving decisions, especially when their identities evoke supportive social norms. Thus, the presence of supportive donor characteristics makes it more likely that a donation will be made.

Although certain donor characteristics are associated with giving, the nature of these relationships are not consistent: none of these associations remain the same (i.e., positive vs. negative vs. no association) under all conditions. To illustrate these inconsistencies, we considered the five most commonly studied sociodemographic predictors of giving: gender, income and wealth, age, religiosity, and education. These sociodemographics are widely believed to impact giving and are therefore included as control variables in many studies. For each article that mentioned one of these sociodemographics in its abstract, we coded the observed effects reported in the article. As can be seen in Figure 5.4.1 all of these associations are volatile: sometimes falling one way, sometimes the other, sometimes being nonsignificant, and sometimes returning contradictory effects. For example, 35% of the studies found that women gave more than men, while 29% found no difference in giving between men and women, and 8% found that men gave more than women. Over a quarter of studies (28%) even found such inconsistencies within their data.

Other donor characteristics are also volatile. Some examples: donors' responsiveness to tax incentives varies substantially across charity sub-types. Anger is not associated with giving in general but does promote giving to politicized causes. And identities are particularly effective when the beneficiary shares an important identity with the donor.

Inconsistencies in observed patterns of association (as illustrated in Figure 5.4.1) reinforce the notion of complex causality and suggest that other

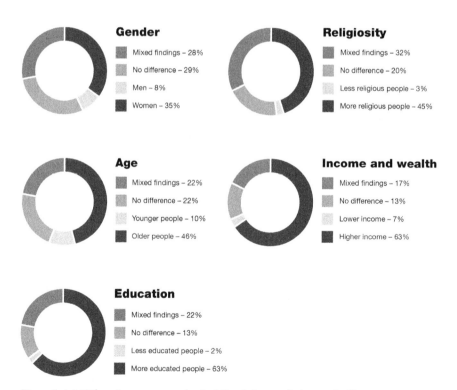

Figure 5.4.1 Who gives more to charity? Breakdown of observed effects across studies considering the effects of gender (*n* = 108), income and wealth (*n* = 94), age (*n* = 94), religiosity (*n* = 74), and education (*n* = 62) on charitable giving.

factors moderate the effects of these donor characteristics. We propose that beneficiaries, fundraisers, and especially the relationships between the three actors can also influence donor decisions. In other words, supportive donor characteristics are necessary *but not sufficient* for understanding donor behavior.

Proposition 2: *Beneficiaries perceived as worthy of care will usually elicit greater levels of charitable support than those deemed unworthy*

Some beneficiaries are more likely to receive help than others. For example, charities supporting children and animals are particularly popular, while charities supporting offenders and prostitutes are comparatively unpopular. Thus, regardless of who is asked to donate, some beneficiary characteristics lead to greater fundraising success than others.

We label the constellation of beneficiary factors that elicit greater support as 'worthiness'. A range of factors appear to contribute to perceptions of beneficiary worthiness. For example, beneficiaries who are younger, more attractive, and perceived as warm receive more help. One the other hand, beneficiaries who are perceived to be responsible for their fate are helped less, possibly due to donors' belief that the world is fair and just. Finally, beneficiaries that are demonstrably more needy elicit the greatest levels of support.

The way that the beneficiary is presented in a fundraising campaign also influences giving responses. Research on the identifiable victim effect demonstrates that including a named and pictured beneficiary leads to greater fundraising success than talking about beneficiaries in the abstract. Paul Slovic's work on psychic numbing also shows that—counterintuitively—people donate more when fewer beneficiaries are impacted. Thus, the number and identifiability of beneficiaries may contribute to perceptions of their worthiness.

Overall, beneficiary characteristics and the ways that beneficiaries are presented in appeals both impact giving: beneficiaries that are perceived as more worthy will generally elicit greater support. However, neediness does not always affect donations and may sometimes even have detrimental effects on giving. Further, identifiable victim effects may only occur when donors are temporally or socially close to the beneficiary. Thus, the effects of beneficiary worthiness also depend on characteristics of and relationships with both donors and fundraisers, as we discuss below.

[…]

Proposition 3: *Fundraisers that are perceived to be more legitimate will usually raise more money.*

We define legitimacy as a higher order construct relating to whether a fundraiser (individual or organization) is seen as a valid and appropriate representative of the cause. Various factors may contribute to perceptions of fundraisers' legitimacy. For individual fundraisers, appearance, professional training, and experience with the cause could all promote legitimacy. For organizational fundraisers, perceptions of legitimacy could be influenced by their track-record for impact, branding, reputation, and general trustworthiness.

Comparatively little is known about how the characteristics of individual fundraisers may enhance or inhibit their effectiveness. Fundraisers are more successful if they are physically attractive, well dressed, and professionally trained. Celebrity endorsement can also promote donation intentions, especially when there is perceived to be a fit between the celebrity and the charity they endorse. These characteristics help make fundraisers seem more legitimate: whether because of their appearance (e.g., well dressed), professionalism (e.g., well trained), or fit with the cause (e.g., well suited to advocate).

Charitable organizations themselves are the fundraisers that donors are most likely to come into contact with: via TV ads, billboards, radio ads, and direct mail. In these cases, it is the brand that does the asking. A number of characteristics of fundraising organizations have been shown to influence charitable giving, and we propose that these organizational characteristics also promote a sense of legitimacy.

Perceptions of fundraising legitimacy can be promoted by the organization's effectiveness (impact on the cause), efficiency (percentage of funds that go toward charitable projects compared to marketing and overheads), alternative sources of funds, and reputation based on factors like size, perceived quality, brand image, accreditation status, or trustworthiness.

As can be seen, characteristics of fundraisers—whether they are individuals or organizations—that make them seem more legitimate will enhance their fundraising success. Once again, however, the fundraising characteristics associated with giving have returned inconsistent results. For example, some studies have shown that charity effectiveness and efficiency are relatively unimportant in determining gifts. Fundraiser legitimacy may therefore usually promote giving but its importance may depend on the particular donor or beneficiary in question, as we discuss below.

[…]

Proposition 4: *Beneficiaries who are similar to donors are generally more likely to generate donations.*

Overall, donors may prioritize helping donors that are similar to them in some way. A sense of similarity could be promoted by any form of commonality between the donor and the beneficiary. For instance, people give more to help beneficiaries that live near them or share an important identity with them. Bekkers even found that simply having a name that starts with a phonetically similar initial as the beneficiary can increase donations.

Yet, although donors may prefer helping similar beneficiaries, they may sometimes also give to dissimilar beneficiaries:

Proposition 5: *Dissimilar beneficiaries may receive aid if there are strategic interests for the donor or the donor's group.*

Helping dissimilar beneficiaries can sometimes be done for strategic reasons, such as to benefit the donor's group or to maintain or establish dominance over another group. For example, when their national identity is threatened people give to help beneficiaries in other countries as a way to restore group-esteem or positive distinctiveness. Further, some high status people help in order to assert their power over others or keep other groups down. Thus, dissimilar beneficiaries may receive help when there are benefits or reputational rewards for the donor.

In addition to the characteristics of each actor, relationships between actors can influence giving. We propose that relational alignment between fundraisers and both donors and beneficiaries can affect donation decisions:

Proposition 6: *Fundraisers that are aligned with either donors or beneficiaries will be more successful, and those aligned with both will be especially successful.*

Donor-fundraiser dyad. Alignment in the form of relationships between donors and fundraisers have been demonstrated to affect giving. When the donor trusts the fundraising organization, they are more likely to donate. Relationships of similarity or shared identity between donors and fundraisers can also impact giving: giving is promoted when donors identify with the fundraising organization, when donors like the fundraiser or share social ties with them, or when a consequential bond exists between donor and fundraiser. People also give more when asked by people that they are personally close with. In sum, a gift appears to be more likely when donors and fundraisers align by, for example, sharing priorities or having existing relationships.

Fundraiser-beneficiary dyad. Very little is known about the way fundraisers and beneficiaries interact to influence giving. Our systematic review uncovered just two relevant articles. One quasi-experiment showed that University fundraisers who had met beneficiaries of the fellowship they were raising money for succeeded in raising more donations than fundraisers who had had no contact with beneficiaries. A second study of stores that fundraise for causes showed that people donated more at checkout if they experienced great service from the fundraising store, but this effect was attenuated when shoppers were asked to give to victims of tragedies rather than to social causes. These two studies show that dynamics between fundraisers and beneficiaries can influence charitable giving, despite the question being largely neglected to date.

The final proposition of our model represents the heart of the triadic approach, but is also the one with the least empirical support to date; a deficit that we hope this article will motivate scholars to soon rectify:

Proposition 7: *The unique interaction between the particular donor, beneficiary, and fundraiser will determine both whether or not a donation will be made and the value of donations.*

Our review uncovered just two studies that considered the full triad of actors in unison. Yinon and Sharon used a 2x2x2 design to simultaneously consider the effects of donor, beneficiary, and fundraiser religion. They found a significant three-way interaction such that Jewish donors were more likely to donate to non-Jewish beneficiary families if they were solicited for donations by a Jewish fundraiser. More recently, Zagefka and colleagues demonstrated another three-way interaction, this time between perceived social norms (donor), neediness (beneficiary), and impact (fundraising organization). They found that the neediness of beneficiaries only promoted giving when donors perceived high organizational impact and low social norms for giving. These two studies show the value of examining how the unique constellation of donor, beneficiary, and fundraiser characteristics interact to influence donation decisions. However, with only two studies having considered triadic relations in giving, future research is needed to illuminate and understand the many inconsistencies observed for direct and dyadic effects outlined above.

[...]

One key theoretical contribution of Charitable Triad Theory is to focus attention on the role of the fundraiser. As mentioned in the introduction, theories of altruism understand it to be dyadic: involving a help giver and a help receiver. In our terms, these approaches consider the dyadic relationships between donors and beneficiaries. However, in the modern world, organizational fundraisers exist to facilitate large-scale helping, often between donors and beneficiaries that are geographically or socially separated. Theories have not yet grappled with the way these intermediaries may affect consumer behavior in the charitable domain. Our triadic theory draws attention to the neglected fundraiser and offers a new theoretical approach to understanding charitable giving that actively considers the three key actors involved in any giving exchange: donor, beneficiary, and fundraiser.

Section 6

TRENDS AND DEBATES ABOUT MAKING FUNDRAISING BETTER

Editors' introduction

Overview

In this final section of the reader we turn to focus on some of the key trends in fundraising and some of the most important debates about making fundraising better. Some authors in this section have helpfully signposted trends to monitor, others suggest tools and techniques to help meet likely demands, whilst a brave few have ambitiously sought to predict the future, its opportunities and pitfalls.

The future is important because fundraisers need to see one step ahead. Planning and delivering appeals and campaigns takes time, a decision today may not impact outcomes for a year or more. Adjusting organisation culture to support fundamental change takes even longer. While fundraising strategies usually project forward three years or more, the nearest we can get to knowing the future is to observe trends and significant influences. Their pattern of evolution can suggest their future trajectory and the impact that they might have on how effective our fundraising delivery is.

Another consideration is where to focus our attention. The previous sections in this reader demonstrate that fundraising is highly dependent on both the internal and external environments. Therefore the choice of where to focus attention must be tailored to each organisation, the nature of its mission and the specific context of its environments. But in this section a number of common key themes emerge including: donor relations; donor behaviour; organisation culture; ethics and regulation; and technology. This list is not exhaustive, and reading these extracts will also offer insights into other trends worth tracking.

As noted in the Editors' introduction to this reader, the role and practice of fundraising is complex and contested, its legitimacy is questioned by some people, and the methods by which some funds are raised also invites critique and concerns. Extracts in this section offer insight into the nature and contours of some of these key debates such as whether the fundraising profession is sufficiently diverse (Zumaya and Martin-John in Section 6.1), whether fundraising practice ought to focus on donors or beneficiaries (Section 6.2), the ethics of using behavioural science to "nudge" potential donors (Croucher et al. in Section 6.4) and how power imbalances affect the relationships between those who are asking and those who have the resources to give (Vu Le in Section

DOI: 10.4324/9781003145936-102

6.1; Bull and Steinberg in Section 6.3). This section – and the Reader – end with trends and predictions for fundraising (Section 6.5). Whilst it is healthy to debate all these topics and more, doing so in a way that is informed by research and reflections on best practice is better still.

6.1 Moving to a mission-aligned fundraising culture

Cynthia Gibson opens this section with an exploration of the impact that the overall internal culture of nonprofits, more so than their strategic plans, has on the capacity to attract and retain donors. Noting the necessity of a "culture of philanthropy" in which everyone – board, leadership and staff – values fund development, Gibson discusses developments that are affecting what this means in practice such as the "rise in people power" enabled by interactive technology; the dominant attitudes and behaviours amongst younger generations; and the ever-fiercer competition to attract the attention of all types of donors.

Gibson also highlights distinguishing features of a successful culture of philanthropy, such as taking a longer-term focus, prioritising donor retention over recruitment, and viewing money as "what we need to do our work" rather than as "dirty". Gibson also identifies four key components found in a fundraising-friendly organisational culture: "shared responsibility for development …; integration and alignment with mission …; a focus on fundraising as engagement …; and strong donor relationships." Whilst, as Gibson admits, these are neither revolutionary nor particularly controversial ideas, she insists their implementation will "eat strategy for breakfast" and enable nonprofit organisations to make the necessary changes rather than continue their fruitless quest of "a miracle-working development director".

Honing in on a specific aspect of fundraising culture Armando Zumaya seeks to identify how we can better achieve racial justice and decolonise philanthropy. Specifically he suggests that the over-emphasis on foundations and major donors as a vehicle to achieve equality fails to acknowledge the importance of the larger proportion of mass philanthropic giving that is "produced by" fundraising. Gibson's view that "all gifts are important" is shared by Zumaya who additionally argues that greater investment in the fundraising function will also advance equality in philanthropy so that "everyone [has] the opportunity to improve their communities and the world. Giving is power. And too often we intentionally give that power only to the rich and white." Zumaya further suggests that one of the reasons donors tend to be "old, straight white men" is because of the lack of diversity in fundraising teams. In the next extract Niambi Martin-John draws on her own experience as a Black fundraiser in Canada to offer insight into why this lack of diversity exists. Martin-John describes the challenges faced in building her fundraising career as a result of what she terms the "white exemption clause" which describes how nonprofit organisational culture permits behaviours and facilitates career progression for white employees, whilst the same opportunities are repeatedly closed to Black people. Martin-John highlights what needs to change to dismantle barriers of power and privilege and to align the culture and practice of the fundraising profession with that of the nonprofit sector it serves.

This sub-section ends with a passionate and humorous piece by Vu Le who writes about another imbalance in power: that between institutional funders (such as charitable trusts and philanthropic foundations) and the non-profits who seek their funding. Vu Le highlights the problematic dynamics in grant application practices whereby honesty from applicant nonprofits may very well not lead to the desired outcomes for the nonprofit. Vu Le usefully reveals flaws in the current grant-making culture which need to be named, acknowledged, and fixed in order to align the practice of grant-making with the mission of the broader philanthropy sector which ought to see fundraisers as partners rather than as duplicitous supplicants. Implied in this extract is a theme emerging from the other authors in this section, that nonprofits have the power to change the culture of fundraising and philanthropy, although this may come at a cost. This is a theme that we will return to in Section 6.3 where Gemma Bull and Tom Steinberg also seek to make sense of the challenging power imbalances between grantmakers and their nonprofit grantees.

6.2 Donor-centric or community-centric fundraising?

This short section presents two contrasting views on our relationship with donors: should fundraising be donor or community centric? Russell James III is an advocate of making the donor the "hero" of the fundraising story by clearly communicating what changed as a result of their gift and ensuring the donor achieves an enhanced identity as a person who has meaningfully acted on their values. James argues that poor donor retention is a direct consequence of not fully engaging donors in the stories they strive to be part of, noting that "Delivering a powerful ask is great. But it's not the same as delivering value to the donor". For James the future of fundraising involves better stewardship for better retention. While in Vu Le's second extract in this section, he sides firmly with the community-centric fundraising movement. Vu Le cautions against privileging donors as heroes because doing so "may be perpetuating the very inequity that we are seeking to address as a sector". Whilst acknowledging many of the tenets of donor-centrism, such as showing appreciation and building relationships, he sets out the unintended problems resulting from putting donors at the centre of fundraising or nonprofit work. These include proliferating the "savior complex" and reinforcing the notion of recipients as marginalised "others" waiting to be saved, rather than fostering communities that are grounded in equity, social justice, belonging and interdependence. Returning to the theme from Section 6.1 of the nonprofit's role in creating and sustaining problematic cultures, Vu Le suggests that donor-centric fundraising leads to "a host of unintended problems ... some of which may be actively preventing us from advancing an equitable society". The answer to whether fundraising should be donor or community centric is likely not a dichotomy, both donors and fundraisers play a key role in fundraising, as also advocated by Chapman et al. in Section 5.4.

6.3 Continuity and change in fundraising approaches

In the first reading of Section 6.1, Cynthia Gibson drew our attention to the real and dramatic impact of technology and social media on donor behaviour. We might therefore think that old analogue communication such as direct mail has had its day. According to Jeff Brooks, fundraising through the letterbox may be changing and less popular with younger generations but it remains "a keystone investment for almost any fundraising program". Brooks offers a research-informed discussion about direct mail's ongoing place within an overall fundraising programme, and how to assess whether or not a direct mail programme remains viable.

By contrast Gemma Bull and Tom Steinberg feel that it is time for change in the grantmaking sector. Their observation that poor grantmakers "are part of the problem of discrimination and marginalisation in society at large, not part of the solution" echoes and extends arguments by authors such as Zumaya, Martin-John, and Vu Le (Section 6.1) by suggesting that grantmakers need to invest more in their own core cost of designing and delivering a better grantee experience. This discussion needs to be handled with care: in Section 3.2 Jung et al. reminded us that grantmakers are not homogeneous, and there is a vanguard of mainly high-value grantmakers consulting grantees and striving to create a better, more equitable, funding experience. But, as Bull and Steinberg illustrate, grantmaking practices can be unintentionally prejudiced against the communities that they claim to be seeking to engage and support.

Danielle Vance-McMullen and Daniel Heist look at a relatively recent development in philanthropy that calls for a new response from the fundraising professional. Welcome the newish kid on the block: the Donor Advised Fund (DAF). The authors of this extract explain how DAFs work, explore some controversies about this giving vehicle, and offer advice on how to approach, cultivate and steward donors who give through DAFs. Whilst there are challenges for fundraisers in understanding this model and responding to its associated critiques, Vance-McMullen and Heist reach a positive conclusion: "Ultimately, DAF donors have made a commitment to charitable giving, and this commitment can benefit nonprofit missions when DAF donors are solicited effectively."

6.4 The impact of science and technology

Behavioural science has been around for over 100 years, but mainstream fundraising has only recently woken up to its relevance. The psychology and ethics of "nudging" donors to give more is explored by Madeleine Croucher, Meredith Niles, Omar Mahmoud and Bernard Ross. This extract opens by inviting fundraisers to view the application of behavioural science as an obligation by informed fundraisers who seek to be "more than *accidentally* good at our work!" The authors then explain how to apply behavioural science-informed fundraising in practice, and offer the acronym, RAISE, to help recall the core strategies for success. This refers to making fundraising nudges

Relevant; Appealing; Intuitive; Social; and Easy. Some behavioural science will seem familiar, some new, but like several other authors in this Reader, Croucher et al. insist that being informed through scientific research, rather than acting on a hunch, will generate better and more effective professional practice.

Crowdfunding takes the age-old fundraising truth – that people give to people – and uses technology, specifically online platforms and social networking, to maximise the number of donors and the amounts raised. Claire van Teunenbroek helps us to understand how philanthropic crowdfunding sits in a wider environment that includes the for-profit sector, and explains how it empowers individuals to support the nonprofit organisations they are passionate about, and also to fundraise directly for individuals they wish to help, including the geographically distant and "unknown crowd". The speed with which this technologically enabled fundraising has emerged, and its potential for engaging new and younger donors, prompts van Teunenbroek's call for greater understanding of how crowdfunding works and how to increase its effectiveness.

Another technological development that is having an impact on the changing face of fundraising is artificial intelligence (AI), which is an umbrella term that can refer to technological advances, including data science, machine learning, and deep learning. Beth Kanter and Allison Fine suggest that AI might enable us to do more of what we are uniquely able to do, get out there and meet donors, echoing the way in which Van Teunenbroek describes crowdfunding as bringing down barriers to connecting with donors. In both instances technology is a mixed blessing. Crowdfunding enables individuals to proactively fundraise to support nonprofits they love, but also to cut-out the nonprofit and fundraise directly for others or themselves. AI can enable more tailored cultivation and stewardship and can free fundraisers from routine administration tasks, but it can also give even greater advantage to asset-rich nonprofits and reinforce prejudices. The two converge when the volumes of data generated by crowdfunding platforms create new opportunities for AI analysis and our progression into what Kanter and Fine describe as "a new disruptive era … that is about to reshape activism and philanthropy".

The next extract focuses on how new technology extends opportunities for fundraising after major disasters, but at the same time has the potential to reinforce problematic stereotypes and power imbalances. Mervi Pantti describes how the YouTube platform allows citizens to create and distribute amateur appeal videos for victims of natural disasters, and explores their impact on the presentation of victims and the mobilisation of solidarity. Interactive functions, whereby viewers can "like" and comment on these videos, reveal significant differences in public concern such that "culturally close" victims in Japan generate more attention than those in Haiti or Africa. As a result these grassroot fundraising efforts can reproduce deep global divisions and reinforce problems highlighted by other authors in this section such as Zumaya, Vu Le, and Martin-John.

6.5 Trends and predictions

The final sub-section in this reader reminds us of the joke: "It's tough to make predictions, especially about the future." The preceding extracts in this section covering developments such as the demands for greater diversity, inclusion, and equality; the application of scientific insights; and the impact of new technology. Combined they can create a dizzying sense that fundraising is changing very rapidly. The extract by Penelope Cagney and Bernard Ross highlights seven "trends to watch" that are unfolding at different speeds with variable global manifestations, including the impact of growing wealth inequality, the emergence of fundraising innovations, and the professionalisation of fundraising. It is reassuring that this text from 2013 includes many trends that are still relevant to watch more than ten years later, pointing to the fact that some aspects of fundraising may be changing at lightning speed, whilst others take their time to unfold.

Mal Warwick's advice to fundraisers on how to survive difficult periods was written in the dark hours of the 2008–9 global financial crisis. His counsel is folksy ("reassess the whole ball of wax", "fish where the big fish are") but remains deeply relevant as we face ongoing economic, social, and political uncertainty driven by the aftermath of the global Covid-19 pandemic, the climate emergency, wars and forced migrations. Reinforcing Jeff Brooks' argument in favour of proven fundraising methods, Warwick encourages nonprofits to "Stick with what works" such as finessing the case for support, providing excellent donor care, and investing in the fundraising function. The final extract in this reader takes a deep look into the crystal ball to ask what fundraising will look like in 2045. Carolyn Cordery, Karen Smith, and Harry Berger review a range of potential trends and developments in demography, technology, government and corporate funding, and individual giving and volunteering, to outline potential future scenarios. Cordery et al. describe the kinds of nonprofit organisations that might emerge in scenarios where marketisation and compassion drive fundraising challenges and possibilities at both the global and local levels.

We cannot know the future with any certainty, but the extracts in this section help us to better understand and respond to change, and in doing so consider how we might evolve our fundraising for the better, to avoid the perils of inequality and neglect, and to optimise the opportunities that society, science, and technology present.

Discussion questions

1. Considering the culture of a fundraising organisation you are familiar with, how does it compare with the philanthropy-friendly, donor-retention aligned models described by Gibson and by James; specifically do you have any suggestions for the organisation you are familiar with?
2. Review the types of equality explored in Sections 6.1 and 6.2, consider the tension between the fundraiser's immediate goal of optimising income and longer-term goal of building strong donor relationships, and sector

wide goals of inclusion and equality; do you believe these three types of goal present irreconcilable conflicts of interest, discuss?

3. Review the grantmaking criteria and application process of a trust or foundation that is either known to you, or that you have researched online. To what extent does it fall foul of Vu Le's critique in Section 6.1, and to what extent has it embraced the good practice advice set out by Bull and Steinberg?

4. Which elements of fundraising do you think are most likely to remain unchanged by developments in technology? Conversely, which technology do you think has truly changed – or will change – the way fundraising functions in the future? What are the advantages of this technology?

5. Kanter and Fine hint at the ways in which technology will enhance donor segmentation and cultivation, whilst Croucher et al describe the application of behavioural science to improve fundraising outcomes. How might these arguments overlap with themes of equality and treating donors equally regardless of gift size? Do you think that advances in technology and behavioural science will ameliorate or exacerbate inequality?

6. Cagney and Ross described "seven trends to watch" in 2013. Using current affairs articles and more recent literature, discuss the evolution of these trends in contemporary fundraising.

6.1 Moving to a mission-aligned fundraising culture

Culture eats strategy for breakfast

Cynthia Gibson, 2016

Generally, a culture of philanthropy is one in which everyone – board, staff and executive director – has a part to play in raising resources for the organization. It's about relationships, not just money. It's as much about keeping donors as acquiring new ones and seeing them as having more than just money to bring to the table. And it's a culture in which fund development is a valued and mission aligned component of everything the organization does.

In the 2013 report, UnderDeveloped, authors Jeanne Bell and Marla Cornelius of CompassPoint wrote that building a culture of philanthropy can help break what they referred to as the "vicious cycle" in nonprofit fund development. Instead of placing all the blame for fundraising challenges on lengthy vacancies and instability in development director positions, the report suggested that nonprofits should pay more attention to the deeper issues of building the capacity, systems and culture to support fundraising success.

Peter Drucker famously wrote that "culture eats strategy for breakfast." Drucker wasn't saying that strategy is irrelevant. Rather, he meant that the strategy a company employs will only be successful if supported by appropriate cultural attributes. Recognizing this, nonprofits with a culture of philanthropy see fundraising less as a transactional tactic and more as a way of operating— one that reflects the definition of philanthropy: A love of humankind and a voluntary joining of resources and action for the public good.

[…]

Nailing down what a culture of philanthropy is will be essential if nonprofits are to make a significant shift in how they think about and approach the work of fund development. What's especially needed are indicators that can help standardize this concept, give organizations a sense of whether they have this kind of culture (or are moving in that direction), and support the field to evaluate whether it's really necessary for successful resource acquisition.

[…]

A rapidly evolving digital landscape is transforming the ways we communicate, work, socialize, and, yes, fundraise. These changes, says Gene Tempel, former fundraiser and president emeritus of Indiana University's Lilly Family School of Philanthropy, are forcing nonprofits to question the traditional wisdom about resource development that may no longer be as applicable to ensuring long-term sustainability. Among the changes that are driving the interest in new models – and a new mindset – for fund development are:

DOI: 10.4324/9781003145936-104

Rise in people power. Today, interactivity, transparency, crowdsourcing, collaboration, and cocreation are giving people access to systems and institutions that were once controlled by experts and other gatekeepers. In the social sector, people are using everything from email and text messaging to YouTube and Snapchat to connect, communicate, and engage in collective action and collaboration in ways that were previously unimaginable. These changes are also transforming philanthropy. In addition to crowdfunding and other online giving platforms that are making it easy for "everyone to be a philanthropist," there is a growing push to democratize traditional philanthropic institutions. Foundations are experimenting with encouraging beneficiary feedback and grantseeker participation in identifying priorities, creating guidelines and making funding decisions. Given the intense competition for financial resources, organizations have to be ready to capitalize on these and other ways people – not just donors – are getting involved in social sector issues and activities. That requires understanding there's no longer a bright line between individual donors and non-donors such as volunteers and activists.

Organizations are changing. The speed and multiple venues through which change now occurs have prompted organizations to adapt structurally. This includes moving from hierarchical systems and rigid department and job assignments (managerial models) to streamlined structures that allow for collaboration, openness, and horizontal decision-making (ecosystem thinking). Some are forgoing physical structures altogether and morphing into virtual entities or networks that can be more cost efficient and nimble. Organizations that continue to operate in traditional, tightly controlled, top-down environments, rather than adapt to more fluid systems and approaches, risk having their relevance and funding dry up.

New generations. Social change work is being reshaped by the attitudes and capacities of young people who've grown up with the Internet and embrace its efficiency, transparency, bottom-up action, and co-creation ethos. Young people are challenging conventional notions of hierarchical leadership, preferring collaboration and horizontal arrangements in which "everyone's a leader." They are also less interested in joining traditional issue-focused membership organizations because they view them as bureaucratic and static. Some argue that millennials, in particular, may be less enamored with larger social movements and more likely to get involved in specific issues, causes or events. As a consequence, some nonprofits are struggling to recruit and sustain a membership base to replenish one that is aging.

Personalized and meaningful communication. Traditionally, organizations crafted and broadcast messages to "educate people." Today, that top-down approach has been upended, with message content being co-created with constituents and the public. This is positioning organizations as distributors of this content rather than gatekeepers of what gets communicated. As a result, organizations have to change the way they engage with their constituents – by seeing them as active partners, rather than just foot soldiers or check writers. It also means that organizations need to spend more time spreading their fundraising and messaging efforts across more outlets, e.g., Facebook, Twitter, magazines, telemarketing, radio, TV, YouTube, etc. Because these and other platforms allow for more input and feedback from the public, organizations have to accept that they won't be able to control their message or brand as much as they used to. Young people especially want more personalized contact with organizations. Nonprofits have to find meaningful ways to involve and "allow young people to co-create experiences with you," says Kari Saratovsky, chief engagement officer of Third Plateau Social Impact Strategies, "because if you don't, they're likely to walk away."

Fierce competition for resources. The growing number of nonprofits has triggered more competition for resources, and the resources that are available are being outstripped by demand. The panoply of new media tools and technologies is increasing the competition for "mind-share," which is leading to "cause fatigue" among people who are overwhelmed by the sheer volume of information and requests they get from organizations.

These trends no doubt contribute to the downward slide in donor retention rates across the sector. According to data generated by Network for Good, at the average U.S. nonprofit, the percentage of first timers who come back to give again the next year is just 27%. That matters, given research showing that retaining and motivating existing donors costs less than acquiring new ones. A recent study from the Association of Fundraising Professionals and the Center on Nonprofits and Philanthropy at the Urban Institute found that for most nonprofits, reducing donor and dollar losses is the least expensive strategy for increasing net funding gains, especially for nonprofits that are sustaining losses or achieving only modest net gains in gifts. Retaining donors, therefore, will be critical if nonprofits, especially smaller and mid-sized organizations, are to survive and thrive.

While there are subtle differences in how people define, practice and assess a culture of philanthropy, the research for this paper turned up four core components.

[...]

1. Shared responsibility for development

In organizations with a culture of philanthropy, fundraising isn't just one person's job or the job of one department or board committee. Everyone—staff, executive director, constituents, board and volunteers—shares responsibility for fund development.

[...]

2. Integration and alignment with mission

In organizations with a culture of philanthropy, fund development is a valued and mission-aligned component of the organization's overall work, rather than a standalone function.

[…]

3. A focus on fundraising as engagement

In organizations with a culture of philanthropy, fund development is no longer separated from engagement. This reflects the fact that people today are connecting with nonprofits via multiple channels (e.g., social media, volunteering, blogs, meet ups, petitions) and engaging with them in multiple ways (e.g., as donors, volunteers, board members, constituents).

[…]

4. Strong donor relationships

In organizations with a culture of philanthropy, donors are seen as authentic partners in the work, not simply as targets or dollar signs. These organizations establish systems to build strong relationships and support donors' connection to the work.

[…]

Table 6.1.1 Fundraising culture versus philanthropy culture

In A Fundraising Culture …	*In A Culture of Philanthropy …*
Philanthropy = grants by institutions or gifts from wealthy individuals.	Philanthropy = love of mankind.
Development staff is responsible for revenue generation.	Everyone in the organization shares some responsibility for revenue generation by serving as ambassadors and building relationships with potential donors and constituents.
It's all about the money.	It's all about the relationships.
Donors = money.	Donors = skills, talents, time and money.
Donors are contacted only when money is needed.	Donors are contacted regularly with invitations to participate in activities, progress updates, and information about how their contributions are helping.
Fundraising and engagement are siloed and have different contact lists.	There is one list for every person who's affiliated with the organization in some way (e.g., volunteering, donating, organizing, etc.).
Fundraising is seen as a one-off or add-on.	Fundraising is incorporated into and across every staff position and activity in the organization.

Table 6.1.1 Cont.

In A Fundraising Culture …	In A Culture of Philanthropy …
Culture is seen as "touchy feely."	Culture is the most important factor in determining an organization's effectiveness.
The board relegates fundraising to the development committee.	The board development committee directs the participation of the entire board in fundraising.
It's about acquiring donors.	It's about keeping donors.
Mission, program goals and operations are separate from revenue generation.	Mission, program goals and operations are aligned with revenue generation.
The focus is on short-term tactics like appeals and events.	The focus is on the longer-term strategy behind the tactics.
The organization functions with a scarcity mindset.	The organization functions with a mindset of abundance.
The organization's leaders make decisions based on what's available.	The organization's leaders make decision based on what the community needs and a shared vision of how to meet that need.
The community isn't engaged.	The community is intentionally engaged and participates as a partner with the organization.
Development staff/directors are relegated to secondary status.	Development staff/directors are part of the leadership team and equal partners with other senior staff; they participate in all planning, strategy, financial and organizational meetings.
Development goals aren't part of everyone's job description.	Development goals are part of everyone's job description.
Board and staff have sporadic contact.	Board and staff have regular opportunities to engage and interact.
The focus is on big gifts.	All gifts are important.
Donations come first.	Donations come after we engage people in our work.
We will win over every donor for our organization.	We will listen and refer donors to other organizations that align more closely with their aspirations.
Money is dirty.	Money is what we need to do our work.
There are rigid lines between organizations' departments, including development.	Job responsibilities and departments are more fluid; more collaboration to meet goals.

[…]

Some guiding questions for organizations seeking to start down the road to building a culture of philanthropy, here are some questions to help guide the process:

- **Do we have staff leadership that believes in a culture of philanthropy?** Monona Yin, a program consultant who leads the Capacity

Building Initiative at the Four Freedoms Fund, has observed that the most important factor in ensuring success in building a culture of philanthropy is having "some kind of leader or person with power in the organization who 'gets it.' You can't just train people in this stuff; you have to make sure they have ongoing support. It's a leadership issue." It's especially important that the executive director is committed to this process because it's impossible to build a strong culture without the executive leading it. According to UnderDeveloped, the director has to be "an instigator, a champion, and a role model to bring fundraising into the heart of the organization and keep it there." Gail Perry agrees: "If it doesn't come from the top, it may not be successful."

- **How can we get the board to become champions of a culture of philanthropy?** Boards need to take responsibility for leading and modeling a culture of philanthropy in the organizations they govern. As Terry Axelrod notes, "You can have great development staff but if the board doesn't care about developing this kind of philanthropic culture, it will become staff-driven and, ultimately, not be as successful." Ask board members what their philanthropic story is. Carve out part of every board meeting to talk about fundraising. Bring in people to help train board members in all aspects of development. Give board members the opportunity to interact with program staff and clients.

- **Beyond our board and staff leaders, do we have other champions in our organization who can model and monitor our progress in developing a culture of philanthropy?** Who are the influential people in the organization who are eager to move a culture of philanthropy— including staff, volunteers and donors? They can help bring others along because "people will start believing in it when they actually see the new behavior at work and working."

- **Is our mission clear and easy to communicate?** While it's good to have a clear mission that reflects shared values, it's just as important that everyone in the organization can communicate it compellingly to potential donors and others involved in your work.

- **Does everyone in the organization understand philanthropy's role in advancing the organization's mission and values and have opportunities to participate in development activities?** Staff need to be able to see how fundraising "fits" with the organization and how fundraising is essential and noble work. The more staff understand that development enables the organization to sustain and strengthen its service of others, the more cooperation and ownership will result. It also helps to provide staff and volunteers with a limited number of clear and simple things each can do to help the development staff take the organization in this new direction. The more hands-on experience people have with these activities, the more they will see how important their participation is in helping the organization get the resources it needs.

- **Do we have a vision of what the organization would look like with a culture of philanthropy that everyone can get behind?** Because change is personal, the change vision has to address people's natural desire to see what's in it for them and how it will enhance the organization's work. Use the mission and vision to remind people of where the organization is headed in its path toward a culture of philanthropy when interest or commitment seem to be lagging. Explore how everyone in the organization, together, would describe the current culture and its personality and how it feels to work there, as well as how it affects people's enthusiasm, commitment, behaviors and interactions. How would people describe a culture that motivates its employees and volunteers, stimulates creativity and respect, and generates enthusiasm and collegiality?

- **How would we nurture and sustain this culture over time?** Culture transformation takes a long time so it's important that organizations designate and assess their progress at regular intervals. What kind of process would help your organization evaluate its organizational culture, define desired changes and make those changes? One core indicator, for example, is that fundraising efforts are donor-centric and focused on building deep relationships over time, not just asking for money when it's needed. How could this be operationalized in your organization?

- **Can we develop policies, procedures and measurable goals for making the plan concrete?** Codifying things in writing conveys that the organization is serious and intentional about changing and provides a more formal blueprint for staff and the board. Put philanthropy on the institutional dashboard and include it in performance measures. Make it a stated part of the values statement. Reward and celebrate progress. And establish clear and measurable goals. For example, if none of the senior program staff give, a goal might be to achieve 100 percent giving by a specific date. Next, create the strategies and tactics you'll use to achieve those goals ... Invite everyone—staff, donors, board, volunteers—to participate in this process and make it the focus of a regularly scheduled meeting.

[...]

The four components of a culture of philanthropy identified in this paper may not sound revolutionary or controversial to some people; indeed, there are many who have been calling for these kinds of changes for years. But taken as a whole, these ideas represent a huge shift in how people are thinking about the work of fund development for nonprofits.

These ideas also can serve as a call to action: At a time when organizations often focus on finding quick fixes or a miracle-working development director to finally turn things around, it may be time to step back and reconsider the core principles and assumptions that drive their fundraising efforts. And, it may be time for the field to dig deeper into the questions of what a culture of philanthropy looks like, how it can help nonprofits achieve sustainable fundraising success, and how to support organizations to make it a reality.

We must invest in fundraising to make it inclusive

Armando E. Zumaya, 2021

I have worked in fundraising for more than three decades so I've heard many views on philanthropy over the years.

Today there is much discussion of racial justice and decolonizing philanthropy. When we talk about this critical need, we should stop and listen carefully. A few chronic misperceptions continue, and some tough things need to be said.

First, foundations only represent a small segment of philanthropy. Many grant makers, nonprofit leaders, and fundraisers seem to assign an outsize amount of clout to foundations. Foundations account for just 18 percent of money going to charity. Individuals account for 70 percent.

So when we talk about making philanthropy more inclusive, if we're only focused on foundations, we've overlooked most charitable giving. To decolonize philanthropy, we must acknowledge the following realities and do something few foundations or big donors ever do: invest in fundraising.

Fundraising produces philanthropy. This bears repeating. The way people talk today implies that philanthropy – even when it's community-centered – comes from well-meaning rich people who just seem to get it in their minds to give, and giant checks magically appear. Sure, that happens sometimes, but most contributions result from the hard work of development officers. If you'd like to understand philanthropy, ask your development officers.

To decolonize philanthropy, we need to create diversity in fundraising. That means that we raise money from the whole community: all colors, all sexual orientation, all religions, all genders, and, yes, all incomes. Right now, raising money is designed to approach and engage old, straight white men – especially in major-gift fundraising. This is true for a range of reasons: racism, implicit bias, and the reality that most nonprofit CEOs and boards are 90 percent white. A diverse fundraising team can begin to change this by reaching out to new and different people in new and different ways. Often the problem is simply missed so no one acts to fix it even though doing so just makes good fiscal sense.

Giving and fundraising are empowering. We must share that power more broadly. That means we should define the Latina single mom giving $25 a month to her local women's shelter as a philanthropist and a priority. Nonprofits give her a means to empower herself. If we are running a children's health organization in Atlanta, for example, then we should have African American

DOI: 10.4324/9781003145936-105

major donors, not just old white people, and the number of women donors should reflect the community.

Often white leaders see working people of color as victims. Real philanthropy means we have given everyone the opportunity to improve their communities and the world. Giving is power. And too often we intentionally give that power only to the rich and white.

Unlocking my authentic voice

Niambi Martin-John, 2021

Whatever we believe about ourselves and our ability comes true for us. – Susan L Taylor

Everyone has a story. The sharing and retelling of those stories, and snippets of our life experiences, is what enables us to relate to others and binds us together as human beings. When we tell our stories, I believe that the shape of our recollections is influenced by the audience with whom we are sharing. Often, we make accommodations for the listener so that we can manage their perceptions of whom we want to be in their eyes. At times, those reconstructions can be beneficial to propel us to find more depth within ourselves – to find a type of freedom. But there are times when we are forced to edit our stories, and by extension ourselves, to make space for the fragility of others, to free others from ancestral guilt, or to imbue a full sense of allyship that hasn't really been earned.

Throughout our lives, we may straddle that place between wanting to tell our stories in our authentic voices and restricting our voices to navigate more easily through the complexities of a society, much of which is unready and often unwilling to hear us. However, I believe the potency of our stories dies a little each time we tell an apocryphal version of our reality. Owning the voice in which we tell our stories and discovering the freedom to do so forcefully and fearlessly, propels us forward unimpeded and empowered – giving rise to greater self-awareness, stronger resolve and increased clarity that, once activated, only serves to generate more stories of activism, change and courage.

In our personal lives, finding the resolve to separate or weed out relationships that require us to 'edit' ourselves can seem less daunting. But in professional settings, we carry a burden of compliance that often compels us to present our stories in the most inauthentic ways.

For years, as I struggled to build a career in fundraising, I felt compelled to compartmentalize my experiences, taking into the workplace only those things that would not threaten, challenge or upset the status quo. This meant that I worked overtime to fit a mold, one that I did not create, contribute to, or identify with. I had to conform in order to be accepted, seen and validated. What occurred to me as I did this complex dance is that my white peers felt no such obligation. They moved in the workplace with an ease, something I interpreted as an air of arrogance and fearlessness that I would never dare to take on. Over the years, as I shared this observation with Black peers, many confirmed what I now call the 'white exemption clause'.

DOI: 10.4324/9781003145936-106

You see, the historical socialization of my white peers in the North American context affords them great power and privileges, including an affirmation that all spaces were created for them. They have permission to not only take up space but to make space for themselves in a way that I simply never could. This type of grooming nurtures and feeds the feeling of superiority and ownership of the process and structure that builds up systemic barriers against Black people. Repeatedly throughout my journey, this issue has emerged.

[...]

Most organizations in the social sector are devoted to improving the lives of people, whether by creating access, funding cures and interventions for diseases or addressing the needs of under-served communities. The result is an assumption that most employees' personal values align with the organisation's mission. The ugly truth, however, is that for most people of colour, the sector is not a safe place. The challenges that we face at the hands of our white peers directly contradicts the image the sector would like to uphold.

To persevere despite the obstacles placed in my way was not easy. And I couldn't do it alone. I knew that to change the trajectory of my career, I needed help from people who would help amplify my voice and open doors. Starting the process of building my support system required deep introspection, a suspension of my ego and careful evaluation about how sponsorship could help me in the work environment. I proceeded to build my network with leaders who saw the value of my work and understood the vision and passion that I offered.

This included gathering a network of white leaders who were willing to, even temporarily, suspend judgement and honestly see the value of my contributions and invest their time in petitioning others to make space for me. In many instances, I couldn't navigate new opportunities without these sponsors because the system is structured so that the validity of my experience and my broad acceptance would never gain traction unless marketed by white people to white people.

As a Black person these relationships can be extremely frustrating because the system is set up to reinforce the white saviour complex. If white people have to repeatedly tell your story you begin to lose ownership of that story. Even though sponsorship suggests that someone is supporting you with no expectation of personal reward in return, it has been my experience that some of the people who helped me progress in my career required my deep gratitude for the favour they did for me. I know with certainty that many times those same people knew my skills and abilities would further their personal and professional agenda. It was in these instances when the return 'favours' would be expected.

There were times when the idea of me in a senior position seemed hard for some to accept, with one co-worker asking me on the eve of a promotion, *"Do you think you are being promoted just so that the organization can have a Black person in a senior role?"*

A real and crippling result of being a Black person on a senior leadership team is that we are often given a nice tidy box along with our promotions.

As long as we stay inside that package of assigned and ascribed behaviours and expectations — saying yes, turning a blind eye to discriminatory behaviour, ignoring inflammatory comments, smiling when someone says or does something that is covertly and even overtly racist so that we can all pretend to be comfortably getting along – all remains well.

However, deciding to imprint your story and build your legacy outside the lines of your portfolio and therefore outside your assigned box can have dire consequences. Like many before me, I have been fired, laid off, demoted, and blackballed for speaking truth, standing up and demanding better. No one will actually tell you why the budget for your role suddenly dried up, or why the restructuring doesn't include you even if they had gone through great pains to let you know how much you were respected and valued in the past. You have to know ahead of time that the consequence of standing up often does not lead to victory in the way that you anticipate – a promotion or being seen as a champion. No, it may very well be the end of the road in an organization, group or association.

But there is freedom in raising your voice.

I have reached that point in my career where I am willing to face the consequences, and I think you will find that many Black people with any measure of success in the sector, had to reach the point where being let go or being the outsider was something they were willing to accept in return for owning their story.

One of my most recent encounters was with a senior leader in my organization. He called me into his office for a chat. He wanted to let me know what an integral part of the organization I was. How my contributions were exceptional, and how much I had taught him about fundraising. He told me that he respected me and that I was one of the smartest people he knew. And then the other shoe dropped, *"However, I am going to need you to tone down your 'smarts'"* he said. *"It makes it difficult for me to keep everyone happy if you are intimidating your peers by knowing and sharing ideas about how they should do their jobs. Could you just not share so much of what you know?"*

Unlike the first time I had experienced this type of deliberate and calculated silencing of my voice, I now had a well-stocked toolkit to help me navigate the conversation. I had become accustomed to being told how excellent my work was only to be treated in the opposite way by my superiors. I was used to being drained of my intellectual power to ensure that others above me looked great while receiving no credit for my contributions.

This time, however, something in me decided this was not going to happen again. What the senior leader was describing as my intimidation of my peers for being "too smart" was, in fact, me creating and taking space for myself. I challenged him to clarify his words by asking if he was requesting that I dumb myself down so that others could feel better about themselves, and less insecure about their lack of knowledge. I then asked him further whether I would have been checked like this if I were a white man or woman?

All around this organization, white men were being celebrated, climbing the professional ladder at alarming rates, while I am told to dumb down my knowledge! It was Shirley Chisholm who said, *"If they don't give you a seat at the table, bring a folding chair."* So here I was, folding chair in hand, taking a seat at a table to which I was reluctantly being accommodated.

I can tell you that no matter how deliberate the actions of your oppressor, they are *never* prepared for you to fight back. They are accustomed to going unchallenged and getting away with bad behaviour. When I challenged this obviously sexist and racist feedback, he immediately backtracked, reminding me that he had complimented me several times during the conversation. He told me how valuable I was to him and to the organization.

It is such a mind trick when this dynamic exists between you and someone who has the power to take your job from you. Do you appease them by pretending to have misunderstood what their real intent was? Or do you stand your ground and force them to admit that they acted poorly?

These are the choices that we must make on a daily basis. Every day, we must decide whether we will be true to ourselves or toe the line so that we can keep our jobs or a work environment peaceful. In my case, I chose to challenge the behaviour when it happened, whether directed at me or others, until it became clear that I was not allowing any incidents of racism, bullying, denigrating speech or actions.

[...]

Working in this sector, I am used to being the only person of colour in a room. In the last few years, however, I have seen more Black people enter the sector, and with that, key leaders and professional associations have started to take note. But there seems to be a decided fear among those in positions of power that we may mobilize.

In one organization I worked, any gathering of Black women caused raised eyebrows – what are you guys plotting? Us Black women would jokingly refer to our social connections as the *"where two or more are gathered"* group because of the strong perception of us gathering in any capacity, meant that we must be planning a revolt. But of course, our white peers were free to gather in large groups, whenever they wanted and as they pleased without comment. In defiance of this, we chose to define ourselves as mentors, friends and empowering partners while also being agitators and change agents choosing to take back the power and characterize ourselves on our own terms.

Black people are indeed gathering and creating networks of support. The fear that such a coming together will upset the imbalance of things and actually challenge the sector to see Black people as competent, capable and worthy of leadership and power is palpable.

As more of us step forward to help shape the sector, some are transitioning out of it, exhausted from the work of either constantly proving yourself to retain roles, or being excluded from roles that we are more than qualified to have. This exodus, though, is cause to build a foundation of support, particularly for Black women who are creating a safe space reinforced by the commonalities of our collective stories.

I had to learn that no one could free me from the cycle of checking myself at the door when I went to work, softening my accent, adjusting my tone, suppressing my creativity, suffocating my Blackness – I had to find my power and stand resolute ready to face whatever came with claiming freedom of self. So I implemented a few rules that helped me to rid myself of the weight of conformity.

First, I gave myself the permission to say "*no*."

If I don't feel comfortable doing something, or if I'm feeling maxed out, I say no. I also learned to determine when my "no" requires me to give an explanation, and when my "no" is simply enough. Someone once asked me to convey a message to an internal stakeholder in a way that I felt was unnecessarily aggressive and did not preserve the dignity of that person. I declined to do so. If this was the only way the message could be conveyed, then I knew I was the wrong person for the job.

Second, I learned to take credit for my work and my contributions and to be loud about it. I found that if I didn't speak up to discuss what I had done, or even the things that I aspired to do, as a Black woman, I would be left in a supportive role. I would be left watching someone else execute the ideas that I cultivated, simply because they knew that they could claim space that I was too timid to take for myself.

I also learned to ask for what I think I am worth instead of what others think I'm worth. As Black people, undervaluing ourselves is something that we have inherited from previous generations. Our ancestors had no choice but to labour in oppressive conditions that offered no reward. And even today, Black people continue to be underpaid, undervalued and economically disadvantaged. This holds true in acute ways in the nonprofit sector. If I want to be compensated in a way that is equitable, I must first ensure that I know what this means and be bold enough to demand it.

At various points along my journey to finding my voice, I was crippled by the fear of the unknown. But fear is the enemy of freedom. One has to be brave to break the chains of fear and grasp freedom for themselves. It is not something that anyone else can do for you. To obtain freedom you must act decisively and courageously, and then use your voice to empower, motivate and safeguard the path that will make freedom more attainable for the next generation. We simply cannot rest. There is much work to be done.

Answers on grant proposals if nonprofits were brutally honest with funders

Vu Le, 2018

A problem that is pervasive in nonprofits is the imbalance of power between funders and nonprofits, which leads to a lot of no-good, very bad things such as the lack of honest communication and feedback between funders and nonprofits.

One area where this shows up is on grant applications. It's not that we nonprofits lie when writing proposals, it's just that … we've been trained to tell funders exactly what we think y'all want to hear, sugarcoating everything in jargon and BS.

A while ago, a colleague imagined what our answers would be like on grant proposals if we nonprofits were allowed to be completely and brutally honest. Here are some of these honest responses, with credit to colleagues across the field, most of whom understandably prefer to remain anonymous; anything in quotes is someone else's direct words. Apologies in advance for the sarcastic, possibly biting tone; the entire sector has been on edge lately:

1. **What is innovative about your program design?** "Our program is entirely innovative. The design is unproven; the approach is untested; the outcomes are unknown. We also have a tried-and-true service delivery model with outstanding results and a solid evidence base to support it. But you funded that last year and your priority is to fund innovative projects. So we made this one up. Please send money."
2. **What is your overhead rate?** "It is too low. We systematically under-invest in human resources, financial management, and program management to keep it that way. By doing so, we have a nice, low overhead number to put on grant applications like this one. Please send money."
3. **How will you sustain this program after this grant runs out?** We will leave you alone and harass other people, continuing to spend half our time trying to convince other foundations that our programs and communities are worth being supported, instead of running and improving the programs that our communities desperately need. Then, after a year or so, when hopefully you forgot that we applied earlier, we'll reapply to your foundation. Please send money.

DOI: 10.4324/9781003145936-107

4. **How does your organization partner with other organizations in the area?** We have an unwritten agreement to sign desperate, last-minute letters of support for one another for grant proposals like this one. Once a while, we go out drinking together, especially when we don't get grants like this one. Please send money.

5. **How will you use the funds if you receive this grant?** We honestly really need this grant to pay for rent and utilities and for wages so our staff can do important work and feed their families, but since you won't allow your funds to be used for those things, we will say that your grant is paying for whatever you will actually fund, then get other funders or donors to give and then tell them that their money is paying for the stuff that they want to fund. We will ultimately waste hundreds of hours every year trying to figure out who is paying for what, hours that could be used to deliver services. Please send unrestricted money.

6. **What is the leadership structure at your organization?** Because of understaffing, our ED is trying to handle too many things all at once and is thus not very competent at any of them. Our board actively undermines or micromanages the staff. The person who is actually holding this whole thing together is our Operations Director Lydia, but she's being laid off because no one wants to fund operations or admin or fundraising. Please send money so we can buy Lydia a cake.

7. **How will your organization align with [so-and-so latest innovative systems-change effort]?** We won't, because we are doing different stuff and because we barely get enough funding to survive, much less actually attend the billions of meetings and do all the work involved in aligning with this effort that has been sucking up all the funding in the region. Please send additional money so we can align or stop asking us to align.

8. **What are other sources of potential funding for this project?** Here below are a bunch of other foundations we are applying to. We are not very confident in many of them, but we figure that the more names we list, the better it makes us look. Some of the foundations won't invest until other foundations make a first move. Please be the one to stop this game of "funding-chicken" by sending money first.

9. **If you receive a partial grant, will you still implement this program?** Likely we will, because the needs are so high, but it will not be the awesome program we envisioned, since we'll have to cut program components, not hire the staff we need, and not be able to serve as many people as we want. But if that's the only choice, we'll reluctantly take it. Then, on some nights, we'll stay awake, staring at the ceiling, crying a single tear that streaks down our worn faces, lit by the moonlight, imagining what could have been. Please send money.

10. **How will you evaluate this program?** Because we have little funding for a formal process with an external evaluator, we will have Edward, our social work practicum student, design a self-report survey. At the beginning and end of the program, we'll administer the survey. We'll put in

lots of numbers and percentages to make it look impressive. This is not very rigorous or valid, due to selection bias, self-report bias, confounding variables, and a host of other issues, but it should be enough to convince you that we have good evaluation data. Please send money so we can buy Edward a cake.

11. **How will the community be transformed as a result of this grant?** Hahahaha, that's a good one! This grant is for $5,000! And people say funders don't have a sense of humor! 5K will allow us to pay for six weeks of rent, which means we can stay open, and who knows what awesome stuff we'll accomplish during those six weeks, am I right? Please add three zeroes if you really want to see transformation.

12. **Besides sending money, what else can the foundation do to support you?:** Please introduce us to other foundations so they can also send money.

Only by being truthful with one another can we hope to better the world.

6.2 Donor-centric or community-centric fundraising?

The donor is the hero of the story

Russell N. James III, 2022

You make the perfect fundraising ask. It works! The donor makes a gift to your charity. Congratulations!

But was the gift a good idea? Four out five new donors say, "No." Data from thousands of charities show new donor retention of 20%. They make a gift. But they don't repeat their mistake. Even a year later, they haven't done it again. The story "worked" to get a gift. But something was missing. It didn't work again.

This causes money problems. A study of more than 10,000 charities found a seriously "leaky bucket." Increased giving from active donors and new gifts from others created gains of $5 billion. Hooray! But wait. Other donors stopped or reduced their giving creating losses of more than $4.6 billion. The researchers explained, "every $100 gained ... was offset by $93 in losses through gift attrition."

Why is this happening? One study explored this question. It interviewed lapsed donors. Why had they stopped giving? The top reasons related to the charity were about impact and gratitude.

It wasn't just that these were weak. It's that they often didn't exist at all. Ex-donors commonly explained, the charity, "Did not inform me how my money had been used." Many said the charity, "Did not acknowledge my support."

We have a story problem

Imagine a story in an interesting setting. The main character has a relatable backstory. A crisis or opportunity builds the tension. Finally, he faces a stark choice: Stay in his original, self-focused world, or go on a demanding adventure to make an impact in the larger world. After some delay, he finally commits. He looks, steely-eyed, at his wise guiding sage and says, "Let's do this!" And then the credits roll. Or the novel ends.

Wait. What? No, no, no! That's not right. That story is awful! I mean, is it even a story? Where's the journey? Where's the climax and victory? Where's the resolution? That was terrible! Would you buy another book from that author? Would you watch another movie by that director? Probably not.

Of course, that's a terrible way to tell a story. Yet, this is often how *actual* fundraising is executed. The storytelling ends at the donation decision. There's

DOI: 10.4324/9781003145936-109

no climax delivering the promised victory. There's no resolution confirming the donor's enhanced identity.

The wrong story

Charities aren't finishing the story. Why not? Often, it's because they weren't *trying* to tell a donor story in the first place. Instead, they were telling the story that *they* wanted to hear. It's a story about them. It's *not* a donation story. It's *not* a donor story. It's a charity *insider* story.

In that story, the charity insiders are the main characters. They're the heroes. The donor is just a bit player. He makes a quick cameo appearance. He is there to honor the heroic administrators. He lays money at their feet (because they're so heroic). Then he disappears.

That story isn't about the donor. It's not about the donor's gift. It's not about the donor's impact. It's about the charity insiders. It's about the administrators. It's about their heroic journey.

This story easily ignores donor retention. Donors are supposed to come back automatically. In this story, donors are there to honor the charity insiders' heroism. So long as charity insiders keep being their heroic selves – and keep reminding donors of this – giving should continue.

Retention, this story suggests, should be easy. It should be automatic. Fundraisers should instead focus elsewhere. They should focus on spreading the charity insiders' fame. They should focus on telling the charity insiders' story to *new* people. They should focus on *new* donors.

The wrong story in metrics

This story bias affects real-world management. One study looked at fundraising accounting metrics. It reviewed their use at hundreds of charities. Out of eleven metrics, which one was most frequently reported to top management? The number of *new* donors recruited.

Some charities tracked costs for both new-donor acquisition and current-donor retention. Even for these charities, internal reporting was different. New-donor acquisition cost was twice as likely to be reported to top management.

What about improving donor commitment and satisfaction? Most fundraisers felt these weren't even "slightly important" to top management.

In math, a dollar is a dollar, whether from new or old donors. But in story, things are different. Top management lives the charity insider hero story. But that story doesn't match with donor retention efforts. In that story, delivering a donor experience *worth* the gift doesn't even make sense. Donors exist to deliver value to the charity insiders, not the other way around.

The right story

For sustainable fundraising, the right story is different. It's the donor's story. The donor's story progresses through:

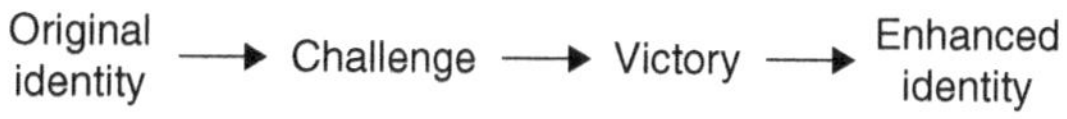

Original
identity ——→ Challenge ——→ Victory ——→ Enhanced
identity

Figure 6.2.1 Original to enhanced identity

- Backstory and setting (*donor's original identity*)
- The inciting incident (*donor's challenge*)
- Climax and resolution (*donor's victory and enhanced identity*).

In the donor's story, the challenge step is the ask. But the effective ask incorporates the full story cycle.

- The ask connects to the donor's original identity (people, values, and history).
- The ask promises a victory.
- The victory promises an enhanced identity. It's personally meaningful. It matches the donor's people, values, and history.

This makes for a great ask. It works. The ask promises a victory. It promises an enhanced identity. But it doesn't deliver them. It doesn't finish the story. A great ask works. But without the rest of the story, it only works once.

Plot means change

A story with no plot fails. A popular guide to screenwriting explains it this way. Films where a character's life at the end is the same as the beginning, "do not tell story." Such films are called "non-plot." They're "non-plot" because they have no change. Instead, "story dissolves into portraiture." There is no story because story requires change.

For a donor, the question is simple: "I made a gift. What changed?" In the donor's story, the victory is the donor's impact. It's the impact of the donor's gift. Charity managers often misunderstand this. To them, a specific donor's impact is vague. It's uncertain. It's also beside the point. Donors are supposed to give because of the *charity's* impact. But here's the problem. If nothing changed *because of* the donor's gift, there's no donation story. There's no donor story. There's no story reason to ever make another gift.

The secret to donor retention: finish the story

Delivering a powerful ask is great. But it's not the same as delivering value to the donor. Delivering value is about what happens *after* the donor says, "Yes." Why don't new donors give again? It's simple. The donor's experience wasn't worth the gift. It failed to deliver value.

The charity didn't finish the donor's story. The donor's story never had a climax. The donor never won a victory. The donor's story never had a resolution. No one ever confirmed the importance of the donor's victory. No one ever recognized the donor's enhanced identity. That's bad story. Few donors will want to repeat that story experience again.

Retention means getting *the next* gift. What's the best way to start that process? Deliver a compelling donor experience for *this* gift. That means finishing the story. It means delivering victory. It means showing the impact from the donor's gift.

Penelope Burk defines the word "Oversolicitation" as "Being asked to give again before they knew their first gift had an impact.

Tom Ahern and Simone Joyaux write, "Donors have one overwhelming interest regarding the charities they support: What did you do with my money? Did I make the world a better place by giving you a gift?"

Finish the story: experimental evidence

The best cultivation for the next gift starts with this one. It starts by delivering a victory. One experiment decided to test this. It tested three appeals to previous donors. One appeal just explained what the requested gift would be used for. A second one also mentioned their past donation. The third instead mentioned how the past donation had been used. The results? The researchers explained, "Providing information on past donation use increases the probability of re-donation compared to both other appeal types."

Why? They explained, "[Reporting] past donation use increases the perceived donation impact, then induces warm glow which translates into a higher intention to donate in future." Reporting past gift usage works. It confirms the donor's victory. It shows a finished story. This induces a "warm glow." It delivers a good experience. Delivering a good experience leads to the next gift. Getting the next gift starts by finishing the last story.

The secret to major gift success: finish the story

Major donors are, of course, critical to fundraising success. Across all charities, the top 13% of donors generate 88% of the money. So, where do we get those magical big donors? The easiest way is simple. Stop *losing* them.

On average, charities lose 4 out of 5 new donors. Improving that only slightly could easily double retention. But how do we know which of these new donors to focus on? How can we tell which ones might be tomorrow's major donors? Sophisticated wealth screening can be great. But for 70% of these top donors (the top 13% generating 88% of the money), the answer is easier. Their *first* gift was $1,000 or more.

Such gifts are our big audition. Can we deliver a donor experience *worth* that initial gift? This first gift is the critical one. After the second gift, retention nearly triples. Passing this initial audition can massively increase our major donors.

Delivering value leads to retention. But it does more. Retention leads to referrals. One secret to *new* major donors is happy *current* major donors.

Charity managers love to dream about the magical new big donor. They think, "One day we'll get that $X million gift." That's fun. But they rarely think, "One day, we'll deliver a donor experience worth that $X million gift." That's not as much fun. That's hard work.

Conclusion

Without a change, there is no plot. Making a gift that doesn't change anything isn't rewarding. It's not an experience donors are likely to repeat. Of course, once we've got the donor's money, we don't have to finish their story. We don't have to deliver their victory. But then we shouldn't expect the donor to return. If we want to keep the donor, we've got to finish their story.

How donor-centrism perpetuates inequity

Vu Le, 2017 [updated 2020]

I think we have a serious problem with the donor-centered approach. Namely that the pervasiveness of this model in our sector may be perpetuating the very inequity that we are seeking to address as a sector.

I believe in many of the tenets of donor-centrism – don't treat donors like ATMs, appreciate every gift of any amount, don't take donors for granted, build relationships, be transparent, etc. I just don't believe that donors should be in the center of nonprofit work, or even the center of fundraising work. Yes, the pervasive donor-centered concept is more nuanced than that, but the name itself, donor-centered, intentionally puts donor right in the middle. And many fundraisers have unconsciously or consciously taken this into account, insisting on treating donors as the most important element of our work. There is so much language now about treating donors like "heroes" or even "superheroes."

An argument can be made that the donor-centered model has been so prevalent in our sector because it works. There are lots of data showing that different donor-centered strategies work. But just because something works does not necessarily mean that it is intrinsically good. Think, for example, of fishing. Data may show that a certain bait works really well. If you use this bait, you will catch more fish, guaranteed. So everyone who can afford it starts using it. What happens then to the fish population, to the pond, to the ecosystem? Just because you can catch a bunch of fish, does that mean that you should?

Of course, that is a very simplistic analogy, and insulting to donors. But in many ways, fundraising in our sector has become like fishing. We treat donors like fish, and we try our best to find the strategies that work, that nets our organizations the most fish/dollars, without worrying about the consequences. But our sector is interconnected, a complex system of interrelated missions. This is a major difference between our sector and the for-profit sector. Cupcakes may have very little to do with shoes or software, but early learning definitely is related to youth development, housing with employment, education with food security, etc. Everything is interrelated in our sector, but we have behaved as if each mission is its own self-sufficient silo, a philosophy that has been reinforced by donor-centrism.

And because of that, a host of unintended problems are created, some of which may be actively preventing us from advancing an equitable society. At its worst, Donor-Centrism:

DOI: 10.4324/9781003145936-110

Perpetuates the Nonprofit Hunger Games: It seems Donor-centrism has resulted in many of us being in competition with one another, using the latest data, to see who can thank people fastest and in the most effective ways, who can tell the best most emotional impact stories, who can be most "accountable" in terms of "overhead" rates and stuff, etc. I've seen workshops like "25 Creative Ways to Thank Your Donors" and "How to Make Thank-You Videos that Stand Out." Has it reached a point now where the iconic handwritten thank-you note is no longer enough? Meanwhile, I attended a workshop where a presenter said, "Most importantly, make sure you have four stars on [charity watchdog site], because donors are comparing you to other nonprofits, and they won't be impressed if you don't have four stars." This is crap, for many reasons, some of which I'll be expanding on in future posts. All of this competition perpetuates the Nonprofit Hunger Games, where instead of working together to solve issues, we nonprofits are forced to fight with one another, resulting in all of us and our community losing.

While those are all serious problems, there are several even more serious issues that our sector and the fundraising field in particular has not really talked about. Without intending to, Donor-Centrism:

Proliferates the Savior Complex: The constant inflating of donors' egos through tactics like the usage of "you" in everything and narratives painting donors as protagonists and heroes saving the day may make them feel good and donate more, but is that what we really want in the long run? Do we really want to further this philosophy that donors are heroes and saviors, that they get nothing in return except appreciation and feel-goods? What is the cost to society when we reinforce the notion that some people are saviors and others are there to be saved, versus getting everyone to understand systemic inequity and their role within it, and how they themselves also benefit from creating a strong community that they live in?

Fuels systemic injustice: So much of our work is to address the challenges caused by wealth disparities, much of which is built on historic and current injustice. To constantly put donors in the center and appeal to their emotion and ego means there is less time and energy devoted to helping our donors understand and navigate the systemic injustice that they may be inadvertently contributing to. By fueling our donors' egos, we unconsciously tell them it's OK, that they don't have to think about the hard stuff, about privilege, about disparities, about racism in the education and criminal justice system contributing to the wealth gap that they may be benefiting from.

Perpetuates the othering of the people we serve: An insidious effect of the Savior complex is that people see other people as "others." "Others" exist in our minds in a binary state, either as enemies, or as those to be helped, never our equals. With this current political climate, we've been seeing a lot of people perceiving and treating fellow human beings as "others/enemies." But the "Others/People-to-be-helped" mindset is also destructive. Donor-centrism is like us standing by the shores of a lake telling donors "You helped us buy bread to feed these ducks. Because of you, 50 ducks didn't go hungry! You are a hero!" instead of getting donors to understand they too are ducks and that their lives and happiness are tied to all the other ducks and to the pond that they share. We cannot build a strong and just society if we reinforce in donors the unconscious perception of the people we help as merely objects of pity and charity to be saved.

Crowds out the voices of people served: As I mentioned in "The Infantilization of marginalized communities must stop" and other posts, there is an assumption that the people receiving services don't know what's good for them or what solutions would work. There is a dissonance in that those we consider "major" donors are often not the people who are experiencing the challenges we are trying to address, but donor-centrism gives them a level of credibility and belief that they hold the solutions. The more we reinforce donors' sense that they are experts when they are not, the more we diminish the voices of those who are most affected by injustice and who thus may have the best solutions to address it.

Further marginalizes already-marginalized communities: A significant number of organizations led by communities of color, LGBTQ communities, communities of disability, rural communities, etc., are small. They are unlikely going to have as robust a development department as larger organizations. But they do some of the most critical and urgent work, often with some of the smallest resources. The more we reinforce in donors' minds that they should be thanked immediately, that they should be communicated with based on their preferences – "I only want newsletters to be emailed to me in November, preferably on a Tuesday" – the more they, and we, see it as normal and expect it. There is no way many organizations led by marginalized communities can meet these expectations with the limited resources they have, which means that the donors may see these organisations as disorganized or incompetent. Larger, more resourced organizations, using principles of donor-centrism have trained donors to expect handwritten thank-you note followed up with phone calls within a day or two of donations. So when a small organization doesn't contact you until two weeks later, it's understandable if donors are not impressed. It doesn't matter that this small organization may not have any development staff, and that it has been using its limited time and funding to prevent people from getting deported or to have conversations with kids of color or people with disabilities about how to protect themselves from bullying and hate crimes in this terrifying political climate.

Reinforces money as the default measure of people's worth: Whether we intend to or not, we still value people who donate more money more. We define "Major Donors" as people who give a certain level, not according to their personal context but according to set thresholds. These donors get extra attention. It's understandable; we need to keep the lights on. But it does unconsciously perpetuate society's ingrained notion that people who have more money deserve special treatment. But what about the smaller gifts? What about the $10 from a student or a $5 from a colleague who is between employment? Are those not considered major gifts? Donor-centrism would say that we appreciate these smaller gifts just the same. But is that really true?

Minimizes other elements needed to do this work well: We know that our work cannot be effective without volunteers, staff, strong board members, funders, consultants, other nonprofits, etc. Placing donors in the center means everyone else must be on the peripheral. Take volunteers, for example. Many of us rely significantly on volunteers, especially around fundraising events. Why don't more organizations have volunteer coordinators? Why does it seem like an expectation for us to send handwritten notes to donors, but it's more a sweet afterthought if we remember to write notes for individual volunteers? The argument that donors don't benefit from donating (but volunteers do benefit from volunteering) is BS and another sign that we have failed to effectively communicate the impact of our work.

Furthers the idea of transactional charity: A tenet of Donor-Centrism, at least of some of the blog posts I've read, is the idea that we need to be accountable in reporting to donors exactly what their donation went to. "Your $1,000 helped 10 kids go to summer camp" or "your $50 bought 20 containers of hummus and five pounds of baby carrots for our preschoolers" or whatever. This is an illusion we tell donors, because the combination of hundreds of elements is needed to make programs successful. This reporting practice allows donors to feel a false sense of cause/effect and accountability, but at the cost of furthering their ignorance about nonprofit work, which is holistic and requires so much more than a single donor's contribution. This ignorance perpetuates the overhead myth and other barriers and harms us and our community in the long-run.

Prevents honest conversations and true partnerships: I've gotten into a couple of friendly arguments on Nonprofit Happy Hour and ED Happy Hour Facebook groups (which you should join, since they're filled with brilliant people) over giving feedback to donors who do or say ridiculous things. Some colleagues, with good reasons, believe we should be very careful about "educating," providing feedback, or outright pushing back when donors say or do things that harm our work or our community. The power dynamics between nonprofits and donors is not as strong as the dynamics between nonprofits and funders, but it is still there. And the more donor-centered people are, I've seen, the more likely they are to believe that it is not our "place" to have honest conversations with our donors. But I don't think we can make progress in many of the issues we're tackling if we cannot build true partnerships with donors, which includes pointing out, respectfully and at the appropriate time, when donors are in the wrong, and helping them shape their thinking and actions.

Short-changes our donors: I know, donor-retention rate is still pretty dismal in our sector. But I'm not sure it's because we're not donor-centered enough and that we need to double-down on it. It might be that donor-centrism might work in the short-run, but in the long run, fails to truly inspire our donors. Think about relationships. The best and happiest ones, the relationships that last, are never ones where one partner is put in the center and constantly heaped with attention and catered to. The best marriages have strong communication, a strong belief in the future, and shared values, but also

vigorous, challenging conversations and disagreements and occasional explosive but cathartic arguments.

Our sector has been talking a lot about equity, diversity, and inclusion. But
not so much in the context of fundraising. As a colleague of mine, James Hong
the ED of the Vietnamese Friendship Association, says,

> We rarely talk about race and equity in fundraising. We always talk about
> race and equity in the context of programs, services, advocacy, etc., …
> never fundraising. Right now, this donor-centered model of fundraising
> isn't designed to build power. It's designed to make money. And frankly,
> you can double the revenues of an organization, increase donations, staff,
> etc., and still fail horribly at your mission.

And this is the critical missing conversation within the work of fundraising
through individuals. With a few exceptions such as the awesome Grassroots
Institute for Fundraising Training (GIFT) and Social Justice Fund Northwest
(SJF), we lag behind in having these discussions, so strong is the drive to
increase revenues. The majority of the conversations I've been a part of around
equity, diversity, and inclusion still focus on how to get people to give: What
strategies do we need to use to get diverse communities to give? How do we
attract diverse development staff … who have the skills and connections to get
diverse people to give? Rarely has the conversation been about the wealth gap,
systemic oppression, and how we can use fundraising principles and practices
to build the power and voice of our community. And this may be a reason why
there are so few development staff of color and why the ones that we have may
be burning out. It's exhausting emotionally and spiritually to constantly have
to ask the people who may not be aware that they benefit from injustice to
contribute to help end it.

Of course, this is not to say that all aspects of donor-centrism are bad and
contributing to injustice. But as our demographics change, as our society's
problems become more numerous and complex, we must look at our fundraising
philosophies and practices through a lens of equity and social justice. We need
a model where we respect donors and build strong relationships with them, but
where they are not in the center. They cannot be in the center. None of us can
be in the center, for all the above and other reasons. The community we serve
and benefit from must be in the center.

I am working with some colleagues to develop a set of principles for what
I'm calling Community-Centric Fundraising, a model that is grounded in
equity and social justice, prioritizes the entire community over individual
organizations, fosters a sense of belonging and interdependence, presents our
work not as individual transactions but holistically, and encourages mutual
support between nonprofits.

6.3 Continuity and change in fundraising approaches

Direct mail: dead, or more alive than ever?

Jeff Brooks, 2019

These are dark times for direct mail fundraising. Response rates are down (and have been trending lower for more than a decade). At the same time, costs of paper, printing, and postage keep going up, usually faster than inflation.

And then there's the M-word: *Millennials*. Everybody knows they don't respond to direct mail. We're not sure they can even find their own mail boxes! So direct mail is dead, right? The sooner you stop using it for fundraising, the better. Right? Not so fast.

A sober and non-panicked look tells us that direct mail isn't dead. It's not even sick. But it's changing, like everything else. If you're profitably using direct mail in your fundraising program, cancelling it might be one of the biggest mistakes you could make.

Have you heard about the grand experiment of the American Cancer Society? One of the biggest direct mail fundraisers in the US looked at the big picture of falling response rates, rising costs, and the looming Millennial Threat. On top of that, the direct mail program was a relatively small source of revenue. It seemed obvious to them: direct mail was fading in importance. So they suspended direct mail donor acquisition. Just acquisition, which is the least profitable and most difficult part of direct mail. They kept their large and thriving direct mail donor cultivation program going. The suspension started in January 2013.

They restarted direct mail donor acquisition about 18 months later because the experiment was a financial disaster. Here's what happened:

- The number of new donors to the Society dropped by 11% — those other channels didn't pick up the slack.
- The massive and successful event, Relay for Life, raised $25 million less than the previous year.
- The estimated five-year impact on income: a loss of $29.5 million

And that doesn't even look at the loss of bequests, which largely come from direct mail donors. That loss is likely only now starting to be felt. And it is going to add millions more in losses over the years.

If an 18-month suspension of direct mail acquisition can do that much damage to an organization with the massive brand recognition and resources of the American Cancer Society, think what it might do to most

DOI: 10.4324/9781003145936-112

fundraisers — the rest of us, who are far smaller and far more dependent on individual donors.

Thing is, even as it grows more expensive and difficult, direct mail is a keystone investment for almost any fundraising program. It is a scalable, reliable source of donors who will do more for you over time. As one American Cancer Society leader said after the experiment, "For every $1 we invest in direct mail acquisition, we bring in $7 over the course of three years."

No question — direct mail is not the cure-all it used to be. The cost has made it unworkable for some organizations.

If you have a viable direct mail program and you shut it down, here are some things that may happen:

• You'll likely lose immediate (first year) revenue.
• Your event revenue may suffer.
• You'll get fewer planned giving prospects.
• Your major donor program will shrink. The large majority of major donors start their giving as direct mail donors.
• Your online giving will probably suffer — direct mail is one of the main drivers of online giving.

But what about the Millennial Threat? Are their different habits and media use going to finally kill off direct mail as a fundraising channel?

Maybe. But that isn't a factor yet. People of that age are not DM-responsive — but they're less responsive to other media too. We thought the same things about Boomers a couple of decades ago. When they were in their 30s and 40s, they were less responsive to direct mail, and all kinds of boys cried all kinds of wolf about the coming doom. But as the Boomers have aged into their 50s, 60s, and even 70s, we see them paying more attention to direct mail. Chances are, the Millennials will do something similar when they reach those ages. But even if they don't, that's years in the future. It's not now.

So how do you know if direct mail is working? There's a pretty easy calculation:

• If your direct mail acquisition is getting a return on investment of less than 0.5:1, it doesn't really work. The cost is so high you will always struggle to make it pay off.
• If that acquisition ROI is 0.65:1 or better, you almost certainly have a viable direct mail program.
• If it's somewhere between 0.5 and 0.65, it might be viable.

And here's the other factor: Direct mail is the best source of major donors and bequest donors. Nothing else comes close. So to really get full value from direct mail, you must have two things:

1. A robust donor upgrade pipeline that encourages donors to increase their giving.
2. A solid bequest marketing and follow-up program.

Without those things, even a solid direct mail program is probably iffy in the long run!

Bottom line: Direct mail is a challenge. And expensive. (And it's getting more so.) Direct mail is important, but it might not be for you just now. Keep your eye on that initial return on investment and make sure you have a way to maximize donor upgrading and bequest marketing!

Modern grantmaking for grant seekers

Gemma Bull and Tom Steinberg, 2021

> The challenge in foundations is that very often they are set up to serve the needs of the board so they can make decisions about how to allocate money rather than the needs of a 'secondary' user group, that is people that are after that money. – Dan Sutch, director of the Centre for the Acceleration of Social Technology

It is quite common for some funders to provide a very good service to their boards but not such a great service to their grantseekers and grantees. In these cases, it is usually because grantmakers regard their boards – rather than their grantseekers and grantees – as the main people they serve. This can result in funders putting time and effort into trying to understand and meet the needs of board members instead of the needs of grantseekers.

Another cause of problems is that it is generally quicker and cheaper for institutions to offer a bad customer experience, and generally more time consuming and expensive for them to offer a good one. Funding organisations, in particular, can be guilty of offering poor experiences because they aren't under any market or political pressure to offer good ones. There's nothing to counterbalance the bureaucratic tendency to put in place yet more questions, attachments, surveys, letters of support, accounts, incorporation documents, budgets, inside leg measurements and so on.

As Sufina Ahmad, director of John Ellerman Foundation, told us, "In the funders I've worked for previously, I've seen time and again a layering or adding of more complexity to processes rather than reviewing wholesale and figuring out what should be removed to make our offer better." Sadly, we aren't surprised. So, given that there's a lack of incentive to offer a good experience, why should a grantmaking organisation … bother to improve things? Why go to the trouble?

For many grantmaking institutions this will be a novel question – one that has never come up before in internal discussions or board meetings. That's because an organisation will analyse and assess the quality of service it offers only if it sees itself as offering a service in the first place. Some traditional funders don't see grantmaking as a service. They see the activity of grantmaking as an act of munificence – the bestowing of gifts on lucky individuals whose only conceivable reaction is delight and gratitude. Just as it would be very rude and ungrateful to complain about your birthday presents, it would be unthinkable

DOI: 10.4324/9781003145936-113

to criticise the nature of grants or the way they are handed out. This, we believe, is not an uncommon view of customer service in funders: *they ain't customers and we ain't providing no freakin' service.*

Attitude-wise, Modern Grantmakers come from a totally different place. ... one of the five key values of Modern Grantmaking is service. This means that Modern Grantmakers see themselves as serving grantseekers and grantees, not as a monarch tossing coins from the window of their gilded coach. Ultimately, there are three reasons why grantmakers should be motivated by a service mindset:

• out of a basic sense of decency and a desire not to cause pain to others;
• out of a sense of equity and a desire to eliminate discriminatory barriers;
• out of a desire to have the greatest possible impact.

Let's dive in to see how these relate to the seemingly prosaic business of customer experience.

What's the connection between a funder's service quality and discrimination?

To see how a funder's quality of service is connected with discrimination, consider [a story] which contains elements drawn from several real-world experiences.

A grantseeker from a disability charity comes up with a project idea that is in line with what your funding organisation has said it wants to fund. This being the 21st century, the grantseeker visits your website to start the online application process. The applicant has a visual impairment, which makes it challenging to use your not particularly accessible website. However, they persevere for a couple of days, slowly and painstakingly cutting and pasting answers into a form that they can't quite see properly and that isn't working very well in the highly magnified view they have to use. It's draining, but they persist.

Eventually, exhausted by the experience, they get to the final page of questions in the application form. And there's a problem – right at the end, there are several additional eligibility questions they hadn't been told about before. They realise with horror that their organisation is not actually eligible for funding, and that all the time they've spent copying and pasting has been for nothing.

The despairing grantseeker slams shut their laptop and then phones a colleague to complain bitterly about how horrible the whole experience has been. Following this complaint the word slowly spreads through the whole community of disability charities that your funder 'doesn't care about people like us'. Gradually your funder receives fewer and fewer applications from disability groups without ever being aware of what's caused this change. A year later your funder convenes an internal meeting, in which your colleagues agonise over the fall in applications from disability organisations. Nobody connects the problem to the application process (because nobody has done any research into user experience), and the problem remains unacknowledged and unresolved.

[...]

Some common problems ... result from funders not taking the time and effort to make grantseekers' and grantees' experiences better. These include:

- The time and energy of people who deserve kindness and respect is sapped and wasted for no justifiable reason.
- Bad news about mistreatment by funders can spread through communities, and a funding organisation can end up suppressing applications from people that it may actually very much want to support.
- Poor service quality can lead to people concluding that funders, overall, are part of the problem of discrimination and marginalisation in society at large, not part of the solution.
- Better connected, more expensively educated and more self-confident grantseekers can overcome almost any application hurdles. This then contributes to an overall skew of funding away from more needy groups and towards organisations run by more privileged people.

When you add these up, bad customer service leads directly to grants that are made to groups that actually need them less. Rubbish application processes lead to inequitable outcomes. This in turn then leads to an overall lower impact

[...]

Put together, these consequences are the exact opposite of why most funders get up and start work in the morning – to help great organisations make big impacts. As Helen Turvey, executive director at the Shuttleworth Foundation, says, 'When it comes to being a nonprofit, necessity is absolutely not the mother of invention. When nonprofit leaders have time and space to think, they just do better work.' Bad, frustrating applicant experiences rob nonprofit leaders of exactly that time and space.

Finally, good-quality customer experiences aren't just about prospective grantseekers. Grantees' quality of life and ability to focus on the things that matter are hugely shaped by the demands placed on them by funders. Just because you've awarded someone free money it doesn't mean that you are not still at risk of wasting their time or of making them feel belittled and worthless. The most common cause of miserable experiences for grantees is progress reporting requirements – especially writing different reports for every funder, in a never-ending cycle of grind.

OK, so what does a Modern Grantmaking customer experience look like?

Modern Grantmakers design funding services that meet the end users' needs and create the kind of flexibility that means people don't have to jump through arbitrary hoops. This requires cultural change and training across everything to empower and support grantmakers with the right skills to become enablers and facilitators versus blockers and gatekeepers. – Ngozi Lyn Cole, experienced senior UK grantmaking executive and board member

Applying for a grant, or managing a current grant, isn't exactly an everyday activity like buying something from a supermarket. However, despite being a somewhat niche activity that only a minority of people will ever engage in, the factors that make it a good or a bad experience are actually very similar to good-quality experiences in other areas of life.

For example, a good shopping experience in a store and a good grant application experience with a funder both have the following characteristics in common:

- They're easy to find.
- You can achieve what you want to quickly and without unnecessary steps.
- It's easy to understand what the whole process is going to look like right from the start.
- While you don't have to speak to a person to achieve your goal, you can do so easily if you need to.
- They're welcoming and accessible to people with different abilities.

[...]

Angela Murray [is] a former staffer at multiple funders who now works for Hyphen8, a company that builds highly accessible grantmaking systems for lots of clients. She summarises the whole situation thus:

A good user experience in grantmaking is when the people applying for funding find it easy to communicate their idea to you and even if they don't get funding they understand why. It's grantmaking where there's a transparent process, where applicants know what's going to happen, when it's going to happen and who's going to make the decision.

[...]

Even invite-only funders should make time and space to explore what it feels like to be a grantee or prospective grantee, and then to improve their experience with you.

Donor advised funds: an important new player in the fundraising sector

Danielle Vance-McMullen and Daniel Heist, 2021

Donor-advised funds (DAFs) are the fastest growing form of philanthropy in the United States, and they are changing the way many donors give to charity. Donor-advised funds are unusual because, although the assets are managed by institutions like community foundations, DAF giving decisions are essentially made by individual donors.

[…]

DAFs function like a charitable checking account. Donors open a fund (or account) by making tax-deductible contributions to a DAF sponsor, a 501(c)(3) public charity that holds and manages the funds [similar frameworks exist in Canada, the EU and UK]. Donors then use advisory privileges to recommend grants from the DAF sponsor to another public charity or private operating foundation. Legally, the sponsor controls the funds, however, the donor recommendations are nearly always followed. In many cases sponsors also give donors discretion on how funds are invested. Each DAF account may have multiple donor advisors authorized to make recommendations. The DAF vehicle provides tremendous flexibility for supporting donors' philanthropic goals.

DAF sponsor organizations can be categorized into three types:

- National – National sponsor organizations serve a broad client base. They include subsidiaries of commercial financial services providers as well as employer-supported workplace giving organizations.
- Community Foundation – Many community foundations (CFs) offer donor-advised funds to local donors. They focus on serving donors within a specific geographic area and promote community-based philanthropy.
- Cause-related – Some donor-advised fund sponsors were organized to serve donors who associate with a specific cause, typically a religious affiliation. We use the term cause-related in lieu of "single-issue" used by National Philanthropic Trust. Many cause-related DAF sponsors facilitate giving to a variety of issues.

Different types of sponsor organizations appear to serve donors with different giving patterns. Overall, the DAF vehicle facilitates a wide variety of philanthropic activity.

[…]

DOI: 10.4324/9781003145936-114

Understanding the average DAF account is more relevant than aggregate national figures for fundraising practice. While some national reports have noted that the mean DAF account size is \$162,556, this number is skewed by a few ultra-large DAF accounts. The assets of a typical DAF account vary somewhat based on the policies of the DAF sponsor, especially policies around minimum opening balances. Fidelity Charitable, which has no minimum contribution, reported a median account balance of \$21,637 in 2020. Silicon Valley Community Foundation, which has a \$5,000 minimum contribution, reported that around 55% of accounts had balances less than \$100,000 in 2019.

Grantmaking

Donor-advised funds granted approximately \$27.8 billion to nonprofits in fiscal year 2019. This figure is approximately one-half of the grantmaking by private (independent) foundations and around 9% of the giving by individuals in 2019, according to Giving USA (2020). While overall the pattern of grants from DAFs seems to follow individual giving, DAF grantmaking is more likely to go to education, public-society benefit, and the arts and a bit less likely to go to religion than the other forms of giving.

Grantmaking by DAFs has increased substantially over time. Over the past 5 years, DAF grants rose by 93%. All growth calculations in this section are in current dollars. In comparison, aggregate individual giving rose 17% over this time. In periods of economic downturns, DAF grantmaking typically remains relatively robust, especially compared to other areas of philanthropic giving by individuals. Moreover, DAF Grantmaking increased significantly in 2020 in response to the COVID-19 pandemic. During the first six months of 2020, a survey of large DAF sponsors found that the number of DAF grants increased by 37.4% and the total value of DAF grants increased by 29.8%, compared to 2019 grants for the same period.

[…]

Opening a DAF account

Starting a DAF is much easier than setting up a private foundation or charitable trust. Many DAF accounts can be set up online in a matter of minutes. Donors choose where to set up their accounts for different reasons. Many choose a commercial sponsor (e.g. Fidelity, Vanguard, Schwab) for ease of use in coordination with an investment account. Others choose a community foundation because of a desire to engage in community-based philanthropy. Still others pick cause-related sponsors, such as a Christian or Jewish organization, to align more closely with their values. Donors also decide how much to contribute and what resources to use. Some DAF sponsors have minimum initial contribution requirements (such as \$5k or \$25k). The initial contribution may be related to a recent or upcoming liquidity event, for which a donor is trying to offset tax liabilities. Once the initial contribution is complete, the donor usually has options for how the money will be invested, ranging from long-term to more short-term investment approaches.

Making grant recommendations

After funding the account, donors "recommend" grants by listing the name or EIN [Employer Identification Number, or charity registration number in the UK] of the charity and the amount of the grant. The DAF sponsor reviews this recommendation and mails a check to the charity. Donors' names are normally included with the check, so the recipient knows who recommended the grant. However, donors can choose to remain anonymous. In the rare occasions when grant recommendations are denied, the legal status of the charity may be in question, or the charity may conflict with the sponsors stated guidelines or IRS regulations, which are described later in this chapter.

[…]

Fundraising approaches for DAF donors

With this understanding of what a DAF is, how donors may be using their DAF, and why, fundraisers can develop strategies for engaging, soliciting, and engaging DAF donors and demonstrating stewardship of their gifts. A recent study showed that "87% of organizations that solicited DAF gifts received a DAF gift in the past 3 years" and even "42% of organizations that did not solicit DAF gifts received a DAF gift" in the same period. Proactive organizations will be more likely to raise money from DAF donors.

Cultivation

There are three groups of DAF donor prospects: 1) current donors who are already using a DAF, 2) current donors who would benefit from using a DAF, and 3) DAF donors who are not current donors. Identifying this last group of donors is often top of mind for fundraisers, but identifying the first two groups will help an organization better prepare for finding the third group. Here are some strategies related to these DAF donor prospects.

1. Ask current donors whether they use a DAF. If so, ask them about their DAF:
   - When did you open your DAF? Where? Why?
   - What assets do you use to contribute to your DAF?
   - How often do you grant from your DAF? What kinds of grants do you make from your DAF?
   - Who are the "donor advisors" on your DAF? Keep track of this data in the donor database to develop solicitation strategies.
2. Talk with current donors about DAFs and share knowledge about the benefits of DAFs. It may seem counterintuitive to help donors set up a DAF because that adds one more step to closing gifts, but remember that fundraising is about long-term relationships. Helping a donor discover the

benefits of DAFs builds a mutually beneficial relationship that will increase the likelihood of future donations.

3. Build relationships with DAF sponsors. Community foundations and cause-related sponsors are sometimes asked to recommend organizations to donors and may also have initiatives to engage their donors with community-based or values-based causes. Sponsors will not provide donor information to a soliciting organization, but they will often provide organizational information to donors.

Solicitation

To start, make it easy for donors to make a DAF grant to your organization. Discuss the use of DAFs on your website and other solicitation materials. List your EIN and mailing address clearly; DAF donors will need this information when making a grant recommendation. Consider using a DAF giving widget, which helps link your giving page with DAF sponsor grantmaking sites.

Next, build strategies for soliciting DAF donors based on the information you gleaned from your engagement questions (listed above). Depending on what strategies donors use for their DAF giving, the following solicitation strategies may be used:

- Annual DAF giving – Ask the donor to consider setting up an automatic grant recommendation to your organization, if offered by the sponsor.
- Bunching DAF giving – Look for short-term projects that the donor can support. Help them envision how they can make a difference to the organization over the next 2–3 years so that they can plan their bunched contributions accordingly.
- Event DAF giving – These donors are likely to have major gift capacity and a major-gift mindset. Follow typical major gift solicitation approaches.
- Long-term DAF giving – If the donor is using the DAF like an endowment, follow the annual DAF giving strategy. Also consider major gift and planned gift opportunities. Remember that donors can name remainder beneficiaries [who receive any funds remaining after fixed value donations are allocated] on DAF accounts.

Acknowledgement and stewardship

Engage DAF donors just like any other donor. While, technically speaking, the check came from the sponsor organization, remember that the donor directed the grant to your organization. Give the donor credit for the grant in your donor database to ensure the donor is properly recognized, engaged, and cultivated for future gifts beginning with demonstration of wise use of previous contributions. Note, however, that donors do not need a receipt for tax purposes, because they received their deduction when contributing to the DAF sponsor. Instead, acknowledge the amount and purpose of the grant received, without mention of tax deductibility. If the grant lacks the donor's name or contact information, some sponsor organizations will transmit acknowledgement and stewardship communications for you. Completely anonymous donors may still be recognized as such in annual reports or donor recognition walls. Report to both those who recommended the grant and the organization from which it came on the use and impact of the grant.

[…]

Critiques of DAFs

The controversies surrounding DAFs are centered on not only concerns about DAFs' outsized role in American philanthropy, but also issues related to gift timing, tax benefits for DAF donations, transparency, and trust.

Speed of grantmaking

Currently, there are no federal regulations regarding how soon or at what rate funds donated into DAF accounts must be granted to operating charities. The rate of donations is measured as a payout rate, which roughly translates to a percent of assets distributed in a year. This rate varies widely by sponsor characteristics and over time. Typical aggregate payout rates tend to hover around 14 to 22%, depending on the calculation method used. Another way of measuring the speed of grantmaking is by looking at "shelf life," or time between contributions and grantmaking. On aggregate, DAF "shelf life" has been estimated at around 4 years.

The time lag between contributions into DAF funds (and tax benefits) and grants from DAF funds has been routinely questioned. Critics have proposed a maximum shelf life for funds. They have also proposed delaying some or all tax benefits to donors until grants are distributed to operating charities. However, others have argued that an immediate tax deduction acts as an important incentive for contributions and flexibility in payout rules allows donors to give more strategically.

Transparency

In addition, critics are concerned about the lack of transparency in giving from DAFs, because there is little reporting required. DAF sponsors report aggregated statistics on the IRS form 990, which means that the public cannot observe which donors made grants to which charities. This anonymity is similar to the privacy afforded to individual donors; foundations' requirements mandate much more transparency. As a result, some private foundations elect to make donations to DAFs to keep their giving anonymous. This behavior has been criticized, largely because these private foundation donations can still be counted as foundation payouts.

Trust and conflicts of interest

Finally, there is a degree of mistrust of DAF sponsors, particularly those with commercial affiliations. Critics are concerned that these institutions benefit from DAF investment and management fees and encourage donors to maintain high asset balances rather than maximize payouts. While the fees from managing DAFs do support operations at DAF sponsors, there is little empirical evidence to support the claim that sponsors purposely encourage donors to maintain high asset balances to maximize fees.

Conclusion

Donor-advised funds play an important role in the modern philanthropic landscape. Development professionals must understand why donors choose to use DAFs as philanthropic vehicles and how to work with donors and their various DAF giving strategies. In addition, development professionals should stay informed of the limitations on DAF giving and the critiques of DAFs to address any concerns that may arise. Ultimately, DAF donors have made a commitment to charitable giving, and this commitment can benefit nonprofit missions when DAF donors are solicited effectively.

6.4 The impact of science and technology

Using behaviour science to nudge donors: does it work and is it ethical?

Madeleine Croucher, Meredith Niles, Omar Mahmoud, and Bernard Ross, 2021

The ethics of using behavioral science in fundraising

The insights from behavioural science are powerful. But anyone who claims to be in the business of pro-social activity must ask "Just because we can learn how to nudge donors to give more, *should* we use this knowledge?"

We would argue that nothing inherent in the use of behavioural nudges is unethical, provided they don't undermine the autonomy or the welfare of the donor. We're guided here by a framework set out by Cass Sunstein in his book *The Ethics of Influence*. Sunstein was a co-author with Richard Thaler, another Nobel laureate, of *Nudge*, one of the most influential books on the subject of behavioural economics and choice architecture. Although Sunstein was writing specifically about the ethics of government applying nudges to influence its citizenry, much of his thinking can be applied to fund raising.

Consider the point about autonomy: autonomy is violated if we take away the donor's ability to make a free choice. Does using any of the insights in this book undermine a donor's free choice? We don't see how it does. Yes, we have an obligation to tell the truth, but that doesn't mean you can't present your truth in the most compelling and attractive way – the beautiful truth, as opposed to the ugly truth. If you know that donors are more likely to respond when you show them that other people have made similar decisions, why not offer this information? Provided everything you say is true, you haven't undermined your donor's ability to make a free choice. In fact, as Lisa Sargent tells us, a really powerful nudge is to remind donors that they are free to choose!

On to the second point: does using any of these insights undermine a donor's welfare? Again, there are other safeguards in place within the framework of existing professional standards to ensure that a donor's giving doesn't harm them. There are protections for vulnerable people who cannot exercise a free choice, and the UK code requires fundraisers to consider whether taking a donation would leave a donor in financial hardship. And an assumption that any incremental gift to a charity must necessarily correspond to a decrease in donor welfare is, in our view, a flawed interpretation of how donors relate to

DOI: 10.4324/9781003145936-116

charities. We aren't playing a zero-sum game with charitable income on one side and donor welfare on the other. There is a large body of evidence that shows gifts to charity, when they are affordable and freely made – conditions that must be met to be compliant with relevant professional standards – increase well-being by making them feel good about themselves, by giving them a sense of agency when confronted with complex problems, etc. So provided you are operating within the relevant professional standards, it is hard to see how using nudges could compromise the welfare of your donor.

But just because an argument makes logical sense it doesn't mean it will be persuasive! So even though we think there is no prima facie case that nudges undermine either donor autonomy or welfare, that doesn't mean that some people won't question their use. One of us authors, Meredith Niles, attended a workshop several years ago exploring the use of behavioural science in marketing, and she remembers a couple of the participants remarking that they often use the techniques the group was exploring, but they felt somehow that knowing the science behind why these techniques work felt "a little suspect." Her heart sank in response, as surely the point is to be more than *accidentally* good at our work!

For fundraisers, this goes further. We believe we have a positive obligation to make our communications as effective as possible. Our beneficiaries need us to deliver results, and our donors trust us to make the best possible use of the money they give us. It costs the same amount of money to mail an effective fundraising letter as it does to send a poor one. Don't our donors expect us to generate the best return on their investment by striving for excellence? And now that you know there is a massive body of peer-reviewed research, conducted at scale by very clever people, including several Nobel laureates, that can help you make your fundraising more effective, isn't it professionally negligent not to try to take advantage of it?!

Trust and confidence are so important to charities, it's always worthwhile pausing to take stock and reflect on whether an action is ethical, as well as effective. We hope we've reassured you that these ideas have an entirely appropriate place in the ethical fundraiser's toolkit.

[…]

How to RAISE more money

There are three key elements to any successful behavioural change project:

1. Define and diagnose your behavioural challenges.
2. Apply behavioural science strategies to effect change.
3. Test, test, test!

First, define your desired behaviour. This can be as simple as defining Who, What, and When. For example, "secure one-off donors (Who) to switch to regular giving (What), when they receive our newsletter email (When)". This seems simple, but the audience, the context, and the timing of a decision-making moment can all influence the outcome. Defining this upfront is key.

Second, we need to understand why the desired behaviour is or isn't occurring, before we start applying behavioural science to try and change things.

[...]

Once you have identified the key barriers to overcome, you're then in a good position to start applying science strategies, or "nudges", to drive your desired behaviour. The techniques you can apply to drive impact are vast and varied. To help, we've distilled these brilliant strategies into a simple summary framework: **RAISE** [as summarised in Table 6.4.1: The RAISE framework].

[...]

Table 6.4.1 The RAISE framework

R-A-I-S-E	Insights	Strategies	Principles
Relevant	We are heavily influenced by how information is framed to us and are more engaged when it resonates strongly on a personal level.	Make supporting more personally meaningful Tap into personal experience Help people visualize the issue and outcome	Framing Self-Identity Theory Concreteness
Appealing	We are more likely to act when we anticipate there will be some kind of intrinsic or extrinsic benefit as a result.	Offer a gift to receive a gift Create a sense of personal achievement Increase perceived value	Reciprocity Goal Gradient Effect Labour Illusion Costly Signaling
Intuitive	Our decision-making is often automatic and is driven by factors outside of our conscious awareness, such as our emotions and senses.	Use imagery to suggest expected behaviors Trigger an emotional response Create mental reference points	Priming Affect Anchoring
Social	Decisions and behavior are often guided by the beliefs and actions of those around us.	Tailor norms to your audience Create shared social identities Use contentiously relevant messengers	Social Norms Social Identity Theory Messenger Theory
Easy	We perceive things more positively and are more likely to act when it requires minimal effort to understand or do.	Put important information upfront Focus on a single request Repeat your request	Cognitive Ease Defaults Information Hierarchy Repetition

Make it relevant

We are heavily influenced by how information is presented to us. The same information can be more or less engaging, depending on how strongly it resonates with our own experiences and values. By better understanding our audience and framing the information we want to communicate in line with their motivations, we can increase the impact of our message … [We] explore three ways we can achieve this: making it personally meaningful, tapping into personal experience, and helping people visualize the issue and/or outcome.

[…]

Natural Language Processing (NLP) can be used to understand the emotions or topics that most resonate with supporters and then deploy this knowledge to tailor content to boost engagement with certain issues. It is interesting to note that what an agency wants to talk about and what a supporter wants to hear are not always the same thing.

Craig Linton explores how different ways of framing monetary donations can drive engagement and income. Knowing that volunteering time, rather than money, can feel more personal and meaningful, he shows how reframing donating money as the equivalent value of your time, i.e. "donate a day's work", drives positive results.

Consider how you can make your cause <u>Relevant</u> by identifying what is most important to supporters and making their contribution feel personal and meaningful.

[…]

Make it appealing

We are more likely to act when we anticipate there will be some kind of extrinsic or intrinsic benefit for doing so. Extrinsic motivations are when we are focused on the outcome and act to gain some type of tangible reward. Intrinsic motivations are when we are focused on the act itself and do something because it is internally satisfying and fills some psychological need. While we like to think that we act purely altruistically, and sometimes we are, often we are more driven by these incentives than we might realise.

Offer a gift to receive a gift

One of the most widely used tactics to make campaigns appealing is reciprocity. Reciprocity explains how we are more likely to do a positive behavior after being on the receiving end of a positive behavior. This simple tactic can be used in a variety of creative ways to drive impact.

At a foundational level this can be as simple as offering a free gift …. Gifts do not have to be material. They could be access to exclusive information, invites to special events, the chance to connect with goodwill ambassadors, etc.

Create a sense of achievement

Another method of encouraging action is by appealing to more intrinsic motivations, such as a sense of personal success. Endowed Progress, also known as the Goal Gradient Effect, explains how we are more motivated to act the closer we get to reaching our goal because the positive feeling that comes with success on a sense of completion is heightened. The most familiar example of this is probably the fundraising thermometer, with donations flooding in the closer we get to the target goal.

[…]

Increase perceived value

Another way of appealing to our audience is by maximizing the perceived value of our cause. As Madeleine Croucher describes, we tend to trust and value messengers more when they have exerted some additional cost of effort … [because] this signals the messenger's belief in, and commitment to, their own cause, subsequently eliciting reassurance and trust from others.

Consider how you can make your cause more Appealing by: understanding the extrinsic and intrinsic motivations of your audience; leveraging reciprocity to encourage behaviours in kind; helping supporters feel a sense of personal achievement; and communicating the effort exerted by your organisation to increase the perceived value of your cause.

Make it intuitive

Our decision-making is often automatic and is driven by factors outside of our conscious awareness such as our emotions and senses.

One phenomenon that encapsulates this effect is known as 'priming' – where our exposure to certain sights, words, and sensations can subconsciously influence our response and nudge us to act. This fascinating effect, while relatively misunderstood, can be executed quite simply, and drive some really impactful results.

[…]

Geoffrey Peters discusses the neuroscience of emotion and some of the ways we can trigger it. Specifically, he shares how the presence of oxytocin is associated with positive emotions such as trust, generosity, compassion and empathy, and is subsequently linked to the likelihood of donating. He reveals how pictures of human/mammals faces and eyes, storytelling, and visuals of human interaction, can all increase oxytocin production and therefore likeliness to donate.

Martin Paul and Karen Armstrong reveal insightful strategies to trigger emotional responses. They successfully prime potential supporters to be open to including a gift in their will to support refugees by asking them a question: what would you take with you if you had to flee at a moment's notice? Those who answered the question were significantly more likely to express interest in leaving a gift in their will. Simply writing a sentence emotionally primed people to support the cause by stimulating reflection and triggering empathy.

Another really interesting way to prime empathy is by using sensory enhancement to help people empathise with the beneficiaries. Christoph Müller-Gattol shows how simulating blindness in direct mail, by blurring out a version of the letter so that it cannot be read, is very effective at helping supporters resonate with an issue that can be difficult to personally identify with, significantly boosting response rates as a result.

[…]

Create mental reference points

We can also prime behaviour by giving people initial reference points to help intuitively guide their decision-making and behaviour, also known as 'anchoring'. Marcelo Iniarra and Ana Paola Pérez reveal interesting and impactful ways of anchoring donation amounts … [One] involves stating a high figure upfront to make subsequent figures mentioned feel relatively small, in this case the cost of taking care of a child for a month, $340. This was followed by a range of donation options, starting with a higher donation option as a second anchor, $60, $50, and $35. The simple inclusion of these reference points made donating gifts closer to $35 feel more reasonable, almost tripling average donations.

[…]

Consider how you can make your desired behaviour feel Intuitive by using imagery and words to suggest that the behaviour is somewhat expected, triggering emotions that drive people to act, such as using reflection to trigger empathy, and appropriate anchor points to drive up donations within reasonable boundaries.

Make it social

Our decision-making and behaviour is often guided by the beliefs and actions of those around us. Deep rooted in evolutionary psychology, this is because the actions of others signal what is beneficial, appropriate, and safe for us to do ourselves.

[…]

Create shared social identities

Our behavior is also driven by the ways in which we associate ourselves with others. We tend to be more persuaded by, or act more in favour of, those we more closely identify with.

Mike Colling describes the benefits of drawing on donors' personal experiences to create a closeness to the cause before asking for support. By giving supporters [of WaterAid] the chance to talk about their own lives on social media in response to the "To be a girl" campaign, they created the capacity for young girls from all around the world to relate to one another. By building these relationships and establishing a shared social identity between the supporter and the beneficiary, [donors] are much more prepared to give.

[…]

Use contextually relevant messages

We are also strongly influenced by who communicates information to us, with authoritative, likable and personally relevant messengers all having the potential to increase the degree to which we pay attention to and act on information. Identifying the messenger who most resonates with your audience and best fits the context in which your message is being delivered can be the difference between a small and big impact.

[…]

Marina Jones reveals how likeable celebrity messengers who elicit trust were more effective in generating support for a theatre company than personally relevant messengers (donors like them), or even direct beneficiaries.

[…]

Consider how you can tap into Social cues to encourage your desired behaviour by understanding the social identities of your audience. Use this understanding to align your messaging with traits or experiences they can identify with, create social norms that most reflect them, and use messengers that feel personally relevant.

Make it easy

We perceive things more positively and are more likely to act when it requires minimal effort to understand or do. While it is last on our list, removing friction and making behaviour easy is in fact one of the simplest and most effective places to start when it comes to applying behavioural science. It sounds obvious, but surprisingly this step is often overlooked.

What do we mean by "removing friction"? Behavioural science tells us that the more easily we can process something, the more likely we are to engage with it and the more positive our associations are towards it. This is because when more mental effort is required to process something or complete a task, we enter a state of cognitive strain which can lead to increased vigilance, negative perceptions and ultimately inaction. Sometimes, the easiest thing we can get supporters to do is nothing at all. This is why having or suggesting a default option often makes it easier for donors to decide.

[…]

Put important information upfront

Make the most important information in your communication immediately obvious and clear so that supporters don't have to expend effort in understanding the ask. The quicker they understand, the more likely they are to act. Madeleine Croucher shows how simply making the purpose of your communication obvious with direct language and iconography [such as] placing 'Appeal. Donation envelope' on the front of the envelope, significantly boosts response rates and average gifts.

Similarly Crawford Hollingworth describes the effectiveness of making key information salient [by] printing large green £2.50 stickers on the front and back of Big Issue [homeless newspaper vendors] tabards. This increased the saliency of the publication's price and reinforced the transactional nature of the purchase, which led to a strong uplift in desired behaviours.

Repeat your request

Expose your audience to your message or ask multiple times to make it more memorable and easier to process. Lisa Sargent shows the impact of repetition in driving conversion and the importance of mixing up how you present your message when repeating it in order to sustain engagement and maximise impact.

Consider how you can make your desired behavior <u>Easy</u>. Put the most important information you want to communicate in the clearest and most obvious place to make sure that it is received. Focus on a single request to avoid confusion and inaction. Repeat this singular request in different ways to make it memorable while keeping your audience engaged.

Conclusion

When you implement behavioural strategies to make your campaign Relevant, Appealing, Intuitive and Social, don't forget to keep it Easy. Above all else, it should remain Easy to understand and do your desired behavior ... Remember to start simple by removing cognitive friction, but more importantly maintain this cognitive ease even as additional strategies are implemented.

What is the potential of crowdfunding?

Claire van Teunenbroek, 2019

A crowdfunding platform provides an internet-mediated place for creators and donors to connect. Therefore, it is both a financial and relation mediator (i.e. social media platform). Donors can connect both with other donors and the creator.

[…]

Key characteristics

Crowdfunding builds on a large group of (private) individuals each donating a small amount online. In exchange for their donation, donors can receive a reward (i.e. reward-based crowdfunding), which ranges from acknowledgements on the developed product to a discount before market launch (e.g. free tickets for a show). A donor can also opt to donate without receiving a reward, i.e. donation-based crowdfunding. Reward- and donation-based crowdfunding are also referred to as philanthropic crowdfunding: the donor's input (i.e. monetary donation) is larger than the output (e.g. rewards). Another type of crowdfunding is equity-based crowdfunding, where backers provide funding for a company and in return, they get a small ownership of the business. The fourth type is lending/loan-based crowdfunding (e.g. peer-to-peer lending), where backers lend capital to companies. Equity- and lending-based crowdfunding focus on crowdfunding projects with a financial incentive: backers expect an economic return; thus, the backer's input is smaller than the expected output.

[…]

Crowdfunding platforms function as an online marketplace for [those] who aim to assemble funding for a specific project, therefore mediating between ideas and donations. Creators share their projects using social media platforms such as Facebook and Twitter.

Project-based, specific and transparent

The creator provides a promotional video, detailed description of the projects aims and the donation amount needed to realize this. Instead of asking for a donation for a general cause (e.g. international aid), with crowdfunding people are asked to donate to specific projects (e.g. digging a water well in a village in Western Kenya). Some projects aim to collect money for one specific person

DOI: 10.4324/9781003145936-117

(e.g. cover the medial expanses of someone's operation). One can question whether the last example still counts as philanthropic, since it does not support a general good but solely has a personal goal. Most platforms include a time limit: the projects run for a few days, which are indicated in advance. The project-based nature of crowdfunding results in a transparent strategy, which provides potential donors with information and control: the donors determine which project is funded rather than the charity.

[...]

Social information

Crowdfunding projects often report statistics about earlier donors, like the number of donors or the average donation amount of earlier donors. The effect of reporting on the donation behavior of other donors is called the social information effect. With crowdfunding, reporting the average donation amount of earlier donors results in an increase in the average donation amount of later donors.

[...]

Developments in crowdfunding worldwide

It is often reported that in recent years, crowdfunding markets experienced a severe growth rate; however, it is important to note that this was mostly among non-philanthropic platforms. Only 15% (about $5.5 billion based on available statistics) of the total amount raised through crowdfunding stems from philanthropic crowdfunding.

[...]

The online nature of crowdfunding supports a broad geographical dispersion: for international platforms, the average distance between creators and donors is about 5,000 kilometres. Meaning that creators and donors are often not from the same country. In this, social media plays an important role since media platforms make it easier for creators to connect with the unknown crowd. It is reported that worldwide, the most popular crowdfunding category covers projects related to healthcare: 27% of the projects worldwide were intended to cover medical expenses.

There are two major platforms on the market for philanthropic crowdfunding that receive donations from all over the world:

- Kickstarter, originated in 2009 in the US, with several very large campaigns over the last few years. Kickstarter offers a vast amount of creative oriented projects. In 10 years, Kickstarter has raised $4.6 billion among 17 million donors.
- Indiegogo, originated in 2008 in the US, approves campaigns for almost anything, except investments. In 10 years, Indiegogo has raised $1.6 billion among 800 thousand donors.

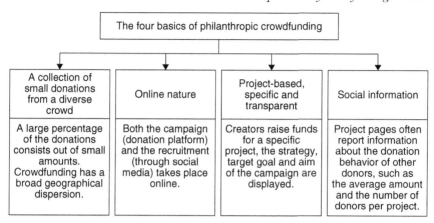

Figure 6.4.1 The four basics of philanthropic crowdfunding

[…]

The US, in comparison with Asia and Europe, has the largest percentage of philanthropic crowdfunding projects: about 18% of the country's total amount raised through crowdfunding comes from philanthropic crowdfunding. One of the world's largest platforms, Kickstarter, is one of the most popular but not per se the most successful platform worldwide. Between 2014 and 2018 about two-third of the projects failed to assemble the target amount.

[…]

China focuses mostly on reward-based crowdfunding. The Chinese sector runs their own crowdfunding platforms with great success, like JD Crowdfunding, Taobao Crowdfunding and Tencent Lejuan. Most of the reward-based platforms are closely branded with e-commerce and large Chinese technology firms where products and services are delivered in return for funding contributions (i.e. reward). Most of the donation-based projects are put forward by non-profit organizations or non-governmental organizations (NGOs). For NGOs, crowdfunding functions as a primary funding source, since NGOs are not allowed to raise money from the public without an affiliation with government projects or special permission from the government.

India mostly uses crowdfunding to fund medical projects. The most popular platform, ImpactGuru, specializes in healthcare related projects. The plat-form reports that since starting in 2015 they have mobilized 20 million euros to help Indians in need. They receive donations from all over the world. In India people must pay for most of their healthcare expenses, thus finances like crowdfunding offer an alternative. The Indian crowdfunding market has witnessed a strong increase now that more people have access to the internet and easier online payments: with 12,000 successful projects in 2018 alone.

In Europe, compared to the US and Asia, philanthropic crowdfunding makes up for the smallest percentage (<10%) of the total crowdfunding market. Philanthropic crowdfunding does not seem to have found their crowd just yet, with negative developments in 2016 and 2017. The nominal growth has fallen back to the 2013 level. Today, the largest crowdfunding markets in Europe are the UK, France, Germany, and the Netherlands. These four countries count as the most mature European crowdfunding markets.

The UK plays a big role in the European crowdfunding landscape in terms of market volume per capita, preferring donation- over reward-based funding. The UK witnessed a strong increase in the number of platforms between 2012 and 2014 .... Despite the [subsequent] decrease in the number of platforms, the donation amount raised continued to grow. This suggests that several platforms have become more successful at attracting donors, at the cost of other platforms. The UK is characterized by an expanding number of niche sites hosting specific projects, such as CrowdJustice (public interest law cases) and DigVentures (archaeology projects).

A popular and one of the older (founded in 2001) platforms is JustGiving, based in the UK and supporting a vast number of categories. The platform hosts more than just crowdfunding projects, like an ambassador model where private individuals raise funds for charities. Since 2019, the platform removed the platform fees from all campaigns, while most platforms expect a certain platform fee from creators for using the platform. In 2019 JustGiving collected over $4.5 billion for public goods since 2001, but it is unclear how much of this originated from crowdfunding projects alone.

France can call itself the second largest dominant force in European crowdfunding. Compared to other European countries, French platforms lead in the amount raised for reward-based projects (126 million euros). French crowdfunding market decreased with 2% in the past year, collecting a total of 81.5 million euros ... The French show a strong preference for reward-based crowdfunding over donation-based crowdfunding: 84% of the total philanthropic amount raised through crowdfunding comes from reward-based crowdfunding projects. France is home to the two largest European reward-based platforms: Ulule (raising €109 million before 2019) and KissKissBankBank (raising €83 million before 2019), both supporting a vast number of categories.

Germany is ranked as the third highest country in Europe. The first German reward-based crowdfunding platform started in 2010. Germany accounts for the largest donation-based crowdfunding percentage in the whole of Europe, but their focus is on financial crowdfunding (i.e. equity or lending-based). German crowdfunding platforms experience strong competition from US-based platforms. For instance, one of the most popular platforms among the Germans is the US based platform Patreon. Patreon not only functions as a crowdfunding platform but also as a social media platform. It applies a unique strategy where donors pay monthly amounts to creators to support them and gain access to their content (i.e. subscription model). The platform supports projects such as podcasts, video creators, gaming creators and writers. The platform was founded in 2013 and within 6 years the platform assembled about $1 billion, donated by 3 million donors to over 100 thousand creators.

There are several successful German crowdfunding platforms which mostly offer projects with a national focus. For instance, Startnext, which achieved a turnover of 1.1 million euros in 2017 … by 2019 they crowdfunded over 60 million euros. The platform offers a broad range of projects, ranging from research to sport, food and theater. Next to Startnext, the Germans prefer Steady, which is a young and upcoming platform founded in 2017 using a similar strategy as Patreon: subscription model. The platform focusses on funding podcasts, videos, arts and nonprofits.

The Netherlands is the fourth highest-ranking country in Europe with regards to online alternative finances by market value. In 2018, crowdfunding raised a total of 32 million euros … The Netherlands counts a fast-growing number of platforms, covering a wide variety of categories (from funding for the arts to science and international projects). Compared to the year before, the total amount raised through crowdfunding grew about 16% in 2018. While this seems promising, it is still a very small percentage (less than 1%) of the total Dutch philanthropic value of about 5.7 milliard euros. The Dutch prefer to fund arts-oriented projects; the largest Dutch crowdfunding platform is the arts-oriented platform Voordekunst.

Crowdfunding in Africa is still a small niche and not much is known about the crowdfunding statistics. However, newly launched crowdfunding services enable individuals to launch crowdfunding projects to raise money for personal expenses. We do know that those who give to crowdfunding projects prefer to give to projects aiming to cover medical expenses, education costs, or volunteer expenses.

Philanthropic crowdfunding deserves more (academic) attention

Few empirical studies have looked specifically at philanthropic crowdfunding projects. The disregard from scientists is unfortunate since there is a need to understand stimulants for donating to crowdfunding projects … to increase the effectiveness of crowdfunding campaigns. For instance, can crowdfunding support the philanthropic sector by attracting a new generation of donors?

How artificial intelligence can help unlock human generosity

Beth Kanter and Allison Fine, 2020

We are very early in the creation of an AI [Artificial Intelligence] for Giving field (AI4Giving) that offers the potential to inform and activate new and existing donors to give more or to give to more causes. The question is whether the interests of the technology providers and the philanthropic community will align as the technology becomes more ubiquitous. Or, as we've seen with social media, whether the commercial interests of the technology platforms will sublimate the philanthropic interests of users.

We are at a tipping point for sector-wide adoption of AI systems and practices. The philanthropic and nonprofit sectors have an opportunity to proactively shape this next era and ensure that at least a significant portion of the technology remains dedicated to the values underpinning philanthropy such as generosity, empathy and transparency. However, this opportunity may be fleeting as AI technologists will inevitably face pressures to monetize their platforms and services.

Our research identified ways AI is and can be used to increase giving to causes and improve the donor experience. AI can:

- Facilitate the connection between everyday givers and nonprofits,
- Advise program officers and major donors on making more-strategic philanthropic investments,
- Support more-efficient stewardship of major and mid-level donors,
- Scale personalized communications for everyday givers,
- Help researchers better understand donors via data collaboratives,
- Automate internal reporting and other administrative tasks.

The most exciting opportunity AI4Good presents is freeing staff from administrative and rote tasks to focus on other activities in order to direct more time and effort to strengthening relationships with doers and donors. However, we found little effort to date on using AI to change the standard model of fundraising that is often transactional and has led to a crisis in donor retention. As Brigitte Hoyer Gosselink, head of product impact for Google.org says, "AI won't fix bad fundraising practices."

Additional challenges include the current constraints of the technology to understand human empathy and the need of AI systems to have enormous sets of clean data to identify patterns. The nonprofit sector has long struggled

DOI: 10.4324/9781003145936-118

to create such data sets. In addition, commercial platforms are unlikely to be transparent about how their algorithms are developed and used. And the technology is racing ahead of ethical concerns about data privacy.

We also note the tendency of larger, better-known nonprofits to have the capacity to take advantage of the new technology, leaving smaller, newer organizations behind. This asymmetry exacerbates the natural tendency of donors to give only to causes with which they are already familiar.

Each of these challenges could be addressed through the use of AI. We envision the expansion of everyday giving spurred by real-time information about local needs modelled on corresponding, existing commercial applications:

- Real-time GoFundMe – To power a system for funding individual needs in real time. For instance, a donor could fund ten beds for homeless individuals for one night.
- Yelp for causes – For peer-to-peer reviews and ratings of giving options.
- Lifestyle app for causes – To ensure that everyday decisions and purchases have an optimal philanthropic benefit.

Our recommendations for the field of philanthropy to support the use of AI to expand generosity include:

- Use AI to expand the giving of everyday donors
- Create a relational model for fundraising
- Support data collaboratives and comprehensive outcomes data
- Convene stakeholders to create ethical approaches to AI principles
- Increase nonprofit fundraisers' capacity to use AI tools

The use of AI to expand philanthropy creates exciting possibilities for broadening who gives and to raise awareness of lesser-known causes. Our greatest hope is that philanthropic leaders will act quickly to invest in immediate needs such as data collaboratives, while also investing in experiments to find ways for AI to increase empathy and connections to a variety of causes.

What is artificial intelligence?

Artificial intelligence (AI) is an umbrella term used to describe different types of technologies. Though AI comes in many flavors and varieties, at its heart AI is the use of computers to help perform tasks automatically that could previously only be done by humans. The intelligent behavior of pattern matching drives the ability to collect, organize and analyze data to generate insights and complete different tasks.

An easy way to understand how AI works is to think about Netflix, which uses machine learning, a form of artificial intelligence, to automatically make recommendations to users on what to watch based on collecting, organizing, and analyzing data on what you and other users have watched on Netflix.

AI requires four components to work successfully: strategy questions (for philanthropy, questions related to increasing or improving giving from the donor's perspective), data (lots of it), algorithms (mathematical models to analyze the data), and tools (computers and software).

[...]

Why artificial intelligence will be a disruptive technology for giving

A disruptive technology forces a fundamental rethinking of existing business models and practices. In addition to creating efficiencies, disruptive technologies remake the relationship between organizations and various stakeholders, which in turn births a new set of business practices and norms.

[...]

If we wind back the clocks to a time twenty years before the age of social media, giving was dramatically different. The cutting-edge technology was direct mail. Donors received a letter on the organization's letterhead asking for a donation or membership to support the mission. Most donors wrote modest, annual checks to their favorite causes. Some may have increased their gift to get a coffee mug or calendar, but for the most part, people gave regular amounts to their favorite nonprofit organizations.

All of that was transformed 15 years ago, when the Internet and social media made person-to-person connecting, sharing, communicating and organizing easy and inexpensive—with or without organizations as intermediaries. This laid the groundwork for movements such as Giving Tuesday, a disaggregated, worldwide phenomenon, and the ALS Ice Bucket Challenge, a people powered viral fundraiser that raised over $125 million in 2014.

P2P (Person-to-Person) Platforms like GoFundMe have also gained popularity with donors giving directly to people rather than to organizations, often to cover extraordinary expenses arising from a medical crisis. GoFundMe, the largest crowdsourced fundraising platform, says people have raised more than $5 billion from 50 million donations in the eight years since it began.

Big social media platforms have helped accelerate the network effect, especially over the last five years. In 2015, Facebook, taking its inspiration from the ALS Ice Bucket Challenge, developed its fundraising platform. According to a Facebook press release, people have raised over $2 billion on Facebook to support the people and causes they care about, with $1 billion of that coming from birthday fundraisers alone. Facebook estimates that over 45 million people have donated to or created a fundraiser on Facebook, a number that has doubled over the past year.

Thus, the Social Media Age fueled the democratization of philanthropic giving. Now a new disruptive era, The Autonomous World [in which new technologies using AI and machine learning are automating human tasks by analyzing enormous amounts of data], has arrived, powered by artificial intelligence. As often occurs with new technologies, it has taken many years to work out the glitches and make AI easily usable and inexpensive. Now that AI is on the cusp of commercial accessibility, it is about to reshape activism and philanthropy.

Using YouTube for disaster fundraising appeals

Mervi Pantti, 2015

The relationship between the fundraiser and its audience takes center stage in this text, which examines how user-created appeals—produced by ordinary people via the YouTube platform—encourage the audience to donate money to help victims of major disasters. The main thrust of the argument is that ordinary people increasingly serve as mediators of humanitarian suffering and as voluntary intermediaries between aid organizations and the general public.

[...]

For instance, after the devastating tsunami in Japan in 2011, Jason, who lives in Japan but was visiting the United States at the time, published a personal video on YouTube entitled 'Help me HELP JAPAN.' The video was recorded in a single close-up shot and describes how bad and helpless he feels at not being able to help and comfort the people in Japan. 'I want to do something positive,' he says, and promises to donate 50 cents to the Japanese Red Cross for each positive comment posted.

[...]

This text asks how do these appeal videos, produced outside the official visibility of humanitarian organizations, function as moral educators? How do their audiences respond to their call to relieve distant suffering? Do their amateur textual strategies and aesthetics help to mobilize solidarity?

[...]

Volunteering in the post-humanitarian world

[...]

Social networking sites have become indispensable platforms for organizing humanitarian fundraising as they allow for the easy peer-to-peer sharing of messages through personal networks on behalf of the fundraisers' cause.

[...]

NGOs' campaigns are said to have increasingly adapted new methods to quell public distrust and the questioning of the authenticity and altruism of humanitarian communication. Ultimately, attempts by humanitarian organizations to gain legitimacy in the eyes of the public have led to a situation in which 'humanitarian organizations refrain from taking a stance and assuming a role as moral educators'. Against these suspicions, it is interesting to examine how grassroots campaigns on YouTube, with its emphasis on authenticity related to

DOI: 10.4324/9781003145936-119

participatory culture and peer-to-peer communication, function as a stage for moral education and whether the ordinariness of these fundraisers affects how their cause is perceived.

Grassroots appeals on YouTube

Combining video production and sharing with social networking features, YouTube enables various forms of interaction such as the possibility to rate, like/dislike and comment on a video. Next to its interactive, participatory potential, it can boast remarkably large audiences, even amateur productions and viral videos can attract tens of millions of views. For this study, 40 user-created disaster appeal videos were selected based on their popularity, the amount of viewer-comments they received and the need to include different forms of videos. Thus, each of the four cases (the 2010 Haiti earthquake, the 2011 Japan earthquake and tsunami, the 2011 East Africa drought and Typhoon Haiyan in the Philippines in 2013) is represented by ten videos. All the selected videos were posted by private individuals and explicitly ask for donations and include links to humanitarian organizations to enable the viewers to do that.

I divided these appeal videos into two broad categories according to how the ordinary humanitarians address their imaginary viewers: directly or indirectly. The first category (vlogs) contains videos either entirely filmed in an intimate shot, in which the poster speaks directly to camera in confessional style about his/her reaction to a disaster and makes his/her plea, or documents a fundraising performance by the YouTuber(s). Videos with an indirect address do not feature the actor but consist of self-made or existing footage, images, words and sound that form a montage. In the following, I identify and explore three elements in the videos and their descriptions: the emotional engagement, the moral agency of the viewer, and the trust-building mechanism.

The emotional engagement

In vlogs, which were the predominant form of video made concerning the tsunami in Japan, the emotional engagement is formed by the authentic emotional expressions and ordinariness of the humanitarian actors and their enthusiastic pleas for help. The victims are usually absent in the visual representation and present only in the textual and verbal descriptions. As a result, we are invited to empathize with the YouTuber, who functions as a proxy witness and representative of the victims. Some western vloggers say that they have been 'hit by the news,' while some Japanese vloggers have been personally affected by the disaster. This emotional turmoil they are experiencing becomes a justification for asking the viewer to share the moral responsibility of providing relief for the victims. An emotional engagement with an appeal vlog also arises from the aesthetic style, which is characterized by unedited close-ups or unprofessional camera movements and the everyday language the vlogger uses. Kevin's vlog entitled 'Haiti Earthquake Victims-Help Support [Donations]' is an exception to the producer-centered vlogs as images of the aftermath of the Haiti quake are seen in the background, while in the foreground Kevin pretends he is reporting from the scene:

> What's up, this is me, Kevin Wei, and I'm here in Haiti, helping people… ish. But I am helping them because I donated money to them so… that they could, like, build their economy and everything like that. And I want you to do it also. So, what I want you to do is grab your cell phone and text the word 'Haiti' to '90999' and what that's gonna do is take ten bucks from your next cell phone account to Red Cross so they could help Haiti.

Montage videos aim to raise funds by placing either the expression of global solidarity or the sufferers of a catastrophe at the center of the narrative. The former elicits a 'fantasy of a moral global community' by focusing on the communion and compassion of people witnessing a disaster, as in a video called 'JAPAN DISASTER Pray for Japan … from New York' that pictures ordinary people from different ethnic backgrounds on the streets of New York, holding a notepad where they have written their greetings to Japanese people such as 'Recover soon!' and 'I think of you.' The latter type of video montage is especially used in the African famine and Haiti appeals that operate within the traditional emotional regimes of humanitarian communication, i.e., empathy, shame, and guilt. As humanitarian narratives, they encourage the audience to act from an empathetic connection with the victims, and also from the notion of taking on moral responsibility in order to help end the suffering presented. In a video titled 'East Africa Appeal' we see heart-wrenching images and hear, in voiceover, the story of a starving baby:

> This is Umi. She's three months old. She weighs 1.7 kilos. That's less than two bags of sugar. She's suffering from hypothermia, pneumonia and severe dehydration. Umi hasn't eaten for five days. Her mother, Amina, is suffering from dehydration too. Her condition is so bad, that she's unable to feed Umi herself. … Many people have donated to the crisis in East Africa but there is still a severe shortfall. Please help children like Umi to survive. Thank you!

Agency of the viewer

The appeal videos mainly approach the viewer as a donor. In addition to the straightforward pleas to donate in the titles or the text of the videos or the address to the viewers, the fundraisers list several links to key humanitarian organizations in the video description—all of which collect money for a specific disaster, thus offering a relatively effortless donation. However, poster-centered vlogs differ from montage videos in that they offer opportunities for action and engagement that go beyond commenting or clicking on a donation link. For example, vloggers ask their audiences to translate their appeals into different languages, post links to the websites of humanitarian relief providers, post positive comments about the victims of the disaster, and so on. They aim to build collective moral agency by engaging their audience in humanitarian action in terms of both 'paying' and active 'speaking' on behalf of the disaster victims.

Some vloggers do this through playful solidarity campaigns which cross the border between the online realm and real world. Nigahiga, the maker of the most viewed video (7.7 million views) of the sample, says not only does he want to help Japan but also to encourage others to do so:

The purpose of this video was not only to support Japan myself, but to encourage others as well. I could have easily donated the money and not made a video about it, but I think it's a lot more important to get support from all over the world.

He promises to donate ten dollars for every honk he gets. We see him next to an intersection in Los Angeles holding a sign 'Honk if you love Japan' and having fun with his friends as people drive by and honk. This video became a trend-setter for amateur fundraising videos as his subscribers took the idea and produced their own 'Honk if you love Japan' video campaigns.

Authenticity and trust-building

In vlogs, the sense of authenticity is reinforced by the ordinariness of the amateur campaigners. This is most pronounced in Whiteboy7thst's video entitled 'HELP JAPAN!!!.' Whiteboy7thst consciously takes on the role of the intermediator between his followers and the victims of the disaster. He says he wants to raise awareness about the disaster among his subscribers (gamers [aged] between 12 and 21 years), who, according to him, are not well-informed because they 'do not follow news.'

While almost all the videos on the East-African famine placed their moral claim on photorealistic images of suffering, in vlogs the main strategy of the video producers for building moral legitimacy is to function as an exemplar of appropriate behavior regarding the disaster, that is, giving their time, effort and money to help those in need. The amateur fundraisers typically start by describing their own donation, or promise to donate in exchange for their audiences' attention and expressions of solidarity towards the cause. Thus, they follow the fundamental principles of fundraising, which say that fundraisers need to convince potential donors that they are deserving of their donations as they are doing volunteer work or have already made their own donations.

In order to understand the legitimacy that these ordinary fundraisers may have in the eyes of their audience, one must consider their profile on YouTube. Most of the authors joined YouTube long before the disaster occurred, and some of them have a large group of followers. Typically, they post videos on topics such as music, games, video-making, beauty, and everyday life. Consequently, the amateur appeals appear as ruptures within the normal YouTube diet of the followers and this, together with the ordinariness of the posters and the amateur aesthetics of the videos, may contribute to their moral weight and legitimacy. Only the authors of the African famine videos, with their societal and spiritual interests, did not have this lifestyle and entertainment-orientation.

While the peer-to-peer nature of amateur humanitarian appeals may help to circumvent the shoot the messenger effect, the distrust of the communication of humanitarian organizations is present in these appeals too, which obviously operate within a broader media context and the broader humanitarian discourse. The distrust is seen, for example, in how the YouTube humanitarians emphasize the legitimacy of the NGOs that they are raising funds for, and in how they try to safeguard their own legitimacy and altruism by showing evidence of their own transaction with an aid agency.

Viewer-comments on the amateur fundraising videos

It is assumed here that comments [posted under the videos by viewers] might give insights into how audiences respond to the moral calls of the videos, and how these responses may vary depending on the case or on the textual and emotional strategies of a video. For each video, the first 100 original comments—or as many as available, excluding comments on the comments— were categorized inductively into [eleven] different categories: (1) Clearly stated intention to donate or statement that donation has been made; (2) Sympathy for the author and appreciation of the author's video; (3) Sympathy for the victims; (4) Distrust related to donation; (5) Annoyance about other users' comments; (6) Annoyance about the topic; (7) Hostility towards the author/video/other users; (8) Hostility towards the topic and donation; (9) Neutral comments; (10) Other users' calls to visit their page/watch video/call a number; (11) Off-topic comments; and [a further category of] Non-classified comments(in languages other than English, unrecognized symbols, etc.)

The total viewer and comment numbers and the number of positive and negative ratings offer initial insights into the reactions of the viewers. The differences between the cases are notable. In total, the videos raising funds for the Japan disaster collected almost 12,500,000 views while the Haiti videos received about 600,000. Moreover, the Japan videos were liked about 275,000 times in comparison to less than 2,000 likes for both the Africa and Haiti videos. The latter have considerably fewer comments than the videos for Japan. The differences in these numbers reveal, on the one hand, the longstanding fact about the geopolitics of suffering: some crises and lives are less deserving of our attention than others, and in this respect citizen appeals on YouTube are no different from other mass media representations. Japanese victims are approached as our equals, while African and Haitian victims are represented as powerless and distant others. It is also important to note that only in the appeals on behalf of Japan and the Philippines did the YouTubers come from the disaster-struck nations and regions, or were of Japanese or Filipino origin. These appeals can be understood as giving a voice to the affected communities. On the other hand, the differences are connected to the hierarchy of the popularity of YouTubers. Almost all of the YouTubers who organized fundraising for Japan have a significant number of subscribers, which obviously predicts a higher number of views.

The study was interested in finding out which narrative strategies and ways to appeal generated the most and the least intentions to donate, and most and least expressions of empathy for the victims of the disasters. The first observation to be made is that the responses were different in every case. What stands out is that the Haiti earthquake received the least comments expressing empathy but generated the most racist comments, echoing the racialized representations of Haitian victims as unorganized and lawless, which were present in the reporting of the disaster in the mainstream media. Overall, the percentage of those who expressed their intention to make a donation is small (5%), especially in comparison to the largest categories of comments, which were sympathy for the poster of an appeal (25%) and off-topic comments (24%). In addition, it is clear that these appeals generated more expressions of sympathy for their makers than for the victims of the disasters (13%).

While the comments differed from case to case, some general trends can be identified. First, celebrity and popular culture driven appeals typically generated an overflow of off-topic comments and respectively very few expressions of compassion. What is also clear is that video montages focusing on the suffering of victims created more empathetic responses than vlogs that centered on the feelings and actions of the self-made humanitarian: this is true for all four disasters. The appeal video which generated most empathetic comments for the victims (87%), the least amount of off-topic comments (2%), and no aggressive reactions is the video montage 'Horn of Africa Drought 2011 – Give me hope that 'help' is coming!' which showed shocking images of suffering. Similarly, in the case of the Haiti quake, the video which earned the biggest share of intentions to donate (17%) was a photorealistic montage of stills depicting the horror of the earthquake's aftermath.

[…]

Conclusion

It has been suggested that YouTube offers a new site of cosmopolitan citizenship due to its (partial) autonomy from commercial media and its rootedness in ordinary experiences and popular discourse, which can lead to enhanced opportunities for participation and public dialogue. While citizens have traditionally volunteered to assist established aid organizations in their disaster responses, self-organized fundraising extends the range of the engagement of citizens conducting humanitarian action. So far, most academic attention regarding digital volunteers responding to a disaster has been given to the practices of the technical volunteer communities. However, there is a need to look at the new citizen roles and actions from a wider perspective and to examine how citizen volunteering and participation in the informal contexts of everyday life may cultivate a cosmopolitan solidarity by constructing a sense of togetherness and collective responsibility.

The specific case of grassroots fundraising on YouTube illustrates such attempts to construct commitment and solidarity. By drawing on a variety of textual strategies and emotional addresses, from shocking photorealistic imagery to playful performances of solidarity, they ask for their viewers' voice and for their money. Thus, they do not entirely correspond with the low-intensity action and emotionality of post-humanitarian appeals, as described by Lilie Chouliaraki, even if they displace the moral 'why' question and, in many videos, center on the campaigners rather than on the victims. Moreover, as we have also seen, they are equally bound by the geopolitically inflected narratives of disasters just like traditional organizers of humanitarian aid are. The fact that the global solidarity enacted in these citizen appeals is rooted in the emotional experiences and life worlds of YouTubers means that culturally close victims are accorded more attention than more distant ones. In addition to reproducing a global hierarchy of human suffering, they also reproduce the deep, global digital divide: whereas the citizens in the Philippines and Japan participate in the donor mobilization, affected people in Haiti and East-Africa do not speak for themselves and remain in the role of the helped.

The appreciation and empathy expressed in the comments suggest that this peer-to-peer moral education may help, to some extent, to get round the widely documented distrust of humanitarian organizations (and the main-stream media). YouTube fundraisers use their own authentic ordinariness to act as intermediaries between aid organizations and the public. However, the impact of these appeals cannot be verified in terms of donations or further action for a humanitarian cause. Nevertheless, this grassroots humanitarianism also allows for hopeful readings of its moral possibilities, in particular regarding its potential to include the voices of the affected communities and to reach unlikely donors, especially youths, while simultaneously bringing the idea of solidarity with distant others into their everyday media use.

6.5 Trends and predictions

Seven trends to watch

Penelope Cagney and Bernard Ross, 2013

Trend 1: There is a continuing growth of great wealth and some of it is being diverted to philanthropy

Great wealth is no longer confined to the developed world – but it is still concentrated in a small number of countries. It is also concentrated in the hands of a small number of people as global inequalities increase. The inequalities exist in many nations – but they raise some significant challenges in territories like those in the Gulf or nations like Russia where there is a more limited commitment to transparency about how wealth is acquired or distributed. For fundraisers the challenge may not simply be securing funds but ensuring that the funds secured will fit with the value and ethical base of their charity.

Regardless of the ethical challenges about who really owns the money, or even how they got it, there is a growing interest among nonprofits in major donors, with increasing numbers of domestic and international NGOs making specialist appointments [of fundraising and development staff] to improve their potential. But this organizational issue in fundraising is not necessarily matched by donor interest in philanthropy. So, although the Giving Pledge has taken off in the United States, it has been less successful in engaging the rich elsewhere. And Carlos Slim – one of the world's richest men – has publicly expressed his frustration at the poor performance of NGOs in addressing the challenges in his native Mexico. Many philanthropists indeed are setting up their own operating agencies or looking for new ways to deliver change. This is a challenge to NGOs that have believed that all philanthropy should be channelled through them.

Even where NGOs are the preferred channel, the culture of philanthropy needs to take root and become more sophisticated to enable fundraisers to do their work well. In parallel we need donors to become more effective in how they invest.

Trend 2: Nonprofit innovations, in fundraising and elsewhere, are no longer coming just from the United States or Europe

There are exciting and challenging innovations growing up in fundraising in India and China and Argentina and Kenya. These innovations are not simply technological, but may relate to recognition of how different cultures can

DOI: 10.4324/9781003145936-121

engage in fundraising and philanthropy. By learning about these developments we may inform our own learning on fundraising.

In Argentina, for example, there are extremely high levels of online giving. This is partly a result of a poor postal system. But that lack of a postal system has driven charities to be more creative and imaginative in the way they engage with donors – moving to online engagement on a scale only dreamed of elsewhere. In Ethiopia we're seeing some of the largest mass participation events in the world, especially marathons but also telethons – creating simple acquisition channels for charities to gain access to potential donors. Hogar de Christo in Chile is a parish and faith-based charity that relies on the world's largest and possibly best-organized team of volunteers and door-to-door collections to deliver fundraising results. At a time when many charities are struggling to engage volunteers, this domestic NGO offers real insights into new ways of gathering and aligning supporters.

In Thailand Cabbages and Condoms avoids donor-based fundraising and instead runs commercial businesses to raise cash for its social projects. (And it does so as a conscious and successful choice.) Thanks to its success as a socially engaged business it not only runs a chain of restaurants and a holiday resort but it uses the significant profits generated to pay for education, HIV work, prison reform projects, and many more. We see the same phenomenon in Kenya where the Red Cross Society, once financially dysfunctional, now successfully runs a chain of hotels that provide income for its relief services. All of these experiments contain important lessons for any fundraiser anywhere in the world.

Trend 3: Indigenous NGOs/NPOs continue to grow in number throughout the world, but there are some leviathans emerging

As the role of the state is challenged worldwide, charities, NPOs (nonprofit organizations) and NGOs are growing in number and increasingly taking on civil society roles in health, education, and social service. So the Red Cross in Kenya has set up and runs a successful ambulance service where the government service is seen as ineffective. This growth – for example, the number of NGOs in the Philippines has grown by 50 percent in the past 10 years – is increasing pressure on fundraisers and fundraising to deliver more money for more causes.

At the same time a small number of large INGOs – Save the Children, UNICEF, World Vision, for example – have broken away in growth terms to form a super league of agencies able to fundraise and operate almost anywhere in the world. They have aggressive market entry strategies, significant investment funds, and teams dedicated to setting up and sustaining fundraising domestic operations. To many domestic NGOs these agencies can seem like Walmart or McDonald's – a form of unwelcome globalization. These super league agencies can invest in developing new markets and are aggressively doing so. Some markets – Brazil, South Korea, India – represent the fundraising equivalent of BRICs. And just as businesses are flocking to BRICs, so INGOs are flocking to these high-growth philanthropic markets.

Most of these agencies are European or North American in origin and act in many ways like commercial multinationals. Surprisingly, perhaps, there are still only early signs of a developing world agency growing to global INGO status. Early candidates like Asia's BRAC [Building Resources Across Communities, an international development organisation based in Bangladesh] and Grameen have grown and work in a number of countries. But both may never really grow to global status as they suffer under significant political pressure as result of their success and growth.

Trend 4: There is considerable debate worldwide about the role of philanthropy and the role of the state

There is certainly a growth in adoption of the capitalist/free-market ideology worldwide generally – despite the recent global financial crisis and the challenges offered by the Occupy movement and other critics. Philanthropy in some areas is a companion ideology to free-market capitalism. An increased role for fundraising is being accelerated by the global financial crisis – philanthropy is being asked to do more as governments have reduced funds and so seek to do less. As noted earlier, specifically there is a perceived growing role for wealthy donors. This approach is shared in the book *Philanthrocapitalism* by Matthew Bishop. It can be summarized as "a new approach to solving social problems based on innovative partnerships between business, nonprofits, and government." In practice the partnership seeks to draw in corporations and wealthy individuals to what has historically been a governmental space in many countries.

But it's important to stress that not everyone agrees with this growth in the role of philanthropy in addressing social challenges. The Gates/Buffett Giving Pledge has not played well in some European and Eastern nations where some millionaires have seen the pledge as potentially undermining the "proper" role of the state in education, in health, and in social security. In this case they may see the proper role for wealthy individuals' philanthropy as more focused in other directions like culture, medical research, and overseas aid.

The growth of philanthropy is also tied to democracy and to the promotion of civil society, home to NPOs and NGOs.

This linkage leads to a troubling trend – as in Ethiopia, Rwanda, Russia, and elsewhere – where "anti-NGO" legislation is currently pending or recently passed at the time of this writing. Where NGOs are not banned outright, defunding through regulation is practiced in many quasi-democracies. There are about four dozen countries where civil society has been threatened over the past few years. Venezuela has a new law, not yet in force at the time of this writing, putting NGOs under permanent surveillance by the state while Zimbabwe simply suspended many of them entirely.

This trend appears even in parts of the world where new democracies have been formed. After the Arab Spring uprisings, a crackdown on U.S. funded pro-democracy groups in Egypt and a bill before parliament that would further restrict nongovernmental organizations inhibited development work and activism. The move against NGOs had been accompanied by personal attacks, threats, and intimidation of activists, particularly women [activists].

This is a troubling trend because NGOs by and large seek to work alongside governments and business. But they need a license to do so.

Trend 5: Fundraising is becoming more professional and professionalized

The explosion in fundraising has fueled a demand for fundraisers with skills and experience. The reality is that there are not enough fundraisers to fill all the posts available. In turn this has led, in many countries, to significant wage inflation for skilled and able fundraisers. This can cause challenges where, for example, senior fundraisers are paid significantly more than senior service staff – or even CEOs. Another implication has been the explosion of interest in qualifications for fundraisers – as organizations seek to "grow their own" and give fundraising stronger theoretical underpinning. In the United States, Canada, and Europe there are now professional qualifications for fundraisers to degree level offered by universities as well as extensive programs of continuous professional development offered by the main professional bodies such as AFP (the U.S.-based Association of Fundraising Professionals) and IoF (the U.K.-based Institute of Fundraising) as well as private providers. Some recent research by the Resource Alliance suggests that there may be 20-plus countries actively involved in developing qualifications in this field with Singapore, for example, a world leader. But note that if you live in Kenya you can also secure an internationally recognized qualification as a fundraiser. And in Mexico there is a boom in courses and programs to respond to the local demand for Spanish-speaking fundraisers. Increasingly fundraising is seen as a genuine career with a development path. This growth brings professionalization and with it regulation and codification.

Trend 6: Everyone agrees that new and social technologies are important, but they disagree on how

Despite many predictions of their demise, "old" technologies in direct marketing are still delivering the most income to charities. And direct mail, telephone, and especially street fundraising like face-to-face (or direct dialogue) fundraising remain the most important sources of donor acquisition for nonprofits worldwide. Some old technologies have been given new life, as when Thunderbird International Graduate School of Management conducted an alumni phonathon, but in keeping with the global nature of its alumni, had multilingual student volunteers call around the clock to connect with people in various time zones. In other instances these established approaches are being combined with newer methodologies – with "telefacing," a combination of door-to-door and telephone giving, being one such idea developed in India and now growing in popularity. Tried and true methods must balance the excitement about online, social, and mobile fundraising. Everyone agrees that these newer approaches are important and will grow in importance. But part of the challenge that is not clear is what their importance will be.

For some the big debate is about "platform" with some agencies focusing on improving their web experience for laptop users while others like Greenpeace are focusing on the mobile experience arguing that the smart phone will soon supplant even laptops, tablets, and so on. For others there are big debates about the proper role of new and social technologies. So, are they simply a means to enhance supporter experience, or a way to link up existing supporters, or as a content-rich and flexible acquisition channel?

Many "gurus" claim to have the answer but the jury is still out in terms of results. What 's clear is that some early successes are emerging. Kiva, with its online micro-credit model has become a model for social engagement in new approaches to philanthropy. Care2Give took the idea and has made it work in Europe more effectively. Interestingly, social media use is not directly related to fundraising success. Brazil has easily the highest penetration of social media use – much greater than the United States. But it is hardly used for fundraising.

Beyond the current inconclusive data there are always inspirational anecdotal examples – many emerging from the Arab Spring. For example, a Tunisian NGO that did a great job raising funds on Facebook, attracting not only individual givers but corporate sponsorship as well. An Australian family raised more than $600,000 with Facebook and Twitter in order to buy a large building where they could live and share their home with asylum seekers and people in desperate need. But it's not always easy to convert desire to cash. So, another example is of the Jordanian family who used Facebook to raise funds to buy the license of a taxi after the driver, their primary source of support, died of leukemia. Seven hundred and fifty friends pledged $8,000 on the site. But these pledges couldn't be collected online because there was no platform for this. The media exists – but you need a secure and tax-efficient vehicle to convert the goodwill to cash.

This lack of a genuinely global platform for giving makes international giving more difficult … Beyond the platform is the issue of tax allowance across borders. The real barrier for most Americans to give internationally has been the expectation of a tax break for their donations to NGOs outside the United States.

[…]

The future will bring even more change. And this change will generate new, and sometimes startling, ethical questions about the use of technology … The biggest question for fundraisers is: How can the Internet and technology be used to nurture a worldwide culture of philanthropy?

Trend 7: Philanthropy thrives best when there are codified civil society structures and regulations for nonprofit agencies

In order for fundraising to flourish donors have to be able to recognize and relate to the special status of NGOs/NPOs.

In some countries this special status is well established with sophisticated regulatory regimes and tax advantages. Even in these sophisticated settings these vary and there are significant distinctions between the U.K. definition of a charity and the U.S. definition of a nonprofit ... Despite these differences it is basically easier to set up and operate as a charity in the United Kingdom, the United States, or most of Europe.

But in other countries and territories such as China, the Gulf, and Russia, these charitable structures are still being developed. (In Russia and elsewhere as noted earlier, some would argue it is becoming increasingly hard to operate independently as an NGO/NPO.)

Many fundraisers and donors consider this lack of a codified approach in their country is significantly hindering the development of a genuinely transparent and sustainable philanthropic culture ... Effective structures and regulatory policies are important to drive trust – one of the key advantages that NGOs have. Donors need to trust that the money will be spent properly – and where it is not, that some judicial process will call the NGO to account. So important is this that UNICEF internationally has a goal to be seen as the most trusted agency in key markets. The belief is that increased trust will help drive increased giving.

There also needs to be agreement about what constitutes good governance – so important to fundraising. Jon Stettner, CEO of Make-a-Wish International, has observed in his work around the world that there is little consistency about board practices and expectations. He has found, for instance, that in some cultures board rotation can be a challenge. Coming off a board suggests that one has not performed well. Remaining on indefinitely means that one is considered a valued board member. In some cultures, board giving is de rigueur – and in other cultures is actively frowned on. The key message here is that philanthropy probably can't change the world on its own. It needs to form part of a group of regulated civil society actors working toward the greater good. And those other actors – government and business – need to know their proper place. And the rules by which each operate need to be explicit.

Surviving the next financial crisis

Mal Warwick, 2009

Our economy is in bad shape and will only get worse. So what can we fundraisers do to minimize the impact of this difficult period on our organizations, and at the same time maximize our income?

Reassess the Whole Ball of Wax. Fundraising, Marketing, and Communications. Accountability mechanisms and systematic evaluation are essential management practices. Unfortunately, the nonprofit sector does not universally employ them. But economic distress has a way of pushing us to assess thoroughly all that we're doing. Now's the time to put in place a regular process that will allow your fundraising, marketing, and communications programs to function at the highest degree of efficiency and effectiveness.

Strengthen Your Case for Giving. Although many of us in the social sector believe the public owes us a living—we've nobly accepted lower pay and longer hours, after all—money doesn't just materialize. It has to be earned. And there's nothing better than a recession to drive this point home. Take the opportunity to re-examine your case for giving. And be certain your donors understand both the more urgent need for your services during tough times and the many concrete steps you're taking to increase your efficiency and effect-iveness. Just be careful not to make a big deal about how your organization's fundraising efforts are suffering. Take it from me: Your donors don't care. They care about how your clients or beneficiaries are faring.

Stick with What Works. Many fundraising consultants and nonprofit managers are enamored with "creativity." But when that word means nothing more than flashy graphics and splashes of brightly colored ink, everyone loses. If the decades-long experience of direct marketers has anything at all to teach the fundraising profession, it's that different isn't always better. An economic downturn does not justify throwing out what has worked in the past. In fact, it's a time for caution and cost cutting.

Cut Costs with a Scalpel, Not an Ax. There are lots of easy ways to cut fundraising costs. You can stop prospecting for new donors. You can elim-inate thank-yous to donors. You can cut out telemarketing efforts, slash the direct mail budget, and reduce the major gift staff. The only problem with this heedless approach is that it's a prescription for bankruptcy.

Business goes on, whatever the economic conditions. You can't not raise funds. You can't treat loyal and responsive donors like statistics. And you can't stop building your donor database. If you do these things, your donor list will

DOI: 10.4324/9781003145936-122

shrink through attrition and your income will slack off to a dribble. The only defensible, business like way to respond to an economic crisis is to recognize that fundraising requires both continuing investment and ongoing care. If the choice arises between cutting back slightly on programs or slashing the fundraising budget, you may shoot yourself in the foot if you opt for the latter. It doesn't take long to destroy an effective fundraising operation – and then where will your programs be?

Fish Where the Big Fish Are. It's obvious to anyone professionally involved in fundraising that it's generally more cost-effective to raise money in big chunks than in little ones. A grant from an institutional funder or a significant gift from an individual major donor rarely comes at a high cost of fundraising. And anyone who's attended even one fundraising conference or workshop has surely become acquainted with the Pareto Principle, or 80/20 rule, which teaches us that a relatively small number of more generous donors account for the lion's share of the net philanthropic revenue our organizations receive. All of this points to the wisdom of focusing more time, effort, and money on generous and responsive donors and less effort on less productive ones.

Yet how many nonprofits truly make use of the simple computer tools that allow us to take advantage of these self-evident truths by grouping donors into distinct segments based on their giving histories? If your organization has the habit of treating all of your donors the same way, it's time to examine how you can fine-tune your program with a well-considered segmentation plan.

If you're already well acquainted with segmentation, then it's time to consider focusing more on mid-level as well as major donors and excluding your least generous supporters from expensive appeals by mail or phone.

Be Attentive to Your Donors. A study of high net worth American donors conducted late in 2008 by the Center on Philanthropy at Indiana University for Bank of America revealed that the No. 1 reason donors stopped giving to a particular charity was "no longer feeling connected to the organization." This is no surprise. All donors need to feel appreciated. They need to feel informed. Their confidence in the charity needs to be constantly reinforced. At no time can a nonprofit operate as though its donors will continue giving no matter how they're treated.

Do Due Diligence. No major gift officer worth her salt would dream of visiting a prospect without attempting to uncover every possible bit of intelligence on the prospect's giving history and personal interests (among many other things). Why, then, is it wrong for a fundraiser who deals with hundreds or thousands of donors at a time – through the mail, by phone, or online – to gather personal information about potential donors before approaching them for gifts? Sadly, most direct response fundraisers act as though this is an unnatural act. We work from bare-bones databases. Generic appeals predominate. We write to our "Dear Friend" or our "Dear Donor" without any inkling of what might interest or motivate that person. Surely, we all understand that such an impersonal approach might be necessary in new-donor acquisition efforts. But don't we know more about our donors than simply that they've given us money once upon a time?

If we have anything more than the most rudimentary of databases, we know how much our donors have given, and how frequently. We know how long they've been giving to us. And we know what sort of appeal triggered their initial gifts, whether it was a letter, a phone call, e-mail, a visit to our Web site, or a conversation with a friend. Even if that's all the information we integrate into our appeals, surely it'll do a better job of securing additional support than a crude "Dear Donor" letter!

Step Up Your Efforts Online. Billions of dollars have been raised online. But the lion's share of that money has gone into the coffers of humanitarian relief organizations such as the American Red Cross, The Salvation Army, and UNICEF; the highest-profile U.S. presidential campaigns, most notably Barack Obama's; and, to a lesser extent, the leading advocacy organizations, such as the Human Rights Campaign, Amnesty International, and Greenpeace. And all those billions, despite how large the numbers might seem, represent a tiny fraction of general philanthropic revenue (somewhere between 1 and 3 percent in the United States, depending on whom you ask).

Online fundraising for its own sake does not represent the salvation of the nonprofit sector in a difficult economy. And yet the online channel has multiple benefits for nonprofit fundraisers, most of them having nothing to do directly with money: attracting younger supporters, providing constituents with opportunities for participation in your work, and reinforcing appeals sent through other channels, to name just three. An enhanced investment in online communications will pay many dividends, reinforcing near-term fundraising efforts and laying the foundation for a more prosperous future.

Break Down the Silos. Here's how fundraising typically goes at major universities: The communications department sends an alumna a magazine. The liberal arts college sends her its solicitations a couple of times a year. The university annual fund enlists students to call her. The history department (her major) is all over her for a gift, too. So is the graduate school of social science (where she received her MA) and the alumni association, which is constantly mailing brochures about exotic trips around the world. And I could go on. Is it any wonder so many universities cry about the low rate of annual fund "participation" by their alumni?

This reality, which also applies to some degree at thousands of nonprofits and institutions, cries out for a referee to minimize the mid-air collisions of all those messages. Some minimal degree of centralized scheduling among all these competing offices would surely reduce donor attrition. Indeed, a truly integrated program of fundraising, marketing, and communications would boost revenue, even under the worst external conditions.

Am I saying that if you follow this recommendation – and all of my others – the recession will go away? Will you achieve fundraising nirvana? Hardly. I offer these suggestions because I believe that if you apply them judiciously, you'll maximize your income in the short run and preserve your capacity for renewed growth once economic conditions improve. At the least, I hope you'll find my optimism reassuring.

What will fundraising look like in 2045?

Carolyn J. Cordery, Karen A. Smith, and Harry Berger, 2017

Recent reports paint a bleak future for charities at the local level, with generosity in decline and volunteers in short supply. Traditional means of philanthropy (such as regular volunteering, grants and street appeals) are being abandoned and, while new forms of giving are emerging, donors and recipients report barriers to finding productive and effective models of giving. Further, fundraising scandals are frequently reported, suggesting regulation is not synchronized with new methods, and controversies arise over, for example, what Kapoor calls 'celebrity humanitarianism'. Charities' preoccupation is with the short-term future, dependent on current political policies and giving models. There are also concerns that increased professionalization of the charity sector has led to higher staff perquisites, diminishing the public benefits available. In addition to local concerns, it appears that few countries are immune from global drivers such as: demographic changes (for example, ageing populations in the developed world), commercialization, and rapidly changing information technology that pushes charities' causes into the 'global stratosphere'. As a response to the changing world, we look forward one generation and ask, what will the charity sector look like in the developed world in 2045?

[...]

Demographic shifts: impacts on local services and volunteers

Demographic shifts are a critical issue to which charitable organizations must respond. In the developed world attention is focused on the ageing population. The final report of the UK's Commission on the Voluntary Sector and Ageing notes that, by 2033, nearly a quarter of the UK population will be aged 65 or older. This should result in more (older) volunteers. Yet, similar to the conclusions of the European Commission, the 2015 Commission notes that these people will be more unequal, significantly impacting the charity sector … Changing demographics do not predict a single future; some older people will struggle financially as pensions become less available, others will seek a carefree retirement where 'having fun' may not necessarily result in an older group of committed volunteers (as is common now), and where those that do volunteer are more likely to want to have a say in the running of the charity. Carney suggests that the "biggest challenge will be in adapting to having a

DOI: 10.4324/9781003145936-123

much larger target group" both in needing to provide care to a larger number of older people and in having a greater population of older people that seek to volunteer and will need to be well managed.

Technological change: global reach and local efficiencies

Technology already disrupts charities' ability to raise funds, primarily by increasing their global reach and allowing for innovation. Saxton et al. note that in 2015, 35% of the United Kingdom (UK) population uses their phones to access the internet, but that this is forecast to rise to 69% by 2020. By 2045, phones may be replaced by other devices, but reliance on technology will continue to increase. The Institute for the Future identified 'crowd-power' as a future force in philanthropy. Here, online platforms are leveraged to gain resources, as seen in the 2015 craze of the ice-bucket challenge. We note that such challenges work only when charities also leverage well-formed partnerships, or respond to viral opportunities in a timely and appropriate manner.

Charities for whom membership is a key input to the business model will also be disrupted by technology. De Cagna identifies the ability to utilize social networks without needing to 'belong' to a charity or other association. Thus, he highlights necessary innovations such as a crowd-sourcing strategy to engage key stakeholders; collaborating digitally; and doing away with a physical presence (The Institute for the Future calls this 'adhocracy'). Such resourcing may not be in local currencies, with bitcoin, credits from game-playing and so on, being mobilized as charity resources. The Institute for the Future notes that such mobilization will also call for 'radical transparency' from charities, as they are accountable for the resources they use.

[…]

Resources: funding from government and corporates

In a recent report of what the future might hold for the charitable sector, Alcock et al. note that a turning point has been reached, in the UK at least. The New Public Management reforms of last century, when charity funding changed from grants to government contracts, were replaced in the 21st century with 'Big Society' and now austerity, to the extent that some wonder if it is the end of the charity sector. In addition, a report from the United States reaffirms the blurring of sectoral boundaries which, along with the failure of many charities in the Global Financial Crisis, confirms the sector is at a cross-road. Charities have responded to these funding disruptions in diverse ways. Larger organizations have professionalized to engage with government and other funders, but smaller, regionally dispersed and voluntary organizations have reduced their engagement. Greater regulations to ensure delivery, accountability and efficiency have arisen as the larger charities in the sector replace government delivery of social services, rather than supplementing services as they did previously. Professionalization has raised questions as to whether the core values of the sector are being undermined by a strategy focusing on where the next dollar is coming from, and whether charities are acting more like government departments or corporates, rather than drawing on charitable, human compassion.

With governments focusing on austerity, charities have been drawn to partnering with corporates to remain sustainable. These partnerships raise the possibility of a 'win–win' as corporates respond to demands for social responsibility through funding and encouraging corporate volunteering. Philanthropy New Zealand and Funding Information Service's report on Business Giving summarizes the means through which firms currently support charities: for example, cause-related marketing, foundation grants, encouraging employee (payroll) giving, sponsorship, donations, pro bono services or goods, scholarships and staff involvement. Nevertheless, corporates report being overwhelmed by calls for help, and charities complain about having to make 'value propositions' when the success of many of their services are extremely hard to measure. Concerns have been raised about the ethics of these relationships, which have to be well managed if they are to succeed. Martinez highlights other negative consequences of alliances that go beyond the corporate merely making grants. These include unethical behaviour by corporates which impacts charities' 'brands' and the power imbalance of corporates in any alliance. On the other hand, a 'parasitic attitude' by charities is likely to result in corporates selecting only the large, well-known and respected charities to work with. For businesses, the main challenge is selecting appropriate social projects.

Yet, corporates' use of their support of a charity as a marketing tool for their brand (and ensuing charity marketization) raises the danger of the charity providing services that are at odds with their mission (known as 'mission drift'), also impairing the charity 'brand'. The UK-based study of McKay et al. argues … that ongoing government austerity will result in a split so that some successful charities will be funded commercially to deliver goods and services, and the remainder through philanthropy and voluntary effort. The former may experience more variable revenue streams.

Resources: support from volunteers

Tighter funding has led to increased demands for volunteers to replace paid staff in professional charities. Nevertheless, paid and unpaid staff are not perfect substitutes, but are often complementary, meaning both are needed. Accordingly, Saxton et al. note that "austerity may be the root of volunteering innovation". We have already noted the rise of corporate partnerships with charities that may also provide volunteers. These are positive moves. As new people are introduced to volunteering, there should be increased investment in voluntary support and positive spin-offs to volunteering outside of work hours. However, Lee suggests that charities' volunteer managers face significant challenges in managing such volunteering. There is other evidence that volunteering is changing. Nichols et al. note a reduction in willingness to volunteer, relating to changes in notions of citizenship within society and reducing engagement in collective action. In contrast to the long term volunteers who commit to a particular organization and regularly volunteer for the same tasks (for example, in sports), Rochester et al. note that episodic or short-term volunteering is a "rapidly growing phenomenon". These episodic volunteers may be interim (over a short period) or temporary (once only).

[…]

Future scenarios for the charity sector in 2045

[…]

These futures are typically exaggerated extremes, representing the potential consequences of a small number of key contextually-specific drivers (including trends and current issues) as a combined set. The real future will likely be found in the overlap between the potential worlds, drawing aspects from all of them.

We have already noted demographic changes, technology and strong trends of resourcing (funding and volunteers) as drivers in the charity sector's future. From these we derived two sets of extremes. The first set of extremes derived from the literature is between increasing globalization through increasing migration and technology; its opposite is local efforts to deliver charity … Charities' resourcing describes the second set of extremes, as the marketization of charities has raised concerns that the charitable sector will be at risk of diverging from its compassionate mission if it is to adopt the values of the market by seeking commercial revenue. This is relevant to government and corporate funding, as the drive for small government (of which austerity is a symptom) has further forced marketization in resolving social needs. Hence, the opposite extreme to marketization is compassion – the value at risk. Milbourne and Murray state this more strongly, noting "competition and profit motives are blatantly inappropriate for welfare and in producing good quality services in supposedly caring services".

[…]

These extremes and four possible future worlds [result in]: Government-funded Elite (Mega Charity), Corporate Cooperation (Charity Ltd), Home Grown (My Charity) and Crowd-Sourced (Our Charity). In each case, we propose an archetypical charity that embodies the dominant features of the scenario.

The first two scenarios concern marketization and show the contrast between global and local extremes.

Government-funded elite

Mega Charity has responded to governments' increasing austerity drives by becoming the provider of choice in an elite group. Therefore, despite austerity, Mega Charity continues to grow, through what Murray and Milbourne term 'predatory behaviours', expanding its services to include those already being offered by smaller charities. Mega Charity takes every opportunity to access government funding, including in the global 'market' following natural disasters and from international aid ...

Corporate cooperation

Charity Ltd leaves the global scale of governmental funding to Mega Charity and instead focuses on corporate funding. Corporates are more likely to seek local impact to increase their market share and could become like 'ministates' as they assume a prominent role in society. Charity Ltd targets corporates for whom the social and environmental agenda has forced fundamental changes to strategy. This agenda is on the rise due to pressures on energy and the environment (as identified by the European Commission, Yeoman, the NIC and the Mowat Centre). Charity Ltd knows that corporates wish to report that they are being more responsible in making their money, and want to show that their staff are actively volunteering for the public good. Nevertheless, such charity revenue can be volatile, as grants and donations are substituted for corporate support, driving Charity Ltd's strategy and delivery further into corporate marketization and away from compassion.

The other two scenarios are driven by compassion rather than marketization. Again we contrast local and global extremes.

Home grown

My Charity is compassionate and has a local focus. Key drivers for My Charity are the rise of individual empowerment and also the ageing population. It is imperative that My Charity captures able, older citizens to volunteer for and donate to its cause, especially since My Charity has become extremely busy serving an increasingly diverse population with urgent social needs (not necessarily age-related) ... My Charity seeks also to foster new models of resourcing which will attract more supporters.

Crowd-sourced

Our Charity harnesses technology, depending on a globally-focused 'crowd-sourced' world. Our Charity ... exploits online platforms (in whatever form they take in 2045), channelling crowd-sourced donations, volunteering, and other support for its charitable purposes. Our charity builds on the increasingly important social capital that sees relationships as key to success. As Our Charity draws on different currencies, crowd-power radically reshapes its resourcing ... Our Charity knows that individuals want to be empowered, which it encourages through storytelling and allowing donors to donate directly to specific individuals or projects.

Discussion and conclusions

[…]

Each scenario has drawbacks, or 'danger zones', which must be mitigated if the scenario, or even elements of the scenario, are realized. If the sector becomes replete with Mega Charities, then their preferential receipt of government income will crowd out smaller, and locally based charities … As charities have traditionally assisted government in linking to local citizens, a government-funded elite will change the face of civil society.

[…]

Will Charity Ltds become merely public relations arms of transnational corporations who wish to be seen as doing good, rather than actually carrying out their charitable missions? This resourcing model is dependent upon corporate resources, and with globalization, will Charity Ltds harness sufficient stable resources to survive and deliver their localized missions?

The danger zone of My Charities is based on the ethos of the sector – relationships. … Despite the compassionate nature of Our Charities, this scenario's danger zone is the dependence on philanthropic support from a global, technologically connected populace. It is likely that Our Charities' donors do not have the view of the whole landscape of social need, and therefore they consider only specific outcomes. How do Our Charities addressing localized need or unglamorous problems attract the attention of a global citizenry? Commentators, like Chomsky, have warned of increasing corporate encroachment on net neutrality and the freedom of the internet, meaning that increased advertising and limits to accessibility are likely to be a feature of technology in 2045. What if maximising Our Charities' donations depends on corporations that control the internet, rather than crowd-power?

[…]

The focus of the futures material studied, and thus our paper, is on the developed world. While the global is a dimension of our scenarios, this is considered within the context of charitable entities based in the developed world. Further research is therefore required on drives of the charitable sector on a global basis, incorporating developing work perspectives. Nevertheless, in offering four possible worlds for 2045, we have highlighted the impact of drivers within these extremes and also the 'danger zones' or drawbacks that could occur if these futures are to become reality.

Sources and copyright information

Ahern, T. (2007) *How to Write Fundraising Materials that Raise More Money: The Art, the Science, the Secrets*. Medfield, MA: Emerson & Church. Copyright © 2007 Emerson & Church. Republished with permission.

Beaton, E. E., LePere-Schloop, M. and Smith, R. (2021) "Whatever it takes": sexual harassment in the context of resource dependence. *Journal of Public Administration Research and Theory* 31(4): 617–633. Copyright © 2021 Oxford University Press. Republished with the permission of Oxford University Press.

Bennett, R. (2019) *Nonprofit Marketing and Fundraising: A Research Overview*. Abingdon, OX: Routledge. Copyright © 2019 Taylor and Francis. Republished with permission.

Bennett, R. and Savani, S. (2011) Sources of new ideas for charity fundraising: an empirical study. *Creativity and Innovation Management* 20(2). Copyright © 2011 John Wiley and Sons. Republished with permission.

Bergeron, A. and Tempel, E. R. (2022) A commitment to ethical fundraising, in G. G. Shaker, E. R. Tempel, S. K. Nathan and B. Stanczykiewicz (eds.), *Achieving Excellence in Fundraising* (5th edn): Wiley. Copyright © 2022 John Wiley and Sons. Reproduced with permission of John Wiley & Sons Inc.

Bhati, A. and Eikenberry, A. M. (2018) A critical fundraising perspective: understanding the beneficiary experience, in A. M. Eikenberry, R. M. Mirabella and B. Sandberg (eds) *Reframing Nonprofit Organisations. Democracy, Inclusion and Social Change*. Irvine, CA: Melvin & Leigh, Publishers. Republished with permission of Melvin & Leigh, Publishers, all rights reserved.

Bhati, A. and Hansen, R. (2020) A literature review of experimental studies in fundraising. *Journal of Behavioral Public Administration*, 3(1). Creative Commons Attribution 4.0.

Botting Herbst, N. and Howard-Dace, L. (2019) *The Complete Fundraising Handbook, 7th edition*, London: Directory of Social Change. Reproduced by kind permission of the publishers, The Directory of Social Change, Suite 103, 1 Old Hall Street, Liverpool, L3 9HG www.dsc.org.uk from whom copies may be purchased.

Breeze, B. (2017) *The New Fundraisers*. Bristol: Policy Press. Copyright © 2017 Policy Press. Re-published with permission of Policy Press (an imprint of Bristol University Press, UK).

Broce, T. E. (1986) *Fund Raising: The Guide to Raising Money From Private Sources* (2nd edn). Norman, OK: University of Oklahoma Press. Copyright © 1986 University of Oklahoma Press. Republished with permission.

Brooks, A. C. (2014) Why fund-raising is fun. *New York Times*, 29 March 2014. Copyright © 2014 The New York Times. Republished with permission.

Brooks, J. (2019) Direct mail: dead, or more alive than ever? www.moceanic.com/2019/direct-mail-dead-or-alive/. Republished with kind permission of the author, all rights reserved.

Bull, G. and Steinberg, T. (2021) *Modern Grantmaking: A Guide for Funders Who Believe Better is Possible*. Great Britain: Modern Grantmaking. Copyright © 2021 Modern Grantmaking. Republished with permission, all rights reserved.

Burlingame, D. and Sargeant, A. (2010) Corporate Giving and Fundraising, in A. Sargeant and J. Shang (eds). *Fundraising Principles and Practice* (1st edn). Hoboken, US: Jossey-Bass. Copyright © 2010 Jossey-Bass. Republished with permission.

Burnett, K. (2002) *Relationship Fundraising* (2nd edn). San Francisco: Jossey Bass. Copyright © 2002 John Wiley and Sons. Republished with permission.

Cagney, P. and Ross, B. (2013) *Global Fundraising: How the World is Changing the Rules of Philanthropy*. Hoboken: Wiley. Copyright © 2013 John Wiley and Sons. Republished with permission.

Carter, P. (2009) *The Complete Special Events Handbook*. London: Directory of Social Change. Reproduced by kind permission of the publishers, The Directory of Social Change, Suite 103, 1 Old Hall Street, Liverpool, L3 9HG www.dsc.org.uk from whom copies may be purchased.

Chapman, C. M., Masser, B. M. and Louis, W. R. (2019) The champion effect in peer-to-peer giving: successful campaigns highlight fundraisers more than causes. *Nonprofit and Voluntary Sector Quarterly* 48(3): 572–592. Copyright © 2019 SAGE. Republished with permission.

Chapman, C. M., Louis, W. R., Masser, B. M. and Thomas, E. F. (2022) Charitable triad theory: how donors, beneficiaries, and fundraisers influence charitable giving. *Psychology and Marketing* 39(9): 1826–1848. Copyright © 2022 John Wiley and Sons. Republished with permission.

Cluff, A. (2009) Dispelling the myths about major donor fundraising. *International Journal of Nonprofit and Voluntary Sector Marketing* 14(4): 371–377. Copyright © 2009 John Wiley and Sons. Republished with permission.

Cordery, C. J., Smith, K. A. and Berger, H. (2017) Future scenarios for the charity sector in 2045. *Public Money & Management*, 37(3), 189–196. © 2017 CIPFA, reprinted by permission of Informa UK Limited, trading as Taylor & Francis Group, www.tandfonline.com on behalf of 2017 CIPFA.

Croucher, M., Niles, M., Mahmoud, O. and Ross, B. (2021) *Change for Better: Behaviour Science Lessons from the World's Top Practitioners*. London: =mc consulting. Copyright ©2021 =mc consulting. Republished with kind permission of the authors.

Cutlip, S. (1965) *Fundraising in the United States: Its Role in America's Philanthropy*. New Brunswick, NJ: Rutgers University Press. Reprinted by permission of Rutgers University Press.

Dale, E. (2017) Fundraising as women's work: examining the profession with a gender lens. *International Journal of Nonprofit and Voluntary Sector Marketing* 22(4). Copyright © 2017 John Wiley and Sons. Republished with permission.

Dean, J. and Wood, R. (2017) "You can try to press different emotional buttons": The conflicts and strategies of eliciting emotions for fundraisers. *International Journal of Nonprofit and Voluntary Sector Marketing*, 22(4): 13–30. Copyright © 2017 John Wiley and Sons. Republished with permission.

Dichter, S. (2008) In Defence of Raising Money, blogpost October 2008, first published at https://sashadichter.com/manifesto-in-defense-of-raising-money/ Reprinted with kind permission of the author, all rights reserved.

Duronio, M. A. and Tempel, E. R. (1997) *Fund Raisers; Their Careers, Stories, Concerns, and Accomplishments*. San Francisco: Jossey-Bass. Copyright © 1997 John Wiley and Sons. Republished with permission.

Elischer, T. (2008) *2008 Expedition: Rediscovering & Climbing the Donor Pyramid*. Think Consulting Solutions. Republished with kind permission of the author's family, all rights reserved.

Fernandez, R. (2010) Fundraising in your own back yard: inviting clients to be donors. *Grassroots Fundraising Journal*. https://nonprofitquarterly.org/fundraising-in-your-own-back-yard-inviting-clients-to-be-donors/. Used with permission from the publisher who has placed the work in the Creative Commons.

Fischer, M. (2000) The colour of ethics, in J. Mordaunt and R. Paton (eds) *Thoughtful Fundraising: Concepts, Issues and Perspectives*. Abingdon, OX: Routledge. Copyright © 2000 Routledge. Reproduced with permission of the licensor through PLSclear.

Garza, A. and Holmes, J. T. (2021) The Fundraiser Bill of Rights. *Advancing Philanthropy*, April 2021. Copyright © 2021 Amelia Garza and Jennifer T. Holmes. All Rights Reserved. Republished with permission.

Gibson, C. M. (2016) Beyond fundraising: what does it mean to build a culture of philanthropy? www.haasjr.org/resources/beyond-fundraising. Used with permission from the publisher who has placed the work in the Creative Commons.

Gow Pettey, J. (2002) Introduction, in J. Gow Pettey (ed.) *Cultivating Diversity in Fundraising*. New York: AFP/Wiley. Copyright © 2002 John Wiley and Sons. Republished with permission.

Greenfield, J. (2013) Rights of donors, in J. Gow Pettey (ed.) *Nonprofit Fundraising Strategy: A Guide to Ethical Decision Making and Regulation for Nonprofit Organizations*, John Wiley & Sons. Copyright © 2013 John Wiley and Sons. Republished with permission.

Greer, L. and Kostoff, L. (2020) *Philanthropy Revolution: How to Inspire Donors, Build Relationships, and Make a Difference*. London: Harper Collins. Copyright © 2020 Lisa Greer and Harper Collins. Reproduced with kind permission of the author and Harper Collins, all rights reserved.

Hansen, R. (2022) Theory in Fundraising, in G. G. Shaker, E. R. Tempel, S. K. Nathan, and B. Stanczykiewicz (Eds.), *Achieving Excellence in Fundraising* (5th edn): Wiley. Copyright © 2022 John Wiley and Sons. Reproduced with permission of John Wiley & Sons Inc.

Harrah-Conforth, J. and Borsos, J. (1991) The evolution of professional fundraising: 1890–1990, in D. F. Burlingame and L. J. Hulse (eds.) *Taking Fundraising Seriously: Advancing the Profession and Practice of Raising Money*. San Francisco and Oxford: Jossey-Bass. Copyright © 1991 John Wiley and Sons. Republished with permission.

Heyman, D. R. (2016) *Nonprofit Fundraising 101: A Practical Guide to Easy to Implement Ideas and Tips from Industry Experts*. Newark, NJ: John Wiley & Sons. Copyright © 2016 John Wiley and Sons. Republished with permission.

James III, R. N. and Routley, C. (2016) We the living: the effects of living and deceased donor stories on charitable bequest giving intentions. *International Journal of Nonprofit and Voluntary Sector Marketing*, 21(2), 109–117. Copyright © 2016 John Wiley and Sons. Republished with permission.

James III, R. (2022) *The Storytelling Fundraiser: The Brain, Behavioral Economics, and Fundraising Story*, www.encouragegenerosity.com: Texas Tech University. Reproduced with kind permission of the author.

Jammeh, F. (2021) My love for philanthropy, in N. Allen, C. V. Nunes Pereira and N. Salmon (eds.) *Collecting Courage: Joy, Pain, Freedom, Love. Anti-Black racism in the Charitable Sector*. Montpelier, VT: Rootstock Publishing. Copyright © 2021 Fatou Jammeh and Rootstock Publishing. Republished with kind permission of the author.

Joyaux, S. (2010) *Involving Your Board Members in Fund Development*. www.simonejoyaux.com/learning-center/board-development/involving-your-board-in-fundraising/ Republished with kind permission of the author's husband, Tom Ahern.

Jung, T., Harrow, J. and Leat, D. (2018) Mapping philanthropic foundations' characteristics: Towards an international integrative framework of foundation types. *Nonprofit and Voluntary Sector Quarterly*, 47(5): 893–917. Copyright © 2018 SAGE. Reprinted by permission of SAGE publications.

Kanter, B. and Fine, A. (2020) *AI4Giving: Unlocking Generosity with Artificial Intelligence: The Future of Giving*. https://ai4giving.org. Reproduced with kind permission of the authors.

Kay-Williams, S. (2000) The five stages of fundraising: a framework for the development of fundraising. *International Journal of Nonprofit and Voluntary Sector Marketing*, 5(3), 220–240. Copyright © 2000 John Wiley and Sons. Republished with permission.

Kelly, K. (1998) *Effective Fund-Raising Management*. Mahwah, NJ: Routledge. Copyright © 1998 Taylor & Francis. Republished with permission.

Klein, K. (2000) Make fundraising your career, in K. Klein and S. Roth (eds.) *Raise more Money: The Best of the Grassroots Fundraising Journal*. Oakland, CA: GFJ Publications. Used with permission from the publisher who has placed the work in the Creative Commons.

Klein, K. (2000) Prospect identification: you already know all the people you need to know to raise all the money you want to raise, in K. Klein and S. Roth (eds.) *Raise More Money: The Best of the Grassroots Fundraising Journal*. Oakland, CA: GFJ Publications. Used and adapted with permission from the publisher who has placed the work in the Creative Commons. Commons license

Le, V. (2018) Answers on grant proposals if nonprofits were brutally honest with funders (part 1). *NonprofitAF.com*, 19 February 2018. Reproduced with kind permission of the author.

Le, V. (2017 [updated 2020]). How donor-centrism perpetuates inequity, and why we must move toward community-centric fundraising. *NonprofitAF.com* 8 June 2020 (updated version). Reproduced with kind permission of the author.

Lewis, J. (2017) *The War for Fundraising Talent and How Small Shops Can Win*. Columbus, OH: Gatekeeper Press. Reproduced with kind permission of the author.

Lindström, E. and Saxton, J. (2013) Inside the mind of a grant-maker: Useful stuff on how grant-making works. https://nfpsynergy.net/inside-the-mind-of-a-grantmaker. Reproduced with kind permission of the authors.

Lord, J. G. (1984) *The Raising of Money: 35 Essentials Every Trustee Should Know*. Cleveland: Third Sector Press. Republished with kind permission of the author. To request a complimentary electronic copy of 25th anniversary edition of the book please contact programs@leadershipphilanthropy.com. Current work: https://leadershipphilanthropy.com/retreats/

MacQuillin, I. (2019) *Fundraising Ethics*. https://sofii.org/article/fundraising-ethics-raise-more-money-while-keeping-your-donors-happy. Reproduced by kind permission of the author.

Marion, B. H. (1994) Decision making in ethics. *New Directions for Philanthropic Fundraising*, Winter 1994, pp. 49–61. Copyright © 1994 John Wiley and Sons. Republished with permission.

Martin-John, N. (2021) Unlocking my authentic voice: a journey to liberating and defining myself, In N. Allen, C. V. Nunes Pereira and N. Salmon (eds.) *Collecting Courage: Joy, Pain, Freedom, Love. Anti-Black racism in the Charitable Sector*. Montpelier, VT: Rootstock Publishing. Copyright © 2021 Niambi Martin-John and Rootstock Publishing. Republished with permission.

Meer, J. (2017) Are overhead costs a good guide for charitable giving?. IZA World of Labor 2017: 329. Republished with kind permission of the author.

Menshenina, I. (2020) Gather people – money will come. *Conscious Fundraising, or Master Book on How to Raise Money for Charity.* Litres.RU. www.litres.ru/irina-menshenina-236/sobiray-ludey-dengi-pridut-osoznannyy-fandrayzing-ili/. Reproduced with kind permission of the author.

Mixer, J. T. (1993) *Principles of Professional Fundraising: Useful Foundations for Successful Practice.* San Francisco: Jossey-Bass Publishers. Copyright © 1993 John Wiley and Sons. Republished with permission.

Moody, M. and Pratt, M. (2020) Tainted money and tainted donors. https://johnsoncenter. org/blog/tainted-money-and-tainted-donors-a-growing-crisis/? Reproduced with kind permission of the Dorothy A. Johnson Center for Philanthropy at Grand Valley State University.

Mullin, R. (2007) Two Thousand Years of Disreputable History, in J. Mordaunt and R. Paton (eds.) *Thoughtful Fundraising: Concepts, Issues and Perspectives*, Abingdon, Oxon: Routledge. Copyright © 2007 Taylor and Francis. Reproduced with permission of the Licensor through PLSclear.

Mullin, R. (1987) *The Fundraising Cycle: The Shortest Book on Fundraising, Ever.* https://sofii. org/article/the-fundraising-cycle-the-shortest-book-on-fundraising-ever. Reproduced with kind permission of SOFII.org.

O'Neill, M. (1994) Fundraising as an ethical act. *New Directions for Philanthropic Fundraising* number 6, Winter 1994: 3–13. Copyright © 1994 John Wiley and Sons. Republished with permission.

Panas, J. (1988) *Born to Raise: What Makes a Great Fundraiser; What Makes a Fundraiser Great.* Chicago, IL: Bonus Books Inc. Reproduced with kind permission of the author's wife, Felicity Panas.

Pantti, M. (2015) Grassroots humanitarianism on YouTube: ordinary fundraisers, unlikely donors, and global solidarity. *The International Communication Gazette* 77(7): 622–636. Copyright © 2015 SAGE Publications. Republished with permission.

Peel, A. (2017) Developing a strategic approach to corporate partnerships, in V. Morton (ed.) *Corporate Fundraising and Partnerships* (5th edn), London: Directory of Social Change. Reproduced by kind permission of the publishers, The Directory of Social Change, Suite 103, 1 Old Hall Street, Liverpool, L3 9HG www.dsc.org.uk from whom copies may be purchased.

Rosen, M. J. (2005) Doing well by doing right: a fundraiser's guide to ethical decision-making. *International Journal of Nonprofit and Voluntary Sector Marketing*, 10(3): 175–181. Copyright © 2005 John Wiley and Sons. Republished with permission.

Rosso, H. (2016) A Philosophy of Fundraising, in E. R. Tempel, T. L. Seiler and D. F. Burlingame (eds) *Achieving Excellence in Fundraising* (4th edn). Hoboken, NJ: Wiley. Copyright © 2015 John Wiley and Sons. Republished with permission.

Rosso, H. A. (1991) Developing a constituency: where fundraising begins, in Rosso, H.A. (Ed) *Achieving Excellence in Fund Raising.* San Francisco: Jossey-Bass. Copyright © 1991 John Wiley and Sons. Republished with permission.

Routley, C. and Sved, R. (2021) *Fundraising Strategy, 3rd edition.* London: Directory of Social Change. Reproduced by kind permission of the publishers, The Directory of Social Change, Suite 103, 1 Old Hall Street, Liverpool, L3 9HG www.dsc.org.uk from whom copies may be purchased.

Sargeant, A. and George, J. (2022) *Fundraising Management: Analysis, Planning and Practice, 4th edition.* London and New York: Routledge. Copyright © 2022 Taylor and Francis. Republished with permission.

Seiler, T. L. (2022) Articulating a Case for Support, in G. G. Shaker, E. R. Tempel, S. K. Nathan, and B. Stanczykiewicz (Eds.), *Achieving Excellence in Fundraising* (5th edn): Wiley. Copyright © 2022 John Wiley and Sons. Reproduced with permission of John Wiley & Sons Inc.

Seymour, H. (1947) *Designs for Giving: The Story of the National War Fund, Inc. 1943–1947.* New York and London: Harper & Brothers. In public domain.

Shaker, G. G. (2021) Are fundraisers givers? *Lilly Family School of Philanthropy blog*, 15 December 2021. Reprinted with kind permission of the author.

Sturtevant, W. (1996) The artful journey: seeking the major gift. *Fundraising Management*, April 1996, pp. 32–35.

Van Teunenbroek C. (2019) Is philanthropic crowdfunding a growing industry? Crowdfunding characteristics and recent developments worldwide. *Alliance Magazine*. Reprinted with permission, first published in Alliance www.alliancemagazine.org/blog/is-philanthropic-crowdfunding-a-growing-industry/

Vance-McMullen, D. and Heist, D. (2021) The Donor Advised Fund (DAF) Revolution, in G. G. Shaker, E. R. Tempel, S. K. Nathan, and B. Stanczykiewicz (Eds.), *Achieving Excellence in Fundraising* (5th edn): Wiley. Copyright © 2022 John Wiley and Sons. Reproduced with permission of John Wiley & Sons Inc.

Wagner, L. (2004) Fundraising, in D. F. Burlingame (ed) *Philanthropy in America: A Comprehensive Historical Encyclopedia*. ABC-CLIO. Copyright © 2004 ABC-CLIO, LLC. Republished with permission.

Warwick, M. (2009) Fundraising in Tough Times. *Stanford Social Innovation Review*, Spring 2009. Copyright © 2009 SSIR. Reproduced with permission.

Warwick, M. (2000) *The Five Strategies for Fundraising Success: A Mission-Based Guide to Achieving Your Goals*. United Kingdom: Wiley. Copyright © 2000 John Wiley and Sons. Republished with permission.

Washington, B. T. (1901) Raising money, In *Up From Slavery: An Autobiography*, New York: Doubleday. In public domain.

Waters, R. D. (2016) The current landscape of fundraising practice, in T. Jung. S. Phillips and J. Harrow (eds.) *The Routledge Companion to Philanthropy*. London: Routledge. Copyright © 2016 Taylor and Francis. Republished with permission.

Wiepking, P. (2022) Understanding individual donors, in G. G. Shaker, E. R. Tempel, S. K. Nathan, and B. Stanczykiewicz (Eds.), *Achieving Excellence in Fundraising* (5th edn), Wiley. Copyright © 2022 John Wiley and Sons. Reproduced with permission of John Wiley & Sons Inc.

Worth, M. J. (2015) *Fundraising: Principles and Practice*: SAGE Publications. Copyright © 2015 SAGE. Republished with permission.

Zumaya, A. E. (2021) To achieve racial justice in philanthropy, we must invest in fundraising and make it inclusive. *The Chronicle of Philanthropy*. Copyright © 2021 Chronicle of Higher Education. Republished with permission.

Index

Note: Page numbers in **bold** refer to tables and *italics* refer to figures

Printed in the United States
by Baker & Taylor Publisher Services